German

With Ease Series

by Maria ROEMER

Adapted for English-speaking learners by
Kerstin Pfeiffer

Illustrated by J.-L. GOUSSÉ

ASSiMiL
The intuitive method

B.P. 25
94431 Chennevières-sur-Marne Cedex
FRANCE

© ASSIMIL 2014
ISBN 978-2-7005-0553-5

Language-learning courses

- Accompanied by optional audio files on CD or in MP3 format
- Now also available as e-courses

Assimil Series

Beginner – Intermediate

Arabic
Chinese With Ease Volume 1
Chinese With Ease Volume 2
Writing Chinese With Ease
Dutch With Ease
New French With Ease*
German
Hebrew**
Hungarian With Ease
Italian With Ease
Japanese With Ease Volume 1
Japanese With Ease Volume 2
Writing Japanese With Ease
Russian*
Spanish
Yiddish

Advanced

Using French

Phrasebooks

French
Italian
Polish
Russian
Spanish

For Kids

Sing Your Way To French

* **e-course** (downloadable) available on www.assimil.com
** Available soon

Contents

Introduction VII
How to use this German course VII
The German alphabet and pronunciation VIII

Lessons 1 to 100
1 Viel Glück! 1
2 Im Hotel 5
3 Das Foto 7
4 Das Frühstück im Café 11
5 Ein Telefongespräch 17
6 Es ist noch nicht spät 21
7 Wiederholung 25
8 Was trinken wir? 29
9 Wer hat Geld? 35
10 Das ist nicht dumm! 39
11 Eine Nachricht 43
12 Bist du's, Janina? 49
13 Ferienende 53
14 Wiederholung 57
15 Entschuldigen Sie bitte, ich habe eine Frage... 61
16 Warum vergeht die Zeit so schnell? 67
17 Zahlen machen müde 73
18 Eine Postkarte aus München 79
19 Essen? Ja gern! Aber was? 83
20 Am Bahnhof 87
21 Wiederholung 93
22 Das Geburtstagsfest 99
23 Eine gute Organisation 103
24 Komm, wir gehen einkaufen! 109
25 Ist Ihr Terminkalender auch zu voll? 113
26 Was machen wir heute Abend, Liebling? 119
27 Na, schmeckt's? 123
28 Wiederholung 129
29 Man kann nicht immer Glück haben 137
30 Dienst ist Dienst und Schnaps ist Schnaps 141

31	Guter Rat ist teuer	147
32	Ein gefährliches Missverständnis	151
33	Die Stadtbesichtigung	157
34	Was man darf und was man nicht darf	161
35	Wiederholung	167
36	Eine gute Partie (1)	173
37	Eine gute Partie (2)	177
38	Alles zu seiner Zeit	183
39	Die Zeiten ändern sich	187
40	Der Autokauf	191
41	Die Stadt Dresden ist eine Reise wert	197
42	Wiederholung	203
43	Die Mücke	209
44	Der 31. Dezember	213
45	In der letzten Minute	219
46	„Der Mensch denkt und Gott lenkt"	223
47	Im Vorzimmer des Chefs	229
48	Ein schwieriger Samstagmorgen	235
49	Wiederholung	239
50	Anzeigen für Ferienwohnungen	247
51	Eine Radiosendung	253
52	Pünktlichkeit ist die Höflichkeit der Könige	259
53	Er ist nicht auf den Mund gefallen (Fortsetzung)	265
54	Kopf hoch!	269
55	„Der Apfel fällt nicht weit vom Stamm"	275
56	Wiederholung	281
57	Wer wird das alles essen?	289
58	Der Hase und der Igel	295
59	Der Hase und der Igel (Fortsetzung)	301
60	Der Hase und der Igel (Fortsetzung und Ende)	307
61	Ein überzeugendes Argument	313
62	Eine schlaue Verkäuferin im Reisebüro	317
63	Wiederholung	323
64	Berlin, die Hauptstadt der Bundesrepublik Deutschland	331
65	Wie wird man reich? Loriot verrät uns das Geheimnis	339
66	Ein perfekter Ehemann	345
67	Und was ist für Sie das Paradies?	349
68	Zehn Fragen zu Ihrer Allgemeinbildung	355
69	Man nimmt sich niemals genug in Acht	361
70	Wiederholung	365

71	„Vater werden ist nicht schwer, Vater sein dagegen sehr"	375
72	Dreimal dürfen Sie raten	379
73	Ein Tierfreund	387
74	„Ich bin von Kopf bis Fuß auf Liebe eingestellt"	391
75	„Was der Bauer nicht kennt, isst er nicht."	399
76	Im Dunkeln geschehen komische Dinge	405
77	Wiederholung	409
78	Der Vorteil flexibler Arbeitszeiten	417
79	Auf der Autobahn	423
80	Eine positive oder negative Antwort?	429
81	Ein nicht ganz alltägliches Vorstellungsgespräch	435
82	Ein nicht ganz alltägliches Vorstellungsgespräch (Fortsetzung)	441
83	Genial oder verrückt?	447
84	Wiederholung	453
85	Wie wird das Frühstücksei gegessen?	461
86	Wie wird das Frühstücksei gegessen? (Fortsetzung)	467
87	Willkommen auf der Wies'n!	473
88	Unsere Vorfahren, die Affen	479
89	Ein Interview im Radio mit Herrn „Stöffche", dem Apfelwein-König	485
90	Ein perfekter Plan	493
91	Wiederholung	499
92	Der verständnisvolle Blumenhändler	505
93	Bewahren Sie die Ruhe, wenn möglich!	511
94	Noch einmal Glück gehabt!	517
95	Wenn sie das gewusst hätte…	521
96	Auf Regen folgt Sonnenschein	527
97	Wenn es doch nur schneien würde!	533
98	Wiederholung	541
99	Ohne Fleiß kein Preis	551
100	Ende gut, alles gut	557

Grammatical appendix	566
Grammatical index	600
Glossaries	607
German–English	608
English–German	654

Introduction

Welcome to *German With Ease*! Whether you're a complete beginner with no previous knowledge of German or have had a bit of exposure to the language, this course is designed to help you learn as painlessly as possible. We will take you through 100 lessons modelled on everyday situations that aim to entertain you while teaching you the essentials of how the language works. With a little perseverance and regular study, you'll gain a conversational knowledge of German within a few months.

How to use this German course

Here's how it works:

- Try to make time to study German each day for approximately 30 minutes.

- Read – and listen to, if you have the recordings – the dialogue at the beginning of each lesson. Then practice reading it out loud, either repeating after the recording or using the phonetic transcriptions to help you pronounce the words. Don't be tempted to translate the text word-for-word into English. After reading the dialogue several times out loud, check the English translation to help you understand what you're reading. This will help you pick up idioms and expressions that can't be translated literally.

- Read the notes, which provide important explanations on aspects of grammar and additional information about vocabulary. After every six lessons, a review lesson summarizes the main grammatical points introduced in that set of lessons. The approach is based on assimilating the grammar progressively, but at any time you can consult the grammatical appendix at the end of the book to review a particular point.

- Do the exercises at the end of each lesson, which will give you the chance to put into practice what you've just learned.

The Assimil method is based on two stages.

Comprehension: the first wave

The first 50 lessons concentrate on comprehension and assimilation of the language. The main goal is to try to understand what you read, and, if you have the recordings, hear. It's the same principle as when a child learns its first language, absorbing it for a while before starting to speak.

Consolidation: the second wave

From lesson 50 on is what we call the 'active phase'. You will continue to study new lessons in the same way as before, but at the same time you will go back to review a previous lesson, starting with lesson 1. This time, however, instead of translating from German to English, try to translate in the other direction: that is, into German. This will consolidate and extend your learning.

Ready to get started? Let's go!

The German alphabet and pronunciation

Alphabet

Here is the German alphabet with the phonetic transcriptions of the letters:
a *ah*, **b** *beh*, **c** *tseh*, **d** *deh*, **e** *eh*, **f** *ef*, **g** *geh*, **h** *hah*, **i** *ee*, **j** *yot*, **k** *kah*, **l** *el*, **m** *em*, **n** *en*, **o** *oh*, **p** *peh*, **q** *koo*, **r** *er*, **s** *es*, **t** *teh*, **u** *oo*, **v** *fow*, **w** *veh*, **x** *iks*, **y** ***ewp****seelon*, **z** *tset*.

The German alphabet also has four additional letters:
ß *es-tset*, **ä** *eh*, **ö** *œ*, **ü** *ew*

Pronunciation

Pronouncing German is easier than it may seem. Once you know the pronunciation rules, there are few exceptions. Some of the sounds are very similar to those in English, while others may sound strange to you at first. It will take a little time to get used to them, but keep practicing by imitating them out loud and you'll soon master them!

• Most words are pronounced as they are spelled. Thus all letters are pronounced, if sometimes only slightly. This latter is particularly true of unstressed endings. For example, in the word **München** *mewnkHuhn* or *mewnkH'n Munich*, the **e** in the **-en** ending is barely audible. This unstressed vowel is similar to the sound in *the* or the initial sound in *about* and is indicated in our phonetic transcriptions by *uh*, or simply by an apostrophe.

• German vowels can be long or short (referring to the duration, or length, of the vowel sound – long vowels are drawn out more). Generally speaking:
- A vowel is long if it is followed by an **h** (which is silent): **ihn** *een him*.
- A vowel is long if it is doubled: **Boot** *boht boat*.
- A vowel is usually long if followed by one consonant: **wen** *wehn whom*.
- A vowel is short if followed by two or more consonants: **offen** *of'n open*.

• Diphthongs (i.e. vowel combinations that glide from one vowel sound to another) in German are **ei** and **ai** (both pronounced *ei*), **eu** and **äu** (both pronounced *oi*) and **au** *ow*. However, note that **ie** isn't a diphthong, but is pronounced like *ee* in *see*: **viel** *feel much*.

• Most of the German consonants are pronounced similarly to English consonants. One combination that is very different and helps to give German its distinctive sound is the **ch**. This can be pronounced in two ways. When **ch** follows the vowels **a**, **au**, **o**, **u**, it is a guttural *kh* like the *ch* in the Scottish *loch*. This sound is made at the very back of the mouth, where *k* is also produced. We've transcribed it as *kh*. When **ch** follows the vowels **i**, **e**, **eu**, **ü**, the sound is produced at the front of the mouth by forcing air through the narrow opening between the tongue and the roof of the mouth. We've transcribed this as *kH* – it is something like the *h* sound in *huge*, but more drawn out.

• When the letters **b**, **d** and **g** occur at the end of a syllable, they are pronounced like **p**, **t** and **k** respectively. The suffix **-ig** at the end of a word is pronounced *ikH*.

• The letter **l** is pronounced a bit differently than in English, with the tip of the tongue against the upper gums and the tongue kept flat.

• The letter **r** is another that gives German its distinctive sound. There are regional differences, but generally when **r** is followed by a vowel, e.g. **Preis** *preis price*, it is 'gargled'. This sound is produced by raising the base of your tongue towards the uvula at the back of your mouth. The resulting guttural sounds a little like the French **r**. However, when **r** follows a vowel, it tends to be pronounced like a neutral vowel, similar to the vowel glide in British English in words such as *here* or *there*. In the phonetic transcriptions, the **r** pronounced as a vowel is indicated by a small superscript [a]: **klar** *klah[a] clear*; **leider** *leid[a] unfortunately*.

• Word stress is important in German. Nearly all German words are stressed on the first syllable or on the first syllable that follows an unstressed prefix. In the phonetic transcriptions, stressed syllables are indicated in bold.

The following overview is a handy pronunciation guide to the sounds that you may need help deciphering.

Letter	Transcription	Example	As in
a	*a*	**als** *als*	h<u>a</u>t
a (long)	*ah*	**Vater** *faht[a]*	f<u>a</u>ther
ä	*e*	**hätte** *hetuh*	l<u>e</u>t
ä (long)	*eh*	**Käse** *kehzuh*	b<u>a</u>ke, w<u>ay</u>
c	*k, ts*	**Cousine** *kooseenuh* **Celsius** *tselseeoos*	<u>c</u>ousin ba<u>ts</u>
e	*e*	**besser** *bes[a]*	l<u>e</u>t
e (long)	*eh*	**Weg** *vehk*	b<u>a</u>ke, w<u>ay</u>
e unstressed/ final	*uh* or *'*	**habe** *hahbuh* **haben** *hahb'n*	th<u>e</u>, <u>a</u>bout
h after a vowel lengthens it		**Sahne** *zahnuh*	p<u>a</u>lm
i	*i*	**Kind** *kint*	h<u>i</u>t
i (long)	*ee*	**wir** *vee[a]*	s<u>ee</u>
j	*y*	**ja** *yah*, **jetzt** *yetst*	<u>y</u>acht, <u>y</u>es
o	*o*	**von** *fon*	<u>o</u>n
o (long)	*oh*	**Moos** *mohs*	s<u>o</u> (with rounded lips)
ö	*œ*	**möchte** *mœkHtuh*	<u>oe</u>uvre, b<u>ur</u>n
ö (long)	*œ*	**Brötchen** *brœt-kH'n*	(a longer version of the above)

q	kv	**Quittung *kvitung***	black <u>v</u>an
s before a vowel	z	**Hase *hahzuh***	wi<u>s</u>e
s before a **p** or **t** (beginning of syllable only)	sh	**streng *shtreng***	<u>sh</u>ip
s (in all other cases)	s	**Thomas *tohmas***	<u>s</u>un
u	u	**Luft *luft***	p<u>u</u>t
u (long)	oo	**gut *goot***	b<u>oo</u>t, m<u>oo</u>n
ü	ew	**Glück *glewk***	p<u>ew</u>, disp<u>u</u>te (pronounced like *oo* with lips pursed)
ü (long)	ew	**kühl *kewl***	(a longer version of the above)
v	f v	**vier *fee*[a]** **Vokabel *voh**kahb**'l***	<u>f</u>atal <u>v</u>ocabulary
w	v	**was *vas***	<u>v</u>ocabulary
y	ew	**Symbol *zewm**bohl***	p<u>ew</u>, disp<u>u</u>te
z	ts	**Zeit *tseit*, zu *tsoo***	ba<u>ts</u>
And:			
ch [1]	kh	**lachen *lakh'n***	Scottish lo<u>ch</u> (guttural)
ch [2]	kH	**ich *ikH***	<u>h</u>uge (but more drawn out)
chs	ks	**Ochse *oksuh***	o<u>x</u>
ng	ng	**streng *shtreng***	si<u>ng</u> (never like in *linger*)
pf	pf	**Pfeffer *pfef*[a]**	ca<u>pf</u>ul
sch	sh	**schon *shohn***	<u>sh</u>ip
ß	ss	**Straße *shtrahssuh***	gra<u>ss</u>

[1] after **a**, **o**, **u**, **au**.
[2] after **e**, **i**, **ü**, **ö**, **ä**, **eu**, **ai**, **ie**, **ei**.

Even if you aren't a complete beginner in German, before starting the lessons, make sure you read the introduction, which contains important information about the approach taken in this book.

1 Erste Lektion *[eh^astuh lektsiohn]*

Viel Glück!

1 – **Gu**ten Tag ①!
2 **Heu**te ist ein **gro**ßer Tag.
3 – Wa**rum**?
4 – Sie ② **ler**nen ③ Deutsch!

Pronunciation
*feel glewk **1** goot'n tahk **2** **hoi**tuh ist ein **grohs**^a tahk **3** varum **4** zee **ler**nuhn doitsh*

Pronunciation notes
To make this first encounter with German pronunciation a little easier for you, the first few lessons will include specific explanations. The numbers indicate the lines that include the words and phrases they refer to. For a more detailed guide to pronunciation, please see the introduction. The bold type in the dialogue indicates where the stress should go – that is, which syllable should be emphasized when you pronounce it.

1, 2, 4, 5 The letter combination *uh* in the phonetic transcription stands for a neutral or unstressed vowel sound that is very

Notes
① You may be wondering why **Glück** *luck, happiness*, **Tag** *day, afternoon* (in the greeting **Guten Tag**) and **Vergnügen** *pleasure, amusement, enjoyment* are written with capital letters. In German, all nouns – that is, the names of people, things, locations or concepts – are capitalized.

② **Sie** is a pronoun that can mean *she*, *they* or, in formal situations, *you*, as here. Like many European languages, German distinguishes between informal and polite forms of address. In writing, the formal **Sie** (*you*) is distinguished from the **sie** meaning *she* or *they* by a capital letter. ▶

1 • **eins** *[eins]*

In the English texts, word-for-word translations from the German are shown in parentheses, whereas words added in English that aren't in the German are shown in square brackets.

First lesson 1

Good luck (*Much luck*)!

1 – Good afternoon (*Good day*)!
2 Today is a big day.
3 – Why?
4 – You are learning (*You[formal] learn*) German.

---

common in German, particularly as the last sound in a word. It equates roughly to the final sound in the English word *the* or the initial sound in *about*: **heute** *hoituh*, **lernen** *lernuhn*. In situations where the letter following a vowel sound requires you to 'swallow' it, so to speak, producing a sound very much like the neutral vowel described above, *uh* has been replaced with an apostrophe: **guten** *goot'n*, **Vergnügen** *fergnewg'n*.

2 The **ei** sound is very common in German and is pronounced like you hear it in 'E**i**nstein' or the long **i** in w**i**ne. We'll usually use the letter combination **ei** to stand for this sound.

2, 5 The unstressed ending **-er**, as well as **r** following a long, stressed vowel, are pronounced almost like a very short, barely articulated **a**: **großer** *grohs*[a], **wir** *vee*[a]. The small [a] will remind you of this.

▶ ③ **Sie lernen** *you* (formal) *learn/are learning*. German is an inflected language, which means that most of the parts of speech (verbs, nouns, pronouns, etc.) change according to their function in the sentence. The basic form of a German verb, the infinitive, usually ends in **-en** or **-n** (e.g. the infinitive *to learn* is **lernen**), but the verb changes its form (conjugates) depending on its person or tense. The form used here, **Sie lernen**, looks like the infinitive, but is actually the third-person plural. Another thing to note about this phrase is that German, unlike English, does not have continuous tense forms (*-ing* forms). **Sie lernen** can thus translate as *you learn* or *you are learning*, depending on the context.

zwei *[tsvei]* • 2

1 5 Wir **wün**schen ④ viel Ver**gnü**gen!

*5 vee^a **vewn**-shuhn feel fer**gnew**g'n*

***

Below are your first exercises. The same types of exercises are included in every lesson, allowing you to remember and assimilate words and phrases you have encountered in the lessons. The first is a translation exercise, and in the second, you need to find the missing words to complete the sentences.

These exercises will not only help reinforce what you've learned, but if you read the sentences out loud, they'll also improve your pronunciation!

Übung 1 – Übersetzen Sie bitte!
Exercise 1 – Please translate!

❶ Sie lernen heute Deutsch. ❷ Guten Tag! ❸ Warum lernen Sie Deutsch? ❹ Wir wünschen viel Glück! ❺ Warum ist heute ein großer Tag?

***

Übung 2 – Ergänzen Sie bitte!
Exercise 2 – Please fill in the blanks!

(Each dot corresponds to one letter.)

❶ Are you (*formal*) learning German?
. . . . Deutsch?

❷ Have fun (*We wish much pleasure*)!
. . . . viel Vergnügen!

❸ Today is a big day.
. . . . . ist ein großer Tag.

❹ We are learning German.
. . . . Deutsch.

3 • **drei** *[drei]*

5 Have fun (*We wish much pleasure*)!

Notes

④ **Wir wünschen** *we wish [you]*. **Wir** *we* is the first-person plural pronoun. The first-person plural verb form takes an **-en** ending, just like the infinitive: **wünschen** *to wish, to desire*.

> Viel Glück!

Answers to Exercise 1

❶ Today you are learning German. ❷ Good afternoon! ❸ Why are you learning German? ❹ We wish you lots of luck! ❺ Why is today a big day?

***

❺ Good afternoon and good luck!
   Guten ... und viel ..... !

Answers to Exercise 2 – Missing words

❶ Lernen Sie – ❷ Wir wünschen – ❸ Heute – ❹ Wir lernen – ❺ – Tag – Glück

---

*Yes, we wish you **viel Glück** and also ... a bit of patience! You'll see that all these strange-sounding words will soon become familiar to you. If you have the recordings, listen to them as often as you like and read the sentences out loud to practice your pronunciation.*

vier *[fee^a]* • 4

2 Zweite Lektion [tsveituh lektsiohn]

Im ① Hotel

1 – **Gu**ten **A**bend!
2 – **Ha**ben Sie ② ein **Zi**mmer frei?
3 – Für **ei**ne Per**son** ③?
4   Sind Sie ④ al**lein**?
5 – Ja, ich bin al**lein**.

Pronunciation
im hotel 1 goot'n ahb'nt 2 hahbuhn zee ein tsim[a] frei 3 few[a] einuh perzohn 4 zint zee alein 5 yah ikH bin alein

Pronunciation notes
1, 4 A final **-d** is pronounced as **-t**: **Abend** *ahb'nt*, **sind** *zint*.
2 Think of the tsetse fly when pronouncing the **z** as in **Zimmer** *tsim[a]*. In German, **z** is never pronounced like the *z* in *crazy*.
5 The **ch** in **ich** is a sound that is a bit tricky for most English

Notes

① **im** is a contraction of the preposition **in** *in, into* and the definite article **dem** *the*. Just note this for now, we'll find out more about this later.

② In a German statement, the subject is usually the first element, while the main verb must be the second element: **Sie haben ein Zimmer.** *You* (formal) *have a room*. In order to form a question, the word order is reversed so the verb comes before the subject: **Haben Sie ein Zimmer?** (literally, 'Have you a room?'). The auxiliary (helping) verb *do/does* that is often used to form questions in English is not used.

③ Now here's a question. Why is it **ein Zimmer** *a room*, but **eine Person** *a person*? The answer is that all German nouns, even those that represent things or ideas, have a grammatical gender: they can be masculine, feminine or neuter. While most ▶

5 • **fünf** *[fewnf]*

Second lesson 2

At (*In-*) the hotel

1 – Good evening!
2 – [Do] you have (*Have you[formal]*) a room available (*free*)?
3 – For one person?
4 Are you on your own (*alone*)?
5 – Yes, I am on my own (*alone*).

speakers. It is produced towards the front of the mouth like the *h* in *huge*, but with a pronounced exhalation of the breath and with the tip of the tongue pushing against the lower teeth. Because the **h** sound is dominant, we have transcribed this phonetically as **kH**. Try not to take the easy way out by simply pronouncing **ich** as *ish*! To practice the **ch** sound, try the following: first, say *ish*. Then press the tip of your tongue firmly against your lower teeth and try to say *ish* without moving the tip of your tongue. If you are doing it correctly, you should be pronouncing *ikH*.

▸ nouns that denote males are masculine, and most that denote females are feminine, the names of inanimate things can be any of the three genders. In German, the grammatical gender of a noun affects the forms of other words associated with it in a sentence: for example, the definite article *the* and indefinite article *a/an*. **Person** is a feminine noun, so its definite article is **die** and its indefinite article is **eine**. **Zimmer** is a neuter noun, so its definite article is **das** and its indefinite article is **ein**. We'll look at masculine nouns in the next lesson.

④ You saw in the previous lesson that the verb form used with the formal **Sie** is like the infinitive: **haben** *to have*, **Sie haben** *you* (formal) *have*. The only exception to this rule occurs with the verb **sein** *to be*, which becomes **Sie sind** *you* (formal) *are*.

sechs [zeks] • 6

3 Übung 1 – Übersetzen Sie bitte!

❶ Guten Tag, haben Sie ein Zimmer frei? ❷ Ein Zimmer für eine Person? – Ja. ❸ Sie haben Glück. ❹ Sarah ist allein. ❺ Warum bin ich allein?

***

Übung 2 – Ergänzen Sie bitte!

❶ Peter is alone.
   Peter ist . . . .

❷ Yes, a room is available (*free*).
   Ja, ... ist frei.

❸ Are you lucky (*Have you[formal] luck*)?
   . . . . Glück?

❹ Good evening, are you (*formal*) alone?
   . . . . , sind Sie allein?

❺ Are you (*formal*) learning German? – Yes.
   . . . . Deutsch? – . . .

---

3 Dritte Lektion *[drituh lektsiohn]*

Das Foto

1 – Wer ist das ①?

Pronunciation
*das **foh**to 1 veh^a ist das*

7 • sieben *[zeeb'n]*

Answers to Exercise 1

❶ Good afternoon, do you have a room available? ❷ A room for one person? – Yes. ❸ You are lucky. ❹ Sarah is alone. ❺ Why am I alone?

***

Answers to Exercise 2 – Missing words

❶ – allein ❷ – ein Zimmer – ❸ Haben Sie – ❹ Guten Abend – ❺ Lernen Sie – Ja

> Warum bin ich allein?

Third lesson 3

The photo

1 – Who is that?

Notes

① **das** is not only the definite article for neuter nouns, but can also function as the word for *this* and *that*: **Das ist Thomas.** *This is Thomas.*

acht *[akht]* • 8

3   **2** – Der Mann ② heißt ③ **Tho**mas Frisch.
     3   Er ④ ist ein Freund aus ⑤ Ber**lin**.
     4 – Und wer ist die Frau ⑥?
     5   Sie ⑦ ist sehr schön.
     6 – Das ist **Ju**lia, **ei**ne **Freun**din ⑧ von **Gi**sela. □

*2 deh__ª__ man heist **toh**mas frish 3 eh__ª__ ist ein froint owss ber**leen** 4 unt veh__ª__ ist dee frow 5 zee ist zeh__ª__ shœn 6 das ist **yoo**lia einuh **froin**din fon **gee**zuhla*

Pronunciation notes
2 The letter **ß** looks like a capital 'B', but is actually pronounced like *ss*. It replaces a double **ss** after a long vowel or diphthong.

Notes
② **der** is the definite article *the* for masculine nouns: **der Mann** *the man*. Like **das** *the* (neuter), it can also mean *this* and *that*. The indefinite article *a/an* for masculine nouns is **ein** (the same as for neuter nouns): **ein Freund** *a friend*.

③ The third-person singular verb form usually ends in **-t**, which is added to the verb stem. So **heißen** *to be called* → **er heißt** *he is called*. (The verb **sein** *to be* is the exception to the rule – the third-person singular form is **ist** *is*.)

④ **er** is the masculine subject pronoun *he* or *it*.

⑤ **aus** can mean *out of*, *made of* and *from*. Here **aus** is used in the sense of *from*: **Peter ist aus Berlin.** *Peter is from Berlin.* The word **von** can also mean *from*, as well as *by*, *of* and *about*. When used with a name, as in line 6, **von** helps to express a relationship between two people or things: **der Freund von Thomas** ('the friend of Thomas'). There are also other ways of indicating relationships, possession and ownership, which we'll come back to later. ▶

***

Übung 1 – Übersetzen Sie bitte!

❶ Das ist ein Foto von Thomas und Julia. ❷ Guten Tag, wer sind Sie? ❸ Die Frau von Thomas heißt Gisela. ❹ Sie ist aus Berlin. ❺ Thomas ist ein Freund.

2 – That (*The*) man is called Thomas Frisch.
3 He is a friend from Berlin.
4 – And who is the woman?
5 She is very beautiful.
6 – That is Julia, a friend of Gisela['s].

2, 6 The stress in the names **Tho**mas, **Ju**lia and **Gi**sela is on the first syllable.
6 Careful! The German **j** is pronounced like the *y* in <u>y</u>es (**Julia yoo**lia), and an initial **g** is always pronounced like the hard *g* in *good* (**Gisela gee**zuhla).

⑥ **Frau** can mean different things in German. Here it means *woman*, but if used with the preposition **von**, as in **die Frau von Thomas**, it means *wife*. With a last name, it means *Mrs/Ms*.

⑦ This is not **Sie** *you* (formal), but **sie** *she* – it is only capitalized because it starts the sentence. We can tell the difference because the verb is in the third-person: **sie ist schön** *she is beautiful*, as opposed to **Sie sind schön** *you* (formal) *are beautiful*. Note that adjectives (words that describe or modify a noun or a pronoun), such as **schön**, can have different forms in German – sometimes the ending changes. When an adjective follows a form of **sein** *to be* (here, **ist**) and modifies the subject of the sentence (here, **sie**), it remains unchanged: that is, it doesn't take an ending. More on this later!

⑧ Many German nouns referring to people have a different form for males and females. The female variant is usually formed by adding the ending **-in** to the male form: **ein Student** *a male student*, **eine Studentin** *a female student*. Note also that the feminine indefinite article ends in **-e**: **ein<u>e</u>** *a/an*, as does the feminine definite article **di<u>e</u>** *the*.

***

Answers to Exercise 1

❶ This is a photo of Thomas and Julia. ❷ Good afternoon, who are you? ❸ Thomas's wife is called Gisela. ❹ She is from Berlin. ❺ Thomas is a friend.

4 Übung 2 – Ergänzen Sie bitte!

❶ Who is Julia's friend (*the friend [f.] of Julia*)?
   ... ist ... . von Julia?

❷ This is Gisela, Thomas's wife (*the wife of Thomas*).
   ... ... Gisela, ... Thomas.

❸ Who is this?
   ... ist ... ?

❹ Thomas's friend (*The friend of Thomas*) is called Peter.
   ... . von Thomas ..... Peter.

❺ Julia is a friend from Berlin.
   Julia ist .... Berlin.

---

4 Vierte Lektion [*feeᵃtuh lektsiohn*]

Das Frühstück ① im Café

1 – Was **wün**schen ② Sie?

> **Pronunciation**
> *das frewshtewk im kafeh 1 vas vewnsh'n zee*
>
> **Pronunciation notes**
> **Title**, **3 das Café** (the place), is written and pronounced as in French; that is, the last syllable is stressed. In contrast, **der**

Notes

① **das Frühstück** *the breakfast* is a neuter noun. Remember that the indefinite article for neuter nouns is **ein** (the same as for masculine nouns). ▶

Answers to Exercise 2

❶ Wer – die Freundin – ❷ Das ist – die Frau von – ❸ Wer – das
❹ Der Freund – heißt – ❺ – eine Freundin aus –

> *Don't worry about all the new words introduced in each lesson. For the time being, the main thing is to understand the German phrases. Try to work on the lessons regularly, repeating them as many times as you like and reading the German aloud. You'll see that this is the best way to familiarize yourself with the language.*

Fourth lesson 4

(*The*) **Breakfast** (*early-piece*) **at the café**

1 – What would you like (*What wish you[formal]*)?

Kaffee (the drink) is pronounced with the stress on the first syllable and a short final **-e**.
1, 2, 5 Here we find the three vowels that can have an umlaut in German: **ä**, **ö** and **ü**. The umlaut changes the vowel sound – **ä** sounds approximately like *e* as in *b<u>e</u>t,* **ö** like *œ* as in *b<u>ur</u>n,* and **ü** like *ew* as in *f<u>ew</u>* (to make the **ü** sound, pronounce *ee* while pursing your lips).

▶ ② **wünschen** *to wish, to desire.* We saw **Wir wünschen viel Vergnügen!** *Have fun!* ('We wish [you] much pleasure!') in lesson 1. The **wir** and the **Sie** forms of this verb are the same as the infinitive. Note that English would use the conditional here, whereas German uses the present tense.

zwölf [tsvœlf] • 12

4

2 – Ich **möch**te **bi**tte ein **Früh**stück mit Ei und zwei **Bröt**chen ③.
3 – **Neh**men Sie **Kaf**fee **o**der Tee ④?
4 – Ich **trin**ke ⑤ Tee.

***

5 – Hier **bi**tte, ein **Früh**stück mit **Bröt**chen, **Kä**se und Wurst ⑥.
6 – **Dan**ke!
7 – **Bi**tte ⑦!
8 – Und das Ei?
9 – Oh ja, das Ei! Es ⑧ kommt ⑨ so**fort**. ☐

---

*2 ikH **mœkh**-tuh **bi**tuh ein **frew**shtewk mit ei unt tsvei **brœt**-shuhn 3 **neh**muhn zee **ka**feh ohd[a] teh 4 ikH **tring**-kuh teh 5 hee[a] **bi**tuh ein **frew**shtewk mit **brœt**-shuhn **keh**zuh unt voorst 6 **dang**-kuh 7 **bi**tuh 8 unt das ei 9 oh yah das ei! es komt zo**fort***

Notes

③ **das Brötchen** *the roll* is a diminutive of **das Brot** *the bread*. A diminutive (a derivative word form that denotes smallness or youth, as in the English word 'pig<u>let</u>', for example) is formed by adding the suffix **-chen** to a noun and adding an umlaut to the stressed vowel (if it is an **a**, **o** or **u**): **die Wurst** → **das Würstchen**. All German diminutives are neuter.

④ **Kaffee** and **Tee** are both masculine: **der Kaffee**, **der Tee**.

⑤ The first-person singular of a verb generally ends in **-e**: **ich trinke** *I drink*, **ich nehme** *I take*.

⑥ **die Wurst** *sausage, cooked meat[s]* exists in countless varieties in German-speaking countries, and it is always feminine. Unfortunately, there is often no apparent logic behind the grammatical gender of German nouns – you just have to memorize them! Thus, **der Käse** (masc.), **die Wurst** (fem.) and **das Brot** (neuter).

▶

2 – I would like (*please*) a breakfast with [an] egg and two rolls (*little-breads*), please.

3 – Would you like coffee or tea (*Take you[formal] coffee or tea*)?

4 – I drink tea.

***

5 – Here you are (*Here please*), a breakfast with rolls, cheese and cooked meats.

6 – Thank you!

7 – My pleasure (*Please*)!

8 – And the egg?

9 – Oh yes, the egg! It's coming (*It arrives immediately*).

4, 6 The **n** sound followed by **k** in ***tring**-kuhn* and ***dang**-kuh* is pronounced almost as if it were written **ngk** *ng-k*. It is a nasal sound similar to the final sound in *singing*.

▶ ⑦ **bitte** has many nuances in German. It can be used to mean *please*, as well as *it's my pleasure, you're welcome*, or even *that's OK* or *don't worry about it* in reply to **bitte** or **danke**. This can result in a polite game of **bitte/danke** ping-pong, which is part of the way of life in German-speaking countries.

⑧ **es** is the neuter personal pronoun, here meaning *it*. It is used to replace neuter nouns, which can be things (as here, **das Ei** *the egg*), or sometimes, people (**das Mädchen** *the girl*).

⑨ **kommen** *to come, to arrive*; **kommt** *it comes, it is coming*. As we've seen, the German present tense can translate into the simple present or continuous present (*to be* + -ing) forms in English. It is also often used to indicate something that is about to happen, especially when an adverb (such as *immediately* in this example) shows that an event will take place soon.

vierzehn *[fee^atsehn]* • 14

4 Übung 1 – Übersetzen Sie bitte!

❶ Ich möchte bitte Tee und zwei Brötchen mit Käse. ❷ Trinkt er Kaffee oder Tee? ❸ Was ist das? – Das ist Wurst. ❹ Das Frühstück im Hotel ist ein Vergnügen. ❺ Ich komme sofort.

***

Übung 2 – Ergänzen Sie bitte!

❶ I would like an egg with cheese, please.
   ... . bitte ... .. mit Käse.

❷ Do you (*formal*) drink coffee or tea?
   .... Kaffee .... Tee?

❸ What would you like (*What wish you[formal]*)? – I['ll] have (*take*) a small sausage with [a] roll.
   Was .... ? – ... . ein Würstchen mit ....

❹ The breakfast will arrive (*arrives*) immediately.
   ... . sofort.

❺ What is this? – This is bread with sausage.
   ... ... ? – Das ist .... mit ....

***

Frühstück: *Germans tend to be early risers, and the word* **Frühstück** *(literally, 'early piece') is proof. Before tackling a long day, many Germans enjoy having a large breakfast consisting of orange juice, a bowl of* **Müsli** *(muesli cereal), a soft-boiled or fried egg,* **Brötchen** *accompanied by cooked meats or cheese, and to top*

Answers to Exercise 1

① I would like tea and two rolls with cheese, please. ② Does he drink tea or coffee? ③ What is this? – This is sausage/cooked meat. ④ The breakfast at the hotel is a pleasure. ⑤ I will come immediately/I'm coming.

***

Answers to Exercise 2

① Ich möchte – ein Ei – ② Trinken Sie – oder – ③ – wünschen Sie – Ich nehme – Brötchen ④ Das Frühstück kommt – ⑤ Was ist das – Brot – Wurst

***

*it off... a croissant! Often a small second breakfast (***ein zweites Frühstück***) at around 10 o'clock is welcome, be it in the office, at home or at school during 'the long (big) break' (***die große Pause***), when pupils who haven't brought their own food to school can buy hot or cold chocolate drinks, sweets or other snacks.*

5 Fünfte Lektion [**fewnf**tuh lek**tsiohn**]

Ein Telefongespräch ①

1 — **Bach**mann.
2 — Ent**schul**digung ②, wie **heiß**en Sie ③?
3 — Klaus **Bach**mann.
4 — Sie sind nicht ④ Herr **Spreng**er?
5 — Nein, mein **Na**me ⑤ ist **Bach**mann.

Pronunciation
*ein tele**fohn**-guh**shpreh**kH **1** **bakh**man **2** ent-**shul**digung vee **hei**suhn zee **3** klows **bakh**man **4** zee zint nikHt her **shpreng**ª **5** nein mein **nah**muh ist **bakH**man*

Notes

① One of the characteristics of the German language is its great capacity for forming compound words. Here is an example of a compound word made up of two nouns: **das Telefon** *telephone* + **das Gespräch** *conversation* becomes **das Telefongespräch** *the telephone conversation, call*. The gender of a compound noun is always that of the last element: **die Wurst** + **das Brot** → **das Wurstbrot** *the sausage sandwich*. We'll have many an occasion to come back to this!

② **Entschuldigung** *apology* is a noun that derives from the verb **entschuldigen** *to excuse, to apologize*. Many German nouns are formed by adding **-ung** to a verb stem. All nouns ending in **-ung** are feminine.

③ There are several ways of asking someone their name in German. You can form a question using **heißen**, which you've already encountered in lesson 3: **Wie heißen Sie?** (literally, ▶

17 • siebzehn *[**zeep**tsehn]*

Fifth lesson 5

A telephone conversation

1 – Bachmann.
2 – Excuse me (*Apology*), what is your name (*how are-called you[formal]*)?
3 – Klaus Bachmann.
4 – You (*formal*) are not Mr Sprenger?
5 – No, my name is Bachmann.

Pronunciation notes
1, **3**, **5** The **ch** in **Bachmann** is the guttural *ch* heard in the Scottish word *lo<u>ch</u>*. It is pronounced at the back of the throat, with the back of the tongue lifted towards the soft palate. We transcribe it as *kh*.
4 At the beginning of a word, **sp** is pronounced as *shp*.

▸ 'How are-called you?'). Alternatively, you can ask **Wie ist Ihr Name?** *What is your* (formal) *name?*

④ Verbs are always negated using **nicht** *not* in German: **Sie sind nicht allein?** *You* (formal) *are not alone?* Note, too, that you can ask a question without inverting the word order of the subject and verb. Just like in English, a rising intonation signals that you're asking a question rather than making a statement: **Sie heißen nicht Sprenger?** *You* (formal) *are not called Sprenger?*

⑤ **der Name** *name* is masculine. As you've seen, the masculine indefinite article is **ein**: **ein Name** *a name*. To say 'my name', you simply put **m** before **ein**: **mein**. **Mein** is used with both masculine and neuter nouns: **mein Name** *my name* (masc.); **mein Frühstück** *my breakfast* (neuter). The form to use with feminine nouns is **meine**: **meine Frau** *my wife*.

achtzehn *[akht*sehn*]* • 18

5
   6 – Oh, ent**schul**digen Sie ⑥ **bi**tte!
   7 Ich **ha**be **ei**ne **fal**sche **Nu**mmer ⑦.
   8 Auf **Wie**derhören.

*6 oh ent**shul**dig'n zee **bi**tuh 7 ikH **hah**buh **ei**nuh **fal**shuh **nu**mᵃ 8 owf **vee**dᵃ-hœr'n*

Notes

⑥ **Entschuldigen Sie!** is a command: *Excuse [me]!* (In German, the 'me' is understood so it isn't necessary to include it.) This is the form to use in situations where politeness is required. The formal **Sie** command uses the same verb form as the present tense, but the word order is reversed – the verb precedes the pronoun: **Kommen Sie!** *Come!* Only the formal command uses the pronoun; it isn't included in informal commands. We'll come back to this later.

***

Übung 1 – Übersetzen Sie bitte!

❶ Entschuldigung, wer sind Sie? ❷ Das ist nicht meine Nummer, das ist eine falsche Nummer. ❸ Frau Bachmann, hier ist ein Telefongespräch für Sie. ❹ Nein, mein Name ist nicht Sprenger. ❺ Entschuldigen Sie, wie heißen Sie?

***

Übung 2 – Ergänzen Sie bitte!

❶ Excuse [me], please, are you (*formal*) Mr Bachmann?
 . . . . bitte, ... Herr Bachmann?

❷ Good evening, my name is Gisela Frisch.
 Guten Abend, ... ist Gisela Frisch.

❸ I am called Julia, and what are you (*formal*) called?
 . . . . Julia, und wie . . . . ?

19 • neunzehn *[nointsehn]*

6 – Oh, please excuse [me].
7 I have the (*a*) wrong number.
8 Goodbye for now (*Until again-to-hear*).

▶ ⑦ As we've mentioned, the grammatical gender of a German noun is often unpredictable. So here's a bit of good advice: learn each noun with its definite article: for example, **die Nummer** *the number* is feminine. If the gender is not mentioned explicitly in a lesson, you can find it in the glossary at the end of the book.

Ein Telefongespräch.

Answers to Exercise 1

❶ Excuse me, who are you? ❷ This is not my number, this is a wrong number. ❸ Mrs Bachmann, there (*here*) is a call for you. ❹ No, my name is not Sprenger. ❺ Excuse me, what is your name?

***

❹ Who is this ? – This is my wife.
 . . . ist das? – Das ist . . . .

❺ No, Thomas is not here.
 . . . . , Thomas . . . . hier.

Answers to Exercise 2

❶ Entschuldigen Sie – sind Sie – ❷ – mein Name – ❸ Ich heiße – heißen Sie ❹ Wer – meine Frau ❺ Nein – ist nicht –

zwanzig [*tsvan*tsikH] • 20

6 | **Andere Länder, andere Sitten**, *literally, 'Other countries, other customs' is a bit like the English saying 'When in Rome, do as the Romans do'. In German-speaking countries, when answering the phone, the person taking the call usually gives his or her family name, and sometimes their first name too, as soon as they pick up the receiver – in other words, before saying hello. The advantages to this custom*

6 Sechste Lektion [zekstuh lektsiohn]

Es ① ist noch nicht spät

1 – Guten **Mor**gen, Frau **Spiel**berg, wie geht es **Ih**nen ②?
2 – Sehr gut, **dan**ke. Und **Ih**nen, Herr Schwab?

Pronunciation
es ist nokh nikHt shpeht **1** *goot'n **mor**g'n frow **shpeel**berk vee geht es **ee**nuhn* **2** *zeh^a goot **dang**-kuh. unt **ee**nuhn her shvahp*

Notes

① As we saw in lesson 4, **es** is the third-person singular personal pronoun used to replace neuter nouns. It is also used as an impersonal subject (i.e. not specifying a particular person or thing): **es ist spät** *it is late*, **es geht gut** *things are going well* ('it goes well').

② **Wie geht es Ihnen?** *How are you?* (formal) ('How goes it for you?') uses the verb **gehen** *to go*. **Ihnen** (with a capital letter) means *you* (formal). <u>Two</u> ways to say *you* in formal situations? What about **Sie**? Well, as we've mentioned, German words can change form depending on their function in a sentence. This variation is called declension, and the form a word takes is called the case. Here, the formal *you* is in the dative case, because it functions as the indirect object in this sentence (and in line 2). Don't worry, all this will be explained soon! For now, just try to remember this useful conversational gambit ▶

21 • **einundzwanzig** *[einunt-tsvantikH]*

are that you don't have to ask to whom you are speaking, and you don't run the risk of saying something not intended for them to hear! At the end of the conversation, rather than using the usual expression for 'goodbye', **auf Wiedersehen**, *which means roughly 'until I see you again' (***wieder** *again,* **sehen** *to see), you say* **auf Wiederhören**, *'until I hear you again' (***hören** *to hear), which is logical, isn't it?*

Sixth lesson 6

It is not yet (*still not*) late

1 – Good morning, Mrs Spielberg, how are you (*how goes it for-you[formal]*)?
2 – Very well, thank you. And (*for-*) you (*formal*), Mr Schwab?

Pronunciation notes
Title Don't be afraid to open your mouth wide in order to say **spät** *shpeht*. The **ä** is a long, open vowel.
1, 2 Just as a final **d** sounds more like a **t**, the consonants **b** and **g** become voiceless at the end of a word. Thus, the **g** in **Spielberg** is pronounced almost like a **k**, ***shpee**lberk*, and the **b** in **Schwab** sounds like a **p**, *shvahp*.

for polite situations, along with the simplest possible response: **Gut, danke, und Ihnen?** *Well, thank you, and you?* To ask informally how someone is (for example, a friend), just say **Wie geht es?** and leave out the **Ihnen**!

zweiundzwanzig [*tsvei*unt-tsvantsikH] • 22

6
3 – Es geht auch gut ③, **dan**ke.
4 Sind die Kol**le**gen ④ noch nicht da?
5 – Nein, **a**ber sie ⑤ **ko**mmen **si**cher gleich ⑥.
6 Sie sind **im**mer **pünkt**lich im Bü**ro**. ☐

*3 es geht owkh goot **dang**-kuh 4 zint dee ko**leh**g'n nokh nikHt dah 5 nein **ah**b[a] zee **ko**muhn zikH[a] gleikH 6 zee zint im[a] **pewngkt**-likH im bew-**roh***

Notes

③ In future lessons, where the English word order doesn't correspond exactly to the German word order, the difference won't be highlighted systematically. But we count on you to look out for this! Take these examples: **es geht gut** *I am fine* ('it goes well'), **es geht auch gut** *I am fine, too* ('it goes also well'), **noch nicht** *not yet* ('still not'). Did you notice these differences? If so, well done! Also, a quick note on German adverbs (words that describe the action of a verb) ... These are not as easily recognizable as English adverbs, which usually end in *-ly*: **sicher** *sure<u>ly</u>*, **gleich** *immediate<u>ly</u>*. But German is simpler, in that most adjectives can be used as adverbs without changing form: **das Ei ist <u>gut</u>** *the egg is good* (adjective); **es geht <u>gut</u>** *I am fine* ('it goes well') (adverb). ▶

***

Übung 1 – Übersetzen Sie bitte!

❶ Guten Tag, Julia, wie geht es? ❷ Es geht gut, danke. ❸ Herr Schwab ist noch nicht da, er ist nicht pünktlich. ❹ Entschuldigen Sie, sind Herr und Frau Spielberg da? ❺ Nein, aber sie kommen gleich.

3 – I am also well (*It goes also well*), thank you.
4 Are your (*the*) colleagues not here yet (*still not there*)?
5 – No, but they are sure to arrive shortly (*they arrive surely immediately*).
6 They are always punctual [about getting to] the office (*in the office*).

▸ ④ **die Kollegen** *the colleagues*, *co-workers* is the plural of **der Kollege** *colleague* (male). A female colleague is **die Kollegin**; pl., **die Kolleginnen** *colleagues* (female). A bit of good news: the definite article for all plural nouns is **die**: **die Männer** *the men*, **die Frauen** *the women*, **die Kinder** *the children*.

⑤ The third-person plural pronoun *they* is **sie** (no capital letter!), and its verb form is the same as the infinitive: **kommen** *to come*, **sie kommen** *they come/arrive*, *they are coming/arriving*. The only exception to this rule is **sein** *to be*: **sie sind** *they are*.

⑥ **gleich** *immediately* is a synonym of **sofort** (see lesson 4).

***

Answers to Exercise 1

❶ Good afternoon, Julia, how are you? ❷ I am fine, thank you. ❸ Mr Schwab is not here yet; he is not punctual. ❹ Excuse me, are Mr and Mrs Spielberg there? ❺ No, but they [will] arrive shortly.

7 Übung 2 – Ergänzen Sie bitte!

❶ It is very late.
Es ist . . . .

❷ My (*The*) colleagues [will] surely arrive shortly.
Die Kollegen . . . . . . sicher . . . .

❸ How are you (*informal*) (*How goes it*)? – Very well, thank you.
. . . . ? – . . . . , danke.

❹ Why are they not here?
Warum . . . . nicht da?

❺ Mrs Spielberg is always punctual.
. . . . Spielberg ist . . . .

---

7 Siebte Lektion *[zeeptuh lektsiohn]*

Wiederholung – Review

As mentioned in the introduction, every seventh lesson is a review that will reinforce grammatical points and vocabulary that have been introduced in the previous six lessons. Read the information carefully, but don't worry about trying to memorize it straightaway. You'll get a chance to take everything in as you progress through the lessons.

1 Verbs and conjugation

Let's recapitulate what we've seen so far.

The infinitive of most German verbs ends in **-en**: **lernen** *to learn*, **kommen** *to come, to arrive*, **haben** *to have*, etc.

Like in English, the verb endings change depending on 'who' is speaking (in grammatical terms, the 'person'): i.e. *I*, *you*, *he/she/it*, *we*, *they*. In German, the appropriate verb ending is added to the verb stem after removing the **-en** (or **-n**) from the infinitive: **lernen** *to learn*, stem: **lern-**.

• To make the first-person singular (*I*), **-e** is attached to the verb stem: **ich lerne** *I learn*.

25 • **fünfundzwanzig** *[fewnfunt-tsvantsikH]*

Answers to Exercise 2

❶ – sehr spät ❷ – kommen – gleich ❸ Wie geht es – Sehr gut – ❹ – sind sie – ❺ Frau – immer pünktlich

> **Wie geht es?** *Are you starting to become familiar with certain words and expressions? Excellent! Continue reading the sentences out loud as you learn them – pretend you're German; it will help your pronunciation! To help consolidate what you've learned, lesson 7 is a review of the points you've seen so far.*

Seventh lesson 7

- To make the third-person singular (*he/she/it*), **-t** is attached to the verb stem: **er/sie/es lernt**.

- The formal second-person (*you*), both singular and plural, and the third-person plural (*they*) are easy! Just use the infinitive form: **Sie lernen** *you* (formal) *learn*, **sie lernen** *they learn*. The only difference is the capital letter in **Sie** *you*. The pronoun **sie** (no capital letter!) also means *she*: **sie lernt** *she learns*. You can tell the difference by the verb ending: **sie lernt** *she learns*, **sie lernen** *they learn*.

- The first-person plural (*we*) also uses the infinitive form: **wir lernen** *we learn*.

2 Grammatical gender and articles ('the, a/an')

Unlike in English, there are various forms for the articles *the* and *a/an*. This is because nouns in German come in three grammatical genders (masculine, feminine and neuter), and the article used with the noun needs to correspond both with its gender and its number, i.e. whether it is singular or plural.

With a singular noun, *the* is **der**, **die** or **das**, and *a/an* is **ein**, **eine** or **ein**.

- masculine: **der/ein Freund** *the/a friend* (male)
- feminine: **die/eine Freundin** *the/a friend* (female)
- neuter: **das/ein Kind** *the/a child*.

With a plural noun, regardless of the gender, *the* is always **die**: **die Freunde** *the friends* (male), **die Freundinnen** *the friends* (female), **die Kinder** *the children*.

The gender of German nouns is not easy to guess, with the exception of nouns for people and animals, which usually (but not always!) follow biological gender – masculine for males, feminine for females. However, neuter is used for children (except **der Junge** *boy*), and inanimate objects could be any one of the three: **der Tag** *the day*, **der Käse** *the cheese,* but **die Wurst** *the sausage* and **das Zimmer** *the room*. Although certain noun endings are characteristic of particular genders, as we will see later, we strongly recommend learning nouns with their gender – that is, with their respective article!

3 Personal pronouns

So far you've seen several different subject pronouns:

- the first-person singular **ich** *I*
- the second-person formal **Sie** *you* (singular and plural)
- the third-person singular: **er** *he, it* (m.), **sie** *she, it* (f.), **es** *it* (n.). (Note that in German you need to use the masculine, feminine or neuter pronoun depending on the gender of the noun it stands in for, regardless of whether it is a person or a thing.)

Das ist der Freund von Julia. Er heißt Thomas.
This is Julia's friend. He is called Thomas.

Frau Berg kommt gleich. Sie ist pünktlich.
Mrs Berg [will] arrive shortly. She is punctual.

Das Zimmer ist schön. Ist es frei? *The room is nice. Is it vacant?*

Der Kaffee ist gut. Er ist heiß. *The coffee is good. It is hot.*

Das Mädchen kommt gleich. Es ist pünktlich.
The girl [will] arrive shortly. She is punctual.

- the third-person plural **sie** *they* (all genders).
<u>Thomas und Klaus</u> lernen Deutsch; <u>sie</u> haben Glück.
Thomas and Klaus are learning German; they are lucky.

<u>Julia und Sarah</u> kommen; <u>sie</u> sind pünktlich.
Julia and Sarah are coming; they are punctual.

<u>Die Zimmer</u> sind schön. Sind <u>sie</u> frei?
The rooms are nice. Are they available?

4 Adjectives and adverbs

Most German adjectives can be used as adverbs (modifying a verb) without changing form:

Julia und Thomas sind pünktlich. *Julia and Thomas are punctual.*

Sie kommen pünktlich. *They arrive punctually.*

Below you'll find a short dialogue that includes the main things covered in the previous six lessons. Listen to it at your leisure and repeat each phrase several times. You'll be surprised at how much you recognize as you listen! Would you have believed you'd be able to do this so soon after starting?

Review exercise

Wer sind Sie?

1 – Guten Tag!
2 – Guten Tag, wie geht es Ihnen, Frau Spielberg?
3 – Gut, danke, aber ich bin nicht Frau Spielberg.
4 – Oh, entschuldigen Sie, bitte!
5 – Bitte.
6 – Ist das nicht das Büro von Frau Spielberg?
7 – Sicher, aber Frau Spielberg ist nicht da.
8 Sie trinkt Kaffee; sie kommt sofort.
9 – Und wie heißen Sie?
10 – Ich bin Julia Bachmann, eine Kollegin.

8 Translation

Who are you?

1 Good afternoon! **2** Good afternoon, how are you, Mrs Spielberg? **3** Well, thank you, but I am not Mrs Spielberg. **4** Oh, excuse me (*please*)! **5** That's OK. **6** Is this not the office of Mrs Spielberg? **7** Certainly, but Mrs Spielberg isn't here (*there*). **8** She is having (*drinks*) coffee; she will arrive (*arrives*) shortly. **9** And what's your name? **10** I am Julia Bachmann, a colleague.

---

8 Achte Lektion [akhtuh lektsiohn]

Was trinken wir?

1 – **Gu**ten Tag, was **möch**ten Sie ①?
2 – Ich **möch**te **bi**tte ein **Känn**chen ② **Ka**ffee.
3 – Und du? Was **trin**kst du ③, **A**lex?

Pronunciation
vas **tring**-k'n **vee**ᵃ **1** **goo**t'n tahk vas **mœkh**-tuhn zee **2** ikH **mœkh**-tuh bituh ein **ken**-kHuhn **ka**feh **3** unt doo? vas **tring**-kst doo **ah**leks

Notes

① **Sie möchten** *you* (formal) *would like*, **ich möchte** *I would like*, are subjunctive forms of **mögen** *to like*. We'll have a closer look at **mögen** soon. For now, just remember that the basic meaning of **mögen** is *to like*, *to want* and the subjunctive **möchte, möchten** means *would like (to)*.

② **das Kännchen** is the diminutive of **die Kanne** *the pot*, *jug* or **die Kaffeekanne** *the coffee pot*, *cafetière*. It refers to a small pot or coffee press that holds two cups (**zwei Tassen**) of coffee. In German-speaking countries, coffee does not tend to be very strong, so you can easily have several cups without risking a sleepless night!

8

That's it! You've finished your first set of lessons! Sit back and relax. There are many interesting things in store for you in the lessons to come!

Eighth lesson 8

What shall we drink (*What drink we*)?

1 – Good afternoon, what would you like (*would-like you[formal]*)?
2 – I would like a small pot [of] coffee, please.
3   And you (*informal*)? What are you drinking, Alex?

▶ ③ Here we have the second-person singular informal form of the verb, which always ends in **-st**: **du trinkst** *you* (informal) *drink*, **du kommst** *you* (informal) *come*, *arrive*, etc. If the verb stem ends in **-ss** or **-ß**, you just add **-t**: **Wie heißt du?** *What are you called? What is your name?* If the verb stem ends in **-t**, however, you have to add an **-e** before the **st** ending: **du möchtest** *you would like.*

dreißig *[dreissikH]* • 30

4 – Ich **neh**me ein Bier.
5   Ist das Bier kalt?
6 – **A**ber na**tür**lich! **Möch**ten Sie auch **et**was **ess**en ④?
7 – Ja, gern.
8 – Gut ⑤, ich **bring**e die **Spei**sekarte und die Ge**trän**ke ⑥ so**fort**.

*4 ikH **neh**muh ein bee^a 5 ist das bee^a kalt 6 **ah**b^a natew^{a}likH! **mœkh**-tuhn zee owkh **et**vas **ess**'n 7 yah gern 8 goot ikH **bring**uh dee **shpei**zuh-kartuh unt dee guh**treng**-kuh zo**fort***

Pronunciation notes
8 • The word **bringe** is pronounced like the English *bring*, but with a final *e* at the end, which is pronounced *uh*.
• **die Speisekarte** is a compound word made up of **die Speise** *food* and **die Karte** *card*. When you come across compound

Notes
④ Although in English we can say either 'something to eat' or 'to eat something', in German, the infinitive is always the very last element in a phrase when it is dependent on another verb: **Ich möchte etwas essen.** *I would like to eat something.* ('I would like something to eat.'). Here **essen** is dependent on **möchte**, so it must come last in the sentence.

⑤ Remember that in German, the same word can be used as an adverb or adjective (lessons 6 and 7). Hence, **gut** means *good* (adjective) and *well* (adverb): **Der Kaffee ist gut.** *The coffee is good.* **Sie sprechen gut Deutsch!** *You speak German well!*

***

Übung 1 – Übersetzen Sie bitte!

❶ Was möchten Sie essen? ❷ Wir nehmen zwei Würstchen mit Brötchen. ❸ Er bringt sofort das Bier und die Speisekarte. ❹ Der Kaffee ist kalt! ❺ Möchtest du etwas trinken? – Nein danke.

4 – I'll have (*I take*) a beer.
5 Is the beer cold?
6 – But of course! Would you also like (*Would-like you also*) something to eat?
7 – Yes, please (*gladly*).
8 – Fine (*Good*), I [will] bring the menu (*food-card*) and the drinks at once.

> words, it is useful to recognize their 'building blocks', as this will help you get the stress right. In this book, stressed syllables are indicated in bold print. In German words, stress generally falls on the first syllable (with some exceptions, of course). In compound words, although the first constituent is stressed, the other elements in the word retain their normal stress patterns. However, they receive only a secondary stress (i.e. they are less stressed) as opposed to the first element, which carries the main stress: **<u>Spei</u>**se**kar**te.

▸ ⑥ **das Getränk** *the drink*, **die Getränke** *the drinks*; here, the plural noun is formed by adding **-e**. Yet the plural of **Speisekarte** is formed by adding **-n**: **die Speisekarten** *the menus*. In previous lessons, we've also seen **der Mann**, **die Männer** *the man*, *the men*, and **die Frau**, **die Frauen** *the woman*, *the women*. Unfortunately, there isn't a general rule for forming plural nouns in German. But the plural is indicated after each noun in the glossary at the end of the book. For example: **das Getränk (-e)**, **die Speisekarte (-n)**, **der Mann (¨er)**, **die Frau (-en)**.

***

Answers to Exercise 1

❶ What would you like to eat? ❷ We'll have two sausages with rolls. ❸ He will bring the beer and the menu right away. ❹ The coffee is cold! ❺ Would you like something to drink? – No, thanks.

zweiunddreißig *[tsveiunt-dreissikH]* • 32

8 Übung 2 – Ergänzen Sie bitte!

❶ Good evening, what would you (*formal*) like?
Guten Abend, was ....?

❷ Are you also having (*Drink you[informal] also*) a beer? – Of course!
.... auch ... .? – .... !

❸ What are you having (*What take you[formal]*)? A small pot of coffee or tea?
Was ....? ... . Kaffee oder Tee?

***

Die Speisekarte
Here is a hot drinks list from a German café menu:

GETRÄNKE *(drinks)*	
Tasse Kaffee	2,20 Euro
Kännchen Kaffee	3,50 Euro
Espresso	2,00 Euro
Cappuccino	2,80 Euro
Tasse Tee	1,60 Euro
Tasse Trinkschokolade	2,50 Euro
Kännchen Trinkschokolade	3,50 Euro
Eine Portion Schlagsahne	0,50 Euro

As you can see, you'll need to specify whether you'd like **eine Tasse Kaffee** *a cup of coffee or* **ein Kännchen Kaffee** *a small pot of coffee. Coffee is usually served with little containers of* **Kaffeesahne***, a pasteurized light cream with approximately 10–15% fat. If you'd like a more milky coffee, say that you would like* **Kaffee mit Milch** *coffee with milk or* **Milchkaffee** *('milk-coffee'). If you prefer your coffee with real cream, you can ask for it* **mit Sahne** *(***die Sahne** *cream). And if you are offered whipped cream (***die Schlagsahne***), don't refuse it! It's really good!*

33 • **drei**unddreißig *[**drei**unt-dreissikH]*

❹ What is your name (*What are-called you[informal]*)?
 – My name is (*I'm called*) Alex.
 Wie . . . . ? – . . . . Alex.

❺ Would you (*formal*) like something to eat?
 – Yes, please (*Gladly*).
 Möchten Sie . . . . ? – . . . . .

Answers to Exercise 2

❶ – möchten Sie ❷ Trinkst du – ein Bier – Natürlich ❸ – nehmen Sie – Ein Kännchen ❹ – heißt du – Ich heiße ❺ – etwas essen – Gern

***

This is the **Brandenburger Tor** *Brandenburg Gate, a monumental archway located in the centre of Berlin and leading onto Boulevard Unter den Linden, which once led to the palace of the Prussian monarchs. The monument is a former city gate, which was rebuilt in the late 18th century by King Frederick William II as a triumphal arch. It was damaged during World War II, though since restored, and has become one of most well-known landmarks in Germany, the backdrop to numerous significant historical events. During the Cold War, it was part of the Berlin Wall that divided the city. Since the fall of the Wall in 1989,* **Brandenburger Tor** *has been considered a symbol of reunification and peace.*

9 Neunte Lektion [nointuh lektsiohn]

Wer hat ① Geld?

1 – **Bi**tte, wir **möch**ten **zah**len.
2   Wie viel ② macht **a**lles zu**sa**mmen, **bi**tte?
3 – Ja, **al**so ein Bier, ein **Känn**chen **Ka**ffee und **zwei**mal ③ **Brat**wurst mit **Po**mmes (Frites),
4   das macht **fünf**zehn **Eu**ro ④ **fünf**zig.

Pronunciation
veh[a] hat gelt **1** *bituh vee[a] mœkh-tuhn tsahl'n* **2** *vee feel makht ales tsuzamuhn bituh* **3** *yah alzoh ein bee[a] ein kenkHuhn kafeh unt tsvei-mahl braht-vurst mit pomuhs* **4** *das makht fewnftsehn oiro fewnftsikH*

Pronunciation notes
3 Pommes Frites, borrowed from the French for 'fried potatoes' or *fries*, is pronounced in German as *pom **frits***. However, colloquially, **Pommes Frites** are more often than not simply

Notes

① You've seen that the third-person singular of a verb is usually formed by adding **-t** to the verb stem: **machen** *to make, to do*, **das macht** *this makes*. But **er hat** *he has* is an exception, as the **b** of **haben** *to have* disappears. The same holds true for the second-person singular: **du hast** *you* (informal) *have*.

② **Wie viel?** *How much?* is followed either by a verb, **Wie viel macht das, bitte?** ('How much makes this, please?'), or immediately by a noun: **Wie viel Geld hat er?** *How much money has he [got]?*

35 • **fünfunddreißig** *[fewnfunt-dreissikH]*

Ninth lesson 9

Who has money?

1 – Excuse me (*Please*), we would like to pay.
2   How much does all this come to (*How much makes all together*), please?
3 – Well then (*Yes, so*), a beer, a small pot [of] coffee and two fried sausages (*twice frying-sausage*) with fries …
4   … that comes to (*makes*) 15 euros 50.

---

referred to as **Pommes po**muhs.
4 According to traditional pronunciation rules, the **-ig** ending ought to be pronounced as if it were written **-ich** *-ikH*: **fünfzig fewnf**ts*ikH*. However, in southern Germany, Austria and German-speaking parts of Switzerland, this is usually pronounced *-k*: **fewnf**ts*ik*. Nobody will hold it against you if you pronounce **-ig** as **-ik**, but try practicing the pronunciation of *-ikH* nevertheless. Numbers are a good opportunity: **zwanzig tsvan**ts*ikH twenty*, **dreißig drei**s*sikH thirty*, **vierzig fee**ᵃts*ikH forty*, etc.

③ **einmal** *once* ('one time'), **zweimal** *twice*, **dreimal** *three times* … Why not continue? **viermal**, **fünfmal** … Use the numbers at the bottom of the pages and just add **mal** *time*.

④ Like many words of foreign origin, **der Euro** *the euro* forms the plural by adding **-s**: **die Euros**. Yet it's **fünf Euro** *five euros* without the **-s**! The rule is simple: when a masculine or neuter noun expressing a unit of measurement or quantity is preceded by a number, it does not become plural: **das Kilo**, **die Kilos**, but **zwei Kilo** *two kilos*; **der Tee**, **die Tees**, but **zwei Tee** *two teas*.

9 5 – Mist ⑤, ich **ha**be kein Geld ⑥.
  6   Hast du Geld?
  7 – Klar, ich be**zah**le ⑦, ich **ha**be ge**nug**. ☐

*5 mist ikH **hah**buh kein gelt 6 hast doo gelt 7 klah[a] ikH buh-**tsah**luh ikH **hah**buh guh**nook***

Notes

⑤ **Mist!** is a frequently used exclamation expressing regret, disappointment or unwelcome surprise and is roughly equivalent to English oaths such as *damn*, *shoot* or *blast*, but its literal meaning is 'dung'!

⑥ **Geld** is neuter: **das Geld** *the money*. We've seen that a noun can have a definite article (**der, die** or **das** in the singular and **die** in the plural), or an indefinite article (**ein, eine, ein**). There is also a negative article: **kein(e)** *no, not a, none, not any*: **Haben Sie kein Geld?** *Have you no money? Don't you have any money?* With plural or feminine nouns, **kein** takes an **-e** ending: **Ich nehme keine Milch.** *I don't take milk.* **Er hat keine Freunde.** *He has no friends.*

***

Übung 1 – Übersetzen Sie bitte!

❶ Ich möchte bitte zahlen. ❷ Gut, zwei Bier und ein Tee, das macht sechs Euro vierzig. ❸ Wie viel Geld hast du? ❹ Sie* haben kein Glück, wir haben kein Zimmer frei. ❺ Das macht zehn Euro fünfzig.

* Out of context, you can't really tell whether this is the formal *you* or *they*. But don't worry, in everyday situations you will always be able to distinguish **sie** *they* and **Sie** *you*.

5 – Blast, I don't have any (*have no*) money.
6   Have you (*informal*) [got any] money?
7 – Of course (*Clear*), I['ll] pay, I have enough.

> Sie haben kein Glück, wir haben kein Zimmer frei.

▶ ⑦ There is no difference in meaning between **zahlen** and **bezahlen** *to pay (for)*. Nevertheless, be wary of prefixes! We'll soon see that the general sense of a word can change when a prefix is added (sometimes completely).

***

Answers to Exercise 1

❶ I would like to pay, please. ❷ Fine, two beers and a tea, that comes to 6 euros 40. ❸ How much money do you have? ❹ You/They have no luck, we don't have a room free. ❺ That comes to 10 euros 50.

> *Don't feel obliged to try to remember all the new words you're learning straight away – it would be surprising if you didn't forget a few! You will come across them again in later lessons, which will help you remember them. For the moment, just be patient!*

achtunddreißig *[akhtunt-dreissikH]*

10   Übung 2 – Ergänzen Sie bitte!

❶ Who will pay (*Who pays*)? I have no money, you (*informal*) have no money, and he has no money.
... ./.....? ... . kein Geld, ... kein Geld und .. ... kein Geld.

❷ Altogether that comes to (*This makes together*) 8 euros 50.
... . zusammen .... Euro ....

❸ What shall we do (*What do we*)? – I would really like to drink a beer (*I would-like gladly a beer to-drink*), and you (*informal*)?
Was .... ? – Ich möchte gern ... . und du?

---

10   Zehnte Lektion *[tsehntuh lektsiohn]*

Das ist nicht dumm!

1 – Was machst du **mor**gen ①, **A**nna?
2 – Ich **geh**e ② mit **Pe**ter in die Stadt.

Pronunciation
*das ist nikHt dum **1** vas makhst doo **mor**g'n ana **2** ikH **geh**-uh mit **peht**ᵃ in dee shtat*

Notes

① The only difference between the words **der Morgen** *the morning* and **morgen** *tomorrow* is the capital letter.

② Like English, German often uses the present tense to convey future meaning when an adverb or the context suggests that something will happen in the future: **Ich gehe morgen in die Stadt.** *I'm going to town tomorrow.* (Literally, 'I go tomorrow to the town.') Practical, isn't it?

39 • **neununddreißig** *[noin*unt-dreissikH*]*

❹ Blast! They don't have any fried sausage here.
. . . . ! Sie haben . . . . hier.

❺ I['ll] pay [for] the beer and you (*informal*) pay [for] the fries.
Ich zahle . . . . . . und . . . . die Pommes.

Answers to Exercise 2
❶ Wer bezahlt/zahlt – Ich habe – du hast – er hat – ❷ Das macht – acht – fünfzig ❸ – machen wir – ein Bier trinken – ❹ Mist – keine Bratwurst – ❺ – das Bier – du zahlst –

Tenth lesson 10

That's not stupid!

1 – What are you (*informal*) doing tomorrow, Anna?
2 – I'm going into (*the*) town with Peter.

Pronunciation notes
2, **3**, **4** The **h** in **gehen**, in **ihr** and in **ansehen** is silent. Its function is simply to lengthen the preceding vowel.

10
3 – Was macht ihr ③ denn ④ dort?
4 – **Geschäf**te **an**sehen ⑤.
5 – Aber **mor**gen ist **Sonn**tag.
6   Die Ge**schäf**te sind ge**schlo**ssen ⑥!
7 – **Glück**licherweise ⑦! Wir **müss**en **spa**ren. □

*3 vas makht ee^a den dort 4 guh-**shef**tuh **an**zehn 5 ahb^a **mor**g'n ist **zon**tahk 6 dee guh-**shef**tuh zint guh**shloss**'n 7 glewklikH^a**vei**zuh! vee^a mewss'n **shpahr**'n*

3 In order not to confuse **ihr** and **er**, pay attention to the initial *ee-* sound in **ihr**. The final *-r* is pronounced without vibrating

Notes

③ Careful, this is not formal address. The formal version would be **Was machen Sie?** *What are you doing?* Here the speaker is referring to two friends: **ihr** *you* is the plural of **du** *you*, or in other words, the second-person plural personal pronoun used for addressing two or more people you know well: **Kinder, kommt ihr?** *Children, are you coming?* In formal address, **Sie** is used regardless of the number of people you are addressing: **Gehen Sie in die Stadt, Herr Schmidt?** *Are you going into town, Mr Schmidt?* or **Gehen Sie in die Stadt, Herr und Frau Schmidt?** *Are you going into town, Mr and Mrs Schmidt?* Note that the second-person plural informal form of the verb ends in **-t** (**ihr geht** *you [all] go*), and is usually the same form as the third-person singular (**er geht** *he goes*). However, there are exceptions. The third-person singular of **müssen** is **er muss** *he has to*, but the second-person plural informal is **ihr müsst** *you [all] have to*. Likewise, the third-person singular of **haben** is **er hat** *he has*, but the second-person informal plural is **ihr habt** *you [all] have*. **Habt ihr Geld?** *Do you [all] have money?*

④ German has many small words whose sole function is to reinforce an emotion, a command or a question. The word ▶

41 • **einundvierzig** *[einunt-fee^{a}tsikH]*

3 – What [will] you (*informal plural*) do (*then*) there?
4 – Check out [the] shops (*Shops to-look-at*).
5 – But tomorrow is Sunday.
6   The shops are closed.
7 – Fortunately! We need to save [money].

---

the vocal cords, like any **r** following a stressed vowel in German. It thus becomes a little 'breath' that sounds almost like a short **-a**: **ihr** *ee*[a]. The same barely articulated 'stifled' **a** occurs in the unstressed **-er** ending: **Peter** *peht*[a], **aber** *ahb*[a].
7 Don't worry about not getting to the end of **glücklicherweise** in one breath. You can pause between **glücklicher** and **weise**.

▸ **denn** is one of these 'flavouring particles', or modal fillers that express or emphasize mood. It is usually used with questions, either to highlight or lessen the sense of surprise (it all depends on pitch and context). **Denn** can be translated as *then*, *now* or *but*, or not at all – which is often the best option: **Wie heißen Sie denn?** *What is your* (formal) *name?*

⑤ **ansehen** *to look at*, derives from **sehen** *to see, to look*; **das Geschäft** is *shop*, *store*, or *business*. Note that in German, the noun comes <u>before</u> the infinitive in formulations like this: **Geschäfte ansehen** *to look at shops*, **Geld sparen** *to save money*.

⑥ **geschlossen** *closed* is the past participle (what in English is sometimes called the *-ed* form) of **schließen** *to close, to shut*.

⑦ **glücklich** *happy, lucky, fortunate* is one of the few adjectives in German that change form when used as an adverb. The adverb is formed by adding **-er** + **-weise** to the adjective (**die Weise** meaning *the way* or *manner*). **Sind Sie glücklich?** *Are you happy?* – **Glücklicherweise, ja!** *Fortunately, yes!*

---

zweiundvierzig [*tsvei*unt-fee[a]tsikH]

11 Übung 1 – Übersetzen Sie bitte!

❶ Was machen Sie Sonntag, Herr und Frau Bachmann? ❷ Wir gehen in die Stadt Kaffee trinken. ❸ Das Café ist heute geschlossen. ❹ Was macht ihr morgen, Kinder? ❺ Ihr spart nicht? Das ist sehr dumm.

***

Übung 2 – Ergänzen Sie bitte!

❶ What are you (*informal plural*) doing today, Anna and Peter?
 – We are learning German!
 Was .... heute, Anna und Peter?
 – ... . Deutsch!

❷ Luckily the shops are not closed today.
 .... sind ... .
 heute nicht ....

❸ Tomorrow is Sunday, and we're going into town to eat fries.
 ...... ist .... und ... . in die Stadt ....

---

11 Elfte Lektion *(elftuh lektsiohn)*

Eine Nachricht

1 **Ha**llo **Thor**sten, hier ist Ja**ni**na.

Pronunciation
*einuh **nakh**rikHt **1 ha**lo **torst**'n hee^a ist ya**nee**na*

Answers to Exercise 1

❶ What are you doing [on] Sunday, Mr and Mrs Bachmann? ❷ We are going into town to have a coffee. ❸ The café is closed today. ❹ What are you going to do tomorrow, children? ❺ You (*pl.*) don't save [money]? That's very stupid.

*****

❹ Why don't you go (*Why go you[informal sing.] not*) with Anna to look at the shops? – I am saving [money].

Warum .... nicht ... Anna die Geschäfte ....? – ... .

❺ What? You (*informal plural*) have to pay and you have no money? Oh, that is stupid!

Was? Ihr ..... zahlen und ... . kein Geld? Oh, ... dumm!

Answers to Exercise 2

❶ – macht ihr – Wir lernen – ❷ Glücklicherweise – die Geschäfte – geschlossen ❸ Morgen – Sonntag – wir gehen – Pommes essen ❹ – gehst du – mit – ansehen – Ich spare ❺ – müsst – ihr habt – das ist –

Eleventh lesson 11

A message

1 Hello Thorsten, this (*here*) is Janina.

Ich habe zwei Plätze für die Oper heute Abend.

11 **2** Sag mal ①, wo bist du ②?
3 Wann kommst du nach **Hau**se?
4 Dein **Han**dy ③ **ant**wortet ④ nicht.
5 Ich **ha**be zwei **Plä**tze ⑤ für die **O**per **heu**te **A**bend ⑥.
6 Ruf mich schnell **an** ⑦!

*2 zahk mahl voh bist doo 3 van komst doo nakh **how**zuh 4 dein **hen**dee **ant**vortuht nikHt 5 ikH **ha**buh tsvei **ple**tsuh few^a dee **ohp**^a **hoi**tuh ahb'nt 6 roof mikH shnel **an***

Notes

① The imperative verb form is used to give commands, offer suggestions or encouragement, or give instructions. There are three imperative forms in German: the second-person singular informal, or '**du**-imperative', is used here. It consists of the verb stem plus **-e**, but, as in this example, the **-e** is often dropped in informal usage: **Sag(e)!** *Say!*; **Komm(e)!** *Come!*; **Ruf(e)!** *Call!* As in an English command, the verb comes first. The polite form ('**Sie**-imperative') is identical to the **Sie**-form of the present tense: **Sagen Sie!** *Say!*; **Kommen Sie!** *Come!* But note that the pronoun **Sie** is always included and follows directly after the verb. We'll find out about the third imperative form later. In German, an imperative is frequently followed by **mal**, an abbreviated form of **einmal** *once* (see lesson 9, note 3). Some say this is to reinforce the command, while others say it is actually to make it sound less forceful.

② This is the second-person singular informal form of **sein** *to be*: **du bist** *you are*.

③ **das Handy, die Handys** *the mobile phone, the mobile phones*. Did you say 'Anglicism'? Spot on! Germans aren't afraid of English words; they even invent new ones! In this case, they've taken an English adjective, capitalized it, given it a neuter gender and turned it into a German noun. Thus, **Handy** is strictly speaking a pseudo-Anglicism, as the word does not in fact exist in English as a term for a mobile phone. ▶

45 • **fünfundvierzig** *[fewnfunt-fee^atsikH]*

2 Hey (*Say once*), where are you (*informal*)?
3 When are you coming home?
4 Your mobile phone just rings (*answers not*).
5 I have two tickets (*places*) for the opera tonight (*today evening*).
6 Call me soon (*quickly*)!

Pronunciation notes
3, 7 You can say **nach Haus** or **nach Hause**, **zu Haus** or **zu Hause**; the final **-e** is optional. But watch out! The final **s** is pronounced *s* (like in *house*), whereas an **s** between two vowels is *z*, so it is ***how***z***uh*** if you opt for the version ending in **-e**.

④ If a verb stem ends in **-t** or **-d**, an **e** has to be inserted between the verb stem and the ending for the second- and third-person singular and the second-person plural: **du antwortest** *you* (informal sing.) *reply*, **er antwortet** *he replies*, **ihr antwortet** *you* (informal plural) *reply*.

⑤ The singular of **die Plätze** is **der Platz**. The word is used here to mean *ticket*, but literally means *place* or *seat* and can also refer to a *town square*.

⑥ **heute Abend** can be translated as *tonight* or *this evening*, whichever you prefer.

⑦ You may be wondering what the word **an** is doing here. It hasn't been translated because it is actually part of the verb – it is what's called a separable prefix, and we have nothing quite like it in English. Let's try to explain: the infinitive **anrufen** means *to call someone on the phone* (**rufen** means *to call* in the sense of 'shout'). The singular informal imperative form of **anrufen** is **Ruf an!** *Call!* The prefix **an** separates from the base verb **rufen** when the verb is conjugated: **ich rufe an** *I call*, **du rufst an** *you* (informal) *call*, etc. If there are other elements in the sentence, these go in between the base verb and the separable prefix, which moves into the final position: **Rufen Sie mich schnell an!** *Call* (formal) *me quickly!* Note also that the stress falls on the separable prefix! We'll be seeing more examples of this soon.

7 Ich **blei**be jetzt zu Haus ⑧.
8 Auf **Wie**derhören!

*7 ikH **blei**buh yetst tsoo hows 8 owf **veed**ᵃ-hœr'n*

Notes

⑧ **das Haus, die Häuser** *the house, the houses.* The expression **nach Hause** or **nach Haus** (the **e** is optional) is used to refer to returning home: **Ich gehe nach Haus(e).** *I am going home.* However, you say **zu Haus(e)** when you are already at home: **Ich bin zu Haus(e).** *I am at home.* We'll soon find out that there are differences in syntax between talking about a place one is going (direction) and talking about a place one happens to ▸

***

Übung 1 – Übersetzen Sie bitte!

❶ Warum sind die Kinder nicht zu Haus?
❷ Entschuldigung, bist du Julia oder bist du Anna?
❸ Haben Sie noch Plätze für die Oper morgen?
❹ Wann müssen wir nach Hause gehen? ❺ Ich bin im Büro, rufen Sie mich an!

***

Übung 2 – Ergänzen Sie bitte!

❶ Where are you (*informal sing.*)? The mobile phone doesn't answer.
Wo . . . . . . ? Das Handy . . . . nicht.

❷ She is calling Thorsten, but he is not at home.
. . . . Thorsten . . , aber er ist nicht . . . . . . (.) .

❸ Hey (*Say once*), do you have a message from Janina?
. . . . . . , hast du . . . . von Janina?

❹ Excuse me, is this (*the*) seat free?
. . . . , ist . . . . frei?

47 • siebenundvierzig *[zeeb'nunt-feeᵃtsikH]*

7 I['ll] stay (*I stay now*) at home.
8 Bye for now (*Until again-to-hear*)!

7 Don't forget that the **z** sounds like *ts* as in *bats*: **zu** *tsoo*.

▸ be (location). **Nach** and **zu** are prepositions, and one meaning of both is *to*. **Nach** is usually used with cities and countries: **Ich gehe nach Deutschland.** *I'm going back to Germany.* **Zu** is used to show movement towards other locations and people: **Wir gehen zu Janina.** *We're going to Janina['s].* So **zu Haus(e)** *at home* is an exception, as it indicates a location rather than movement.

***

Answers to Exercise 1

❶ Why are the children not at home? ❷ Excuse me, are you Julia or are you Anna? ❸ Do you still have tickets for the opera tomorrow? ❹ When do we have to go home? ❺ I am at the office – call me!

***

❺ He goes home and learns German.
   Er geht .... (.) und ..... Deutsch.

Answers to Exercise 2

❶ – bist du – antwortet – ❷ Sie ruft – an – zu Haus(e) ❸ Sag mal – eine Nachricht – ❹ Entschuldigung – der Platz – ❺ – nach Haus(e) – lernt –

> *Half an hour of German a day is all we ask of you! The most important thing is to read and/or listen to a lesson every day, repeating the German phrases aloud several times. Don't try to translate the German into English at this stage, just stick to trying to understand the gist of it.* **Morgen ist auch noch ein Tag!** *'Tomorrow is also still a day' or* Tomorrow is another day!

achtundvierzig *[akhtunt-fee^atsikH]* • 48

12 Zwölfte Lektion [tsvœlf-tuh lektsiohn]

Bist du's ①, Janina?

1 – **Gu**ten Tag! Hier ist der **An**rufbe**ant**worter von Ja**ni**na **Fisch**er ②.
2 **Lei**der **ha**be ich ③ im Mo**ment kei**ne Zeit ④.
3 Hinter**lass**en ⑤ Sie **bi**tte **ei**ne **Nach**richt!

Pronunciation
bist doos yaneena 1 goot'n tahk! hee^a ist deh^a anroof-buhantvort^a fon yaneena fish^a 2 leid^a hahbuh ikH im moment keinuh tseit 3 hint^alass'n zee bituh einuh nakhrikHt

Notes

① Like in English, the apostrophe indicates the contraction of two words by the omission of a letter. Here, the apostrophe replaces the **e** of the neuter pronoun **es** *it*: **Bist du's?** = **Bist du es?** *Is it you?* (Literally, 'Are you it?'). Since the last German spelling reform, the apostrophe is no longer obligatory, and you can simply attach the **s** to the preceding word without an apostrophe: **Bist dus?** Whereas in English this type of expression is impersonal (e.g. *it's me/you/us*), in German, the person speaking is the subject, so **sein** *to be* has to be conjugated accordingly: **ich bin es** (or **ich bin's/ich bins**) *it is me*; **er ist es** (**er ist's/ists**) *it is him*; **wir sind es** (**wir sind's/sinds**) *it is us*, etc.

② **der Anrufbeantworter von Janina Fischer** *the answerphone of Janina Fischer* or *Janina Fischer's answerphone*. In English, possession or a close relationship can be shown by adding *'s* to a noun or by using a phrase with *of*. In spoken German, the construction **von** + proper name is often used in a similar way to *'s*: **der Hund von Peter** *Peter's dog*.

③ The word order of the subject and verb is inverted (i.e. the verb comes before the subject) in several situations – for ▶

Twelfth lesson   12

Is that you (*Are you-it*), Janina?

1 – Good afternoon! This is (*Here is*) the answerphone (*call-responder*) of Janina Fischer.
2 Unfortunately, I am busy at the moment (*have I at-the moment no time*).
3 Leave (*Behind-leave[formal]*) a message, please.

Pronunciation notes
2 In **der Moment,** unlike in English, the stress falls on the second syllable: *mo**ment***.
2, 4, 6 The final **e** of the first-person singular is often swallowed: **hab' ich** *hap ikH,* **ich ruf'** *ikH roof,* **ich komm' gern** *ikH kom gern*. Note that if the final **e** is swallowed, a final **b** is pronounced as *p*: **ich habe** *ikH **hah**buh*, but **ich hab'** *ikH hap*.

▸ imperatives: **Gehen Sie!** *Go!*, for questions: **Bist du zu Hause?** *Are you at home?* and also in statements in which the first word of the sentence is not the subject, as here: **Leider bist du nicht zu Hause.** *Unfortunately, you are not* ('are you not') *at home.* This allows the conjugated form of the verb to stay in its usual place, as the second element in the sentence.

④ **Ich habe Zeit.** *I have time. I am free (to do something).* **Ich habe keine Zeit.** *I have no time. I am busy.* Note that the negative article takes an **-e** ending here (**keine Zeit**) because **die Zeit** is a feminine noun.

⑤ **hinterlassen** *to leave behind* ('behind-leave') is used only in the sense of something definitively left behind: **Sie hinterlassen viel Geld.** *They [will] leave behind a lot of money* (i.e. when they die). Otherwise, simply use **lassen** *to leave*: **Lass die Kreditkarte zu Hause, wir müssen sparen!** *Leave the credit card at home; we have to save [money]!*

fünfzig *[**fewnft**sikH]* • 50

12 4 Ich **ru**fe zu**rück** ⑥. **Dan**ke und bis bald!
5 – **Hal**lo, Ja**ni**na, ich bin's, **Thors**ten.
6 Ich **kom**me gern **heu**te Abend **mit** ⑦.
7 **Al**so bis **spä**ter! Tschüs.

*4 ikH **roo**fuh tsu**rewk**. **dang**-kuh unt bis balt 5 **hal**oh ya**nee**na ikH bins **tors**t'n 6 ikH **ko**muh gern **hoi**tuh ahb'nt mit 7 **al**zoh bis **shpeht**ᵃ! tshews*

Notes

⑥ Like **anrufen** *to call on the phone*, **zurückrufen** *to call back* is a separable-prefix verb; hence, the prefix **zurück** separates from the base verb when it is conjugated. By itself, **zurück** means *back*, *backwards* or *behind*. A separable prefix can attach itself to many verbs, for example: **zurückkommen** *to come back*, **zurückgehen** *to go back*, etc. In each case, **zurück** separates from its base verb when conjugated and becomes the final element in the sentence: **Wann kommst du zurück?** *When will you come back* ('When come you back')?

***

Tschüs oder Auf Wiedersehen? Bye or Goodbye?
Since the 1990s, **Tschüs!** *Bye! See you! has had remarkable success in Germany. A major daily newspaper even published an article entitled* **Die Deutschen nehmen Abschied vom "auf Wiedersehen"!** *The Germans take leave of 'auf Wiedersehen'!* **Tschüs** *was long considered an informal way of saying farewell to someone, but today it has replaced* **auf Wiedersehen** *not only within families, but even at the hairdresser or the bank. The origin*

***

Übung 1 – Übersetzen Sie bitte!

❶ Warum hast du keine Zeit? ❷ Wir gehen in die Stadt, kommt ihr mit? ❸ Frau Fischer ist leider nicht zu Hause. ❹ Ich bleibe bis heute Abend hier, rufen Sie mich bitte zurück! ❺ Sind Sie's, Herr Spielberg? – Ja, ich bin's.

4 I [will] call back. Thank you and bye for now (*until soon*)!
5 – Hello, Janina, it's me (*I am-it*), Thorsten.
6 I'd love to come with [you] tonight (*I come gladly today evening with*).
7 See you (*So until*) later! Bye.

▶ ⑦ And another example: here, **mit** is a separable prefix (from **mitkommen** *to come with (someone), to come along, to accompany*), not the preposition **mit** *with*. Whereas a preposition must be followed immediately by a noun (**Ich trinke Tee mit Milch.** *I drink tea with milk.*), a separable prefix is either attached to the base verb or found at the end of a phrase. **Kommt ihr mit?** *Are you* (informal plural) *coming with [us]?* **Nein**, **wir kommen nicht mit.** *No, we are not coming with [you].*

***

of **Tschüs** *or* **Tschüss** *(the spelling depends on the length of the* **ü**, *which varies from area to area and from person to person) derives, believe it or not, from the Spanish* **adiós** *or the French* **adieu**. *Would you have guessed it? Well, say* **adiós**, **adiós** *very quickly, replacing* di *with* dj, *and* **adiós** *turns into* **adjüs**. *This is how it was pronounced in Low German, the variety of German historically spoken in northern Germany. At the beginning of the 20th century, adjüs became* **atschüs**, *from which* **tschüs** *derives.*

***

Answers to Exercise 1

❶ Why don't you have any time? ❷ We are going into town; are you (*pl.*) coming with [us]? ❸ Ms Fischer is unfortunately not at home. ❹ I [will] stay here until tonight/this evening – call me back, please! ❺ Is that you, Mr Spielberg? – Yes, it's me.

13 Übung 2 – Ergänzen Sie bitte!

❶ Hello, Thomas, it's me, Julia – call (*informal*) me back, please!
Hallo, Thomas, ...'s, Julia, ... mich bitte
.......!

❷ The answerphone responds (*answers*) – they are not at home.
... . antwortet – ... .
nicht zu Hause.

❸ Unfortunately, she is busy (*has no time*) on Sunday.
...... hat sie Sonntag ....

❹ Are you coming (*Come you[informal sing.]*) with [me] to drink a beer? – Of course, I'm coming (*with*).
.... ein Bier trinken? – Natürlich
....

❺ Please leave (*formal*) a message. Bye and see you soon!
.... bitte ....!
Tschüs und bis ....!

---

13 Dreizehnte Lektion [dreitsehntuh lektsiohn]

Ferienende

1 – Wo seid ihr ①, **Kin**der?

Pronunciation
fehriuhn-enduh 1 voh zeit ee^a kind^a

Pronunciation notes
Title Pay attention to where the break lies in compound words, which is signalled by a dash in the phonetic transcription: **Ferienende** *fehriuhn-enduh*.
1, 3, 7 The **-d** at the end of **seid** and **sind** is pronounced as a *-t*.

53 • dreiundfünfzig [*dreiunt-fewnftsikH*]

Answers to Exercise 2

❶ – ich bin – ruf – zurück ❷ Der Anrufbeantworter – sie sind – ❸ Leider – keine Zeit ❹ Kommst du mit – komme ich mit ❺ Hinterlassen Sie – eine Nachricht – bald

Thirteenth lesson 13

The end of the holidays (*Holidays-end*)

1 – Where are you, children?

Notes

① **sein** *to be* is an irregular verb, as you have already seen. The second-person plural is **ihr seid** *you are*. Put your mind at rest, it's the only verb with irregular plural forms in the present tense: **wir sind** *we are*, **ihr seid** *you* (informal pl.) *are*, **sie sind** *they are*. Even the plural of **haben** *to have* is regular: **wir haben** *we have*, **ihr habt** *you have*, **sie haben** *they have*.

vierundfünfzig *[fee^aunt-fewnftsikH]* • 54

13 2 Kommt ② schnell, das **Ta**xi **war**tet ③.
3 – Wir sind **fer**tig, **a**ber der **Ko**ffer schließt nicht.
4 – Wie ist das **mög**lich?
5 Zeigt mal!
6 Iiii, was ist das denn?
7 – **Vor**sicht, das sind die **Kra**bben ④ – die ⑤ **le**ben noch!

*2 komt shnel das **ta**ksi **var**tuht 3 vee[a] zint **fer**tikH ahb[a] deh[a] kof[a] shleest nikHt 4 vee ist das **mœ**klikH 5 tseikt mahl 6 ee vas ist das den 7 **fohr**zikHt das zint dee **kra**buhn dee **leh**buhn nokh*

Notes

② The second-person plural informal imperative ('**ihr**-imperative') is identical to the second-person plural of the present tense, you just omit the personal pronoun: **ihr kommt** *you come*, **Kommt!** *Come!* Remember that the polite form (singular and plural) of the imperative is **Kommen Sie!** *Come!*

③ Note the **-e** placed between the verb stem and the ending in the second- and third-person singular and the second-person plural: **warten** *to wait* (verb stem = **wart-**) conjugates to **du wartest** *you* (informal sing.) *wait*, **er wartet** *he waits* and **ihr wartet** *you* (informal pl.) *wait* (see lesson 11, note 4).

④ The singular of **Krabben** *crabs* is **die Krabbe**, which is a feminine noun, like many German nouns referring to animals ▶

***

Übung 1 – Übersetzen Sie bitte!

❶ Wartet hier! Ich rufe ein Taxi. ❷ Sie haben Krabben? Zeigen Sie mal! ❸ Warum seid ihr noch nicht fertig, Kinder? ❹ Vorsicht! Dort kommt eine Krabbe. ❺ Das ist leider nicht möglich, wir haben keine Zeit.

2 Come (*informal pl.*) quickly, the taxi is waiting.
3 – We're ready, but the suitcase won't shut (*shuts not*).
4 – How is that possible?
5 Show [me]! (*Show[informal pl.] once!*)
6 Yuck, what is that (*then*)?
7 – Careful, they are (*these are the*) crabs – they are alive (*these live still*)!

6 Iiii! is an exclamation expressing distaste. The degree of distaste is conveyed by the tone and insistence with which it is uttered. As the saying goes, **Der Ton macht die Musik!** *It's not what you say, but how you say it!*

7 v is normally pronounced as *f*: **viel** *feel*, **vier** *fee*^{a} (except in words of foreign origin: **bravo** ***brah****vo*).

▸ whose gender isn't obvious. For example, **die Ratte** can refer to a male or a female rat. With regard to cats, **die Katze** *the cat* is used, unless it is clear that the cat is undoubtedly male, in which case it would be **der Kater** *the tomcat*. Nearly all feminine nouns referring to animals end in **-e** and form the plural by adding **-n**: **die Katze, die Katzen, die Ratte, die Ratten**. Good news, isn't it?

⑤ Here **die** is the demonstrative pronoun *these* or *those*. Most forms of this pronoun are identical to those of the definite article. In spoken German, it is often used instead of the personal pronoun (e.g. *he, she, they*, etc.): **Die Kinder? Die sind nicht zu Hause.** *The kids? They* (These) *are not at home.* **Klaus? Der ist nicht hier!** *Klaus? He* (This-one) *is not here!*

***

Answers to Exercise 1

❶ Wait *(pl.)* here! I'll call a taxi. ❷ You have [some] crabs? Show me! ❸ Why are you not ready yet, children? ❹ Careful! Here comes a crab. ❺ That is unfortunately not possible; we don't have time.

sechsundfünfzig *[zeks*unt-*fewnftsikH]*

14   Übung 2 – Ergänzen Sie bitte!

❶ Children, why are you alone? Where is Mum?
   Kinder, warum .... allein? .. ist Mama?

❷ I won't eat these crabs (*I eat the crabs not*); they are still alive (*these live still*).
   ... . die Krabben nicht, die ..... noch.

❸ Hurry up (*Make [informal pl.] quickly*), the taxi is coming right away.
   ...., das Taxi ..... gleich.

❹ Yuck, what is that (*then*)? Show (*informal pl.*) [me]!
   Iiii, ... denn? ..... mal!

❺ The suitcase is very big and it closes well.
   ... . ist sehr groß und .. .. gut.

---

14   Vierzehnte Lektion *(fee^atsehntuh lektsiohn)*

Wiederholung – Review

1 Verb conjugation

While English has dropped most of its verb endings over the centuries, German has retained specific endings that link the verb with the subject in terms of person (first-, second- or third-person) and number (singular or plural). First-person refers to who is speaking (**ich** *I*; **wir** *we*); second-person to who is spoken to (**du** *you* [sing.]; **ihr** *you* [plural]); and third-person to who or what is being spoken about (**er/sie/es** *he/she/it*; **sie** *they*). For formal address, German uses the third-person plural **Sie** (with a capital **S**) for *you*, singular and plural.

The conjugations are formed by adding a verb ending to the stem of the verb after taking off the infinitive ending **-en**. In the present tense, the first-person singular ends in **-e**, the second-person in **-st** and the third-person in **-t**. In the plural, the first- and third-person verb forms are identical to the infinitive, and the second-person

57 • siebenundfünfzig *[zeeb'nunt-fewnftsikH]*

Answers to Exercise 2

❶ – seid ihr – Wo – ❷ Ich esse – leben – ❸ Macht schnell – kommt –
❹ – was ist das – Zeigt – ❺ Der Koffer – er schließt –

Coming up in the next lesson is your second review. If you have time, read the German in the last six lessons out loud before moving on. The more you practice, the better. You could note down new vocabulary words, but don't forget to include the article for each new noun so you can remember its gender. Use the glossary if you need any help.

Fourteenth lesson 14

verb form ends in **-t** (just like the third-person singular). However, notice the irregularities in **haben** and **sein** below:

	kommen *to come*	**warten** *to wait*	**haben** *to have*		**sein** *to be*
ich	komme	warte	habe	but	bin
du	kommst	wartest	hast		bist
er, sie, es	kommt	wartet	hat		ist
wir	kommen	warten	haben		sind
ihr	kommt	wartet	habt		seid
sie	kommen	warten	haben		sind
Sie	kommen	warten	haben		sind

Remember that the second-person plural, **ihr** *you*, is used to address several people informally; in formal situations (no matter how many people you're addressing), use **Sie**!

2 The nominative case of articles

In lesson 6, we briefly mentioned that certain words in German change form, or 'decline', depending on their function in a sentence. To explain this further, remember that a noun, for example, can function in a sentence as a subject, a direct object, an indirect object, or it can denote possession or a close relationship. Each of these functions corresponds to a particular case in German. If a noun is the subject of a sentence or phrase, it is in the nominative case. If it is the direct object, it is in the accusative case. Altogether, there are four cases in German. The complete set of inflections (or variations) of a word in a particular case is called a declension. There is more information about this in the grammatical appendix.

By now you will be starting to get to grips with the three grammatical genders in German, and the impact of a noun's gender on other words associated with it, such as articles. Case adds yet another layer of complexity to this, but don't be discouraged – we'll take it slowly! When a noun is in the nominative case, the definite article (*the*) associated with it is either **der** (m.), **die** (f.) or **das** (neuter) in the singular; in the plural, there is only one definite article (**die**) for all three genders in the nominative case. As for the indefinite article (*a/an*) with a singular nominative noun, **ein** and the negative **kein** *no*, *not a/an*, *not any*, are the same in the masculine and neuter – the feminine forms are **eine** and **keine**.

Nominative case:

	Singular			Plural
	masc.	fem.	neuter	
definite article	der	die	das	die
indefinite article	ein	eine	ein	-
negative article	kein	keine	kein	keine

Unfortunately, the gender of a German noun is rarely predictable or intuitive: **der Platz** *the place*, **die Zeit** *the time*, **das Haus** *the house* … Hence, don't forget to learn nouns with their respective articles.

3 Negation

In German, there are a number of ways of making a statement or question negative. One of them, mentioned above, is the negative article **kein(e)**, which is used to negate a noun and can have different nuances of meaning, depending on context: *no, not a, none, not any, no one, nobody*: **Hat er ein Haus?** *Does he have a house?* – **Nein, er hat kein Haus.** *No, he has no house.* (In English, in this example, we would often make the verb negative instead: 'No, he doesn't have a house.') In short, **kein(e)** is used to negate a noun that – in a positive sentence – would be preceded by an indefinite article or no article.

However, if a noun is preceded by a definite article, **nicht** *not* is used as negation. **Nicht** can occupy different positions. It can occur at the end of the sentence (**Ich mache die Übungen nicht.** *I do not do the exercises.*) or before the word (or group of words) being negated: **Der Platz ist nicht frei.** *The place is not free.* **Wir gehen nicht in die Oper.** *We're not going to the opera.*

The question when to use **nicht** or **kein(e)** may seem daunting, but the rule for applying them is really quite simple:

• no article or indefinite article + noun → **kein(e)**
Das sind Katzen. *These are cats.*
Nein, das sind keine Katzen. *No, these are not cats.*
Das ist eine Katze. *This is a cat.*
Nein, das ist keine Katze. *No, this is not a cat.*

• definite article + noun → **nicht**
Ist das die Katze von Peter? *Is this Peter's cat?*
Nein, das ist nicht die Katze von Peter. *No, this is not Peter's cat.*

Nicht is also used to negate verbs, but we'll find out more about this later. Also, note that unlike in English, the combination *not + a/an* does not exist in German!

That's enough grammar for the time being. Perhaps you still have some questions? Don't worry, that's normal! We still have a lot more interesting lessons to come! You can relax now and enjoy the final dialogue. Nothing beats practice when it comes to learning a language. **Wir wünschen Ihnen viel Vergnügen!** We wish you 'much pleasure'!

15 Review exercise
Warum bleibt er allein?

1 – Was machst du denn heute, Thomas?
2 – Ich gehe in die Stadt.
3 – Gehst du allein?
4 – Nein, Julia kommt mit.
5 – Ihr habt Glück, ihr seid zusammen.
6   Ich bin immer allein. Warum?
7 – Also komm mit!
8 – Ja, warum nicht?
9   Was machen wir denn dort?
10 – Geschäfte ansehen, ein Bier trinken, oder zwei …
11 – Ach, ich habe kein Geld.
12   Ich bleibe zu Haus und lerne Deutsch.

---

15   Fünfzehnte Lektion *[fewnftsehntuh lektsiohn]*

Entschuldigen Sie ① bitte, ich habe eine Frage…

1 – Wo ist bitte eine U-Bahn-Station ②?

Pronunciation
entshuldig'n zee bituh ikH habuh einuh frahguh 1 voh ist bituh einuh oo-bahn-shtatsiohn

Notes

① Remember that in the formal imperative, the pronoun **Sie** must be included and must directly follow the verb: **Entschuldigen Sie!** *Excuse [me]!* (the 'me' is understood). **Warten Sie!** *Wait!* However, informal imperatives are formed without a pronoun: **entschuldige** *excuse [me]* is the second-person singular ▶

Translation
Why does he stay alone?

1 What are you doing *(then)* today, Thomas? **2** I'm going into town. **3** Are you going on your own *(alone)*? **4** No, Julia is coming along *(comes with)*. **5** You *(pl.)* are lucky, you are together. **6** I am always alone. Why? **7** So come with [us]! **8** Yes, why not? **9** What [will] we do there? **10** Check out [the] shops, drink a beer or two … **11** Oh, I don't have [any] money. **12** I [will] stay at home and learn German.

Tschüs und bis morgen! *Bye and see you tomorrow!*

Fifteenth lesson 15

Excuse [me], please, I have a question …

1 – Where is [there] a subway station, please?

▶ informal ('**du**-imperative') and **entschuldigt** *excuse [me]* is the second-person plural informal ('**ihr**-imperative').

② The **U** in **U-Bahn** *subway, underground* comes from **der Untergrund** *the underground* and **die Bahn** means *the train, track* or *road*. So **die U-Bahn** is literally 'the underground train' and **die Straßenbahn** *the tram*, 'the street train'.

zweiundsechzig *[tsveiunt-zekHtsikH]* • 62

15   2 – **A**ber hier gibt es ③ **kei**ne **U**-Bahn, nur **ei**ne **Straß**enbahn.
   3 – **A**ch so! Wo ist denn dann **bi**tte die **Straß**enbahn**hal**testelle?
   4 – **Al**so, da **geh**en Sie ④ **gerade**aus und die **zwei**te **Straß**e rechts,
   5   dann die **ers**te **Straß**e links ⑤ und dort **seh**en Sie schon die **Hal**testelle.
   6 – **Vi**elen Dank ⑥ für die **Aus**kunft.
   7 – **Kei**ne **Ur**sache!

---

2 ahb^a hee^a gipt es keinuh oo-bahn noo^a einuh shtrahss'n-bahn 3 akh zoh! voh ist den dan bituh dee shtrahss'n-bahn-haltuh-shteluh 4 alzoh dah geh-uhn zee guhrahduh-ows unt dee tsveituh shtrahssuh rekHts 5 dan dee eh^astuh shtrahssuh links unt dort zeh-uhn zee shon dee haltuh-shteluh 6 feel'n dank few^a dee owskunft 7 keinuh oo^azakhuh

Pronunciation notes
3 Don't be afraid of long compound words! Try pronouncing them element by element first: **Straßen-bahn-halte-stelle**.

Notes

③ The impersonal expression **es gibt** *there is*, *there are* (literally, 'it gives') is more common in English than in German, which often just uses **sein** *to be* or other verbs instead: **Ist hier keine U-Bahn-Station?** *Is [there] no subway station here?* The expression **es gibt** contains the third-person singular form of **geben** *to give*, which is an irregular verb; the vowel in the verb stem changes. In the present tense, this change only occurs in the second- and third-person singular forms: **ich gebe** *I give*, but **du gibst** *you give* and **er/sie/es gibt** *he/she/it gives*. The plural forms are regular.

④ Remember that in German the verb comes before the subject not only in imperatives and questions, but also when the first element in a statement is not the subject: **Dann gehst du geradeaus.** *Then you go straight ahead.* ('Then go you straight ▶

63 • dreiundsechzig *[drei*unt-zekHtsikH*]*

2 – There is no subway here (*But here there is no subway*), just a tram.
3 – Oh, I see! In that case, where is (*Where is in-that-case then*) the tram stop (*street-train-stopping-place*), please?
4 – Well, you go (*there go you[formal]*) straight ahead and [you take] the second street [on the] right,
5 then the first street [on the] left and there you [will] see (*already*) the stop.
6 – Many thanks for the information.
7 – You're welcome (*No cause*).

Remember, in compound nouns, the first constituent carries the primary (i.e. main) stress: **Stra**ßenbahn**hal**testelle (see lesson 8).
4 geradeaus consists of **gerade** and the preposition **aus**, which you have already come across. Here, the main stress is on **aus**.
4, 5 Remember the letter **ß** replaces a double **ss** after a long vowel and is pronounced *ss* (see lesson 3).
5 At the beginning of a word, **st** is pronounced *sht*: **Straße shtrah**ssuh. However, when **st** occurs in the middle of a word, it is normally pronounced *st*: **erste eh**ᵃ*stuh*.

ahead.') This keeps the verb in the second position. Another example of what is called 'inverted word order', i.e. when something other than the subject is in the first position and the subject follows the verb, can be found in the statement **hier gibt es keine U-Bahn** in line 2. It begins with an expression of place (**hier**), followed by the verb (**gibt**) and the subject (**es**). We'll come back to this later.

⑤ Normally, **links** *[on or to the] left* and **rechts** *[on or to the] right* are used without prepositions in German. **Links ist die Oper und rechts sehen Sie das Café Kranzler.** *[On the] left is the opera, and [on the] right you['ll] see the Café Kranzler.*

⑥ Unlike **danke** *thank you*, the noun **der Dank** *the thanks* doesn't end in **-e**.

vierundsechzig *[fee*ᵃ*unt-zekHtsikH]* • 64

15 Übung 1 – Übersetzen Sie bitte!

❶ Entschuldigen Sie, wo ist bitte die Oper? ❷ Gehen Sie die zweite Straße links. ❸ Gibt es hier keine U-Bahn? ❹ Die Straßenbahnhaltestelle ist gleich rechts. ❺ Die U-Bahn-Station ist heute geschlossen.

***

Übung 2 – Ergänzen Sie bitte!

❶ Here there is no subway, but a tram.
Hier .... .. keine U-Bahn, aber ....

❷ Excuse (*formal*) [me], I have a question – where is there a café here (*where is here a café*)?
...., ich habe .... – .. ... hier ein Café?

❸ You go right and then [keep] (*always*) straight ahead.
Sie gehen ...... und dann immer ....

❹ Many thanks for the information.
Vielen .... für ... .

❺ Take (*Go*) the second street [on the] left; the opera is just [on the] right.
Gehen Sie ... . links, die Oper ... . rechts.

Answers to Exercise 1

❶ Excuse me, where is the opera, please? ❷ Take (*Go*) the second street on the left. ❸ Is there no subway here? ❹ The tram stop is immediately to the right. ❺ The subway station is closed today.

***

Answers to Exercice 2

❶ – gibt es – eine Straßenbahn ❷ Entschuldigen Sie – eine Frage, wo ist – ❸ – rechts – geradeaus ❹ – Dank – die Auskunft ❺ – die zweite Straße – ist gleich –

Don't be too perfectionist in the first few lessons. Just repeat the sentences in each lesson aloud several times and try to understand them. You don't have to construct sentences yourself just yet. This will come in the second part of the book.

16 Sechzehnte Lektion [zekHtsehntuh lektsiohn]

Warum vergeht die Zeit so schnell?

1 – Um wie viel Uhr fährt dein Zug **ab** ①?
2 – In drei Mi**nu**ten, um **sech**zehn Uhr **acht**zehn ②, Gleis zwölf.
3 – Das ist hier.
4   Komm, steig schnell **ein** ③!
5 – „**Ach**tung ④ an Gleis zwölf, die **Tü**ren **schließen**.

Pronunciation
*varum fer**geht** dee tseit zoh shnel **1** um vee feel oo[a] feh[a]t dein tsook **ap 2** in drei mi**noo**t'n um **zekH**-tsehn oo[a] **akht**-tsehn gleis tsvœlf **3** das ist hee[a] **4** kom shteik shnel **ein 5 akh**tung an gleis tsvœlf dee **tew**ruhn **shlee**ss'n*

Notes

① **fahren** *to drive*, *to go by train*, *car or other means of transport* (but not on foot!); **abfahren** *to leave*, *to depart*, *to take off*. The separable prefix **ab** often expresses a sense of detachment, distance or removal from something. Note that the vowel **a** in the verb stem changes to **ä** in the second- and third-person singular: **du fährst**, **er/sie/es fährt**. The other present-tense forms are entirely regular: **ich fahre**, etc.

② German numbers from 13 to 19 follow a similar pattern to English. They are formed by adding **-zehn** (*ten*) to the appropriate number: **dreizehn** ('three-ten' = *thirteen*), **vierzehn**, etc. For more information on numbers, take a quick glance at review lesson 21. Note that 'am' and 'pm' are not used. The 24-hour clock is the norm for timetables and official schedules, while the 12-hour clock is often used in everyday language. So, 4 pm would be **sechzehn Uhr** ('sixteen clock') ▶

Sixteenth lesson 16

Why does time pass (*Why passes the time*) so quickly?

1 – What time does your train leave? (*At how much clock leaves your[informal sing.] train?*)
2 – In three minutes, at sixteen (*clock*) eighteen, [on] platform twelve.
3 – That's here.
4 Come, get in quickly (*get quickly in*)!
5 – "Attention at platform twelve, the doors are closing.

Pronunciation note
1, **4**, **6** Note that in spoken German, the stress falls on the separable prefix, as we see in these sentences with the verbs <u>**ab**</u>**fahren** and <u>**ein**</u>**steigen**: **Der Zug fährt <u>ab</u>, steigen Sie bitte <u>ein</u>!** This is because the prefix determines the meaning of the verb.

▶ or **vier Uhr** ('four clock'). In order to express an exact time, you need the word **um**: **um fünfzehn Uhr** *at three o'clock* ('at fifteen clock'). The same holds true for asking the time: **Um wie viel Uhr?** *At what time?* ('At how much clock?').

③ This dialogue has several examples of the second-person singular informal imperative ('**du**-imperative'), as it's a conversation between a couple. It is formed by dropping the final **-en** from the infinitive: **Komm!** *Come!* **Steig ein!** *Get on! Board!* (e.g. the train). One could add a final **-e** to the verb here, but this is increasingly left out. The opposite of **einsteigen** is **aussteigen**. **Steig aus!** *Get off! Alight!* See how important the separable prefix is?

④ **die Achtung** *the attention* is synonymous with **die Vorsicht** when trying to direct someone's attention to a possible danger. **Achtung!** or **Vorsicht!** *Careful!*

achtundsechzig *[akht*unt-zekHtsikH] • 68

6 Der Zug nach Han**no**ver fährt **ab**."

7 – **Gu**te **Rei**se! Und ver**giss** ⑤ nicht: ich **lie**be dich ⑥!

8 – **War**te ⑦, gib mir noch **ei**nen Kuss ⑧!

6 deh^a tsook nakh hanoh^fa feh^at ap 7 gootuh reizuh! unt fergiss nikHt ikH leebuh dikH 8 vartuh gip meer nokh einuhn kuss

Notes

⑤ **vergessen** *to forget* is an irregular verb. Just as with **geben** *to give*, the vowel of the verb stem changes to **i** in the second- and third-person singular and the singular informal imperative: **Vergiss!** *Forget!* **Gib!** *Give!* If there is a stem-vowel change from **e** to **i** or **ie** in the second- and third-person singular forms of a verb, the singular informal imperative has this vowel change, too, but never has a final **-e**: **Sieh mal!** *Look (once)!*

⑥ **du** *you* (informal sing.) becomes **dich** in the accusative case, i.e. when used as a direct object (the person or thing that directly receives the action of the verb).

⑦ If a verb stem ends in **-t**, the singular informal imperative must include a final **-e**: **Warte!** *Wait!*, **Antworte!** *Reply!*

⑧ **ich** *I* becomes **mich** in the accusative case, i.e. when used as a direct object, and **mir** in the dative case, i.e. when used as ▶

***

Übung 1 – Übersetzen Sie bitte!

❶ Um wie viel Uhr fährt der Zug nach Berlin ab? ❷ Thomas hat einen Platz für die Oper heute Abend. ❸ Gute Reise! Ruf mich von Berlin an! ❹ Gibst du mir noch einen Kuss? ❺ Warte! Ich nehme auch den Zug nach Hannover.

6 The train to Hanover is departing (*leaves*)."
7 – [Have a] good journey! And don't forget: I love you!
8 – Wait, give (*to-*) me another kiss!

▶ an indirect object (what indirectly receives the action of the verb, usually a person): **Gib mir einen Kuss.** *Give* (informal sing.) *me a kiss*. (The function of the object pronouns is easier to understand if this is rephrased: 'Give a kiss to me.') **Kuss** *kiss* is a masculine noun, so its definite article is **der** and its indefinite article **ein** when it is the subject of a sentence (i.e. in the nominative case): **Ein Kuss ist nicht genug.** *A kiss is not enough*. However, when a noun functions as a direct object in a sentence, it is in the accusative case, as are any articles used with it: **ein** becomes **einen** and **der** changes to **den**: **Ich möchte bitte einen Kuss.** *I would like a kiss, please*. **Nehmen Sie den Zug?** *Are you taking the train?* The good news is that only the singular masculine articles change in the accusative. The articles **die** (f. sing. & all plurals), **eine** (f.) and **das**, **ein** (n.) don't change in the accusative.

***

Answers to Exercise 1

❶ What time does the train for Berlin leave? ❷ Thomas has a ticket (*place*) for the opera this evening. ❸ [Have a] good journey! Call me from Berlin! ❹ [Will you] give me another kiss? ❺ Wait! I'm also taking the train to Hanover.

16 Übung 2 – Ergänzen Sie bitte!

❶ Attention, the doors are closing, board (*formal pl.*) [the train] quickly, please!

......., die Türen ...., ... bitte schnell ... !

❷ Don't forget me! I love you!

.... mich .....! ... . dich!

❸ The train for Cologne leaves at 3:14 [pm] (*fifteen clock fourteen*).

... ... nach Köln ..... um fünfzehn Uhr vierzehn ...

❹ We get the train at 4:15 [pm] (*sixteen clock fifteen*) – that's in ten minutes.

Wir nehmen ... ... um .... Uhr ...., das ist .. ..

❺ What time (*At how much clock*) are you travelling to Hanover?

.. .. fahren Sie .... Hannover?

***

A republic of states
The city of Hanover is considered part of northern Germany, though it is located roughly 300 kilometres south of Hamburg. Destroyed during World War II, Hanover is neither particularly big nor particularly famous today. However, it is the capital of a **Land**, *which is a state. When you look at a map of Germany, you'll see many internal borders: they delineate the 16* **Länder**, *or states of the* **Bundesrepublik Deutschland** *the Federal Republic of Germany. Each* **Land** *has its own capital city. Thus* **Hannover** *Hanover is the capital of* **Niedersachsen** *Lower Saxony,* **München** *Munich is the capital of* **Bayern** *Bavaria, and* **Hamburg** *is the*

Answers to Exercise 2

❶ Achtung – schließen, steigen Sie – ein ❷ Vergiss – nicht – Ich liebe – ❸ Der Zug – fährt – ab ❹ – den Zug – sechzehn – fünfzehn – in zehn Minuten ❺ Um wie viel Uhr – nach –

***

capital of ... **Hamburg**. *It is one of three cities that are states in their own right:* **Hamburg**, **Bremen** *and* **Berlin**. *The* **Länder** *each have their own constitutions, but they are also required to abide by federal law. Although you can cross the borders between the* **Länder** *without realizing it, when you're in a pub (***eine Kneipe***) in Berlin, Dresden, Munich or Frankfurt, the differences are quite noticeable – and above all audible. Each city has its distinct terms for bread rolls, beer and* **Schnaps** *(a clear alcoholic beverage distilled from fruit or grain), its own way of welcoming you, and so on. If you're visiting the different* **Länder**, *look out for what makes them distinctive!*

17 Siebzehnte Lektion [zeeptsehntuh lektsiohn]

Zahlen ① machen ② müde

1 Ein Jahr hat zwölf **Mo**nate.
2 Ein **Mo**nat hat **drei**ßig **o**der **ein**und**drei**ßig ③ **Ta**ge.
3 Pro Tag schläft man ④ acht **Stun**den ⑤.

> **Pronunciation**
> tsahluhn makh'n mewduh **1** ein yah[a] hat tsvœlf **moh**natuh
> **2** ein **moh**nat hat **drei**ssikH od[a] **ein**-unt-**drei**ssikH **tah**guh
> **3** proh tahk shlehft man akht **shtun**duhn

Notes

① **die Zahl** *the number, numeral* is a feminine noun. Always try to learn a noun with its definite article! By the way, **bezahlen** or **zahlen** *to pay* derive from **Zahl**, as does **zählen** *to count*.

② **machen** *to do, to make* can be used with adjectives: **müde machen** *to make tired, to tire*, **glücklich machen** *to make happy*, etc.

③ One of the biggest difficulties English speakers experience with German numbers is that the numbers between 21 and 99 appear to be formed 'backwards'. What in English is *twenty-six* is **sechsundzwanzig** in German: 'six-and-twenty'. The smaller number comes first, followed by **und**, and then the larger number: **einundzwanzig** ('one-and-twenty'), **fünfundachtzig** ('five-and-eighty'). To make a number above 100 all you do is add the word for 100, 200, 300, etc. in front: **dreihundertfünf-undsechzig** *three hundred and sixty-five* ('three-hundred-five-and-sixty'). There's more about numbers in lesson 21. ▶

Seventeenth lesson 17

Numbers make [you] tired

1. A year has twelve months.
2. A month has thirty or thirty-one (*one-and-thirty*) days.
3. One sleeps eight hours per day (*Per day sleeps one eight hours*).

Ein Jahr hat zwölf Monate und dreihundertfünfundsechzig Tage.

④ The indefinite or impersonal pronoun **man** is usually used when the subject is unknown or you don't want to define it. In English, 'one', 'people' and the impersonal 'you' are used for this purpose: **Man macht das nicht.** *One doesn't/You don't do that.*

⑤ **die Stunde** *the hour* expresses a time span: **Eine Stunde hat sechzig Minuten.** *An hour has sixty minutes.* As we saw in the last lesson, **die Uhr** *the clock*, *watch* can also mean 'hour', but only in the sense of giving the time: **um fünf Uhr** *at five o'clock*. Whenever you're talking about the time, you should use **Uhr**, which is always singular in this case. In contrast, **Stunde** becomes plural if you talk about durations of more than one and a half hours: **eineinhalb Stunden**.

vierundsiebzig *[fee^aunt-zeeptsikH]* • 74

17

4 **Neun**zig **Ja**hre ⑥, das macht **neun**zigmal **dreihun**dert**fünf**und**sech**zig **Ta**ge:
5 **al**so **zwei**und**drei**ßigtausend**acht**hundert-und**fünf**zig, und man schläft ⑦…
6 Mensch ⑧ bin ich **mü**de!
7 Ich **zäh**le **mor**gen **wei**ter ⑨.
8 **Gu**te Nacht!

---

*4 **noin**tsikH **yah**ruh das makht **noin**tsikHmahl **drei**-hund^{a}t-**fewnf**unt-**zekH**tsikH **tah**guh 5 **al**zoh **tsvei**unt-**drei**ssikH-**tow**zuhnt-**akht**-hund^{a}tunt-**fewnf**tsikH unt man shlehft 6 mensh bin ikH **mew**duh 7 ikH **tseh**luh **mor**g'n veit^a 8 **goo**tuh nakht*

Pronunciation notes
4, 5 Numbers – even long ones, as you can see in this lesson – are usually written out as one word in German. In compound words

Notes

⑥ **das Jahr** *the year*, **der Monat** *the month*, **die Stunde** *the hour*. Remember that the definite article in the plural is always **die**: **die Jahre**, **die Monate**, **die Stunden**. Use the glossary at the end of the book if you need to check the gender and the plural forms of nouns.

⑦ **schlafen** *to sleep* is conjugated like **fahren** (lesson 16, note 1): **ich schlafe**, but **du schläfst**, **er/sie/es schläft**.

⑧ **Mensch** is a widely used familiar interjection that allows you to express – depending on the intonation – all emotions and feelings known to humankind … in fact, **der Mensch** means ▶

4 Ninety years, that makes ninety times three hundred and sixty-five days:
5 so, thirty-two thousand eight hundred and fifty, and one sleeps …
6 Boy (*Man*), am I tired!
7 I['ll] continue counting tomorrow (*I count tomorrow further*).
8 Good night!

there is usually one syllable that carries the primary stress while others receive a secondary stress. In contrast, long numbers (i.e. those with more than one element) may have several equal stresses, e.g. in **zwei**und**drei**ßig**tau**send**acht**hundert**fünf**zig, which is far from being the longest possible number, by the way ... We'll come back to this in review lesson 21.
7 Note that the two dots above the **a** (the **Umlaut**) are the sole difference between **zählen** and **zahlen**. Make sure to pronounce the **ä** as a long, open vowel.

mankind or *humankind*. German distinguishes between 'man' in general (i.e. a human being, a person): **der Mensch** (plural: **die Menschen**), and a man: **der Mann** (plural: **die Männer**). The interjection **Mensch!** can mean many things depending on the context: *Man!*, *Boy!*, *Hey!* and even *Come on!*

⑨ As a separable prefix, **weiter** (literally, 'further') translates as *continue to*: **zählen** *to count* → **weiterzählen** *to continue to count*; **schlafen** *sleep* → **weiterschlafen** *to continue to sleep*, **weitermachen** *to continue to do* (or simply 'to continue').

sechsundsiebzig *[zeksunt-zeeptsikH]* • 76

Übung 1 – Übersetzen Sie bitte!

❶ Wir machen die Übungen morgen weiter. ❷ Ein Jahr hat zwölf Monate und dreihundertfünfundsechzig Tage. ❸ Man schläft zweihundertvierzig Stunden pro Monat. ❹ Kinder, ich zähle bis drei und dann schlaft ihr! ❺ Mensch, macht schnell, der Zug wartet nicht!

***

Übung 2 – Ergänzen Sie bitte!

❶ One doesn't do that (*That does one not*).
Das .... nicht.

❷ I would like (*gladly*) to sleep. Good night!
Ich möchte gern .... !

❸ A day has twenty-four hours.
Ein Tag hat ....

❹ He sleeps twelve hours per night, and at the office he continues to sleep.
.. .. zwölf Stunden ... Nacht und im Büro ....

❺ Seven is a lucky number (*The number seven brings luck*).
... . sieben ...... Glück.

Answers to Exercise 1

❶ We [will] continue the exercises tomorrow. ❷ A year has twelve months and three hundred and sixty-five days. ❸ One sleeps two hundred and forty hours per month. ❹ Children, I [will] count to three and then you [will] sleep! ❺ Come on (*Man*), hurry up (*make quickly*) – the train won't wait!

***

Answers to Exercise 2

❶ – macht man – ❷ – schlafen – Gute Nacht ❸ – vierundzwanzig Stunden ❹ Er schläft – pro – schläft er weiter ❺ Die Zahl – bringt –

Are you disappointed because you thought you'd be practicing the accusative in this lesson and you haven't come across a single example? In fact you have! This lesson has a number of nouns in the accusative, for example: **Ein Jahr hat zwölf <u>Monate</u>.** *If you haven't spotted them, it's because feminine, neuter and plural nouns don't change in the accusative.*

18 Achtzehnte Lektion [akhtsehntuh lektsiohn]

Eine Postkarte aus München

1 **Lie**be ① **Mu**tti ②! Wie geht's dir?
2 Hier läuft ③ **al**les fan**tas**tisch.
3 Mein **Zim**mer ist groß und schön und die **Uni** ④ ist nicht weit.
4 **Näch**ste ⑤ **Wo**che **seh**e ich **mei**nen ⑥ Pro**fes**sor.

> **Pronunciation**
> *einuh **post**-kartuh ows **mewn**kH'n **1 lee**buh **mu**ti! vee gehts dee^a **2** hee^a loift **al**es fan**tas**tish **3** mein **tsim**^{a} ist grohs unt shœn unt dee **u**ni ist nikHt veit **4 nekH**stuh **vo**khuh **zeh**-uh ikH **mei**nuhn pro**fes**sor*

Notes

① **lieb** *dear*, *sweet*, *good* (in the sense of well behaved) derives from the verb **lieben** *to love*, but used as a form of address in a letter or postcard, **Liebe** means 'Dear …' (when addressing a woman – see the information at the end of the lesson).

② **Mutti** is an abbreviation for **die Mutter** *the mother*; likewise **Vati** is an abbreviation for **der Vater**. **Mama** and **Papa** are also commonly used.

③ **laufen** can mean *to run*, *to go*, *to walk* but also *to work* (e.g. a machine or a plan), depending on the context. It is conjugated like **fahren** and **schlafen** (see note 7, lesson 17). It is also possible to say **Hier geht alles gut.** *All is going well here.*

④ **Uni** is a colloquial abbreviation for **die Universität**.

⑤ In lesson 3, we mentioned that adjectives (words that describe, modify or qualify a noun or a pronoun) can appear in different ways in German. We've already seen examples of adjectives that occur after forms of **sein** *to be* and do not change (i.e. do not take endings). These are called 'predicate adjectives'. ▶

Eighteenth lesson   18

A postcard from Munich

1   Dear (*f.*) Mum! How are you (*How goes-it for-you[informal]*)?
2   Here, everything is going brilliantly (*runs all fantastically*).
3   My room is big and lovely (*beautiful*), and the university isn't far.
4   Next week, I [will] see (*see I*) my professor.

Pronunciation notes
3, 7 Note that the **ö**-sound in **schön** *shœn* and the **ü**-sound in **Grüße** *grewssuh* are long here.
4 nächst- is often pronounced *nekst-* instead of *nekHst-* .

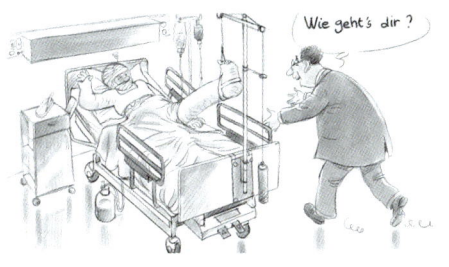

> There are also 'attributive adjectives', which are adjectives that precede the nouns they modify. Attributive adjectives do have endings: **nächste Woche** *next week*. We'll look at adjective endings in more detail later. For now, just note that an attributive adjective takes an **-e** ending: **nette Kollegen** *nice colleagues*, whereas a predicate adjective does not: **Die Kollegen sind nett.** *The colleagues are nice.*

⑥ In the same way that **ein** *a/an* becomes **einen** in the masculine accusative, **mein** *my* becomes **meinen** (in this sentence **Professor** is a direct object, so takes the accusative).

achtzig *[akhtsikH]* • 80

5 Man sagt, er sieht gut aus ⑦ und ist nett.
6 Ich bin ein **biss**chen **auf**geregt.
7 **Vie**le **lie**be **Grü**ße ⑧,
8 **Dei**ne **Me**lani.

*5 man zahkt eh^a zeet goot ows unt ist net 6 ikH bin ein **biss**-kH'n **owf**guhrehkt 7 **fee**luh **lee**buh **grew**ssuh 8 **dein**uh **me**lani*

Notes

⑦ **aussehen** *to look* (as in *to appear*) derives from **sehen** *to see, to behold*. The stem vowel **e** changes to **ie** in the second- and third-person and in the singular informal imperative: **Sieh mal!** *Look!* **Du siehst müde aus.** *You look tired.* **Sie sieht gut aus.** *She looks good.* or *She is good-looking.* Note that this phrase can mean either that someone is attractive or that they look well at a particular point in time.

***

Übung 1 – Übersetzen Sie bitte!

❶ Frau Bachmann sieht heute sehr gut aus. ❷ Wir fahren nächste Woche in Ferien. ❸ Wie geht es dir, Melanie? ❹ Wann siehst du deinen Professor das nächste Mal? ❺ Das Hotel ist gut, die Zimmer sind schön.

***

Übung 2 – Ergänzen Sie bitte!

❶ Why are you (*informal sing.*) running (*then*)? Are you in a hurry (*Have you no time*)?
   Warum . . . . denn? . . . . . . keine Zeit?

❷ Next week we [will] see (*see we*) the professor (*m.*).
   . . . . sehen wir . . . .

❸ Dear Mrs Spielberg, how are you (*formal*)?
   . . . . . Frau Spielberg, ... Ihnen?

81 • einundachtzig *[ein*unt-akhtsikH*]*

5 People say [that] he's good-looking (*looks good*) and is nice.
6 I am a little nervous (*excited*).
7 Love (*Many dear greeting*s),
8 (*Your[f.]*) Melanie.

6 It is often said that **bisschen** isn't easy to pronounce. That's not true! First, say **biss** without thinking about the ending **-chen**. Then say **-chen**: ***biss**-kH'n*. That's it!

***

⑧ When **viel** *much, many, a lot* is used before an uncountable noun in the singular, it doesn't take an ending: **Er hat nicht viel Geld.** *He doesn't have much money.* However, when used with a countable noun in the plural, it takes an ending: **Sie haben viele Freunde.** *They have many friends.* We'll come back to this later. The noun **der Gruß**, **die Grüße** *the greeting, the greetings* comes from **grüßen** *to greet, to welcome*.

***

Answers to Exercise 1

❶ Mrs Bachman looks very good today. ❷ We [will] go (*drive*) on holiday next week. ❸ How are you, Melanie? ❹ When will you next see your professor? ❺ The hotel is good; the rooms are lovely (*beautiful*).

***

❹ You (*informal sing.*) look tired – sleep a little!
.. .. müde ..., schlaf ... . !

❺ See you soon! Love (*Many greetings*), (*your [m.]*) Thomas.
Bis bald! ...., ... Thomas.

Answers to Exercise 2

❶ – läufst du – Hast du – ❷ Nächste Woche – den Professor ❸ Liebe – wie geht es – ❹ Du siehst – aus – ein bisschen ❺ – Viele Grüße, dein –

zweiundachtzig *[tsveiunt-akhtsikH]* • 82

19 | *Salutations in letters*
The standard way of addressing friends in personal correspondence is **Liebe Susanne** *(to a woman),* **Lieber Paul** *(to a man),* **Liebe Freunde** *(to more than one person), i.e.* Dear … *More colloquially, you can write* **Hallo Susanne**, **Hi Paul**. *If this is still too traditional or stuffy for you, you'll have to wait a bit until your knowledge of German allows you to be more imaginative.*

Salutations at the end of a letter equally vary depending on who you are addressing and the relationship you have with them. The standard expression is **viele Grüße**, *which means 'many greetings'. From there, you can give free rein to your imagination. You could,*

19 Neunzehnte Lektion *[nointsehntuh lektsiohn]*

Essen? Ja gern! Aber was?

1 – Jetzt **lau**fen wir schon zwei **Stun**den. ①
2   Sag mal, hast du **kei**nen **Hung**er ②?
3 – Doch ③, na**tür**lich, und auch Durst ④.

Pronunciation
ess'n? yah gern! **ahb**ᵃ *vas?* **1** *yetst* **lowf**'n veeᵃ *shon tsvei* **shtun**duhn **2** *zahk mahl hast doo* **kei**nuhn **hung**ᵃ **3** *dokh* na**tew**ᵃlikH *unt owkh durst*

Notes

① In previous lessons we've seen that the German present tense can function as the simple present ('I walk') as well as the present progressive ('I am walking') in English. Or when used with expressions such as **morgen** or **nächstes Jahr**, it can express that an action will take place in the future: **Ich komme morgen.** *I [will] come tomorrow.* In addition, to express continuing action (something that started in the past but is still going on), German often uses the present tense and words such as **schon** *already* or **seit** *since/for* where English uses the present perfect tense: **Ich arbeite seit zwei Stunden.** ('I work since two hours.') *I have been working for two hours.* ▶

for example, reinforce your greeting quantitatively: **Tausend Grüße** [A] thousand greetings, **Eine Million Grüße** A million greetings, *or you could reinforce it qualitatively:* **Liebe Grüße** Dear greetings, **Herzliche Grüße** Affectionate/Warm greetings. *Or you can combine the two:* **Tausend herzliche Grüße**, *etc. Moreover,* **herzlich** affectionate, warm *contains the word* **das Herz** the heart, *which you can be creative with:* **Viele tausend ♥-liche Grüße**. *Whatever you choose, don't forget to include* **dein** *your (if you're male),* **deine** *your (if you're female) or* **Ihr(e)** *your (formal masc./fem.), used when you're not on familiar terms with someone, before your name.*

Nineteenth lesson 19

Eat? Yes, gladly! But what?

1 – We've been walking for two hours now (*Now walk we already two hours*).

2 Say (*once*), aren't you hungry (*have you no hunger*)?

3 – Yes, of course (*naturally*), and [I'm] thirsty, too (*and also thirst*).

② Certain expressions without articles are negated using the negative article **kein**: **Zeit haben** *to have time*, **keine Zeit haben** *not to have time*, **Hunger haben** *to be hungry*, **keinen Hunger haben** *not to be hungry*. The **-en** ending in **keinen** tells you that **Hunger** is a masculine noun. The feminine ending is **-e** (**keine Zeit**). With a neuter noun, there is no ending: **kein** (**kein Geld**).

③ **Doch** *yes* is only used in response to a negative question. **Heißen Sie nicht Sonja?** *Aren't you called Sonja?* **Doch, natürlich, ich bin Sonja.** *Yes, of course, I am Sonja.* Otherwise, *yes* is **ja**.

④ **Durst** *thirst*, like **Hunger**, is a masculine noun. German frequently uses **haben** *to have* + noun in expressions that are constructed in English with *to be* + adjective: **Er hat Durst.** *He is thirsty.* **Er hat keinen Durst.** *He isn't thirsty.*

19
4 – Also, was **m**achen wir?
5 – **Kau**fen wir etwas zu ⑤ **e**ssen!
6 – Wo denn? Hier gibt es ⑥ **kei**nen **Su**permarkt, **kei**ne **Knei**pe – nichts.
7 – **Su**chen wir ⑦ eine **Tank**stelle!
8 – **Wozu** ⑧?
9 – Dort **fin**den wir **si**cher was ⑨.

*4 al*zoh vas **makh**'n vee^a *5 kowf*'n vee^a etvas tsoo **ess**'n *6* voh den? hee^a gipt es **kei**nuhn **zoo**p^a-markt **kei**nuh **knei**puh nikHts *7 zoo***kH**'n vee^a **ei**nuh **tank**-shteluh *8 vot***soo** *9* dort **fin**duhn vee^a **zikH**^{a} vas

Notes

⑤ When used immediately before an infinitive, **zu** means *to*. **Wir haben keine Zeit zu schlafen.** *We don't have time to sleep.* **Sie haben nichts zu trinken.** *They have nothing to drink.*

⑥ **es gibt** *there is/are* (the same expression is used in the singular and plural) requires the accusative case. **Es gibt einen Zug nach Berlin.** *There is a train to Berlin.* Did you notice that the order is swapped (line 6) to keep the verb in the second position? You may also have noticed from their articles that **Supermarkt** is masculine and **Kneipe** is feminine.

⑦ As you can see here, German has yet another form of the imperative: the '**wir**-imperative'. It is equivalent to the English 'Let's …' rather than being an order. It is formed very much like the formal imperative ('**Sie**-imperative'). You simply take the **wir** form of the present tense and put the pronoun directly after it: **Gehen wir!** *Let's go!* Like with the **Sie**-imperative, the pronoun can't be omitted.

85 • **fünfundachtzig** *[fewnfunt-akhtsikH]*

4 – Well, what are we going to do (*what do we*)?
5 – Let's buy (*Buy we*) something to eat.
6 – Where (*then*)? (*Here*) there is no supermarket, no pub – nothing.
7 – Let's look for (*Search we*) a service station.
8 – What for?
9 – There we['ll] certainly find (*find we certainly*) something.

Pronunciation notes
6 Only the final **-s** distinguishes **nichts** from **nicht**. So don't overlook it!
7 **die Tankstelle** is composed of the noun **die Stelle** (*the place*) and the verb **tanken** (*to fill up* [with petrol], *to (re)fuel*). Don't forget to pronounce the initial **s** of **stelle** as *sh*.

⑧ **Wozu?** *What for? For what? Why?* is often replaced by **warum** *why*. However, if the aim is to know the reason or purpose for something, you use **wozu**: **Wozu lernen Sie Deutsch?** *Why* (for what reason) *are you learning German?* – **Ich möchte in Berlin arbeiten.** *I would like to work in Berlin.* Remember that an infinitive that is dependent on another verb is always placed at the very end of a phrase (see lesson 8).

⑨ **was** is frequently used instead of **etwas** *something*: **Möchten Sie was trinken?** *Would you like something to drink?*

20 Übung 1 – Übersetzen Sie bitte!

❶ Hast du keinen Hunger? – Doch! ❷ Was gibt es heute zu essen? ❸ Komm, kaufen wir etwas zu trinken! ❹ Ich warte schon eine Stunde, warum kommst du so spät? ❺ Die Kneipe ist geschlossen, was machen wir jetzt?

***

Übung 2 – Ergänzen Sie bitte!

❶ Would you like something to drink? – Certainly (*Surely*)!
Möchten Sie .... ? – ...... !

❷ No, thanks, I'm not hungry.
Nein ....., ich habe ....

❸ Let's stay another week (*still a week*)! – For what? (*Here*) there is nothing to see.
Bleiben wir noch .... ! – .... ? Hier .... .. nichts .. ..

---

20 Zwanzigste Lektion *[tsvantsikHstuh lektsiohn]*

Am Bahnhof ①

1 – **Ha**llo **Ga**bi! Ich bin am **Bahn**hof in Köln.

Pronunciation
*am **bahn**-hohf **1 ha**lo **gah**bi! ikH bin am **bahn**-hohf in kœln*

Note

① **der Bahnhof** *the train station* is a compound noun made up of a word we've come across already, **die Bahn** *the train*, *the track* and **der Hof** *the yard*, *the court*. Remember that the last element in a compound noun determines its grammatical gender. The word **am** is a contraction of the preposition **an** and the article **dem**. We'll come back to this.

Answers to Exercise 1

❶ Aren't you hungry? – Yes [I am]! ❷ What is there to eat today? ❸ Come, let's buy something to drink! ❹ I've been waiting for an hour already, why are you so late? ❺ The pub is closed; what [will] we do now?

***

❹ Is there a supermarket here? I don't see a (*see no*) supermarket.
   Gibt es hier . . . . ? Ich sehe
   . . . .

❺ The service station isn't far, we['ll] find (*there find we*) something to eat there.
   . . . . ist nicht weit, dort . . . . . .
   . . . etwas . . . .

Answers to Exercise 2

❶ – etwas trinken – Sicher ❷ – danke – keinen Hunger ❸ – eine Woche – Wozu – gibt es – zu sehen ❹ – einen Supermarkt – keinen Supermarkt ❺ Die Tankstelle – finden wir – zu essen

Twentieth lesson 20

At the train station

1 – Hello Gabi! I'm at the train station in Cologne.

Am Bahnhof.

2   Ich **habe** den **An**schluss nach **Ham**burg ver**passt** ②.
3 – Oh, das ist **scha**de! **Wel**chen ③ Zug nimmst du denn jetzt?
4 – Ich **neh**me den ICE ④ um fünf vor sechs.
5   Kommst du mich **ab**holen ⑤?
6 – Na**tür**lich **hol**e ich dich **ab**.
7   Um wie viel Uhr kommt dein Zug ge**nau an**?
8 – Ich **glau**be um **zwan**zig nach zehn ⑥.

*2 ikH **hah**buh dehn **an**shluss nahkh **ham**burk fer**past** 3 oh das ist **shah**duh! **vel**kHuhn tsook nimst doo den yetst 4 ikH **neh**muh dehn ee-tseh-eh um fewnf foh^a zeks 5 komst doo mikH **ap**hohl'n 6 na**tew**^{a}**lik**H **hohl**(uh) ikH dikH **ap** 7 um vee feel oo^a komt dein tsook guh-**now an** 8 ikH **glow**buh um **tsvan**tsikH nahkh tsehn*

Notes

② **verpasst** *missed* is the past participle of **verpassen**. This sentence includes our first example of the present perfect, the tense most commonly used in conversational German to refer to past actions or states. It is formed here with the auxiliary verb **haben** *to have*, which is conjugated, and a past participle: **ich habe verpasst** *I have missed*. In English, the past participle is often referred to as the -ed form (although there are many irregular past participles, such as 'eaten'). For the time being, make a mental note of the fact that in German, the past participle appears at the end of the sentence or phrase.

③ The question word (interrogative adjective) **welcher**, **welche**, **welches** *which*, *what* declines in exactly the same way as the definite article **der**, **die**, **das**. In the masculine accusative, it takes an **-en** ending: **Welchen Käse möchten Sie?** *Which cheese would you like?* **Der Student sieht den Professor.** *The student sees the professor.*

④ **ICE** is the abbreviation for **I**nter**c**ity-**E**xpress, a German high-speed train.

2 I've missed the connection to Hamburg (*I have the connection to Hamburg missed*).
3 – Oh, that's a pity! So what train are you getting now (*What train take you then now*)?
4 – I['ll] get (*take*) the ICE at five to (*before*) six.
5 [Will] you come [and] pick me up (*Come you me up-pick*)?
6 – Of course, I['ll] pick you up (*pick I you up*).
7 What time does your train arrive exactly (*comes your train exactly at*)?
8 – I believe at twenty past (*after*) ten.

Pronunciation notes

2, 3 Make sure you differentiate the vowel length in the masculine article **den** and the adverb **denn**. The **e** of the former is a long *eh*, while the **e** in **denn** is short because of the double consonant that follows.

3, 4 The **e** in the verb stem of **nehmen** is long. It changes to a short **i** in the second- and third-person singular: **du nimmst**.

6, 7 The separable prefix at the end of each of these sentences is in bold because it carries the sentence stress: **Holst du mich ab?** Don't forget that you have to 'reattach' the separable prefix in front of the infinitive if you are looking up a verb with a separable prefix in a dictionary ... e.g. **abholen, ankommen**.

▸ ⑤ **abholen** can mean *to pick up someone or something*, *to meet someone* (e.g. at a train station) or *to get*, *to fetch*: **Sie holt Thomas am Bahnhof ab.** *She is picking Thomas up at the train station.* **Holen Sie mich ab?** *[Will] you pick me up?* Just as **du** becomes **dich** in the accusative, **ich** changes to **mich**.

⑥ In everyday language, **nach** *after* and **vor** *before* are used for giving the time (see lines 4 and 8). **Es ist zehn nach acht**. *It's ten past* ('after') *eight*. **Es ist zwanzig vor sieben.** *It is twenty to* ('before') *seven*. As in English, **sieben** *seven* could be am or pm here. The 12-hour clock is often used in everyday speech, but on the radio, on television or in reference to timetables, in the morning you'd be more likely to hear **acht Uhr zehn** *8:10,* and in the evening **zwanzig Uhr zehn** *20:10* (8:10 pm).

neunzig *[noin*tsikH*]*

20   9 – **Pri**ma ⑦! Ich **freu**e mich ⑧.

*9 pree**ma**! ikH **froi**uh mikH*

Notes
⑦ Enthusiasm can be conveyed with a variety of informal words in German: **prima**, **toll**, **super**, **klasse**, etc. Like anywhere else, the choice of expression is a question of trends and age. ▶

***

Übung 1 – Übersetzen Sie bitte!

❶ Peter kommt um zwanzig nach fünf in Köln an. ❷ Nehmen Sie den ICE um achtzehn Uhr fünf! ❸ Um wie viel Uhr kommt der nächste Zug aus Hamburg an? ❹ Warten Sie am Bahnhof, ich hole Sie ab. ❺ Ich komme um sechzehn Uhr in Hannover an.

***

Übung 2 – Ergänzen Sie bitte!

❶ (*At*) what time are you coming to pick me up (*come you me up-pick*)?

.. .. kommst du mich ....?

❷ I believe there are two trains to Bonn; which are you getting (*take you*)?

... . zwei Züge .... Bonn, ... nimmst du?

❸ Pity, the ICE at 7:04 [am] doesn't run today (*travels today not*).

......, der ICE .. .. fährt heute nicht.

91 • einundneunzig *[ein*unt-n**oin**tsikH*]*

9 – Great! I'm glad.

▶ ⑧ **sich freuen** *to be glad/happy/pleased* is a frequently used verb that we'll look at in more detail soon. For now just remember the first-person singular: **ich freue mich** *I'm happy, I'm glad*.

***

Answers to Exercise 1

❶ Peter arrives in Cologne at twenty past five. ❷ Take the ICE at five past six (*18:05*)! ❸ What time does the next train from Hamburg arrive? ❹ Wait at the train station, I['ll] pick you up. ❺ I arrive in Hanover at 4pm (*16:00*).

***

❹ She has missed the connection (*the connection missed*) – she arrives an hour later.
Sie hat . . . . verpasst, ...
eine Stunde später . . .

❺ Of course, we['ll] pick you up at the train station.
– Great, I'm glad.
Wir holen dich . . . . am Bahnhof . . .
– Prima, ...

Answers to Exercise 2

❶ Um wie viel Uhr – abholen ❷ Ich glaube es gibt – nach – welchen – ❸ Schade – um sieben Uhr vier – ❹ – den Anschluss – sie kommt – an ❺ – natürlich – ab – ich freue mich

21 Einundzwanzigste Lektion
[einunt-tsvantsikHstuh lektsiohn]

Wiederholung – Review

1 Verbs in the present tense – some peculiarities

In the past six lessons, we've seen that certain German verbs deviate somewhat from the standard pattern of verb conjugation that we encountered in lessons 1 to 14. These include: a) verbs that have a stem-vowel change in the second- and third-person singular present tense and b) separable-prefix verbs.

1.1 Irregular (or strong) verbs

Verbs are called irregular or 'strong' if they conjugate differently from the normal patterns. In German, these divergences from the standard patterns include, for example, a change in the vowel in the verb stem or the addition of an umlaut. In the present tense, such a change only occurs in the second- and third-person singular. The first-person singular and the plural forms of the verb don't deviate from the normal patterns (with the exception of **sein** *to be* – see the conjugation table in lesson 14).

There are several possible changes:

- **a → ä**: **schlafen** *to sleep* → **ich schlafe** but **du schläfst, er/sie/es schläft**

- **au → äu**: **laufen** *to run* → **ich laufe** but **du läufst, er/sie/es läuft**

- **e → i**: **geben** *to give* → **ich gebe** but **du gibst, er/sie/es gibt**

- **e → ie**: **sehen** *to see* → **ich sehe** but **du siehst, er/sie/es sieht**.

We'll point out further examples of changes and deviations as the lessons progress.

Some verbs follow slightly more complicated rules and patterns, but you'll become familiar with them as you encounter them: **nehmen** *to take* is a good example → **du nimmst, er nimmt**.

Twenty-first lesson 21

Only verbs whose stem vowel changes from **e** to **i** or **ie** have this vowel change in the '**du**-imperative': **Gib!** *Give*! **Nimm!** *Take!* **Sieh!** *Look* (see)*!* They never take an **-e** ending, unlike the second-person singular imperative of other verbs.

Let's take this opportunity to review how other verbs (i.e. those without stem-vowel changes) form the imperative. In general, the imperative is formed by adding the endings **-(e)**, **-t**, **-en**, **-en** to the verb stem:

- **du**-imperative (2nd-person sing. informal): **Lern(e)!** *Learn!*
- **ihr**-imperative (2nd-person pl. informal): **Lernt!** *Learn!*
- **Sie**-imperative (2nd-person formal sing./pl.): **Lernen Sie!** *Learn!*
- **wir**-imperative (1st-person plural): **Lernen wir!** *Let's learn!*

1.2 Separable-prefix verbs

We can't really hide the fact that separable-prefix verbs are very important in German; you'll have to get used to them as quickly as possible. In fact, it shouldn't seem so strange – in English there are a lot of verbs used with a preposition that changes the verb's meaning: e.g. *to pick* and *to pick up*. This preposition can move away from the verb: *to pick up* becomes *I'll pick you up* – so it's not so different! For the time being, make sure to check if there is a little word 'trailing' at the end of a sentence or phrase: if there is, (re)attach the prefix to the verb to find the infinitive. If you'd like to practice this a little, try to answer the following questions:

- What is the infinitive of the verb in the following sentence? **Machen Sie bitte die Tür auf!** *Open the door, please!* Found it? Well done! It's **aufmachen** *to open* – not **machen** *to do, to make*.

- What does the following sentence mean? **Sie gibt viel Geld aus.** No, this does not translate as 'she gives a lot of money', but 'she <u>spends</u> a lot of money': **geben** *to give*, **ausgeben** *to spend*. Once again, you can see the crucial difference a separable prefix can make to the meaning of a verb!

vierundneunzig *[fee^aunt-nointsikH]* • 94

2 The accusative case of articles

Let's look again at the variations articles undergo in different cases, i.e. depending on the function they (and the noun they are associated with) fulfil in a sentence:

• An article is in the nominative case when the noun that it precedes is the subject of the sentence or when it follows a form of the verb **sein**. **Sein** functions as a kind of equalizer in terms of case. Have a look at this example: **Der Professor ist ein Freund von Claudia.** *The professor is a friend of Claudia['s].* Here, **ein Freund** is not an object because **ist** is not an action that's being done to **Freund** by **der Professor**, but a state.

In the nominative case, the masculine definite article (singular) is **der** *the*; the indefinite article is **ein** *a/an*.

• An article is in the accusative case when the noun it precedes functions as the direct object (i.e. the person or thing that directly receives the action of the verb).
Der Student sieht den Professor. *The student sees the professor.*
Der Professor trinkt einen Kaffee. *The professor drinks a [cup of] coffee.*

In the accusative case, the masculine definite article (singular) is **den**; the indefinite article is **einen**.

The feminine (sing.) article **die** and the neuter (sing.) article **das**, as well as the plural article **die**, don't change in the accusative.

	Singular			Plural
	masc.	fem.	neuter	
nominative	der/ein	die/eine	das/ein	die
accusative	den/einen	die/eine	das/ein	die

At this point, let's just add that the negative articles **kein(e)** *no, not a/an*, and the possessive adjectives **mein(e)** *my*, **dein(e)** *your* (informal), etc. decline (i.e. change) in the same way as **ein(e)**:
Thomas hat keinen Koffer. *Thomas doesn't have a suitcase.*
Er nimmt immer meinen Koffer. *He always takes my suitcase.*

3 Cardinal numbers

If you've been looking carefully at the page numbers in the book, you'll already have a good idea of the numbers in German. The numbers from 1 to 12 are: **eins** *eins*, **zwei** *tsvei*, **drei** *drei*, **vier** *fee[a]*, **fünf** *fewnf*, **sechs** *zeks*, **sieben** *zeeb'n*, **acht** *akht*, **neun** *noin*, **zehn** *tsehn*, **elf** *elf*, **zwölf** *tsvœlf*.

But let's look again at some important aspects of pronunciation.

• In German, all the letters are pronounced. This is important, as one letter can make a difference in meaning. For example, **ein** is the indefinite article *a/an* (masc./neut.), whereas **eins** is the number one.

• The initial sound in **zwei**, **zehn**, **zwölf** is a bit tricky for most English speakers. Resist the temptation to pronounce this like the English letter 'z'. The German **z** is pronounced like *ts* at the end of words such as *bats* or *plots*. Think of the hissing sound an old-fashioned whistling kettle or a pressure cooker makes. By the way, *to hiss* is **zischen** – a nice example of onomatopoeia.

• The **v** in **vier** is pronounced like the **f** in **fünf**.

• **sechs** and **Sex** are sometimes both pronounced *zeks* (depending on the region).

• Saying **acht** gives you a chance to clear the frog in your throat!

• For **zehn** *tsehn*, pronounce a long *eh*, then add -**n**.

The numbers from 13 to 19 are formed 'backwards', that is, the smaller number comes first, followed by the bigger number (the ten): **dreizehn**, **vierzehn**, **fünfzehn**, **sechzehn**, **siebzehn**, **achtzehn**, **neunzehn**. Careful with **sechzehn** and **siebzehn**, as **sechs** changes to **sech-** and **sieben** to **sieb-**.

The German equivalent of the English suffix -*ty* for the numbers from 20 to 90 (as in for<u>ty</u>, six<u>ty</u>, etc.) is -**zig**: **zwanzig**, **dreißig**, **vierzig**, **fünfzig**, <u>**sech**</u>**zig**, <u>**sieb**</u>**zig**, **achtzig**, **neunzig**. As you can see, there is only one exception to the rule and that's **dreißig** *thirty*, which ends in -**ßig**. Remember -**ig** at the end of a word is pronounced -*ikH*, except in southern Germany, where it's pronounced -*ik*. You could always try to pass for someone from the south if you prefer!

21 The numbers from 21 to 99 follow the pattern of the nursery rhyme 'Sing a Song of Sixpence' with its four-and-twenty blackbirds: **einundzwanzig**, **zweiundzwanzig**, etc., up to **neunundneunzig**.

For numbers greater than 100 (**hundert**), the word for the hundred(s) comes first, followed by the units and the tens: **(ein) hundertsiebenundachtzig** *187*, **dreihundertfünfundvierzig** *345*. The thousands work in the same way: **(ein)tausend** *1000*, **siebentausend** *7000*, **viertausendvierhundertfünfzig** *4450*, etc. Note that in the hundreds and thousands, **sechs** and **sieben** are used, not their shortened forms.

Some concluding remarks:

Note that **eins** *one* becomes **ein-** when followed by another numeral: **einundsiebzig** *71*. Moreover, it declines when followed by a noun: **Wir bleiben einen Tag.** *We are staying for one day.*

ein is often omitted at the beginning of a hundred or a thousand: **tausendvierhundertfünfzig** *1450*, but never in the middle: **tausendeinhundertfünfzig** *1150*.

Let's stop here for today. Just one more quick question: can you write out the number 969,897 in German?

Answer:
Neunhundertneunundsechzigtausendachthundertsieben-undneunzig
noinhundᵃt-noinuntzekHtsikH-towzuhnt-akhthundᵃt-zeebuhn-unt-nointsikH
It's a mouthful, isn't it?

Out of breath? Well, now it's time to relax while listening to the following conversation. Take your time! You're not the one who's got a train to catch ...

Review exercise 21

Die Bahnhofsauskunft

1 – Guten Morgen, um wie viel Uhr fährt der nächste Zug nach Hamburg, bitte?
2 – Ein ICE fährt um dreizehn Uhr zweiunddreißig.
3 – Was? In sechs Stunden? So spät?
4 Gibt es keinen Zug heute Morgen?
5 – Doch, einen Schnellzug, aber der fährt in vier Minuten ab.
6 – Prima, den nehme ich.
7 Sagen Sie schnell, welches Gleis?
8 – Gleis zehn, Sie gehen rechts und dann immer geradeaus!
9 – Vielen Dank! Sie sind sehr nett.
10 – Keine Ursache, aber verpassen Sie nicht den Zug!
11 Laufen Sie! Die Zeit vergeht schnell!

Translation

Station information

1 Good morning, what time does the next train to Hamburg leave, please? **2** An ICE leaves at 13:32. **3** What? In six hours? That late? **4** Isn't there a train this morning? **5** Yes, an express train, but it *(m.)* leaves in four minutes. **6** Great, I ['ll] take it. **7** Tell [me] quickly, which platform? **8** Platform ten – you go right and then [keep] straight on. **9** Many thanks! You are very kind. **10** It's nothing *(No cause)*, but don't miss the train! **11** Run! *(The)* time passes quickly!

22 Zweiundzwanzigste Lektion
[tsveiunt-tsvantsikHstuh lektsiohn]

Das Geburtstagsfest ①

1 – Was für **ein**e ② **Hit**ze!
2   Die **Schü**ler **ha**ben Glück, sie **ha**ben **hit**zefrei.
3 – Ja, wir sind zu ③ alt, für ④ uns ist das vor**bei**.
4 – Sag mal, wie alt ⑤ bist du **ei**gentlich?
5 – Ich bin **fünf**und**zwan**zig, **a**ber nicht mehr ⑥ **lang**e.
6 – Wa**rum**? Wann ist denn dein Ge**burts**tag?

Pronunciation
*das guh**boo**ᵃts-tahks-fest* **1** *vas fewᵃ **ein**uh **hit**suh* **2** *dee **shew**lᵃ **hah**buhn glewk zee **hah**buhn **hit**suh-frei* **3** *yah veeᵃ zint tsoo alt fewᵃ uns ist das fohᵃ**bei*** **4** *zahk mahl vee alt bist doo **eig**'ntlikH* **5** *ikH bin **fewn**funt-**tsvan**tsikH **ah**bᵃ nikHt mehᵃ **lang**uh* **6** *va**rum**? van ist den dein guh**boo**ᵃts-tahk*

Notes

① The compound noun **das Geburtstagsfest** *the birthday celebration* contains the words **der Geburtstag** *the birthday* – which is itself a compound noun – and **das Fest** *the celebration, party*. (Another word for *party* is **die Party** – see line 9.) In this compound noun, an **s** is inserted between each of the nouns it consists of: **die Geburt** + **der Tag** → **der Geburtstag** and **der Geburtstag** + **das Fest** → **das Geburtstagsfest**. There are also other ways of joining two words, as we'll see.

② The expression **Was für ein(e) …** *What (a/an) …!, What kind of …?* can be used as an exclamation or a question: **Was für ein Tag!** *What a day!* **Was für einen Mann suchen Sie?** *What kind of man are you looking for?* Note in these examples that **ein(e)** declines (i.e. changes in the different cases), and remember that there is no plural indefinite article: **Was für Probleme hat er?** *What kinds of problems does he have?*

Twenty-second lesson

The birthday celebration

1 – What (*for a*) heat!
2 The schoolchildren are lucky, they are off on account of the heat (*they have heat-free*).
3 – Yes, we're too old; for us that's (*is that*) over.
4 – Tell [me], how old are you in fact?
5 – I'm twenty-five, but not for much longer (*not more long*).
6 – Why? When is (*then*) your birthday?

Das Geburtstagsfest

③ **zu** followed by an adjective or an adverb translates as 'too': **Es ist zu heiß.** *It is too hot.* We've already seen **zu** *to, towards, at, on* with the infinitive (lesson 19): **Ich habe nichts zu essen.** *I don't have anything to eat* ('I have nothing to eat'), and in the expression **zu Haus(e)** *at home* (if one is there), as opposed to **nach Haus(e)** *home* (if one is going there).

④ **für** *for* requires the accusative case: **uns** *us* is the accusative form of the subject pronoun **wir** *we*.

⑤ Many questions concerning quantity or measurements are formed with **wie** *how* + adjective (in its base, i.e. unchanged, form): **Wie alt sind Sie?** *How old are you?* **Wie groß ist er?** *How tall is he?*

⑥ **nicht mehr** means *no longer, not any longer, not anymore*: **Er trinkt nicht mehr.** *He doesn't drink anymore.*

22

7 – Am 4. August ⑦ **wer**de ich **sechs**und**zwan**zig.
8 – Mensch, das ist **Sams**tag!
9 Weißt du ⑧ was, wir **ge**ben **ei**ne Ge**burts**tags**par**ty für dich!

*7 am **fee**ᵃtuhn ow**gust** vehᵃduh ikH **zeks**unt-**tsvan**tsikH
8 mensh das ist **zams**tahk 9 veist doo vas veeᵃ **gehb**'n **ei**nuh guh**boo**ᵃts-tahks-**pah**tee fewᵃ dikH*

Notes

⑦ In both written and spoken German, ordinal numbers are used to indicate dates. In writing, a full stop after the number shows that it is ordinal: **am 4. August** *August 4th* is literally **am vierten August** 'on the fourth August'; and **am 15. Mai** *May 15th* is literally **am fünfzehnten Mai** 'on the fifteenth May'. We'll come back to this in review lesson 28. For now, the main ▶

***

Summer in Germany

Contrary to popular belief, the weather in Germany is not at all unpleasant during the summer months. On average there are fewer hours of sunshine per year than in more southerly latitudes, and the summer is shorter, limited to the months of July and August. Even so, it can get very hot. In Baden-Württemberg and Bavaria, the temperatures can easily reach 30 °C (86 °F) or over. And if the temperature in the shade does indeed climb that high during school hours, students are sent home on account of the heat. It's worth noting that almost no schools in Germany (or in Austria or Switzerland for that matter) are air-conditioned. In the north

***

Übung 1 – Übersetzen Sie bitte!

❶ Weißt du was, ich trinke nicht mehr. ❷ Wie alt sind die Kinder? ❸ Am 19. (neunzehnten) August gebe ich eine Party, kommen Sie? ❹ Was für ein Geburtstagsfest und was für eine Hitze! ❺ Samstag gibt Thorsten eine Geburtstagsparty für Janina.

7 – On the fourth [of] August, I will be (*become I*) twenty-six.
8 – Hey (*Man*), that's Saturday!
9 You know what (*Know you something*)? We [will] give a birthday party for you!

things to remember are that you have to use the contraction **am** (**an** + **dem**) when giving a precise date, and that the day always precedes the month.

⑧ Meet the irregular verb **wissen** *to know*, which does not at all follow the conjugation rules we've already seen. Its conjugations in the singular present tense are **ich weiß, du weißt, er/sie/es weiß**. We'll come back to this again later. In the expression **Weißt du was?** *You know what?*, **was** is an abbreviation of **etwas** *something*.

***

of Germany, **die Hitzewellen** *heatwaves are less frequent. People make the most of every ray of sunshine. As soon as it's possible to go outside, people migrate to their (always well-kept) gardens to work, eat, bask in the sun (even if this requires wearing a winter coat) or give parties:* **Gartenfeste** *or* **Grillfeste**. **Grillen** *to grill, to barbecue has become something of a national sport (***Volkssport***) in Germany since the 1950s. The Germans are undoubtedly among the most enthusiastic grillers in Europe – well, German men at least. Cooking chunks of meat over an open fire in the garden has long been an almost exclusively male pastime and can easily give rise to hour-long debates over the right cuts, equipment and seasoning.*

***

Answers to Exercise 1

❶ You know what? I don't drink anymore. ❷ How old are the children? ❸ On August 19th, I'm giving a party – are you coming? ❹ What a birthday celebration and what heat! ❺ On Saturday, Thorsten is giving a birthday party for Janina.

hundertzwei • 102

23 Übung 2 – Ergänzen Sie bitte!

❶ What a day! Why aren't we off on account of the heat (*have we not heat-free*)?

... ... Tag! ..... haben wir nicht .... ?

❷ You are no longer tired? – But no, that's over!

Sie sind .... müde? – Aber nein, ... !

❸ The fries are for us, not [just] for you (*informal sing.*) (*alone*).

Die Pommes Frites sind ... ..., nicht ... . allein.

23 Dreiundzwanzigste Lektion
[dreiunt-tsvantsikHstuh lektsiohn]

Eine gute Organisation

1 – **Möch**test du im **Gar**ten **o**der im Haus **fei**ern?
2 – Im **Gar**ten. Ich mag ① **Gar**tenfeste.
3 – Gut! Wen ② **la**den wir **ein**?

> **Pronunciation**
> *einuh gootuh organizatsiohn 1 mœkh-tuhst doo im gartuhn ohdᵃ im hows feiᵃn 2 im gartuhn. ikH mahk gartuhn-festuh 3 goot! vehn lahduhn veeᵃ ein*

Notes

① **ich mag** *I like* is the first-person present tense of the verb **mögen** in the indicative mood. The indicative is used in statements that are factual or likely: **Ich mag Schokolade.** *I like chocolate.* We've already seen **mögen** in its subjunctive form: **ich möchte, du möchtest, Sie möchten** *I would like, you would like*, etc. The indicative and subjunctive are examples of what are known as 'grammatical moods' – verb inflections

❹ Anna's birthday is on the 16th of August (*On-the 16th August is the birthday of Anna*).
.. 16. (sechzehnten) ...... ist ... .
von Anna.

❺ How old are you in fact? Thirty-one or thirty-two?
... ... sind Sie .... ? Einunddreißig
oder .... ?

Answers to Exercise 2

❶ Was für ein – Warum – hitzefrei ❷ – nicht mehr – das ist vorbei ❸ – für uns – für dich – ❹ Am – August – der Geburtstag – ❺ Wie alt – eigentlich – zweiunddreißig

---

Twenty-third lesson 23

(*A*) **Good organization**

1 – Would you like to celebrate in the garden or in the house (*Would you like in-the garden or in-the house to-celebrate*)?
2 – In the garden. I like garden parties.
3 – Good! Whom [shall] we invite (*invite we*)?

that allow the speaker to indicate their attitude towards what they are saying. In German, the subjunctive is used to talk about hypothetical situations or to express wishes or polite requests. We'll come back to this later. As you can see, **mögen** is irregular. It belongs to a category of verbs called modal verbs, which indicate an attitude rather than an action. We'll be looking at **mögen** more closely soon.

② The interrogative pronoun (question word) **wer** *who* declines like the masculine definite article **der** *the*. When it functions as a direct object, **wer** becomes **wen** *whom* in the accusative case: **Wen laden wir ein?** *Whom do we invite?* (The verb for *to invite* is **einladen** – did you spot the separable prefix?)

hundertvier • 104

4 – Klaus und **sein**e ③ **Freun**din, **Son**ja und **ih**ren ④ Mann, **dein**e **Schwes**ter und **ih**re Fa**mi**lie, **mein**e **Brü**der ⑤, das Or**ches**ter …
5 – Wird ⑥ das nicht zu viel?
6 Das wird **teu**er.
7 – Nein, das wird **lus**tig ⑦.
8 Alle **bring**en **et**was zu **es**sen **o**der zu **trin**ken **mit** ⑧. ☐

---

*4 klows unt **sein**uh **froin**din **zon**ya unt **ee**ruhn man **dein**uh **shvest**ᵃ unt **ee**ruh fa**mee**lyuh, **mein**uh **brewd**ᵃ das or**kest**ᵃ
5 virt das nikHt tsoo feel 6 das virt **toi**ᵃ 7 nein das virt **lus**tikH
8 **a**luh **bring**uhn **et**vas tsoo **ess**'n **ohd**ᵃ tsoo **trink**'n mit*

Notes

③ In lessons 5 and 11, you were introduced to two possessive adjectives: **mein** (first-person singular: *my*) and **dein** (second-person singular informal: *your*). In this lesson, there are two more: **sein** *his, its* and **ihr**: *her, its* (both third-person singular). In German, the choice of possessive adjective depends first of all on who the 'possessor' is (which can be a person or a thing). In the third-person, you use **sein** if the possessor is masculine (or neuter): **sein Hund** *his dog*; and **ihr** if the possessor is feminine: **ihr Hund** *her dog*. In this respect, they are very much like English possessive adjectives (apart from *its*, which in German needs to correspond to the grammatical gender of the possessor). However, German possessive adjectives can also take endings, which are determined by the gender, number and case of the owned object. These endings are the same as for **kein**: e.g. <u>**Sein**</u> **Geburtstag** (masc. sing. possessor of a masc. sing. nominative noun) **ist am 4. Mai und <u>ihr</u> Geburtstag** (fem. sing. possessor of a masc. sing. nominative noun) **ist einen Tag später.** *His birthday is on the 4th of May and her birthday is a day later.* However, **Ich sehe sein<u>en</u> Hund und sein<u>e</u> Katze.** *I see his dog and his cat.* Here **seinen Hund** and **seine Katze** are in the accusative as they are direct objects. We'll come back to this in review lesson 28.

4 – Klaus and his girlfriend, Sonja and her husband (*man*), your sister and her family, my brothers, the band …
5 – Isn't that getting (*Becomes that not*) too much?
6 That [will] be (*becomes*) expensive.
7 – No, it [will] be fun (*becomes funny*).
8 Everybody [will] bring (*All bring*) something to eat or to drink (*with*).

- By the way, using a possessive adjective before **Freund** or **Freundin** often signals that one isn't referring to any old friend, but to a girlfriend or boyfriend, especially if no proper name is mentioned: so **mein Freund** can mean *my boyfriend*, **deine Freundin** *your girlfriend* (note how the ending of the possessive adjective changes to agree with the feminine **Freundin**). Likewise, **ihr Mann**, 'her man', is *her husband*.

④ In this reply, all the nouns are direct objects of **einladen** *to invite*, and hence all articles and possessive adjectives are in the accusative: **Wir laden ihren Freund, seine Schwester, das Orchester und alle Freunde ein.** *We're inviting her boyfriend, his sister, the band and all [our] friends.*

⑤ **Brüder** (with an umlaut) is the plural of **der Bruder** *the brother*. However, **die Schwester** forms the plural by adding **-n**: **die Schwestern**. The word **die Geschwister** is used for *brothers and sisters* or *siblings*.

⑥ The irregular verb **werden** (**ich werde, du wirst, er/sie/es wird**) has a number of uses in German; its basic meaning is *to become*. When used with an adjective or adverb, **werden** expresses a notion of change or evolution: **Das wird zu viel.** *It is getting too much.* ('That becomes too much.') **Ich werde müde.** *I am starting to get tired.* ('I become tired.') **Es wird kalt.** *It is getting cold.* ('It becomes cold.') It can also refer to a future situation, as here where the speakers are referring to something that will be too much, too expensive, too fun.

⑦ **lustig** can mean *funny*, *hilarious*, *amusing*, *merry* or *cheerful*, depending on the context. It's a multipurpose word for describing something that's entertaining!

⑧ **mitbringen** *to bring*, *to bring along* is a separable-prefix verb.

hundertsechs • 106

Übung 1 – Übersetzen Sie bitte!

❶ Daniels Bruder ist neunzehn und seine Schwester dreiundzwanzig. ❷ Am 5. (fünften) Mai feiern wir den Geburtstag von Anna. ❸ Klaus lädt Sonja und ihre Schwester ein. ❹ Bringt nichts mehr mit! Das wird zu viel. ❺ Sie sieht ihren Freund um fünfzehn Uhr im Café.

***

Übung 2 – Ergänzen Sie bitte!

❶ Whom are you (*pl.*) inviting? Anna and her brothers and Thomas and his girlfriend.
... ladet ihr ein? Anna und .... und Thomas und ....

❷ Would you (*informal sing.*) like a party in the garden or in the house?
.... ein Fest .. .. oder .. ..?

❸ Anna and Klaus are inviting us (*invite us*) for Saturday evening; it's surely going to be fun (*that becomes surely funny*).
Anna und Klaus ..... uns für Samstagabend ..., ... sicher lustig.

❹ She picks her brother and her sister up at the train station.
Sie holt .... und .... am Bahnhof ab.

❺ The party will not be (*becomes not*) expensive – everybody is (*all are*) bringing something (*with*).
Das Fest .... nicht ....., alle .... etwas ....

Answers to Exercise 1

❶ Daniel's brother is 19 and his sister is 23. ❷ On the 5th of May, we will celebrate Anna's birthday. ❸ Klaus is inviting Sonja and her sister. ❹ Don't bring anything else! It's getting too much. ❺ She sees her boyfriend in the café at 3 pm *(15:00)*.

***

Answers to Exercise 2

❶ Wen – ihre Brüder – seine Freundin ❷ Möchtest du – im Garten – im Haus ❸ – laden – ein – das wird – ❹ – ihren Bruder – ihre Schwester – ❺ – wird – teuer – bringen – mit

24 Vierundzwanzigste Lektion
[*fee^aunt-tsvantsikHstuh lektsiohn*]

Komm, wir gehen einkaufen! ①

1 – Wir **ha**ben das **Grill**fleisch, die Kar**to**ffeln und den **Ap**felsaft ②.
2 Was **brau**chen ③ wir noch?
3 – Nichts, das ist **a**lles.
4 – Gut, dann **geh**en wir **zah**len.
5 – Halt, wir **ha**ben den Sekt ④ ver**ge**ssen ⑤.

Pronunciation
*kom vee^a **geh**uhn **ein**kowf'n 1 vee^a **hahb**'n das **gril**-fleish dee kar**tof**'ln unt dehn **apf**'l-zaft 2 vas **brow**kh'n vee^a nokh 3 nikHts das ist **a**les 4 goot dan **geh**uhn vee^a **tsahl**'n 5 halt vee^a **hahb**'n dehn zekt fer**gess**'n*

Notes

① **einkaufen gehen** *to go shopping*. In this construction with two verbs, only **gehen** declines – **einkaufen** remains an infinitive: **ich gehe einkaufen** *I go shopping*, **du gehst einkaufen** *you go shopping*, **wir gehen einkaufen** *we go shopping*.

② **der Saft** *juice*, **der Apfel** *apple*. **Apfelsaft** is yet another example of a compound noun. Remember that the gender of a compound noun depends on the gender of the last element: **der Apfel** + <u>**der**</u> **Saft** = <u>**der**</u> **Apfelsaft**; **die Orange** + <u>**der**</u> **Saft** = <u>**der**</u> **Orangensaft**.

③ **brauchen** *to need, to require* is used with the accusative because what is 'needed' is a direct object: **Ich brauche den Saft.** *I need the juice.* The definite article **den** is in the accusative case.

④ **der Sekt** *sparkling wine* is a vital ingredient of any serious celebration in Germany. Even though it is generally less expensive

Twenty-fourth lesson   24

Come [on], we're going shopping!

1 – We have the barbecue meat, the potatoes and the apple juice.
2 What [else] do we need (*need we still*)?
3 – Nothing, that's all.
4 – Good, then let's go pay.
5 – Stop, we've forgotten the sparkling wine (*have the sparkling-wine forgotten*).

than French **Champagner** (*shampany*), it is considered a luxury item. Germany has a long tradition of producing **Sekt**, which is mostly made from white grape varieties. Most **Sekt** is produced by medium-sized to large **Sektkellereien** ('sparkling wine cellars'). However, in winegrowing areas of Germany, you will often find **Winzersekt** *winegrower's Sekt*. This is produced in small quantities from the producer's own vineyards.

⑤ The past participle of **vergessen** *to forget* (i.e. *forgotten*) takes the same form as the infinitive. But this isn't always the case! Think back to **schließen** *to close* → **geschlossen** *closed*. We'll look at participles in more detail soon. For now, simply note that the past participle comes at the end of a phrase, while the conjugated auxiliary verb (here, **haben**) occupies the usual place of the verb – that is, the second position: **Er hat alles vergessen.** *He has forgotten everything.* ('He has all forgotten.')

6 – Stimmt! Ich **hol**e ⑥ ihn ⑦.
7 – **Okay**, ich **geh**e schon mal an ⑧ die **Ka**sse und **steh**e **Schlang**e ⑨.

> **6** shtimt! ikH **hoh**-luh een **7** o**keh** ikH **geh**-uh shon mahl an dee **ka**ssuh unt **shteh**-uh **shlang**uh

Notes

⑥ **holen** – like **abholen** – can mean *to get*, *to fetch* or *to pick up*: **Ich hole Brot.** *I['ll] get bread* or *I'm getting bread*. The separable prefix **ab** can express a sense of detachment, but also frequently implies a notion of waiting for something: **Freunde am Flughafen abholen** *to pick up friends from the airport*, **ein Paket abholen** *to pick up a parcel*.

⑦ As we've mentioned, the pronoun *it* has to agree with the grammatical gender of the noun it replaces. Here, 'it' refers to the masculine noun **der Sekt**. In the accusative case, **er** *he*, *it* (m.) becomes **ihn** *him*, *it* (m.): **Sie liebt ihn.** *She loves him.* But note that the feminine and neuter personal pronouns, **sie** (f.) and **es** (neuter) don't change in the accusative case: **Er liebt sie.** *He loves her.* **Wo ist das Brot? – Ich hole es.** *Where is the bread? – I['ll] get it.*

***

Übung 1 – Übersetzen Sie bitte!

❶ Sie brauchen Ferien, Herr Spielberg, das ist alles. ❷ Ich mag nicht Schlange stehen. ❸ Sie kauft einmal pro Woche ein. ❹ Haben Sie keinen Sekt? – Doch, ich hole ihn. ❺ Was möchten Sie? Zwei Kilo Kartoffeln?

6 – True! I['ll] get it (*m.*)
7 – OK, I['ll] go (*already once*) to the checkout and queue up (*stand snake*).

> Ich mag nicht Schlange stehen.

⑧ **an** is a preposition meaning *at*, *to*, *on*: **Ich gehe an die Kasse.** *I'm going to the checkout.* **Wir fahren ans Meer.** *We go to the seaside* ('sea'). In the last example, **ans** is a contraction of **an** and the neuter article **das**.

⑨ In German, one doesn't stand in a queue or a line, but in a 'snake'. **Schlange stehen** *to queue up*, *to stand in line* consists of **die Schlange** *the snake* and **stehen** *to stand*.

***

Answers to Exercise 1

❶ You need a holiday (*holidays*), Mr Spielberg, that's all. ❷ I don't like standing in line/queuing up. ❸ She goes shopping once a (*per*) week. ❹ Don't you have any sparkling wine? – Yes, I['ll] get it. ❺ What would you like? Two kilos of potatoes?

hundertzwölf • 112

25 Übung 2 – Ergänzen Sie bitte!

❶ Why have you forgotten the potatoes (*the potatoes forgotten*) and not the beer?

Warum hast du ... . vergessen und nicht ... .?

❷ What do you need? – Nothing, thanks.

... brauchen Sie? – ......, danke.

❸ She goes to the checkout, and he quickly gets (*he gets still quickly*) the sparkling wine.

Sie geht .. .., und .. .... noch schnell den Sekt.

❹ I would like an orange juice, please, and that is all.

Ich möchte bitte .... und das ist ......

---

25 Fünfundzwanzigste Lektion
[fewnfunt-tsvantsikHstuh lektsiohn]

Ist Ihr ① Terminkalender ② auch zu voll?

1 Ich bin Ver**tre**ter für Com**pu**ter.

Pronunciation
*ist ee^a ter**meen**-ka**lend**^a owkh tsoo fol **1** ikH bin fer**treht**^a few^a com**pyoot**^a*

Notes

① **Ihr** – with a capital letter – is the possessive adjective *your* (m./f.) in formal situations. With this possessive adjective you don't need to worry about the gender of the possessor, however it does need to agree with what is possessed. **Ihr** is used with ▶

❺ When are you (*pl.*) going shopping? I need something to drink.
Wann geht ihr .... ? Ich brauche
..... zu trinken.

Answers to Exercise 2

❶ – die Kartoffeln – das Bier ❷ Was – Nichts – ❸ – an die Kasse
– er holt – ❹ – einen Orangensaft – alles ❺ – einkaufen – etwas –

If you're feeling a bit overwhelmed that there are too many new things to take on board, remember that you're not expected to retain everything at once. Just keep on reading the German in each lesson aloud and repeating it several times over. There is also a grammatical appendix at the end of the book that you can refer to whenever you need to. And most importantly, don't forget: **Es ist noch kein Meister vom Himmel gefallen.** *'No master has fallen from the sky yet.'* – No one is born a master.

Twenty-fifth lesson 25

Is your (*formal*) diary too full as well?

1 I am [a] computer sales representative (*for computers*).

singular masculine or neuter nouns in the nominative case. **Ihre** is used with feminine or plural nominative nouns.

② **der Terminkalender** *appointments calendar*, *diary* is a compound noun consisting of **der Termin** *appointment*, *date*, *deadline* and **der Kalender** *calendar*, *diary*. The word **Termin** is used for official appointments, e.g. at the doctor's: **Freitag hat er einen Termin bei Doktor Schmidt.** *[On] Friday, he has an appointment with Dr Schmidt.*

hundertvierzehn • 114

25

2 Am **Mon**tag **flie**ge ich ③ nach Barce**lo**na.
3 **Diens**tag**nach**mittag ④ **ko**mme ich zu**rück**.
4 **Mitt**woch**vor**mittag **ha**ben wir **ei**ne **Sit**zung ⑤.
5 **Do**nnerstag ⑥ **tre**ffe ich **Kun**den.
6 Ich **ho**ffe, **ih**re ⑦ Ma**schi**nen funktio**nie**ren.
7 Am **Frei**tag **ar**beite ich im Bü**ro**.
8 Und am **Sams**tag repa**rie**re ich zu **Hau**se … den Com**pu**ter. ☐

---

*2 am **moon**tahk **flee**guh ikH nahkh bartsuh**loh**na
3 **deens**tahk-**nakh**mitahk **ko**muh ikH tsoo**rewk** 4 **mit**vokh-**foh**ᵃ mitahk **hah**buhn veeᵃ **ei**nuh **zit**sung 5 **don**ᵃstahk **tre**fuh ikH **kun**duhn 6 ikH **ho**fuh **ee**ruh ma**shee**nuhn funktsyo**nee**ruhn
7 am **frei**tahk **ar**beituh ikH im bew**roh** 8 unt am **sams**tahk repa**ree**ruh ikH tsoo **how**zuh… dehn com**pyoot**ᵃ*

Notes

③ Remember that in a statement, the conjugated verb is always in position 2 – whether the subject occupies position 1 or not. Compare **Ich fliege am Montag nach Barcelona** and **Am Montag fliege ich nach Barcelona**, or even **Nach Barcelona fliege ich am Montag**. The verb is considered in the second position in all of these sentences. In examples 2 and 3, the subject follows the verb because position 1 is filled by an expression of time and place respectively. We could spend a long time telling you about German sentence structure, but we'd rather let you get used to it in context first. You'll find yourself beginning to pick it up without even realizing it!

④ **Dienstagnachmittag** consists of **Dienstag** *Tuesday* and **der Nachmittag** *afternoon* (**nach** *after* + **Mittag** *noon*). Likewise, **der Vormittag** *morning*, literally means 'before-noon' (**vor** *before* + **Mittag** *noon*). Remember that **nach** doesn't only mean 'after', but also 'to' when used with a verb that conveys movement. **Er fliegt nach Barcelona.** *He flies to Barcelona.*

⑤ **die Sitzung** *meeting* derives from the verb **sitzen** *to sit*. Many German nouns are formed by adding the suffix **-ung** to the stem

2 On Monday, I fly (*fly I*) to Barcelona.
3 Tuesday afternoon, I come back (*come I back*).
4 Wednesday morning (*Wednesday-before-noon*), we have (*have we*) a meeting.
5 Thursday, I meet (*meet I*) customers.
6 I hope their machines work.
7 On Friday, I work (*work I*) at the office.
8 And on Saturday, I repair (*repair I*) … the computer at home.

Pronunciation note
6, 8 There are a lot of verbs of Latin or French origin in modern German. These end in **-ieren** and the stress is on the syllable containing the **ie** sound: **funktionieren** *funktsyoneeruhn*, **reparieren** *repareeruhn*, **studieren** *shtudeeruhn*, **telefonieren** *telefoneeruhn*, etc.

▸ of a verb. You already know one of them, **die Entschuldigung** *excuse*, from **entschuldigen** *to excuse*. All nouns that end in **-ung** are feminine, and they form the plural by adding **-en**: **die Sitzungen** *meetings*.

⑥ To refer to a day of the week, one can say either just **Donnerstag** *Thursday* or **am Donnerstag** *on Thursday*.

⑦ We've seen that the feminine singular and third-person plural subject pronoun are the same: **sie trinkt Kaffee** *she drinks coffee*, **sie trinken Kaffee** *they (m./f.) drink coffee*. The same holds true for the possessive adjective: **ihr(e)** – with a small letter – which means *her* as well as *their* (m./f.). As with **Ihr** in note 1, **ihr** needs to agree with what is possessed. **Ihr Freund ist groß.** *Her/their friend* (m.) *is tall*. **Ihre Freundin ist nett.** *Her/their friend* (f.) *is nice*. **Die Kinder treffen ihre Freunde.** *The children meet their friends* (pl.). Be careful to distinguish between **Ihr(e)** *your* (formal) and **ihr(e)** *her*, *their*. The capital letter is crucial here.

25 Übung 1 – Übersetzen Sie bitte!

❶ Am Dienstag fahren wir nach Berlin. ❷ Haben Sie nächste Woche Zeit? ❸ Am Mittwoch arbeitet sie zu Hause. ❹ Fliegen Sie Freitagvormittag nach München? ❺ Ich möchte bitte einen Termin mit Doktor Bachmann.

***

Übung 2 – Ergänzen Sie bitte!

❶ What are you doing on Saturday? – I have a meeting.
   Was machen Sie .. .. ? – Ich habe
   ....

❷ Klaus comes back from Barcelona [on] Friday evening (*Klaus comes Friday-evening from Barcelona back*).
   Klaus ..... Freitagabend aus Barcelona ....

❸ When do you (*formal sing.*) meet your customers? – Monday.
   Wann .... Kunden? – ....

❹ Her computer doesn't work any longer – he is repairing it.
   ... Computer .... nicht mehr –
   .. .. ihn.

***

Die Wochentage: the days of the week
All the names for the days of the week have a history, which may make it easier to remember them:
• **Sonntag** *is the day of the sun (***die Sonne** *the sun).*
• **Montag** *is the day of the moon (***der Mond** *the moon).*
• *Contrary to popular opinion,* **Dienstag** *has nothing to do with* **der Dienst** *service. It is the day of Tiw (also Tyr; Ziu), the ancient Germanic god of war. The word* **Dienstag** *as it is used now probably derives from* **thingstag**, *the day of the* **Thing** *(governing assembly), of which Tiw was the protector.*
• **Mittwoch** *is the day in the middle of the week:* **die Mitte** *middle and* **die Woche** *week.*

Answers to Exercise 1

❶ On Tuesday, we go to Berlin. ❷ Do you have time next week? ❸ On Wednesday, she works at home. ❹ Do you fly to Munich on Friday morning? ❺ I would like an appointment with Dr Bachmann, please.

❺ On Wednesday, my diary is (*is my diary*) too full, but Thursday morning I am free (*have I time*).

Am . . . . ist mein . . . . zu voll, aber . . . . habe ich Zeit.

Answers to Exercise 2

❶ – am Samstag – eine Sitzung ❷ – kommt – zurück ❸ – treffen Sie Ihre – Montag ❹ Ihr – funktioniert – er repariert – ❺ – Mittwoch – Terminkalender – Donnerstagvormittag –

***

• *Donar (Þunar; Thor), the ancient Germanic god of thunder (**der Donner** thunder) has lent his name to **Donnerstag** (as well as to 'Thursday' in English).*
• *And finally, one day of the week is dedicated to a goddess – Frija (Freya; Frig), the goddess of fertility and marriage and the wife of Wotan or Wodan, the Germanic 'god of gods'. (By the way, Wodan himself is the origin of the English 'Wednesday'.)*
• *The origins of **Samstag** are less easy to pin down. One thing is for sure: it doesn't take its name from a Germanic god. **Samstag** is more commonly used in the south of Germany; in the north, people say **Sonnabend**, which means 'the evening before Sunday'.*

hundertachtzehn • 118

26 Sechsundzwanzigste Lektion
*[zeks**unt**-ts**van**tsikHstuh lek**tsiohn**]*

Was machen wir heute Abend, Liebling ①?

1 – Hast du Lust ②, ins ③ The**a**ter zu **geh**en?
2 – Nein, ich **fin**de The**a**ter zu **an**strengend.
3 – Wir **kön**nen **ei**nen Spa**zier**gang ④ **ma**chen.
4 – Ach nein, es **reg**net ⑤ **si**cher bald.

> **Pronunciation**
> *vas **mak**huhn vee[a] **hoi**tuh ahb'nt **leep**ling **1** hast doo lust ins teaht[a] tsoo **geh**-uhn **2** nein ikH **fin**duh teaht[a] tsoo **an**shtrenguhnt **3** vee[a] **kœ**nuhn **ei**nuhn shpat**see**[a]gang **mak**huhn **4** akh nein es **rehg**nuht zikH[a] balt*

Notes

① **Liebling** *darling* may be used for men or women, though the word itself is masculine: **der Liebling**.

② Certain expressions such as **Lust haben** *to feel like, to be in the mood for*, **Zeit haben** *to have time*, **sich freuen** *to be glad/pleased*, require what is called a dependent infinitive preceded by **zu**. The construction '**zu** + infinitive' functions as a kind of 'attachment' that completes the main clause: **Er hat Lust eine Pizza zu essen.** *He feels like eating a pizza.* Such dependent infinitives exist in English as well, and they are also preceded by *to*: **Ich lerne zu fahren.** *I learn to drive.* However, certain verbs in English are followed by a gerund (also known as an *-ing* word) rather than an infinitive – the example *to feel like* is one of them: *He feels like eating a pizza.* Note also that in German, the '**zu** + infinitive' occurs at the end of the sentence. If the infinitive is a separable-prefix verb, the **zu** comes between the prefix and the base verb: **Hast du Lust ein**zu**kaufen?** *Do you feel like shopping?* Since the last spelling reform, it is no longer obligatory to set off the infinitive phrase by a comma ▶

Twenty-sixth lesson 26

What are we doing tonight, darling?

1 – Do you feel like going to the theatre (*Have you desire in-the theatre to go*)?
2 – No, I find [the] theatre too tiring.
3 – We can go for a walk (*can a walk do*).
4 – Ah no, it [will] surely rain soon (*it rains surely soon*).

Pronunciation notes
1 Like all unstressed **-er** endings, the **-er** of **Theater** is pronounced like the neutral vowel [a].

▶ (as in line 1), but many people still do, either out of habit or for clarity: **Ich freue mich(,) Sie zu sehen.** *I am glad to see you.*

③ **ins** is a contraction of the preposition *in* **in** and the article **das**. Note that in German the preposition *in* is used to express going 'to' the theatre.

④ Did you notice that **der Spaziergang** *walk* is masculine? If it were neuter, it would have been **ein**, and if it were feminine, **eine**! Yes, that's it, **einen** is the singular masculine accusative. Also note that dependent infinitives used with modal verbs (verbs that indicate likelihood, ability or obligation, such as *can*) are never preceded by **zu**, although they are also relegated to the end of the sentence: **Wir können eine Pizza <u>essen</u>.** *We can eat a pizza.* ('We can a pizza eat.')

⑤ Like verbs whose stem ends in **-t** or **-d**, verbs whose stem ends in a consonant followed by **n** or **m** also insert an **-e** before the conjugation ending: **regnen** *to rain* (stem **regn-**), **es regnet** *it rains*. It's easy to understand why: just try to say 'regnt'!

hundertzwanzig • 120

5 – Wir **neh**men **ei**nen **R**egenschirm ⑥ mit.
6 – Och, ich **ha**be **kei**ne Lust.
7 – Dann **blei**ben wir zu Haus und **la**ssen ⑦ **Pi**zzas **ko**mmen,
8   was meinst ⑧ du?
9 – Au ja, **das** ist **ei**ne **gu**te **I**dee.

---

*5 vee^a **neh**muhn **ei**nuhn **reh**g'n-shirm mit **6** okh ikH **hah**buh **kei**nuh lust **7** dan **blei**b'n vee^a tsoo hows unt **la**ss'n **pit**sas **ko**muhn **8** vas meinst doo **9** ow yah **das** ist **ei**nuh **goo**tuh i**deh***

Notes

⑥ One often hears **der Schirm** rather than **der Regenschirm** *umbrella*, which literally means 'rain-protection'. Note that it is **der Regen** *rain*, but **re**g**n**en *to rain*.

⑦ **lassen** can mean *to allow, to permit*, but also *to leave (behind)* and *to have something done*: **Sie lässt das Kind ins Theater gehen.** *She allows the child to go to the theatre.* **Sie lässt ihren Regenschirm zu Haus.** *She leaves her umbrella at home.* **Sie lässt ihren Computer reparieren.** *She is having her computer repaired.*

⑧ **meinen** *to think, to consider* as in 'to be of the opinion'. Another meaning of **meinen** is *to mean*.

***

Übung 1 – Übersetzen Sie bitte!

❶ Machen wir einen Spaziergang! ❷ Habt ihr keine Lust, ein Bier zu trinken? ❸ Lassen Sie bitte ein Taxi kommen! ❹ Es regnet und ich habe keinen Regenschirm! ❺ Einkaufen ist anstrengend!

5 – We [will] take an umbrella.
6 – Oh, I don't feel like it (*have no desire*).
7 – Then let's stay at home and have pizzas delivered (*let pizzas come*),
8 what do you think?
9 – Oh yes, that is a good idea.

> **6, 9 Och** is an interjection conveying weariness; **au ja**, in contrast, expresses joyful approval. Thus they require completely different intonations!

***

Answers to Exercise 1

❶ Let's go for a walk! ❷ Don't you [all] feel like drinking a beer? ❸ Please phone a taxi (*let a taxi come*)! ❹ It's raining and I have no umbrella! ❺ Going shopping is tiring!

27 Übung 2 – Ergänzen Sie bitte!

❶ Do you (*informal sing.*) have time to go shopping? – Yes, sure.
...., einkaufen zu gehen? – Ja, ...

❷ Can we not stay at home?
Können wir nicht .. .. ?

❸ She doesn't feel like going to the theatre (*She has no desire in-the theatre to go*).
Sie hat .... Theater .. gehen.

---

27 Siebenundzwanzigste Lektion
*[zeeb'nunt-**tsvan**tsikHstuh lek**tsiohn**]*

Na, schmeckt's ①?

1 – Sehr gut! Das **Es**sen ② ist **wirk**lich **aus**ge**zei**chnet.
2 – Ja, die **Vor**speisen ③ **schme**cken **köst**lich.

Pronunciation
*na shmekts **1** zeh^a goot! das **ess**'n ist **virk**likH ows guh**tseik**Hnuht
2 yah dee **foh**^{a}-shpeizuhn **shmek**'n **kœst**likH*

Notes

① **Schmeckt's?** *Are you enjoying your food? Do you like your meal?* or **Wie schmeckt's?** *How is your meal?* ('How does it taste?') are probably among the most frequently asked questions in German. They are usually asked when you're eating, since **schmecken** means *to taste* as well as *to taste good*. Hence **Das schmeckt!** can mean *That's/It's nice!, This/It tastes good!* or *That's/It's tasty!* Feel free to add **gut** *good*, **sehr gut** *very good*, **ausgezeichnet** *excellent*, etc. for reinforcement.

123 • **hundertdreiundzwanzig**

❹ What would you like to do this evening (*today evening to-do*), darling?

... möchtest du .... machen, ... ?

❺ It isn't raining anymore – we don't need an umbrella.

.. .. nicht mehr, wir brauchen ....

Answers to Exercise 2

❶ Hast du Zeit – sicher ❷ – zu Haus bleiben ❸ – keine Lust, ins – zu – ❹ Was – heute Abend – Liebling ❺ Es regnet – keinen Regenschirm

Twenty-seventh lesson 27

Well, are you enjoying your meal (*does-it-taste*)?

1 – [It's] very good! The meal is really excellent.
2 – Yes, the starters are (*taste*) delicious.

② Every German infinitive may be used as a noun. All that is needed is a capital letter: **essen** *to eat* → **das Essen** *the food, the meal*, **lesen** *to read* → **das Lesen** *the reading*, etc. Note that the English equivalent is often a gerund (the *-ing* verb form that functions as a noun). An infinitive used as a noun is always neuter: **das** Lesen, **das** Essen, **das** Arbeiten.

③ **die Vorspeise** *starter* literally means 'the before-food'. Likewise, *dessert* is **die Nachspeise** ('the after-food') or **der Nachtisch** ('the after-table'). But note that **der Nachtisch** is masculine because **der Tisch** *table* is masculine.

27

3 – Und die **Haupt**speisen ④ sind noch **be**sser!
4 – Aber ich **fin**de die Por**tio**nen zu groß.
5 – Ich auch, ich bin schon to**tal** satt ⑤.
6 – Wie **bit**te? Wollt ⑥ ihr **kei**nen **Nach**tisch?
7   Der Schokoladenkuchen schmeckt hier so gut!
8 – Nein **dan**ke, ich kann nicht mehr.
9 – Ich auch nicht ⑦, ich **neh**me auch **kei**nen.
10 – Ich ver**steh**e euch ⑧ nicht.
11 Der **Nach**tisch ist das **Bes**te ⑨!

---

*3 unt dee **howpt**-shpeizuhn zint nokh **bess**ᵃ **4 ahb**ᵃ ikH **fin**duh dee por**tsioh**nuhn tsoo grohs **5** ikH owkh ikH bin shon to**tahl** zat **6** vee **bit**uh? volt eeᵃ **kei**nuhn **nahkh**tish **7** deᵃ shoko**lah**duhn-kukh'n shmekt heeᵃ zoh goot **8** nein **dang**-kuh ikH kan nikHt mehᵃ **9** ikH owkh nikHt, ikH **neh**muh owkh **kei**nuhn **10** ikH fer**shteh**uh oikH nikHt **11** dehᵃ **nahkh**tish ist das **bes**tuh*

Notes

④ **die Hauptspeise** *main course* is a compound word made up of **das Haupt** *head* and **die Speise** *food, fare*. **das Haupt** is only used in a figurative sense: **Opa ist das Haupt der Familie.** *Granddad is the head of the family.* In compound words it signifies 'principal, central, main': **der Hauptbahnhof** *the main station*, **die Hauptstadt** *the capital*.

⑤ **Ich bin total satt.** *I'm really full.* This expression should only be used in informal situations. A more polite way of declining food would be **Nein danke, ich habe keinen Hunger mehr.** *No thank you, I'm not hungry anymore.*

⑥ **wollen** *to want, to wish* is another modal verb, and its present tense forms are irregular. You'll find an overview of the forms of **wollen** in review lesson 35.

3 – And the main courses are even better!
4 – But I find the portions too big.
5 – Me too (*I also*), I am already really full (*totally satisfied*).
6 – What (*How please*)? Don't you want any dessert (*Want you[pl.] no dessert*)?
7 The chocolate cake here is (*tastes here*) so good!
8 – No thanks, I can't [eat] any more (*I can no more*).
9 – Neither can I (*I also not*), I won't have any (*I take also none*).
10 – I don't understand you (*pl.*).
11 The dessert is the best [thing]!

Pronunciation note
6, 9 Germans often barely articulate the final **-e** in first-person singular verbs, and sometimes they even leave it out entirely. The same holds true for the ending **-en** of the masculine definite and indefinite articles in the accusative case and the negation **kein(e)**. So, for example, it wouldn't be unusual to hear **ich nehm' kein' Nachtisch** instead of **ich nehme keinen Nachtisch**.

⑦ The word for *neither* (and *not either*) is very logical in German: just negate **auch** 'also' → **auch nicht** 'also not'. **Du verstehst das nicht? Ich auch nicht!** *You don't understand this? – Neither do I!/I don't either!*

⑧ **euch** is the accusative of **ihr** *you* (pl.). Remember that **ihr** and **euch** are used when addressing more than one person informally: **Kinder, wo seid ihr? Ich sehe euch nicht.** *Children, where are you? I don't see you.*

⑨ **das Beste** *the best* means 'the best bit/thing'.

27 Übung 1 – Übersetzen Sie bitte!

❶ Schmeckt der Apfelkuchen gut? ❷ Guten Tag, entschuldigen Sie, verstehen Sie Deutsch? ❸ Nein, danke, wir nehmen keinen Nachtisch. ❹ Das schmeckt köstlich, ich möchte bitte ein bisschen mehr. ❺ Ich nehme keine Vorspeise, und du?

***

Übung 2 – Ergänzen Sie bitte!

❶ Mrs Spielberg, your (*formal*) chocolate cake is (*tastes*) really excellent.
Frau Spielberg, ...
schmeckt wirklich . . . .

❷ The starters here are the best; I['ll] have (*take*) two.
. . . . sind hier . . . ., . . .
. . . . . zwei.

❸ Why don't you (*pl.*) want to eat, children? Doesn't it taste [good]?
Warum . . . . nicht essen, Kinder?
. . . . nicht?

❹ He doesn't understand her: the portions are small, but she finds them too big.
. . . . sie nicht: . . . . sind klein, aber . . . . sie . . . .

❺ Many thanks, I don't want any (*would-like no*) dessert. – Neither do I (*I also not*), I'm full.
Vielen Dank, ich möchte . . . .
– Ich . . . ., ich bin . . . . .

127 • **hundertsiebenundzwanzig**

Answers to Exercise 1

❶ Does the apple cake taste good? ❷ Good afternoon, excuse me, do you understand German? ❸ No thanks, we won't have any dessert. ❹ That is delicious – I would like a little more, please. ❺ I won't have a starter, and you?

***

Answers to Exercise 2

❶ – Ihr Schokoladenkuchen – ausgezeichnet ❷ Die Vorspeisen – das Beste, ich nehme – ❸ – wollt ihr – Schmeckt es – ❹ Er versteht – die Portionen – sie findet – zu groß ❺ – keinen Nachtisch – auch nicht – satt

Before moving on to the review lesson, we strongly recommend rereading the dialogues in the past six lessons, as exposure to the living language is as important as grammatical explanations. And don't forget to try to put what you're learning into practice as much as possible!

28 Achtundzwanzigste Lektion

[**akht**unt-**tsvan**sikHstuh lek**tsiohn**]

Wiederholung – Review

1 Personal pronouns in the nominative and accusative case

You're hopefully getting used to the accusative (the case for direct objects), which you've seen in the last few lessons. Now you just need to practice which to use when. To help you, here is a table with the personal pronouns in the nominative and the accusative.

	Nominative	Accusative
1st-person sing.	**ich** *I*	**mich** *me*
2nd-person sing.	**du** *you*	**dich** *you*
3rd-person sing.	**er** *he*, *it* (m.) **sie** *she*, *it* (f.) **es** *it* (neuter)	**ihn** *him*, *it* (m.) **sie** *her*, *it* (f.) **es** *it* (neuter)
1st-person pl.	**wir** *we*	**uns** *us*
2nd-person pl.	**ihr** *you*	**euch** *you*
3rd-person pl.	**sie** *they*	**sie** *them*

Formal		
	Nominative	Accusative
2nd-person (sing. and pl.)	**Sie** *you*	**Sie** *you*

At the risk of being repetitive, let's review some useful rules:

- The feminine (**sie**), neuter (**es**) and plural (**sie**) third-person personal pronouns don't change in the accusative case. The formal pronoun **Sie** doesn't change either. It is only distinguished from the third-person plural by its capital letter.
- The second-person plural pronoun **ihr** *you* is used to address two or more people informally.
- Just like the definite article, the masculine singular personal pronoun in the accusative ends in **-n**: **ihn** *him*, *it* (m.).

Twenty-eighth lesson 28

- In the third-person, when the pronoun refers to a thing rather than a person (i.e. *it*), the pronoun has to correspond with the grammatical gender of the noun it replaces.

2 Possessive adjectives

Possessive adjectives describe a noun by showing ownership, possession or relationship. They are somewhat more complicated in German than in English, as they decline not just according to the possessor, but also to the gender, case and number of what is possessed. Don't worry, we'll learn the forms gradually!

In English:
A possessive adjective only identifies the possessor. It does not change according to the object(s) possessed. For example:
Is this Melanie's? – Yes, it is her cake/house/dog.
Are these Peter's? – Yes, they are his books/clothes/papers.

In German:
A German possessive adjective also identifies the possessor. You've encountered seven so far:

Singular possessor			
1st person		**mein-**	*my* (m./f.)
2nd person	informal	**dein-**	*your* (m./f.)
	formal	**Ihr-**	*your* (m./f.)
3rd person		**sein-**	*his*, *its* (m.)
		ihr-	*her*, *its* (f.)
		sein-	*its* (neuter)
Plural possessor			
3rd person		**ihr-**	*their* (m./f.)

However, a possessive adjective in German also needs to agree in case, gender and number with the noun possessed. So to choose the correct possessive adjective you have to:

hundertdreißig • 130

- identify the possessor
- determine the case, gender and number of the noun possessed
- provide the appropriate ending that corresponds to the case, gender and number of the noun possessed. These endings are the same as for the forms of **ein**.

Here's an overview for the nominative case (the same endings are used for **dein**, **Ihr**, **sein** and **ihr**):

	What is possessed (when the subject of the sentence)			
	Singular			Plural
	masc.	fem.	neuter	
Possessor (m./f.)	mein Bruder	meine Schwester	mein Kind	meine Kinder

Examples:
Mein Hund heißt Fido. *My dog is called Fido.* (**der** Hund)
Deine Katze ist süß! *Your cat is cute!* (**die** Katze)
Seine Frau ist in Ferien. *His wife is on holidays.*
Ihr Mann ist in Deutschland. *Her husband is in Germany.*
Sind das **Ihre** Bücher? *Are those your books?*

And don't forget that in the third-person, the form of *its* you choose depends on both the grammatical gender of the possessor, as well as the gender, number and case of what it possesses:

Die Sonne und ihr Licht *The sun and its light*
(**ihr** because **die Sonne** is feminine and **das Licht** is neuter sing.)

Die Sonne und ihre Planeten *The sun and its planets*
(**ihre** because **die Sonne** is feminine and **die Planeten** is plural)

We'll look at the other grammatical cases later.

3 Asking questions: *Wer? Welcher? Was für (ein)?*

Certain question words also decline.
• **Wer?** *Who?* declines for case like the masculine definite article **der** *the*:
Wer ist das? *Who is that?*
(nominative: when 'who' is the subject)

131 • **hunderteinunddreißig**

Wen treffen sie um fünfzehn Uhr? *Whom do they meet at 3:00?*
(accusative: when 'whom' is the direct object)

- **Welcher?** *Which?* declines for gender, number and case. It declines like **der, die, das**:

Welcher Zug fährt nach Bonn? *Which train goes to Bonn?*
(**der** Zug – masc. nominative)

Welche Vorspeise nimmst du? *Which starter are you having?*
(**die** Vorspeise – fem. accusative)

Welches Buch ist das Beste? *Which book is the best?*
(**das** Buch – neuter nominative)

Welchen Freund triffst du Sonntag? *Which friend are you meeting on Sunday?* (**den** Freund – masc. accusative)

Welche Bücher magst du? *Which books do you like?*
(**die** Bücher – neuter accusative)

- 'Which?' in the sense of 'What kind of?' translates as **Was für …?** / **Was für ein(e) …?** Note that **ein** declines:

Was für eine Sitzung haben Sie morgen?
What kind of meeting do you have tomorrow? (**die** Sitzung – fem.)

Was für ein Fest ist das?
What kind of celebration is this? (**das** Fest – neuter)

Was für einen Nachtisch möchtest du?
What kind of dessert would you like? (**den** Nachtisch – m. acc.)

But there is no plural form of **ein**:
Was für Vorspeisen magst du? *What kind of starters do you like?*

Was für ein … ! can be used as an exclamation: **Was für eine Idee!** *What an idea!* **Was für ein Tag!** *What a day!*

4 The position of the verb

Let's go over some of the sentence structures we've seen so far. We'll discover more in later lessons.

4.1 Conjugated verb in first position

This occurs (just like in English):
- in a yes/no question: **Haben Sie Hunger?** *Are you hungry?*

• in a command: **Machen Sie schnell!** *Make haste! Hurry up!*
(A yes/no question is one that can be answered simply with 'yes', 'no', 'maybe', etc. Yes/no questions are usually distinguished from questions that ask for specific information. An informational question begins with a question word: see 4.2)

4.2 Verb in second position

It is not immediately obvious what is meant by 'the second position' in a sentence. In order to define this, it is necessary to determine what constitutes the first position. This might be a single word or a group of words: for example, a phrase that acts as a subject, a direct object, an adverb or adverbial phrase, an expression of time or place, etc. The second position is hence the position <u>after the introductory element</u>.

The verb is in the second position in the following cases:

• in a question that starts with a question word (as in English):
Wie heißen Sie? *What is your name?*
Wer trinkt keinen Kaffee? *Who doesn't drink coffee?*
Wann kommt Ihr Zug an? *When does your train arrive?*

• in a statement (that is, a sentence that establishes a fact and is neither a question nor a command):
Thomas arbeitet heute nicht. *Thomas doesn't work today.*
Heute arbeitet Thomas nicht. *Today, Thomas doesn't work.*
Seine Freundin arbeitet auch nicht.
His girlfriend doesn't work either.
Morgen Abend gehen sie in die Oper.
Tomorrow evening they are going to the opera.

There are some exceptions, as we'll see later.

4.3 A dependent infinitive

Unlike in English, when two verbs are used to express something in a German sentence, they are not found together. The infinitive (preceded by **zu** or not) is placed at the end of the sentence (in the last position).

Ich möchte im Garten Geburtstag feiern.
I would like to celebrate [the] birthday in the garden. ('I would like in the garden birthday to celebrate.')

Er hat keine Lust, nach Hause zu gehen.
He doesn't feel like going home. ('He has no desire to home to go.')

Sometimes German sentence structure may seem a bit complicated, but don't worry. With practice, you'll get used to it!

5 Ordinal numbers and dates

5.1 Ordinal numbers

The ordinal numbers between 1 and 19 are formed by adding the suffix **-te** to the numeral. The only exceptions are: **der erste** *the first*, **der dritte** *the third*, and **der siebte** *the seventh*.

1st	**erste**	*11th*	**elfte**
2nd	**zweite**	*12th*	**zwölfte**
3rd	**dritte**	*13th*	**dreizehnte**
4th	**vierte**	*14th*	**vierzehnte**
5th	**fünfte**	*15th*	**fünfzehnte**
6th	**sechste**	*16th*	**sechzehnte**
7th	**siebte**	*17th*	**siebzehnte**
8th	**achte**	*18th*	**achtzehnte**
9th	**neunte**	*19th*	**neunzehnte**
10th	**zehnte**		

The ending **-ste** is added to numbers beyond 19: **der zwanzigste** *the twentieth*, **der einundzwanzigste**, *the twenty-first* etc.

The endings **-te** and **-ste** decline in certain circumstances. In the accusative singular, for example, **-te** and **-ste** change to **-ten** and **-sten** respectively:

Er ist der erste. *He is the first.* (nominative)
Er hat den ersten Platz. *He is in first place.* (accusative)

5.2 Dates

In German, there are two ways to express dates:

• using the verb **sein** *to be*:
Heute ist Dienstag, der 25. Mai.
Today is Tuesday, the 25th [of] May.

hundertvierunddreißig • 134

(The number is pronounced **'fünfundzwanzig<u>ste</u>'** because there is a period after the number, which indicates that it is an ordinal. This period is required in dates.)

- using the verb **haben** *to have*:
Heute haben wir den 25. Mai. *Today is the 25th [of] May.*
(The number is pronounced **'fünfundzwanzig<u>sten</u>'** with -n because the date is in the accusative here.)

The preposition **am (an + dem)** is used to give a precise date:
Wann ist Ihr Geburtstag? *When is your birthday?*
Am 3. (dritten) September. *On the 3rd [of] September.*

To figure out how to give your own birthday, here are the twelve months of the year:
Januar, Februar, März, April, Mai, Juni, Juli, August, September, Oktober, November, Dezember.

And here are the names of the four seasons:
der Frühling *spring*, **der Sommer** *summer*,
der Herbst *autumn/fall*, and **der Winter** *winter*.

> *Now sit back and enjoy the review exercise to soak in all that you've just learned.*

Review exercise

Die Geburtstagsparty von Melanie

1 – Guten Abend, ich bin Sonja, eine Freundin von Melanie.
2 – Die Party ist super, finden Sie nicht?
3 – Stimmt, aber was für eine Hitze!
4 – Ach, ich glaube, es regnet bald.
5 – Möchten Sie etwas trinken?
6 – Au ja, das ist eine gute Idee.
7 – Warten Sie, ich hole ein Glas Sekt für Sie.
8 Ich komme gleich zurück.

***

135 • **hundertfünfunddreißig**

9	Hallo, wo sind Sie? Hier ist Ihr Sekt!
10 –	Vielen Dank. Sie trinken keinen?
11 –	Nein, ich fahre, ich trinke Apfelsaft.
12 –	Sind Sie der Bruder von Melanie?
13 –	Nein, ich bin ihr Kollege, wir arbeiten zusammen.
14 –	Ach, <u>Sie</u> sind das, jetzt verstehe ich.
15 –	Was verstehen Sie?
16 –	Melanie findet ihren Kollegen sehr nett.
17 –	Ach wirklich? Das ist lustig.
18	Sie findet ihre Freundin auch prima...

Translation
Melanie's birthday party

(*The speakers use formal address.*)

1 Good evening, I'm Sonja, a friend of Melanie['s]. **2** The party is great, don't you think? **3** True, but it's so hot! **4** Unfortunately, I believe it [will] rain soon. **5** Would you like something to drink? **6** Oh yes, that's a good idea. **7** Wait, I['ll] get a glass [of] sparkling wine for you. **8** I'll be back in a moment (*I come at-once back*). **9** Hello, where are you? Here is your sparkling wine! **10** Many thanks. You aren't having any (*You drink none*)? **11** No, I'm driving, I'm drinking apple juice. **12** Are you Melanie's brother? **13** No, I'm her colleague, we work together. **14** Oh, it's <u>you</u> (*you are that*), now I understand. **15** What do you understand? **16** Melanie finds her colleague very nice. **17** Oh really? That's funny. **18** She also finds her friend *(f.)* great ...

> *See what sort of conversation you could have if you attended a* **Gartenparty** *tomorrow? It comes in very handy to know a bit of small talk for all sorts of situations. We don't know how this particular story will end, but we do know one thing – we're sure to see you again soon.* **Bis morgen!**

29 Neunundzwanzigste Lektion
[*noinunt'**tsvan**tsikHstuh lek**tsiohn**]*

Man kann ① nicht immer Glück haben

1 – Sag mal, ist es noch weit ②?
2 – Nein, viel**leicht** noch **fünf**zehn Kilo**me**ter.
3 – Gott sei Dank, die Ben**zin**uhr ③ ist auf null.
4 – Seit wann? Schon **lange**?
5 – **Un**gefähr **zwan**zig Kilo**me**ter ④.
6 – Dann **kön**nen wir es theo**re**tisch **scha**ffen ⑤.

Pronunciation
By now you're becoming familiar with the pronunciation of certain words. So from this lesson on, we'll only give you the phonetic transcriptions for words you haven't seen yet – or only infrequently. This will allow you to spot the new words in the lesson at a glance.

Notes
① The infinitive of **kann** *can* is **können** *to be able to, to know how to*. **können** is one of six so-called modal verbs. These indicate an attitude towards an action; they don't express the action itself. In a sentence containing a modal verb, the verb that expresses the action is in the infinitive form and is in the last position, while the modal verb is conjugated and is in the second position: **Man kann Glück haben.** *One can be lucky.* ('One can luck have.') We'll look at the conjugation of modal verbs in detail in lesson 35.

② **weit** can mean *far* or *wide*.

③ **die Benzinuhr** is a compound word made up of **das Benzin** *petrol, fuel* and **die Uhr** *clock, watch*.

④ The majority of masculine nouns ending in **-er** form the plural simply by adding an umlaut: **der Vater**, **die Väter** *father*,

137 • **hundertsiebenunddreißig**

Twenty-ninth lesson 29

One can't always be lucky

1 – Tell [me], do we still have far to go (*is it still far*)?
2 – No, maybe (*still*) 15 kilometres.
3 – Thank God (*God be thanks*), the petrol gauge is on empty (*zero*).
4 – Since when? A long time (*Already long*)?
5 – [For] about 20 kilometres.
6 – Then we could theoretically manage it (*Then can we it theoretically manage*).

... kan ... **1** ... veit **2** ... feel-**leikHt** ... kilo**meht**ᵃ **3** got zei ... ben**tseen**-ooᵃ ... nul **4** zeit van? ... **lang**uh **5 un**guh-fehr ... **6 kœ**nuhn ... teo**reh**tish **shaf**'n

fathers. Sometimes, they don't change at all in the plural: **das Zimmer**, **die Zimmer** *room, rooms*; **der Kilometer**, **die Kilometer** *kilometre, kilometres*. Speaking of which, remember that masculine and neuter nouns used as units of measurement generally do not change in the plural: **ein Euro, zehn Euro** (and NOT 'Euros').

⑤ **schaffen** is a verb with multiple meanings. Here it is used in the sense of *to achieve, to manage, to cope with something*. It is a transitive verb, which means that it always takes a direct object (here, **es** *it*). In German the direct object is always in the accusative case: **Er schafft den Nachtisch nicht.** *He can't manage [to eat] the dessert.* ('He manages the dessert not.') **Sie schafft ihre Arbeit.** *She is coping with her work.* **Ich schaffe es nicht.** *I can't manage it.*

7 Warum hältst du denn an ⑥?
8 – Es ist Schluss ⑦, wir haben kein Benzin mehr.
9 – Verflixt ⑧, das ist der Unterschied zwischen theoretisch und praktisch.

7 ... heltst... 8 ... shlu'ss ... 9 ferflikst ... unt^esheet tsvish'n ... praktish

Notes

⑥ You already know **Halt!** *Stop!* The verbs **anhalten** and **halten** *to stop, to halt* are both used to describe the voluntary stopping of something in motion. The stem vowel **a** changes to **ä** in the second- and third-person singular: **du hältst, er/sie/es hält**. But note that **anhalten** is a separable-prefix verb and that the prefix moves to the last position in present tense sentences: **Der Zug hält an.** *The train is stopping.*

⑦ **der Schluss** *end, ending, closure* is related to **schließen, geschlossen** *to close, closed*. **Schluss** and **geschlossen** are written with **ss** because the preceding vowel is short; after a long vowel, as in **schließen**, you have to use **ß**.

⑧ **Verflixt!** is a familiar interjection along the lines of **Mist!** (lesson 9, note 5). It is also an adjective that can mean *accursed, darned* or *blasted*: **Die verflixte Benzinuhr funktioniert nicht!** *The darned petrol gauge doesn't work!* Did you notice the **-e** ending of the adjective in this example? In lesson 18 we ▶

***

Übung 1 – Übersetzen Sie bitte!

❶ Schaffen Sie das allein oder brauchen Sie mich? ❷ Seit wann funktioniert die Benzinuhr nicht mehr? ❸ Theoretisch kann er das, aber praktisch ist er zu dumm. ❹ Halten Sie bitte an, ich möchte einen Kaffee trinken. ❺ Der Unterschied zwischen „Mist" und „verflixt" ist nicht sehr groß.

7 Why are you stopping then?
8 – It's finished (*end*), we have no petrol left (*more*).
9 – Darn, that's the difference between theory (*theoretically*) and practice (*practically*).

Pronunciation note
9 das is in bold here to show that the sentence stress falls on it.

> Schaffen Sie das allein oder brauchen Sie mich?

saw that predicate adjectives (which follow nouns and a form of **sein**) are invariable: **Julia und Thomas sind pünktlich.** *Julia and Thomas are punctual.* But if the adjective precedes the noun it modifies, it is an attributive adjective and must decline to agree with the number, gender and case of the noun. Its ending also depends on what kind of article precedes the noun, if any. We will explain adjective endings in detail in the review lesson.

***

Answers to Exercise 1

❶ Can you manage this on your own or do you need me? ❷ Since when has the petrol gauge not been working? ❸ In theory he can [do] this, but in practice he is too stupid. ❹ Stop please, I would like to have a coffee. ❺ The difference between 'blast' and 'darn' isn't very big.

hundertvierzig • 140

30 Übung 2 – Ergänzen Sie bitte!

❶ It isn't far now (*It is now not more far*).
Es ist jetzt ....

❷ Darn, I have no petrol left (*more*), and there (*here*) is no petrol station.
Verflixt, ich habe ...., und hier ist ....

❸ Let me [be], I can manage this on my own (*this alone manage*).
Lass mich, ... das allein ....

---

30 Dreißigste Lektion [*dreissikHstuh lektsiohn*]

Dienst ist Dienst und Schnaps ist Schnaps ①

1 – Ich **bi**tte Sie, **blei**ben Sie doch ② noch ein **we**nig ③!
2 Es ist nicht spät.

Pronunciation
deenst ... shnaps ... **1**... **veh**nikH

Notes

① This saying literally translates as 'Duty is duty and schnapps is schnapps' (**der Dienst** *service, duty*; **der Schnaps** *schnapps, spirits*), in the sense of 'You can't mix business and pleasure'.

② We've seen **doch** as *yes* in response to a negative question (lesson 19). However, it can also function as a particle like **denn**. **Doch** can be added for amplification or to convey a sense of invitation or exhortation, as in *just* or *do*: **Kommen** ▶

141 • hunderteinundvierzig

❹ Since when have you been learning German? – Not (*Still not*) long, about four weeks.
.... lernen Sie Deutsch? – Noch nicht
....., ... vier Wochen.

❺ When will we stop (*stop we*)? I'd like to have a coffee.
Wann ....? Ich möchte .....
....

Answers to Exercise 2

❶ – nicht mehr weit ❷ – kein Benzin mehr – keine Tankstelle
❸ – ich kann – schaffen ❹ Seit wann – lange, ungefähr –
❺ – halten wir an – einen Kaffee trinken

Thirtieth lesson 30

There's a time and place for everything

1 – Please (*I ask you*), do stay a little [longer] (*stay you just still a little*)!
2   It isn't late.

Sie doch mit! *Just come along! Do come along!* It can also be used to emphasize a request: **Sprich doch nicht so laut!** *Don't speak so loudly, will you?* or to intensify a statement: **Das sehe ich doch!** *I do see that! I see that after all!*

③ **wenig** means *little* or *not much*: **ein wenig** is synonymous with **ein bisschen**.

30

3 – Ich weiß, **a**ber ich muss ④ **mor**gen früh **auf**stehen ⑤.

4 – Wa**rum müs**sen Sie denn so früh **auf**stehen?

5 – **Mor**gen ist **Diens**tag ⑥ und **diens**tags ⑦ kontro**lliert** mein Chef per**sön**lich die **An**kunftszeit.

6 – **A**ber nein, **mor**gen ist nicht **Diens**tag, **son**dern ⑧ **Mitt**woch.

7 Sie **kön**nen noch **blei**ben!

8 – Ach, **Diens**tag, **Mitt**woch **o**der **Don**nerstag, das ist das**sel**be ⑨ für **mei**nen Chef ⑩.

9 **Wis**sen Sie, für ihn ist **je**der ⑪ Tag „**Dienst**-tag".

---

3 ... mus ... owf**sh**tehn 4 ... mewss'n ... 5 ... deens**t**aks ko'ntrol**eert** ... per**zoen**likH ... ankunfts-tseit 6 ... zond^{a}n ... 8 ... das-**zel**buh ... 9 ... yehd^e ...

Notes

④ The infinitive of **muss** *must* is **müssen** *to have to, to be obliged to, to need to*. **Müssen** is another modal verb, and its stem vowel changes from **ü** to **u** in all three forms of the singular: **ich muss, du musst, er/sie/es muss**.

⑤ **aufstehen** *to get up* is another separable-prefix verb: **ich stehe auf** *I get up*, **du stehst auf** *you get up*, etc.

⑥ Many people assume – wrongly – that **Dienstag** comes from 'service day' or 'day of duty', just like they assume that **Freitag** means 'free day' or 'day off'. There's no truth in this. Remember the information about the origins of the names of the days of the week in lesson 25?

⑦ The name of a day of the week (e.g. **Dienstag**) or the name for a part of the day (e.g. **der Abend**) may be used as an adverb to indicate repetition or habitual action. An **-s** is then added to the noun. But remember that adverbs – unlike nouns – are ▶

143 • **hundertdreiundvierzig**

3 – I know, but I have to get up early tomorrow (*must tomorrow early up-get*).
4 – Why do you have to get up so early (*Why must you then so early up-get*)?
5 – Tomorrow is Tuesday, and Tuesdays my boss personally checks our (*the*) arrival time.
6 – But no, tomorrow isn't Tuesday, but Wednesday.
7 You can (*still*) stay!
8 – Ah, Tuesday, Wednesday or Thursday, it's [all] the same for my boss.
9 You know (*Know you*), for him every day is (*is every day*) 'service-day'.

➤ not capitalized in German: **Dienstag** *Tuesday* → **dienstags** *every Tuesday, on Tuesdays*; **der Morgen** → **morgens** *every morning, in the morning*; **Freitag** → **freitags** *every Friday, on Fridays* → **freitagabends** *every Friday evening, on Friday evenings*, etc.

⑧ In general, *but* is **aber** in German. However, after a negative clause (involving **nicht** or **kein**), **sondern** is used. **Sondern** is a coordinating conjunction and expresses a contrast or contradiction. It is equivalent to *but, on the contrary, instead, rather*: **Er kommt nicht aus Italien, sondern aus Frankreich.** *He is not from Italy, but from France.* **Das ist kein Kaffee, sondern Tee.** *This isn't coffee, but tea.*

⑨ **dasselbe** means *the same (thing)*: **Es ist immer dasselbe!** *It's always the same!* It is the neuter form of the demonstrative pronoun **derselbe** (m.), **dieselbe** (f.) *the same*. **Derselbe**, **dieselbe** and **dasselbe** always refer back to a person or a thing already mentioned. Here **dasselbe** refers to the neuter pronoun **es** in the impersonal expression **Es ist immer dasselbe!**

⑩ False friend alert! **Chef** in German means *boss, head*, not a professional cook!

⑪ **jeder**, **jede**, **jedes** *every, all, everyone, anyone* declines.

hundertvierundvierzig

30 **Übung 1 – Übersetzen Sie bitte!**

① Sonntags essen wir nicht zu Hause. ② Jede Woche trifft sie einmal ihre Freundin. ③ Es ist immer dasselbe, sie steht zu spät auf! ④ Ich muss leider gehen, meine Frau wartet schon lange. ⑤ Trinken Sie nicht zu viel Schnaps!

***

Übung 2 – Ergänzen Sie bitte!

① He has to go home, it is already late and he is on duty at six o'clock (*he has at six o'clock duty*).

.. .... nach Haus gehen, es ist schon .... und er hat um sechs Uhr ....

② Please (*I ask you* [acc.]), do stay (*stay just still*) a little [longer], every minute is a pleasure for me.

... . dich, ... doch noch ... ., ... ist ein Vergnügen ... mich.

③ Today isn't Wednesday, but Thursday.

Heute ist ...., ... Donnerstag.

④ It's always the same: every morning one goes (*goes one*) to the office, and every evening one is (*is one*) tired.

Es ist immer ....: ...... geht man ins Büro, und ...... ist man .....

⑤ Get (*formal*) up please, I have to inspect you (*I must you check*).

.... bitte ..., ... Sie ....

145 • hundertfünfundvierzig

Answers to Exercise 1

❶ On Sundays we don't eat at home. ❷ Every week she meets her friend (*f.*) once. ❸ It's always the same – she gets up too late! ❹ Unfortunately, I have to go, my wife has been waiting a long time (*waits already long*). ❺ Don't drink too much schnapps!

***

Answers to Exercise 2

❶ Er muss – spät – Dienst ❷ Ich bitte – bleib – ein wenig, jede Minute – für – ❸ – nicht Mittwoch, sondern – ❹ – dasselbe – morgens – abends – müde ❺ Stehen Sie – auf, ich muss – kontrollieren

31 Einunddreißigste Lektion

Guter ① Rat ist teuer

1 – **Tho**mas, Sie **so**llen ② zum ③ Chef **ko**mmen!
2 – Soll ich **o**der muss ich?
3 – Das **müs**sen Sie **wis**sen ④!
4 – **Ich** weiß nur, dass der Chef will ⑤, dass Sie **ko**mmen.
5 – Halt, **war**ten Sie, das ⑥ ist nicht so **ein**fach.
6 Hat er **gu**te **Lau**ne **o**der **schlech**te **Lau**ne?
7 – **E**her **schlech**te **Lau**ne, **den**ke ich.

Pronunciation
goot[e] raht ... **1** ... zol'n ... **5** ... einfakh **6** ... gootuh lownuh ... shlekHtuh ... **7** eh[a] ... denkuh ...

Notes

① If a noun is preceded by an adjective rather than an article or a possessive pronoun, the adjective must show the noun's gender and/or case. The adjective takes the same endings as the definite article (with the exception of the masculine and neuter genitive, but we won't worry about that just now): **guter Rat** *good advice* (**der** Rat [m.]), **gute Laune** *good mood* (**die Laune** [f.]) (line 6).

② **sollen** *to be supposed to, to be meant to* expresses an obligation towards someone or something, to society, or to one's own conscience – one 'should' do something. However, **sollen** is less binding than **müssen**, which conveys a sense of compulsion – one 'must' do something. **Müssen oder sollen wir Geld verdienen?** *Do we have to earn money or are we [just] supposed to?*

Thirty-first lesson 31

It's hard to know what to do
(*Good advice is expensive*)

1 – Thomas, you are supposed to go and see the boss (*to-the boss come*).
2 – Am I supposed to or do I have to?
3 – That's for you to say (*That must you know*)!
4 I only know that the boss wants you to go and see him (*wants that you come*).
5 – Stop, wait, that's not so easy.
6 Is he in [a] (*Has he*) good mood or [a] bad mood?
7 – More likely [a] bad mood, I think (*think I*).

③ The preposition **zu** *to, towards* is normally used with verbs expressing movement. The only exception is **zu Hause sein** *to be at home*. **zum** is a contraction of **zu + dem**. We'll find out more about the article **dem** soon.

④ **wissen** *to know* is the only non-modal verb that follows the same conjugation pattern as the modal verbs (see lesson 35). In the present tense singular, the stem vowel changes from **i** to the diphthong **ei**, and the first- and third-person forms are the same: **ich weiß, du weißt, er/sie/es weiß**. The plural forms follow the regular present-tense pattern.

⑤ **ich will, du willst, er/sie/es will** are the singular forms of the modal verb **wollen** *to want, to wish, to intend to*.

⑥ Did you spot the difference in spelling between the conjunction **dass** *that* (line 4) – with a double **s** – and the pronoun **das** *it, this, that*?

31   8   Er scheint **ziem**lich nerv**ös** zu ⑦ sein.
      9 – **Seh**en Sie, jetzt ist **all**es klar:
   10   ich **muss hin**gehen ⑧,
   11   ich **hab**e **kein**e Wahl.

8 ... sheint **tseem**likH nerv**œs** ... 10 ... **hin**gehn 11 ... vahl

Notes

⑦ **scheinen** *to seem, to appear* is always followed by an infinitive preceded by **zu**: **Sie scheint müde zu sein.** *She appears to be tired.* ('She seems tired to be.')

⑧ The particle **hin** shows motion away from the speaker. It can be translated as *there*, but we often leave this out in English: **Du gehst morgen in die Oper? Ich gehe auch hin.** *You're going to the opera tomorrow? I'm going (there), too.*

***

Muss es sein? – Ja, es muss sein! *Is it necessary? – Yes, it is!*
This literally translates as 'Must it be? – Yes, it must be!' These words are normally spoken with conviction as they are meant to express an absolute necessity or compulsion, something inescapable, rather than one of several options. Saying **es muss sein** *conveys that there is only one decision to make.*

The problem is, of course, that the perception of true necessity is in the eye of the beholder. Imagine a situation where a father says to his children: **Ihr müsst jetzt schlafen!** *You must [go to] sleep now! To which the children reply:* **Wir müssen aber unser Spiel zu Ende machen!** *But we have to finish our game! We'll leave the outcome of this scenario to your imagination ...*

***

Übung 1 – Übersetzen Sie bitte!

❶ Frau Spielberg, Sie sollen Ihren Mann anrufen!
❷ Müsst ihr wirklich schon nach Hause gehen?
❸ Sie scheinen sehr nervös zu sein, was haben Sie? ❹ Es muss leider sein, Sie haben keine Wahl.
❺ Die Kinder sollen zum Essen kommen!

8 He seems to be quite nervous (*seems quite nervous to-be*).
9 – You see, now everything is clear:
10 I have to go (*there*),
11 I have no choice.

> Sehen Sie, jetzt ist alles klar.

***

Or another example: Your partner says **Wir müssen einkaufen gehen!** *We must go shopping! You could, of course, mount an attempt at defence by asking:* **Muss das wirklich sein?** *Is that really necessary? ('Must that really be?') If the answer is* **Das muss sein!** *then you've got little choice but to give in.*

Interestingly, nowadays people say **Ich muss arbeiten** *I have to work, whereas not too long ago they would have said* **Ich soll arbeiten** *I should work;* **müssen** *is increasingly replacing* **sollen**. *Might this be a sign that we've become more accepting of the obligations we're faced with?*

***

Answers to Exercise 1

❶ Mrs Spielberg, you should phone your husband! ❷ Must you really go home already? ❸ You seem to be very nervous, what's wrong (*what have you*)? ❹ Unfortunately, it is necessary (*It must unfortunately be*) – you have no choice. ❺ The children should come and eat (*to-the meal come*)!

hundertfünfzig • 150

32 Übung 2 – Ergänzen Sie bitte!

❶ Careful, the boss is in a bad mood today (*has today bad mood*).
Vorsicht, ... hat heute ....

❷ Why don't you (*informal sing.*) want to go to the party?
Warum .... nicht ... . gehen?

❸ That's not easy, but we have no choice.
Das ist ...., aber wir haben .....
..... .

❹ They don't seem to know that he is quite nervous (*quite nervous is*).
... . nicht .. .., dass er
.... ist.

---

32 Zweiunddreißigste Lektion

Ein gefährliches Missverständnis ①

1 – Oh, der ist süß ②!

Pronunciation
... guh**fehr**likHes **mis**fershtentnis **1** ... zews

Notes

① **das Missverständnis** *misunderstanding, disagreement* is a neuter noun; we can tell because of the **-es** ending of the adjective **gefährlich** *dangerous* (the indefinite article **ein** could indicate a masculine or neuter noun). Neuter nominative adjectives end in **-es**, and masculine nominative adjectives end in **-er**. You saw the **-er** ending in lesson 31: **guter Rat** *good advice* or **ein guter Rat** *a good piece of advice*. Note as well that the prefix **miss-** (like 'mis' in English) expresses a negative idea. So **das Verstädnis** means *comprehension*,

❺ Are you supposed to or do you have to do one lesson per day?   32
...... oder ...... Sie eine Lektion pro Tag
......?

Answers to Exercise 2

❶ – der Chef – schlechte Laune ❷ – willst du – zum Fest – ❸ – nicht einfach – keine Wahl ❹ Sie scheinen – zu wissen – ziemlich nervös – ❺ Sollen – müssen – machen

As you know, we recommend that you do a lesson a day. It's for you to decide whether this is an absolute or a relative obligation! In the first case, you'll probably say **Ich muss eine Lektion pro Tag machen.** *And in the second,* **Ich soll eine Lektion pro Tag machen.** *Whatever the case may be, we're glad to see that you've reached the end of lesson 31. Keep up the good work!*

Thirty-second lesson   32

A dangerous misunderstanding

1 – Oh, he is cute!

Sind Sie verrückt?

understanding, appreciation: **verstehen** *to comprehend, to understand*; **missverstehen** *to misunderstand.*

② **süß** *means sweet or cute*: **Das ist ein süßes Kind.** *That's a cute child.* **Der Nachtisch ist zu süß.** *The dessert is too sweet.*

hundertzweiundfünfzig • 152

2 Wie alt ist der ③?
3 Darf ④ ich den **strei**cheln?
4 – Wenn Sie **wol**len.
5 – Au, der beißt ja ⑤, au, **au**a!
6 Mensch, das tut weh!
7 **Hal**ten Sie doch **end**lich **Ih**ren Hund zu**rück**!
8 Sie **dür**fen so **ei**nen Hund nicht frei **lau**fen **las**sen ⑥!
9 Sind Sie ver**rückt**?
10 – Tut mir Leid ⑦, ich **ke**nne den Hund nicht.

---

3 darf ... **shtrei**kH'ln **4** ven ... **5** ow ... beist yah ... **ow**ah
6 ... toot veh **7** ... **ent**likH... **8** ... **dewrf**'n ... **9** ... fe**rrewkt**
10 ... leit ... **ke**nuh...

Notes

③ **der, die** and **das** are often used as demonstrative pronouns. They are identical to the definite article (except in the genitive, which we'll get to later). A demonstrative pronoun is used instead of a personal pronoun (e.g. **er, sie, es**) when the pronoun is to be emphasized. **Wie alt ist der?** *How old is him.* **Den kenne ich nicht.** *I don't know him.* **Was macht die hier?** *What's she doing here?* (See also lesson 13, note 5.)

④ The infinitive of **darf** *may* is **dürfen** *to be allowed to*. In contrast to **können** *to be able to*, **dürfen** indicates that an action depends on authorization from someone else rather than possibility: **Ich kann in Ferien fahren.** *I can go on holiday.* (I have the means or opportunity to do so); **Ich darf in Ferien fahren.** *I may go on holiday.* (I have permission to do so). In the same way, **dürfen** in the negative, as in line 8's **nicht dürfen**, means *not to be allowed to* in the sense of *mustn't*: **Er darf nicht trinken.** *He mustn't drink.* Be careful not to use

153 • **hundertdreiundfünfzig**

2 How old is he?
3 May I stroke him?
4 – If you like (*want*).
5 – Ouch, but he bites (*yes*), ouch, ow!
6 Gosh, that hurts!
7 For goodness sake, hold back your dog, will you (*Hold you will-you at-last your dog back*)!
8 You mustn't let a dog like that run free (*such a dog free run let*)!
9 Are you crazy?
10 – I'm sorry, I don't know this (*the*) dog.

Pronunciation note

5 au and **aua** are cries of pain. The greater the pain, the longer the **u** *oo* is drawn out after the **a**: *a-oooo*... However, don't confuse **aua** and **au ja**, an interjection expressing enthusiastic consent (see lesson 26).

nicht müssen in this context, which means 'not to have to': **Er muss nicht trinken.** *He doesn't have to drink.*

⑤ **ja** *yes* is also used as a particle that reinforces a statement or question and conveys surprise: **Es regnet ja!** *But it's raining!*

⑥ Note the word order: **laufen lassen** ('to run let'). In contrast with English, **lassen** *to let, to allow, to have something done* always comes second when paired with another infinitive. **Man muss Kinder spielen lassen.** *One must let children play.* **Wo kann ich bitte mein Handy reparieren lassen?** *Where can I have my mobile phone repaired, please?* (lesson 26).

⑦ **Tut mir Leid** or **Das/es tut mir Leid** *I am sorry* literally means 'This does to me suffering.' The verb **tun** *to do* is synonymous with **machen**, and is used in many a useful expression. We've just seen one: **Das tut weh!** *That hurts!* ('That does pain!')

hundertvierundfünfzig • 154

32 11 Das ist nicht **mei**ner ⑧.

11 ... meinᵃ

Notes

⑧ Possessive pronouns replace a noun and indicate ownership: *mine, yours, his, hers, its, ours, theirs*. You won't be surprised to hear that German possessive pronouns not only have to indicate the owner, but also have to agree in gender, number and case with what is possessed. They are formed by taking the appropriate possessive adjective and adding the ending

***

Übung 1 – Übersetzen Sie bitte!

❶ Mama, warum dürfen wir den Apfelkuchen nicht essen? ❷ Er hat ein Handy, aber er nimmt immer meins. ❸ Achtung! Mein Hund beißt! ❹ Oh, das Kind ist süß! ❺ Tut mir Leid, Sie dürfen hier nicht telefonieren.

***

Übung 2 – Ergänzen Sie bitte!

❶ I'm sorry, my dog bites everyone (*all*).

.. .., mein Hund ..... alle.

❷ May I call you tomorrow? – If you want.

.... Sie morgen anrufen? – Wenn ... .

❸ Yuck, my cake is too sweet; and how is yours (*informal sing.*)?

Iiii, mein Kuchen ist .. ..., und wie ist ......?

155 • **hundertfünfundfünfzig**

11 It isn't mine.

that agrees with the noun it replaces: **meiner** (m.), **meine** (f.), **meins** (neuter): **Ist das dein Hund? – Ja, das ist meiner**. *Is this your dog? – Yes, it is mine.* **Die Tasche hier, ist das deine?** *This bag here, is this yours?* **Ist das sein Haus? – Ja, das ist seins.** *Is this his house? – Yes, it is his.*

***

Answers to Exercise 1

❶ Mum, why aren't we allowed to eat the apple cake? ❷ He has a mobile, but he always uses mine. ❸ Careful! My dog bites! ❹ Oh, the child is cute! ❺ I'm sorry, you may not make calls (*may not telephone*) here.

***

❹ May he let his dog run free (*his dog free run let*)?
.... .. seinen Hund frei .... ?

❺ But there's been (*this is*) a misunderstanding! He isn't dangerous, he is just (*only*) a little excited!
Aber das ist ... . ! Er ist
nicht ...., er ist nur ... .
.... !

Answers to Exercise 2

❶ Es tut mir Leid – beißt – ❷ Darf ich – Sie wollen ❸ – zu süß – deiner ❹ Darf er – laufen lassen ❺ – ein Missverständnis – gefährlich – ein wenig aufgeregt

hundertsechsundfünfzig • 156

33 Dreiunddreißigste Lektion

Die Stadtbesichtigung ①

1 **Mei**ne **Da**men und **Her**ren,
2 **ge**gen**ü**ber ist der **Bahn**hof,
3 und links **seh**en Sie den **Köl**ner Dom ②.
4 Wir **müs**sen jetzt **aus**steigen und zu Fuß ③ **wei**tergehen.
5 Um ④ den Dom ist **ei**ne **Fuß**gängerzone ⑤.
6 Wir **wol**len zu**erst** den Dom be**sich**tigen und dann die **Alt**stadt.
7 Zum Schluss **dür**fen Sie ein „Kölsch" ⑥ **trin**ken, das **ty**pische Bier von hier.

Pronunciation
dee **shtat**-buhzik**H**tigung **1** ... **dah**muhn ... **heruhn 2 gehg**'n-ewb^a ... **3** ... **kœln**^{a} dohm **4** ... tsoo foos ... **5** ... **foos**-geng^a-tsohnuh **6** ... tsoo-**eh**^{a}st ... buhzik**H**tig'n ... **alt**-shtat ... **7** ... **kœ**lsh ... **tew**pishuh ...

Notes

① Remember that nouns ending in **-ung** are always feminine (lesson 25, note 5). The noun **die Besichtigung** *visit* derives from the verb **besichtigen** *to visit*. **Die Besichtigung** and **besichtigen** are used when referring to visiting places. The verb **besuchen** is used to talk about visiting people: **Ich besuche meine Freundin.** *I visit my friend* (f.).

② Another way of saying **der Dom von Köln** is **der Kölner Dom**. As a general rule, you add **-er** to the name of a city or a region to signal that something (or someone) is from there: **die Berliner Universität** *the University of Berlin*, **die Frankfurter Würstchen** *sausages from Frankfurt* or simply *Frankfurters*. In these examples, **Berliner** and **Frankfurter** are actually adjectives. Note that such adjectives are invariable:

157 • **hundertsiebenundfünfzig**

Thirty-third lesson 33

Sightseeing (*The city-visit*)

1 (*My*) Ladies and gentlemen,
2 [just] opposite is the train station,
3 and on the left, you see (*the*) Cologne Cathedral.
4 We have to get off now and continue on foot (*on foot further-go*).
5 Around the cathedral [there] is a pedestrian zone.
6 We will (*want*) first visit the cathedral and then the old town.
7 Finally (*At-the end*), you may drink a 'Kölsch', the local beer (*the typical beer from here*).

they always end in **-er**, no matter what the gender, number or case. Moreover, they're always capitalized: **Ich kann den Mainzer Dom sehen!** *I can see Mainz Cathedral!*

③ **der Fuß**, **die Füße** *foot, feet*; **zu Fuß** *on foot*.

④ Here **um** means *around* and it requires the accusative case: **um den Dom** *around the cathedral.* We've already seen that the preposition **um** can also mean *at* when used with a specific time: **um drei Uhr** *at 3 o'clock*.

⑤ **die Zone** *zone*, **der, die** (pl.) **Fußgänger** *pedestrian(s)*. Remember that masculine nouns ending in **-er** don't change in the plural, except for some that take an umlaut: **der, die Arbeiter** *worker(s)*, but **der Bruder**, **die Brüder** *brother(s)*.

⑥ Note that you say **ein** or **das** '**Kölsch**' because it refers to a type of beer and **das Bier** is a neuter noun in German.

hundertachtundfünfzig • 158

8 Und wer ⑦ kein Bier mag ⑧, be**ko**mmt ein Glas **Ap**felschorle.

> 8 ... bu**ko**mt ... **ap**f'l-shorluh

Notes

⑦ We've seen **Wer?** *Who?* as a question word. However, here **wer** is an indefinite relative pronoun meaning *whoever* or *anyone who*. It relates to a person or persons who are not clearly defined: **Wer viel liest, lernt viel.** *[He] who reads a lot learns a lot*. When **wer** is used in this way it introduces a subordinate clause, and so the conjugated verb comes in the last position: **Und wer kein Bier <u>mag</u>** ('And whoever no beer <u>likes</u>'). Also note that in German the subordinate clause is always separated from the main clause by a comma.

***

Übung 1 – Übersetzen Sie bitte!

❶ Wir fahren nächstes Wochenende nach Köln.
❷ Wer nicht zu Fuß gehen will, nimmt die U-Bahn.
❸ Zum Schluss wollen wir den Dom besichtigen.
❹ Ich mag keine Frankfurter Würstchen und Sie?
❺ Sie müssen hier aussteigen.

***

Übung 2 – Ergänzen Sie bitte!

❶ She doesn't like beer; she would like a glass [of] wine.

... ... kein Bier, ... ein Glas Wein.

❷ We're now coming into the pedestrian zone and, of course, we'll continue on foot (*and go naturally on foot further*).

Wir kommen jetzt in ... .
und gehen natürlich .. ... weiter.

❸ Do you know the old town [of] Hamburg?

Kennen Sie die .... ?

8 And whoever doesn't like beer gets a glass [of] 'Apfelschorle'.

⑧ In lesson 23, we saw **ich mag** *I like* and its infinitive **mögen**. Like *like*, the meaning of **mögen** is less strong than 'love' and is often used to express a taste (see lesson 23): **ich mag kein Bier** *I don't like beer*, **ich mag Rap** *I like rap*, but can also express a feeling, as in **ich mag dich** *I like you* (a bit more restrained than **ich liebe dich** *I love you*). Remember that **ich möchte** (the subjunctive of **mögen**) means *I would like* and is similar to **ich will** *I want*: **Ich möchte ein Bier.** *I would like a beer.* **Ich will kein Bier.** *I don't want any beer.*

***

Answers to Exercise 1

❶ We're going to Cologne next weekend. ❷ Anyone who doesn't want to go on foot takes the underground/subway. ❸ Finally, we will (*want to*) visit the cathedral. ❹ I don't like frankfurter sausages, and you? ❺ You have to get off here.

***

❹ Tomorrow I can't, I'm going sightseeing (*I make a city-visit*).
Morgen .... nicht, ich mache ....
. . . .

❺ Whoever wants to visit Cologne Cathedral has to get off here (*must here off-get*).
... den Kölner Dom ....,
muss hier ....

Answers to Exercise 2

❶ Sie mag – sie möchte – ❷ – die Fußgängerzone – zu Fuß – ❸ – Hamburger Altstadt ❹ – kann ich – eine Stadtbesichtigung ❺ Wer – besichtigen will – aussteigen

hundertsechzig • 160

34 | Apfelschorle und Bier, die deutschen Nationalgetränke
'Apfelschorle' and beer, Germany's national drinks

In contrast to cider **(der Apfelwein** *'apple-wine'),* **Apfelschorle** *is a non-alcoholic mixture of apple juice and* **Sprudel,** *sparkling mineral water.* **Apfelschorle** *is nice and refreshing, so almost everyone drinks it in summer ... except, perhaps, those who prefer beer. Germany has a tradition of beer-brewing that goes back centuries. It also has the world's largest number of breweries (around 1,300), which includes a long list of famous brands. Nowhere else do you find greater choice (a selection of about 5,000 different beers). In theory you could try a different beer every day for almost 13.5 years!*

German brewers still abide by the famous **Reinheitsgebot** *– literally, 'Purity Order' – the oldest food safety law still in force in the world. The* **Reinheitsgebot** *has its origins in a 1516 ducal decree issued by William IV of Bavaria that restricted the ingredients in beer-making to water, barley and hops. The role of yeast in the brewing process wasn't clear at the time, but yeast was added to the list of permitted ingredients in the subsequent incarnations of this regulation that have made their way into German law.*

During the Middle Ages, the centre of German beer production lay in the north, in Hamburg and in Lower Saxony. The most famous

34 Vierunddreißigste Lektion

Was ① man darf und was man nicht darf

1 – Man darf nicht bei Rot ② die **Straß**e **ü**ber**que**ren.

Pronunciation
*1 ... roht ... **ewbᵃkvehr**uhn*

Notes

① Like in English, **was** *what* can be a question word: **Was machst du?** *What are you doing?* or an indefinite relative pronoun: **Was sie macht, ist verboten.** *What she does is forbidden.*

areas for beer production today – the Rhine Valley and Bavaria – were mostly known as wine-growing areas. But a taste for beer rapidly spread south, and from the 17th century onwards, Munich and Dortmund became the beer capitals of what is now Germany. Having said that, there is still a lot of regional variety in beers. For example, 50 kilometres south of Dortmund, people tend to drink **Kölsch**, *a pale beer (***helles Bier***) that is only brewed in Cologne. However, in Düsseldorf,* **Alt** *or* **Altbier**, *an amber-coloured dark beer (***dunkles Bier***) is the most popular brew. And in Thuringia and Saxony you can find various kinds of* **Schwarzbier** *('black beer')*.

Thirty-fourth lesson 34

What one may and (*what one*) mustn't [do]

1 – One mustn't cross the road at a red light (*at red the road cross*).

Pronunciation note
1 Careful! In German, **qu** is pronounced *kv*.

In the latter case, **was** refers to something without specifically defining it and has the meaning 'that which'.

② In the expression **bei Rot gehen/fahren** *to cross on foot/drive through a red light*, **rot** *red* is capitalized because it is used as a noun, 'the colour red'.

2 – Man darf nicht be**trun**ken **Fahr**rad **fah**ren ③.

3 – Man darf nicht **sa**gen, dass **je**mand ver**rückt** ist ④.

4 – Aber man darf in Shorts spa**zie**ren **geh**en,

5 – und man darf San**da**len mit **So**cken **tra**gen!

6 – **Ei**gentlich darf man **al**les **ma**chen, was ⑤ die **an**deren nicht stört ⑥.

7 – Ja, man darf nach zehn Uhr **a**bends **we**der ⑦ laut ⑧ Mu**sik hö**ren noch Sa**xo**fon **spie**len.

8 – Kurz, man darf **ma**chen, was er**laub**t ⑨ ist, und nicht **ma**chen, was ver**bo**ten ist … ☐

---

2 … buh**trunk**'n **fah**ᵃraht … 3 … **yeh**mant … 4 … shorts … 5 … zan**dahl**'n … **zok**'n **trah**g'n 6 … an**duh**ruhn … **shtœrt** 7 … **vehd**ᵃ lowt moo**zik** … zakso**fohn shpeel**'n 8 kurts … er**lowp**t … fer**boh**tuhn …

Notes

③ Instead of **das Fahrrad** *bicycle, bike*, people often simply say **das Rad** *wheel*, particularly to avoid repetition, such as in the expression **Fahrrad fahren** *to cycle*.

④ In a subordinate clause introduced by a conjunction – here, **dass** *that* – or by a relative pronoun (see note 1), the verb is in the last position: **Ich weiß, dass du verrückt bist.** *I know that you are crazy* ('that you crazy <u>are</u>'). Don't forget that in German a comma is required to separate the main clause (**Ich weiß**) from the subordinate clause (**dass du verrückt bist**), or that dependent infinitives are in the last position in the sentence, which occurs a lot in this lesson: **Man darf nicht betrunken <u>fahren</u>.** *One mustn't drive drunk* ('drunk <u>drive</u>').

⑤ When **was** is used after indefinite nouns and pronouns such as **alles** *all, everything, anything*, **nichts** *nothing*, **etwas** *something* or **das Beste** *the best*, it best translates to *that* (which is often optional in English). **Machen Sie nichts, was** ▶

2 – One mustn't cycle drunk (*drunk bicycle drive*).
3 – One mustn't say that somebody is crazy.
4 – But one may go for a walk in shorts,
5 – and one may wear sandals with socks!
6 – Actually, one may do anything (*everything*) that doesn't bother others (*that the others not bothers*).
7 – Yes, after ten o'clock in the evening, one must neither listen to loud music nor play the saxophone (*neither loudly music listen nor saxophone play*).
8 – [In] brief, one may do what is allowed, and [may] not do what is forbidden ...

Sie nicht wollen! *Don't do anything (that) you don't want [to do]!* **Es gibt nicht vieles, was sie nicht weiß.** *There isn't much (that) she doesn't know.*

⑥ **stören** *to disturb, to bother*: **Bitte nicht stören!** *Please don't disturb!* **Das stört mich nicht.** *That doesn't bother me.*

⑦ **weder ... noch** *neither... nor.*

⑧ The opposite of **laut** *loud, noisy, boisterous* is **leise** *muted, low, gentle, quiet*. **Die Musik ist zu laut.** *The music is too loud.* Here, **laut Musik hören** can be translated as 'to listen to loud music' or 'to play music loudly'. Note that German uses an adverb + verb construction – **laut hören** ('loudly listen') – whereas English uses an adjective + noun – 'loud music'.

⑨ **erlaubt** and **verboten** are respectively the past participles of **erlauben** *to permit, to allow* and **verbieten** *to forbid, to prohibit, to ban*. We'll look at forming past participles soon.

hundertvierundsechzig • 164

34 Übung 1 – Übersetzen Sie bitte!

❶ Ihr dürft alles machen, was ihr wollt, Kinder.
❷ Es ist verboten, die Straße bei Rot zu überqueren.
❸ Thomas hat weder Zeit noch Lust Rad zu fahren.
❹ Man darf die anderen nicht stören. ❺ Hallo, ist hier jemand?

***

Übung 2 – Ergänzen Sie bitte!

❶ Do you (*formal*) wear sandals with socks?
.... Sandalen ... . ?

❷ You (*informal sing.*) mustn't do that (*may this not do*), that is (*after ten o'clock*) not permitted after 10 o'clock.
.. .. das nicht ......, das ist ....
.... nicht ....

❸ Do what you want, it (*that*) doesn't bother me.
Machen Sie, ..., das .....
mich ......

❹ He is drunk and is cycling – that's forbidden!
Er ist .... und ...., das ist
.... !

❺ Please don't disturb [me], I don't want any (*I want no*) breakfast.
Bitte nicht ......, ... kein Frühstück.

Answers to Exercise 1

❶ You may do anything (*that*) you want, children. ❷ It is prohibited to cross the street at a red light. ❸ Thomas has neither [the] time nor [the] desire to cycle. ❹ One mustn't disturb the others. ❺ Hello, is anyone there (*is here somebody*)?

***

Answers to Exercise 2

❶ Tragen Sie – mit Socken ❷ Du darfst – machen – nach zehn Uhr – erlaubt ❸ – was Sie wollen – stört – nicht ❹ – betrunken – fährt Rad – verboten ❺ – stören, ich will –

35 Fünfunddreißigste Lektion

Wiederholung – Review

1 Modal verbs

The six modal auxiliary ('helping') verbs in German are **können** *to be able to, to know how to* ('can'); **wollen** *to want to, to wish to, to intend to*; **sollen** *to be supposed to* ('should'); **müssen** *to have to* ('must'); **dürfen** *to be permitted to* ('may'); and **mögen** *to like*. They have certain characteristics in common with the (non-modal) verb **wissen** *to know* in that they are irregular in the singular forms of the present tense.

- The first-person (**ich**) and third-person (**er/sie/es**) singular forms are identical – the verb stem takes no ending. The second-person singular (**du**) takes the regular -st ending.

- With the exception of **sollen**, the stem vowel changes in the singular.

Here's an overview:

	können	wollen	sollen	müssen	dürfen	mögen
ich	kann	will	soll	muss	darf	mag
du	kannst	willst	sollst	musst	darfst	magst
er sie es	kann	will	soll	muss	darf	mag
wir	können	wollen	sollen	müssen	dürfen	mögen
ihr	könnt	wollt	sollt	müsst	dürft	mögt
sie	können	wollen	sollen	müssen	dürfen	mögen

- Modal verbs indicate an attitude about an action; they don't express the action itself. Hence they usually occur with a so-called dependent infinitive. In German, this infinitive is in the last position in the sentence:
Er kann morgen nicht kommen. *He can't come tomorrow.*
Wir müssen jetzt nach Hause gehen. *We have to go home now.*

Thirty-fifth lesson   35

• The modal verb is conjugated and occurs in the position normally occupied by the conjugated verb, that is:
- the second element in a statement:
Leider <u>kann</u> er morgen nicht kommen.
Unfortunately, he <u>can't</u> come tomorrow.

- the first element in a yes/no question:
<u>Müssen</u> wir wirklich nach Haus gehen?
Do we really <u>have to</u> go home?

- the second position in questions introduced by a question word:
Warum <u>dürfen</u> wir kein Bier trinken, Mama?
Why aren't we <u>allowed to</u> drink beer, Mum?

2 The meanings of modal verbs

• The difference between **müssen** 'must' and **sollen** 'should' is similar to that in English. While **müssen** is used to express an obligation that theoretically leaves no room for alternatives, **sollen** is used when one feels obliged to do something either by someone else or by one's own conscience. However, watch out when using **müssen** with the negation **nicht**, which translates not as 'must not' but as *not to be obliged to* or *not to have to*. The expression that corresponds to 'mustn't' as in 'not allowed to' is **nicht dürfen**, whereas if you'd rather soften the proscription into a request or advice, use **nicht sollen** 'should not':
Du musst das nicht machen. *You don't have to do that.*
Du sollst das nicht machen. *You're not supposed to do that.*
Du darfst das nicht machen. *You mustn't do that.*

• **Ich möchte** *I would like* is the subjunctive of the modal verb **mögen** *to like* and expresses a wish or a desire, while **ich mag** is used to express a general fondness (or dislike, if used with **nicht**) for someone or something:
Ich mag Schokoladenkuchen. *I like chocolate cake.*
Ich möchte Schokoladenkuchen essen. *I would like to eat chocolate cake.*

Don't worry, these differences will come naturally with practice.

hundertachtundsechzig • 168

3 Adjectives and adjective endings

Let's take a closer look at what's known as 'adjective declension'. Adjectives can appear in two positions in a sentence: following the noun they describe (predicate adjectives) or preceding the noun they describe (attributive adjectives).

Predicate adjectives are easy because they are invariable – that is, they don't take endings:
Der Hund ist süß. *The dog is cute.*
Die Katze ist süß. *The cat is cute.*
Das Baby ist süß. *The baby is cute.*

In contrast, attributive adjectives do take endings, which are determined by two main factors:

• whether or not the adjective is preceded by another qualifying word (an article, possessive pronoun, etc.)
• the gender, number and case of the noun that the adjective describes.

3.1 Preceded adjectives

In German, if an article or pronoun (*the*, *those*, *a*, *my*, etc.) is used with an adjective, one or the other or both have to reflect the gender, number and case of the noun they modify.

In the case of a definite article preceding an adjective, the article clearly indicates the gender and/or case of the noun, so the adjective ending doesn't need to change for each gender. In the nominative, the adjective simply takes an **-e** ending:
der süße Hund *the cute dog*
die süße Katze *the cute cat*
das süße Baby *the cute baby*

In the case of an indefinite article, because the masculine and neuter nominative and accusative forms don't have endings and therefore don't show the gender of the noun unequivocally, the adjective has to take on this function by adding the markers for masculine (**-er**) and neuter (**-es**):
ein süßer Hund *a cute dog*
eine süße Katze *a cute cat*
ein süßes Baby *a cute baby*

3.2 Unpreceded adjectives

If an adjective is not preceded by an article or pronoun, it needs to take an ending that indicates the gender, number and/or case of the noun it modifies. Let's take the adjective **gut** *good* as an example. In order to say *Good wine is expensive*, you'd need to know that **der Wein** is a masculine singular noun and that in this sentence it is in the nominative case because it is the subject. So you add the nominative masculine **-er** ending to the adjective: **gut** + **er** → **Guter Wein ist teuer.** Or if you wanted to say *Good chocolate is rare* (**selten**), you'd have to bear in mind that **Schokolade** *chocolate* is a feminine singular noun and it is nominative in this sentence. Therefore, you have to add the feminine marker **-e** to the adjective: **gut** + **e** → **Gute Schokolade ist selten.**

In other words, in the absence of a preceding modifying word, the adjective ending needs to indicate the gender and case of a noun. Here's an overview for the endings of unpreceded adjectives in the nominative case:
süßer Wein *sweet wine* (masc.)
süße Marmelade *sweet jam* (fem.)
süßes Brot *sweet bread* (neuter)

Ultimately, adjective declension is actually quite handy as it gives you more opportunities to recognize – and to remember – the gender of a noun, even if it may seem complicated at first.

4 Word order in dependent (subordinate) clauses

A dependent or subordinate clause is a clause that cannot stand alone; it must be combined with a main clause to express a complete idea. In German, a dependent clause is separated from the main clause by a comma. Dependent clauses are often introduced by a subordinating conjunction such as **dass** *that* or **wenn** *if, when*, by a relative pronoun, or by a question word. The conjugated verb is in the last position in the dependent clause.

Wir wissen, dass Sie Deutsch <u>lernen</u>.
We know that you're learning German.
Sie müssen ein bisschen warten, wenn Sie nicht alles <u>verstehen</u>.
You have to wait a little if you don't understand everything.

35 **Heute wissen wir nicht, was morgen <u>kommt</u>.**
Today we don't know what comes tomorrow.
Können Sie uns sagen, warum Sie kein Bier <u>mögen</u>?
Can you tell us why you don't like beer?

5 Days of the week and times of day

Die Woche hat sieben Tage: Montag, Dienstag, Mittwoch, Donnerstag, Freitag, Samstag (oder Sonnabend) und Sonntag.
The week has seven days: Monday, Tuesday, Wednesday, Thursday, Friday, Saturday and Sunday.

Der Tag teilt sich in: der Morgen, der Vormittag, der Mittag, der Nachmittag, der Abend und die Nacht.
The day is divided into [early] morning, morning (literally, 'forenoon'), *midday, afternoon, evening and night.*

The name of the day can be used on its own or with the preposition **am** + the day (see also lesson 28, section 5):
(Am) Montag fahre ich nach Deutschland.
On Monday I'm going to Germany.
(Am) Samstagabend feiere ich meinen Geburtstag.
On Saturday evening I [will] celebrate my birthday.

By adding **-s** to the name of a day or a time of day, you can convey the idea of 'every':
Montags arbeite ich. *On Mondays I work.*
Abends bleibe ich zu Hause. *Every evening I stay at home.*
Und was machen Sie sonntags? *And what do you do on Sundays?*

Note that in this case the word is not capitalized (except at the beginning of a sentence) because it has changed into an adverb and only nouns are capitalized in German.

> **Wir wollen jetzt die Grammatik ein bisschen vergessen! Hier kommt unser Dialog!** *Now let's forget a little [about] grammar! Here is our review exercise!*

Review exercise 35

Ein netter Mann

1 – Sagen Sie mal, ist das Ihr Hund?
2 – Ja, das ist meiner, warum?
3 – Hunde dürfen nicht in den Dom.
4 – Aber mein Hund beißt nicht.
5 – Das macht keinen Unterschied: verboten ist verboten.
6 – Aber ich komme von weit und möchte den Dom besichtigen.
7 – Das können Sie auch, aber ohne Ihren Hund.
8 Sie haben keine Wahl.
9 – Vielleicht können Sie ihn fünf Minuten nehmen?
10 – Sind Sie verrückt? Ich bin im Dienst!
11 Und er kennt mich nicht.
12 – Das macht nichts, er mag jeden. Danke. Bis gleich! (wau, wau, wau …)
13 – Halt, halt das ist nicht so einfach, warten Sie, warten Sie doch!
14 – He, Sie da! Sprechen Sie leise!
15 Und Hunde sind hier verboten!

Translation

A nice man

1 Tell [me], is that your dog? **2** Yes, it's mine. Why? **3** Dogs aren't allowed into the cathedral. **4** But my dog doesn't bite. **5** That makes no difference: forbidden is forbidden. **6** But I come from far [away] and would like to visit the cathedral. **7** You can do that (*That can you also*), but without your dog. **8** You have no choice. **9** Maybe you can take him [for] five minutes? **10** Are you crazy? I'm on duty. **11** And he doesn't know me. **12** That doesn't matter (*makes nothing*), he likes everyone. Thanks. See you in a minute! (woof, woof, woof …) **13** Stop, stop, that's not so easy; wait, wait, will you! **14** Hey, you there! Talk quietly! **15** And dogs are forbidden [in] here!

36 Sechsunddreißigste Lektion

Eine gute Partie

1 – Guck ① mal, **Clau**dia, kennst du den Mann dort?
2 – Den da? Den **gro**ßen **blon**den?
3 – Ja, den. Sprich ② doch nicht so laut!
4 Er soll ③ **schreck**lich reich sein.
5 – Wo**her** ④ weißt du das?
6 – Ich **ha**be es **ges**tern ge**hört** ⑤.

Pronunciation
... par**tee** 1 kuk ... kenst ... 2 ... **blon**duhn 3 ... sh**prik**H ... 4 ... **shrek**likH reikH ... 5 vo**heh**ᵃ ... 6 ... guh-**hœ**ᵃ**t**

Pronunciation notes
Title In **die Partie**, the stress is on the second syllable (par**tee**) while in **die Party**, the first syllable is stressed – **pah**tee. The stress patterns reflect the different origins of these two words.

Notes

① **gucken** is often used in everyday language in the sense of *to look*, but it can also translate as *to peek, to peer* or *to watch*.

② **Sprich!** is the informal second-person imperative (the 'du-imperative') of **sprechen** *to speak, to talk*.

③ The most common use of **sollen** is to express an obligation, as in *to be supposed to*: **Ich soll einkaufen gehen.** *I am supposed to go shopping.* However, **sollen** can also be used to relate a rumour or a report, as in 'It is said that …': **Es soll regnen.** *It is supposed to rain.* **Er soll alt sein.** *He is meant to be old.* Remember that the dependent infinitive of a modal verb always occurs in the last position.

④ **Woher?** *Where from? From where?* is used to ask about provenance or origin: **Woher kommt sie?** *Where does she come from?* In everyday speech, **woher** often separates into **wo** and **her**: **Wo kommt sie her?** *Where does she come from?*

173 • **hundertdreiundsiebzig**

Thirty-sixth lesson 36

A good match

1 – Look, Claudia, do you know the man [over] there?
2 – Him (*there*)? The tall blonde [one]?
3 – Yes, him. Don't speak so loudly, will you (*Speak will-you not so loudly*)!
4   He is meant to be terribly rich.
5 – How do you know (*Where-from know you that*)?
6 – I heard it yesterday (*I have it yesterday heard*).

die Partie *match*, *part*, *game* is of French origin, **die Party** *party* is borrowed from English.
1 The initial **g** of **gucken** is often pronounced *k*: **kuk'n**.
1, **2**, **3**, **7**, **11** Remember that the vowel in **den** *dehn* is long, whereas the vowel in **denn** is short: *den*.
6, **8**, **9** Like all inseparable prefixes, the **ge-** prefix of the past participle is never stressed.

⑤ **gehört** *heard* is the past participle of **hören** *to hear, to listen*. The past participle of regular (weak) German verbs is normally formed by adding the prefix **ge-** and the ending **-t** to the verb stem: **spielen** → **ge** + **spiel** + **t** → **gespielt**. The **-t** ending is **-et** in verbs whose stem ends in **-d** or **-t** and in some verbs whose stem ends in **-m** or **-n**: **arbeiten** → **gearbeitet**; **regnen** → **geregnet**. A number of regular verbs lack the **ge-** prefix in the past participle, but we'll come back to this later. The past participle (along with a present tense form of **haben** or **sein**) is needed to form the present perfect tense. This is one of several past tenses in German. It is commonly used in conversation to refer to past actions or states: **Ich habe sie gesehen.** *I have seen her* or *I saw her*. The past participle is the last element in the phrase: **Ich habe sie gestern in der Stadt gesehen.** *I saw her in town yesterday*. Note that in German, the present perfect tense refers to all actions or states in the past, whereas English uses the simple past (*I saw*) for completed actions and the present perfect tense for uncompleted actions (*I have seen*).

36
7 – Wo denn?
8 – Zwei **Mäd**chen **ha**ben im **Su**permarkt **ü**ber ⑥ ihn ge**re**det ⑦.
9 – Und was **ha**ben sie ge**sagt**?
10 – Sie **fin**den, dass er **ei**ne interes**san**te **Beu**te ist: reich, **le**dig, ein **biss**chen alt, **a**ber nicht zu **häss**lich.
11   He, **war**te! Wo**hin** ⑧ willst du denn?   □
(Fortsetzung folgt)

---

8 … gu**hreh**duht **9** … guh**zahkt 10** … intuh**res**san**tuh boi**tuh … **leh**dikH … **hes**likH **11** heh … vo**hin** … **fort**zetsung folkt

Notes

⑥ The preposition **über** (here meaning 'about') is part of the prepositional verb **reden über** *to talk about* (which is synonymous with **sprechen über**). Both **reden über** and **sprechen über** are followed by the accusative case: **Sie sprechen über den Hund.** *They talk about the dog.* As a spatial preposition, **über** means *over* or *above*. Prepositions often fulfil several functions – we'll come back to this.

⑦ **geredet** is the past participle of **reden** *to speak, to talk*, which is synonymous with **sprechen** – with one notable exception. With regard to speaking languages, only **sprechen** is used: **Ich spreche kein Spanisch.** *I don't speak Spanish.*

⑧ **Wohin?** *Where (to)?* is used to ask about direction or a change of location: **Wohin geht sie?** *Where is she going?* (or **Wo geht sie hin?**, as we saw with **woher** in note 4). As **wohin** in

***

Übung 1 – Übersetzen Sie bitte!

❶ Kennen Sie die Frau dort? ❷ Seine Frau soll viel Geld haben. ❸ Wohin gehen wir heute Abend? Ins Theater oder in die Oper? ❹ Was hast du gesagt? Warum sprichst du so leise? ❺ Haben Sie gehört, wohin er fährt?

7 – Where (*then*)?
8 – Two girls were talking about him in the supermarket.
9 – And what did they say (*what have they said*)?
10 – They think (*find*) that he is an interesting catch: rich, single, a little old, but not too ugly.
11 Hey, wait! Where are you off to (*Where-to will you then*)?
(To be continued ('Continuation follows')...*)*

itself expresses a change of location, it doesn't always require a verb of movement, especially with a modal verb: **Wohin wollt ihr?** *Where do you want to go?* ('To-where want you?'). Sometimes a modal verb isn't even needed: **Das Restaurant ist geschlossen. Wohin jetzt?** *The restaurant is closed. Where to now?* Remember that to ask the position of something, i.e. if neither origin nor direction/movement are implied, use **wo**: **Wo ist der Bahnhof?** *Where is the station?*

✽✽✽

Answers to Exercise 1

❶ Do you know the woman [over] there? ❷ His wife is meant to have a lot of money. ❸ Where are we going tonight? To the theatre or to the opera? ❹ What did you say? Why are you speaking so softly? ❺ Have you heard where he is going?

hundertsechsundsiebzig • 176

37 Übung 2 – Ergänzen Sie bitte!

❶ Where (*Where-from*) do you know this from? I haven't heard anything.
..... wissen Sie das? Ich .... nichts ....

❷ Look! That is a big cake.
...... Sie mal! Das ist ... .

❸ We have spoken about everything.
... . über alles ....

❹ Wait (*formal*), will you! Where(-*to*) do you want [to go] then?
.... doch! ..... wollen Sie denn?

---

37 Siebenunddreißigste Lektion

Eine gute Partie
(Fortsetzung)

1 – Sie geht **wirk**lich **hin** ①.
2 Das darf nicht wahr sein!
3 Und jetzt spricht sie ihn so**gar an**!

Pronunciation
2 ... vah^a ... 3 ... zo**gah** ...

Notes

① Remember **hin** and **her** (in **wohin** and **woher**)? These adverbs are often called 'direction particles' as they indicate the direction of movement. Broadly speaking, **hin** expresses motion away from the speaker, and **her** towards the speaker: *there* and *here* respectively. They can be used as separable prefixes with many verbs, e.g. **herbringen** *to bring here* or

5 Don't speak (*informal*) so loudly – we can be heard (*one can hear us*)!
...... nicht .. ...., man kann uns .....!

Answers to Exercise 2

1 Woher – habe – gehört **2** Gucken – ein großer Kuchen **3** Wir haben – geredet **4** Warten Sie – Wohin – **5** Sprich – so laut – hören

Are you reading the text in the dialogues and exercises out loud? Great! Don't worry about speaking too loudly as you're practicing. Try to listen to your pronunciation – if you're only half liking what you're hearing, repeat the texts as many times as you like. Little by little you'll start to hear the difference ...

Thirty-seventh lesson 37

A good match
(Continuation)

1 – She is really going over there (*She goes really there*).
2 It can't be true (*That must not true be*)!
3 And now she's even speaking to him!

Pronunciation notes
1, 3, 5 The sentence stress is on the last word because these are separable prefixes: **hingehen**, **ansprechen** and **anbieten**.

hinfahren *to go there*: **Mein Vater wohnt in Berlin. Wir fahren hin.** *My father lives in Berlin. We go there.* However, with verbs that don't express coming or going, **hin** and **her** can correspond to a range of adverbs that don't indicate direction in the same way: **Setz dich doch hin!** *Do sit down!*

37

4 Was kann sie ihm ② **sa**gen?
5 Er lacht, er **bie**tet ihr ③ **ei**nen Platz **an**.
6 Sie setzt sich ④ **ne**ben ihn, ganz nah!
7 Sie ist to**tal ü**bergeschnappt ⑤.
8 Sie unter**hal**ten sich, er sieht hier**her** ⑥.
9 Was **ma**che ich nur? Sie **win**ken mir ⑦.

4 ... eem 5 ... lakht ... beetuht ee^a ... 6 ... zetzt zikH nehbuhn een gants nah 7 ... total ewb^a-guhshnapt 8 ... unt^{a}haltuhn zikH ... zeet hee^{a}heh^a 9 ... vink'n mee^a

Notes

② **ihm** *him, to him* is the dative form of **er** *he*. The dative is the third German case we'll talk about (after the nominative and the accusative). The dative has a wide range of functions in German, but its main role is to mark the indirect object. This is usually a person and indicates to whom or for whom the direct object (in the accusative case!) is intended: **Sie zeigt ihm die Stadt.** *She shows the city to him.* **Sie gibt ihm den Kuchen.** *She gives the cake to him.* We'll look at the dative forms of pronouns and articles in lesson 42. Here's just a little hint: the **-m** ending also occurs with masculine articles in the dative.

③ **ihr** *her, to her* is the dative of **sie** *she*. **Er bietet ihr einen Kaffee an.** *He offers a coffee to her.* As we see in the translation of line 5, often in English the indirect object pronoun can also come directly after the verb, avoiding the use of 'to': **Er bietet ihr einen Platz an.** *He offers her a seat.* This can make it a bit trickier to identify the indirect object, but just ask yourself if the word indicates to whom or for whom the direct object is intended. As above, note the pronoun ending: **-r**. The feminine definite article in the dative also has this ending: **Er bietet der Frau einen Kaffee an.** *He offers the woman a coffee.* More about this soon!

④ **sich setzen** *to sit (oneself) down* is an example of a reflexive verb. These are verbs that include a pronoun (here, the third-person **sich**) to indicate that the subject is equally the object of the verb's action. In English, this concept is expressed with *myself, herself, ourselves*, etc., as in 'we enjoyed ourselves'.

4 What can she be saying to him?
5 He's laughing, he's offering her a seat (*place*).
6 She's sitting (*herself*) [down] next to him, really (*completely*) close!
7 She has gone (*is*) completely crazy.
8 They're talking to each other, he's looking over (*here-to*).
9 What shall I do (*do I only*)? They're waving to me.

However, German sometimes uses the reflexive for verbs that aren't reflexive in English. In line 8, we see another use of a reflexive verb: **sich unterhalten** *to speak to each other*. Reflexive pronouns can also be used to indicate reciprocal action, i.e. *to each other*. We'll find out more about reflexive verbs in the coming lessons.

⑤ **übergeschnappt** is the past participle of **überschnappen** *to go crazy*. **überschnappen** is a separable-prefix verb: **ich schnappe über** *I am going crazy*. In the past participle, the prefix remains joined to the verb stem, with the **ge-**prefix inserted between them: **über-ge-schnappt**.

⑥ **hin** and **her** can also combine with other adverbs such as **hier** to form compound words: **Komm hierher.** *Come here!* or *Come this way!* **Hierhin will ich nicht gehen.** *I don't want to go there* or *I don't want to go in this direction.*

⑦ **mir** *me, to me* is the dative of **ich** *I*: **Gib mir bitte den Käse!** *Give me the cheese, please!* ('Give the cheese to me, please!') In line 11, we see **dir** *you, to you*, the dative of **du** *you*.

hundertachtzig • 180

37 **10** Ich muss zu **ih**nen ⑧ **geh**en.
11 – **Hal**lo, **An**ja, darf ich dir **mei**nen **Va**ter **vor**stellen?
12 Er wohnt in Bra**si**lien und ver**bringt sei**nen **Ur**laub ⑨ in Eu**ro**pa. □

*11 ... **an**ya ... dee^a ... foh^a**shtel**'n **12** ... vohnt in bra**zee**lyuhn ... fer**brinkt zei**nuhn oo^{a}lowp in oi**roh**pa*

Notes

⑧ **ihnen** *them, to them* is the dative of **sie** *they*. The dative is always required after **zu** *to, for*. There are other prepositions that always require the dative, as well as some that always require the accusative, such as **für** *for* (see lesson 22, note 4).

✷✷✷

Übung 1 – Übersetzen Sie bitte!

❶ Hallo, Thomas, wohin gehst du? ❷ Kann ich dir etwas zu trinken anbieten? ❸ Anja, kannst du bitte herkommen? ❹ Wo verbringen Sie Ihre Ferien? In Europa oder in Brasilien? ❺ Der Chef winkt mir, das darf nicht wahr sein!

✷✷✷

Übung 2 – Ergänzen Sie bitte!

❶ May I introduce my friend to you (*May I to-you[informal] my friend[f.] introduce*)?
Darf ich ... meine Freundin .... ?

❷ They're waving to you; you have to go over there (*there-go*)!
... . dir, du musst .... !

❸ She speaks nothing but (*speaks only still*) German; she is crazy.
... . nur noch Deutsch, sie ist ....

181 • **hunderteinundachtzig**

10 I have to go [over] to them (*I have-to to them go*).

11 – Hello, Anja, may I (*to-you*) introduce my father to you?

12 He lives in Brazil and is spending his vacation in Europe.

> **12** The diphthong **eu** in **Europa** is pronounced *oi: oirohpa*.

And there even are some that can take either the dative or the accusative! But don't panic, we'll come back to this.

⑨ **der Urlaub** *holiday*, *vacation* is used in the singular, whereas **die Ferien** *holidays* is always plural.

***

Answers to Exercise 1

❶ Hello, Thomas, where are you going? ❷ May I offer you something to drink? ❸ Anja, can you come here, please? ❹ Where do you spend your holidays? In Europe or in Brazil? ❺ The boss is waving at me – it can't be true!

***

❹ Why don't you sit [down] (*Why sit you[formal] yourself not*)? The seat is not taken (*free*).

Warum . . . . sich nicht? . . . . ist frei.

❺ What did you say to him (*have you[informal] to-him said*)?

Was . . . . . . ihm . . . . . . ?

Answers to Exercise 2

❶ – dir – vorstellen ❷ Sie winken – hingehen ❸ Sie spricht – übergeschnappt ❹ – setzen Sie – Der Platz – ❺ – hast du – gesagt

38 Achtunddreißigste Lektion

Alles zu seiner Zeit

1 – **Gu**ten Tag, kann ich **Ih**nen ① **helf**en?
2 – Ja, ich **su**che **ei**nen **fest**lichen **An**zug.
3 – **Schau**en Sie mal, hier **ha**ben wir **ei**nen **Smo**king ②.
4 Der Preis ist sehr **güns**tig.
5 – Nein, ich will **kei**nen **Smo**king, ich **ha**be nach ③ **ei**nem **An**zug ge**fragt**!
6 – Darf ich **fra**gen, für **wel**che Gelegenheit?
7 – Ich will **hei**raten ④.
8 – Oh, wann denn? Ich gratu**lie**re ⑤.
9 Was trägt denn **Ih**re **zu**künftige Frau?
10 – Ich weiß nicht, ich **ken**ne sie noch nicht.

Pronunciation
1 ... helf'n *2* ... festlikHuhn antsook *3* show'n ... smohking *4* ... preis ... gewnstikH *5* ... guhfrahkt *6* ... guhlehg'nheit *7* ... heiratuhn *8* ... gratooleeruh *9* ... tsookewnftiguh ...

Notes

① **Ihnen** *you, to you* (with a capital letter!) is the dative of the formal **Sie** *you*. In German, **helfen** *to help* requires the dative case: **Ich helfe der Frau.** *I help the woman.*

② Did the article **einen** alert you to the fact that both **Anzug** and **Smoking** are masculine nouns: **der Anzug** and **der Smoking**? The latter comes from the English 'smoking jacket'.

③ Here, **nach** (followed by the dative) has neither a spatial nor a temporal meaning. It is just a preposition that accompanies **fragen** *to ask* to introduce an object: **Die Touristen fragen nach dem Weg.** *The tourists ask (for) the way.* You'll come across other verbs followed by a preposition (e.g. **gratulieren**

Thirty-eighth lesson   38

All in good time (*All at its time*)

1 – Good afternoon, can I help you?
2 – Yes, I am looking for (*I search*) a formal (*festive*) suit.
3 – Look, here we have a tuxedo.
4   The price is very reasonable (*favourable*).
5 – No, I don't want a tuxedo, I asked for a suit (*I have for a suit asked*)!
6 – May I ask for which occasion?
7 – I want to get married.
8 – Oh, when (*then*)? Congratulations (*I congratulate*).
9   What will your future wife be wearing (*What wears then your future wife*)?
10 – I don't know. I don't know her yet.

zu, note 5). These verb + preposition constructions are wholly idiomatic, so they have to be learned together: **fragen nach** (+ dative) *to ask for/about*.

④ **heiraten** *to marry, to get married*: **Er hat eine reiche Frau geheiratet.** *He has married a rich woman*. (But *I am married* is **ich bin <u>ver</u>heiratet**.)

⑤ **gratulieren** *to congratulate* can be used for all occasions: birthdays, marriages, exams, etc. It is followed by the preposition **zu** + dative: **Wir gratulieren Ihnen zum Geburtstag.** *We congratulate you on your birthday*. (**zum** is a contraction of **zu dem**, and **dem** is the dative of the masculine definite article **der**!)

hundertvierundachtzig • 184

38 **11** Ich **su**che sie, wenn ich den **An**zug **ha**be ⑥.
12 Eins ⑦ nach dem **an**deren.

> **12** eins nakh dehm **an**duhruhn

Notes

⑥ **habe** is in the last position because – as you may remember – the conjugated verb is always in the last position in a dependent, or subordinate, clause (which is introduced by a conjunction and is separated from the main clause by a comma). Note that **wenn** can have the temporal meaning 'when' or 'whenever', but it can also introduce a conditional clause, meaning 'if': **Ich komme, wenn ich kann.** *I [will] come when/if I can.* Normally the context tells whether **wenn** is used in a conditional or a temporal sense. In contrast, **wann** *when* is always temporal (see line 8): **Wann haben Sie Zeit?** *When [will] you have time?* **Ich weiß nicht, wann er kommt.** *I don't know when he [will] come.*

⑦ **eins** or **eines** is the neuter form of the pronoun **einer**, which can mean *one*, *someone* or *anyone*. **eins** can also mean 'one thing', particularly in everyday speech: **Eins möchte ich noch sagen.** *I'd like to add one [more] thing.* It is also possible to use **einer, eine, ein(e)s** as an adjective with the definite article; these are commonly used with a form of **der andere**, corresponding to 'the one ... the other': **Der eine Mann schaut her, der andere**

***

Übung 1 – Übersetzen Sie bitte!

❶ Guten Abend, darf ich Ihnen meinen Mann vorstellen? ❷ Wann heiraten Sie? Nächste Woche? ❸ Sie suchen einen Anzug? Für welche Gelegenheit? ❹ Sie haben mich nach dem Weg zur Oper gefragt. ❺ Liebling, ich gratuliere dir zum Geburtstag.

11 I [will] look for her when I have the suit.
12 First things first (*One-thing after the other*).

nicht. *One man looks over, the other doesn't.* **Die eine singt, die andere spielt.** *One (f.) sings, the other plays.* **Das eine funktioniert, das andere ist kaputt.** *One (n.) works, the other one doesn't.* The neuter **das andere** can be used in the sense of 'the other thing' or 'another thing'. Note that the definite article declines, as we see in line 12 where it is in the dative case: **dem anderen**. We'll explain why it ends in **-n** here in the upcoming lessons.

***

Answers to Exercise 1

❶ Good evening, may I introduce my husband to you? ❷ When are you getting married? Next week? ❸ You are looking for a suit? For what occasion? ❹ They asked me (*for*) the way to the opera. ❺ Darling, I wish you a happy birthday (*I congratulate you on your birthday*).

39 Übung 2 – Ergänzen Sie bitte!

❶ I don't know who this is; I don't know him!

... ., wer das ist, ... ihn nicht!

❷ I [will] quickly ask the woman there (*here*) for the way, and then we can go to the cinema. – Not so quickly, one thing at a time (*one-thing after the other*).

Ich ..... schnell die Frau hier .... dem Weg, und dann ...... wir ins Kino ...... – Nicht so ...., eins ....

❸ What are you looking for (*search you[formal]*)? Can I help you?

Was ....? Kann ich ....?

---

39 Neununddreißigste Lektion

Die Zeiten ändern sich ①

1 – Wem ② **schrei**bst du, wenn ③ ich **fra**gen darf?

Pronunciation
... end^e n ... **1** vehm **shrei**pst ...

Notes

① **(sich) ändern** means *to change* in the sense of 'to modify', 'to amend' (and not 'to replace'). **ändern** can be followed by an object that indicates what is changing: **Er ändert seine Pläne.** *He changes his plans.* Or it can be used with a reflexive pronoun to indicate that the subject itself is changing: **Ich ändere mich!** *I [will] change!* ('I change myself!') The reflexive pronoun refers back to the subject and may be either in the accusative or the dative, depending on its function in the sentence. We'll look at the forms of reflexive pronouns and their uses in more detail in lessons to come.

④ I [will] take the suit, the price is reasonable (*favourable*).   **39**
Ich nehme ... ., der Preis ist ....
⑤ May I introduce my boss *(m.)* to you?
.... Ihnen meinen .... vorstellen?

Answers to Exercise 2

❶ Ich weiß nicht – ich kenne – ❷ – frage – nach – können – gehen – schnell – nach dem anderen ❸ – suchen Sie – Ihnen helfen ❹ – den Anzug – günstig ❺ Darf ich – Chef –

Thirty-ninth lesson   39

Times are changing
(*The times change themselves*)

1 – To whom are you writing (*To-whom write you*), if I may ask?

② Notice the lack of a preposition here. In German, declension fulfils the function of the preposition 'to' before an indirect object. **Wer?** *Who?* declines like the masculine definite article, so in the dative, **wer** changes to **wem?** *to whom?*

③ Here **wenn** is used in a conditional sense and translates as 'if': **Wenn ich fragen darf.** *If I may ask.* Note that the conjugated verb – not the infinitive – is in the last position in the subordinate (dependent) clause introduced by **wenn**. Don't forget the comma separating the main and subordinate clause!

hundertachtundachtzig • 188

39
2 – **Meinem Onkel** ④ in **A**merika.
3 – Du hast **einen Onkel** in **A**merika?
4 – **Kl**ar, **alle haben** doch ⑤ **Verwan**dte ⑥ dort.
5 – **Auß**er mir ⑦, ich **ha**be **nie**mand dort.
6 – Das ist **wirkl**ich Pech!
7 – **Wa**r**um** denn? Ich ver**stehe** dich nicht.
8 – Na, wem schickst du denn **Brie**fe, wenn ⑧ du Geld brauchst?
9 – Kein Pro**bl**em! Ich **schrei**be **mei**ner **Tan**te ⑨ in **Chi**na. ☐

2 meinuhm onk'l ... amehrika 4 ... fervantuh ... 5 owss^a ... neemant ... 6 ... pekH 8 ... shikst ... breefuh ... 9 ... problehm ... tantuh ... kHeena

Notes

④ Again, note that the indirect object isn't preceded by a preposition – instead, it is in the dative: **Er schreibt sein<u>em</u> Onkel.** *He writes <u>to</u> his uncle.* Like the indefinite article **ein**, the possessive adjectives (**mein/dein/sein/ihr/Ihr**) take the ending **-em** in the dative masculine and neuter singular.

⑤ We've already seen that **doch** can be used in a number of ways. Firstly, it can be an affirmative answer to a negative question: **Du gehst heute nicht ins Kino? – Doch!** *You're not going to the cinema today? – Yes, I am!* Secondly, it can be added for amplification or to convey a sense of invitation or exhortation: **Gehen Sie doch ins Kino!** *Do go to the cinema!* (lesson 30). When **doch** is not stressed, like in the example in the dialogue, this can have the effect of turning a statement into a question that expects a positive answer. In this case, it translates as 'surely' or as a question tag: **Du kannst mir doch helfen.** *You can help me, can't you?* **Das machst du doch nicht.** *Surely you don't do that.*

⑥ The word **Verwandte** refers to all relatives: **Onkel** *uncle*, **Tante** *aunt*, **Großmutter** *grandmother*, etc. In contrast, **die Familie** only includes **Vater, Mutter und Kinder** *father,*

189 • **hundertneunundachtzig**

2 – To my uncle in America.
3 – You have an uncle in America?
4 – Of course (*Clear*), everyone has (*all have surely*) relatives there.
5 – Except [for] me – I have no one there.
6 – That's really bad luck!
7 – Why (*then*)? I don't understand you (*understand you not*).
8 – Well, to whom do you send (*then*) letters when you need money?
9 – [That's] no problem! I write to my aunt in China.

> Man muss sie nehmen, wie sie ist, sie ändert sich nicht mehr.

mother and children. Note that **Verwandte** is a plural noun and hence requires a plural verb form; **Familie**, however, is a collective noun in the singular.

⑦ The preposition **außer** *except (for)*, *apart (from)*, *besides* is followed by the dative: **Alle haben Geld außer meinem Bruder.** *Everybody has money except (for) my brother.*

⑧ Here, **wenn** is used temporally: *when*, *whenever* (see lesson 38, note 6).

⑨ The dative feminine singular ending is always **-r**, whether it's a definite article, an indefinite article or a possessive adjective: **Er schreibt der/einer/seiner Freundin.** *He writes to the/a/his friend* (f.).

Übung 1 – Übersetzen Sie bitte!

① Sie ändert sich nicht mehr. ② Mein Onkel aus China verbringt immer seinen Urlaub in Europa. ③ Wem schreiben Sie? Ihrem Chef? ④ Sagen Sie mir, wenn Sie Geld brauchen. ⑤ Alle außer ihm haben Verwandte in Amerika.

***

Übung 2 – Ergänzen Sie bitte!

① My aunt helps me when I need money.
Meine Tante . . . . , wenn . . . .
. . . .

② We spend our holidays in China.
. . . . unsere Ferien . . . .

③ I don't understand what you are saying.
. . . . , was Sie sagen.

---

40 Vierzigste Lektion

Der Autokauf

1 – **Gu**ten Tag, Herr **Fi**scher, **ha**ben Sie **ei**nen **neu**en **Wa**gen ①?

Pronunciation
... *owto-kowf* **1** ... *noi-uhn vahg'n*

Pronunciation note
Title Remember that **au** is pronounced *ow*: **Autokauf** *owto-kowf*.

Notes

① Did you spot that this is the accusative masculine? **der Wagen** is masculine, which is why one says **der Mercedes**, **der BMW** *beh em veh*, etc. However, **das Auto** *car* is neuter, like most words of foreign origin.

Answers to Exercise 1

❶ She won't change anymore. ❷ My uncle from China always spends his vacation in Europe. ❸ To whom are you writing? To your boss? ❹ Tell me if you need money. ❺ Everyone except him has relatives in America.

***

❹ To whom are you writing? Do I know the person?
... schreiben Sie? .... die Person?

❺ I have many relatives, but Klaus has only an uncle.
Ich habe viele ...., aber Klaus hat nur
....

Answers to Exercise 2

❶ – hilft mir – ich Geld brauche ❷ Wir verbringen – in China ❸ Ich verstehe nicht – ❹ Wem – Kenne ich – ❺ – Verwandte – einen Onkel

---

Fortieth lesson 40

The car purchase

1 – Good afternoon, Mr Fischer, do you have a new car?

Fahrräder sind umweltfreundlich, sie fahren ohne Benzin.

40
2 – Ja, den ② **ha**be ich **letz**ten **Mo**nat ge**kauft**.
3 – Ge**fällt** ③ er Ihnen?
4 – Und wie! Der ist **wirk**lich **gro**ße **Klas**se.
5 – Den **an**deren **Freun**den ④ ge**fällt** er auch sehr gut.
6 – Der ist doch **si**cher sehr **teu**er, nicht wahr?
7 – Stimmt ⑤, er ist nicht **bil**lig.
8 **A**ber ich **ha**be den **Wa**gen von ⑥ **mei**ner Frau ver**kauft** ⑦.
9 – Und was macht **Ih**re Frau jetzt?
10 – Sie hat ein **neu**es **Fahr**rad ge**kriegt** ⑧.
11 Das ist **um**weltfreundlicher ⑨. ☐

---

*2 ... **guhkowft** 3 **guhfelt** ... 4 ... **klassuh** 5 **dehn anduhruhn froin**duhn ... 7 ... **bi**likH 8 ... **ferkowft** 10 ... **guhkreekt** 11 ... **um**velt-frointlikHᵃ*

Notes

② **den** is a demonstrative pronoun here. One could say **ich habe den gekauft** 'I have bought this (m.)' or **ich habe ihn gekauft** 'I have bought it (m.)'; however, in spoken German, the demonstrative is often used. (Note that masculine pronouns – **er** *he/it*, **ihn** *him/it*, etc. – are used to refer to the masculine noun **Wagen** *car*, whereas the neuter noun **Auto** would be referred to with the neuter pronoun **es**.)

③ **gefällt** is the third-person singular present tense of **gefallen** *to appeal to, to like*. When using **gefallen**, keep in mind the construction of 'to appeal to': what one likes is the subject of the sentence (and thus in the nominative case), while the person doing the liking is in the dative case: **Das Haus gefällt mir.** *I like the house.* ('The house appeals to me.') It is also common for sentences with **gefallen** to start with the dative: **Dem Mann gefällt der Anzug nicht.** *The man doesn't like the suit.* ('To-the man appeals the suit not.')

④ The plural definite article **die** *the* changes to **den** *(to) the* in the dative: **die Freunde** *the friends*, **den Freunden** *to the friends*. ▶

2 – Yes, I bought it last month (*this have I last month bought*).
3 Do you like it (*Appeals it[m.] to-you*)?
4 – You bet (*And how*)! It is really fantastic (*great class*).
5 – My other friends also like it very much (*To-the other friends appeals it also very good*).
6 – It is (*yet*) surely very expensive, isn't it (*not true*)?
7 – That's right (*Correct*), it isn't cheap.
8 But I have sold my wife's car.
9 – And what does your wife do now?
10 – She has a new bicycle (*got*).
11 It's more environmentally friendly (*environment-friendly*).

Note in the dative plural, an **-n** is also added to the noun (if it doesn't already end in **-n**).

⑤ **stimmt** is the third-person singular of **stimmen** *to be right/correct/true*: **das stimmt** or simply **stimmt** is a common expression for *[That's] true*, *[That's] right* (lesson 24).

⑥ The preposition **von** *of* must always be followed by the dative.

⑦ **verkauft** *sold* is the past participle of **verkaufen** *to sell*. The past participles of inseparable-prefix verbs don't take a **ge-** prefix. But note that the past participle of **kaufen** *to buy* (a regular verb) does: **gekauft** *bought* (line 2).

⑧ **kriegen** is perhaps one of the most frequently used verbs in spoken German. Its meanings range from *to get*, *to receive* to *to begin to have* and *to catch*: **Ich kriege im Sommer einen Hund.** *I [will] get a dog in the summer.* **Krieg keinen Husten!** *Don't catch a cough!*

⑨ **umweltfreundlich** *environmentally friendly*. **die Umwelt** *environment* consists of **um** *round, about* and **die Welt** *world*; **freundlicher** with the ending **-er** is a comparative form of **freundlich** *friendly*. We'll look at comparisons soon.

Übung 1 – Übersetzen Sie bitte!

❶ Ich finde den neuen Kollegen sehr nett, er gefällt mir. **❷** Mir gefällt er auch, er gefällt allen. **❸** Wir haben unser Auto verkauft und Fahrräder gekauft! **❹** Fahrräder sind umweltfreundlich, sie fahren ohne Benzin. **❺** Er hat von seinen Eltern zum Geburtstag einen Anzug gekriegt.

***

Übung 2 – Ergänzen Sie bitte!

❶ Where is your car? – I have sold it (*it sold*).

.. ... dein Wagen? ... . ihn ....

❷ What did you get for [your] birthday (*What have you[informal] then for-the birthday got*)?

Was .... .. denn zum Geburtstag ....?

❸ I like your suit (*Your suit appeals to-me*), Mr Berg. Where did you buy it (*have you[formal] it bought*)?

Ihr Anzug ...., Herr Berg. Wo .....
... den ....?

***

Das „Kult-Objekt" Auto The car as 'cult object'
*The car has long played an important role in Germany and has, in many ways, become part of the national identity. Germany is the third-biggest car manufacturer in the world, with some 850,000 people employed in the car industry. Who hasn't heard of famous German makes such as Audi, Mercedes and BMW (**Bayrische Motoren-Werke** Bavarian Motor Works), not to mention VW, the famous **Volkswagen** (People's Car)?*

*On the surface, Germany is obsessed with cars – the bigger, the better. In the decades after the Second World War, you knew you had it made in Germany when you were able to buy a Mercedes or a BMW, and even now the car is often still a prestige object. As a result, people take great care of their vehicles, accessorizing them with all kinds of things found in the **Automarkt**, a sort of specialized supermarket for motoring-related products. Moreover, the lack of speed limits on the **Autobahn** motorway, freeway is*

Answers to Exercise 1

❶ I find the new colleague very nice. I like him (*He appeals to me*). ❷ I like him too – everybody likes him. ❸ We have sold our car and bought bicycles! ❹ Bicycles are environmentally friendly; they run without petrol. ❺ For his birthday, he got a suit from his parents.

***

❹ That's expensive. – That's true, it's not cheap.

Das ist ...... – Das stimmt, das ist .....
....

❺ Bring another beer for my friends (*to-my friends still a beer*)! I'm paying.

Bringen Sie meinen .... noch ein Bier!
Ich ......

Answers to Exercise 2

❶ Wo ist – Ich habe – verkauft ❷ – hast du – gekriegt ❸ – gefällt mir – haben Sie – gekauft ❹ – teuer – nicht billig ❺ – Freunden – zahle

***

one of the sacred cows of German motoring. Summed up in the catchphrase **'Freie Fahrt für freie Bürger'** *'Free [unrestricted] speed for free citizens', the ability to put one's foot down on the accelerator is inviolable to many drivers, and it draws a number of speed-obsessed tourists to Germany.*

Yet caring for one's car isn't simply a pastime in Germany, it's also to a certain degree a necessity, as vehicle inspections are rather strict. Every two years, cars have to pass the **'TÜV'** *(***Technischer Überwachungsverein***) test. The* **TÜV** *validates the safety of all kinds of products, but nowadays is mainly known for checking the roadworthiness and emissions of vehicles.*

While an object of desire for some, the car does have its enemies in Germany, particularly among environmentalists. In cities from Freiburg im Breisgau to Berlin, more and more people are swapping their cars for bikes. Moreover, public transportation in Germany is efficient and very popular.

41 Einundvierzigste Lektion

Die Stadt Dresden ist eine Reise wert ①

1 – Wir **möch**ten **Deutsch**land **bes**ser **ken**nen **ler**nen.
2 **Wo**hin **sol**len wir **fah**ren?
3 **Kannst** du uns **ei**nen Rat ② geben?
4 – **Si**cher! Ihr müsst **un**bedingt nach **Dres**den **fah**ren!
5 – Wo liegt ③ das denn?
6 – Im **Os**ten ④. **Dres**den ist die **Haupt**stadt von **Sach**sen.

Pronunciation
... **drehs**duhn ... **veh**ᵃt 1 ... **doitsh**-lant **bess**ᵃ ... 3 ... raht ...
4 ... **un**buhdinkt ... 5 ... leekt ... 6 im **os**tuhn ... **howpt**-shtat
... **zaks**'n

Notes

① **wert sein** *to be worth*: **Das ist viel wert.** *That is worth a lot. It is really worth it.* **Das ist nichts wert.** *That is worth nothing. It isn't worth anything.* The noun **der Wert** means *worth, value*.

② In this sentence, **der Rat** *advice, piece of advice* is in the accusative as it is the direct object. The indirect object **uns** *(to) us* is in the dative case. Many German verbs, such as **geben** *to give*, **bringen** *to bring*, etc., take both direct and indirect objects: **Sie gibt dem Kind einen Apfelsaft.** *She gives the child (indirect object) an apple juice (direct object).* Don't forget that in German the case signals whether a noun or a pronoun is a direct or indirect object; a preposition is never used in front of an indirect object. Also a quick word on word order: if the direct object is a noun, it usually comes after the indirect object. If it is a pronoun, it comes before the indirect object: **Sie gibt ihn dem Kind.** *She gives it to the child.*

Forty-first lesson 41

The city [of] Dresden is worth a visit
(*a visit worth*)

1 – We would like to get to know Germany better (*Germany better to-know to-learn*).
2 Where(-*to*) should we go?
3 Can you give us some advice?
4 – Sure! You absolutely must go to Dresden.
5 – Where is that (*is-located that then*)?
6 – In the east. Dresden is the capital of Saxony.

③ Here, **liegen** means *to be situated/located*.

④ We've seen that **im** is a contraction of the preposition **in** + the definite article **dem**. And we've learned that **dem** is dative masculine or neuter: **der Osten** *the east*, **im Osten** *in the east*. **In** is one of nine 'two-way prepositions'; spatial prepositions that can take either the dative (as here) or the accusative, depending on context. The dative is used to refer to positions in space (where?); the accusative to refer to movements through space (to where?). **Wo wohnen Sie?** *Where do you live?* **Im Zentrum.** *In the centre.* But **Wohin fahren Sie?** *(To) where are you going?* – **In die Stadt.** *Into town.*

hundertachtundneunzig • 198

41 7 – Und was gibt es ⑤ dort zu **seh**en?
  8 – Viel. Es ist eine **al**te Ba**rock**stadt mit **lang**er ⑥ Ge**schich**te.
  9 Ich **schwö**re euch ⑦, die **Rei**se lohnt ⑧ sich. ☐

> 8 ... **al**tuh ba**rok**-shtat ... **lang**ᵉ guh**shikH**tuh 9 ... **shvœ**ruh oikH ... lohnt zikH

Notes

⑤ We've already encountered the expression **es gibt** *there is/there are*. Here it occurs with a dependent infinitive preceded by **zu** at the end of the sentence. German has a number of constructions in which an infinitive is preceded by the particle **zu**, which can often be translated as 'to' in English: **Es gibt hier nichts zu sehen.** *There is nothing to see here.* But remember that modal verbs don't require **zu**: **Ich kann dich sehen.** *I can see you.* Moreover, when **es gibt** is followed by a noun, this has to be in the accusative: **Gibt es hier keinen Supermarkt?** *Is there no supermarket here?*

⑥ **die Geschichte** means *history* as well as *story*. The preposition **mit** *with* always requires the dative. Since the noun has no

***

Übung 1 – Übersetzen Sie bitte!

❶ Ich möchte München besser kennen lernen. ❷ Du musst unbedingt in den Englischen Garten gehen. ❸ Wo liegt Sachsen? – Im Osten von Deutschland. ❹ Ich gebe euch einen Rat, erzählt mir keine Geschichten! ❺ Was gibt es denn hier zu sehen?

7 – And what is there to see (*there*)?
8 – A lot (*Much*). It is an old baroque city with [a] long history.
9 I swear to you, the journey is worth it.

> **Pronunciation note**
> 8 Some people find **Geschichte** tricky to pronounce because it contains both **sch** and **ch**. But just think of **ich** and then pronounce *sh* before it: *shikH*.

article, the adjective shows the case by taking the dative feminine ending **-er**: **lang** *long*, but **mit langer Geschichte** *with [a] long history*.

⑦ **euch** *(to) you* is the dative of the informal plural **ihr** *you*. The formal address would be **Ihnen** *(to) you*.

⑧ The reflexive verb **sich lohnen** – which derives from **der Lohn** *remuneration, wages* – is used mainly in the expression **Das lohnt sich./Das lohnt sich nicht.** *It is/isn't worth it.* **sich lohnen** can be translated as *to be rewarding, to be worth it*, as well as *to pay*.

***

Answers to Exercise 1

❶ I would like to get to know Munich better. ❷ You absolutely have to go to the English Garden. ❸ Where is Saxony? – In the east of Germany. ❹ I['ll] give you some advice; don't tell me stories! ❺ What is there to see here then?

41 Übung 2 – Ergänzen Sie bitte!

❶ We are looking for a good restaurant; can you give us some (*an*) advice?

... . ein gutes Restaurant, könnt ihr ... . ?

❷ It's not worth it, there is (*there*) nothing to see.

Das .... nicht, ... dort ...... zu sehen.

❸ Where(*-to*) are you going? To Dresden? Where is(*-located*) that (*then*)?

..... fahren Sie? Nach Dresden? .. .. das denn?

Besichtigen Sie Dresden! Visit Dresden!
The picturesque baroque city of Dresden lies in southeastern Germany. It is often called the 'Florence of the North' due to its magnificent architecture, its mild climate and its fertile soil. Situated at the crossroads between the Catholic south, the Protestant north, the Roman west and the Slavic east, Dresden has been an important centre since its foundation 800 years ago. The city's golden age was the first half of the 18th century, during the reign of **Friedrich August der Starke** *(Frederick Augustus I or Augustus II the Strong), Elector of Saxony and King of Poland. Some of the most beautiful baroque buildings, such as the* **Dresdner Zwinger**, *a palace used for court festivities, Pillnitz Castle and the Dresden Cathedral (***Dresdner Frauenkirche***), date to this period. Today the* **Zwinger** *houses the Old Masters Picture Gallery, containing the royal art collection, as well as a remarkable porcelain collection that includes Asian pieces alongside the most beautiful china*

❹ In the east of Germany – it is the capital of Saxony.
．．．．．．．． von Deutschland, das ist ．．．
．．．．．．．．．． von Sachsen.

❺ Why have you (*informal*) bought this? It's worth nothing.
Warum ．．．．．． das ．．．．．．．? Das ist ．．．．．．
．．．．．

Answers to Exercise 2

❶ Wir suchen – uns einen Rat geben ❷ – lohnt sich – es gibt – nichts – ❸ Wohin – Wo liegt – ❹ Im Osten – die Hauptstadt – ❺ – hast du – gekauft – nichts wert

produced in **Meißen** *since the inception of porcelain production there in 1708.**

Dresden prospered during the 19th century and became one of the richest cities in Germany, thanks to its high-quality manufacturing industry and its geographical situation. Today Dresden still boasts some of the most beautiful mansions in Germany, luxurious symbols of its splendid past. The city has miraculously withstood the twists of fate: wars have left their marks on the city, but despite even the vast destruction of the Second World War, Dresden has preserved, or in some cases regained, its fascinating allure. After seeing all the sights the city has to offer, don't miss a trip down the Elbe in a restored paddle steamer. You won't just get an unforgettable view of the city and the mansions and castles along the banks, but also experience one of the most beautiful river landscapes in Europe.

* *The town of* **Meißen** *is 20 kilometres northwest of Dresden.*

42 Zweiundvierzigste Lektion

Wiederholung – Review

1 The dative: articles and personal pronouns

In addition to the nominative and the accusative cases, German has a dative case (there are four cases in all). The main function of the dative is to indicate an indirect object.

Der Mann gibt dem Hund den Käse.
The man gives the cheese to the dog.

- The subject is in the nominative: **der Mann**.
- The direct object ('What does the man give?') is in the accusative: **den Käse**.
- The indirect object ('To whom does he give it?') is in the dative: **dem Hund** *to the dog*.

As you know, German word order sometimes differs from English. In German, the direct (accusative) object determines the order of objects in a sentence.

- If the direct object (here, **Käse** *cheese*) is a noun, it comes <u>after</u> the indirect (dative) object:

Der Mann gibt dem Hund <u>den Käse</u>.
The man gives the dog the cheese.
The Mann gibt ihm <u>den Käse</u>. *The man gives him the cheese.*

- If the direct object (here, **ihn** *it* [m.]) is a personal pronoun, it comes <u>before</u> the indirect object:

Der Mann gibt <u>ihn</u> dem Hund. *The man gives it to the dog.*
Der Mann gibt <u>ihn</u> ihm. *The man gives it to him.*

The following sections give the declensions for the articles and personal pronouns, expanded to include the dative case.

Forty-second lesson 42

1.1 Definite and indefinite articles

	Singular			Plural
	masc.	fem.	neuter	
Nominative	der/ein	die/eine	das/ein	die/ –
Accusative	den/einen	die/eine	das/ein	die/ –
Dative	dem/einem	der/einer	dem/einem	den/...-**n**

Some brief remarks about articles in the dative:

• The masculine and neuter singular articles are the same.

• In the plural, not only the article takes the ending **-n**, but the noun also adds an **-n** (unless the plural already ends in **-n** or **-s**):
Der Vater gibt den Kindern Schokolade. *The father gives chocolate to the children.* (nominative plural: **die Kinder**)
Claudia schreibt den Freunden einen Brief. *Claudia writes a letter to the friends.* (nominative plural: **die Freunde**)
But:
Anja erklärt den Frauen den Weg. *Anja explains the way to the women.* (nominative plural: **die Frauen**)
Das macht den Autos nichts! *This doesn't do anything to the cars.* (nominative plural: **die Autos**)

1.2 Personal pronouns

	Nominative	Accusative	Dative
1st-person sing.	**ich** *I*	**mich** *me*	**mir** *(to) me*
2nd-person sing.	**du** *you*	**dich** *you*	**dir** *(to) you*
3rd-person sing.	**er** *he, it* (m.) **sie** *she, it* (f.) **es** *it* (neuter)	**ihn** *him, it* **sie** *her, it* **es** *it*	**ihm** *(to) him, it* **ihr** *(to) her, it* **ihm** *(to) it*
1st-person pl.	**wir** *we*	**uns** *us*	**uns** *(to) us*
2nd-person pl.	**ihr** *you*	**euch** *you*	**euch** *(to) you*
3rd-person pl.	**sie** *they*	**sie** *them*	**ihnen** *(to) them*

And the formal personal pronouns:

Formal			
	Nominative	Accusative	Dative
2nd-person (sing. / pl.)	**Sie** *you*	**Sie** *you*	**Ihnen** *(to) you*

Remember that in German the third-person personal pronouns **er/sie/es** may refer to people or things (the choice depends on the grammatical gender of the noun):
Die Frau ist klein. → **Sie ist klein.** *She is small.*
Die Tasche ist klein. → **Sie ist klein.** *It is small.*

2 The past participle of regular (weak) verbs

The majority of German verbs form the past participle by adding **-t** to the infinitive stem (the equivalent of *-ed* in English). The **-t** ending is **-et** when the verb stem ends in **-d** or **-t**. Some verbs whose stems end in **-m** or **-n** also take the **-et** ending. Most regular (weak) verbs also add the prefix **ge-** in the past participle. So the 'construction manual' for the past participle of regular verbs is:
ge- + verb stem + **-t** = past participle

machen *to do, to make* → **gemacht** *done, made*
sagen *to say* → **gesagt** *said*
reden *to talk* → **geredet** *talked*
arbeiten *to work* → **gearbeitet** *worked*

But careful! Inseparable-prefix verbs don't take the prefix **ge-**:
verkaufen *to sell* → **verkauft** *sold*
erzählen *to tell* → **erzählt** *told*

A present tense form of **haben** or **sein** + the past participle of the verb are used to form the present perfect tense.
Present tense: **Ich spiele Tennis.**
Present perfect tense: **Ich habe Tennis gespielt.** *I have played tennis. / I played tennis.*

We'll look in more detail at past participles (e.g. of separable-prefix verbs) and at the present perfect tense in future lessons. For now, just remember that German commonly uses the present perfect in everyday speech to refer to past actions or states.

3 *Wo?* 'Where?' *Wohin?* '(To) where?' *Woher?* 'From where?'

When expressing 'where', German distinguishes between:

• a position, i.e. a place where someone or something is (**Wo?**)
Wo sind Sie? *Where are you?*

• a change of location, i.e. a place where someone or something moves to (**Wohin?**)
Wohin gehen Sie? or **Wo gehen Sie hin?** *Where are you going (to)?*

• the provenance or origin, i.e. where someone or something comes from (**Woher?**)
Woher kommen Sie? or **Wo kommen Sie her?** *Where are you from?*

Hin and **her** thus show direction. **Hin** expresses motion away from the speaker (*to*), **her** expresses motion towards the speaker (*from*). Both are combined not only with **wo** in questions, but with other parts of speech, such as adverbs, in responses:
Ich bin hier, ich bin dort. *I am here, I am there.*
Ich gehe hierhin, ich gehe dorthin. *I go (to) here, I go (to) there.*
Ich komme hierher, ich komme dorther. *I am from here, I am from there.*

4 The points of the compass & the 16 *Bundesländer*

der Norden / *North*

der Westen / *West*   **der Osten** / *East*

der Süden / *South*

42

1 Schleswig-Holstein
2 Hamburg
3 Bremen
4 Nordrhein-Westfalen
5 Mecklenburg-Vorpommern
6 Brandenburg
7 Berlin
8 Rheinland-Pfalz
9 Saarland
10 Thüringen
11 Sachsen-Anhalt
12 Sachsen
13 Niedersachsen
14 Hessen
15 Baden-Württemberg
16 Bayern

Review exercise

Die Welt ist klein

1 – Thomas! Das darf nicht wahr sein!
2   Was machst du hier in Dresden im Smoking?

207 • zweihundertsieben

3 Wohin gehst du denn?
4 Woher kommst du?
5 Was hast du die ganze Zeit gemacht?
6 Wie geht's dir?
7 Hast du meine Briefe nicht gekriegt?
8 Du musst mir unbedingt sagen, wo du wohnst …
9 – Sicher, Melanie, aber warte, lass mich dir antworten.
10 Eins nach dem anderen.
11 Also: mir geht's sehr gut.
12 Ich bin mit meinem Orchester für zwei Tage hier.
13 Wir spielen heute Abend in der Oper.
14 Ich habe deine Briefe leider nicht gekriegt.
15 Wir haben die letzten sechs Monate in China gespielt.
16 Aber hör mal: ich freue mich sehr, dich zu sehen!
17 Du siehst fantastisch aus!
18 Du gefällst mir wirklich.
19 Warum lachst du? Ich bin ledig und nicht hässlich.
20 Und ich schwöre dir, bald bin ich reich.

Translation

The world is small

1 Thomas! It can't be true! 2 What are you doing here in Dresden wearing (*in*) [a] tuxedo? 3 Where are you going? 4 Where [have] you come from? 5 What have you been doing all this time (*have you the complete time done*)? 6 How are you? 7 Didn't you get my letters? 8 You absolutely have to tell me where you live … 9 Sure, Melanie, but wait, let me answer you. 10 One thing at a time (*One thing after the other*). 11 Well, I am very well. 12 I am here with my orchestra for a couple of (*two*) days. 13 We [will] play in the opera tonight. 14 Unfortunately, I didn't get your letters. 15 We have been playing in China for the past 6 months (*have the past 6 months in China played*). 16 But listen: I am very happy to see you! 17 You look fantastic! 18 I really like you (*You appeal to me really*). 19 Why are you laughing? I am single and not ugly. 20 And I swear to you, soon I will be (*am I*) rich.

43 Dreiundvierzigste Lektion

Die Mücke

1 — Warum hast du das Licht angemacht ①?
2 — Ich kann nicht schlafen.
3   Ich habe eine Mücke gehört.
4 — Oh nein! Wo ist sie?
5 — Sie sitzt ② auf der Lampe.
6 — Schnell, gib mir die Zeitung! (*klatsch!*)
7   Schade, zu spät, sie ist weggeflogen ③.
8 — Wohin denn? Siehst du sie?
9 — Ja, dort, jetzt fliegt sie auf die ④ Lampe zurück.

Pronunciation
... *mewkuh* **1** ... *likHt anguhmakht* **5** ... *zitst* ... *lampuh*
6 ... *tseitung* **7** *shahduh* ... *wekguhflohg'n*

Notes

① **angemacht** *switched on* is the past participle of the separable-prefix verb **anmachen**. The **ge-** prefix of the past participle comes between the separable prefix and the participle stem: **an** + **ge** + **macht**. The opposite of **anmachen** is **ausmachen** *to switch off* (line 13). Its past participle is **ausgemacht**: **Ich habe das Licht ausgemacht.** *I switched off the light.*

② **sitzen** means *to be sitting*.

③ **weggeflogen** is the past participle of **wegfliegen** *to fly away*. The **ge-** prefix again comes between the separable prefix (**weg**) and the stem of the past participle. Moreover, the stem vowel changes: **wegfliegen** (infinitive) → **weggeflogen** (past participle). The past participle also ends in **-en**. The reason

Forty-third lesson 43

The mosquito

1 — Why did you switch on the light (*have you the light on-switched*)?
2 — I can't sleep.
3 I heard a mosquito (*have a mosquito heard*).
4 — Oh, no! Where is it?
5 — It is (*sitting*) on the lamp.
6 — Quick, give me the newspaper! (*Splat!*)
7 [What a] pity, too late, it has flown away (*is away-flown*).
8 — Where to (*then*)? Do you see it?
9 — Yes, there, now it is flying back to the lamp (*flies it on the lamp back*).

Pronunciation notes
1, 7, 9, 11, 13 The stress falls on the separable prefix: **an**gemacht, **weg**geflogen, **zurück**fliegen, **run**terfallen, **aus**machen.

for this is that **fliegen** is a strong verb. Did you also notice that **wegfliegen** uses **sein** instead of **haben** to form the present perfect (rather than *has flown away*, 'is flown away')? This is the case for verbs of motion that don't have a direct object, such as **fliegen** or **fahren**, and verbs that express a change in condition or state, such as **aufstehen** *to get up*: **Ich bin gestern nach Hamburg gefahren.** *I went to Hamburg yesterday.* **Ich bin um 7 Uhr aufgestanden.** *I got up at 7 o'clock.*

④ Here the spatial preposition **auf** *on* is followed by the accusative: **auf die Lampe** *on the lamp*. However, in line 5, **auf** is followed by the dative: **auf der Lampe**. The difference arises from the fact that in line 5 the mosquito is already on the lamp (its position), whereas in line 9 it is heading towards the lamp (its goal or direction). More on this in lesson 49.

43
10 **Dies**es ⑤ Mal ent**komm**t sie mir nicht!
11 – **Vor**sicht, fall nicht **run**ter ⑥! (*klatsch!*)
12 – Ich **ha**be sie! **End**lich **ha**be ich ⑦ sie.
13 – Dann **kön**nen wir ja ⑧ das Licht **aus**machen.
14 **Gu**te Nacht! □

10 deezes mahl entkomt ... **11** ... runtᵃ **12** ... entlikH ...

Notes

⑤ The demonstrative **dieser** (m.), **diese** (f.), **dieses** (neuter) principally refers to something nearby in time or space, corresponding to *this*: **Diese Tasche gefällt mir nicht.** *I don't like this bag*. It follows the declension pattern for the definite article **der, die, das**.

⑥ **runter** *down* is a colloquial short form of **herunter**. It can be added to a verb as a separable prefix: **runterfallen** *to fall down*, **runtergehen** *to go down* (e.g. the stairs), **runtergucken** *to look down*.

⑦ This is a good example of inverted word order. If an element other than the subject occupies the first position in a sentence, the subject follows the verb, which remains in its usual second position: **Ich habe sie endlich.** = **Endlich habe ich sie.**

***

Übung 1 – Übersetzen Sie bitte!

❶ Onkel Klaus sitzt mit der Zeitung im Garten. ❷ Wir fliegen nicht, wir fahren mit dem Auto nach Italien. ❸ Mach bitte das Licht aus, die Mücken kommen. ❹ Im Sommer sind sie nach Brasilien geflogen. ❺ Was machst du auf dem Auto? Komm sofort runter!

10 This time it won't escape me (*escapes it me not*)! 43
11 – Careful, don't fall down! (*Splat!*)
12 – I have it! At last, I have it.
13 – Then we can (*yes*) switch off the light.
14 Good night!

> **10** Inseparable prefixes are never stressed: ent**komm**en.

Die Mücke

⑧ As we've seen, **ja** can mean more than simply *yes*. Embedded in a statement, **ja** indicates that both the speaker and listener know something is correct or obvious: **Dann können wir ja gehen.** *So we can go then.* It can also reinforce an exclamation (lesson 32, note 5), conveying a sense of surprise: **Da sitzt ja eine Mücke!** *[But] there is a mosquito [here]!*

***

Answers to Exercise 1

❶ Uncle Klaus is sitting in the garden with the newspaper. ❷ We aren't flying, we're going by (*with the*) car to Italy. ❸ Please switch off the light, the mosquitos are coming. ❹ This summer they flew to Brazil. ❺ What are you doing on the car? Come down immediately!

44 Übung 2 – Ergänzen Sie bitte!

❶ Please switch on the light (*Switch[informal] please the light on*), I don't see anything (*I see nothing*).
.... bitte das Licht .., ... nichts.

❷ Where is (*sitting*) the mosquito? – On the lamp.
.. sitzt ... . ? – Auf ... .

❸ This time, it hasn't flown away; I have it at last.
.... ist sie nicht ...., ...
.... sie endlich.

---

44 Vierundvierzigste Lektion

Der 31. Dezember ①

1 – Es ist fünf vor zwölf ②, hol schnell den Cham**pagn**er.
2 – Wo ist er denn?

Pronunciation
... *einunt-dreissikstuh deh**tsemb**[a] **1** ... sham**pany**[a]* ...

Notes

① Remember that dates are given with ordinal numbers in German, and that ordinal numbers are indicated by a full stop after the number: **der einunddreißigste Dezember** *the thirty-first [of] December*.

② **fünf vor zwölf** 'five before twelve', or *five to twelve*. In everyday speech, **zwölf** *twelve* can refer to either midday or midnight. If it is important to be more precise, you can say

213 • zweihundertdreizehn

④ They have switched off the light (*the light off-switched*); they want to sleep.

Sie haben ... ., sie wollen
....

⑤ Do you (*informal*) have the crab at last? Careful, don't let it escape!

.... .. endlich die Krabbe? ...., lass sie nicht ....!

Answers to Exercise 2

① Mach – an, ich sehe – ② Wo – die Mücke – der Lampe ③ Dieses Mal – weggeflogen, ich habe – ④ – das Licht ausgemacht – schlafen ⑤ Hast du – Vorsicht – entkommen

Forty-fourth lesson 44

The 31st [of] December

1 – It is five to (*before*) 12 – get the champagne, quickly.
2 – But where is it?

Wo ist die Zeitung?

zwölf Uhr mittags *noon* or **zwölf Uhr nachts** *midnight*. Other words for *midnight* are **Mitternacht** or **vierundzwanzig Uhr** 'twenty-four o'clock' or **null Uhr** 'zero o'clock'.

44
3 – Er steht ③ natürlich im **Kühl**schrank ④.
4 – Da ist er nicht, ich **ha**be **ü**berall **nach**gesehen ⑤.
5 – Das kann nicht sein!
6 – Liegt er oder steht er im **Kühl**schrank?
7 – Ich bin **si**cher, ich **ha**be ihn in die Tür vom **Kühl**schrank ge**stellt** ⑥.
8 – In der Tür steht nur **ei**ne **Fla**sche Oli**ve**nöl.
9 Seit wann stellst du Öl in den **Kühl**schrank?
10 – Ach, jetzt weiß ich, wo**hin** ich den Cham**pagn**er ge**stellt ha**be ⑦!

---

*3 ... shteht ... **kewl**-shrank **4** ... ew^bªal **nakh**-guhzehn **6** leekt ... **7** ... tew^a ... guh**shtelt 8** ... o**leev**'n-œl*

Notes

③ In English, *to be* is often used to denote a general location (e.g. 'It is in ...'), whereas German often gives a more specific position: **stehen** *to stand, to be standing* is used to describe something upright; **liegen** *to lie, to be lying* describes something in a horizontal position: **Die Flasche steht im Kühlschrank.** *The bottle stands in the fridge.* **Die Flasche liegt im Kühlschrank.** *The bottle lies in the fridge.*

④ **kühl** *cool*; **Schrank** *cupboard*.

⑤ **nachgesehen** is the past participle of **nachsehen** (literally, 'after-look') *to look, to check, to verify.*

⑥ German also uses more specific verbs to describe movement to a position, conveyed in English with the general *to put* (e.g. 'I put it in ...'). For example, **stellen** *to put/place upright*

215 • zweihundertfünfzehn

3 – It is (*standing*) in the fridge, of course.
4 – It isn't there (*There is it not*), I've checked everywhere.
5 – That can't be [true]!
6 – Is it lying or is it standing in the fridge?
7 – I am sure I put it in the fridge door (*have it in the door of-the fridge placed-upright*).
8 – In the door there is (*standing*) only a bottle [of] olive oil.
9 Since when have you been putting (*place-upright you*) oil in the fridge?
10 – Ah, now I know where I put the champagne!

44

Pronunciation note
8 The **v** in **Olive** is pronounced like an English *v* as the word is of foreign origin.

(past participle **gestellt**) specifies that the object was placed standing up. Remember that spatial prepositions are followed by the accusative case when the verb expresses movement towards a specific goal: **Er stellt die Flasche auf den Tisch.** *He puts the bottle on the table.* (see lesson 43, note 4).

⑦ **habe** occurs in the last position here because it is part of a dependent clause. In this sentence, **wohin** introduces an indirect question (the direct question would have been **Wohin habe ich den Champagner gestellt?** *Where did I put the champagne?*), which is dependent on the main clause, **jetzt weiß ich** *now I know*. In subordinate clauses, the conjugated verb is in the final position. As you know, the subordinate clause is separated from the main clause by a comma.

44 **Übung 1 – Übersetzen Sie bitte!**

❶ Wohin habt ihr die Flaschen gestellt? ❷ Kannst du bitte nachsehen, wie viel Uhr es ist? ❸ Wo ist die Zeitung? Liegt sie auf dem Kühlschrank? ❹ Es ist fünf vor sechs und wir haben noch kein Brot geholt. ❺ Holen wir Champagner, wir müssen das feiern!

***

Übung 2 – Ergänzen Sie bitte!

❶ I [will] put (*I place-upright*) the bottle in the fridge; we [will] drink it this evening.
Ich . . . . . . die Flasche . . . . ,
wir trinken sie . . . .

❷ When is our appointment? – Wait (*formal*), I have to check.
. . . . ist unser Termin? – . . . . , ich
muss . . . .

❸ I can't remember (*I know not more*) where I put the champagne (*placed-upright have*).
. . . . . . nicht mehr, wohin ich den
Champagner . . . .

❹ I am sure – the potatoes are (*lying*) in the cupboard.
Ich bin . . . . . . , die Kartoffeln . . . .
. . . .

❺ Quick, get me (*Get[informal] me quickly*) the newspaper! – Since when are you my boss?
. . . mir . . . . die Zeitung! – . . . .
bist du . . . . ?

Answers to Exercise 1

❶ Where did you put the bottles? ❷ Can you please check what time it is? ❸ Where is the newspaper? Is it lying on the fridge? ❹ It is five to 6 and we haven't bought (*fetched*) any bread yet. ❺ Let's get champagne; we have to celebrate this!

***

Answers to Exercise 2

❶ stelle – in den Kühlschrank – heute Abend ❷ Wann – Warten Sie – nachsehen ❸ Ich weiß – gestellt habe ❹ – sicher – liegen im Schrank ❺ Hol – schnell — Seit wann – mein Chef

Are you starting to feel more comfortable with German past participles? It's simply a matter of getting used to them, just like the declensions and separable-prefix verbs. You're becoming increasingly familiar with the special features of the German language, **nicht wahr**? *Right?*

45 Fünfundvierzigste Lektion

In der letzten Minute

1 – Wo warst ① du denn so **lang**e?
2 – Auf dem Klo ② war ③ eine **Schlang**e.
3 – **Hoff**entlich ④ hat das Stück noch nicht **an**gefangen ⑤.
4 – Wo **sit**zen ⑥ wir? **Un**ten **o**der **o**ben?
5 – **Un**ten, ganz vorn, in der **zwei**ten **Rei**he. Komm!
6 – Oh, es ist schon **dun**kel.
7 – Ich **glau**be, hier sitzt **nie**mand.

> **Pronunciation**
> 1 ... vahᵃst ... 2 ... kloh vahᵃ ... 3 hof'ntlikH ... anguhfang'n
> 4 ... untuhn ... ohb'n 5 ... forn ... rei-uh 6 ... dunk'l

Notes

① **du warst** *you were* is the second-person singular simple past tense of **sein** *to be*. The simple past, like the perfect tense, is used to refer to events in the past. We've seen that the use of the perfect is rather different to its use in English; in German, it can be used to relate fully completed actions in the past, particularly in conversational and informal contexts. However, the simple past is used more frequently for the verb **sein** (as well as **haben** and the modal verbs) in all contexts.

② **das Klo** or **die Toilette** (in the singular) *the bathroom, the toilets*: **Ich muss aufs** (= **auf das**) **Klo** or **Ich muss auf (die) Toilette**. *I have to [go to] the bathroom.* (In colloquial usage, the verb **gehen**, **kommen** or **fahren**, depending on the context, is understood and is often omitted.) **Wo ist das Klo?** *Where is the bathroom?* **Klo** is short for **Klosett**, from the English

Forty-fifth lesson 45

At the last minute

1 – Where were you (*then*) [for] so long?
2 – There was a queue in the bathroom.
3 – I hope (*Hopefully*) the play (*piece*) hasn't started yet.
4 – Where are we sitting? Downstairs (*Below*) or upstairs (*above*)?
5 – Downstairs, right in front (*completely front*), in the second row. Come [on]!
6 – Oh, the lights are already dimmed (*it is already dark*).
7 – I believe no one is sitting here.

Pronunciation notes
4, 8 Take care when pronouncing the stem vowels in **sitzen** and **setzen**. They make all the difference in these two verbs.

'water-closet' (the abbreviation **WC** is also used – pronounced *veh tseh* in German).

③ In the simple past, the third-person singular of **sein** *to be* does not take the usual **-t** ending: **er/sie/es war** *he/she/it was*.

④ **hoffentlich** *hopefully* is an adverb that derives from **hoffen** *to hope*. It can be replaced with **ich hoffe** *I hope* or **wir hoffen** *we hope*: **Ich hoffe, das Stück hat noch nicht angefangen.** *I hope the play hasn't started yet.* When it is assumed that everyone hopes for the same thing, **hoffentlich** can mean *let's hope*: **Hoffentlich regnet es nicht.** *Let's hope it won't rain.*

⑤ **angefangen** is the past participle of **anfangen** *to start, to begin*. Mind the prefix! By itself, **fangen** means *to catch*.

⑥ **sitzen** *to sit, to be sitting* is another verb that indicates a specific position (like **stehen** *to be standing* and **liegen** *to be lying*). Its past participle is **gesessen** (line 13).

45   **8**   **Set**zen wir uns ⑦ bis zur ⑧ **Pau**se **hier**hin.
       9 – **Hil**fe! Oh, ent**schul**digen Sie **bit**te!
     10 – Pst! **Kön**nen Sie nicht still sein? **Ru**he, **bit**te!
     11 – Was war denn? (*geflüstert*)
     12   Wa**rum** hast du ge**schrien** ⑨?
     13 – Auf **mei**nem Platz hat schon **je**mand ge**ses**sen!   ☐

---

8 zets'n ... bis tsoo^a powzuh ... **9 hilfuh** ... **10** pst ...shtil zein? **roo**-uh ... **11** ... (guh**flewst**^et) **12** ... guh**shreen** **13** ... **yeh**mant guh**zes**'n

13 Remember that **j** is pronounced *y*: **jemand yeh**mant.

Notes

⑦ Remember that **sich setzen** *to sit down* is a reflexive verb in German ('to sit oneself'). Reflexive constructions are used more frequently in German than in English. A reflexive pronoun always indicates the same person or thing as the subject. It may be in either the accusative or the dative case, depending on its function in the sentence: with **sich setzen**, it is in the accusative. The reflexive pronouns are the same as the personal pronouns in most of the persons (so in the accusative, **mich** *myself*, **dich** *yourself*, **uns** *ourselves*, **euch** *yourselves*), apart from the third-person singular and plural and the formal, which are all **sich**. <u>**Ich**</u> setze <u>**mich**</u>. *I sit down.* ('<u>I</u> sit <u>myself</u>'.) <u>**Du**</u> setzt <u>**dich**</u>. *You sit down.* <u>**Er**</u> setzt <u>**sich**</u>. *He sits down.* **Sie**

***

Übung 1 – Übersetzen Sie bitte!

❶ Ich bin müde, ich setze mich fünf Minuten hierhin. ❷ Können wir anhalten? Ich muss aufs (auf das) Klo. ❸ Komm schnell, hoffentlich gibt es keine Schlange. ❹ Thomas hat ganz allein unten gesessen und Musik gehört. ❺ Kommt da jemand? – Nein, da kommt niemand.

8 Let's sit (*Sit we ourselves*) [down] here until the interval (*pause*).
9 – Help! Oh, excuse me, please!
10 – Shush! Can't you be quiet (*quiet be*)? – Silence, please!
11 – What was [that] then? (*whispered*)
12 Why did you shout?
13 – There was already someone sitting in my seat (*In my seat has already someone sat*)!

Ich bin müde, ich setze mich fünf Minuten hierhin.

haben sich gesetzt. *They have sat down.* **Bitte setzen Sie sich doch.** *Please sit down* (formal).

⑧ **bis zu** *until*; **zur** is a contraction of **zu + der**. Remember that the preposition **zu** *to* is always followed by the dative. So **die Pause** *interval, intermission* is feminine.

⑨ **geschrien** is the past participle of **schreien** *to shout, to cry out*. The **ei** in an infinitive often changes to **ie** in the past participle.

***

Answers to Exercise 1

❶ I'm tired ... I['ll] sit down here [for] five minutes. ❷ Can we stop? I have to [go] to the bathroom. ❸ Come quickly, hopefully there is no queue. ❹ Thomas sat downstairs all by himself (*completely alone*) and listened to music. ❺ Is there somebody coming (*Comes there someone*)? – No, there is nobody coming.

46 Übung 2 – Ergänzen Sie bitte!

❶ I believe the play has already started.

... ., das Stück ... schon ....

❷ Don't sit down (*Sit yourself[informal] not*) in (*on*) my seat or I [will] shout!

.... nicht auf .... oder ... .!

❸ Excuse me (*formal*), you are sitting in my seat.

...., Sie sitzen ... .

---

46 Sechsundvierzigste Lektion

„Der Mensch denkt und Gott lenkt"

1 – **Ha**ben Sie **schö**ne **F**erien ver**bra**cht ①, Herr Sturm?
2 – Nein, das kann man nicht **sa**gen.
3 – Oh, das tut mir Leid für Sie.
4 Was ist denn pas**sie**rt ②?

Pronunciation
... *lenkt* **1** ... *fer***brakht** ... *shturm* **4** ... *pas***see**ᵃ*t*

Notes

① **verbracht** *spent* is the past participle of **verbringen** *to spend* (time). It is irregular in that it doesn't add the **ge-** prefix and there is a vowel change in the verb stem. It is an inseparable-prefix verb; these never add the **ge-** prefix in the past participle. However, the past participle of **bringen** *to bring, to deliver*

④ Where were you (*informal*)? Now we have to wait until the interval (*pause*).

Wo . . . . ? Jetzt müssen wir . . . . . .
. . . . . warten.

⑤ Help! – Why did you (*formal*) shout then? I hope (*Hopefully*) you are well.

. . . . . ! – Warum . . . . denn . . . . ?
. . . . geht es Ihnen gut.

Answers to Exercise 2

① Ich glaube – hat – angefangen ② Setz dich – meinen Platz – ich schreie ③ Entschuldigen Sie – auf meinem Platz ④ – warst du – bis zur Pause – ⑤ Hilfe – haben Sie – geschrien – Hoffentlich –

Forty-sixth lesson 46

'Man proposes, God disposes'
(*The human thinks and God directs*)

1 – Did you have a nice holiday (*Have you nice holidays spent*), Mr Sturm?
2 – No, one can't [really] say that.
3 – Oh, I'm sorry (*for you*).
4 Tell me, what happened?

is **ge**bracht, and that of the separable-prefix verb **mitbringen** *to bring along* is **mitgebracht**. Note that in German you ask if someone 'spent' a nice time, weekend, holiday, etc., rather than if they 'had' a nice time.

② **passiert** is the past participle of **passieren** *to happen*. Verbs that end in **-ieren** never take the **ge-** prefix.

zweihundertvierundzwanzig • 224

46
5 – Wir sind in die **Ber**ge ge**fah**ren ③ wie **je**des Jahr um **die**se Zeit.
6 **Nor**malerweise ist im **Ju**ni das **Wet**ter sehr schön.
7 **A**ber **die**ses Jahr hat es in den **Ber**gen ④ nur ge**reg**net.
8 Die **ers**ten **Ta**ge sind wir **trotz**dem **raus**gegangen ⑤.
9 **A**ber nach vier **Ta**gen **Re**gen **hat**ten ⑥ wir ge**nug**.
10 Wir sind nach **Hau**se ge**fah**ren.
11 Und kaum zu **Hau**se **an**gekommen ⑦, war der **Him**mel blau und das **Wet**ter **herr**lich ⑧!

> 5 ... **berg**uh guh**fahr**uhn ... **yeh**des ... 6 nor**mah**lªveisuh ... **yoo**ni... **vet**ª ... 7 ... guh**rehg**nuht 8 ... **trots**dehm **rows**-guhganguhn 9 ... **rehg**uhn ha**tuhn** ... guh**nook** 11 ... kowm ... **an**'guhkomuhn ... **him**uhl blow ... **her**likH

Notes

③ Watch out! Remember that all verbs that indicate movement or a change of state form the present perfect tense with **sein** *to be* rather than **haben** *to have*: **Ich bin nach Köln gefahren.** *I have gone to Cologne.* The same is true for **passieren** in line 4: **Was ist passiert?** *What has happened?*

④ **in den Bergen** *in the mountains* is dative plural: **der Berg** *mountain*, **die Berge** *mountains* (nominative/accusative). Remember that plural nouns in the dative take the ending **-n**. The dative is needed here because a position is given: **Wo hat es geregnet?** *Where did it rain?* – **in den Bergen** (location). However, in line 5 the accusative is needed because the mountains are a destination: **Wohin fahren wir?** *Where(-to) are we going?* – **in die Berge** (direction).

⑤ **rausgegangen** is the past participle of **rausgehen** *to go out, to go outside*. **raus** is a common abbreviation for **heraus** *out*, just

225 • zweihundertfünfundzwanzig

5 – We went to (*in*) the mountains, like every year at this time.
6 Normally the weather is very nice in June.
7 But this year there was nothing but rain in the mountains (*has it in the mountains only rained*).
8 The first [few] days, we went outside all the same (*are we nevertheless gone-outside*).
9 But after four days [of] rain we had enough.
10 We drove home (*are to home driven*).
11 And as soon as we arrived home (*And scarcely at home arrived*), the sky was blue and the weather splendid!

Pronunciation notes
5, 7 Remember that **ie** is pronounced as a long *ee*: **diese** *deezuh*; **dieses** *deezuhs*. However, **ei** is always pronounced *ei* as in Einstein: **die Zeit** *dee tseit*.
8, 11 The diphthong **au** in **raus** and **blau** is pronounced *ow*.

like **runter** is an abbreviation of **herunter** *down* (lesson 43). Here, **raus** functions like a separable prefix: **Ich gehe raus.** *I go outside.* Hence, the **ge-** prefix of the past participle inserts itself between **raus** and the verb stem.

⑥ **wir hatten** *we had* is the simple past of **haben** *to have*. You'll find the full conjugation in lesson 49. For now just remember that there isn't much of a difference in meaning between the present perfect and the simple past in German. One could say either **wir hatten genug** *we had enough* or **wir haben genug gehabt** *we'd had enough*. It's a question of style, really. The simple past is more often used for narrating a series of events in the past, as well as in formal writing (e.g. newspapers).

⑦ **angekommen** is ... you've probably guessed ... the past participle of **ankommen** *to arrive*.

⑧ **herrlich** can mean *splendid*, *fine*, *magnificent* or *wonderful*.

46 Übung 1 – Übersetzen Sie bitte!

❶ Ich habe meine Ferien zu Hause verbracht.
❷ Wir sind wie jedes Jahr nach Italien gefahren.
❸ Wir hatten herrliches Wetter. ❹ In den Bergen hat es die ganze Zeit geregnet. ❺ Diese Woche bin ich nicht rausgegangen.

***

Übung 2 – Ergänzen Sie bitte!

❶ Last year we flew to Barcelona.
.... Jahr .... wir nach Barcelona ....

❷ They went to the mountains in June.
... . im Juni .. ..

❸ Where have you (*informal*) spent the night? What has happened?
Wo .... .. die Nacht ....? Was ist denn ....?

❹ Scarcely arrived, they went home again.
Kaum ...., sind sie wieder .... gefahren.

❺ In the mountains, the weather was magnificent, but in Munich, there was nothing but rain (*has it only rained*).
.. .. war das Wetter ...., aber in München ... es nur ....

Answers to Exercise 1

❶ I spent my holidays at home. ❷ We went to Italy, like [we do] every year. ❸ We had splendid weather. ❹ In the mountains it rained the whole time. ❺ This week I didn't go outside.

***

Answers to Exercise 2

❶ Letztes – sind – geflogen ❷ Sie sind – in die Berge gefahren ❸ – hast du – verbracht – passiert ❹ – angekommen – nach Hause – ❺ In den Bergen – herrlich – hat – geregnet

*The progress you're making is **herrlich**! Keep reading out loud and repeating the text in each lesson several times. This will help you assimilate the language without too much effort.*

47 Siebenundvierzigste Lektion

Im Vorzimmer des Chefs ①

1 – **Gu**ten Tag, ich **möch**te **bi**tte Herrn ② **Dok**tor ③ **Han**sen **spre**chen ④.
2 – Ja, **gu**ten Tag, wen darf ich **mel**den?
3 – Ich bin **Dok**tor **Büch**ner von der **Fir**ma **Schnei**der & Co.
4 Ich **ha**be um 14 (**vier**zehn) Uhr mit ihm **ei**ne Ver**ab**redung.
5 – **Set**zen Sie sich ⑤ doch **bi**tte! Ich bin gleich zu**rück**.

***

Pronunciation
... **foh**ªtsimª des shefs **1** ... hern **dok**tohª **hans**'n ... **2** ... **mel**duhn **3** ... **bewkH**nª ... **shnei**dª unt koh **4** ... fer**a**prehdung

Notes

① **des Chefs** is in the genitive case, which is the fourth (and final!) case we'll be looking at. It is used to show possession or other close relationships. In English this is shown by adding *'s* to a noun (*Peter's car*) or with *of* (*the colour of the car*), while in German it is indicated by the genitive case. The genitive usually follows the noun it modifies: **das Vorzimmer des Chefs** 'the waiting room of the boss'. The definite articles **der** (m.) and **das** (neuter) change to **des** in the genitive, and an **-s** is added to the noun. In spoken German, the genitive of possession has almost died out. It is usually replaced with **von** + dative: **das Vorzimmer vom (von + dem) Chef**.

② **Herr** *Mr* ends in **-n** here because it is in the accusative case (see note 4): **Herr Büchner ist ein Kollege.** *Mr Büchner is*

Forty-seventh lesson 47

In the boss's waiting room (*before-room*)

1 – Good afternoon, I would like to speak to Dr Hansen, please.
2 – Yes, good afternoon, who shall I say is here (*whom may I announce*)?
3 – I am Dr Büchner from the firm Schneider & Co.
4 I have an appointment with him at 2 pm (*14:00*).
5 – Please, do sit down! I'll be back in a moment (*immediately*).

***

a colleague. But **Kennen Sie Herrn Büchner?** *Do you know Mr Büchner?* Certain masculine nouns, referred to as 'weak nouns' or 'masculine n-nouns', take the ending **-n** or **-en** in all cases but the nominative singular. **Der Junge ist klein.** *The boy is small.* **Ich kenne den Jungen nicht.** *I don't know the boy.* Don't worry, there aren't very many of these nouns!

③ In German-speaking countries, titles still matter and are considered part of one's name. Hence they need to be included in formal contexts. Formal address begins with **Herr** or **Frau**, followed by titles such as **Doktor** or **Professor**, and finally the family name: **Frau Professor Bachmann** (*Mrs*) *Professor Bachman*. If you have an academic title, you should mention it when introducing yourself formally to someone, and others will expect you to take theirs into account when addressed.

④ **sprechen** is here used in the sense of *to speak to someone*. The 'someone' in question directly receives the action of the verb, so is a direct object and requires the accusative: **Der Chef will dich sprechen.** *The boss wants to speak to you.*

⑤ Here, **sich** is the reflexive pronoun of the formal *you*: **Setzen Sie sich bitte!** *Please sit down!* ('Sit you yourself please!')

47   6   Herr **Dok**tor **Han**sen, **Dok**tor **Büch**ner ist ger**a**de ⑥ ge**kom**men.
       7 – Oh, ich **ha**be mein **Ves**perbrot noch nicht ge**ges**sen.
       8   **Ge**ben Sie mir noch eine **Vier**telstun**de**.

***

       9 – Herr **Dok**tor **Büch**ner, tut mir Leid, **Dok**tor **Han**sen ist noch nicht vom **Mit**tagessen ⑦ zu**rück**gekommen.
   10   **Kön**nen Sie sich **bit**te **ei**nen **Au**genblick ⑧ ge**dul**den ⑨? □

---

7 ... fesp^a-broht ... guh**ges**s'n   8 ... fee^atuhl-**shtun**duh
9 ... **mit**ahk-ess'n   10 ... owg'n-blik guh**dul**duhn

Notes

⑥ We've seen **gerade** meaning *straight* and **geradeaus** *straight ahead* (lesson 15). It can also mean *just*, as in 'a little time ago': **Ich bin gerade angekommen.** *I have just arrived.*

⑦ **das Mittagessen** *lunch* ('noon-meal'), **das Abendessen** *dinner* ('evening-meal'), but **das Frühstück** *breakfast* ('early-piece'). **vom** is the contraction of **von** + **dem**. The preposition **von** always takes the dative case.

⑧ **der Augenblick** ('eyes-glance') is synonymous with **der Moment** *moment*. Note that the time expression here is in the

***

Übung 1 – Übersetzen Sie bitte!

❶ Unsere Verabredung ist um 16 Uhr. ❷ Frau Büchner ist leider noch nicht da. ❸ Setzen Sie sich bitte, der Chef kommt gleich zurück. ❹ Wen möchten Sie sprechen? Herrn Hansen? ❺ Gedulden Sie sich bitte eine Viertelstunde.

6 Dr Hansen, Dr Büchner has just arrived.
7 – Oh, I haven't eaten my sandwiches yet.
8 Give me another quarter [of an] hour.

***

9 – Dr Büchner, I'm sorry, Dr Hansen is not yet back from lunch (*from-the lunch back-come*).
10 Could you wait a moment, please (*Can you yourself please a moment be-patient*)?

accusative case and there is no preposition: **Ich bleibe nur einen Augenblick.** *I'm only staying [for] a moment.*

⑨ Did you notice the **sich** after **Sie**? Yes, **sich gedulden** *to be patient* is another example of a reflexive verb: **Du musst dich gedulden.** *You have to be patient.* In line 10, it is synonymous with **warten** *to wait*.

***

Answers to Exercise 1

❶ Our appointment is at 4 pm. ❷ Mrs Büchner is unfortunately not yet here. ❸ Please sit down, the boss will be right back (*comes immediately back*). ❹ Who would you like to speak to? Mr Hansen? ❺ Please wait [for] a quarter of an hour.

47 Übung 2 – Ergänzen Sie bitte!

1 I've waited [for] a quarter of an hour; I['ll] come back tomorrow.
Ich habe .... gewartet, ...
..... morgen ....

2 The boss's car hasn't arrived yet, please wait (*be-patient you [formal] yourself*) a moment!
Der Wagen ... . ist noch nicht ....,
.... bitte einen Moment!

3 Can I speak to Mr Schneider, please? – I'm sorry, he has just gone outside.
Kann ich bitte ..... Schneider ....?
– ... ..., er ist ...... rausgegangen.

Eating habits

In southern Germany (particularly in **Schwaben** *Swabia),* **das Vesper** *is a meal or snack consisting of bread, cold cuts, and/or cheese that is usually eaten between breakfast and lunch or in the evening. The word* **Vesper** *comes from the Latin* ***vespera***, *evening, and* **die Vesper** *can also refer to the evening prayer service held at sunset in many churches. In other areas of Germany, mid-morning snacks have different names, such as* **(die) Brotzeit** *('bread-time' in Bavaria) or* **(die** *or* **das) Imbs** *(in Rheinhessen, a picnic in the vineyards around noon).*

In German-speaking countries, the evening meal was long considered less important than lunch and was more like a snack than what qualifies as dinner in Anglo-American culture. An old proverb encapsulates this attitude quite neatly: **'Morgens essen wie ein Kaiser, mittags wie ein König und abends wie ein Bettelmann'**

④ At what time is our appointment? At 3 o'clock (*15:00*)?

Um wie viel Uhr ist . . . . ?
. . fünfzehn . . . ?

⑤ Do sit down (*formal*).

. . . . doch.

Answers to Exercise 2

① – eine Viertelstunde – ich komme – zurück **②** – des Chefs – angekommen – gedulden Sie sich – **③** – Herrn – sprechen – Tut mir Leid – gerade – **④** – unsere Verabredung – Um – Uhr **⑤** Setzen Sie sich –

'In the morning eat like an emperor, at noon like a king, and in the evening like a beggar'. Though this tradition lives on in many homes where dinner consists of soup or bread and cold cuts or cheese, things have changed for many people. There are several reasons for this, above all the fact that **das Mittagessen** lunch *is no longer a communal meal in many families. Many children attend school in the mornings (school tends to finish at 1pm in Germany), yet they often don't all come home at the same time and thus just find themselves something to eat in the fridge. Among adults, only 1 in 6 eats lunch at home, 1 in 4 in a canteen, 1 in 10 in a restaurant or fast-food outlet, and 2 in 5 take a packed lunch. Consequently, people tend to be hungry in the evening. Quite apart from that, there are increasing numbers of households in which both parents work, so neither is around to cook two hot meals per day.*

48 Achtundvierzigste Lektion

Ein schwieriger Samstagmorgen

1 – Wo kommen nur alle diese Autos her?
2　Warum müssen alle Leute am Samstagmorgen einkaufen fahren ①?
3 – Wahrscheinlich aus demselben ② Grund wie wir, Papa.
4 – Werde nicht frech ③! Ich parke jetzt hier.
5 – Aber das geht nicht, das ist die Ausfahrt der Polizei ④.
6 – Das ist mir egal.
7　Samstags arbeiten die sowieso nicht, und wir sind in einer halben Stunde zurück.

Pronunciation
... **shvee**rig^a ... 3 vah^a**shein**likH ... dehm**zel**buhn grunt ...
4 **veh**^aduh ... frekH! ... **par**kuh ... 5 ... **ows**fah^at deh^a poli**tsei**
6 ... e**gahl** 7 ... zovi**zoh** ... **hal**buhn ...

Notes

① **einkaufen gehen** or **fahren** *to go shopping (on foot* or *by car)*, **kaufen** *to buy*, **verkaufen** *to sell* ... See the importance of prefixes?

② Do you remember **dasselbe** *the same, the same thing* (lesson 30)? In **demselben**, we recognize **selb-**, which means 'same'. The variations **derselbe, dieselbe, dasselbe** (m., f., neut.) include the definite article **der, die, das** and the adjective **selb-** combined in a single word ('the-same'). However, both the definite article and **selb-** decline as if they were two separate words. Hence, **aus demselben Grund** *for the same reason*, because **der Grund** is masculine and the preposition **aus** takes the dative case. With regard to **selb-**, it takes the ending **-en** in all cases except the nominative singular, in which the ending

Forty-eighth lesson 48

A difficult Saturday morning

1 – Where are all these cars coming from (*Where come only all these cars from*)?
2 Why does everybody (*all people*) have to go shopping on a Saturday morning?
3 – Probably for (*of*) the same reason as us (*we*), Dad.
4 – Don't be (*Become not*) cheeky! I [will] park (*now*) here.
5 – But you can't (*that works not*) – this is the exit for (*of*) the police.
6 – I don't care (*That is to-me equal*).
7 On Saturdays, they don't work anyway, and we will be (*are*) back in half an hour.

Ein schwieriger Samstagmorgen

is always **-e**. Phew! Sometimes the theory is more complicated than the practice. We'll see the adjective declensions in lesson 56 ... by then, it will already seem familiar!

③ **frech** *cheeky, impertinent, insolent.*

④ **der Polizei** is the genitive of **die Polizei**. The genitive and dative feminine articles are the same. Note that *the police* is singular in German and so requires a third-person singular verb: **Die Polizei kommt!** *The police are coming* ('comes')*!*

48

8 *Zehn Minuten später im Großmarkt.*
9 – Der Besitzer des **Fahr**zeugs ⑤ HH ⑥ – DY – 349 soll **bi**tte so**fort sei**nen **Wa**gen **weg**fahren.
10 Sein **Fahr**zeug blo**ckiert** die **Ein**fahrt der Polizei**wa**gen ⑦!

---

8 … *grohs*-markt **9** … *buhzits*ᵃ *des fah*ᵃ*-tsoiks hah hah – deh ewp*silon – *dreihund*ᵃ*tnoinuntfee*ᵃ*tsikH* … **10** … *blokee*ᵃ*t* … *einfah*ᵃ*t* …

Notes

⑤ **des Fahrzeugs** is the genitive of **das Fahrzeug** *vehicle*. The neuter and masculine definite articles in the genitive are the same: the article ends in **-es** and the noun takes the ending **-s**: **das Ende des Regenwetters** *the end of the rainy weather* ('rain-weather'). More on this in lesson 49.

***

Shopping in Germany
In Germany, **das Ladenschlussgesetz** *('shop-end-law') regulates when shops are required to be closed to the public. Opening hours are permitted between 6 am and 8 pm on weekdays, but shops must remain closed on Sundays and public holidays (of which there are rather a lot in some areas). Since 2006, the individual* **Länder** *are free to regulate weekday opening hours, so there is some variation, although the ban*

***

Übung 1 – Übersetzen Sie bitte!

❶ Hier dürfen Sie nicht parken, das ist eine Ausfahrt! ❷ Werden Sie nicht frech, oder ich rufe die Polizei! ❸ Die Freunde der Kinder kommen in einer halben Stunde. ❹ Eine alte Frau ist die Besitzerin des Großmarkts. ❺ Samstags bleibe ich aus demselben Grund wie Sie zu Hause.

8 *Ten minutes later in the superstore.*
9 – The owner of the vehicle [registered] HH–DY–349 should (*please*) immediately remove his car (*his car drive-away*).
10 The (*His*) vehicle is blocking the entrance of the police cars!

⑥ The first letters on German vehicle number plates indicate the city or region where the vehicle is registered. **HH** stands for **Hansestadt Hamburg** *Hanseatic city [of] Hamburg*.

⑦ Here, **der Polizeiwagen** is genitive plural. The plural definite article in the genitive case is **der**; the noun doesn't change. The nominative singular is equally **der Polizeiwagen**, because **der Wagen** is a masculine noun. Don't worry about confusing the two, as genitives are always preceded by another noun.

***

on opening on Sundays and holidays remains in effect everywhere. And old habits die hard. Until 2003, when the latest version of the **Ladenschlussgesetz** *was passed, shops up and down the country closed at 6 or 6:30 pm on weekdays and around 1 pm on Saturdays. In small towns and rural areas, most small businesses still observe these opening hours, although supermarkets normally don't. Nevertheless, some people still do their weekly shop Saturday morning.*

***

Answers to Exercise 1

❶ You aren't allowed to park here – this is an exit! ❷ Don't be (*become*) cheeky or I['ll] call the police! ❸ The children's friends are coming in half an hour. ❹ An old lady is the owner of the superstore. ❺ Every Saturday, I stay at home for the same reason as you.

49 Übung 2 – Ergänzen Sie bitte!

❶ The mother of my friend (*f.*) goes shopping on Mondays.
Die Mutter .... geht montags
....

❷ The police car blocks the entrance to the superstore.
... . blockiert die Einfahrt ...
....

❸ They have the same car as us? I don't care (*That is to-me equal*).
Sie haben .... wie wir? Das ist
... .

---

49 Neunundvierzigste Lektion

Wiederholung – Review

1 The genitive case

The genitive is the fourth case in the German system of declension. Its main function is to link nouns or noun phrases to express possession or close relationships: **das Haus des Professors** *the professor's house*; **die Abfahrt des Zuges** *the departure of the train*. The genitive usually follows the noun it describes: **der Wagen des Chefs** *the boss's car* ('the car of-the boss'). The only exception is when a proper name is used in the genitive: **Petras Freund** *Petra's friend*; **Frau Bachmanns Haus** *Mrs Bachmann's house*. (No apostrophe!) Here are the articles in all four cases:

	Singular			Plural
	masc.	fem.	neuter	
Nominative	der/ein	die/eine	das/ein	die/ –
Accusative	den/einen	die/eine	das/ein	die/ –
Dative	dem/einem	der/einer	dem/einem	den/...-n
Genitive	des/eines ...-(e)s	der/einer	des/eines ...-(e)s	der/ –

239 • zweihundertneununddreißig

❹ Why are you so insolent? You aren't the boss of the firm.
Warum bist du so ..... ? Du bist nicht ...
.... der Firma.

❺ The owner of the vehicle is probably in the supermarket.
... . des Fahrzeugs ist ....
im Supermarkt.

Answers to Exercise 2

❶ – meiner Freundin – einkaufen ❷ Der Polizeiwagen – des Großmarkts ❸ – denselben Wagen – mir egal ❹ – frech – der Chef – ❺ Der Besitzer – wahrscheinlich –

Forty-ninth lesson   49

There are three important points concerning the genitive case:

• In the singular, the genitive masculine and neuter articles are the same, and the genitive noun takes an **-es** or **-s** ending. Which ending? Here are some rules of thumb.

• One-syllable masculine and neuter nouns normally add **-es**:
der Rat des Freundes *the friend's advice*
das Fahrrad des Kindes *the child's bike*
die Tür des Hauses *the door of the house*

• Multi-syllable masculine and neuter nouns normally add **-s**:
der Erste des Monats (genitive masculine of **der Monat**)
the first of the month
die Tür des Büros (genitive neuter of **das Büro**)
the door of the office

• The feminine articles in the genitive case are the same as the dative case; the noun doesn't change:
das Kind der (genitive) **Frau** *the woman's child*
Er spricht mit der (dative) **Frau.** *He speaks with the woman.*

• In the plural, the genitive article **der** is the same as the masculine singular nominative article and the feminine articles in the dative

and genitive. You won't confuse them: a noun in the genitive is always dependent on a preceding noun:
der Tag der Männer *the men's day*
der Tag der Frauen *the women's day*
der Tag der Kinder *the children's day*

Don't worry, this is less complicated than it seems, particularly since the genitive is often replaced with **von** + dative in everyday speech: **das Büro von dem (vom) Chef** *the boss's office*.

2 The past participle

2.1 The past participle of irregular verbs

Before we talk about irregular verbs, a brief reminder that regular ('weak') verbs form their past participles the following way:
ge- + verb stem + **-(e)t**:
parken → **geparkt**
kaufen → **gekauft**
melden → **gemeldet**

Irregular ('strong') verbs form their past participle differently:

• Their past participles generally end in **-en**, e.g.:
fahren *to drive, to go by car* (→ **gefahren**)
kommen *to come* (→ **gekommen**)
schlafen *to sleep* (→ **geschlafen**)

• Sometimes there is a vowel change in the stem, e.g.:
gehen *to go* (→ **gegangen**)
sitzen *to be sitting* (→ **gesessen**)
schreien *to shout, to cry* (→ **geschrien** or **geschrieen**)

Don't worry about memorizing the past participles of irregular verbs right now. You'll pick them gradually since you'll encounter them quite often.

2.2 Past participles of verbs with separable and inseparable prefixes

• Separable-prefix verbs form their past participle by adding **ge-** between the separable prefix and the verb stem:

anmachen *to switch on, to light* → **an**ge**macht** *switched on, lit*
runterfallen *to fall down* → **runter**ge**fallen** *fallen down*
zurückkommen *to return* → **zurück**ge**kommen** *returned*

(Remember that separable-prefix verbs are verbs whose prefix separates from the stem and moves to the last position in present tense statements. The separable prefix carries the main stress because it gives meaning to the verb: **Ich mache das Licht an.** *I switch the light on.* **Ich mache das Licht aus.** *I switch the light off.*)

In contrast, inseparable-prefix verbs don't take the prefix **ge-**:
erlauben *to permit, to allow* → **erlaubt** *permitted, allowed*
verbieten *to forbid* → **verboten** *forbidden*
bekommen *to receive* → **bekommen** *received*
(**er-**, **ver-**, **be-** are inseparable prefixes, which replace the prefix **ge-** of the past participle.)

• Other verbs that don't take the **ge-** prefix are those whose infinitive ends in **-ieren**.
studieren *to study* → **studiert** *studied*
telefonieren *to phone* → **telefoniert** *phoned*

3 The simple past of *sein* and *haben*

The simple past is often used interchangeably with the perfect tense in German to relate something that happened in the past. There is a general tendency, particularly in spoken usage, to use the perfect tense. Hence, **ich habe mir letztes Jahr das Bein gebrochen** 'I have broken my leg last year' is perfectly acceptable in German, whereas the simple past would be used in English: *I broke my leg last year.* However, even in conversational contexts, **sein** and **haben** are normally used in the simple past.

Here are their simple past tense forms:

	sein	haben
ich	war	hatte
du	warst	hattest
er/sie/es	war	hatte
wir	waren	hatten
ihr	wart	hattet
sie/Sie	waren	hatten

As you can see, all forms except the first- and third-person singular of **sein** add verb endings. This is a feature shared with the modal verbs, whose first- and third-person forms are also alike (see lesson 35). We'll come back to the past tense soon.

4 Two-way prepositions

We've seen that in German it matters a lot if the relationship between a noun and a verb is one of motion towards or away from the noun (direction) or one describing position (location).

In questions, the difference is reflected in the choice of question words. **Wo?** *Where?* is used to ask where something is; **Wohin?** *Where to?* is used to ask the direction something is taking.

In answers, the locational or directional relationship is reflected either in the choice of preposition or in the choice of case after the preposition.

Sometimes different prepositions are needed to give a location or a direction:
Ich wohne in Deutschland. *I live in Germany.* (location)
but: **Ich fahre nach Deutschland.** *I go to Germany.* (direction)

Die Kinder sind zu Hause. *The children are at home.* (location)
but: **Die Kinder gehen nach Hause.** *The children go home.* (direction)

Most German prepositions require that the object is in a particular case. For instance, **nach** and **zu** always take an object in the dative case; **durch** *through* always takes an object in the accusative case. However, there are also what are called two-way prepositions. These can take an object in either the accusative or dative case – but they don't do so at random. When such a preposition answers the question **Wohin?** (direction), it takes the accusative case. When answering the question **Wo?** (location), it takes the dative case. There are nine two-way prepositions: **an** *at, on, to*; **auf** *at, to, on, upon*; **hinter** *behind*; **in** *in, into*; **neben** *next to, beside, near*; **über** *above, across, over, about*; **unter** *under, below, among*; **vor** *in front of*; **zwischen** *between*. (The meaning of a two-way preposition may depend on whether it takes an object in the dative or the accusative.)

The change in case is very helpful in situations where the same preposition has different meanings in different contexts, since the case of the object indicates whether the relationship is one of location or direction:
Wir sitzen in dem* (dative) **Garten.** *We are sitting in the garden.* (location) * One could also say **im Garten** (**im** = **in** + **dem**).
Gehen wir in den (acc.) **Garten.** *Let's go to the garden.* (direction)
in der Stadt *in the city* (location)
in die Stadt *to the city* (direction)

This feature of German means that verbs that express motion can be omitted in sentences containing modal verbs:
Ich muss schnell ins Büro. *I have to [go] to the office quickly.*
('I must quickly to-the office.')
Wohin musst du? *Where do you have to [go]?*
('To-where must you?')

5 Demonstratives: *dieser, diese, dieses*; pl. *diese*

Demonstratives indicate what is being referred to – in English, *this*, *that*, *these*, *those* are demonstratives. They can be used as pronouns, replacing a specific person, idea or thing that has usually been mentioned before (e.g. *This is crazy.*). They can also be used as determiners or adjectives to modify a noun (e.g. *This pear is juicy.*).

The demonstratives meaning *this*, *these* in German are **dieser** (m.), **diese** (f.), **dieses** (neut.), **diese** (pl.), however, in spoken usage, the definite articles **der**, **die**, **das**, pl. **die** are also often used as demonstratives. Note that demonstratives have to agree in gender, number and case with the noun they replace or modify; they decline like the definite article.

Dieser Hund ist jung. *This dog is young.*
Or **Der Hund ist jung.** (The stress falls on **der**.)

Ich habe diesen Mann noch nicht gesehen.
I have not seen this man before.
Or **Ich habe den Mann noch nicht gesehen.** (stress on **den**)

49 *That's enough grammar for today! Let's finish with a dialogue that will let you practice what you've learned in this set of lessons.*

Review exercise

Gesagt ist gesagt

1 – Du bist sicher, dass der Besitzer des Hauses nicht da ist?
2 – Ganz sicher, der verbringt seine Ferien immer im Juni in den Bergen.
3 – Ich weiß nicht. Wie viel, sagst du, liegt im Geldschrank?
4 – Jedes Jahr um diese Zeit ist der Geldschrank bis oben voll.
5   Er ist gerade aus Südamerika zurückgekommen,
6   und hat einen Koffer voll Geld mitgebracht.
7 – Und wo steht der Geldschrank?
8 – Auf dem Klo, gleich neben der Tür.
9 – Um Gottes willen! Warum hat er ihn dorthin gestellt?
10 – Er glaubt sicher, niemand sucht ihn dort.
11   Ich schwöre dir, es ist wirklich nicht schwierig.
12 – Ach nein, lass mal, ich will nicht wieder anfangen.
13 – Mensch, nur noch dieses Mal: einmal ist keinmal.
14 – Nein, tut mir Leid, ich kann wirklich nicht.
15   Wir haben eine herrliche Zeit zusammen verbracht.
16   Aber ich habe der Mutter meiner Kinder gesagt, ich fange nicht wieder an.

Translation
[What is] said is said

1 You are sure that the owner of the house isn't here? **2** Absolutely sure, he always spends his holidays in the mountains in June. **3** I don't know. How much do you say is (*lying*) in the safe (*money-cupboard*)? **4** This time every year (*Every year at this time*) the safe is full to the top (*until above full*). **5** He has just returned from South America, **6** and has brought [back] a suitcase full [of] money. **7** And where is (*standing*) the safe? **8** In the bathroom, right (*immediately*) next to the door. **9** Oh my God! Why has he put it there (*it there-to placed-upright*)? **10** He surely believes nobody [will] look for it there. **11** I swear to you, it is really not difficult. **12** Ah no, leave [it] be – I don't want to start again. **13** Listen (*Man*), only one more time (*still this time*): once doesn't count (*one-time is no-time*). **14** No, I'm sorry, I really can't. **15** We've had (*spent*) a great time together. **16** But I told the mother of my children [that] I [will] not start again.

The second wave – **Die zweite Welle**
In the lessons so far, we've asked you simply to listen and read (aloud if possible) and to translate from German into English. You've now completed this so-called 'passive' phase of your learning. With the next lesson, we'll enter the 'active' phase. What does this entail? Well, you will simply 'actively' apply what you've come to understand 'passively'. From the next lesson on, you'll go back to a previous lesson, starting with lesson 1. Covering up the German text, you will translate the dialogue from English into German – aloud, of course. This will help you consolidate vocabulary and grammar by revisiting texts, while building on your knowledge with the information in the new lessons. Going back will make you realize how far you've already come – you'll be amazed how much progress you've made. At the end of each new lesson, we'll indicate which lesson you should go back to. **Viel Spaß!** Have fun! (*'Much pleasure!'*)

50 Fünfzigste Lektion

Anzeigen ① für Ferienwohnungen

1 – Hör mal, wie **find**est du das?
2 **Wun**derschöne **Lux**us-**Fe**rienwohnung in **Spa**nien zu ver**mie**ten.
3 **Herr**lich an der **Küs**te ge**le**gen ②.
4 **Son**niges ③, **groß**es **Wohn**zimmer, zwei **Schlaf**zimmer, **hel**le **Kü**che und Bad.
5 **Gro**ßer Bal**kon** (**Süd**seite) mit **schö**ner ④ **Aus**sicht auf das Meer.
6 Sie **brau**chen kein **Spa**nisch.

> **Pronunciation**
> antseig'n ... **feh**riuhn-**voh**nung'n 2 vundᵃ-shœnuh luksus-...
> fermeetuhn 3 ... kewstuh guh**leh**g'n 4 zoniges grohses
> **vohn**-tsimᵃ ... shlahf-tsimᵃ heluh kewkHuh ... baht
> 5 ... bal**kong** (**zewt**-zeituh) ... shœnᵃ ows-zikHt ... mehᵃ
> 6 ... shpahnish

Notes

① **die Anzeige** *advertisement*; one can also say **die Annonce** *anongsuh*. Remember that the majority of words ending in **-e** are feminine and form the plural by adding **-n** (**die Anzeigen**, **die Annoncen** *advertisements*). The word **Ferienwohnungen** consists of **die Ferien** *holidays* + **die Wohnung** *apartment*.

② **gelegen**, translated here as *located*, is the past participle of **liegen** *to lie, to be lying*. We'll come back to this in lesson 56.

③ We've seen that attributive adjectives decline depending on the gender and case of the noun they precede and the presence (or absence) of an article. If there is no article, the adjective ending tells you the gender of a noun. For example, **sonniges**

Fiftieth lesson 50

Advertisements for holiday apartments

1 – Listen, how does this sound to you (*find you that*)?
2 Gorgeous luxury holiday apartment in Spain to rent.
3 Magnificent location on the coast (*Magnificently at the coast located*).
4 Sunny, large living room, two bedrooms, bright kitchen and bathroom.
5 Large balcony (south side) with beautiful view[s] of the sea.
6 You don't need [to speak] Spanish.

Pronunciation notes
2 In **wunderschön**, the main stress is on the first syllable **vund**[a], but one can also stress **schön**, which has a reinforcing effect.
5, 8 In words of French origin, the last syllable is stressed: **der Balkon** *bal**kong***, **der Frisör** *fris**œ**[a]*.

signals that **das Wohnzimmer** is neuter; likewise **helle** shows that **die Küche** is feminine; and in the next line, **großer** tells you that **der Balkon** is masculine.

④ Here is another adjective that has declined because it isn't preceded by an article: **schön** here takes the dative feminine ending **-er** because the preposition **mit** is always followed by the dative, and **die Aussicht** *view* is a feminine noun. If there were an article, the article would decline to the dative case, while the adjective would take the ending **-en**, which is often considered a 'weak' adjective ending: **mit einer schönen Aussicht** *with a nice view*. We'll come back to this.

zweihundertachtundvierzig • 248

50 7   Die **Spa**nier ⑤ **spre**chen sehr gut Deutsch.
8   Es gibt so**gar ei**nen **deut**schen **Zahn**arzt und Fri**sör**.
9 – Das klingt gut, **a**ber sie **sa**gen nicht, wie viel die **Woh**nung **kos**tet.
10   **Au**ßerdem **möch**te ich nach ⑥ **Spa**nien, um **Spa**nisch zu ⑦ **ler**nen…

---

7 ... *shpah*ni*ª* ... 8 ... *doit*sh'n *tsahn*-ahtst ... *fris*œ*ª*
10 ... *owss*ª*dehm*...

Notes

⑤ **der Spanier, die Spanier** *Spaniard, the Spanish*; however, the language is **das Spanisch** *Spanish*. While English uses adjectives to indicate nationalities ('I am English/American/Canadian', etc.), German uses a noun without an article: **Er ist Engländer.** *He is English.* ('He is Englishman.'); **Sie ist Engländerin.** *She is English.* ('She is Englishwoman.'). The vast majority of nouns that indicate a female's nationality end in **-in**. The major exception is an important one though: **Er ist Deutscher.** *He is German.* **Sie ist Deutsche.** *She is German.* To refer to a language, use the adjective with a capital letter: **Ich spreche Deutsch.** *I speak German.* Stay tuned to find out other nationalities and languages.

***

Übung 1 – Übersetzen Sie bitte!

❶ Meine Wohnung hat ein großes Wohnzimmer. ❷ Er geht nach Südamerika, um Spanisch zu lernen. ❸ Zu vermieten: großes Haus am Meer mit vier Schlafzimmern. ❹ Unser Zahnarzt wohnt jetzt in Spanien. ❺ Er hat ein Haus mit herrlicher Aussicht auf das Meer gekauft.

7   The Spanish speak German very well.
8   There is even a German dentist (*tooth-doctor*) and hairdresser.
9 – That sounds good, but they don't say how much the apartment costs.
10 Besides, I'd like [to go] to Spain in order to learn Spanish …

---

8 **Arzt** can be pronounced either with a long **a** *[ahᵃtst]* or with a short **a** followed by **r** *[artst]*. Be careful with the spelling! Although the end of the word is pronounced *tst*, it is written with only a single **t** (at the end); the other **t** you hear is part of **z** *ts*.

---

⑥ **Ich möchte nach Spanien …** *I'd like [to go] to Spain …*
Remember, **gehen** *to go* isn't needed here because the preposition **nach** itself indicates that there is movement from one place to another.

⑦ **um … zu** translates as *in order to*, *to*; **um** introduces a subordinate clause, and the infinitive preceded by **zu** moves to the end of the sentence: **Ich bin gekommen, um Sie zu sehen.** *I have come (in order) to see you.*

***

Answers to Exercise 1

❶ My apartment/flat has a large living room. ❷ He is going to South America in order to learn Spanish. ❸ To rent/let: large house at the sea[side] with four bedrooms. ❹ Our dentist now lives in Spain. ❺ He bought a house with a magnificent view of the sea.

50 Übung 2 – Ergänzen Sie bitte!

1 How many rooms does their apartment have? – A large living room and five bedrooms.
Wie viele Zimmer hat .... ? – Ein ...... Wohnzimmer und fünf ....

2 And in addition, they have a large balcony with a magnificent view.
Und außerdem haben sie .... mit ....

3 The house is located at the coast and doesn't cost much (*costs not much*).
Das Haus ... an der Küste .... und ...... nicht viel.

4 We are renting out our luxury apartment in Spain in May and June.
... . unsere Luxuswohnung .. .. im Mai und ..... .

5 I need Spanish in order to work in Spain.
Ich brauche .... , .. in Spanien .. ..

251 • zweihunderteinundfünfzig

Answers to Exercise 2

❶ – ihre Wohnung – großes – Schlafzimmer ❷ – einen großen Balkon – einer herrlichen Aussicht ❸ – ist – gelegen – kostet – ❹ Wir vermieten – in Spanien – Juni ❺ – Spanisch um – zu arbeiten

Second wave: 1st lesson

51 Einundfünfzigste Lektion

Eine Radiosendung

1 **Gu**ten **A**bend, **mei**ne **Da**men und **Her**ren!
2 **Herz**lich will**kom**men bei **un**serer ①
   Sendung „Be**rühm**te **Deut**sche ②".
3 Wir **möch**ten Ihnen **heu**te **ei**nen sehr
   be**deu**tenden **Dich**ter ③ **vor**stellen.
4 Er ist im **Jah**re ④ 1749
   (**sieb**zehn**hun**dert**neun**und**vier**zig) in
   Frankfurt ge**bo**ren ⑤.
5 Er hat in **Straß**burg und **Leip**zig **Ju**ra
   stu**diert**.
6 Mit **sei**nem **ers**ten Ro**man** „Die **Lei**den ⑥
   des **jun**gen **Wer**ther" ist er be**rühmt**
   ge**wor**den ⑦.

Pronunciation
... rahdio-**zen**dung **2** ... vil**kom**uh ... buh**rewm**tuh ... **3** ...
buh**doi**tuhnduh **dikH**tᵃ ... **4** ... **zeep**tsehn-**hund**ᵃt-**noin**unt-
feeᵃtsikH ... guh**boh**ruhn **5** ... **shtrahs**burk ... **leip**tsikH
yoora shtu**dee**ᵃt **6** ... ro**mahn** ... **lei**duhn des **yung**uhn **vert**ᵃ
... guh**vor**duhn

Notes
① The preposition **bei** has several meanings: *by, at, with, to,* etc. It is always followed by the dative. We've seen that the feminine article **die** changes to **der** in the dative. Likewise, **unsere** *our* (f.) takes the ending **-r** in the dative singular: **bei unserer Sendung**.

② As the adjective here is not preceded by an article, it takes the ending **-e** to indicate the nominative plural (like **die**, the plural definite article): **berühmte Deutsche** *famous Germans*. However, if the definite article is included, the adjective takes

Lesson fifty-one 51

A radio programme

1. Good evening, (*my*) ladies and gentlemen!
2. (*Cordially*) Welcome to our programme 'Famous Germans'.
3. Today, we would like to introduce you to a very important (*significant*) poet.
4. He was born in Frankfurt in the year 1749 (*is in the year 1749 in Frankfurt born*).
5. He studied law in Strasbourg and Leipzig.
6. He became famous with his first novel 'The Sorrows of Young Werther' (*is he famous become*).

the 'weak' ending **-en**: **die berühmten Deutschen** *the famous Germans*. For now just take note of the different adjective endings – they'll gradually become familiar.

③ **der Dichter** can mean both *poet* and *writer*, but is usually used only for poets these days.

④ The final **-e** in **im Jahr(e)** *in the year* is optional. It is a somewhat antiquated dative ending. In order to give a year, one can either say **im Jahr(e)** followed by the year, or simply the year without a preposition: **Ich bin 1982 (neunzehnhundertzweiundachtzig) geboren.** *I was born [in] 1982.*

⑤ The past participle **geboren** *born* is used here like an adjective describing the state of the subject: **Goethe ist in Frankfurt geboren.** *Goethe was born in Frankfurt.* However, **geboren** is strictly speaking part of a passive construction formed with the verb **sein** *to be*, much like its English equivalent *to be born*. We'll come back to passive constructions later.

⑥ **die Leiden** *sufferings*, *sorrows* is the plural of **das Leid**, which can also mean *distress* or *agony*.

⑦ **geworden** is the past participle of **werden** *to become*.

zweihundertvierundfünfzig • 254

51
7   Aber sein **Le**benswerk war „Faust".
8   Er **hat**te viel **Ein**fluss auf **sei**ne Genera**ti**on und die Genera**ti**onen da**nach** ⑧.
9   Die **deut**sche **Kla**ssik hat mit ihm **auf**gehört ⑨.
10 Er ist am 22. (**zwei**und**zwan**zigsten) März 1830 (**acht**zehn**hun**dert**drei**ßig) ⑩ in **Wei**mar ge**stor**ben ⑪.

7 ... lehb'ns-verk ... fowst 8 ... einflus ... generatsyohn ... 9 ... klassik ... owfguh-hœ^at 10 ... tsveiunt-tsvantsikHstuhn merts akht'tsehn-hund^at-dreissikH ... veimar guhshtorb'n

Notes

⑧ **danach** translates as *afterwards* or *thereafter*: **Ich gehe ins Theater und danach gehe ich nach Hause.** *I'm going to the theatre, and afterwards I'll go home.*

⑨ **aufgehört** is the past participle of **aufhören** *to stop*, *to cease*. In the previous lesson, we saw **hören** *to hear*, *to listen*. See the difference a prefix can make?

⑩ With regard to word order, note that expressions of time generally come before expressions of place in German: **Ich gehe morgen ins Kino.** *I'm going to the cinema tomorrow.*

⑪ **sterben** *to die*; **gestorben** *died*. Remember that past participles occur in the last position in the sentence: **Wann ist Goethe gestorben?** *When did Goethe die?*

***

Übung 1 – Übersetzen Sie bitte!

❶ Darf ich mich vorstellen? Ich bin Thomas Büchner. ❷ Ihre Kinder sind groß geworden! ❸ Wann sind Sie geboren? Am 1. April? ❹ Es hat seit drei Wochen nicht aufgehört zu regnen. ❺ Ich lerne eine Viertelstunde Deutsch und danach gehe ich essen.

7 But his life's work was 'Faust'.

8 He had a lot of influence on his generation and (*the*) subsequent generations (*afterwards*).

9 (*The*) German Classicism ended with him (*has with him stopped*).

10 He died in Weimar on 22 March 1830.

> **Pronunciation note**
> 7 In **Lebenswerk** *lehb'ns-verk*, the **-s** linking the two nouns **Werk** and **Leben** is attached to **Leben**.

Wann sind Sie geboren?

***

Answers to Exercise 1

❶ May I introduce myself? I am Thomas Büchner. ❷ Your children have grown (*are big become*)! ❸ When were you born? On the 1st of April? ❹ It hasn't stopped raining for three weeks. ❺ I['ll] study German [for] a quarter of an hour and afterwards I['ll] go eat.

zweihundertsechsundfünfzig • 256

51 Übung 2 – Ergänzen Sie bitte!

❶ (*Cordially*) Welcome to our city!
   .... in unserer Stadt!

❷ This radio programme was very interesting.
   .... sehr interessant.

❸ This man is very important and he has a lot of influence.
   Dieser Mann ist .... und er hat ....

❹ My grandmother was (*is*) born in 1917 and died in 1998.
   Meine Großmutter ist 1917 .... und 1998 ....

***

Johann Wolfgang von Goethe

Goethe is without a doubt one of the most important figures in German literature. In almost every German town, there is a **Goetheplatz** *or a* **Goethestraße** *or a* **Goetheschule**. *Often you'll find all three. Goethe was and is considered by many a universal genius. A novelist, poet, playwright and philosopher, he is best known today as one of the greatest contributors to Weimar classicism. He also acted as chief advisor to the Duke of Saxe-Weimar-Eisenach. However, Goethe also produced a sizeable body of scientific work that focused on such diverse topics as plants, colour, clouds, weather, morphology and geology. His 'Theory of Colours' (***Farbenlehre***), published in 1810, was one of the earliest descriptions of the nature and perception of colours.*

   Goethe himself considered his scientific contributions of greater value to humankind than his literary works, and thus it is perhaps surprising that his literary masterpiece raises the question about

❺ Good evening, Mr Hansen, may I introduce you to my wife (*to-you[formal] my wife introduce*)?
.... Herr Hansen, darf ich ..... meine Frau ....?

Answers to Exercise 2

❶ Herzlich willkommen – ❷ Diese Radiosendung war – ❸ – sehr bedeutend – viel Einfluss ❹ – (neunzehnhundertsiebzehn) geboren – (neunzehnhundertachtundneunzig) gestorben ❺ Guten Abend – Ihnen – vorstellen

***

the value of scientific knowledge. In 'Faust', the eponymous hero exclaims: **'Ich habe, ach, Philosophie, Juristerei* und Medizin, und leider auch Theologie, durchaus studiert, mit heißem Bemühen. Da steh' ich nun, ich armer Tor, und bin so klug als wie zuvor.'** *'I've studied, alas, philosophy, the law and medicine, and even, more's the pity, divinity, with ardent effort, through and through. And here I am now, poor fool, and no wiser today than I ever was.' In his despair, Faust makes a pact with the devil, Mephistopheles, offering him his soul should he reveal to him the secrets and pleasures of the world and manage to make him love life ...*

* *By choosing the expression* **die Juristerei** *instead of* **die Jura** *or* **die Jurisprudenz**, *Goethe adds a mocking tone to 'law' here.*

Second wave: 2nd lesson

52 Zweiundfünfzigste Lektion

Pünktlichkeit ① ist die Höflichkeit der Könige

1 – Was ist denn pass**ie**rt?
2 Du bist nicht **zu**verlässig.
3 Wir **wa**ren um **Vier**tel vor acht ②
   ver**a**bredet ③.
4 Und du kommst fünf nach acht.
5 – Ich weiß, ent**schul**dige **bi**tte.
6 Ich **konn**te ④ erst ⑤ halb acht ⑥ aus dem
   Bü**ro** weg ⑦.
7 Dann **wa**ren na**tür**lich über**all** die **Stra**ßen
   ver**stopft**.

> **Pronunciation**
> *pewnktlikHkeit ... hœflikHkeit deh^a kœniguh* **1** *... passee^{a}t*
> **2** *... tsooferlessikH* **3** *... fee^{a}tuhl foh^a akht ...* **6** *... kontuh ...*
> *wek* **7** *... fershtopft*

Notes

① Some nouns are formed from adjectives by adding **-keit**: **pünktlich** *punctual* → **die Pünktlichkeit** *punctuality*; **höflich** *polite* → **die Höflichkeit** *politeness*. Such nouns are feminine and form the plural by adding **-en**, like those ending in **-ung** (lesson 50). Adjectives ending in **-lich** are themselves derived from a noun: here, **der Punkt** *point* and **der Hof** *court*.

② **Viertel vor acht** literally means 'quarter before eight'. We've already encountered **fünf vor zwölf** *five to twelve*. German uses **vor** *before* (instead of 'to') and **nach** *after* (instead of 'past') to give the time: **Viertel nach acht** *a quarter past 8*; **fünf nach acht** *five past 8* (line 4).

③ **verabredet sein** *to arrange to meet, to have an appointment/meeting with someone*.

259 • zweihundertneunundfünfzig

Fifty-second lesson 52

Punctuality is the politeness of kings

1 – What happened (*then*)?
2 One can't count on you (*You aren't reliable*).
3 We were [supposed] to meet at quarter to 8 (*We were at quarter before 8 arranged-to-meet*).
4 And you get here at five past 8.
5 – I know, I'm sorry.
6 I could only get out of the office at half past seven (*I could only half eight from the office away*).
7 [And] then, of course, the streets were jammed everywhere.

④ **ich konnte** *I could* is the past tense of **können** *can, to be able to*. Remember that in the past tense, the first- and third-person singular forms are the same: **er/sie/es konnte** *he/she/it could*.

⑤ Referring to time, **erst** implies that it is later or earlier than expected or desirable, corresponding to *only*, *not ... until* or sometimes *as late as*. **Er ist erst um 10 Uhr gekommen.** *He didn't arrive until 10:00.* **Es ist erst 15 Uhr.** *It's only 3pm.*

⑥ **halb acht** 'half eight' – but be careful! This translates to *half past seven*. Unlike in English, **halb** indicates the hour to come rather than the preceding hour: **halb sieben** *half past six*, **halb drei** *half past two*, **halb elf** *half past ten*, etc. It's a bit tricky, but you'll soon get used to it!

⑦ **weg** by itself indicates *gone*, *left* or *departed*. It's often used with **gehen** or **sein**: **Der Kuchen ist weg!** *The cake is gone!* **Der Zug ist weg.** *The train has left.* **Ich kann jetzt nicht weg.** *I can't leave right now.* It can also be a separable prefix: **weggehen** *to go away* → **ich gehe weg** *I'm going away*.

52 8 Und **schließ**lich bin ich 10 (zehn) Mi**nu**ten he**rum**gefahren ⑧, um **ei**nen **Park**platz zu **fin**den.
9 – **Wohin** hast du denn das **Au**to ge**stellt**?
10 – Mach dir **kei**ne **Sor**gen, es ist **al**les in **Ord**nung.
11 Komm, die **lass**en **nie**mand mehr rein ⑨, wenn es **ein**mal **an**gefangen hat ⑩. ☐

(Fortsetzung folgt)

---

8 ... shleeslikH ... herumguhfah^an ... 10 ... zohrg'n ... in ortnung 11 ... rein ...

Notes

⑧ Instead of **herumfahren**, one can simply say **rumfahren** (see the next note).

⑨ **rein** is a colloquial short form of either **herein** or **hinein**. Remember that **her** indicates movement towards the speaker (a bit like *here*), whereas **hin** expresses movement away from the speaker (a bit like *there*). But this is not always easy to determine. The phrase in line 11 could read **die lassen niemand mehr herein** (referring to the people inside the concert hall not letting those outside come towards them – 'here'), or it could read **die lassen niemand mehr hinein**

***

Übung 1 – Übersetzen Sie bitte!

❶ Natürlich waren am Sonntag alle Autobahnen verstopft. ❷ Um wie viel Uhr waren wir verabredet? ❸ Er ist schließlich um neun Uhr gekommen. ❹ Wir sind eine Stunde rumgefahren, um das Hotel zu finden. ❺ Wir lassen Sie nicht rein, wenn Sie nicht pünktlich kommen.

8 And finally I drove around [for] 10 minutes in order to find a parking space.
9 – Where(-*to*) did you park (*put*) the car then?
10 – Don't worry (*Make yourself no worries*), everything is fine (*it is all in order*).
11 Come [on], they don't let anyone (*more*) in after (*when*) it (*once*) has started.

(To be continued)

(if one takes the perspective of those outside the concert hall not being allowed to go 'there'). So **rein** can be a useful way to avoid specifying the direction of movement!

⑩ As you know, the conjunction **wenn** 'when' or 'if' causes the conjugated verb to move to the last position in the subordinate clause. This holds true even if there is a past participle: **Wir können nicht mehr reingehen, wenn sie angefangen haben.** *We can't go in once they have started.* ('We can no more go in when they started have.')

***

Answers to Exercise 1

❶ Of course, all the motorways/freeways were jammed on Sunday. ❷ At what time were we [supposed] to meet? ❸ He finally arrived at nine o'clock. ❹ We drove around for an hour in order to find the hotel. ❺ We won't let you in if you don't come on time.

Übung 2 – Ergänzen Sie bitte!

① Don't worry (*Make yourself no worries*), he is reliable – he is (*comes*) always punctual(*ly*).

Machen Sie sich . . . . , er ist
. . . . , er kommt immer . . . .

② What has happened? – Nothing, everything is fine (*in order*).

Was ist denn . . . . ? – Nichts, alles ist . .
. . . .

③ I have an appointment with Mr Hansen at half five. – I'm sorry, he has (*is*) already gone.

Ich bin um . . . . mit Herrn Hansen
. . . . – Tut mir Leid, ... schon
. . . .

④ No one can [go] in when it has started.

. . . . darf . . . . , wenn es . . . .

⑤ Finally, she arrived at a quarter to four (*is she at quarter before four come*).

. . . . ist sie um . . . .
gekommen.

***

> **Pünktlichkeit und Zuverlässigkeit** punctuality and reliability *are – along with willingness to work – the main virtues associated with German-speaking countries, if one relies on cultural generalizations. They are closely linked: someone who isn't punctual isn't considered reliable either! When you've received a dinner or party invitation, make sure you're there on time, unless 'c.t.' is written at the bottom of the invitation: 'c.t.' stands for* **cum tempore** *(Latin 'with time'), and it is a means of allowing people to be a quarter of an hour late. Otherwise, being late is considered negligent if not outright disrespectful to your host. Persistent lateness may cause all kinds of problems, not only at*

Answers to Exercise 2

❶ – keine Sorgen – zuverlässig – pünktlich ❷ – passiert – in Ordnung ❸ – halb sechs – verabredet – er ist – weg ❹ Niemand – rein, angefangen hat ❺ Schließlich – Viertel vor vier –

Er ist schließlich um neun Uhr gekommen.

***

work, but also in people's private lives, leading to the breakdown of friendships, and sometimes even marriages. Having said this, punctuality is often an aspiration as much as anything else, even in Germany ...

*But do you know who coined the phrase '**Pünktlichkeit ist die Höflichkeit der Könige**'? Nope, it wasn't a German, but Louis XVIII of France (1755–1824)!*

Second wave: 3rd lesson

53 Dreiundfünfzigste Lektion

Er ist nicht auf den Mund gefallen ①
(Fortsetzung)

1 – Ich bin schon **lange** nicht mehr in **ei**nem so **gu**ten ② **Konzert** gewesen ③.
2 Hat es dir auch ge**fal**len ④?
3 – Ja, es war **traum**haft ⑤.
4 – Komm, ich **ha**be einen **Bären**hunger ⑥.
5 Dort steht **un**ser **Au**to.
6 – **Gu**ten Abend, Polizei! Ist das Ihr **Wa**gen?
7 – Der hier? Eh, nein, den **ha**be ich nie ge**se**hen. Wa**rum** denn?
8 – **Sei**en Sie ⑦ froh, für den Be**sit**zer wird das **teu**er.

Pronunciation
... munt ... **1** ... zoh **goo**tuhn kon**tsert** guh**veh**zuhn **3** ... **trowm**haft **4** ... beh**ruhn-hung**ª **8 zei**-uhn ... froh ...

Notes

① **gefallen** is the past participle of **fallen** *to fall*.

② The preposition **in** *in, inside, into, to* is here followed by the dative because a location is being given (the concert). **das Konzert** *concert* is neuter, and the dative of the neuter indefinite article is **einem**. Since the article shows the case and the gender of the noun here, the adjective, **gut** *good*, doesn't have to and thus takes the 'weak' ending **-en**: **in einem guten Konzert** (lesson 50, note 4).

③ The verb **sein** is more often used in the simple past (e.g. *was, were*) than in the perfect tense (e.g. *has/have been*), but the latter does exist. As we see here, the auxiliary of **sein** in the perfect tense is also **sein** (rather than **haben** *to have*), resulting

Fifty-third lesson 53

He has the gift of the gab
(*He hasn't fallen on the mouth*)
(Continuation)

1 – It's a long time since I've been to such a good concert (*I am already long not more in a so good concert been*).
2 Did you like it, too (*Has it to-you also appealed*)?
3 – Yes, it was fantastic (*dreamlike*).
4 Come [on], I'm ravenous (*I have a bear's-hunger*).
5 There's (*There stands*) our car.
6 – Good evening. Police. Is this your car?
7 – This one here? Er, no, I've never seen it [before]. Why (*then*)?
8 – Consider yourself lucky (*Be glad*); for the owner this'll be (*becomes this*) expensive.

in: **ich bin gewesen** *I have been*, **du bist gewesen** *you have been* ('I am been', 'You are been', etc.).

④ The past participles of **fallen** *to fall* and **gefallen** *to like*, *to enjoy* (but constructed like 'to appeal to' – see lesson 40) are the same. There's little risk of confusing them though, as the two verbs take different auxiliaries to form the perfect tense: **haben** for **gefallen** *to like*, and **sein** for **fallen** *to fall*: **Der Film hat mir gefallen.** *I liked the film.* **Er ist aus dem Fenster gefallen.** *He fell from the window.*

⑤ The root word in **traumhaft** is **der Traum** *dream*. The suffix **-haft** is an ending by which adjectives are derived from nouns or verbs: **das Kind ist lebhaft** *the child is active* ('lively').

⑥ **der Bär** *bear* and **der Hunger** *hunger*.

⑦ **Seien Sie!** *Be!* is the formal imperative of **sein** *to be*.

zweihundertsechsundsechzig • 266

53 9 – Ach ja? Der **Ar**me ⑧! Na dann, **gu**te Nacht!
10 – Du bist gut, und wie **fah**ren wir nach **Hau**se?
11 – Das weiß ich im **Au**genblick noch nicht.
12   **Geh**en wir erst ⑨ mal **es**sen.
13   Mit **lee**rem ⑩ **Ma**gen kann ich nicht **nach**denken. □

9 ... armuh ... 13 ... lehruhm mahg'n ... nakh'denk'n

Notes

⑧ **der Arme** *the poor [man/person]* is actually the adjective **arm** *poor* used as a noun. Many adjectives can be used as nouns. Adjectival nouns decline like adjectives, retaining their endings as though a noun were there: **der Arme (Mann)** *the poor (man)*, **den Armen (Mann)** *the poor (man)* (acc.). They are usually capitalized.

⑨ **erst** here comes from **zuerst** *first, at first, first of all, not until*.

⑩ The declension here is **mit leerem Magen** because **der Magen** *stomach* is masculine and **mit** is followed by the dative. But if there is an article (including a negative article: **kein, keine, kein,** pl. **keine**) before the noun phrase, the article takes the dative ending, and the adjective a 'weak' ending: **mit ei**n**em lee**r**en Magen** *on* ('with') *an empty stomach*.

***

Übung 1 – Übersetzen Sie bitte!

❶ Bist du schon in Deutschland gewesen? ❷ Er kann zu Hause nicht nachdenken. ❸ Kennen Sie diesen Mann? – Den da? Nein. ❹ Wann essen wir? Ich habe einen Bärenhunger! ❺ Hat Ihnen dieser Abend gefallen? – Ja, es war traumhaft.

9 – Oh, really (*yes*)? Poor them (*The poor [one]*)! Ah well, good night!
10 – You're a clever one (*You're good*) – and how [will] we get (*drive*) home?
11 – (*That*) I don't yet know at the moment.
12 Let's go eat first (*Go we first once to-eat*).
13 I can't think (*think-it-over*) on an empty stomach.

***

Answers to Exercise 1

❶ Have you already been to Germany? ❷ He can't think at home. ❸ Do you know this man? – The one [over] there? No. ❹ When are we eating? I'm ravenous! ❺ Did you enjoy this evening? – Yes, it was fantastic.

54 Übung 2 – Ergänzen Sie bitte!

❶ Where is (*stands*) our car? I can't see it.

. . . . . . unser Wagen? Ich sehe . . . nicht.

❷ I don't know, I have to think about it.

. . . ., ich muss . . . .

❸ The concert was fantastic (*dreamlike*), but now I am ravenous (*have I a bears-hunger*).

Das Konzert war . . . ., aber jetzt habe ich . . . .

❹ Where have you (*formal*) put (*-upright*) the champagne? I've been looking for it for a long time (*I search it already long*).

. . . . den Champagner . . . .?
Ich suche ihn . . . .

---

54 Vierundfünfzigste Lektion

Kopf hoch!

1 Hand aufs ① Herz, Sie **ha**ben die **Na**se voll?
2 Man hat **Ih**nen Sand in die **Au**gen ge**streut** und **gol**dene **Ber**ge ver**spro**chen ②?

> **Pronunciation**
> *kopf hohkh* **1** *hant owfs herts … nahzuh …* **2** *… zant … owg'n guhshtroit … golduhnuh … fershprokh'n*

Notes

① **aufs** is the contraction of **auf + das**. The verb **legen** *to put, to lay* is implied here – the full phrase would be: **die Hand aufs Herz legen** 'to lay the hand on the heart'. The expression means *admit it, be honest*. You may remember **liegen** *to be lying, to lie* (lesson 44) referring to the position of something?

5 Consider yourself lucky (*Be you[formal] glad*) you don't have an empty stomach.

. . . . , Sie haben keinen . . . .

Answers to Exericse 2

1 Wo steht – ihn – **2** Ich weiß nicht – nachdenken **3** – traumhaft – einen Bärenhunger **4** Wohin haben Sie – gestellt – schon lange **5** Seien Sie froh – leeren Magen

*The progress you've made is **traumhaft**! Well done – this hasn't happened on its own! Don't be intimidated by the adjective endings, which are admittedly a little complex. Instead, just do what the Germans do and swallow the endings ...*

Second wave: 4th lesson

Fifty-fourth lesson   54

Chin up (*Head high*)!

1 Be honest (*Hand on-the heart*), are you fed up (*you have the nose full*)?
2 Someone's pulled the wool over your eyes (*One has to-you sand in the eyes strewn*) and promised [you] the moon (*golden mountains*)?

The verb **legen** also implies a horizontal position, but refers to the <u>action</u> of laying something down: **Ich lege die Hand auf das Herz.** *I put* ('lay') *my hand on my heart*, but **Die Hand liegt auf dem Herz.** *My hand is* ('lies') *on my heart*. Note that **auf** is a two-way preposition: with **legen** it takes the accusative (direction) and with **liegen** it takes the dative (position).

② **versprochen** is the past participle of **versprechen** *to promise*. **gesprochen** is the past participle of **sprechen** *to speak*, *to talk*.

54 3 Und Sie **ha**ben den Kopf ③ ver**lor**en ④?
4 Jetzt **schä**men Sie sich und **den**ken na**tür**lich, dass **al**les zu **En**de ist?
5 **Hö**ren Sie, wir **wol**len uns ja nicht in **Ih**re **An**gelegenheiten **mi**schen …
6 Aber **Träu**me **hän**gen an ⑤ **ei**nem **sei**denen ⑥ **Fa**den, der ⑦ kann leicht **rei**ßen.
7 Dann spinnt man **ei**nen **neu**en!
8 Sie **mei**nen, wir **ha**ben nichts ka**piert** ⑧?
9 Sie **ir**ren sich, wir **ha**ben Sie sehr gut ver**stan**den, denn ⑨ auch wir sind schon **trau**rig und ver**zwei**felt ge**we**sen.
10 **Ma**chen Sie also kein Ge**sicht** wie drei **Ta**ge **Re**genwetter, **son**dern **gie**ßen Sie sich einen **hin**ter die **Bin**de ⑩.

---

3 … ferlohruhn 4 … shehmuhn … 5 hœᵃn … anguhleg'nheituhn mish'n 6 … troimuh heng'n … zaiduhnuhn fahduhn … reisuhn 7 … shpint … 8 … kapeeᵉt 9 … ir'n … trowrikH … fertsveifuhlt … 10 … guhzikHt … geesuhn … hintᵃ … binduh

---

Notes

③ Did you notice the genders of nouns describing parts of the body: **der Kopf** *head*, **der Mund** *mouth*, but **die Nase** *nose*, and **das Auge** *eye*? Their respective plural forms are: **die Köpfe, die Münder, die Nasen, die Augen**.

④ **verloren** is the past participle of **verlieren** *to lose*.

⑤ **hängen an** *to hang on/from, to be hanging on/from*. The preposition **an** means 'on' or 'from': **Die Lampe hängt an der Decke.** *The lamp is hanging from the ceiling.* The verb can also be used in the active sense: **Ich hänge das Bild an die Wand.** *I hang the picture on the wall.*

3 And you've lost your (*the*) head?

4 Now you're ashamed and think, of course, that everything is over (*all at end is*)?

5 Listen, we don't want to meddle (*mix us*) in your affairs …

6 But dreams hang on a silk string, which (*this*) can easily tear.

7 So one spins a new one!

8 You think (*consider*) we haven't got a clue (*have nothing got*)?

9 You're mistaken (*You err*), we've understood you very well, because we, too, have been sad and desperate.

10 So don't have a long face (*Make therefore no face like three days rain-weather*), but knock one back (*pour yourself one behind the tie*).

⑥ The adjective **seiden,** which comes from **die Seide** *silk*, here takes an **-en** ending because the article **einem** indicates the gender and case of **der Faden** (masculine dative).

⑦ Remember that **der, die** and **das** are often used as demonstrative pronouns (*this*, *that*, etc.). Here, **der** stands in for **ein seidener Faden**.

⑧ **kapieren** *to catch on, to get it* is a colloquial term for **verstehen** *to understand*: **Er kapiert sehr schnell.** *He gets [it] very quickly.*

⑨ The conjunction **denn** *because, for* is synonymous with **weil** *because, as, since*. But watch out for word order! **weil** starts a subordinate clause in which the conjugated verb moves to the last position. In contrast, **denn** coordinates two main clauses, which means it doesn't affect word order: **Sie lächelt, denn er hat ihr goldene Berge versprochen.** *She smiles because he has promised her the moon.*

⑩ **die Binde** *bandage* comes from **binden** *to bind, to attach, to link*. It's an antiquated word for what is usually called **die Krawatte** *necktie* today.

54 11 Bald **lächelt** Fortu**na** ⑪ **wie**der, **a**ber **Vor**sicht, dass Sie **mor**gen **kei**nen **Ka**ter ⑫ **ha**ben!

11 ... lekhlt fortoona ... kaht^e ...

Notes
⑪ **Fortuna** is the Roman goddess of fate and the personification of luck. If she smiles on you, you're lucky ...

***

Übung 1 – Übersetzen Sie bitte!

❶ Es ist besser, nicht den Kopf zu verlieren. ❷ Ich bin sicher, dass du nichts kapiert hast. ❸ Irren Sie sich nicht, er lächelt immer, aber er ist oft traurig. ❹ Ich finde, dass er dir zu viel Sand in die Augen streut. ❺ Hand aufs Herz, haben Sie manchmal die Nase voll von Deutsch?

***

Übung 2 – Ergänzen Sie bitte!

❶ Careful, the picture is hanging only from a string: it could (*can*) fall down!

Achtung, das Bild ..... nur .. .., es kann .... !

❷ You (*formal*) are mistaken, he hasn't lost his (*the*) head; he has (*is*) always been like this (*so been*).

... ., er hat nicht ... . verloren, ... immer so .... !

❸ Don't have a long face – nothing is lost (*at end*)!

Mach .... wie drei Tage ...., nichts ist .. .. !

11 Soon lady luck [will] smile [on you] again, but [be] careful that you don't have a hangover (*tomcat*) tomorrow!

⑫ **der Kater** *tomcat* is the masculine form of **die Katze** *cat* (female). Remember that German uses the female form as a default if the sex of the cat in question isn't known. However, if you're hungover, you're most definitely dealing with *a tomcat*, **einen Kater** …

***

Answers to Exercise 1

❶ It is better not to lose one's head. ❷ I'm sure that you didn't get it at all. ❸ Don't be mistaken – he always smiles but he is often sad. ❹ I think that he's really pulling the wool over (*strews too much sand in*) your eyes. ❺ Be honest, are you sometimes fed up with German?

***

❹ He promises her the moon (*golden mountains*) and she smiles.
. . . . ihr goldene Berge und . . .
. . . .

❺ Yesterday he was desperate because he lost a lot of money, and today he has a hangover.
Gestern war er . . . . , denn . . . . . viel Geld . . . . , und heute hat er . . . .

Answers to Exercise 2

❶ – hängt – an einem Faden – runterfallen ❷ Sie irren sich – den Kopf – er ist – gewesen ❸ – kein Gesicht – Regenwetter – zu Ende ❹ Er verspricht – sie lächelt ❺ – verzweifelt – er hat – verloren – einen Kater

Second wave: 5th lesson

55 Fünfundfünfzigste Lektion

„Der Apfel fällt nicht weit vom Stamm"

1 – Wa**rum** hast du dich ① in **mei**nen **S**essel ge**setz**t, **Dan**iel?
2 Los ②! Steh auf!
3 Du weißt ge**nau**, das ist mein **S**essel, wenn wir **fern**sehen ③.
4 – Wa**rum** denn? Ich sit**ze heu**te hier. Dort steht ein **an**derer Stuhl.
5 – Mach **kei**nen Quatsch und hau ab ④!
6 – Nee, der Film fängt gleich **an**, und ich **blei**be hier **sit**zen.
7 – Das **wer**den wir gleich **seh**en ⑤!

Pronunciation
... **apf**'l ... shtam **1** ... **mei**nuhn **z**esl guh**zetz**t **dahn**yel **2** lohs shteh owf **3** ... **fern**zeh'n **4** ... **and**'rᵃ shtool **5** ... kvatsh ... how ap **6** neh ... film ...

Notes

① Remember that **sich setzen** *to sit down* is a reflexive verb in German: **Er hat sich gesetzt.** 'He has himself sat down.'

② **los**, used by itself, is an injunction signalling a need to hurry up or to get on with something. Its meaning depends on the context: **Wir müssen los!** *We have to get going!* **Es ist spät, los!** *It is late, hurry up!* **Los!** *Let's go!*

③ **fernsehen** *to watch TV* consists of **fern** *far* and **sehen** *to see*. It is a separable-prefix verb: **Wir sehen heute fern.** *We're watching TV today.* Note that in a dependent clause like **wenn wir fernsehen**, the separable prefix is reattached to the base verb, which is in the final position.

Fifty-fifth lesson 55

Like father, like son
(The apple doesn't fall far from the trunk)

1 – Why have you (*yourself*) sat down in my armchair, Daniel?
2 Come on! Get up!
3 You know [very] well (*exactly*) [that] this is my armchair when we watch TV.
4 – Why (*then*)? I'm sitting here today. There is another chair [over there].
5 – Don't be silly (*Make no nonsense*) and get lost!
6 – No, the film is about to start (*starts immediately*), and I'm staying here (*seated*).
7 – We will see [about] that right now.

Pronunciation note
6 nee is a very common colloquial form of **nein**. The *eh* can be drawn out as long as you wish, thus allowing you to emphatically convey anything from a categorical refusal to astonishment, disgust or anything in between.

④ **abhauen** *to beat it, to push/buzz/clear off* is, obviously, colloquial. Without a prefix, **hauen** means *to hit* or *to beat*. If you want to say **Hau ab!** *Get lost!* more politely, you could use: **Geh bitte!** or **Gehen Sie bitte!** *Please go!*

⑤ Introducing the German future tense ... Yes, it really does exist; it's just frequently replaced by the present. And yet there's hardly anything simpler: **werden** + infinitive of the main verb = future. Note that **werden** takes the usual place of the conjugated verb, and the infinitive occurs in the final position: **Wir werden das Futur in Lektion 56 sehen.** *We will see the future tense in lesson 56.*

55 8 – Spinnst ⑥ du? Hör auf mich zu **schla**gen! Lass mich in **Frie**den!
Au, **au**a, au, au!
9 – Was ist denn hier los ⑦? Seid ihr ver**rückt** ge**wor**den?
10   Hört so**fort** mit **eu**rem Ge**schrei** ⑧ auf!
11 – Oh, **hal**lo, **Pa**pa, du bist schon zu**rück**?
12 – Ja, wie ihr seht. Steh auf, **A**lex, du weißt ge**nau**, dass das mein **Ses**sel ist! ☐

8 ...freeduhn! ow ow-a ow 10 ... oiruhm guhshrei ...

Notes

⑥ The basic meaning of **spinnen** is 'to spin' (e.g. yarn or a thread) (see previous lesson); however, it is also used in the sense of *to be crazy*. How's that? Well, **die Spinne** is a *spider*, and when you say **Du spinnst doch!** *But you're crazy!* the implication is that like a spider spins a web, the person is spinning a web of strange thoughts.

⑦ This **los** is used differently from the **los** in line 2. Here it's part of a very useful expression: **Was ist los?** *What's going on?*

***

Übung 1 – Übersetzen Sie bitte!

❶ Setzt euch ins Auto! Wir müssen los! ❷ Komm! Wir müssen schnell abhauen! ❸ Die Kinder wissen genau, dass das der Sessel ihres Vaters ist. ❹ Dieses Geschrei muss sofort aufhören! ❺ Daniel und Alex spinnen, sie sehen den ganzen Tag fern.

8 – Are you crazy? Stop hitting me! Leave me in peace! Ouch, ouch, ouch, ouch!
9 – What is (*then*) going on here? Have (*Are*) you gone insane?
10 Stop shouting at once (*Stop at-once with your [pl.] shouting*)!
11 – Oh, hi, Dad, you're back already?
12 – Yes, as you [can] see. Get up, Alex, you know [very] well that this is my armchair!

Daniel und Alex spinnen, sie sehen den ganzen Tag fern.

⑧ **das Geschrei** *shouting, yelling, outcry*; **der Quatsch** *nonsense, rubbish*. The possessive adjective **euer**, **eure** *your* is the second-person plural (the plural of **dein** *your*, used when speaking to more than one person informally). The formal would be: **Hören Sie auf mit Ihrem Geschrei!** *Stop shouting!*

***

Answers to Exercise 1

❶ Get (*Sit yourselves*) in the car! We have to get going! ❷ Come on! We have to clear off fast! ❸ The children know very well that this is their father's armchair! ❹ This shouting has to stop at once! ❺ Daniel and Alex are crazy – they watch TV all day.

55 Übung 2 – Ergänzen Sie bitte!

1 Don't be silly (*Make no nonsense*), children, your (*informal*) parents will soon be back (*back be*).

...., Kinder, ... Eltern ...... bald ....

2 Leave me in peace, Alex and Daniel, I want to watch TV.

Lasst mich .. .., Alex und Daniel, ich will ....

3 Get up, children, it's already half six.

...., Kinder, es ist schon ....

4 Sit (*formal*) down quickly; the film has already started.

.... sich schnell, der Film ... schon ....

5 What's going on [over] there? – You (*formal*) will see right now.

... ... dort ...? – Das .... gleich ......

Answers to Exercise 2

❶ Macht keinen Quatsch – eure – werden – zurück sein ❷ – in Frieden – fernsehen ❸ Steht auf – halb sieben ❹ Setzen Sie – hat – angefangen ❺ Was ist – los – werden Sie – sehen

> **Note on gender**
> *We'd like to draw your attention again to the gender of nouns, at the risk of boring you. But the aim is to help you identify the gender of a noun yourself. In the dialogue for this lesson, there are two nouns whose gender you can't determine because nothing gives you any hints:* **der Frieden** *peace is masculine and* **das Geschrei** *shouting is neuter. But were you able to work out the genders of* **Sessel**, **Stuhl** *and* **Quatsch**? *You may have figured out that* **der Sessel** *is masculine because Alex says* **du hast dich in meinen Sessel gesetzt** *you sat down in my armchair, and* **meinen** *is accusative masculine. Ditto for* **der Stuhl** *chair, as Daniel says* **ein anderer Stuhl steht dort** *there is another chair over there, and the* **-er** *ending is the nominative masculine ending. The feminine would be* **eine andere**, *and the neuter* **ein anderes**. *Finally,* **der Quatsch** *[kvatsh] must be masculine, because Alex says* **mach keinen Quatsch**, *and* **keinen** *is the accusative masculine. See, you're getting there!*

Second wave: 6th lesson

56 Sechsundfünfzigste Lektion

Wiederholung – Review

1 Adjective declension

The declension of attributive adjectives depends on whether or not the adjective is preceded by an article and whether this article shows the gender and case of the noun unequivocally. If the article indicates the gender and case, the adjective simply takes an **-e** or **-en** ending (often called 'weak endings'). If not, the adjective has to take an ending that indicates both gender and case.

1.1 Adjectives preceded by a definite article

The definite article always carries markers for case and gender:

Case of noun	Gender/number of noun	
	masc. sing.	fem. sing.
Nom.	**der alte Mann** *the old man*	**die junge Frau** *the young woman*
Acc.	**den alten Mann**	**die junge Frau**
Dative	**dem alten Mann**	**der jungen Frau**
Genitive	**des alten Mann(e)s**	**der jungen Frau**

Case of noun	Gender/number of noun	
	neuter sing.	plural (m./f./n.)
Nom.	**das kleine Kind** *the small child*	**die guten Freunde** *the good friends*
Acc.	**das kleine Kind**	**die guten Freunde**
Dative	**dem kleinen Kind**	**den guten Freunden**
Genitive	**des kleinen Kind(e)s**	**der guten Freunde**

So, when an adjective is preceded by a definite article, it takes the ending **-en**, except in the nominative singular (masculine, feminine and neuter) and in the accusative singular (feminine and neuter), when it takes the ending **-e**.

Fifty-sixth lesson 56

1.2 Adjectives preceded by the indefinite article *ein* or the negative article *kein*

These adjectives decline just like adjectives preceded by the definite article. The only exceptions are the nominative singular (masculine, feminine and neuter) and the accusative singular (feminine and neuter); in these cases it takes the same endings as the definite article (**der**, **die**, **das**):

Case of noun	Gender/number of noun	
	masc. sing.	fem. sing.
Nom.	(k)ein alter Mann *an/no old man*	(k)eine junge Frau *a/no young woman*
Acc.	(k)einen alten Mann	(k)eine junge Frau
Dative	(k)einem alten Mann	(k)einer jungen Frau
Genitive	(k)eines alten Mann(e)s	(k)einer jungen Frau

Case of noun	Gender/number of noun	
	neuter sing.	plural (m./f./n.)
Nom.	(k)ein kleines Kind *a/no small child*	keine* guten Freunde *no good friends*
Acc.	(k)ein kleines Kind	keine guten Freunde
Dative	(k)einem kleinen Kind	keinen guten Freunden
Genitive	(k)eines kleinen Kind(e)s	keiner guten Freunde

* In the plural, there is no indefinite article, only a negative article.

1.3 Unpreceded adjectives

In cases where no article is used, the adjective must take the endings of the article – refer to the definite articles in 1.1 – except in the genitive singular (masculine and neuter), as the following tables show.

zweihundertzweiundachtzig • 282

Case of noun	Gender/number of noun	
	masc. sing.	fem. sing.
Nom.	**alter Mann** *old man*	**junge Frau** *young woman*
Acc.	**alten Mann**	**junge Frau**
Dative	**altem Mann**	**junger Frau**
Genitive	**alten Mann(e)s**	**junger Frau**

Case of noun	Gender/number of noun	
	neuter sing.	plural (m./f./n.)
Nom.	**kleines Kind** *small child*	**gute Freunde** *good friends*
Acc.	**kleines Kind**	**gute Freunde**
Dative	**kleinem Kind**	**guten Freunden**
Genitive	**kleinen Kind(e)s**	**guter Freunde**

2 The future tense

We've seen that German usually uses the present tense to indicate a future action, especially when a time expression already shows that the event takes place in the future:
Er kommt morgen zurück. *He's coming back tomorrow.*
Wir fahren nächstes Jahr nach Italien.
We're going to Italy next year.

However, German does have a future tense; it is just not used as frequently as in English. The future tense is mainly used if the present tense could be misunderstood, i.e. when it is not clear from the context that an event will take place in the future. It can also indicate probability.

The future is a compound tense, which means it is formed by using a present tense form of the auxiliary verb (in this case, **werden**) and the infinitive of the verb in question:
Ich werde einen Brief bekommen. *I will get a letter.*
Es wird wohl regnen. *It will probably rain.*

Note that the infinitive of the main verb in the future tense should always be placed at the end of a clause or sentence:
Sie werden das leicht schaffen. *You will manage easily.*

Unser Rat *Our advice*: Remember that while in the future tense **werden** functions only as an auxiliary, as a main verb it means *to become* or *to get*. Thus **werden** expresses a change of state, which in itself can have a future sense. It is often translated with the present progressive tense in English:
Es wird dunkel. *It is getting dark.* ('It becomes dark.')

To form the future tense of **werden**, it appears twice, as both the auxiliary and the main verb:
Es wird bald dunkel werden. *It will soon get dark.*

In the upcoming lessons, you'll get used to the different uses of **werden**: **Sie werden es selbst sehen.** *You'll see it for yourself.*

3 Possessive adjectives

Lesson 28 contained an overview of all the possessive adjectives, with two exceptions: the first- and second-person plural. Here they are:

Plural possessor	
1st person	**unser-**	*our* (m./f.)
2nd person	**euer-**	*your* (m./f.)

Remember that a possessive adjective also needs to agree in case, gender and number with the noun possessed.
Unser König (m.) **ist nicht euer König.** *Our king is not your king.*
Unsere Welt (f.) **ist nicht eure Welt.** *Our world is not your world.*
Aber euer Glück (n.) **ist unser Glück.** *But your luck is our luck.*
Und eure Freunde (pl.) **sind auch unsere Freunde.** *And your friends are our friends.*

Note: When **euer** has an ending, the **e** preceding the **r** is usually omitted: **euer** → **eure**.

Possessive adjectives decline like the indefinite article in the singular and like the negative article **kein** in the plural: **Siehst du unseren Hund** (masc. acc.)? *Do you see our dog?* **Kinder, geht bitte in eure Zimmer** (neuter acc.). *Children, please go to your rooms.*

4 Verbs indicating 'position' or 'action'

4.1 Verbs indicating position

German has several verbs that describe the position of things where English usually uses *to be*. The four most important are:

• **stehen** *to stand, to be standing*:
Der Mann steht auf der Straße. *The man stands/is standing on the street.*

• **sitzen** *to sit, to be sitting*:
Die Frau sitzt auf dem Stuhl. *The woman sits/is sitting on the chair.*

• **liegen** *to lie, to be lying*:
Der Mann liegt in seinem Bett[1]. *The man lies/is lying in his bed.*

• **hängen** *to hang, to be hanging*:
Das Kind hängt am Trapez[2]. *The child hangs/is hanging from the trapeze.*

[1] **das Bett (-en)** *bed*
[2] **das Trapez (-e)** *trapeze*

Note: When a position is indicated, the preposition is followed by the dative case, answering the question **Wo?** *Where?*
Wo liegt die Zeitung? – Auf dem Stuhl.
Where is ('lies') the newspaper? – On the chair.

When talking about people or certain types of objects, choosing an appropriate verb normally isn't difficult:
Eine Tasse steht auf dem Tisch[3]. *A cup is standing on the table.*
Das Buch liegt auf dem Tisch. *The book is lying on the table.*
Der Mantel hängt an der Garderobe[4]. *The coat is hanging on the coat rack.*

[3] **der Tisch (-e)** *table*
[4] **die Garderobe (-n)** *cloakroom, coat rack, dressing room*

But what about a plate – does it stand or lie on a table? In German, a plate stands on the table:
Der Teller steht auf dem Tisch.
While a book lies on the table, but stands in a library:
Das Buch liegt auf dem Tisch, aber es steht in der Bibliothek.

One more thing: verbs indicating position are intransitive (i.e. they don't take a direct object) and are usually irregular (strong). Their past participles are: **stehen → gestanden, sitzen → gesessen, liegen → gelegen** and **hängen → gehangen**. We'll see these in future lessons.

4.2 Verbs indicating action (movement to a position)

Along with verbs specifying the position or location of something, German has a corresponding set of verbs that express the action of moving something to a position or location, where English often simply uses *to put, to place*:

- **stellen** *to stand something upright*
- **setzen** *to set something down*
- **legen** *to lay something down*
- **hängen** *to hang something up*

Das Kind stellt die Puppe auf den Stuhl.
The child places (upright) the doll on the chair.
Das Kind setzt die Puppe auf den Tisch.
The child puts (sets) the doll on the table.
Das Kind legt die Puppe in das Bett.
The child puts (lays) the doll in the bed.
Das Kind hängt die Puppe über das Bett.
The child hangs the doll over the bed.

Note: When movement to another location is indicated, the preposition is followed by the accusative case, answering the question **Wohin?** *Where to?*
Wohin legst du die Zeitung? – Auf den Tisch.
Where are you putting the newspaper? – On the table.

German verbs expressing a change of location are transitive (i.e. they always take a direct object) and are regular (weak). They form their past participles like other weak verbs: **gestellt, gesetzt, gelegt** and **gehängt**.

56 *Phew!* **Kopf hoch!** *That's enough grammar for today! Now all that's left to do is read the following dialogue and realize how much progress you've made!*

Review exercise

Traum und Wirklichkeit

1 – Hand aufs Herz, haben Sie schon eine so wunderschöne Aussicht gesehen?
2 Ich liebe diese Aussicht: blaues Meer, blauer Himmel, goldene Berge in der Sonne.
3 Was braucht man mehr?
4 Nur diese Leute überall, ich kann sie nicht mehr sehen.
5 Ich bin 1957 (neunzehnhundertsiebenundfünfzig) geboren, da war kein Mensch hier.
6 Generationen haben hier ruhig und in Frieden gelebt.
7 Dann sind die ersten Touristen* gekommen.
8 Unser traumhaftes Plätzchen ist berühmt geworden.
9 Und jetzt sind die Straßen verstopft.
10 Man muss Stunden herumfahren, um einen Parkplatz zu finden.
11 – Ja, das ist verrückt. Sie haben immer hier gewohnt?
12 – Natürlich nicht. Mit 20 bin ich abgehauen, ich hatte die Nase voll.
13 Hier war nichts los, keine Arbeit, keine Kneipe, kein Kino …
14 Ich bin 25 (fünfundzwanzig) Jahre nicht hier gewesen.
15 – Wo wohnen Sie denn jetzt?
16 – Hier. Ich bin der Besitzer dieses Hotels.

17 Ich besitze noch drei andere Hotels hier.
18 Wollen Sie etwas trinken?
19 Kommen Sie, ich lade Sie ein.

* **der Tourist** *tourist*. Although the word is borrowed from English, the stress falls on the second rather than the first syllable.

Translation

Dream and reality

1 Honestly, have you ever seen such a gorgeous view? 2 I love this view: blue sea, blue sky, golden mountains in the sun … 3 What [else] does one need (*more*)? 4 Only these people everywhere, I can't [put up with] (*see*) them anymore. 5 I was (*am*) born [in] 1957, [back then] there was no one (*no person*) here. 6 Generations lived here quietly and in peace. 7 Then, (*are*) the first tourists arrived. 8 Our fantastic little place became famous. 9 And now, the streets are jammed. 10 One has to drive around [for] hours in order to find a parking space. 11 Yes, that's crazy. Have you always lived here? 12 Of course not. At (*with*) 20, I cleared off, I was fed up. 13 There was nothing going on here, no work, no pub, no cinema … 14 I wasn't here [for] 25 years (*I am 25 years not here been*). 15 Where do you live now then? 16 Here. I am the owner of this hotel. 17 I own (*still*) three other hotels here. 18 Would you like something to drink? 19 Come [on], I'm paying (*I invite you*).

> Irren Sie sich nicht, er lächelt immer, aber er ist oft traurig.

Second wave: 7th lesson

zweihundertachtundachtzig • 288

57 Siebenundfünfzigste Lektion

Wer wird das alles essen?

1 Mögen Sie Mozartkugeln?
2 Wissen Sie, diese runden Nougatpralinen, die so heißen, weil Mozart sie so gern gegessen hat?
3 Wenigstens sagt man das, aber leider kann es nicht stimmen.
4 Mozart war nämlich ① schon lange tot, als ② der Salzburger Konditor *Paul Fürst* 1890 (achtzehnhundertneunzig) das „Mozartbonbon" erfunden hat.
5 Die größte ③ Mozartkugel-Schachtel hat einen Inhalt von 2500 (zweitausendfünfhundert) Stück und allein der Deckel wiegt 120 (einhundertzwanzig) Kilogramm.

Pronunciation
1 ... mohtsart-kooguhln 2 ... runduhn noogat-praleenuhn ... guhgess'n ... 3 vehnikstuhns ... 4 ... toht als ... zaltsburgᵃ

Notes

① **nämlich** *after all*, is usually used in statements that further explain what has just been said. It's thus similar to **denn** *because, for*. But in contrast to the conjunction **denn**, **nämlich** never introduces a justification; it generally comes after the conjugated verb: **Er weiß das; er war nämlich da.** *He knows this; he was, after all, there.* = **Er weiß das, denn er war da.** *He knows this because he was there.* Often, the most natural way to express this in English is with a clause beginning with *as* or *because*, like the German '**denn**' sentence. But remember, **nämlich** comes after the conjugated verb.

② The conjunction **als** *when* introduces a clause concerned with a single event or block of time in the past: **Wir haben in**

Fifty-seventh lesson 57

Who will eat all this?

1. Do you like 'Mozartkugeln'?
2. You know, those round chocolates that are so named because Mozart liked to eat them so much (*them so gladly eaten has*)?
3. At least, that's what they say (*At-least says one that*), but unfortunately it can't be true (*can it not be-true*).
4. Mozart was, after all, (*already*) long dead when the Salzburg confectioner Paul Fürst invented the 'Mozartbonbon' [in] 1890 (*1890 the 'Mozartbonbon' invented has*).
5. The largest box of 'Mozartkugeln' contains (*has a content of*) 2,500 pieces, and the lid alone weighs 120 kg.

*kon**di**tohr powl fewrst ... -bongbong er**fun**duhn ... **5** ... gr**œ**stuh ... -**shakh**tuhl ... **in**halt ... **dek**'l veekt ...*

Salzburg gewohnt, als ich Kind war. *We lived in Salzburg when I was a child.*

③ **größte** is the superlative of **groß** *big*. The superlative of an adjective is generally formed by adding **-st** to the base form: **klein** → **kleinst-**. Note that if it precedes a noun, it takes adjective endings: **die kleinste Praline** *the smallest chocolate*. The **-st** ending is **-est** if the adjective stem ends in **-d**, **-t**, or a sibilant such as **-s**: **der weiteste Fluss** *the widest river*. Many monosyllabic adjectives with the stem vowels **a**, **o** or **u** also add an umlaut in the superlative: **kalt** → **kältest-**; **groß** → **größt-**. Note that **groß** only takes a **-t** ending as it ends in **ß** – which, as you know, replaces a double **s** after a long vowel.

zweihundertneunzig • 290

57 6 Noch viel **schwer**er ④ ist **a**ber die **höch**ste ⑤ **Eis**torte ⑥ der Welt (sie ist drei **Me**ter **vier**zig hoch!).
7 Ein **Eis**kon**di**tor**mei**ster und **sei**ne Ge**sell**en **ha**ben sie in **sie**ben **Ta**gen bei **Mi**nus 30 (**drei**ßig) Grad ⑦ ge**baut**.
8 **Den**ken Sie jetzt **a**ber nicht, dass sich in **deut**schen **Lan**den ⑧ **al**les um das **Es**sen dreht ⑨!

---

6 ... shvehrᵃ ... hœkhstuh (or: hœks-tuh) eis-tortuh ...
7 ... eis-konditohr-meistᵃ ... guhzel'n ... minus ... graht guhbowt 8 ... doitsh'n landuhn ... dreht

Notes

④ **schwerer** is the comparative of **schwer** *heavy, difficult*. The comparative is formed by adding **-er** to the base form of the adjective. Adjectives that take an umlaut in the superlative also take one in the comparative: **groß → größer**, **schön → schöner**, etc.

⑤ **höchste** is the regular superlative of **hoch** *high, tall*. But be careful! **hoch** is one of five 'irregular' adjectives because it loses its **c** in the comparative: **höher**. If you're curious, take a brief look at lesson 63 where this is explained further.

⑥ **Falls Sie das Rezept interessiert: Sie brauchen 1 200 Liter Milch, 155 Liter Sahne, 27 Kilogramm Kakao, 85 kg Schokolade, über 100 kg Erdbeeren und ungefähr 15 kg Himbeeren.**
[... re**tsept** intuhres**see**ᵃt; towz'nt-**tsvei**hundᵃt litᵃ ... **hund**ᵃt-**fewnf**unt**fewnf**tsikH ... **zee**buhnunt-**tsvan**tsikH ... ka**kow fewnf**unt-**akht**sikH ... **ert**-behruhn ... **him**behruhn]
In case you're interested in the recipe, you need 1,200 litres of milk, 155 litres of cream, 27 kg of cocoa, 85 kg of chocolate, more than 100 kg of strawberries and around 15 kg of raspberries.

6 But much heavier still is (*Still more heavier is but*) the tallest ice-cream cake in the (*of-the*) world (it is 3.40 m high!).

7 A master ice-cream confectioner and his assistants constructed it in seven days at minus 30 degree[s] [Celsius].

8 But don't now think that everything revolves around food in German-speaking countries (*that itself in German lands all around the food revolves*)!

> Der Rhein ist der größte Fluss in Deutschland.

⑦ **der Grad** *degree* remains in the singular when used as an expression of measurement. Note that in Germany the temperature is usually given in degrees Celsius!

⑧ The plural of **das Land** *country* is **die Länder**. **Lande** is a poetic plural used mainly in the expression **in deutschen Landen** (the final **-n** marks the dative plural) in order to avoid confusion between 'in German-speaking countries' (which potentially include Austria and parts of Switzerland) and 'the **Länder** (federal states) of Germany'.

⑨ **sich drehen um** (+ acc.) *to centre on, to revolve around* is a reflexive verb. It's usually used in the impersonal construction **es dreht sich um** *it centres on, it concerns, it is about*.

zweihundertzweiundneunzig • 292

57 Übung 1 – Übersetzen Sie bitte!

❶ Was ist schwerer? Ein Kilo Sand oder ein Kilo Papier? ❷ Mozart ist im Jahr siebzehnhunderteinundneunzig gestorben. ❸ In unserer Familie dreht sich alles um die Kinder. ❹ Es hat nicht geregnet, weil es bei minus 4 Grad nicht regnet. ❺ Der Rhein ist der größte Fluss in Deutschland.

***

Übung 2 – Ergänzen Sie bitte!

❶ What are these round chocolates called that you like to eat so much (*so gladly eat*)?

... . diese ...... Pralinen, die Sie so ....?

❷ What are you thinking (*What think you[informal]*)? At minus 30 degrees, one doesn't eat ice cream!

Was ....? ... . 30 Grad isst man ....!

❸ Do you (*formal*) know who invented 'Mozartkugeln'?

...., ... die Mozartkugeln ....?

Answers to Exercise 1

❶ What is heavier? A kilo of sand or a kilo of paper? ❷ Mozart died in 1791. ❸ In our family, everything revolves around the children. ❹ It didn't rain, because it doesn't rain at minus 4 degrees. ❺ The Rhine is the biggest river in Germany.

***

❹ Today everything revolves (*revolves itself all*) around money.
Heute .... alles .../.. ... Geld.

❺ My grandfather was already long dead when I went to Berlin.
Mein Großvater ... schon lange ..., ... ich .... bin.

Answers to Exercise 2

❶ Wie heißen – runden – gern essen ❷ – denkst du – Bei minus – kein Eis ❸ Wissen Sie, wer – erfunden hat ❹ – dreht sich – ums / um das – ❺ – war – tot, als – nach Berlin gegangen

Second wave: 8th lesson

58 Achtundfünfzigste Lektion

German usually uses the simple past tense for narration. However, taking into consideration the trouble the Brothers Grimm went to to make their stories accessible, we're retelling the following tale in the perfect tense, as this is used more frequently in everyday

Der Hase und der Igel
(nach einem Märchen der Brüder Grimm)

1 An einem schönen Sonntagmorgen haben sich der Igel und der Hase auf einem Feld getroffen ①.
2 Der Igel hat höflich gegrüßt und den Hasen gefragt ②:
3 „Ach, Sie gehen auch bei diesem schönen Wetter spazieren ③?"
4 Der Hase hat das sehr lustig gefunden und geantwortet: „Ja, ich gehe spazieren, aber was machen Sie mit Ihren krummen Beinen?"
5 Diese Worte ④ haben den Igel tief verletzt:

Pronunciation
... **hah**zuh ... **eeg**'l ... (... **meh**ᵃkH'n ... **brew**dᵃ grim) **1** ... felt guh**trof**'n **2** ... guh**grewst** ... **hahz**'n guh**frahkt 4** ... guh-**ant**vortuht: ... **krum**uhn ... **5** ... **vor**tuh... teef fer**letst**

Notes
① **getroffen** is the past participle of **treffen** *to meet*. Here it's used reflexively: **treffen sich** *to meet each other*.

295 • zweihundertfünfundneunzig

Fifty-eighth lesson 58

speech. Note that German uses a colon and double quotation marks to signal direct discourse in writing. Opening quotation marks are placed below the line of writing, closing ones above.

The hare and the hedgehog
(Based on a folktale by the Brothers Grimm)

1 One (*On a*) beautiful Sunday morning, the hedgehog and the hare met in (*on*) a field.
2 The hedgehog greeted [the hare] politely and asked (*the hare*):
3 'Ah, you're also going for a walk in (*with*) this nice weather?'
4 The hare found this very funny and responded: 'Yes, I'm going for a walk, but what are you doing with your crooked legs?'
5 These words deeply hurt the hedgehog:

---

② **fragen** *to ask*: **Er fragt den Hasen.** *He asks the hare* (acc.). Note that **der Hase** *hare* (often also erroneously used for *rabbit*) is a 'weak noun' or 'masculine n-noun' and takes an **-n** ending in the accusative case (see lesson 47).

③ **spazieren gehen** *to go for a walk* (**spazieren** is rarely used by itself). The first of these two infinitives moves into the last position, like a separable prefix: **Wir gehen jeden Sonntag spazieren.** *We go for a walk every Sunday.*

④ **das Wort** *word* has two plural forms: **die Worte** refers to the words someone says: **Er macht viele Worte.** *He talks a lot.* However, **die Wörter** refers to countable words: **ein Satz mit sechs Wörtern** *a sentence with six words.*

58   6   „Was **wol**len Sie **da**mit **sa**gen?", hat er ge**ru**fen. „**Ich** kann **schnel**ler **lau**fen als ⑤ Sie!"
   7   Da hat der **Ha**se laut ge**lacht**:
   8   „Sie? **Schnel**ler **lau**fen als ich? Da **la**che ich mich ja tot ⑥."
   9   „**Okay**", hat der **I**gel ge**sagt**, „**we**tten wir, dass ich **schnel**ler **lau**fe als Sie!"
   10 Der **Ha**se ist vor **La**chen fast er**stickt**: „**Ein**verstanden, **ma**chen wir **ei**nen **Wett**lauf, und wer ge**winnt**, be**kommt ei**nen **Gold**taler ⑦ und **ei**ne **Fla**sche Schnaps.
   11 **Fan**gen wir gleich **an**!"
   12 „**Halt, ei**nen Mo**ment**", hat der **I**gel erwidert, „ich muss nur schnell nach **Hau**se ⑧ und **mei**ner Frau Be**scheid sa**gen ⑨.
   13 Ich bin gleich zu**rück**."
(Fortsetzung folgt)

6 ... guh**roof**'n ... sh**nel**ᵃ ... 9 o**keh** ... ve**tuhn** ... 10 ... er**shtikt**: ein**fersht**andᵃ'n ... **vet**-lowfᵃ ... guh**vint** ... **golt**-tahlᵃ ... 12 ... buh**sheit** ...

Notes

⑤ The conjunction **als** can mean different things. In comparisons **als** is equivalent to *than*: **Ich laufe schneller als du.** *I run faster than you.* **Er ist kleiner als ich.** *He is smaller than me.* But remember from the previous lesson that **als** can also have a temporal function: **Als der Hase das gehört hat, ist er vor Lachen fast erstickt.** *When the hare heard this, he almost choked with laughter.*

⑥ **sich totlachen** literally translates as 'to dead-laugh oneself'. **Ich habe mich totgelacht.** *I was dying of laughter.*

⑦ **ein Goldtaler** *a gold taler* was a coin used in the early 1800s (when the Brothers Grimm were writing) in what is today Germany, Austria and Switzerland.

6 'What do you mean by that (*What want you with-that to-say*)?' he cried. 'I can run faster than you!'
7 Then (*There*) the hare laughed loudly:
8 'You? Run faster than me (*I*)? Well now I'm laughing myself to death (*There laugh I myself yes dead*).'
9 'Okay,' said the hedgehog, 'let's bet that I [can] run faster than you!'
10 The hare almost choked with laughter: 'All right (*Agreed*), let's have (*make*) a race, and whoever wins will get (*gets*) a gold taler and a bottle of schnapps.'
11 'Let's start right now (*immediately*)!'
12 'Wait (*Stop*), one moment,' the hedgehog replied. 'I just have to [go] home quickly to (*and*) let my wife know.
13 I'll be back right away.'

(To be continued)

> Er ist kleiner als seine Schwester, aber er läuft schneller als sie.

⑧ As you know, **gehen** isn't needed in **ich muss nach Haus(e)** *I have to [go] home*, because **nach** on its own indicates movement towards **das Haus**.

⑨ **Bescheid sagen** or **geben** ('to tell or to give information') is a commonly used expression for *to get back to someone, to let someone know*: **Wenn ich zurück bin, sage ich dir Bescheid.** *When I'm back, I['ll] let you know.* **Geben Sie uns Bescheid, wenn Sie mehr wissen.** *Get back to us when you know more.*

58 Übung 1 – Übersetzen Sie bitte!

❶ Sie haben sich auf der Terrasse eines Cafés getroffen. ❷ Er ist kleiner als seine Schwester, aber er läuft schneller als sie. ❸ Können Sie mir bitte Bescheid geben, wenn Sie zurück sind? ❹ Der Igel war tief verletzt, weil der Hase sich fast totgelacht hat. ❺ Dieser Mann hat mich gegrüßt, aber ich kenne ihn nicht.

***

Übung 2 – Ergänzen Sie bitte!

❶ [Shall] we bet (*Bet we*) that I [can] run faster than you (*inf.*)?

. . . ., dass ich . . . . laufe . . . . . ?

❷ [Shall] we meet (*Meet we ourselves*) next Friday at (*in*) the same café? – All right.

. . . . nächsten Freitag in demselben Café? – . . . .

❸ We['ll] let you know (*We tell/give you information*) when we start.

. . . . Ihnen . . . ., wenn . . . .

***

Wer kennt nicht die Märchen der Brüder Grimm? Who doesn't know the fairy tales by the Brothers Grimm?
The brothers Jacob and Wilhelm Grimm published their first collection of fairy tales in 1812. Jacob was the King of Westphalia's librarian and a professor of medieval history at Göttingen, where Wilhelm, one year his junior, also worked as an assistant librarian.

As children, they loved to listen to popular stories. Later, influenced by an interest in medieval German stories, they started to collect folktales and transcribe them in accessible language, while remaining as true to the original story as possible. Their aim was to save a cultural legacy from oblivion. Popularizing literature

Answers to Exercise 1

❶ They met each other on the terrace of a café. ❷ He is smaller than his sister, but he runs faster than her. ❸ Can you please let me know when you're back? ❹ The hedgehog was deeply hurt because the hare almost died of laughter. ❺ This man greeted me, but I don't know him.

***

❹ We have to [go] home quickly, because we bet (*we bet have*) that we would be the first home (*that we the first to home are*).
Wir müssen schnell . . . . , weil . . .
 . . . . , dass wir die ersten . .   . .
sind.

❺ She asked him what his name was (*what he is called*), but he didn't answer.
Sie hat . . .   . , wie er . . . . . , aber er hat nicht . . . .

Answers to Exercise 2

❶ Wetten wir – schneller – als du ❷ Treffen wir uns – Einverstanden ❸ Wir sagen/geben – Bescheid – wir anfangen ❹ – nach Hause – wir gewettet haben – zu Hause – ❺ – ihn gefragt – heißt – geantwortet

***

as they did earned them much criticism from some contemporary poets. However, the public enthusiastically received their tales (including 'Hansel and Gretel', 'Cinderella', 'Rapunzel' and 'Snow White'), which are still popular to this day.

Their fairy tales have been so successful that they have eclipsed the other major contributions the Brothers Grimm – both brilliant linguists – made in the study of the German language and its origins. These include an influential text on German grammar, as well as a dictionary.

Second wave: 9th lesson

59 Neunundfünfzigste Lektion

Der Hase und der Igel
(Fortsetzung)

1 Der Igel ist schnell nach Hause gelaufen ①.
2 Seine Frau war beim Kochen ②, als er zu Hause angekommen ist.
3 Aber er hat nur gerufen: „Lass das, Frau, zieh dich an ③ und komm schnell mit!
4 Ich habe mit dem Hasen gewettet, dass ich schneller laufen kann als er".
5 „Oje, oje", hat da die Frau gejammert.
6 „Habe keine Angst! Wenn du mir ④ hilfst, geht alles ⑤ gut", hat der Igel sie beruhigt.

Pronunciation
2 ... beim kokh'n ... 3 ... tsee dikH an ... 5 oyeh ... guhyam^at
6 ... angst ... hilfst ... buhrooikt

Notes

① **gelaufen** is the past participle of **laufen** *to run, to walk*. Remember that <u>all</u> verbs expressing movement or a change in location form the perfect tense with the auxiliary **sein** *to be* rather than **haben** *to have*: **Ich bin gelaufen, weil es geregnet hat.** *I ran because it rained.*

② **kochen** can mean *to cook* as in 'to prepare food', as well as *to boil*. **der Koch, die Köchin** is *chef* (m., f.). The construction **beim** (or **bei dem**) + an infinitive (used as a noun) indicates that an action is ongoing: **Wir waren beim Essen, als Freunde angerufen haben.** *We were eating ('with-the eating') when our friends called.* English uses '-ing' forms for this purpose.

③ **sich anziehen** *to get dressed, to dress oneself*: **ich ziehe mich an** *I'm getting dressed*, etc. The second-person singular

301 • dreihunderteins

Fifty-ninth lesson 59

The hare and the hedgehog
(Continuation)

1 The hedgehog ran home quickly (*is fast to home run*).
2 His wife was cooking when he arrived home.
3 But he only shouted: 'Leave that (*wife*), get dressed and come with [me] quickly (*come fast with*)!
4 I bet (*with*) the hare that I can run faster than him.'
5 'Oh dear, oh dear,' (*then*) the wife lamented.
6 'Don't worry (*Have no anxiety*)! If you help me, all will be well (*goes all well*),' the hedgehog reassured (*calmed*) her.

imperative ('**du**-imperative') is formed the usual way, i.e. without a personal pronoun in the nominative and without the second-person ending **-st**: **Zieh dich an!** *Get dressed!*

④ **helfen** requires the dative: **jemandem helfen** *to help someone*, as in 'to give help to someone'; **Sie hilft ihrer Mutter.** *She helps her mother.* (**ihrer** is the possessive adjective *her*, *its* in the dative feminine singular.)

⑤ When a sentence starts with a subordinate (dependent) clause, the word order in the main clause is inverted, i.e. the verb moves into the first position, and the subject into the second: **Wenn ich gewinne, bekomme ich eine Flasche Champagner.** *If I win, I [will] get* ('get I') *a bottle of champagne.* Remember that the conditional **wenn** translates as 'if', and the temporal **wenn** as 'when', 'whenever'.

7 „Siehst du den **groß**en **A**cker ⑥ dort?
8 Wir **lau**fen dort **un**ten los ⑦, der **Ha**se in **ei**ner **Fur**che und ich in **ei**ner **an**deren.
9 Du ver**steckst** dich **o**ben am **A**cker, und wenn der **Ha**se **an**kommt, dann rufst du: Ich bin schon da!
10 Hast du ver**stan**den?"
11 Die **I**gelfrau hat nur mit dem Kopf ge**nickt** ⑧.
12 „**Gu**t, **al**so geh schnell auf **dei**nen Platz, der **Ha**se **war**tet auf ⑨ mich."

(Fortsetzung folgt)

---

7 ... zeest ... ak^a ... **8** ... fu^akhuh ... and'ruhn **9** ... fershtekst ... **11** ... eeguhl-frow ... guhnikt

Notes

⑥ **der Acker** is a cultivated field or plot of farmland, while a field more generally is **das Feld**.

⑦ As an adverb, **los** signals detachment or separation: **Es ist spät, wir müssen los!** *It is late, we have to go!* As a separable prefix, **los** often indicates the beginning of something: **Um wie viel Uhr fahren wir los?** *What time are we going?*, as in 'What time will we start driving?' (lesson 55).

✳✳✳

Übung 1 – Übersetzen Sie bitte!

❶ Wenn wir um acht Uhr losfahren, kommen wir um zwölf Uhr an. ❷ Die Kinder waren beim Fernsehen, als die Mutter sie gerufen hat. ❸ Ich muss los, meine Kollegen warten auf mich. ❹ Ich kann mich nicht allein anziehen, kannst du mir bitte helfen? ❺ Als ich sie gefragt habe: „Sprechen Sie Deutsch?", hat sie genickt.

7	'Do you see the large field there?
8	We [will] start running down there (*there below*), the hare in one furrow and I in another.
9	You hide (*yourself*) at the top of the field, and when the hare arrives, (*then*) you shout: "I'm already here!"
10	Do you understand (*Have you understood*)?'
11	The hedgehog's wife (*hedgehog-woman*) simply (*with the head*) nodded.
12	'Good, so go quickly to your place, the hare is waiting for (*on*) me.'

(To be continued)

⑧ **mit dem Kopf nicken** – or simply **nicken** – *to nod*; its opposite is **mit den Kopf schütteln** *to shake one's head*.

⑨ One says **warten auf jemanden** or **etwas** (with the accusative) *to wait for someone* or *something*: **Er wartet auf seinen Freund.** *He waits for his friend.* **Ich warte auf den Bus.** *I wait for the bus.*

***

Answers to Exercise 1

❶ If we leave at 8 o'clock, we [will] arrive at noon. ❷ The children were watching TV when their (*the*) mother called them. ❸ I have to go, my colleagues are waiting for me. ❹ I can't dress myself alone; can you please help me? ❺ When I asked her, 'Do you speak German?', she nodded.

59 Übung 2 – Ergänzen Sie bitte!

1 Wait (*informal*) for me! I can't run so fast (*so fast run*)!

....! Ich kann nicht so ....!

2 If you agree (*agreed are*), nod (*you with the head*).

.... Sie .... sind, nicken Sie ... ...

3 'Don't worry (*Have you no anxiety*), I [will] help you,' he reassured her (*has he her calmed*).

„Haben Sie ...., ... Ihnen", hat er sie ....

4 The dog is hiding under the armchair (*has himself under the armchair hidden*), don't you (*informal*) see him?

Der Hund ... . unter dem Sessel ...., ... ihn nicht?

5 Getting dressed, she listened to 'Eine Kleine Nachtmusik' by Mozart (*She has with-the dressing 'A Little Night-music' of Mozart listened*).

Sie hat .... „Eine Kleine Nachtmusik" ... Mozart ....

Answers to Exercise 2

❶ Warte auf mich – schnell laufen ❷ Wenn – einverstanden – mit dem Kopf ❸ – keine Angst, ich helfe – beruhigt ❹ – hat sich – versteckt, siehst du – ❺ – beim Anziehen – von – gehört

Die Kinder waren beim Fernsehen, als die Mutter sie gerufen hat.

Second wave: 10th lesson

60 Sechzigste Lektion

Der Hase und der Igel
(Fortsetzung und Ende)

1 „Hier bin ich **wie**der, wir **kön**nen **an**fangen."
2 „Gut, **fang**en wir **an**", hat der **Ha**se ge**sagt** und **an**gefangen, bis drei zu **zäh**len ①: eins, zwei …
3 Bei drei ist er **los**gelaufen so schnell wie ② er **konn**te.
4 Der **I**gel da**ge**gen hat nur ein paar ③ **Schri**tte ge**macht**.
5 Dann ist er **sit**zen ge**blie**ben und hat **ru**hig ge**war**tet.
6 Als der **Ha**se **o**ben **an**gekommen ist, hat die **I**gelfrau ge**ru**fen: „Ich bin schon da!"
7 „Noch **ein**mal", hat der **Ha**se to**tal** ver**wirrt** ④ ge**schrien**.
8 Aber **un**ten **an**gekommen hat der **I**gel ge**ru**fen: „Ich bin schon da."

Pronunciation
2 … tsehl'n… 4 … da**geh**g'n … pah^a **shri**tuh …
5 … guh**blee**buhn … 7 … fer**virt** …

Notes

① Don't confuse **zählen** *to count* (with an umlaut) and **zahlen** *to pay* (without an umlaut)!

② **so … wie** is used to compare the equality of two things. Its equivalent in English is *as … as*: **Ich bin so groß wie du.** *I am as tall as you.* Remember that comparisons of inequality use **als** *than*: **Er ist viel jünger als seine Frau.** *He is much younger than his wife.* (lesson 58)

307 • dreihundertsieben

Sixtieth lesson 60

The hare and the hedgehog
(Continuation and end)

1 'Here I am again, we can start.'
2 'Good, let's start,' said the hare, and [he] started to count to three (*until three to count*): one, two …
3 On three, he started to run as fast as he could.
4 The hedgehog, however, only walked a few paces (*only a couple steps made*).
5 Then he sat down (*sitting stayed*) and waited patiently (*calmly*).
6 When the hare arrived at the top [of the field] (*above arrived*), the hedgehog's wife called out: 'I'm already here!'
7 'One more time (*Again once*)!' the hare shrieked, completely baffled.
8 But [when he] arrived at the bottom (*below arrived*) the hedgehog called out: 'I'm already here!'

③ **ein paar** *a few, a couple of*. But careful, **das Paar** with a capital letter means *the couple*, and **ein Paar** *a pair*.
④ **verwirrt** *baffled, confused* from **verwirren** *to confuse*.

dreihundertacht • 308

60 9   Der **Ha**se, der **im**mer **wü**tender ⑤
geworden ist, ist **drei**und**sieb**zigmal ⑥
ge**lau**fen.
10 Beim **vier**und**sieb**zigsten Mal ist er vor
Er**schöp**fung tot **um**gefallen ⑦.
11 Der **I**gel und **sei**ne Frau sind ver**gnügt** ⑧
nach Haus ge**gang**en.
12 Ja, was **nüt**zen die **läng**sten ⑨ **Bei**ne, wenn
man **ei**nen **kur**zen Ver**stand** ⑩ hat? ☐

---

9 ... *vewtuhnd*ᵃ ... *drei*unt*zeep*tsikH-*mahl* ... **10** ...
*feer*unt*zeep*tsikH*stuhn* ... *foh*ᵃ er*shœ*pfung ... *um*guhfal'n

Notes

⑤ **wütend** derives from the verb **wüten** *to rage* and the noun **die Wut** *anger, fury, rage*. You already know that **werden** often indicates a change of state: **müde werden** *to become tired*; **wütend werden** hence translates as *to become enraged*. The combination of **immer** + comparative signifies 'more and more': **immer wütender** *to become more and more enraged*, **immer kälter** *colder and colder*, etc.

⑥ As with **einmal** *once* or **fünfmal** *five times*, **mal** can be added to any number. However, apart from **einmal**, the same thing can be expressed with an ordinal number and **Mal**: **Der Igel hat einmal gerufen, dann ein zweites Mal und dann ein**

***

Übung 1 – Übersetzen Sie bitte!

❶ Warum läufst du immer schneller? ❷ Der Hase war ganz verwirrt, als er die Igelfrau gesehen hat. ❸ Er hat längere Beine als sie, aber einen kürzeren Verstand. ❹ Seine Freundin hat am Bahnhof auf ihn gewartet. ❺ Bei diesem schönen Wetter können wir nicht zu Hause sitzen bleiben.

9 The hare, who was getting more and more enraged, ran 73 times (*is 73 times run*).
10 (*At-*) The 74th time, he dropped dead with exhaustion (*is he with exhaustion dead fallen-over*).
11 The hedgehog and his wife merrily went home.
12 Well, what is the use of (*are-of-use*) the longest legs when one has a small (*short*) mind?

---

*11... fer**gnewkt** ... guh**gang**'n 12 ... **new**ts'n ... **leng**stuhn ... ku^atsuhn fer**shtant** ...*

---

drittes Mal. *The hedgehog called once, [and] then a second time and then a third time.*

⑦ **tot umfallen** *to drop dead.* **umfallen** *by itself means to fall over, to topple.*

⑧ Remember **das Vergnügen** *pleasure, amusement*?

⑨ **lang** *long,* **länger** *longer,* **der/die/das längste** *the longest.* Comparative and superlative adjectives decline in the normal way: **der längste Fluss Europas** *the longest river in Europe,* **die längsten Flüsse der Welt** *the longest rivers in the world.*

⑩ **der Verstand** covers lots of things in English, from *mind* to *understanding, reason* and *sense*.

***

Answers to Exercise 1

❶ Why do you run faster and faster? ❷ The hare was completely baffled when he saw the hedgehog's wife. ❸ He has longer legs than her, but a smaller (*shorter*) mind. ❹ His girlfriend waited for him at the station. ❺ With this beautiful weather, we can't sit around at home.

60 Übung 2 – Ergänzen Sie bitte!

❶ I [will] count to three, and then we start running! Do you understand (*Have you understood*)?

... . bis drei, und dann ....!
Habt ihr .... ?

❷ You must not get angry (*angry become*) when you don't win.

Ihr ..... nicht ...., wenn ihr nicht ....

❸ He screamed as loudly as he could (*He has so loud screamed as he could*), but nobody came (*is come*).

.. ... so laut .... er konnte, aber niemand ... .

***

Ein vielseitiges Tier A versatile animal
Despite this tale by the Brothers Grimm, the hare is considered an intelligent and friendly animal in Germany. He is the teacher **Meister Lampe** *in children's books, for example. For many centuries, the hare and its cousin, the rabbit, were also revered for their ability to reproduce. The hare was associated with the goddesses of fertility and love among the ancient Greeks, Romans and Germanic tribes alike. This association later led the Roman Catholic Church to condemn it as a symbol of 'fornication' and 'lust'*. In the 8th century, one pope went as far as prohibiting the consumption of hare and rabbit meat!*

However, the hare's reputation was rehabilitated during the 17th century when it became associated with the spring religious festival of Easter. In some areas it was claimed that the **Osterhase** *Easter hare (which we know as the Easter Bunny) brought* **die Ostereier** *the Easter eggs. It wasn't such a silly idea: you hardly*

4 When did you (*formal*) start to learn German?
Wann ...., Deutsch zu ..... ?

5 They arrived at home merrily because the hare dropped dead.
... ... vergnügt zu Haus ...., weil der Hase ... .

Answers to Exercise 2

1 Ich zähle – laufen wir los – verstanden **2** – dürft – wütend werden – gewinnt **3** Er hat – geschrien wie – ist gekommen **4** – haben Sie angefangen – lernen **5** Sie sind – angekommen – tot umgefallen ist

***

ever see it and it is faster than a hen – and anyway, even children know that hens don't lay coloured eggs. But the Easter hare had competitors: for example, the fox in Brandenburg, the cuckoo in Berlin and the cock in Thuringia. In the predominantly Catholic areas of southern Germany, it was even said that church bells fly to Rome on Good Friday and bring back eggs and sweets for the children when they return on Easter Sunday. Yet the **Osterhase** *eventually ousted his opponents. Today no one would dispute his existence. Every year more than 12,000 tons of* **Schokoladenosterhasen** *are sold. In terms of kilograms of chocolate, the Easter Bunny even beats Santa Claus!*

* *In medieval church art, the hare often lies at the feet of the Virgin Mary as a symbol of her victory over lasciviousness.*

Second wave: 11th lesson

61 Einundsechzigste Lektion

Ein überzeugendes ① Argument

1 – Restau**rant Schloss**garten, **gu**ten Tag.
2 – **Gu**ten Tag, ich **möch**te für **Diens**tagabend **nächs**ter Woche **ei**nen Tisch reser**vie**ren ②.
3 – Für wie **vie**le ③ Per**so**nen?
4 – Für zwei Per**so**nen. Ist es **mög**lich, **drau**ßen zu **sit**zen?
5 – Selbstver**ständ**lich ④, wenn uns das **Wet**ter **kei**nen Strich ⑤ durch die **Rech**nung macht.
6   Um wie viel Uhr **wün**schen Sie zu ⑥ **es**sen?
7 – Um neun Uhr.

Pronunciation
... ewbᵃ**tsoig**'nduhs argu**ment** 1 ... **shlos**-gahtuhn ... 2 ... rezer**vee**ruhn 3 ... per**zoh**nuhn 5 ... zelpst-fer**shtent**likH ... **shtrikH** durkH ... **rekH**nung ...

Notes

① **überzeugend** *convincing* is the present participle of **überzeugen** *to convince, to persuade*. Present participles are usually formed by adding the ending **-d** to the infinitive. As in the lesson title, they can be used like adjectives, in which case they take endings like all other adjectives. **das Argument** is neuter, so its indefinite article is <u>ein</u> Argument. Hence we have to say: **ein überzeugend<u>es</u> Argument** (see lesson 56).

② **reservieren** *to reserve, to book.*

③ **viel Zeit** *a lot of time*, **viel<u>e</u> Argumente** *many arguments*. **wie viel** *how much, how many* can take an **-e** ending (like other plural adjectives), but in everyday speech this is often left out: **Wie viel Uhr ist es?** *What time is it?* **Wie viele** (or **viel**) **Leute sitzen draußen?** *How many people are sitting outside?*

313 • dreihundertdreizehn

Sixty-first lesson   61

A convincing argument

1 – Restaurant Schlossgarten (*castle-garden*), good afternoon.
2 – Good afternoon, I would like to book a table for Tuesday evening next week.
3 – For how many people (*persons*)?
4 – For two (*persons*). Is it possible to sit outside?
5 – Of course, if the weather doesn't thwart the plan (*if to-us the weather no line through the calculation makes*).
6   (*At*) What time do you wish to eat?
7 – At nine o'clock.

④ **selbstverständlich** consists of **selbst** *itself* (as well as *myself, yourself, himself*, etc.) or *in person*: **ich mache das selbst** *I['ll] do this myself*; and **verständlich** *understandable*. So **das ist selbstverständlich** means 'this is self-evident', 'that goes without saying', and **selbstverständlich** often translates simply as *of course* or *naturally*.

⑤ **einen Strich machen** *to draw (make) a line*, but **einen Strich durch die Rechnung machen** has the figurative meaning of *to thwart something, to upset one's plans*. **die Rechnung** can mean *bill* and *calculation*. It derives from the verb **rechnen** *to calculate, to count*.

⑥ The infinitive after **wünschen** *to wish* is here preceded by **zu**: **Wünschen Sie sofort zu essen?** *Do you wish to eat at once?* This is very polite, but also slightly antiquated. **wünschen** is most often used without an infinitive: **Ich wünsche Ihnen ein schönes Wochenende.** *I wish you a nice weekend.*

61 8 – Das ist **et**was ⑦ spät, die **Kü**che schließt in der **Wo**che um 22 (**zwei**undzwanzig) Uhr 30 (**drei**ßig).
  9   Und das ist **scha**de, wenn Sie **ei**nen **un**serer **köst**lichen **Nach**tische ver**su**chen **wol**len.
 10 – Wenn wir um 20 Uhr 30 **kom**men, ist der **Nach**tisch nicht mehr in Ge**fahr**?
 11 – Nein, dann **ha**ben wir ge**nug** Zeit. Auf **wel**chen **Na**men ⑧ darf ich reser**vie**ren?
 12 – Mein **Na**me ist Ralf **Buch**holz.
 13 – Gut, Herr **Buch**holz, der Tisch ist für 20 Uhr 30 reser**viert**. **Al**so bis **Diens**tag.
 14 – Ich **dan**ke Ihnen ⑨, auf **Wie**derhören. □

*9 ... ferzukh'n ... 10 ... guh**fah**ª 12 ... **book**hholts*

Notes

⑦ **etwas** not only means *something*, but also *a little*.

⑧ **der Name** *name* is a weak masculine noun (lesson 47, note 2).

⑨ **danken** *to thank* requires the dative case for the person who is being thanked, as in 'to give thanks to': **Wir danken unseren Freunden.** *We thank our friends.* **danken** is often used with the preposition **für**: **Ich danke Ihnen für die Auskunft.** *I thank you for the information.*

***

Übung 1 – Übersetzen Sie bitte!

❶ Deine Argumente überzeugen mich leider nicht. ❷ Das Wetter hat uns einen Strich durch die Rechnung gemacht. ❸ Ich danke dir für deine Hilfe. ❹ Selbstverständlich können Sie draußen essen, wenn Sie es wünschen. ❺ Auf welchen Namen haben Sie reserviert?

8 – That's a little late – the kitchen closes at 10:30 pm during the week.
9 And that's a pity if you want to try one of our delicious desserts.
10 – If we come at 8:30, is the dessert no longer at risk (*in danger*)?
11 – No, in that case (*then*) we [will] have enough time. In what name shall I make the reservation (*On what name may I reserve*)?
12 – My name is Ralf Buchholz.
13 – Fine, Mr Buchholz, the table is booked for 8:30 pm. So see you (*until*) Tuesday.
14 – (*I*) Thank you, goodbye.

Auf welchen Namen haben Sie reserviert?

***

Answers to Exercise 1

❶ Unfortunately, your arguments don't convince me. ❷ The weather upset our plans. ❸ I thank you for your help. ❹ Of course you can eat outside if you wish to (*you it wish*). ❺ In which name did you book?

dreihundertsechzehn • 316

Übung 2 – Ergänzen Sie bitte!

❶ Good evening, for how many people did (*have*) you book (*reserved*)?
Guten Abend, ... haben Sie ....?

❷ That is not [a] convincing argument; we have to try to find a better one (*a better-one to find*).
Das ist ...., wir müssen ...., ein besseres .. ..

❸ We thank you for your help. – But of course (*this is self-evident*)!
... . für Ihre Hilfe. – ...., das ist doch ....!

❹ If you (*formal*) don't come immediately, we [will] not have enough time.
Wenn ... nicht sofort ......, ... nicht ..... Zeit.

---

62 Zweiundsechzigste Lektion

Eine schlaue Verkäuferin im Reisebüro

1 – **Gu**ten **Tag**, ich **möch**te **ei**ne **Rei**se in die **Son**ne **bu**chen ①.
2 – Oh, da kann ich **Ih**nen **ei**nige **Schnäpp**chen ② **an**bieten.

Pronunciation
... *shlowuh ferkoifuhrin* ... 1 ... *bookh'n* 2 ... *shnepkH'n anbeet'n*

317 • dreihundertsiebzehn

❺ Bring the bill, please, we would like to pay.
Bringen Sie bitte ... ., wir möchten ....

Answers to Exercise 2

❶ – für wie viele Personen – reserviert ❷ – kein überzeugendes Argument – versuchen – zu finden ❸ Wir danken Ihnen – Aber – selbstverständlich ❹ – Sie – kommen, haben wir – genug – ❺ – die Rechnung – zahlen

Have you been going back to revisit a previous lesson every day? Don't forget to read it out loud and, even more importantly, to cover up the German text and try to translate the English into German – this will allow you to apply what you've learned. The first step is to recognize words when you see them, but the real goal is to be able to use them. **Wir hoffen, dieses Argument überzeugt Sie!** We hope this argument convinces you!

Second wave: 12th lesson

Sixty-second lesson 62

A clever sales assistant at the travel agency

1 – Good afternoon, I'd like to book a trip to somewhere sunny (*in the sun*).
2 – Oh, (*there*) I can offer you some [great] deals.

Notes

① **buchen** *to book*, *to reserve* is used for trips, flights, hotel rooms, etc. Its basic meaning is 'to enter something in the books', 'to record something' (book = **das Buch**).

② **das Schnäppchen** is a great *bargain* or *deal*. It comes from the verb **schnappen** *to snap up*, *to grab*, *to snatch*. **einige** means *some*, *a few*.

3 Wie **lange wol**len Sie denn **blei**ben und wann **wol**len Sie **los**fliegen?
4 – **Flie**gen? Wer hat denn von **Flie**gen ge**spro**chen?
5 – Ach, Sie **flie**gen nicht gern ③?
6 – Nicht gern? Ich **ha**sse es!
7 **Wis**sen Sie nicht, wie **vie**le **Flug**zeuge **letz**tes Jahr **ab**gestürzt ④ sind?
8 – Nein, und ich **möch**te es lieber ⑤ nicht **wis**sen,
9 ich **flie**ge **näm**lich übermorgen in die **Son**ne, nach **Ku**ba, zu **ei**nem fan**tas**tischen Preis!
10 **Stel**len Sie sich vor ⑥, **al**les **in**begriffen: Flug, **Un**terkunft mit **Voll**pension, so**gar** die Fahrt vom **Flug**hafen zum Ho**tel**.
11 – Das klingt **wir**klich interes**sant**!

---

*4 ... guh**sh**pro**kh**'n 6 ... **ha**ssuh ... 7 ... **flook**-tsoiguh... **ap**guhshtewrtst ... 8 ... **leeb**ᵃ ... 9 ... **koo**ba ... 10 ... **in**buhgrif'n ... **unt**ᵃkunft ... **fol**-pangsyohn (or -pensyohn) ... **flook**-hahf'n ...*

Notes

③ **gern** (or **gerne** with **-e**) is often used with verbs in the sense of 'to like', 'to enjoy': **ich reise gern(e)** *I like travelling* (literally, 'I travel gladly').

④ **abstürzen** *to fall, to plunge, to crash* indicates a fall from a great height (the separable prefix **ab** often signals movement away or down). **stürzen** without the prefix means *to fall, to topple*: **Er ist von seinem Rad gestürzt.** *He fell off his bike.*

⑤ **lieber** ('more-gladly') is the comparative of **gern** *gladly*. Its English equivalent is *prefer* or *would rather*: **Ich reise lieber**

3 So how long do you want to stay and when do you want to fly (*off-fly*)?
4 – Fly? Who said anything about flying (*has then of flying spoken*)?
5 – Ah, you don't like flying (*you don't fly gladly*)?
6 – Not like (*Not gladly*)? I hate it!
7 Don't you know how many airplanes crashed last year (*last year crashed are*)?
8 – No, and I would prefer (*would-like it more-gladly*) not to know,
9 as I'm flying (*I fly after-all*) somewhere sunny the day after tomorrow, to Cuba, at a fantastic price!
10 Imagine (*you yourself*), all inclusive (*included*): flight, accommodation with full board, even the trip from the airport to the hotel.
11 – That sounds really interesting!

---

mit dem Zug als mit dem Flugzeug. *I prefer to travel* ('I travel more-gladly') *by train than by plane.*

⑥ When **sich vorstellen** is used in the sense of 'to imagine something', the reflexive pronoun is in the dative: **Stell dir vor, wir gewinnen!** *Imagine (to yourself), we're winning!* In contrast, **sich vorstellen** in the sense of 'to introduce oneself' requires an object (the reflexive pronoun) in the accusative: **Darf ich mich vorstellen?** *May I introduce myself?* (lesson 37, line 11 and lesson 51, line 3). The infinitive after **sich vorstellen** *to imagine* is preceded by **zu**: **Sie stellen sich vor die Besten zu sein.** *They imagine themselves to be the best.*

62 **12** – Ja, das ist **un**ser **bes**tes ⑦ **An**gebot, aber **scha**de, für Sie kommt es nicht in **Fra**ge.
13 – **War**ten Sie mal, viel**leicht** kann ich **ein**mal eine **Aus**nahme **ma**chen.
14 **Schließ**lich ist **Flie**gen laut Sta**tis**tik am **si**chersten ⑧.

---

12 ... **bes**tuhs **an**guhboht ... 13 ... **ows**'nahmuh ...
14 **shlees**likH ... lowt shta**tis**tik am **zi**kH\u1D43stuhn

Notes

⑦ **gut** *good*, **besser** *better*, **beste** *best*. Like in English, the superlative is used to compare more than two things: **das beste Angebot von allen** *the best offer of all*, but **das bessere Angebot (von zwei)** *the better offer (of two)*.

⑧ **am sichersten** *safest*: the superlative of adverbs and predicate adjectives is formed by inserting **am** in front of the adverb or adjective and adding the ending **-(e)sten** to it: **Im Sommer arbeitet Frau Bachmann am längsten.** *In the summer Mrs Bachmann works longest.* **Am sichersten ist es zu Hause zu bleiben.** *It is safest* ('The safest is it') *to stay at home*.

***

Übung 1 – Übersetzen Sie bitte!

❶ Wir haben zu einem fantastischen Preis eine Reise nach Marokko gebucht. ❷ Nehmen Sie lieber den Zug oder das Auto, um in die Ferien zu fahren? ❸ Er ist gestern Nachmittag auf der Straße gestürzt. ❹ Haben Sie keine Angst, wenn Sie fliegen? ❺ Unsere Schnäppchen sind die besten die es auf dem Markt gibt.

12 – Yes, it's our best offer, but [what a] pity [that] for you this is out of the (*comes it not in*) question.
13 – Wait, maybe I can [just this] once make an exception …
14 After all (*Finally*), flying is safest according to statistic[s].

***

Answers to Exercise 1

❶ We booked a trip to Morocco at a fantastic price. ❷ Do you prefer to take the train or the car to go on holiday? ❸ He fell in the street yesterday afternoon. ❹ Aren't you afraid (*Have you no fear*) when you fly? ❺ Our bargains are the best that there are on the market.

63 Übung 2 – Ergänzen Sie bitte!

❶ I can't imagine a cleverer sales assistant (*I can to-me no cleverer sales assistant imagine*).
Ich kann ... keine .... Verkäuferin ....

❷ I would like to book a room with full board.
... . ein Zimmer ... .

❸ Do you (*formal*) prefer to drink beer or water?
.... Bier oder ...... ?

❹ [The] flight, [the] accommodation and even the drinks are included in the price.
...., ... und ..... die Getränke sind im Preis ....

---

63 Dreiundsechzigste Lektion

Wiederholung – Review

1 Irregular (strong) verbs and their past participles

There are several types of irregular (strong) verbs. Some have stem vowel changes in the present tense and/or the past participle.

1.1 Irregular (strong) verbs with stem vowel *a*

a changes to **ä** in the second- and third-person singular present tense, but the stem vowel remains **a** in the past participle:
schlafen *to sleep* → **schläfst, schläft** → **geschlafen** *slept*
fahren *to go by car* → **fährst, fährt** → **gefahren** *gone by car*

1.2 Irregular (strong) verbs with stem vowel *e*

• **e** changes to **i** or **ie** in the second- and third-person singular present tense, but remains **e** in the past participle:

5 Your (*formal*) offer sounds very good, but unfortunately my husband doesn't like flying (*flies unfortunately not gladly*).
... . klingt ...., aber mein Mann ...... leider nicht .....

Answers to Exercise 2

1 mir – schlauere – vorstellen **2** Ich möchte – mit Vollpension buchen **3** Trinken Sie lieber – Wasser **4** Flug, Unterkunft – sogar – inbegriffen **5** Ihr Angebot – sehr gut – fliegt – gern

Second wave: 13th lesson

Sixty-third lesson 63

geben *to give* → **gibst, gibt** → **gegeben** *given*
sehen *to see* → **siehst, sieht** → **gesehen** *seen*

• **e** changes to **i** in the second- and third-person singular present tense and to **o** in the past participle:
helfen *to help* → **hilfst, hilft** → **geholfen** *helped*
sprechen *to speak* → **sprichst, spricht** → **gesprochen** *spoken*

1.3 Irregular (strong) verbs with stem vowel *ei*

• **ei** changes to **ie** in the past participle; there is no change in the present tense:
schreien *to scream, to shout* → **geschrien** *screamed, shouted*

• **ei** changes to **i** (short) in the past participle; there is no change in the present tense:
beißen *to bite* → **gebissen** *bitten*

1.4 Irregular (strong) verbs with stem vowel *i*

• **i** changes to **u** in the past participle; there is no change in the present tense:
trinken *to drink* → **getrunken** *drunk*
finden *to find* → **gefunden** *found*

• **i** changes to **o** in the past participle; there is no change in the present tense:
beginnen *to begin, to start* → **begonnen** *begun, started*

1.5 Irregular (strong) verbs with stem vowel *ie*

ie changes to **o** in the past participle; there is no change in the present tense:
fliegen *to fly* → **geflogen** *flown*
verbieten *to forbid* → **verboten** *forbidden*

1.6 Exceptions

There are some verbs that don't follow any of these patterns:
kommen *to come* → **gekommen** *come* (in the simple past: **ich kam, du kamst, er kam** *I came, you came, he came,* etc.)
sein *to be* → **gewesen** *been*
liegen *to lie* (*to be lying down*) → **gelegen** *lain*
sitzen *to sit* → **gesessen** *sat*
stehen *to stand* (*to be standing up*) → **gestanden** *stood*, etc.

As you can see, there are quite a few exceptions. The only option is to learn them by heart! You don't have to try to memorize these in lists, just carry on working through the lessons and you'll learn them effortlessly as you see them in different contexts.

2 Comparisons (adjectives and adverbs)

2.1 Comparatives and superlatives

• **General rule**
The comparative of an adjective is formed by adding **-er** to the base form, the superlative by adding **-ste***:

* More precisely, it is formed by adding **-st** + the appropriate adjective ending, as the comparative and superlative forms decline

like attributive adjectives (see lesson 56): **das schnellste Auto** *the fastest car*, but **die schnellsten Autos** *the fastest cars*.
schnell *fast* → **schneller** *faster* → **schnellste** *fastest*
schön *nice* → **schöner** *nicer* → **schönste** *nicest*
klein *small* → **kleiner** *smaller* → **kleinste** *smallest*

- **Special cases**
- Some adjectives/adverbs add an umlaut in the comparative and superlative:
jung *young* → **jünger** *younger* → **jüngste** *youngest*
arm *poor* → **ärmer** *poorer* → **ärmste** *poorest*

The same goes for **groß** *big, tall*, **dumm** *stupid*, **stark** *strong*, **schwach** *weak*, **kalt** *cold*, **warm** *warm*, **lang** *long*, **kurz** *short*, **alt** *old*. (This list isn't complete; you'll see other examples soon.)

- The majority of adjectives ending in **-d**, **-t**, **-s**, **-ß**, **-x** or **-z** insert an **e** before the ending **-ste** in the superlative to aid pronunciation:
berühmt *famous* → **berühmter** *more famous* → **berühmteste** *most famous*
heiß *hot* → **heißer** *hotter* → **heißeste** *hottest*

After **-sch**, the **e** is optional:
frisch *fresh* → **frischer** *fresher* → **frisch(e)ste** *freshest*

But:
groß *big, tall* → **größer** *bigger, taller* → **größte** *biggest, tallest*

- **Irregular forms**
There are only a few adjectives and adverbs that have irregular comparative and superlative forms:
gut *good* → **besser** *better* → **beste** *best*
viel *a lot* → **mehr** *more* → **meiste** *most*
hoch *high* → **höher** *higher* → **höchste** *highest*
nah *close* → **näher** *closer* → **nächste** *closest, next*

2.2 Uses of the comparative and superlative

- Comparisons of equality: **so** (or **ebenso**) **... wie** *as ... as*:
Er ist ebenso schlau wie du. *He is as clever as you.*
Daniel ist noch nicht so groß wie sein Vater. *Daniel is not yet as tall as his father.*

63
- Comparisons of inequality: the comparative form of an adjective or adverb and **als** *than*:
Peter ist schlauer als du. *Peter is cleverer than you.*
Der Eiffelturm ist höher als der Turm von dem Kölner Dom.
The Eiffel Tower is higher than the spire of Cologne Cathedral.

- Comparisons involving more than two things (the superlative):
Der Kölner Dom ist die größte gothische Kathedrale in Deutschland.
Cologne Cathedral is the largest Gothic cathedral in Germany.
Trier ist die älteste Stadt in Deutschland.
Trier is the oldest city in Germany.

Note: the construction **am** + adjective + **-sten** is used for adverbs (example 1) and predicate adjectives (example 2):
1) **Petra singt am schönsten.** *Petra sings the best* ('prettiest').
2) **Im Frühling ist das Wetter hier am schönsten.** *The weather here is nicest in spring.*

This form can also be used with **sein** *to be*:
Die kleinsten Blumen sind am schönsten.
The smallest flowers are prettiest.

There are some irregular adverbial forms such as:
gern *gladly* → **lieber*** *more gladly* → **am liebsten** *most gladly*

* This can also be the comparative of **lieb** *dear, nice*: **lieber, liebste**.

Superlative adjectives that refer to a noun that is understood but not directly expressed are preceded by **der, die, das**. The superlative adjective therefore takes an ending:
Die kleinsten Blumen sind die schönsten. *The smallest flowers are the prettiest* (flowers).
Du bist der beste. *You're the best* (person).

3 The temporal conjunctions *als* and *wenn*

Als and **wenn** are both equivalent to *when*, but in German they are used in different contexts and are not interchangeable.

- **als** is used to introduce a clause concerned with a single event in the past or a block of continuous time in the past:
Als ich am Bahnhof angekommen bin, haben meine Freunde auf mich gewartet. *When I arrived at the station, my friends were waiting for me.*
Als er jung war, hat er ein Jahr in Amerika gearbeitet. *When he was young, he worked in America for a year.*

- **wenn** is used:

- to introduce a clause concerned with repeated events in the past. One can say **jedes Mal, wenn** *every time* or **wenn** *whenever*:
Jedes Mal, wenn/Wenn sie sich getroffen haben, waren sie glücklich. *Every time/Whenever they met, they were happy.*
Jedes Mal, wenn/Wenn er nach Amerika geflogen ist, haben ihn seine Freunde am Flughafen abgeholt. *Every time/Whenever he flew to America, his friends picked him up from the airport.*

- to introduce a clause concerned with events or possibilities in the present or future.
Ruf mich an, wenn du in Köln bist! *Call me when you're in Cologne!*
Wenn Sie ihn sehen, grüßen Sie ihn von mir.
When* you see him, say hello from me ('greet you him from me').

* Remember that **wenn** can also mean 'if'. Thus this phrase can also be translated as *If you see him* ... The meaning should be clear from the context.

- Finally, don't forget that **wann** *when* is only used in direct and indirect questions.
Wann kommt ihr Zug an? *When does your train arrive?*
Ich frage mich, wann wir uns wiedersehen.
I wonder ('ask myself') when we [will] see each other again.

> *Do you find all this grammar heavy going? Don't worry, you can always refer to the grammatical appendix if you need reminders as you're doing the lessons.*

63 Review exercise

To finish this set of lessons, we now offer you a second tale by the Brothers Grimm so you can apply all you've learned. Before you start, here are four words you've not yet encountered: **das Pferd** *horse,* **die Kuh** *cow,* **melken** *to milk and* **das Schwein** *pig.*

Hans im Glück
(nach den Brüdern Grimm)

1. Hans hatte sieben Jahre bei einem Meister gearbeitet, als er zu ihm gesagt hat: „Ich bin gern hier, aber ich möchte meine Mutter wiedersehen, die immer älter wird."
2. Der Meister hat ihm für seine Dienste ein Goldstück gegeben, das so groß wie der Kopf von Hans war, und Hans hat sich damit so schnell wie er konnte auf den Weg gemacht.
3. Aber das Gold war so schwer, dass er vor Erschöpfung fast umgefallen ist.
4. Gott sei Dank hat er einen Mann mit einem Pferd getroffen, der ihn freundlich gegrüßt hat.
5. „Sie haben mehr Glück als ich. Sie haben nämlich ein Pferd", hat er zu ihm gesagt, „und so sind Sie viel schneller als ich und weniger müde."
6. „Ich mache dir ein Angebot", hat der Mann geantwortet, "ich gebe dir mein Pferd, wenn du mir dein Goldstück gibst."
7. „Nichts lieber als das", hat Hans erwidert und hat sich sofort auf das Pferd gesetzt.
8. „Ich bin der glücklichste Mensch auf der Welt", hat er sich gesagt und hat lustig „hopp, hopp" geschrien.
9. Da ist das Pferd so schnell losgelaufen, dass Hans runtergefallen ist.
10. In diesem Moment ist ein Mann mit einer Kuh gekommen.

11 „Sie haben Glück", hat Hans gerufen, „eine Kuh ist ruhiger als ein Pferd und außerdem gibt sie Milch."
12 „Wenn du willst, nehme ich dein Pferd für meine Kuh", hat der Mann angeboten.
13 Hans war sofort einverstanden und beim Weitergehen hat er sich gesagt: „Ich bin wirklich der glücklichste Mensch auf der Erde."
14 Ein paar Stunden später hatte er großen Durst.
15 Also ist er mit der Kuh stehen geblieben und hat versucht, die Kuh zu melken.
16 Aber die Kuh ist immer wütender geworden und hat ihm Angst gemacht.
17 In diesem Augenblick hat Hans einen Mann gesehen, der mit seinem Schwein zum Markt gegangen ist.
18 „Schade", hat er zu ihm gesagt, „ich möchte auch lieber ein Schwein haben als eine so dumme Kuh."
19 Sie können sich sicher vorstellen, wie die Geschichte weitergeht…
20 Als Hans nach Hause gekommen ist, hatte er nichts mehr, aber er war überzeugt, der glücklichste Mensch auf der Welt zu sein.

Translation

Lucky Hans (*Hans in luck*)
(based on [a story by] the Brothers Grimm)

1 Hans had worked with a master for seven years when he said to him: 'I like being here (*am gladly here*), but I would like to see my mother again who is getting older and older (*always older becomes*).' **2** For his services, the master gave him a piece of gold (*gold-piece*) that was as big as Hans's head, and Hans went on his way with it as fast as he could. **3** But the gold was so heavy that he nearly fell over with exhaustion. **4** Thank the Lord, he met a man with a horse who greeted him kindly. **5** 'You are luckier (*have more luck*) than I, as you have (*you have after all*) a horse,' he said to him, 'and so you are much faster than me (*I*) and less tired.' **6** 'I [will] make you an offer,' responded the man. 'I [will] give you my horse if you give me your piece of gold.' **7** 'There's nothing I'd like better (*Nothing more-gladly than that*),' replied Hans and [he] immediately sat on the horse. **8** 'I'm the luckiest person (*human being*) in the world,' he said to himself and cheerfully cried 'Giddy up!' **9** Then the horse started running so fast that Hans fell off. **10** At the same time (*is*) a man with a cow came along. **11** 'You're lucky,' Hans called, 'a cow is calmer than a horse and besides it gives milk.' **12** 'If you want, I['ll] take your horse [in return] for my cow,' the man offered. **13** Hans agreed immediately

---

64 Vierundsechzigste Lektion

Berlin, die Hauptstadt der Bundesrepublik Deutschland

1 Ber**lins** ① Ver**gan**genheit ist – wie Sie **wis**sen – sehr **auß**erge**wöhn**lich.

2 Fast **drei**ßig **Jah**re lang war **die**se Stadt durch **ei**ne **Mau**er in zwei ge**teilt**.

Pronunciation
... b**und**uhs-repu**pleek** ... **1** ber**leens** fer**gan**guhnheit ... **ow**ss-guh**vœn**likH **2** ... **mow** ... guh**teilt**

Notes

① Possession can be expressed in different ways in German. Normally, the 'possessor' follows the noun it modifies, but proper names may come first (as in English), with the ending **-s** <u>without an apostrophe</u>: **Giselas Vergangenheit** *Gisela's past*. But if there is an article, the possessive proper name must follow the noun: **die Vergangenheit Giselas** 'the past of-Gisela'. If in doubt, you can always avoid the possessive by using **von** (+ dative): **die Vergangenheit von Gisela**. The possessive is also known as the genitive case.

(*was immediately agreed*), and continuing on his way, he said [to] himself: 'I really am the luckiest person on (*the*) Earth.' **14** A few hours later he was very thirsty (*had he big thirst*). **15** So he stopped (*standing stayed*) with the cow and tried to milk it (*the cow*). **16** But the cow got more and more angry and made him scared (*to-him fear made*). **17** At this moment Hans saw a man who was going to the market with his pig. **18** '[What a] pity,' he said to him. 'I would also prefer to have a pig [rather] than such a (*so*) stupid cow.' **19** You can surely imagine how the story continues … **20** When Hans arrived at home, he had nothing left (*nothing more*), but he was convinced [he was] the luckiest person on the planet (*to be*).

Bis morgen! *See you tomorrow!*

Second wave: 14th lesson

Sixty-fourth lesson 64

Berlin, the capital of the Federal Republic [of] Germany

1 Berlin's past is – as you know – very extraordinary.
2 [For] almost 30 years (*long*), this city was divided in two by a wall (*in two divided*).

Ich habe das noch nie gehört, das ist eine außergewöhnliche Geschichte.

3 Am 9. (**neun**ten) Novem**ber** 1989 ② fiel ③ die **Mau**er.

4 **Ost-** und **West**berliner ④ **konn**ten ⑤ sich **end**lich **wie**der in **ih**rer Stadt frei bewegen.

5 Ein Jahr spät**er**, am 3. (**dri**tten) Ok**to**ber 1990 **fei**erte ⑥ man ⑦ die Ver**ei**nigung von **Ost-** und **West**deutschland.

6 Seit**her** ⑧ ist der **dri**tte Ok**to**ber der **deut**sche Natio**nal**feiertag.

---

3 ... nointsehn-hund^at-noinunt-akhtsikH feel ...
4 ... buhvehg'n **5** ... nointsehn-hund^at-nointsikH fei^atuh ... fereinigung ... **6** zeitheh^a ... natsionahl-fei^a-tahk

Notes

② Dates are given with ordinal numbers: **am neunten November**, **der dritte Oktober**. Years before 2000 are expressed as follows: **neunzehnhundertneunundachtzig** 'nineteen hundred eighty-nine'; **neunzehnhundertneunzig** 'nineteen hundred ninety'. Note that, whereas the word **hundert** can be omitted in English, it is always included in German, but without an 'and'. After the year 2000, you simply say **zweitausend** *two thousand* plus the number of years that follow: **zweitausendeins** 'two thousand one', **zweitausendsiebzehn** 'two thousand seventeen', etc.

③ **fiel** is the third-person singular simple past tense of **fallen** *to fall*. As we've seen, this past tense is less common than the present perfect, and is mainly used in formal written texts (e.g. novels, police reports, newspaper articles). We'll be looking more at the conjugation of the simple past in this set of lessons. For now, just note that this is an irregular (strong) verb, in which the stem vowel changes and there is no **-t** ending in the third-person singular.

④ The term for the inhabitants of a particular place is normally formed by adding an ending to the name of the town, **-er** (m.), or **-erin** (f.): **Berlin** → **der Berliner** *the man from Berlin*, **die Berlinerin** *the woman from Berlin*, **die Berliner** *the people*

3 On [the] 9th [of] November, 1989, the wall fell.
4 East and West Berliners could finally move (*themselves*) freely in their city again.
5 One year later, on [the] 3rd [of] October, 1990, (*celebrated one*) the [re]unification of East and West Germany was celebrated.
6 Since then, the third [of] October has been (*is*) the German national holiday (*celebration-day*).

of Berlin. In some instances, the final vowel in the name of the city disappears when **-er/-erin** is added: **München** → **der Münchner**, **Dresden** → **der Dresdner**. Occasionally, there are other changes such as **Bremen** → **der Bremer**, **die Bremerin**, and of course there are a number of exceptions. Note that no indefinite article is used when saying where one is from: **Ich bin Berliner.** 'I am citizen-of-Berlin (m.).' Using an indefinite article can change the meaning – for example, **ein Berliner** is short for **ein Berliner Pfannkuchen** 'a Berlin pancake', which is a jam-filled doughnut!

⑤ **konnten** *they were able to*, *they could* is the third-person plural simple past tense of **können**. Modal verbs with an umlaut in the infinitive lose it in this tense.

⑥ Regular (weak) verbs form the simple past by adding the endings **-te**, **-test**, **-te**, **-ten**, **-tet**, **-ten** to the verb stem: **machen** *to make* → **du mach<u>test</u>** *you made*. Note that the first- and third-person have the same endings: **feiern** → **ich feier<u>te</u>** *I celebrated*, **er feier<u>te</u>** *he celebrated* and **wir feier<u>ten</u>** *we celebrated*, **sie feier<u>ten</u>** *they celebrated*.

⑦ Constructions with **man** *one* normally translate to the passive voice in English, as they avoid identifying the subject: **Man reparierte das Auto schnell.** ('One repaired the car quickly.') *The car was repaired quickly*.

⑧ **seither** *since then* is equivalent to **seit dieser Zeit** *since that time* (the preposition **seit** requires the dative).

dreihundertvierunddreißig

64

7 Ber**lin wur**de ⑨ die **Haupt**stadt der **neu**en **Bun**desrepublik.

8 **Heu**te ist **die**se Stadt **gleich**zeitig ein Sym**bol** für Zer**stö**rung und **Wie**deraufbau, **Tren**nung und Ver**ei**nigung.

9 **Zö**gern Sie nicht, nach Ber**lin** zu ⑩ **ko**mmen.

10 Mit **je**dem Schritt er**le**ben ⑪ Sie ein Stück Ge**schich**te, **Welt**geschichte! ☐

---

7 ... vurduh ... 8 ... gleikH-tseitikH ... zewmbohl tsershtœ'rung ... veed^a'owfbow trenung ... 9 tsœg^an ... 10 ... erlehbuhn ...

Pronunciation note
8 The **y** – called **ypsilon** *ewpsilon* in German – is pronounced as a long *ew* (as in *pew*): **das Symbol** *z<u>ew</u>mbohl*.

***

Übung 1 – Übersetzen Sie bitte!

❶ Ich habe das noch nie gehört, das ist eine außergewöhnliche Geschichte. ❷ Meine Mutter ist mit 5 Jahren nach Westdeutschland gekommen. ❸ Wissen Sie, warum der 3. Oktober der Nationalfeiertag Deutschlands ist? ❹ Claudias Bruder fiel von einer Mauer und konnte sich nicht mehr bewegen. ❺ Berlin ist ein Symbol für die Vereinigung* zwischen Ost und West.

335 • dreihundertfünfunddreißig

7 Berlin became the capital of the new Federal Republic.
8 Today this city is both (*at-the-same-time*) a symbol of (*for*) destruction and reconstruction, separation and [re]unification.
9 Don't hesitate to come to Berlin.
10 With every step, you [will] experience a bit (*a piece*) [of] history – world history!

Notes

⑨ **wurde** is the third-person (and first-person) singular simple past of **werden** *to become*.

⑩ **zögern** *to hesitate* used with a verb requires **zu** before the dependent infinitive: **Er zögert(,) das Auto zu nehmen.** *He hesitates to take the car.* (The comma is optional.)

⑪ **erleben** *to experience, to undergo something*.

***

Answers to Exercise 1

❶ I've never heard this before; this is an extraordinary story. ❷ My mother came to West Germany at the age of five. ❸ Do you know why the third of October is Germany's national holiday? ❹ Claudia's brother fell from a wall and couldn't (*himself*) move anymore. ❺ Berlin is a symbol of (*for*) the [re]unification of (*between*) East and West.

* The official term for the historical event in 1990 is **Deutsche Wiedervereinigung** *German reunification*.

64 Übung 2 – Ergänzen Sie bitte!

❶ As you (*formal*) know, Berlin is the capital of Germany.

... ..., ist Berlin ... . Deutschlands.

❷ East and West Berlin were divided by a wall [for] almost 30 years (*were almost 30 years by a wall divided*).

... - und .... waren fast dreißig Jahre ....

❸ Gisela's sister is from Berlin; she has been living in Berlin since 1990.

.... Schwester ist ....; sie wohnt .... in Berlin.

***

> **Die Bundesrepublik Deutschland**
> The Federal Republic of Germany
> *In 2009, Germany commemorated two important historical events: firstly, the 60th anniversary of the enactment of* the Basic Law (**das Grundgesetz**) *which marked the foundation of the West German state; and secondly, the 20th anniversary of* the fall of the Berlin Wall (**der Mauerfall**) *which led to German reunification and put an end to over 40 years of separation. In 1990, the 11* **Länder** *of the West German Federal Republic (FRG) were joined by five 'new'* **Länder*** *of the former German Democratic Republic (GDR): Brandenburg, where Potsdam is located; Mecklenburg-Western Pomerania, with its more than 2,000 lakes; Saxony, with its capital Dresden; Saxony-Anhalt, the birthplace of well-known Germans such as Martin Luther and Georg Friedrich Handel; and finally Thuringia, with its famous city of Weimar. East and West Berlin were reunited to form a new city-state. Since the reunification, 3 October has been the national holiday:* **der Tag der deutschen Einheit** Day of German Unity.

④ She hesitates to take another piece of cake (*still a piece cake to take*).

... ., noch ... . Kuchen .. nehmen.

⑤ This man's past is extraordinary; he has really experienced a lot.

... . dieses Mannes ist ....; .. ... wirklich viel ....

Answers to Exercise 2

① Wie Sie wissen – die Hauptstadt – ② Ost – Westberlin – durch eine Mauer geteilt ③ Giselas – Berlinerin – seit neunzehnhundertneunzig – ④ Sie zögert – ein Stück – zu – ⑤ Die Vergangenheit – außergewöhnlich; er hat – erlebt

***

Germany is a federal state, which means that each **Land** *has a certain amount of sovereignty. The Basic Law lays out which issues fall within the ambit of the federal government and which devolve to the states. The head of state is the* **Bundespräsident** *Federal President. He or she is elected by the Federal Assembly every five years, and unlike in the United States, for example, his or her role is largely a ceremonial one. The guidelines of government policy are laid down by the* Federal Chancellor **Bundeskanzler** *(m.)* or **Bundeskanzlerin** *(f.). The chancellor is elected by the* **Bundestag**, *the German Parliament, and in turn chooses ministers to form* **die Bundesregierung** *the Federal Government. In 2001, the* **Bundestag** *and* **Bundesregierung** *left the former West German capital, Bonn, to move to the* **Reichstag** *in Berlin, next to the Brandenburg Gate.*

* For the **Länder** (states), see lesson 42.

Second wave: 15th lesson

65 Fünfundsechzigste Lektion

Wie wird man reich?
Loriot verrät uns das Geheimnis ①

1 Das Geheimnis, warum nur so wenige ② reich sind, ist eigentlich keines ③.
2 Jeder versteht mit ein bisschen Überlegung, dass reich werden Geld kostet.
3 Deshalb ④ sind nämlich nur wenige reich.
4 Wenn ich einen Friseursalon eröffnen will ⑤, brauche ich nicht nur ein Diplom, einen Kamm und guten Willen ⑥, sondern auch Kapital.
5 Wenn das Kapital fehlt, muss ich meine Kunden auf dem Gehweg oder im Wald ⑦ frisieren.

Pronunciation
... lorioh ferreht ... guhheimnis **1** ... kein's **2** ... ewbᵃlehgung ... **4** ... frizœᵃ-zalong erœfnuhn ... diplohm ... kam ... viluhn ... kapitahl **5** ... fehlt ... geh-vehk ... valt frizeeruhn

Notes
① **ein Geheimnis verraten** *to reveal, to tell a secret.* Note that **das Geheimnis** can be a *mystery* or a *secret*.
② **wenige** implies **Leute/Personen**: **Nur wenige haben Glück im Leben.** *Only few are lucky in life.*
③ **keines** (or **keins**) *no, not any, none* is neuter here because it refers back to a neuter noun (**das Geheimnis**).
④ **deshalb** *hence, therefore, thus* answers the question **Warum?** or **Weshalb?** *Why?*

Sixty-fifth lesson   65

How does one get (*becomes one*) **rich?**
Loriot reveals (*betrays to-us*) **the secret**

1. The mystery why so few people are rich isn't really a mystery (*is actually none*).
2. Everyone understands, with a little reflection, that getting rich costs money.
3. This is why so few are rich (*Therefore are after-all only few rich*).
4. If I want to open a hairdressing salon, I need not only a certificate, a comb and good will, but also funds (*capital*).
5. If [sufficient] capital is lacking, I [will] have to style the hair of my clients on the sidewalk (*walk-way*) or in the forest.

Pronunciation notes
1 The **e** at the end of **keines** is often almost silent. It can also be written as **keins**.
4 der Friseur can also be spelled **Frisör**. **der Salon** can be pronounced *zalohn* or *zalong*.

⑤ Note the word order in a statement introduced by **wenn** *if*. The conjugated verb moves to the last position in the subordinate clause: **Wenn du nicht kommen kannst ...** *If you can't come*, and in the main clause that follows, the subject and verb are inverted: **... muss ich allein essen.** *I have to eat alone.*

⑥ **der Wille** *will* is a weak masculine noun, taking an **-n** ending in all cases except the nominative singular (lesson 47, note 2).

⑦ **der Wald** *forest*, **die Wälder** *forests*. Do you check the gender and plural form of nouns every now and then?

dreihundertvierzig • 340

65 6 Und das ist **stre**ssig.
7 Ich wieder**ho**le **also**: Man muss reich sein, um es zu **wer**den.
8 Ich emp**feh**le **Ih**nen **des**halb, bei **Ih**rer Ge**burt** reich zu sein.
9 **Je**der **an**dere Ver**such,** reich zu **wer**den ⑧, ist sehr **müh**sam und kann **Ih**nen die **Lau**ne und die Ge**sund**heit ver**der**ben ⑨. □

---

6 ... shtre**ssikH 7** ... veed^a**hoh**luh ... **8** ... emp**feh**luh ...
9 ... **mew**zam ... guh**zunt**heit fer**der**buhn

Notes

⑧ Infinitives dependent on verbs other than modals (or some verbs of perception such as **sehen** and **hören**) are usually preceded by **zu**: **Es hat angefangen zu regnen.** *It started to rain.* In addition, an infinitive in a phrase that completes the meaning of a noun requires **zu**. The infinitive phrase functions much like a dependent clause, except that it never has a subject. It is usually set apart by a comma in order to avoid confusion: **Alle Versuche, Deutsch zu sprechen, sind ausgezeichnet.** *All attempts at speaking German are excellent.*

***

Übung 1 – Übersetzen Sie bitte!

❶ Wenn Sie nicht verstehen, müssen Sie es sagen. ❷ Reisen kostet Geld, deshalb bleibe ich zu Hause. ❸ Sie können sehen, dass dieses Problem eigentlich keins ist. ❹ Wir können noch kein Restaurant eröffnen: das Kapital fehlt uns. ❺ Mit dem Fahrrad darf man nicht auf dem Gehweg fahren.

6 And that's stressful.

7 Hence I repeat: one has to be rich in order to get rich (*it to become*).

8 I [would] advise you, therefore, to be rich at (*with your*) birth.

9 Any (*Every*) other attempt to become rich is very arduous and can drag you down and harm your health (*can to-you the mood and the health spoil*).

⑨ **die Laune verderben** ('the mood to-spoil') *to drag someone down*, *to dampen someone's spirits*. Note that the person whose parade is being rained on is in the dative: **Das verdirbt <u>mir</u> die Laune!** *This drags me down!*

***

Answers to Exercise 1

❶ If you don't understand, you [just] have to say so (*it*). ❷ Travelling costs money, hence I stay at home. ❸ You can see that this problem isn't actually one (*none is*). ❹ We can't open a restaurant yet: we lack capital. ❺ One mustn't ride a bike on the sidewalk.

65 Übung 2 – Ergänzen Sie bitte!

❶ I mustn't reveal this to you; it's a secret.
Ich darf euch das nicht ....; das ist ....

❷ Do you know how to get rich (*one rich becomes*)? – With a little reflection and good will!
Wissen Sie, ... reich wird? – ... ein bisschen .... und gutem ......!

❸ If you like forests, visit the Black Forest!
.... Sie ...... mögen, ... den Schwarzwald!

***

Loriot* *(real name Bernhard Victor Christoph Carl von Bülow) was in many ways the uncrowned king of comedy in post-war Germany. A cartoonist, comedian, actor and writer, he was born the son of a Prussian officer in Brandenburg an der Havel on 12 November 1923 and died on 22 August 2011. Loriot said of his father, a serious and distinguished man, that he could laugh at his own dignity and the failures resulting from it. It is on him that Loriot modelled his trademark cartoon character the* **Knollennasenmännchen** *– a small man with a bulbous nose.*

Loriot had a gift for pointing out the absurdities of life and the emptiness of conventions and etiquette. In his work, mundane, everyday activities such as eating in a restaurant, going to a concert – not to mention office work – regularly descend into chaos, albeit a well-mannered middle-class kind of chaos. Many of his jokes touched on key German stereotypes, and he poked fun at German

❹ Please repeat (*formal*), I believe I didn't understand correctly.
.... bitte, ich glaube, ...
nicht richtig ....

❺ I won't let bad weather drag me down (*I let to-me by bad weather not the mood spoil*).
Ich lasse ... von schlechtem ...... nicht
die ....

Answers to Exercise 2

❶ – verraten – ein Geheimnis ❷ – wie man – Mit – Überlegung – Willen ❸ Wenn – Wälder – besuchen Sie – ❹ Wiederholen Sie – ich habe – verstanden ❺ mir – Wetter – Laune verderben

***

earnestness and devotion to formality. One of the most famous examples is the animation **'Zwei Herren im Bad'** *'Two men in the bath'. It features two men in a hotel bath, Herr Müller-Lüdenscheid and Herr Doktor Klöbner, one of whom is clearly there by mistake. Regardless of the intimacy of the situation, the two engage in an absurdly formal conversation (about rubber ducks among other things) and address each other with full honorifics at all times. It is scenes like this that made Loriot a household name in Germany and earned him the accolade of the person who taught Germans to laugh at themselves.*

* **Loriot** *is French for 'oriole', the bird in his family coat of arms.*

Second wave: 16th lesson

66 Sechsundsechzigste Lektion

Ein perfekter Ehemann ①

1 – **Gu**ten **A**bend, Schatz! Bin ich froh, **end**lich zu **Hau**se zu sein!
2 Ich **hat**te **ei**nen sehr **an**strengenden ② Tag. Und wie geht's dir?
3 – Och, ich **ha**be die **Na**se **ziem**lich voll.
4 – Wa**rum** denn? Was ist denn los?
5 – Seit **Ta**gen ver**su**che ich im Restau**rant** **Schloss**garten **an**zurufen ③, **a**ber es ist **im**mer be**setzt**.
6 Ich **woll**te **ei**nen Tisch für **un**seren **Hoch**zeitstag **ü**bermorgen reser**vie**ren ④,
7 da**mit** ⑤ wir ihn dort **fei**ern, wo wir uns **ken**nen ge**lernt** ⑥ **ha**ben.
8 **Heu**te **A**bend ist das Restau**rant** ge**schlos**sen und **mor**gen ist es **si**cher zu spät.
9 – Na**tür**lich bist du jetzt **fürch**terlich ent**täuscht**, nicht wahr?

Pronunciation
... per**fekt**ᵃ **eh**uh-man **1** ... shats ... **2** ... **an**shtrenguhnduhn ... **5** ... buh**zetst** **6** ... **hokh**tseits-tahk ... rezer**vee**ruhn **9** ... **fewrkHt**ᵃlikH ent-**toisht** ...

Notes

① **die Ehe** *marriage*, in the sense of the relationship, whereas the ceremony is **die Hochzeit** (line 6) *wedding*.

② **ein anstrengender Tag** *a tiring day* ('an effortful day'): **die Anstrengung** *effort*, **(sich) anstrengen** *to make an effort*.

③ **versuchen** *to try* takes a dependent infinitive preceded by **zu**. Here, the infinitive is the separable-prefix verb **anrufen** *to call*.

345 • dreihundertfünfundvierzig

Sixty-sixth lesson 66

A perfect husband

1 – Good evening, darling (*treasure*)! Am I glad to be home at last!
2 I had a very tiring day. And how are you?
3 – Oh, I'm a bit fed up (*I have the nose quite full*).
4 – But why? What's wrong?
5 – For days I've been trying (*try I*) to phone (*in-*) the Schlossgarten restaurant, but [the line] (*it*) is always engaged (*occupied*).
6 I wanted to book a table for our wedding anniversary (*wedding-day*) the day after tomorrow,
7 so we [can] celebrate it (*there*) where we met each other (*where we ourselves know learned have*).
8 This evening the restaurant is closed and tomorrow it will surely be (*is*) too late.
9 – Of course you're terribly disappointed now, aren't you (*not true*)?

---

to phone, so **zu** comes between the prefix and the base verb: **Er versucht an<u>zu</u>rufen, aber niemand antwortet.** *He tries to call, but no one answers.*

④ Dependent infinitives used with modal verbs are <u>never</u> preceded by **zu**: **Wollen Sie das bitte nicht vergessen?** *Would you please not forget this?*

⑤ The conjunction **damit** *so, so that* introduces a subordinate clause and causes the verb to move to the last position.

⑥ **kennen lernen** literally means 'to-know to-learn'. It is usually used with people in the sense of *to get to know, to meet*.

66 10 – Klar, ich **ha**tte mich so da**rau**f ge**freu**t ⑦,
mit dir **wie**der dort**hin** zu **geh**en.
11 – **Al**so, wenn es nur das ist, mein **Lieb**ling,
dann hast du **kei**nen Grund **trau**rig zu sein!
12   Hast du ver**ges**sen, dass du mit **ei**nem
Supermann ver**hei**ratet bist?
13   Ich **ha**be na**tür**lich schon vor ⑧ **ei**ner **Wo**che
ge**nau** dort **ei**nen Tisch reser**vier**t …   □

---

10 … guh**froi**t … 11 … grunt **trow**rikH … 12 … zoopᵃman fer**hei**ratuht …

Notes

⑦ **sich freuen** *to be glad, to be pleased* is a frequently used verb: **Ich freue mich, Sie zu sehen.** *I am glad to see you.* **sich auf etwas/jemanden freuen** means *to look forward to something.* **darauf** replaces **auf das** ('on this'): **Ich freue mich darauf, Sie morgen zu treffen.** *I'm looking forward to meeting you tomorrow.* (Note that **ich hatte mich so darauf gefreut** *I had so looked forward to this* is the past perfect tense. We'll come back to this tense later.)

⑧ Note that **vor Tagen** *days ago* refers to a particular point in the past, whereas **seit Tagen** *for days* indicates a time span. When used temporally, **vor** translates as *ago*: **Vor einer Stunde war sein Telefon besetzt.** *An hour ago, his phone was engaged.* The word **seit** can mean *since* or *for*; when used with the

***

Übung 1 – Übersetzen Sie bitte!

❶ Sie hat ihren Freund vor drei Jahren in Berlin kennen gelernt. ❷ Die Kinder freuen sich auf die nächsten Ferien. ❸ Sie haben keinen Grund, enttäuscht zu sein. ❹ Seit Wochen hat er sehr anstrengende Tage. ❺ Wann haben Sie versucht, mich anzurufen?

10 – Sure, I had [been] so looking forward to going there again with you (*I had myself so on-this been-glad with you again to-there to go*).
11 – Well, if it's only that, my darling, then you have no reason to be sad!
12 Have you forgotten that you are married to (*with*) a superman?
13 I have naturally already booked a table (*exactly*) there a week ago …

present tense, it expresses an action that started in the past, but is continuing into the present (in English, we use perfect tenses when giving time spans). **Er wohnt seit Montag in Hamburg.** *He has been living* ('lives') *in Hamburg since Monday.* **Seit einer Stunde ist sein Telefon besetzt.** *His phone has been* ('is') *engaged for an hour.*

***

Answers to Exercise 1

❶ She met her boyfriend in Berlin three years ago. ❷ The children are looking forward to the upcoming *(next)* holiday. ❸ You have no reason to be disappointed. ❹ He has been having very tiring days for weeks. ❺ When did you try to call me?

67 Übung 2 – Ergänzen Sie bitte!

❶ I am very pleased to meet you (*you to-know to learn*).
... . mich sehr, Sie ...... zu ....

❷ They met each other six weeks ago, and today they are already celebrating [their] wedding.
Sie haben sich ... sechs ...... kennen gelernt, und heute .... schon ....

❸ He is glad to be home at last; the day was very tiring.
Er ist ...., zu Haus .. ...., der Tag war ....

❹ So he doesn't feel (*isn't*) disappointed or sad, she phones him every evening.
.... nicht .... oder .... ist, ... sie ihn jeden Abend ...

---

67 Siebenundsechzigste Lektion

Und was ist für Sie das Paradies?

1 – **Al**so, Sie sind der ① **Mei**nung, dass es **zwi**schen ② den Nationali**tä**ten **kei**ne **Un**terschiede gibt?

2 Ich ver**ste**he Sie nicht. Da ③ bin ich ganz **an**derer **Mei**nung.

Pronunciation
... para**dees** 1 ... **mei**nung ... natsionali**teh**tuhn ...

Notes

① This is the genitive singular feminine article of **die Meinung** *opinion*. **Ich bin Ihrer Meinung.** *I am of your opinion.* **Ich bin der Meinung, dass Spanien das schönste Land Europas ist.** *I am of the opinion that Spain is the most beautiful country in Europe.* Like most nouns ending in **-ung**, **Meinung** derives from a verb: **meinen** *to be of the opinion*, and also *to mean* (see line 4).

349 • dreihundertneunundvierzig

❺ If it's only this, then he has no reason not to speak to her for days (*for days not with her to speak*). 67

. . . . es nur das . . . , dann hat er . . . . . .
. . . . nicht mit ihr . . . .

Answers to Exercise 2

❶ Ich freue – kennen – lernen ❷ – vor – Wochen – feiern sie – Hochzeit ❸ – froh, endlich – zu sein – sehr anstrengend ❹ Damit er – enttäuscht – traurig – ruft – an ❺ Wenn – ist – keinen Grund seit Tagen – zu sprechen

Second wave: 17th lesson

Sixty-seventh lesson 67

And what is paradise for you?

1 – So, you are of the opinion that there are no differences between the nationalities?
2 I don't understand you. (*There*) I have a completely different (*am I completely of-another*) opinion.

Pronunciation notes
Title In **das Paradies** the stress is on the last syllable: *para**dees***.

② Here **zwischen** *between* is used with the dative: **Zwischen dir und mir gibt es einen großen Unterschied.** *There is a big difference between you and me.*
③ **da** *there* is often used in the sense of 'in this case': **Da laufe ich lieber.** *In this case I prefer to walk.*

3 Kennen Sie nicht die Geschichte vom Paradies und der Hölle?

4 – Welche meinen Sie? Erzählen Sie mal!

5 – Das Paradies ist dort, wo der Koch Franzose ④, der Automechaniker Deutscher ⑤, der Bankier Schweizer, der Liebhaber Italiener und der Polizist Engländer ist.

6 – Ah ja ⑥? Das ist ja sehr interessant. Aber warum denn?

7 – Warten Sie, die Geschichte ist noch nicht zu Ende ⑦.

8 Die Hölle ist dagegen dort, wo der Koch Engländer, der Automechaniker Franzose, der Bankier Italiener, der Liebhaber Schweizer und der Polizist Deutscher ist.

9 – Ach, wissen Sie, für mich ist das Paradies da, wo meine Mutter kocht, unser Nachbar Automechaniker ist, wo es keine Polizei gibt, und ich selbst Bankier und Liebhaber bin …

---

3 … hœluh **4** velkHuh … **5** … kokh frantsohzuh … owtomekHahnik[a] doitsh[a] … banki-eh shveits[a] … leephahb[a] … englend[a] … **9** … nakhbah …

Notes

④ In German, nouns are used used for nationalities (**Er ist Franzose.** *He is [a] Frenchman.*) rather than adjectives (**französisch** *French*) (lesson 50). These nouns are formed in different ways: **der Engländer** *the Englishman*, but **der Deutsche** *the German*. We'll come back to this in the review lesson.

351 • dreihunderteinundfünfzig

3   Don't you know the story of paradise and hell?
4 – Which [one] do you mean? [Go on], tell [it]!
5 – Paradise is (*there*) where the cook is French, the car mechanic German, the banker Swiss, the lover Italian, and the policeman English.
6 – Oh, really? That's very interesting. But why?
7 – Wait, the story isn't finished yet.
8   Hell, in contrast, is (*there*) where the cook [is] English, the car mechanic French, the banker Italian, the lover Swiss, and the policeman German.
9 – Well, you know, for me paradise is (*there*) where my mother cooks, our neighbour is [a] car mechanic, where there are (*is*) no police and I myself am [a] banker and [a] lover ...

5 der Bankier derives from French and is pronounced with the stress on the second syllable. Also note the pronunciation of **ie** here: ban**ki-eh**.

⑤ Careful! **der Deutsche** *the German* is an adjectival noun and declines like an attributive adjective: **ein Deutscher**, but **eine Deutsche** *a German woman*.

⑥ **Ah ja?** can express surprise or doubt: *Oh, really?* However, **Ah ja!** or **Ach ja!** with an exclamation mark signals that one has (finally) understood something: *Oh, yes!* In statements, **ja** may either reinforce or challenge a declaration. Depending on intonation, the statement **Sie sind ja intelligent!** *Aren't you clever!* can be a genuine compliment or pure irony.

⑦ **das Ende** *the end*, **zu Ende sein** *to be finished, to be over*. But note: **am Ende sein** can also mean *to be at the end of one's resources* (physically, mentally, financially, etc). It's difficult to overstate the importance of prepositions in German!

67 Übung 1 – Übersetzen Sie bitte!

❶ Sie möchte einen Bankier heiraten, weil sie Geld liebt. ❷ Engländer und Franzosen sind oft ganz anderer Meinung. ❸ Meinen Sie, dass es zwischen den Ländern große Unterschiede gibt? ❹ Meine Mutter kochte sehr gut, meine Frau leider nicht! ❺ Man sagt, die Deutschen leben, um zu arbeiten und die Franzosen arbeiten, um zu leben.

***

Übung 2 – Ergänzen Sie bitte!

❶ She has the choice of (*between*) a German [man] and an Italian, but she would like a Swiss [man].

... ... die Wahl zwischen ....
und ....; aber sie möchte .....
....

❷ Let's wait a little! It seems that this story is not yet finished.

.... ein bisschen! Es scheint, dass
.... noch nicht .. .. ist.

❸ I think (*am of-the opinion*) that there is a big difference between this car and your (*informal sing.*) car.

Ich bin ... ., dass es ....
diesem .... und .... einen großen
Unterschied gibt.

❹ What are you talking about (*What tell you* [informal sing.] *there*)? I don't understand this.

Was .... da? Das ....
nicht!

❺ Which language do you (*formal*) like better? English or German?

...... Sprache gefällt ..... besser? ....
oder ....?

Answers to Exercise 1

❶ She would like to marry a banker because she loves money.
❷ The English (*Englishmen*) and the French (*Frenchmen*) are often of completely different opinion[s]. ❸ Do you think that there are big differences between the countries? ❹ My mother cooked very well; unfortunately, my wife doesn't! ❺ It is said that (*One says*) the Germans live in order to work, and the French work in order to live.

***

Answers to Exercise 2

❶ Sie hat – einem Deutschen – einem Italiener – einen Schweizer ❷ Warten wir – diese Geschichte – zu Ende – ❸ – der Meinung – zwischen – Auto – deinem Auto – ❹ – erzählst du – verstehe ich – ❺ Welche – Ihnen – Englisch – Deutsch

Sie möchte einen Bankier heiraten, weil sie Geld liebt.

Second wave: 18th lesson

68 Achtundsechzigste Lektion

Zehn Fragen zu Ihrer Allgemeinbildung ①

1 Wer erfand ② die Relativitätstheorie?
   a. Newton b. Einstein c. Galilei
2 Wen nannte ③ man den eisernen Kanzler?
   a. Otto von Bismarck b. Konrad Adenauer
   c. Helmut Kohl
3 Wem brachten ④ die Griechen ein Pferd vor die Stadttore ⑤?
   a. den Germanen b. den Trojanern
   c. den Römern
4 Wessen ⑥ Frau war die Kaiserin „Sissi"?
   a. Kaiser Franz Josephs b. Philipps des Zweiten ⑦ c. Peters des Großen
5 Wann kamen ⑧ die Gartenzwerge nach Deutschland?
   a. im 18. Jahrhundert b. im 19. Jahrhundert
   c. im 20. Jahrhundert

Pronunciation
... alguh**mein**-bildung **1** ... er**fant** ... relativi**tehts**-teo**ree 2** ... **nant**uh ... **eiz**ᵃ**nuhn kants**lᵃ **3** ... **brakh**tuhn ... **greek**H'n ... **shtat**-tohruh ... ger**mah**nuhn ... tro**yahn**ᵃn ... **rœm**ᵃn **4** ves'n ... **keiz**uhrin ... **keiz**ᵃ ... **yoh**zefs ... **fil**ips des **tsveit**'n ... **5** ... **kah**muhn ... **gart**'n-ts**ver**guh ... **akht**'tsehntuhn yah-**hund**ᵃt

Notes
① **allgemein** *common, general*; **die Bildung** *education, culture, instruction, formation.*
② **erfand** is the simple past tense of **erfinden** *to invent*. One way to learn irregular verbs is to memorize all the main forms together: infinitive, simple past tense, past participle: **erfinden, erfand, erfunden**. Not a bad idea, **nicht wahr**?

Sixty-eighth lesson 68

10 questions on your general knowledge

1. Who invented the theory of relativity?
   a. Newton b. Einstein c. Galileo
2. Who was called (*called one*) the Iron Chancellor?
   a. Otto von Bismarck b. Konrad Adenauer
   c. Helmut Kohl
3. To whom did the Greeks bring a [wooden] horse to the city gates?
   a. the ancient Germans b. the Trojans
   c. the Romans
4. Whose wife was the Empress Sissi?
   a. Emperor Franz Joseph's b. Philip II's
   c. Peter the Great's
5. When did (*the*) garden gnomes arrive in Germany?
   a. in the 18th century b. in the 19th century
   c. in the 20th century

③ **nannte** is the simple past of **nennen** *to call, to name something*.

④ **brachten** is the simple past of **bringen**; the past participle is also irregular: **gebracht** *brought*.

⑤ **das Tor** is a large *gate*, whereas **die Tür** is a *door*: **das Brandenburger Tor** *the Brandenburg Gate*.

⑥ **Wessen?** *Whose?* is the genitive interrogative pronoun, used to ask who something belongs to. It is always followed directly by a noun: **Wessen Buch ist das?** *Whose book is this?*

⑦ In the nominative, **Philipp II.** is **Philipp der Zweite** 'Philip the Second'. But the article and ordinal number decline for case: **Mary war die Frau Philipps II. (des Zweiten).** *Mary was the wife of Philip II.* **Sie war mit Philipp II. (dem Zweiten) verheiratet.** *She was married to Philip II.*

⑧ **kamen** is the simple past of **kommen** *to come, to arrive*.

dreihundertsechsundfünfzig • 356

6 Wo saß ⑨ die Lore**lei**?
  a. in **ei**nem Schiff b. auf **ei**nem **Fel**sen
  c. am **U**fer
7 Wo**her stamm**ten ⑩ die Teu**to**nen?
  a. aus **Süd**deutschland und der Schweiz
  b. aus **Ost**deutschland und **Po**len
  c. aus **Nord**deutschland und **Dä**nemark
8 **Wel**che der **fol**genden **O**pern kompo**nier**te ⑪ **Beet**hoven?
  a. Fi**de**lio b. die **Zau**berflöte
  c. die **Lus**tige **Wit**we

Die Antworten finden Sie am Ende dieser Lektion.

---

6 ... zahs ... lohruh**lei** ... shif ... felz'n ... uf⁽ᵃ⁾ **7** ... shtamt'n ... teu**toh**nuhn **8** ... kompo**neer**tuh **beht**'hohf'n ... tsowbᵃ-flœtuh ... **lus**tiguh **vit**vuh

Notes

⑨ **saß** is the simple past of **sitzen** *to sit, to be seated*. Remember that **sitzen** indicates a position rather than movement, and that the preposition following it therefore takes the dative case: **sie sitzt am (= an dem) Ufer** *she is sitting on the shore*.

***

Übung 1 – Übersetzen Sie bitte!

❶ Die Kaiserin Elisabeth lebte von achtzehnhundertsiebenunddreißig bis achtzehnhundertachtundneunzig. ❷ Wem haben Sie die Blumen gebracht? Der Frau des Kanzlers? ❸ Mozart, der aus Salzburg stammte, komponierte die Zauberflöte. ❹ Die Lorelei saß auf einem Felsen und kämmte* ihre langen, blonden Haare. ❺ Können Sie mir sagen, wessen Ehemann Philipp der Zweite war?

* Remember **der Kamm** *comb*? **kämmen** is the verb.

6 Where did the Lorelei sit?
a. in a ship b. on a rock c. on the shore
7 Where did the Teutons come from?
a. southern Germany and Switzerland
b. eastern Germany and Poland
c. northern Germany and Denmark
8 Which of the following operas did Beethoven compose?
a. Fidelio b. The Magic Flute
c. The Merry Widow

You'll find the answers at the end of this lesson.

⑩ **stammten** is the simple past of **stammen** *to come from (originally), to hail from, to originate from.*

⑪ The simple past of verbs ending in **-ieren** is regular. Consequently, the third-person singular ends in **-te**: **er komponierte** *he composed.*

***

Answers to Exercise 1

❶ The Empress Elisabeth lived from 1837 to 1898. ❷ [For] whom did you bring the flowers? For the wife of the chancellor? ❸ Mozart, who hailed from Salzburg, composed The Magic Flute. ❹ The Lorelei sat on a rock and combed her long, blonde hair. ❺ Can you tell me whose husband Philip II was?

dreihundertachtundfünfzig • 358

Übung 2 – Ergänzen Sie bitte!

❶ Do you perhaps know who invented (*the*) garden gnomes and in which century?

Wissen Sie vielleicht, ... die Gartenzwerge ...... und .. . .?

❷ Where did your grandparents [originally] come from? From Germany or [from] (*the*) Switzerland?

Woher .... eure Großeltern? Aus .... oder aus ... .?

❸ Which of Beethoven's symphonies do you think is (*find*) the most beautiful? – I like the fifth best.

...... der Symphonien .... finden Sie .. ..? – Ich mag ... . am liebsten.

❹ Whom did you (*informal*) call Sissi when you were small? Peter's friend or Helmut's sister?

... . Sissi, ... du klein warst? ...... Freundin oder .... Schwester?

❺ The Greeks brought a horse to (*before*) the city gates so that the Trojans [would] come out of the city (*out of-the city came*).

Die Griechen .... ein Pferd ... ..., damit ... . aus der Stadt ......

Answers to Exercise 2

❶ – wer – erfand – in welchem Jahrhundert ❷ – stammten – Deutschland – der Schweiz ❸ Welche – Beethovens – am schönsten – die fünfte – ❹ Wen nanntest du – als – Peters – Helmuts – ❺ – brachten – vor die Stadttore – die Trojaner – kamen

Answers to lesson dialogue: 1) b **2)** a **3)** b **4)** a **5)** c **6)** b **7)** c **8)** a

Second wave: 19th lesson

69 Neunundsechzigste Lektion

Man nimmt sich niemals genug in Acht ①

1 – Ent**schul**digen Sie, ich **su**che den **Haus**meister.
2 – Da **ha**ben Sie Pech ②, es gibt schon **lang**e **kei**nen ③ mehr bei uns.
3 – So was **Dum**mes ④! Ich muss **dring**end mit einem **Mie**ter **spre**chen.
4 – Zu wem ⑤ **wol**len Sie denn?
5 – Zu Herrn **Wör**le, **ken**nen Sie ihn?
6 – Mmm …, der **Na**me ist mir nicht ganz **un**bekannt.
7 Was **wol**len Sie denn von ihm?
8 – Das ist ver**trau**lich, das darf ich ihm nur per**sön**lich **sa**gen.
9 – Ich ver**steh**e. Ist es **et**was sehr **Schlim**mes?
10 – Schlimm? Aber nein! **G**anz im **G**e**g**enteil!

Pronunciation
*3 … **dring**'nt … **meet**ᵃ … 5 … **vœ**ᵃluh … 8 … fer**trow**likH … per**zœn**likH … 9 … **shlim**es*

Notes

① **sich in Acht nehmen** *to be careful, to take care, to look after oneself*; so the title literally means 'One takes never enough care of oneself'. **Acht** is an old Germanic word also found in **Achtung** *attention*.

② **das Pech** *pitch* (the tarry substance) also means *bad luck*.

Sixty-ninth lesson 69

One can never be careful enough

1 – Excuse me, I am looking for the caretaker.
2 – You're out of luck there (*There have you bad-luck*), we've not had one for a long time (*there is already long not anymore with us*).
3 – Oh, that's a nuisance (*Such something stupid*)! I must urgently speak with a tenant.
4 – To whom do you want [to speak]?
5 – To Mr Wörle, do you know him?
6 – Hmm ... the name isn't completely unknown to me.
7 What do you want from him then?
8 – That's confidential; (*this*) I can only tell him in person (*personally*).
9 – I understand. Is it something very bad?
10 – Bad? (*But*) no! Completely the *(in)* opposite!

③ **keinen** *no, not a, not any, none* is the accusative masculine of the negative article **keiner, keine, keins**.

④ **So was (etwas) Dummes!** *That's annoying!* The adjective **dumm** *stupid, silly* is turned into a neuter noun by adding the ending **-es** and a capital letter. The same is the case in **etwas Schlimmes** *something bad*, where the adjective **schlimm** *bad* is used as a noun expressing an abstract concept.

⑤ Although in English we would say 'To whom do you want to speak?', the understood verb here is **gehen**: 'To whom do you want to go?'. Remember that **gehen** doesn't have to be stated in German, as the preposition **zu** already indicates movement.

69
11 Unter uns – aber sagen Sie es niemandem weiter – er hat im Lotto gewonnen ⑥.
12 – Was sagen Sie da? Hören Sie, ich bin Herr Wörle.
13 Wie viel ist es denn?
14 – Leider nicht viel, Herr Wörle, verzeihen Sie mir bitte die Lüge!
15 In Wahrheit komme ich nämlich ⑦ vom Finanzamt ⑧ und muss mich mit Ihnen ein bisschen unterhalten.

11 … loto guvonuhn 14 ... fertsei'n … lewguh 15 … vah{ª}heit … finants-amt ...

Notes

⑥ **gewonnen** is the past participle of **gewinnen** *to win* (the **ge-** is already there in the present tense): **Wer wagt, gewinnt!** ('Who dares wins!') *Nothing ventured, nothing gained.*

⑦ Remember **nämlich**? Like **denn** *because, as*, it justifies what has just been said. **Das darf ich nicht sagen, das ist nämlich vertraulich = denn das ist vertraulich.** *I mustn't tell, as this is confidential.* (lesson 57, note 1)

⑧ **das Amt** is a public office, an official agency: **das Arbeitsamt** *job centre, employment office* ('the work-office'), **das Zollamt** *customs office*, etc.

***

Übung 1 – Übersetzen Sie bitte!

❶ Was suchen Sie? Einen Zahnarzt? Hier gibt es keinen mehr. ❷ Was ich Ihnen jetzt sage, ist vertraulich! ❸ Der Name ist mir leider unbekannt. ❹ Nimm dich in Acht! Der Mann scheint vom Finanzamt zu kommen. ❺ Ich muss Sie dringend persönlich sprechen.

11 [Just] between us – but don't tell anyone (*tell you it to-no-one further*) – he has won the lottery.
12 – What are you saying (*there*)? Listen, I am Mr Wörle!
13 So how much is it?
14 – Unfortunately not much, Mr Wörle, please forgive me [for] the lie!
15 In truth I am (*come*) actually from the tax office and I must have a little talk with you (*must myself with you a little discuss*).

Was suchen Sie? Einen Zahnarzt?

***

Answers to Exercise 1

❶ What are you looking for? A dentist? There isn't one here anymore. ❷ What I am telling you now is confidential! ❸ Unfortunately, this name is unknown to me. ❹ Be careful! This man seems to come from the tax office. ❺ I urgently have to talk to you personally.

dreihundertvierundsechzig • 364

70 Übung 2 – Ergänzen Sie bitte!

❶ Excuse (*formal*) [us], we're looking for the caretaker; is there not one here?

...., wir suchen ...
..........; gibt es hier ......?

❷ That's a lie! Be careful (*Take you yourself in care*), as we all know the truth.

Das ist ....! Nehmen Sie sich .. ....,
wir kennen nämlich alle ... .

❸ I urgently have to [go to see] Mr Wörle. Do you (*formal*) know him?

Ich muss .... Wörle. ......
... ...?

---

70 Siebzigste Lektion

Wiederholung – Review

1 The simple past tense

The simple past tense, like the present perfect tense, is used to refer to events in the past. It is often called the narrative past because it recounts a series of connected events in the past. It is more common in formal writing such as literature, newspaper articles, etc. (The present perfect tense is usually used in conversational contexts.) It corresponds to both the English simple past (*I went*) and the past progressive (*I was going*).

1.1 Conjugation

Note that the first- and third-person singular forms are the same in this tense. Hence the third-person singular never ends in **-t**, unlike in the present tense.

④ I have to speak to you personally; I have something very interesting to tell you.
Ich muss Sie .... , ich habe Ihnen .... zu sagen.

⑤ I know that she has won the lottery, but we have to keep this [just] between us (*this must under us stay*).
Ich weiß, dass ... im Lotto ...., aber das muss .... bleiben.

Answers to Exercise 2

① Entschuldigen Sie – den Hausmeister – keinen ② – eine Lüge – in Acht – die Wahrheit ③ – dringend zu Herrn – Kennen Sie ihn ④ – persönlich sprechen – etwas sehr Interessantes – ⑤ – sie – gewonnen hat – unter uns –

Second wave: 20th lesson

Seventieth lesson   70

• **Regular (weak) verbs**
These add the endings **-te**, **-test**, **-te**, **-ten**, **-tet**, **-ten** to the verb stem. Weak verbs with a stem ending in **-d**, **-t** or **-n** insert an **-e** before these endings.

	fragen *to ask*	antworten *to answer*	öffnen *to open*
ich	fragte	antwortete	öffnete
du	fragtest	antwortetest	öffnetest
er/sie/es	fragte	antwortete	öffnete
wir	fragten	antworteten	öffneten
ihr	fragtet	antwortetet	öffnetet
sie (and **Sie**)	fragten	antworteten	öffneten

- **Irregular (strong) verbs**

These undergo a stem vowel change, and the tense marker **-te** is not added. All forms except the first- and third-person singular add verb endings to the simple past tense stem:

	kommen *to come*	gehen *to go*	nehmen *to take*	ziehen *to pull*
ich	kam	ging	nahm	zog
du	kamst	gingst	nahmst	zogst
er/sie/es	kam	ging	nahm	zog
wir	kamen	gingen	nahmen	zogen
ihr	kamt	gingt	nahmt	zogt
sie (and Sie)	kamen	gingen	nahmen	zogen

- **Mixed verbs**

These are regular verbs that have a stem vowel change – and occasionally a consonant change – as well as add the simple past tense marker **-te** to the stem (for this reason they are often called irregular weak verbs). There are only eight:
– **bringen** *to bring* → **ich brachte, du brachtest,** etc.
also: **denken** *to think*
– **nennen** *to call, to name* → **ich nannte, du nanntest,** etc.
also: **brennen** *to burn*, **kennen** *to know*, and **rennen** *to run*
– **wenden** *to turn* → **ich wandte, du wandtest,** etc. (or **ich wendete**)
also: **senden** *to send*

Note that these verbs form the past participle by adding the **ge-** prefix and a final **-t** to the simple past tense stem: **gebracht** *brought*, **genannt** *called*, **gewandt** *turned*.

- **Modal verbs**

These take the same simple past endings as regular (weak) verbs, adding these to the stem after dropping the umlaut (**mögen** also has a consonant change). The verb **wissen** equally takes these endings, but also has a stem vowel change. Note the difference with the modal verb stems in the present tense (see lesson 35).

Infinitive	1st-person past	1st-person present
können *can, to be able to*	ich konnte	ich kann
müssen *must, to have to*	ich musste	ich muss
sollen *should, to be supposed to*	ich sollte	ich soll
dürfen *may, to be permitted to*	ich durfte	ich darf
wollen *to want, to wish, to intend to*	ich wollte	ich will
mögen *to like, to want to*	ich mochte*	ich mag
wissen *to know*	ich wußte	ich weiß

* Be careful to pronounce **ich mochte** with an **o** followed by a guttural **ch** *[**mokh**tuh]* and not to confuse it with the subjunctive **ich möchte** *I would like*, which is pronounced **mœkH***tuh*.

1.2 Stem vowel changes

In the last review lesson we looked at typical stem vowel changes in the past participles of irregular verbs. Now we can complete this overview with the stem changes in the simple past tense. You'll find the main irregular verbs in the grammatical appendix:

Infinitive	1st-person simple past	Past participle
schlafen *to sleep*	schlief	geschlafen
geben *to give*	gab	gegeben
sprechen *to speak*	sprach	gesprochen
bleiben *to stay*	blieb	geblieben
trinken *to drink*	trank	getrunken
beginnen *to begin*	begann	begonnen
verbieten *to forbid*	verbot	verboten

Although there are some rules, the stem vowel change in the simple past tense cannot always be predicted, so it is best to learn the verbs one by one. (Fortunately, the number of irregular verbs is relatively small.) For our part, we'll make sure to point them out as often as possible. You could also copy them on post-its and put them on the fridge door or somewhere else you'll see them several times a day. You could even practice them in the shower ... in which case you might want to laminate the list!

2 The interrogatives *Wer?*, *Was?* and *Welcher?*

• **Wer?** *Who?* declines like the masculine definite article (except in the genitive):

<u>nominative</u>: **Wer?** *Who?* (subject) →
Wer bist du? – Karl. *Who are you? – Karl.*

<u>accusative</u>: **Wen?** *Whom?* (direct object) →
Wen liebst du? – Sylvia. *Whom do you love? – Sylvia.*

<u>dative</u>: **Wem?** *To whom?* (indirect object) →
Wem zeigst du die Stadt? – Sylvia.
To whom are you showing the city? – To Sylvia.

<u>genitive</u>: **Wessen?** *Whose?* (possession) →
Wessen Freund bist du? – Sylvia̲s Freund/der Freund <u>von</u> Sylvia. *Whose friend are you? – Sylvia's friend.*

All these forms refer to people and are often answered with a person's name. Proper names don't decline, except in the genitive, when they take an **s** ending (but <u>no apostrophe</u>): **Sylvias Freund** *Sylvia's friend.*

If the answer is not a proper name, the article mirrors the case of the interrogative pronoun:

Wer **spricht gut Deutsch?** *Who speaks German well?*
– der **Onkel aus Amerika**

Wen **treffen Sie um 15 Uhr?** *Whom [will] you meet at 3 pm?*
– den **Onkel aus Amerika**

Wem schreiben Sie einen Brief? *To whom are you writing a letter?*
– **dem Onkel aus Amerika**

Wessen Auto ist das? *Whose car is this?*
– **das Auto des Onkels* aus Amerika** or **das Auto von dem Onkel aus Amerika**

* Note that the genitive is usually accompanied by a noun (here **das Auto**).

- **Was?** *What?* refers to things or ideas and has only one form:
Was ist das? *What is this?*
Was essen Sie? *What are you eating?*

- **Welcher?** (m.), **Welche?** (f.), **Welches?** (neuter) *Which?* decline like the definite article. (But note that the genitive of **welcher** is no longer used.)

Welcher Bahnhof ist in der Nähe? *Which station is nearby?*
Welche U-Bahn fährt dorthin? *Which subway goes there?*
Welches Gleis suchen Sie? *Which platform are you looking for?*
Welchen Zug nehmen Sie? *Which train are you taking?*
Von welchem Gleis? *From which platform?*

Finally, remember that in indirect questions, the conjugated verb occurs in the last position:
Frag Papa, wen man „Sissi" nannte.
Ask Dad who was called 'Sissi' ('whom one 'Sissi' called').
Wissen Sie, wessen Freundin sie ist?
Do you know whose friend she is?
Er will wissen, welches der Bücher am interessantesten ist.
He wants to know which of the books is most interesting.

Once again, don't worry! You aren't expected to retain all this information immediately. The aim is to reveal the workings of the language to you gradually.

3 Countries and their inhabitants

Let's look at **die Länder und ihre Einwohner**. The names of countries and continents are normally neuter, and they are used without an article.

Österreich liegt im Süden Mitteleuropas. Es hat neun Bundesländer. *Austria is situated in the south of Central Europe. It has nine federal states.*

A small number of countries are exceptions to these rules:
• <u>masculine</u>: **der Libanon** *Lebanon*, **der Sudan** *Sudan*, **der Irak** *Iraq*, **der Iran** *Iran*
• <u>feminine</u>: **die Bundesrepublik** *the Federal Republic*, **die Tschechische République** (or **Tschechien**) *the Czech Republic*, **die Slowakische Republik** (or **die Slowakei**) *Slovakia*, **die Schweiz** *Switzerland*, **die Türkei** *Turkey*, **die Antarktis** *Antarctica*
• <u>plural</u>: **die USA** = **die Vereinigten Staaten** *the United States*, **die Niederlande** *the Netherlands*.

Nationalities are derived from the names of countries and follow several patterns. To state a person's nationality, a noun (rather than an adjective) is used, directly after a form of **sein** (with no indefinite article): **Ich bin Ire.** *I am Irish.* ('I am Irishman.')

Here's a quick overview:

• The vast majority of nouns indicating male inhabitants of a country are formed by adding the suffix **-er**. They don't change in the plural: **der/die Amerikaner, der/die Australier, der/die Italiener, der/die Japaner, der/die Schweizer** (*Swiss*), **der/die Österreicher** (*Austrian*), **der/die Iraner**, etc.

Some nouns take an umlaut: **England → der Engländer, Thailand → der Thailänder, Neuseeland → der Neuseeländer** (*New Zealander*).

In some instances, **-er** is added to a modified form of the country: **Wales → der/die Waliser** (*Welshman*), **Kanada → der/die Kanadier** (*Canadian*).

To indicate a female inhabitant, the additional suffix **-in** (singular) or **-innen** (plural) is added to the **-er** suffix: **die Amerikanerin/die Amerikanerinnen, die Italienerin/Italienerinnen, die Engländerin/Engländerinnen, die Japanerin/Japanerinnen, die Waliserin/die Waliserinnen,** etc.

371 • **dreihunderteinundsiebzig**

- Many other nouns denoting male inhabitants of a country end in -e. These are weak masculine nouns ('n-nouns') and thus add an -n in all cases (except the nominative singular) as well as in the plural: **der Schwede/die Schweden** (*Swede/Swedes*), **der Schotte/die Schotten** (*Scotsman/Scotsmen*), **der Franzose/die Franzosen, der Chinese/die Chinesen, der Pole/die Polen, der Grieche/die Griechen** (*Greek/Greeks*). (**der Ungar** *the Hungarian* and **der Zypriot** *the Cypriot* also fall into this category, even though they don't end in -e.)

The female equivalent drops the -e and adds -in (singular) or -innen (plural) and is, of course, not weak: **die Französin** (note the umlaut!)/**die Französinnen; die Chinesin/die Chinesinnen, die Polin/die Polinnen, die Griechin/die Griechinnen**.

- The noun for male inhabitants of some countries ends in -i and forms the plural by adding -s:
der Israeli(-s), der Pakistani(-s) (or **der Pakistaner**), **der Somali(-s)**

The feminine form adds an -n in the singular and -nnen in the plural: **die Israelin, die Israelinnen**.

- The big exception to the rules above is the adjectival noun **der Deutsche** *the German* (masc. sing.), the female equivalent being **die Deutsche** and the plural **die Deutschen**. An adjectival noun takes exactly the same endings as an adjective. The difference between **der Deutsche** and **der Schwede**, for example, may not immediately meet the eye, but add the indefinite article and it becomes apparent: **ein Schwede** but **ein Deutscher**; **eine Schwedin** but **eine Deutsche**. There is no feminine plural form, but you can always work around this by saying **die deutschen Frauen** *the German women*.

And now, after all this grammar, finish up with the review exercise to put into practice what you've learned.

70 Review exercise

Woher stammen eigentlich die Germanen?

1. Viele Deutsche fahren in den Ferien nach Italien, Frankreich, Griechenland oder Spanien.
2. Ich habe das auch fast zwanzig Jahre lang gemacht.
3. Ich dachte, man erlebt mehr, wenn man in ein anderes Land fährt.
4. Heute bin ich anderer Meinung.
5. Eigentlich habe ich es schon immer anstrengend gefunden, am Meer zu sitzen und nichts zu tun.
6. Meine Frau hat das nie verstanden, im Gegenteil!
7. Wenn sie am Meer saß, Zeitung las und Eis aß, fühlte sie sich wie im Paradies.
8. Aber als wir vor zwei Jahren nach Mallorca gefahren sind, war sie auch enttäuscht.
9. Sie sagte: „Wenn alle Nachbarn Deutsche sind, kann ich ebenso gut in Deutschland bleiben."
10. Deshalb wollen meine Frau und ich unseren 24. Hochzeitstag nicht auf den Balearen feiern, sondern im Teutoburger Wald.
11. Dort hat nämlich der Germane Hermann – die Römer nannten ihn Arminius – mit ein bisschen Überlegung die Römer geschlagen.
12. Ja, die Römer hatten Pech.
13. Unsere Geschichte ist wirklich sehr interessant.
14. Ich kann Ihnen nur empfehlen, auch Ihre nächsten Ferien in Deutschland zu verbringen.
15. Außerdem ist es sehr gut für die Allgemeinbildung…

Translation
Where do the ancient Germans actually come from?

1 Many Germans go on holiday to Italy, France, Greece or Spain. **2** I have also done so (*this*) [for] almost 20 years. **3** I thought one experiences more when one goes to another country. **4** Today, I am of another opinion. **5** In fact, I have (*already*) always found it tiring to sit by (*at*) the sea and do nothing. **6** My wife never understood this – on (*in*) the contrary! **7** When she sat by the sea, reading a newspaper and eating an ice cream (*newspaper was-reading and ice cream was-eating*), she felt (*herself*) like [she was] in (*the*) paradise. **8** But when we went to Majorca two years ago, she was disappointed, too. **9** She said: 'If all [our] neighbours are Germans, then I might (*can*) as well stay in Germany.' **10** Therefore my wife and I are not going (*want not*) to celebrate our 24th wedding anniversary on the Balearic Islands, but in the Teutoburg Forest. **11** As [it is] there that the ancient German *Hermann* – the Romans called him *Arminius* – defeated the Romans with a little reflection. **12** Yes, the Romans had bad luck. **13** Our history is really very interesting. **14** I can only advise you to spend your next holiday in Germany as well. **15** Moreover, it's very good for [one's] general knowledge …

***

Der Teutoburger Wald is a low mountain range (**ein Mittelgebirge**) *in Westphalia, in northwestern Germany, between Kassel and Hanover. The Battle of the Teutoburg Forest (***die Schlacht im Teutoburger Wald*** *or* ***die Varusschlacht****) took place near Kalkriese in 9 CE when an alliance of Germanic tribes led by Arminius of the Cherusci ambushed and defeated three Roman legions. Later, this ancient battle would have a profound effect on German nationalism. In the 19th century, Germany was still divided into many states, but Germans came to identify the Germanic tribes as shared ancestors of one 'German people' and to associate forces such as Napoleonic France and the Austro-Hungarian Empire with the invading Romans. To commemorate the battle, the* **Hermannsdenkmal**, *a monument to Hermann surmounted by a 53.46 m (173.39 ft) statue, was erected in a forested area near Detmold. It was completed in 1875 and is still a very popular tourist attraction.*

Second wave: 21st lesson

71 **Einundsiebzigste Lektion**

„Vater werden ist nicht schwer,
Vater sein dagegen sehr."

1 – **Kin**der, wacht auf ①!
2 Es ist halb **sie**ben ②, ihr müsst **auf**stehen.

Nach einer Viertelstunde

3 Wo bleibt ihr denn? Ich **ha**be euch vor **ein**er **Vier**telstunde ge**weck**t ③.
4 Los, raus aus den **Bet**ten, sonst kann ich euch nicht in die **Schu**le **mit**nehmen!
5 Be**eilt** euch! Ich muss **spä**testens zehn nach **sie**ben los ④.

*Zehn Mi**nu**ten später*

6 Hört mal! Es ist fast **sie**ben und ihr habt euch noch nicht mal ⑤ ge**wa**schen.
7 Ich ver**steh**e nicht, was mit euch los ⑥ ist.

Pronunciation
1 ... vakht owf *3* ... guh**vekt** *4* ... be**tuhn** zonst ... **shoo**luh ... *5* buh-**eilt** ... **shpeh**tuhstuhns ... *6* ... guh**va**sh'n

Notes

① **aufwachen** *to wake up* and **aufstehen** *to get up* are separable-prefix verbs: **ich wache auf** *I wake up*, **wir stehen auf** *we get up*.

② Remember that **halb sieben** means *half past six* in German because the half hour is counted in relation to the following hour, as if there were a 'to'. So **halb zwei** *one-thirty* ('half [to] two'), **halb fünf** *four-thirty* ('half [to] five'), etc.

③ **jemanden wecken** *to wake someone*; **der Wecker** *alarm clock* (literally, 'the waker').

375 • dreihundertfünfundsiebzig

Seventy-first lesson 71

**'Becoming a father isn't hard;
but being one is (*very*).'**

1 – Children, wake up!
2   It's half past six (*half [to] seven*), you have to get up.

A quarter of an hour later
3   Where are (*remain*) you? I woke you a quarter of an hour ago.
4   Come on, get out of bed (*the beds*), otherwise I can't take you to school (*not into the school with-take*).
5   Hurry up! I have to [leave] – at the latest – at ten past seven (*away*).

Ten minutes later
6   Listen! It's nearly seven and you haven't even (*have yourselves not yet once*) washed.
7   I don't understand what's wrong with you.

④ When used with a modal verb, **los** means 'to leave': **Wir müssen los.** *We have to leave.*

⑤ Careful! **nicht mal** (the colloquial version of **nicht einmal**) means *not even*. 'Not once' would be **nicht ein einziges Mal** *not one single time*.

⑥ You know the expression **Was ist los?** *What's up? What's wrong?* Here we have a 'personalized' version: **Was ist los mit dir (euch, ihm,** etc.**)?** *What's up with you (you [pl.], him,* etc.*)?* By itself, **los** can also mean *Come on!* or *Let's go!*

dreihundertsechsundsiebzig • 376

71 8   Habt ihr **kei**ne Lust **auf**zustehen oder seid ihr **ein**fach **wie**der **ein**geschlafen ⑦?
   9 – Nee, **Pa**pa, das ist es nicht.
  10 – So? Was ist es denn dann?
  11 – Wir **geh**en ab **heu**te nicht mehr in die **Schu**le.
  12 – Wie **bi**tte? ⑧ Wann habt ihr denn das be**schlos**sen ⑨?
  13 – **Ges**tern Abend, als du uns er**klärt** hast, dass das **Le**ben die **bes**te **Schu**le ist.
  14   Wir **fin**den das auch.

---

8 ... ein**guh**shlahf'n **12** ... buh**shloss**'n **13** ... er**klehrt** ...

Notes

⑦ **einschlafen** *to fall asleep* is also a separable-prefix verb: **ich schlafe ein** *I fall asleep*. Note that **aufwachen** and **einschlafen** denote a change of state and therefore form the present perfect tense with **sein**: **ich bin eingeschlafen** *I have fallen asleep, I fell asleep*.

⑧ **Wie bitte?** *Pardon?, I beg your pardon?, Sorry?, Excuse me?*

⑨ **beschlossen** is the past participle of **beschließen** *to decide*. Don't confuse it with **schließen** *to close* and its past participle **geschlossen**.

***

Übung 1 – Übersetzen Sie bitte!

❶ Er ist um halb fünf aufgewacht, aber gleich wieder eingeschlafen. ❷ Ich finde nicht, dass Deutsch schwer ist. ❸ Beeilen Sie sich bitte! Wir müssen in fünf Minuten los. ❹ Können Sie mich bitte morgen früh um Viertel vor sieben wecken? ❺ Sie haben mir nicht einmal „Guten Tag" gesagt!

8 Don't you feel like getting up or have you just fallen asleep again?
9 – No, Dad, it's not that.
10 – Well, what is it then?
11 – From today, we aren't going to school anymore.
12 – Pardon? When did you decide this then?
13 – Yesterday evening, when you explained to us that life is the best school.
14 We agree with you (*We find that too*).

> Er ist um halb fünf aufgewacht, aber gleich wieder eingeschlafen

***

Answers to Exercise 1

❶ He woke up at 4:30, but fell asleep again immediately. ❷ I don't think that German is difficult. ❸ Hurry up, please! We have to leave in five minutes. ❹ Could you (*Can you*) wake me at a quarter to seven tomorrow morning (*tomorrow early*), please? ❺ They didn't even say 'Good afternoon' to me!

Übung 2 – Ergänzen Sie bitte!

❶ When did you get up today?
Wann .... heute ....?

❷ Hurry up (*you*[inf. sing.]), otherwise we[′ll] arrive too late.
...., ... kommen wir zu spät.

❸ Come on, you have to get up; it is already 7:30.
..., ihr müsst ...., es ist schon ....
.....

❹ When did you (*formal*) decide not to go to the office anymore?
Wann ...., nicht mehr
ins Büro .. ..?

Zweiundsiebzigste Lektion

Dreimal dürfen Sie raten

1 Wer ist der **Schrift**steller,
2 a) der oft **eine Bas**kenmütze trug, ob**wohl** ①
er **Deut**scher war?
3 b) den **kei**ne **Un**gerechtigkeit **gleich**gültig
ließ ②?

Pronunciation
1 ... **shrift**-shtel[a] **2** ... **bas**k'n-mewtsuh ... op**vohl** ...
3 ... **un**guhrekHtikHkeit ... **gleikH**'gewltikH lees

Notes

① **obwohl** *although, even though.* Remember the subject and the verb in the main clause are inverted if a sentence starts with a subordinate clause: **Obwohl er sehr müde ist, geht er nicht ins Bett.** *Even though he is very tired, he doesn't go to bed.*

⑤ Three days ago, I couldn't wake up, and today I can't fall asleep, do you (*informal*) understand this?

... ... konnte ich nicht ....
und heute kann ich nicht ....,
....?

Answers to Exercise 2

❶ – sind Sie/seid ihr – aufgestanden ❷ Beeil dich, sonst – ❸ Los – aufstehen – halb acht ❹ – haben Sie beschlossen – zu gehen ❺ Vor drei Tagen – aufwachen – einschlafen – verstehst du das

Second wave: 22nd lesson

Seventy-second lesson

You have three guesses
(*Three-times may you guess*)

1 Who is the writer:
2 a) who often wore a beret even though he was German?
3 b) whom no injustice left indifferent (*indifferent left*)?

② **ließ** is the third-person singular simple past of **lassen** *to let, to permit*; the past participle is **gelassen** *let, permitted*.

72 4 c) dem man 1972 (**neun**zehn**hun**dert**zwei**-
und**sieb**zig) den **No**bel**p**reis für Litera**tur**
ver**lieh** ③?

5 d) **de**ssen ④ **Kriegs**erzählungen **Tau**sende
zu ⑤ Pazifisten **mach**ten?

6 Wer ist die **blon**de **Schau**spielerin,
7 a) die als **Lo**la in dem Film „Der **blaue**
Engel" berühmt **wur**de?
8 b) die nicht nur die **Män**ner, **son**dern auch
viele **Frau**en vergötterten?
9 c) der die **größ**ten Regis**seu**re **Haupt**rollen
anboten ⑥?
10 d) **de**ren **Stim**me noch **heu**te leicht
zu er**ken**nen ist, weil sie ein **we**nig
„**rau**chig ⑦" klingt?

---

*4 ... nointsehn-hund^at'tsvei'untzeeptsikH ... nobel-preis ...
lit'ratu^a ferlee 5 dess'n kreeks-ertsehlung'n ... patsifistuhn
... 6 ... showshpeeluhrin 7 ... eng'l ... 8 ... fergœt^atuhn
9 ... rezhisœruh ... 10 dehruhn shtimuh ... rowkhiKH ...*

Notes

③ The infinitive of **verlieh** is **verleihen** *to award*, and the past participle is **verliehen**.

④ The singular forms of the relative pronoun are the same as the definite article (**der**, **die**, **das**, etc.), except in the genitive: **dessen** (m.), **deren** (f.) and **dessen** (neuter) *whose*. Another feature of genitive relative pronouns is that they are always followed directly by a noun: **Das ist ein Schriftsteller, dessen Bücher niemanden gleichgültig lassen.** *This is a writer whose books leave no one indifferent.*

4 c) to whom the Nobel Prize for Literature was awarded in 1972?
5 d) whose war stories made thousands [in]to pacifists?

6 Who is the blonde actress:
7 a) who became famous as Lola in the film 'The Blue Angel'?
8 b) whom not only men but also many women adored?
9 c) to whom the greatest directors offered leading roles?
10 d) whose voice is still (*today*) easy to recognize because it sounds a little husky?

Pronunciation note
9 der Regisseur is a loan word from French, so the 'g' retains its original French pronunciation, like the *zh* sound in *vision*. The final **-e** of the plural **die Regisseure** must be pronounced: *rezhisœruh*.

⑤ **jemanden zu etwas machen** *to make someone into something*: **Sie machte ihn zu ihrem Liebhaber.** *She made him (into) her lover.* Remember that **zu** always takes the dative case.

⑥ **anboten** is the third-person plural simple past of **anbieten** *to offer*. In a subordinate clause introduced by a conjunction or a relative pronoun, the separable prefix – here **an** – reattaches itself to the verb: **Der Kaffee, den er uns anbietet, ist gut.** *The coffee that he offers us is good.* In contrast, in a main clause, the separable prefix occurs in the last position: **Er bietet uns Kaffee an.** *He offers us coffee.*

⑦ **rauchig** *smoky*, here in the sense of *husky*, derives from **rauchen** *to smoke*.

11 Wie **heiß**en die **bei**den ⑧ **deut**schen **Dich**ter,
12 a) die sich **Hun**derte von **Brie**fen **schrie**ben?
13 b) die man „die **groß**en **deut**schen **Kla**ssiker" nennt?
14 c) von **de**nen ⑨ **a**lle **Schul**kinder **min**destens ein Werk stu**die**ren **müs**sen?
15 d) **de**ren **Sta**tue vor dem The**a**ter in **Wei**mar steht? ☐

Die Lösungen finden Sie am Ende der Lektion.

*11 ... **bei**duhn ... 14 ... **deh**nuhn ... **min**duhstuhns ... verk ...*
*15 ... **shtah**tu-uh ...*

Notes

⑧ **die beiden** *the two* can also be used without the article: **beide** *both*.

⑨ **denen** is the dative plural relative pronoun.

***

Übung 1 – Übersetzen Sie bitte!

❶ Sie erkennt sofort die Stimme des Mannes, der sie anruft. ❷ Wissen Sie, wer den letzten Nobelpreis für Literatur bekommen hat? ❸ Heinrich Böll wurde durch seine Kriegserzählungen berühmt. ❹ Wie heißt der deutsche Dichter, dessen Namen alle Schulkinder kennen? ❺ Marlene Dietrich, deren Geburtsstadt Berlin ist, ist in Paris gestorben.

11 What are the names of the two German poets: **72**
12 a) who wrote each other hundreds of letters?
13 b) who are known as 'the great German classics' (*whom one '…' calls*)?
14 c) of whose works all schoolchildren have to study at least one (*by whom all schoolchildren at-least one work study must*)?
15 d) whose statue stands in front of the theatre in Weimar?

You['ll] find the answers at the end of the lesson.

> Wissen Sie, wer den letzten Nobelpreis für Literatur bekommen hat?

***

Answers to Exercise 1

❶ She immediately recognizes the voice of the man who phones her. ❷ Do you know who received the last Nobel Prize for Literature? ❸ Heinrich Böll became famous for his war stories. ❹ What is the German poet called whose name all schoolchildren know? ❺ Marlene Dietrich – whose birthplace was (*is*) Berlin – died in Paris.

Übung 2 – Ergänzen Sie bitte!

❶ Who is the woman whose photo is (*stands*) on your desk?

Wer ist ... ., ... auf deinem Schreibtisch .....?

❷ The actor, whose name I've forgotten, has played the leading role in many films.

... ., ... Namen ich vergessen habe, hat in vielen Filmen ...

....

❸ Who was the writer who wrote 'Faust'?

... war ... ., ... „Faust" .... hat?

***

Heinrich Böll

Heinrich Böll (1917–85) is one of the most widely known German authors of the post-World War II period. He was awarded the Nobel Prize for Literature in 1972. Böll grew up in a Catholic family in Cologne and began writing before World War II. His early published works, such as **Der Zug war pünktlich** *The Train Was on Time (1949) and* **Wo warst du Adam?** *And Where Were You, Adam? (1951), as well as the short story collection* **Wanderer, kommst du nach Spa…*** *Passer-by, If You Come to Spa... (1950), centre on the war and the devastating material and psychological effects it had on ordinary people. In the period of the 'economic miracle' (1950s–70s), Böll made his name not only as a bestselling author, but also as a socially engaged, and at times controversial, commentator on the state of Germany. His novels* **Billiard um halb zehn** *Billiards at Half-past Nine,* **Ansichten eines Clowns** *The Clown and* **Gruppenbild mit Dame** *Group Portrait with Lady contain often biting critiques of what he perceived as the conformism, lack of courage, and abuse of power by authority figures in government, business and the church in post-war West*

❹ He still has (*today still*) friends to whom he writes a letter at least once a year.
Er hat .... Freunde, ... er
.... einmal im Jahr .... schreibt.

❺ Even though she has never smoked, she has a husky voice.
...... sie nie ...., hat sie ....
....

Answers to Exercise 2

❶ – die Frau, deren Foto – steht ❷ Der Schauspieler, dessen – die Hauptrolle gespielt ❸ Wer – der Schriftsteller, der – geschrieben – ❹ – heute noch – denen – mindestens – einen Brief – ❺ Obwohl – geraucht hat – eine rauchige Stimme

Answers to lesson dialogue: 1) Heinrich Böll **2)** Marlene Dietrich **3)** Johann Wolfgang von Goethe und Friedrich Schiller

***

Germany. Böll was also the main German intellectual involved in the 1970s debates concerning the terrorism of the left-wing Red Army Faction, which provided the backdrop to one of his best-known novels, **Die verlorene Ehre der Katharina Blum** The Lost Honour of Katharina Blum *(1974).*

* *The title is a reference to an epigram by Simonides that was inscribed on a commemorative stone placed on top of the burial mound of the Spartans at Thermopylae. The epigram is usually translated as:*
   Go tell the Spartans, stranger passing by,
   that here obedient to their laws we lie.

Are you worried about the increasing amount of new vocabulary? Don't be! Simply go through the lessons at your own pace and don't tie yourself in knots trying to memorize every last thing. You'll come across many of these words and expressions again in upcoming lessons, which will help you to remember them.

Second wave: 23rd lesson

73 Dreiundsiebzigste Lektion

Ein Tierfreund ①

1 – Wenn ich **rich**tig ver**stan**den **ha**be, **spre**chen Sie **al**so zwölf **Fremd**sprachen **flie**ßend ②?
2 **Darf** ich Sie **nach** ③ **Ih**rem **Wun**dermittel **fra**gen?
3 – **Wun**dermittel **ha**be ich gar keins ④.
4 **Mei**ne Me**tho**de ist die **ein**fachste, die man sich **vor**stellen kann:
5 Sie **spre**chen, **hö**ren, **le**sen und **den**ken – das ist sehr **wich**tig – nur in der **Spra**che, die Sie **ler**nen.
6 – Sie **mei**nen, Sie **fah**ren in das Land, **des**sen **Spra**che Sie **ler**nen?
7 – **A**ber nein! Ich **blei**be zu **Hau**se, ich bin doch nicht von **ges**tern!
8 Wo**zu le**ben wir in **ei**ner Welt, in der es **Ka**belfernsehen und **In**ternet gibt?

Pronunciation
... tee^a-froint **1** ... **fremt**-shprah-kh'n **flees**'nt **2** ... **vund**^a-mit'l ... **3** ... gah^a ... **4** ... me**toh**duh ... **8** ... **kahb**'l-fern'zehn ... **int**^anet ...

Notes
① Although **das Tier** *animal* is neuter, **der Tierfreund** is masculine because of **der Freund** *friend*. Many German nouns that indicate a preference for something are constructed with -freund: **der Menschenfreund** *philanthropist*, **der Musikfreund** *music lover*, **der Käsefreund** *cheese lover*, etc.

Seventy-third lesson 73

An animal lover (*animal-friend*)

1 – If I understood correctly (*right*), (*so*) you speak 12 foreign languages fluently?
2   May I ask (*you*) your magic formula (*after your miracle-means*)?
3 – Magic formula[?] I have none (*at all*).
4   My method is the easiest you (*one*) can (*oneself*) imagine:
5   you speak, listen, read and think – that's very important – only in the language (*that*) you're learning.
6 – You mean, you go to the country whose language you're learning?
7 – But no! I stay at home – I wasn't born (*I am not from*) yesterday!
8   Why (*What-for*) are we living in a world where (*in which*) there is cable TV and [the] internet?

② **fließend** *flowing* is the present participle of **fließen** *to flow*; in the context of speaking languages it means *fluent*. It can be used as an adverb or an adjective: **Sie spricht fließend Englisch.** *She speaks English fluently.* **Er antwortet mir in fließendem Deutsch.** *He replies to me in fluent German.*

③ Remember that with **fragen** *to ask*, the person who is being asked is always in the accusative: **sie fragt den Mann/die Frau** *she asks the man/the woman*. However, when the object of the question is preceded by the preposition **nach**, it requires the dative case: **Sie fragt die Frau nach dem Weg.** *She asks the woman* ('after') *the way*.

④ **gar** reinforces a negation and translates as 'at all'. The indefinite pronoun **keins** (or **keines**) *no, not a, none* is neuter here as it refers to a neuter noun: **das Wundermittel**.

dreihundertachtundachtzig • 388

73

9 – **O**kay, **a**ber wie **ma**chen Sie das kon**kret** im **All**tag?
10   Ich **stel**le mir das **schwie**rig vor ⑤.
11 – Da **ha**ben Sie ganz **recht** ⑥!
12   **Mei**ne **ers**te Frau ist mir **weg**gelaufen, als ich Ita**lie**nisch ge**lernt ha**be, und **mei**ne **zwei**te, als ich **an**gefangen **ha**be, Chi**ne**sisch zu **ler**nen.
13   Ich **ha**be mir dann **ei**nen Papa**gei** ge**kauft**, der be**gei**stert ist, wenn ich mit mir selbst **re**de. □

---

9 ... kon**kreht** ... 12 ... ita**lyeh**nish ... kHi**nehz**ish ... 13 ... papa**gei** (or **pa**pagei) ... buh**geist**ᵃt ...

Notes

⑤ We've seen **sich vorstellen** with the meaning *to introduce oneself*, but it can also mean *to imagine*. **Ich stelle mich vor** *I introduce myself*, but **Stell dir mal sein Gesicht vor!** *Just imagine his face!* In the second example, the reflexive pronoun is in the dative because what is imagined is in the accusative case (see lessons 62 and 77).

***

Übung 1 – Übersetzen Sie bitte!

❶ Sie haben vor zehn Wochen angefangen, Deutsch zu lernen. ❷ Unser Großvater hat fünf Sprachen gelernt, als er Kind war. ❸ Es ist schwierig, sich ein Leben ohne Fernsehen und Internet vorzustellen. ❹ Sie hat sich diese Schuhe in dem Geschäft gekauft, dessen Besitzer der Vater ihres Freundes ist. ❺ Er hat mich in fließendem Chinesisch nach dem Weg gefragt.

9 – OK, but how do you do this concrete[ly] in [your] daily life?
10 I imagine (*to-myself*) this [is] difficult.
11 – You are completely right there!
12 My first wife left me (*is from-me away-run*) when I was learning Italian, and my second [wife] when I started learning Chinese.
13 Then I bought (*myself*) a parrot, who is excited when I talk to myself (*when I with me myself talk*).

> Er hat mich in Fließendem Chinesisch nach dem Weg gefragt.

⑥ **das Recht** *law, right*; **das Unrecht** *injustice, wrong*. Note that in German you 'have' rather than 'are' right or wrong: **recht haben** *to be right* and **unrecht haben** *to be wrong*.

***

Answers to Exercise 1

❶ They/You started learning German ten weeks ago. ❷ Our grandfather learned five languages when he was [a] child. ❸ It is difficult to imagine a life without television and [the] internet. ❹ She bought herself these shoes in the shop whose owner is her friend's father. ❺ He asked me the way in fluent Chinese.

74 Übung 2 – Ergänzen Sie bitte!

❶ In order to speak a language fluently, one has to go to the country whose language one is learning.

Um eine Sprache .... zu sprechen, muss man in ... . fahren, ... man lernt.

❷ He's old-fashioned (*is from yesterday*); he knows neither cable TV nor [the] internet.

Er ist ... .; er kennt weder .... noch Internet.

❸ I am so sorry to hear that your cat ran away last week.

Es tut mir so Leid .. .., dass deine Katze ...... Woche ....

---

74 Vierundsiebzigste Lektion

„Ich bin von Kopf bis Fuß auf Liebe eingestellt" ①

1 – Stell doch mal ② das **Ra**dio ab und den **Fern**sehapparat an ③!

Notes

① This is a line from a famous song that Marlene Dietrich performed as Lola in **Der Blaue Engel**. It continues ... **und das ist meine Welt, und sonst gar nichts** ... *and that's my world, and nothing else.* The English version is 'Falling in Love Again (Can't Help It)', which has been covered by The Beatles, among others.

391 • dreihunderteinundneunzig

❹ Don't you (*informal*) think that more and more people talk to themselves (*with them themselves speak*)? – Yes, (*there*) you're right.

.... nicht, dass immer mehr Leute mit sich .... ? – Ja, da ....

❺ Why (*What-for*) are you doing this? If I understood you correctly, this isn't important at all.

.... machen Sie das? Wenn ich Sie .... verstanden habe, ist das ... nicht ....

Answers to Exercise 2

❶ – fließend – das Land – dessen Sprache – ❷ – von gestern – Kabelfernsehen – ❸ – zu hören – letzte – weggelaufen ist ❹ Denkst du – selbst reden – hast du recht ❺ Wozu – richtig – gar – wichtig

Second wave: 24th lesson

Seventy-fourth lesson 74

'From head to toe (*foot*), I'm ready for (*tuned into*) love'

1 – Switch off the radio and [turn] on the TV, [will you]?

② Adding **doch mal** to an imperative 'softens' it, making the order a request: **Komm doch mal her!** *Come here, will you?*

③ **anstellen** *to switch/turn on* and **abstellen** *to switch/turn off* are usually used in reference to machines or electrical devices. They are synonymous with **anmachen** and **ausmachen**.

dreihundertzweiundneunzig • 392

2 Im **Zwei**ten ④ kommt gleich **eine Sen**dung über Marlene **Diet**rich, die ich gern **seh**en **möch**te.

3 – Hat die nicht die "**Kam**eliendame" ge**spielt**?

4 – Nein, du ver**wechs**elst sie mit **Gre**ta **Gar**bo, **ih**rer ⑤ **größ**ten Rivalin.

5 – Ach ja, jetzt weiß ich, wer das ist: ihr hat der **Schwa**nenfedermantel ge**hört** ⑥, den wir im **Film**museum ge**seh**en **ha**ben!

6 – Ja, ganz **rich**tig. **A**ber es ist er**staun**lich, dass du dich noch an den **Man**tel er**inn**erst ⑦.

7 Du warst **da**mals erst ⑧ acht **Jah**re alt.

8 – Ich er**inn**ere mich auch an das **fleisch**farbene ⑨ Kleid, das sie **un**ter dem **Man**tel ge**tra**gen hat.

Pronunciation
2 ... **zen**dung ... 3 ... ka**meh**lyuhn-dahmuh ... 4 ... fer**vek**suhlst ... ri**vah**lin 5 ... **shvah**nuhn-fehdᵃ-mantuhl ... **film**-mu**zeh**-um ... 6 ... er**shtown**likH ... **erin**ᵃst 8 ... e**rin**'ruh ... **fleish**-fahbuhnuh kleit ...

Notes

④ One can say **im zweiten Programm** or simply **im Zweiten** or **im ZDF**, which is the abbreviation for **im Zweiten Deutschen Fernsehen**, the German public-service TV broadcasting service on channel 2.

⑤ **ihrer** is in the dative (fem.) because of the preposition **mit**, even if the preposition isn't repeated.

⑥ Note that the infinitive **gehören** *to belong* already has a **ge-** prefix; its past participle is therefore the same as that of **hören** *to hear, to listen*: **gehört**. But you won't confuse the two

2 On channel 2 there is going to be (*In-the second comes immediately*) a programme about Marlene Dietrich that I'd (*gladly*) like to watch.

3 – Didn't she play the 'Lady of the Camellias'?

4 – No, you're confusing her with Greta Garbo, her greatest rival.

5 – Oh yes, now I know who she (*that*) is: the swansdown coat that we saw in the film museum belonged to her (*to-her has the swan-feather-coat belonged that we ...*)!

6 – Yes, absolutely right. But it is astonishing that you still remember the coat.

7 You were (*then*) only 8 years old then.

8 – I also remember the flesh-coloured dress that she wore underneath the coat.

> Unsere Geschichte ist wirklich sehr interessant.

because **gehören** *to belong* always requires a dative object: **das Buch gehört mir** *the book belongs to me*.

⑦ **sich an etwas/jemanden erinnern** *to remember something/someone*. Here **an** is a preposition rather than a separable prefix. Did you spot that **sich erinnern** is a reflexive verb?

⑧ **erst** *only* is used here in the sense of *merely, just* – indicating the belief that something isn't much: **er ist erst zehn Jahre alt** *he's only 10 years old* (i.e. he is young!).

⑨ **das Fleisch** *flesh, meat*; **-farben** derives from **die Farbe** *colour*, but it only occurs as part of compound words.

dreihundertvierundneunzig

9 Wenn sie **ihren Man**tel **auf**gemacht ⑩ hat, hat man zu**erst** ge**dacht**, sie ist nackt da**run**ter ⑪.
10 – Ja, das war be**ein**druckend.
11 **A**llerdings ist das, was sie in **ih**rem **Le**ben ge**leis**tet hat, noch be**ein**druckender.
12 Ich **glau**be, sie war **wirk**lich sehr **mu**tig. ☐

---

9 ... nakt da**runt**ᵃ **10** ... buh-**ein**druk'nt **11** all'ᵃdings ... guh**leis**tuht ... buh**ein**druk'ndᵃ **12** ... **muh**tikH

Notes

⑩ **auf**machen and **zu**machen are respectively synonyms for **öffnen** *to open* and **schließen** *to close*.

⑪ **darunter** *underneath* replaces **unter dem Mantel** *under the coat* here. Compounds consisting of **da-** + preposition are generally used to refer to things and ideas (for people, you use the preposition + a pronoun). **Erzählt Paula viel von ihrem**

***

Übung 1 – Übersetzen Sie bitte!

❶ Gleich kommt eine interessante Sendung über die österreichische Literatur. ❷ Er hat im Kino mit seiner Schwester den „Blauen Engel" gesehen. ❸ Er erinnert sich nicht an die „Kameliendame", obwohl ihm dieser Film gut gefallen hat. ❹ Ich glaube, Sie verwechseln diesen Mann mit einem anderen. ❺ Wem gehörte der Mantel, der aus Schwanenfedern gemacht war?

9 When she opened her coat, it looked (*one thought*) at first [that] she was (*is*) naked underneath.
10 – Yes, that was impressive.
11 However, what (*that which*) she accomplished in her life is even more impressive.
12 I believe she was really very brave.

Mann? – Ja, sie erzählt viel <u>von</u> <u>ihm</u>. *Does Paula talk a lot about her husband? – Yes, she talks a lot <u>about</u> <u>him</u>.* However: **Erzählt Paula viel von ihrer Arbeit im Kino? – Ja, sie erzählt viel <u>davon</u>.** *Does Paula talk much about her work in the cinema? – Yes, she talks a lot <u>about it</u>.* **Da-** expands to **dar-** when the preposition begins with a vowel: **Sie erinnert sich nicht <u>daran</u>.** *She doesn't remember it.*

***

Answers to Exercise 1

❶ There is going to be (*Immediately comes*) an interesting programme about Austrian literature. ❷ He saw 'The Blue Angel' at the cinema with his sister. ❸ He doesn't remember 'The Lady of the Camellias' even though he liked the film a lot (*to-him the film well appealed has*). ❹ I believe you're confusing this man with another. ❺ To whom did the coat made from swansdown belong?

74 Übung 2 – Ergänzen Sie bitte!

❶ Can you (*formal*) tell me why so many people confuse 'right' and 'left'?

. . . . sagen, warum so viele Leute „rechts" und „links" . . . . ?

❷ To whom does the red coat belong? To you (*informal*) or to your sister?

Wem . . . . . . der . . . . Mantel? . . . oder . . . . ?

❸ Why didn't you (*informal*) open the door? – I was already asleep.

Warum . . . . . . nicht die Tür . . . . ?
– Ich war . . . .

***

> **Marlene Dietrich** *is still considered one of Germany's biggest international stars, an actress and performer to whose unique charm men and women succumbed in equal measure. Marlene, real name Marie Magdalene, was born in Schöneberg, which is now part of Berlin, in 1901. In 1930, Josef von Sternberg offered her the role of the cabaret singer Lola in 'The Blue Angel', the breakthrough that made her famous worldwide. She went to Hollywood with von Sternberg and there had a series of box-office successes, becoming one of the most highly paid actresses of her time. In 1939, she took US citizenship after the Nazi regime sought to entice her back to Germany. During World War II, she toured extensively for the Allied effort and was later awarded the Medal of Freedom by the US Government and the Légion d'honneur by the French Government as recognition for her wartime work.*
>
> *Dietrich still made occasional films in the post-war years, but she spent most of the 1950s to the 1970s touring the world as a*

④ Do you (*informal*) remember the actor who played the leading role in the film *M – A City Seeks a Murderer*?
.... den Schauspieler, ... die Hauptrolle in dem Film „*M – eine Stadt sucht einen Mörder*" ....?

⑤ May I switch on the TV? I'd like to watch (*see*) a programme about Heinrich Böll.
Darf ich ... . ? Ich möchte .... über Heinrich Böll ....

Answers to Exercise 2

① Können Sie mir – verwechseln ② – gehört – rote – Dir – deiner Schwester ③ – hast du – aufgemacht – schon eingeschlafen ④ Erinnerst du dich an – der – gespielt hat ⑤ – den Fernseher anstellen – eine Sendung – sehen

***

successful show performer. However, her health declined during this period, and she became increasingly dependent on alcohol and painkillers in her later years. Always conscious of her image, she spent the last 13 years of her life in seclusion in her Paris apartment, and the last 11 years largely in bed. Yet although she had withdrawn from the public eye, she maintained active phone and correspondence contact with friends and public figures.

Marlene Dietrich died in 1992 and was buried in Berlin-Friedenau Cemetery. The **Filmmuseum** *in Berlin now holds most of her personal effects, including costumes and many personal letters from friends, colleagues and lovers. It is among the most complete collections of any 20th-century artist.*

Second wave: 25th lesson

75 Fünfundsiebzigste Lektion

„Was der Bauer nicht kennt, isst er nicht."

1 – Sie **ko**mmen auch aus **Nord**deutschland, nicht wahr? Ich **hö**re es an ① **Ih**rem Ak**zent**.
2 – Ja, ich **ko**mme aus Kiel, **a**ber ich **woh**ne schon ② zehn **Jah**re hier in **Mün**chen.
3 – Ach, schon so **lang**e? Ich bin erst zwei **Jah**re hier.
4 Ich bin **mei**nem Mann ③ ge**folg**t, als er die **Fir**ma ge**wech**selt hat.
5 – Sie **schei**nen darüber nicht **glück**lich zu sein, **ha**ben Sie sich hier nicht gut **ein**gelebt ④?
6 – Na ja, wie Sie **wis**sen ist es für **Nord**deutsche nicht leicht **un**ter ⑤ **Bay**ern zu **le**ben.

Pronunciation
... bow^a ... **1** ... aktsent **2** ... keel ... **4** ... firma guveks'lt ...
5 ... glewklikH ... eingulehpt **6** ... bei^an ...

Notes
① **hören an** + dative *to hear [something] in ...* : **ich höre es an deiner Stimme** *I hear it in your voice.*
② **schon** *already* is used here to indicate the opposite meaning of **erst** *only, just* that we saw in the last lesson – that is, in the sense that something has been going on a long time. **Er wohnt schon zwanzig Jahre in Kiel, aber sie wohnt erst fünf Jahre dort.** *He has been living in Kiel for 20 years now, but she has only been living there for 5 years.* Note that the present tense

399 • dreihundertneunundneunzig

Seventy-fifth lesson 75

'What the farmer doesn't know, he doesn't eat.'

1 – You're also from northern Germany, aren't you? I hear it in your accent.
2 – Yes, I'm from Kiel, but I've been living for 10 years now (*I live already 10 years*) here in Munich.
3 – Oh, that (*already so*) long? I've been (*I am*) here only 2 years.
4 I followed my husband when he changed jobs (*the company*).
5 – You don't seem to be happy about that. Have you not settled in well here?
6 – Well, as you know it isn't easy for northern Germans to live among Bavarians.

is often used in German to talk about how long something has been going on (in English, this requires the present perfect continuous tense).

③ The object of **folgen** takes the dative: **er folgt dem Mann** *he follows the man.*

④ **sich einleben** *to settle in, to adapt* is a reflexive separable-prefix verb: **Ich lebe mich langsam in Deutschland ein.** *I am slowly settling in Germany.* **Er hat sich schnell in dem neuen Land eingelebt.** *He settled quickly in the new country.*

⑤ The preposition **unter** means *under, underneath*, but also *among*. In the sense of *among*, it is always followed by the dative: **Wir waren unter Freunden.** *We were among friends.*

75 7 – Oh, ich **ha**be mich schnell an die **bay**rische **Le**bensart ge**wöhnt** ⑥.

8 Ich **tra**ge zwar **im**mer noch **kei**ne **kur**zen **Le**derhosen ⑦, aber zum **Bei**spiel auf **Weiß**würste oder **Schweins**haxen **möch**te ich nicht mehr ver**zich**ten.

9 – Was? Sie **es**sen **die**se „**Schweine**rei**en**" ⑧? Das ist ja **ek**lig!

10 – **Ha**ben Sie schon **ein**mal eine **Weiß**wurst pro**biert**? Nein? Das **ha**be ich mir ge**dacht**.

11 **Kom**men Sie, wir **geh**en in den **Bier**garten ⑨ hier. Ich **la**de Sie ein.

12 Wir **trin**ken **ein** oder, **bes**ser noch, zwei **Weiß**bier da**zu**.

13 Und ich garan**tie**re Ihnen, Sie **wer**den die **Bay**ern mit **an**deren **Au**gen **seh**en.

---

*7 ... leh**b**'ns-art guh**vœnt** 8 ... tsvah[a] ... leh**d**[a]-hohz'n ... tsum bei**sh**peel ... **veis**-vewrstuh ... **shveins**-haks'n ... fer**tsikH**-tuhn 9 ... shveinuh**rei**'n ... **ehk**likH 13 ... garan**teer**uh ...*

Notes

⑥ **sich an etwas** (acc.) **gewöhnen** *to get used to something, to adjust to something*: **Sie kann sich nicht an deutsches Essen gewöhnen.** *She can't get used to German food.*

⑦ **Lederhosen** ('leather-breeches') are traditional men's clothing in Bavaria and Tyrol. They are usually worn together with a hat that has a tuft of chamois (mountain goat) fur. The female equivalent is the **Dirndl**, a traditional dress consisting of a bodice, blouse, full skirt and apron.

⑧ This is a pun. Although it makes reference to pigs, **die Schweinerei** actually means *rubbish*, *filth*, *mess* and has nothing to do with pork products, which translate roughly as '**alles vom Schwein**'.

7 — Oh, I quickly got used to the Bavarian way of life (*life-manner*).
8 Admittedly, I still don't wear (*I wear admittedly still no*) short leather breeches, but, for example, I would no longer like to do without veal and pork sausages and knuckle of pork (*would-like I not more to-forgo*).
9 — What? You eat this rubbish (*pork stuff*)? But that's disgusting!
10 — Have you ever (*already once*) tried a veal and pork sausage? No? That's what I thought (*This have I to-myself thought*)!
11 Come, we['ll] go to the beer garden here. It's on me (*I invite you*).
12 We['ll] drink one or, better yet, two wheat beers with it.
13 And I assure (*guarantee*) you, you'll see the Bavarians in a new light (*with other eyes*).

Was der Bauer nicht kennt, isst er nicht.

⑨ **der Biergarten** is a popular kind of open-air pub where drinks and local food are served. They originated in Bavaria and are particularly popular there.

75   Übung 1 – Übersetzen Sie bitte!

❶ Mein Mann war sehr glücklich über die Lederhosen, die ich ihm mitgebracht habe. ❷ Sie war die einzige Süddeutsche unter den Leuten, die eingeladen waren. ❸ Erinnerst du dich an den Biergarten, wo wir unsere erste Weißwurst gegessen haben? ❹ Er wohnt zwar schon zehn Jahre hier, aber er scheint die Stadt nicht gut zu kennen. ❺ Es ist nicht immer leicht, sich an andere Lebensarten zu gewöhnen.

***

Übung 2 – Ergänzen Sie bitte!

❶ I assure you (*formal*) he is from southern Germany (*south-Germany*); you can hear it in (*this hears one in*) his accent.

Ich garantiere . . . . . , er ist . . . . ;
das . . . . seinem Akzent.

❷ In Munich, you have to try wheat beer and eat a veal and pork sausage with it.

. . . . müssen Sie das Weißbier . . . .
und dazu . . . . essen.

❸ When I changed jobs (*the company*), my husband followed me to northern Germany.

. . . ich die Firma . . . . , ist . . .
mein Mann nach Norddeutschland . . . .

Answers to Exercise 1

❶ My husband was very happy about the leather breeches I brought back for him. ❷ She was the only southern German among the people who were invited. ❸ Do you remember the beer garden where we ate our first veal and pork sausage? ❹ Admittedly, he has been living here for 10 years now, but he doesn't seem to know the city well. ❺ It isn't always easy to get used to other ways of life.

***

❹ She quickly got used to the German way of life even though she is from southern Europe (*south-Europe*).
... ... schnell .. die deutsche Lebensart ...., obwohl sie ... . kommt.

❺ They have only been living (*They live only*) here [for] 6 months, but they have already settled in well.
Sie leben .... sechs Monate ...., aber ... . schon gut ....

Answers to Exercise 2

❶ – Ihnen – aus Süddeutschland – hört man an – ❷ In München – probieren – eine Weißwurst – ❸ Als – gewechselt habe – mir – gefolgt ❹ Sie hat sich – an – gewöhnt – aus Südeuropa – ❺ – erst – hier – sie haben sich – eingelebt

Second wave: 26th lesson

vierhundertvier • 404

76 Sechsundsiebzigste Lektion

Im Dunkeln ① geschehen komische Dinge

1 – Na, wie ② hat dir der Film gefallen?
2 – Ich habe ihn ziemlich lang gefunden, um nicht zu sagen langweilig ③.
3 – Ich gar nicht! Das ist der spannendste Krimi ④, den ich seit langem gesehen habe.
4 Bis zur letzten Minute habe ich mich gefragt, ob ⑤ es wirklich Selbstmord war.
5 Das Ende hat mich total überrascht, auch wenn es mir jetzt ganz logisch erscheint.
6 – Ich glaube, ich muss mir den Film ein zweites Mal ansehen.
7 Ich habe von dem, was passiert ⑥ ist, nicht viel mitgekriegt ⑦.

Pronunciation
... dunk'ln guhshehn kohmishuh dinguh 2 ... tseemlikH ... langveilikH 3 ... shpanuhntstuh krimi ... 4 ... zelpst-mort ... 5 ... ewbª'rasht ... lohgish ersheint 7 ... mit'guhkreekt

Notes

① **das Dunkel** is the adjective **dunkel** *dark* turned into a noun: *the dark*. **Im Dunkeln** takes the ending **-n** because it retains adjective endings even though it is a noun! One can also say **die Dunkelheit** *darkness*.

② **Wie gefällt dir ...?** is synonymous with **Wie findest du ...?** *How do you like ...? What do you think of ...?*

③ **langweilig** *boring* derives from the verb **sich langweilen** *to be bored*: **Er hat sich den ganzen Abend gelangweilt.** *He was bored the whole evening.*

Seventy-sixth lesson 76

Strange things happen in the dark
(*In-the dark happen funny things*)

1 – Well, how did you like the film?
2 – I thought it was (*found it*) quite long, if not to say boring.
3 – I didn't (*I not at all*)! It was (*This is*) the most captivating thriller that I've seen in a long time.
4 Up to the last minute, I asked myself whether it was really suicide (*self-murder*).
5 The end completely surprised me, even though it seems totally logical now.
6 – I think (*believe*) I have to watch (*to-me*) the film a second time.
7 I didn't catch much of what happened.

④ **der Krimi**: abbreviation of **der Kriminalfilm** *detective film, thriller* or **der Kriminalroman** *crime novel, murder mystery*.

⑤ **ob** *whether* is used to introduce an indirect question (i.e. a question within a statement). In English, *if* and *whether* are used interchangeably in this context, but German requires **ob**. As it introduces a dependent clause, a comma separates it from the main clause: **ich frage mich, ob**…, *I ask myself if/whether*…, **ich weiß nicht, ob**… *I don't know if/whether*…, **ich will wissen, ob**… *I would like to know if/whether*…

⑥ **passieren** *to happen* is synonymous with **geschehen** (see title): **Was ist denn passiert/geschehen?** *What happened?* The present perfect is formed with **sein** rather than **haben**.

⑦ **mitkriegen** *to 'get', to catch on* (literally, 'with-receive') is the colloquial form of **mitbekommen** *to understand*.

8 Jedes Mal, wenn du mich ge**weck**t hast, **wa**ren **ir**gendwelche ⑧ Schläge**rei**en im Gang.
9 Sag mal, hast du mich nicht **schla**fen **las**sen ⑨, weil du Angst **hat**test?
10 – Quatsch! Ich **ha**be nicht ein**mal** ge**merk**t, dass du ge**schla**fen hast.
11 – Was sagst du da? Wer hat mich denn dann **je**des Mal am Ohr ge**kit**zelt?
12 – Ich wars ⑩ auf **al**le **Fäl**le nicht.

*8 ... irg'nt'velkhuh shlehguh**rei**'n ... gang 10 ... guh**merk**t ...*
*11 ... guh**kit**s'lt 12 ... **fe**luh ...*

Notes

⑧ Like *some-* in English, the prefix **irgend-** can be added to many different articles and pronouns (**einer, eine, welche, wer, was, jemand,** etc.) to signal a degree of vagueness or uncertainty: **Wir wollen irgendwo in Italien Urlaub machen.** *We want to holiday somewhere in Italy.* **Ich habe gestern irgendeinen Krimi gesehen.** *I watched some thriller [or other] yesterday.*

⑨ Were you wondering why the modal verb **lassen** is an infinitive here rather than a past participle? When preceded by an infinitive, it must keep the infinitive form. This rule is called the 'double infinitive': **er hat sich gehen lassen** (not gelassen).

***

Übung 1 – Übersetzen Sie bitte!

❶ Jedes Mal, wenn man mich kitzelt, glaube ich zu sterben. ❷ Es ist schon dunkel und ich habe das nicht einmal gemerkt. ❸ Alle haben sich gefragt, ob es Mord oder Selbstmord war. ❹ Welcher Film willst du sehen? – Irgendeinen Krimi, der spannend ist. ❺ Warum haben Sie mich so lange schlafen lassen?

8 Whenever you woke me there was some [kind of] fight(s) going on (*in motion*). 76
9 Tell me, did you not let me sleep because you were scared?
10 – Nonsense! I didn't even realize (*notice*) that you were sleeping.
11 – What are you saying (*there*)? [So] who kept tickling my ear then (*Who has me after-all then every time on-the ear tickled*)?
12 – It wasn't me in any case (*I was-it ... not*).

> Welchen Film willst du sehen?

he let himself go. This is true for all modal verbs: **er hat nicht kommen können** (<u>not</u> **gekonnt**) *he couldn't come.*

⑩ **wars** – also spelled **war's** – is a contraction of **war es**: **ich war es** ('I was it') *it was me*. We've already seen similar cases such as **Wie geht es?** *How are you?* ('How goes it?'), which can also be written as **Wie geht's?** or **Wie gehts?**

***

Answers to Exercise 1

❶ Every time someone (*one*) tickles me, I believe I'm dying. ❷ It is already dark and I didn't even realize it (*this not even noticed*). ❸ Everyone asked themselves whether it was murder or suicide. ❹ Which film do you want to see? – Some thriller that is captivating. ❺ Why did you let me sleep so long?

77 Übung 2 – Ergänzen Sie bitte!

❶ I liked the film very much (*To-me has the film very well appealed*). And how did you (*formal*) like it?

Mir ... ... sehr gut .... Und ... hat er ....?

❷ I asked you (*informal*) three times whether you wanted to watch this film or some other [film].

Ich habe .... dreimal ...., .. du diesen Film sehen wolltest oder .... anderen.

❸ In any case, I prefer to see (*see I more-gladly*) films without fights.

... . sehe ich lieber Filme ohne ....

---

77 Siebenundsiebzigste Lektion

Wiederholung – Review

1 Relative pronouns

1.1 Definite relative pronouns: *der, die, das, die*

The forms of the German relative pronoun are the same as the definite article, except for the dative plural and all genitive forms.

	Singular			Plural
	masc.	fem.	neuter	
Nominative	der	die	das	die
Accusative	den	die	das	die
Dative	dem	der	dem	denen
Genitive	dessen	deren	dessen	deren

409 • vierhundertneun

❹ I haven't seen such strange (*funny*) things for a long time (*Since long have I not* ...); I didn't even get (*the*) half [of it].
.... habe ich nicht mehr so ....
.... gesehen, ... nicht mal die Hälfte
....

❺ This is the most boring film that I've seen in the past [few] years.
Das ist ... ., den ...
in den letzten Jahren ....

Answers to Exercise 2

❶ – hat der Film – gefallen – wie – Ihnen gefallen ❷ – dich – gefragt, ob – irgendeinen – ❸ Auf alle Fälle – Schlägereien ❹ Seit langem – komische Dinge – ich habe – mitgekriegt ❺ – der langweiligste Film – ich – gesehen habe

Second wave: 27th lesson

Seventy-seventh lesson 77

A relative pronoun is used to introduce a clause that provides additional information about a noun or pronoun that has already been mentioned (e.g. *who, that, which, whose,* etc.).

• **The choice of relative pronoun**

The form to use depends on two things:

• Firstly, the gender and number of the noun to which it refers:
Der Schriftsteller, der die Blechtrommel schrieb, war Günter Grass. *The author who wrote* The Tin Drum *was Günter Grass.*
Die Schauspielerin, die so gut singt, heißt Hildegard Knef. *The actress who sings so well is called Hildegard Knef.*
Das Mädchen, das einen roten Pullover trägt, ist meine Schwester. *The girl who is wearing a red sweater is my sister.*
Die meisten Leute, die in München leben, sprechen fließend bayrisch. *Most people who live in Munich speak Bavarian fluently.*

- Secondly, the case depends on its grammatical function in the relative clause (i.e. whether it is a subject, direct or indirect object, the object of a preposition, etc.):
Der Film, <u>den</u> (accusative masc.) **wir gesehen haben, hat uns gut gefallen.** *We liked the film that we saw a lot.*
Die Frau, <u>der</u> (dative fem.) **ich gerade Guten Tag gesagt habe, ist unsere Hausmeisterin.** *The woman to whom I just said hello is our caretaker.*
Der Schriftsteller, <u>dessen</u> (genitive masc.) **Namen* ich immer vergesse, ist in Köln geboren.** *The author whose name I always forget was born in Cologne.*

* As the genitive indicates possession, the relative pronoun in the genitive is always directly followed by a noun (without an article): **dessen Namen**. However, an adjective can precede the noun: **Sonja, <u>deren</u> kleiner Bruder in München wohnt, fährt oft in die bayrische Hauptstadt.** *Sonja, whose younger ('little') brother lives in Munich, often goes to the Bavarian capital.*

- **Other characteristics**

- The relative clause can be introduced by a preposition followed by a relative pronoun:
Ist das nicht der Mann, mit dem Anja gestern ins Kino ging?
Isn't this the man with whom Anja went to the cinema yesterday?
Wo ist die Firma, bei der Sie arbeiten?
Where is the company where ('for which') you work?

- Since a relative clause is a subordinate (dependent) clause, the conjugated verb occurs in the last position.
Ist das der Mann, den Sie gesehen haben?
Is this the man that you saw?

- In English, a relative pronoun may or may not be stated. In German, the relative pronoun must always be stated.
Das ist das Auto, das ich kaufen möchte.
This is the car I want to buy.

- Relative clauses are set off by commas in German.

1.2 Indefinite relative pronouns: *wer, was*

Indefinite relative pronouns are used when the antecedent (the 'relative' part) is unknown, undefined or not specific. **Wer** is used for people, **was** is used for objects.

Wer nicht für mich ist, ist gegen mich.
Whoever is not for me is against me.
Ich habe leider nicht gesehen, was sie gekauft hat.
Unfortunately, I didn't see what she bought.

was is also used after **alles** *everything*, **etwas** *something*, **nichts** *nothing*, **vieles** *much*, and after neuter superlatives:
Es gibt vieles, was er nicht weiß. *There is much he doesn't know.*
Das Beste, was ich in den Ferien gegessen habe, war die Schweinshaxe. *The best [thing] I ate during the holidays was the pork knuckle.*
but: **Ich habe die schönsten Ferien erlebt, die man sich vorstellen kann.** *I had* (experienced) *the best holidays* (that) *one can imagine.*

2 Reflexive pronouns

2.1 Forms of the reflexive pronoun

A reflexive pronoun indicates the same person or thing as the subject, so its form must reflect this. It can occur in the accusative or dative case depending on its grammatical function in the sentence. Its forms differ from the personal pronouns only in the third-person singular and plural, which are all **sich**.

	Accusative	Dative
1st-person sing.	**mich** *myself*	**mir** *(to) myself*
2nd-person sing.	**dich** *yourself*	**dir** *(to) yourself*
3rd-person sing.	**sich** *himself, herself, itself, oneself*	**sich** *(to) himself, herself, itself, oneself*
1st-person pl.	**uns** *ourselves*	**uns** *(to) ourselves*
2nd-person pl.	**euch** *yourselves*	**euch** *(to) yourselves*
3rd-person pl.	**sich** *themselves*	**sich** *(to) themselves*

And the formal reflexive pronouns:

Formal		
	Accusative	Dative
2nd-person (sing. and pl.)	**sich** *yourself, yourselves*	**sich** *(to) yourself, yourselves*

For example, have a look at the conjugation of **sich waschen** *to wash*. The reflexive pronoun is in the accusative when it functions as a direct object and in the dative when the verb has a different direct object:

sich waschen *to wash oneself*
(reflexive pronoun in the accusative)
ich wasche mich *I wash myself*
du wäschst dich *you wash yourself*
Claudia wäscht sich *Claudia washes herself*
wir waschen uns *we wash ourselves*
ihr wascht euch *you wash yourselves*
sie waschen sich *they wash themselves*

sich etwas waschen *to wash something*
(reflexive pronoun in the dative)
(Note that when referring to parts of the body, German often uses a definite article and a reflexive pronoun, while English uses a possessive adjective.)
ich wasche mir die Augen *I wash my eyes*
du wäschst dir die Haare *you wash your hair*
Claudia wäscht sich das Gesicht *Claudia washes her face*
wir waschen uns die Hände *we wash our hands*
ihr wascht euch die Füße *you* (pl.) *wash your feet*
sie waschen sich die Ohren *they wash their ears*

2.2 The position of the reflexive pronoun

In a main clause, the reflexive pronoun occurs after the verb even when the subject and verb are inverted:
Er erinnert sich gut an seine erste Freundin.
He remembers his first girlfriend well.
Nach vielen Jahren erinnert er sich noch an seine erste Freundin. *After many years, he still remembers his first girlfriend.*

2.3 Reflexive verbs in German vs English

And one last point: there are very few verbs in English in which a reflexive pronoun is required (e.g. *to perjure oneself*). But reflexive constructions are more frequent in German. Keep in mind that some verbs have a reflexive pronoun as part of the verb construction where their English equivalents do not:

• **sich ändern** *to change*:
die Zeiten haben sich geändert *the times have changed*

• **sich bewegen** *to move*:
Hat er sich bewegt? *Has he moved?*

• **sich fühlen** *to feel*:
Fühlst du dich nicht wohl? *Don't you feel well?*

You'll see it's not all that complicated. Just make a mental note when you see a verb with a reflexive pronoun and you'll soon pick them up.

3 Translating 'if': *wenn* or *ob*?

• When 'if' introduces a condition, it is translated as **wenn**:
Wenn du um zwölf Uhr nicht da bist, esse ich allein.
If you're not here at 12, I['ll] eat by myself.
Ich gehe mit Ihnen, wenn Sie wollen.
I['ll] go with you if you want.

• When 'if' introduces an indirect question without a question word (i.e. when you could also say *whether*) it is translated as **ob**.
Direct question: **Kommt Paul zu deiner Party?**
Is Paul coming to your party?
Indirect question: **Weißt du, ob Paul zu deiner Party kommt?**
Do you know if/whether Paul is coming to your party?

Wissen Sie, ob der Goetheplatz rechts oder links von uns liegt?
Do you know if Goethe Square is to our right or to our left?
Er überlegt, ob es besser ist, den Zug zu nehmen oder das Flugzeug. *He considers whether it would be ('is') better to take the train or the plane.*

To check whether something is an indirect question, just add **oder nicht** *or not*:
Sie fragt sich, ob er verheiratet ist (oder nicht).
She asks herself whether he is married (or not).

77 *You're almost done! To finish, listen to (or read out loud) the story of a dream that will show you just how much you've learned in this set of lessons.*

Review exercise

Manchmal können noch Wunder geschehen

1. Als Klaus um halb fünf am Morgen aufwachte, wusste er nicht mehr, wo er war.
2. Er konnte sich weder an das Zimmer noch an die Person, die neben ihm schlief, erinnern.
3. Langsam gewöhnten sich seine Augen an die Dunkelheit.
4. Aber alles, was er sah, war ihm fremd.
5. Nein! Nicht alles! Dort an der Tür hing der Schwanenfedermantel von Marlene Dietrich.
6. In diesem Moment erinnerte er sich wieder an das Wunder, das ihm passiert war.
7. Er war gestern Abend allein im Biergarten gewesen.
8. An einem anderen Tisch saßen ein paar Männer, die schon ziemlich viel getrunken hatten.
9. Unter ihnen war eine einzige Frau, die sich zu langweilen schien.
10. Sie war wunderschön und sehr blond.
11. Er glaubte zu träumen, aber als er den Schwanenfedermantel sah, den sie trug, war er sicher:
12. Es war die Schauspielerin Marlene Dietrich, die er vergötterte!
13. Eine Verwechslung war unmöglich.
14. Er hatte zwar schon zwei Bier getrunken, aber sein Kopf war immer noch klar.
15. Und dann… ist die Frau aufgestanden und zu ihm gekommen!
16. „Guten Abend", hat sie mit ihrer rauchigen Stimme gesagt, „darf ich mich zu Ihnen setzen?"

17 „Aber natürlich, gern", hat er überrascht und glücklich geantwortet.
18 Sie sprach fließend Deutsch, aber mit leichtem amerikanischen Akzent.
19 Sie haben eine Viertelstunde geredet und am Ende hat sie einfach gesagt: „Kommen Sie! Ich nehme Sie mit zu mir."
20 Und er hat sich nicht lang gefragt, ob er ihr folgen sollte…
21 Alles war also ganz logisch.
22 Vorsichtig bewegte er sich im Bett und sagte zu der Frau, deren blonde Haare ihn an der Nase kitzelten: „Marlene, Liebling!"
23 „Wach auf, Klaus! Es ist halb sieben.
24 Du musst die Kinder in die Schule mitnehmen."

Translation
Sometimes miracles can still happen

1 When Klaus woke up at 4:30 in the morning, he didn't know (*more*) where he was. **2** He could remember neither the room nor the person who was sleeping next to him. **3** Slowly, his eyes adjusted to the darkness. **4** But everything that he saw seemed (*was*) strange (*foreign*) to him. **5** No! Not everything! There, on the door, hung Marlene Dietrich's swansdown coat. **6** At this moment, he remembered (*again*) the miracle that [had] happened to him. **7** He had been in the beer garden last night, by himself. **8** At another table sat a few men who had already drunk quite a lot. **9** Among them was a single woman who seemed to be bored. **10** She was gorgeous and very blonde. **11** He thought (*believed*) he was dreaming (*to dream*), but when he saw the swansdown coat she was wearing, he was sure: **12** This was the actress Marlene Dietrich, whom he adored! **13** There was no confusion possible (*A confusion was impossible*). **14** Admittedly, he had already drunk two beers, but his head was (*always*) still clear. **15** And then … the woman got up and came over to him! **16** 'Good evening,' she said in (*with*) her husky voice. 'May I sit with you?' **17** 'But of course, it's my pleasure (*gladly*),' he replied, surprised and happy. **18** She

spoke fluent German, but with a slight (*light*) American accent.
19 They spoke for a quarter of an hour and then (*at the end*) she just said: 'Come! I'll take you home with me.' **20** And he didn't wonder for long (*asked himself not long*) whether he should follow her … **21** So everything was completely logical. **22** Carefully, he moved in the bed and said to the woman whose blonde hair tickled

---

78 Achtundsiebzigste Lektion

Der Vorteil flexibler Arbeitszeiten

1 – **Mahl**zeit ① und bis **spä**ter.
2 – Was? Du machst schon **Mit**tagspause?
3   Wie spät ist es denn? ②
4 – Es ist fünf vor halb zwölf ③, **a**ber ich **ha**be schon um **sie**ben **an**gefangen.
5   Nach **vier**einhalb ④ **Stun**den **Ar**beit tut mir der Kopf weh und **au**ßerdem knurrt ⑤ mein **Ma**gen.

Pronunciation
... *for*teil fle*ksee*bl^a *arbeits*-tseituhn **1** *mahl*-tseit ...
5 ... *fee*ª*einhalp* ... *knurt* ... **mah**g'n

Notes

① The primary meaning of **die Mahlzeit** (literally, 'mealtime') is *meal*, derived from **das Mahl**, an archaic word for *meal*: **Das war eine ausgezeichnete Mahlzeit.** *That was an excellent meal.* But in many parts of Germany, **Mahlzeit!** is used as a greeting around midday, whether you're at the table or not.

② The question **Wie spät ist es?** ('How late is it?') is synonymous with **Wie viel Uhr ist es?** *What time is it?*

③ **fünf Minuten vor halb zwölf** – or just **fünf vor halb zwölf** – (i.e. 'five minutes before half twelve') means 11:25 because

417 • **vierhundertsiebzehn**

his nose: 'Marlene, darling!' **23** 'Wake up, Klaus. It's 6:30. **24** You have to take the kids to school.'

> *Do you realize the progress you've made since you started? Congratulations!* **Schönen Tag und bis morgen!** *Have a nice day and see you tomorrow!*

Second wave: 28th lesson

Seventy-eighth lesson 78

The advantage [of] flexible working hours
(*work-times*)

1 – Enjoy your lunch and see you later.
2 – What? Are you taking (*You make*) [your] lunchbreak already?
3 What time is it (*How late is it then*)?
4 – It's 11:25, but I (*already*) started at 7:00.
5 After four-and-a-half hours [of] work my head aches (*does to-me the head pain*) and, besides, my stomach is growling.

halb zwölf is 11:30 ('half [to] twelve'), and five minutes before this is ... 11:25. Logical, isn't it? In any case, this is much more widely used than **fünfundzwanzig nach elf**.

④ **viereinhalb** *four and a half* is written as one word, as are **eineinhalb, zweieinhalb, dreieinhalb** *one and a half, two and a half, three and a half*, etc. These expressions don't decline: **Sie wartet schon dreieinhalb Stunden.** *She has already been waiting for three and a half hours.* Remember that **die Stunde** is the word for *hour* (a period of 60 minutes); **die Uhr** refers to a specific time, similar to *o'clock*: **Es ist ein Uhr.** *It is 1:00.*

⑤ **knurren** *to growl, to snarl* is first and foremost what a dog does when you try to take a bone away from it.

6 Ich **brau**che **dring**end **fri**sche Luft und was ⑥ zu **es**sen.

7 – **Fri**sche Luft? **Da**von gibt es **drau**ßen ge**nug** bei der **Käl**te!

8 Ich **geh**e bei dem **Sau**wetter ⑦ nicht raus: mir ist hier **drin**nen schon kalt.

9 – Auch nicht, wenn ich dir **sa**ge, dass ich zu **Hen**kels ⑧ in die „**Al**te **Müh**le" **geh**e, und dass es bei **de**nen ⑨ **heu**te **haus**gemachte Kar**tof**felknödel ge**füllt** mit **Le**berwurst gibt?

10 – Das ist na**tür**lich was **an**deres.

11 Wa**rum** hast du das nicht gleich ge**sagt**?

12 Halt mir **ei**nen Platz frei! Ich **ko**mme in zehn Mi**nu**ten nach ⑩.

---

6 ... *frishuh luft* ... **7** ... *keltuh* **8** ... *zow-vet[a]* ... **9** ... *henk'ls* ... *mewluh* ... *kartof'l-knœd'l guhfewlt* ... *lehb[a]-vurst* ...

Notes

⑥ In everyday German, **was** often replaces **etwas** *something*. See also line 10: **was anderes** or **etwas anderes** *something different, something else*.

⑦ **das Sauwetter** *bad weather* consists of **das Wetter** *weather* and **die Sau** *sow*. German is extraordinarily rich in pig-related metaphors and expressions, which is hardly surprising given the ubiquity of everything to do with pork. While many have negative connotations, others don't: **Ich glaube, mein Schwein pfeift!** ('I believe my pig is whistling!') expresses great surprise (as pigs are not in the habit of whistling), and **Schwein haben** means *to be lucky*.

⑧ As in English, an **s** is added to make a last name plural, but in German no definite article is used to refer to the family. **Henkels sind gute Freunde von uns.** *[The] Henkels are good friends of ours.*

419 • **vierhundertneunzehn**

6 I urgently need fresh air and something to eat.
7 – Fresh air? There's enough of that outside in this cold (*That-of there is outside enough with this cold*)!
8 I'm not going out in this beastly weather (*sow-weather*): I'm already cold in(*side*) here.
9 – Not even (*Also not*) if I tell you that I'm going to [the] Henkels in the 'Old Mill' and that they are serving (*there is at them*) homemade potato dumplings filled with liver sausage today?
10 – That's of course completely different (*something other*).
11 Why didn't you say so (*that*) before (*at-once*)?
12 Save a seat for me (*Hold to-me a place free*)! I'll be there (*I come*) in 10 minutes (*after*).

⑨ **bei denen** here means something like 'at theirs', with **denen** the demonstrative pronoun *them* in the dative, referring to the Henkels. The preposition **bei** can have various meanings: **Sie wohnt bei ihrer Freundin.** *She lives with her girlfriend* ('at her girlfriend's'). **Tom arbeitet bei Siemens.** *Tom works at Siemens.* **Wir bewerben uns auch bei einer großen Firma.** *We'll also apply to a large company.* **Der Laden ist bei der Kirche.** *The shop is by the church.* **Ich kann bei dieser Hitze nicht schlafen.** *I can't sleep in this heat.*

⑩ **nachkommen** *to follow* ('to come after').

Übung 1 – Übersetzen Sie bitte!

❶ Um wie viel Uhr haben Sie angefangen zu arbeiten? ❷ Sie haben eineinhalb Stunden Mittagspause, von zwölf bis halb zwei. ❸ Seit Tagen tut ihr der Kopf weh, sie braucht dringend Ruhe. ❹ Ich muss was essen; mein Magen hört nicht auf zu knurren. ❺ Ist Ihnen kalt? Soll ich das Fenster schließen?

***

Übung 2 – Ergänzen Sie bitte!

❶ What are we eating today? My stomach is already growling.
... . heute? Mein Magen ......
.....

❷ Let's stay inside; outside it's too cold.
Lass uns .... bleiben, ... ist es ..
.....

❸ Could (*Can*) you save me a seat (*place*), please?
Können Sie ... bitte .... ?

***

Wie ist die Kartoffel nach Deutschland gekommen?
How did the potato get to Germany?
The potato is for Germany what rice is for Asia or pasta for Italy. It is hard to imagine German cooking without it. Potatoes were first brought to Europe in the 1500s by Spanish conquistadores, who discovered them in the Andes, where they were cultivated by the native population. At first, the plants only attracted the attention of botanists because of their pretty white or purple flowers, which came to adorn royal gardens. But in the mid-18th century, Frederick the Great, King of Prussia, ordered potatoes to be planted throughout his kingdom as a means of preventing famine. His propaganda campaigns for the potato, aimed at winning over distrustful Prussian farmers, are almost as famous as the wars he waged.

Answers to Exercise 1

❶ At what time did you start working? ❷ They have [a] one-and-a-half hour (*hours*) lunchbreak, from 12:00 to 1:30. ❸ For days her head has been aching – she urgently needs rest (*quiet*). ❹ I have to eat something; my stomach won't (*doesn't*) stop growling. ❺ Are you cold? Should I close the window?

***

❹ Why didn't you say straight away that you don't like dumplings?
. . . . nicht gleich . . . . . . , dass Sie . . . . . . nicht mögen?

❺ In this cold, I don't go out. – Not even (*Also not*) if I come along?
Bei dieser Kälte . . . . nicht . . . . . – . . . . , . . . ich mitkomme?

Answers to Exercise 2

❶ Was essen wir – knurrt schon ❷ – drinnen – draußen – zu kalt ❸ – mir – einen Platz freihalten ❹ Warum haben Sie – gesagt – Knödel – ❺ – gehe ich – raus – Auch nicht, wenn –

***

Since then, the potato has been a staple food in Germany, and it still makes up a large part of the German diet. Potatoes are prepared in many ways, from **Pellkartoffeln** *'peel potatoes', potatoes boiled in their skins, to* **Salzkartoffen** *'salt potatoes', peeled potatoes boiled with salt,* **Kartoffelsalat** *potato salad, of which there are countless varieties,* **Kartoffelpfannkuchen** *potato pancakes,* **Bratkartoffeln** *pan-fried potatoes,* **Kartoffelklöße** *or* **Kartoffelknödel** *potato dumplings,* **Kartoffelsuppe** *potato soup and* **Schupfnudeln**, *finger-thick noodles made from mashed potato, similar to Italian gnocchi. Needless to say,* **Pommes frites** *chips or French fries are also very popular.*

Second wave: 29th lesson

79 Neunundsiebzigste Lektion

Auf der Autobahn

1 – Bis jetzt **ha**ben wir Glück ge**habt**, **Kin**der.
2   Drückt die **Dau**men ①, dass ② es so **wei**ter geht.
3   Wenn kein Stau ③ kommt, sind wir in fünf **Stun**den am Strand.
4 – Du, Karl, ich weiß, es ist nicht der Mo**ment**, **a**ber kannst du **bi**tte an der **näch**sten **Rast**stätte ④ kurz **an**halten?
5   Ich muss **drin**gend auf Toilette.
6 – Ist das **wirk**lich **nö**tig? Seit wir auf der **Au**tobahn sind, **fah**re ich im Schnitt ⑤ **hun**dert**fünf**zig ⑥.

Pronunciation
... *owto-bahn* **2** *drewkt ... dowmuhn* ... **3** ... *shtow ... shtrant*
4 ... *rast-shtetuh* ... **5** ... *toiletuh* **6** ... *nœtikH ... shnit* ...

Notes

① **die Daumen drücken** ('the thumbs to press/squeeze') *to cross one's fingers*: **ich drücke dir die Daumen** *I'm crossing my fingers for you* means the same as **ich wünsche dir viel Glück** *I wish you good luck*.

② **dass** can be used in the sense of **damit** *so, so that, in order that*: **Beeilen wir uns, damit/dass wir nicht zu spät kommen.** *Let's hurry, so we won't be too late.*

③ **der Stau** *traffic jam* forms the plural with **-s**, like many other nouns that end in a vowel (except for those ending in **-e**): **die Staus** *traffic jams*, **die Autos** *cars* – but **die Toiletten** *toilets*.

Seventy-ninth lesson 79

On the motorway

1 – We've been lucky so far, children.
2 Keep your fingers crossed (*Press the thumbs*) that it'll continue like this (*it so further goes*).
3 If there isn't a traffic jam (*no traffic-jam comes*), we'll be (*are we*) at the beach in five hours.
4 – (*You*) Karl, I know it's not good timing (*the moment*), but can you stop briefly at the next rest area, please?
5 I urgently need the toilet (*I must urgently onto toilet*).
6 – Is this really necessary? Since we've been (*are*) on the motorway, I've been going (*drive I*) on average 150 [kph].

④ **die Raststätte** is a motorway service area or rest stop with a service station and a restaurant or cafeteria. The word consists of **die Rast** *rest, break* and **die Stätte** *place, site*. If there's no eating option, one says **der Rastplatz** or **der Parkplatz**.

⑤ **im Schnitt** is short for **im Durchschnitt**: **der Durchschnitt** *average*. The noun is related to **schneiden** (**schnitt**, **geschnitten**) *to cut*. Note that as elsewhere in continental Europe, speeds in Germany are indicated in kilometres per hour: 150 kph is about 93 mph.

⑥ There is no general speed limit on German motorways. Incidentally, the German word for 'speed limit' is rather impressive: **die Geschwindigkeitsbegrenzung** (from **die Geschwindigkeit** *speed* and **die Begrenzung** *limitation*).

7 Kannst du nicht **war**ten, bis wir an der **Gren**ze sind?

8 – Papa, wir **mü**ssen aber auch mal ⑦!

9 – Es ist zum Ver**rückt**werden ⑧! So**bald** wir auf die **Au**tobahn **ko**mmen, muss **al**le Welt aufs Klo.

10 Könnt ihr nicht ein **ein**ziges Mal zu **Hau**se **da**ran ⑨ **den**ken?

11 – Reg dich doch nicht auf ⑩, **Pa**pa! Wir **ko**mmen **des**halb nicht **spä**ter an.

12 Lass **Ma**ma **da**nach **fah**ren, die holt die ver**lo**rene Zeit schnell **wie**der auf.

---

7 … *grentsuh* … **9** … *ferrewkt-veh^{a}d'n! zobalt* … **10** … *eintsiguhs* … **11** *rehk* … *owf* … **12** … *ferlohr'nuh* …

Notes

⑦ **Ich muss mal** is short for **ich muss mal auf (die) Toilette/aufs Klo (gehen)**. Remember that **müssen** always conveys the notion of compulsion: when you have to go, you have to go!

⑧ **das Verrücktwerden** is an infinitive used as a noun. It derives from **verrückt werden** *to go crazy*. Note that all infinitives used as nouns are neuter. The English equivalent is often

***

Übung 1 – Übersetzen Sie bitte!

❶ An vielen Grenzen in Europa muss man nicht mehr anhalten. ❷ Ich habe dir den ganzen Morgen die Daumen gedrückt. ❸ Die Deutschen fahren auf der Autobahn so schnell sie können. ❹ Regen Sie sich nicht auf! Der Stau ist nicht lang. ❺ Sobald Papa vor dem Fernsehapparat sitzt, schläft er ein.

7 Can't you wait until we're at the border?
8 – But Dad, we also need to go (*we must but also once*)!
9 – It's [enough] to drive you mad! As soon as we get to the motorway, everybody (*all world*) has to [go] to the toilet.
10 Can you not just once think about this at home?
11 – Don't get worked up [about it], Dad, will you! We won't arrive any later [just] because of this.
12 Let Mum drive afterwards; she'll quickly make up the lost time (*she makes the lost time quickly again up*).

a gerund; that is, the -*ing* form of the verb used as a noun: **das Fahrradfahren** *cycling*, **das Autowaschen** *carwashing*, **das Insbettgehen** *going to bed*, etc. However, this particular example wouldn't be expressed in English with a gerund.

⑨ **daran** translates as 'about this' here because **denken an** is *to think about*: **ich denke daran (an das)** *I think about this*.

⑩ The meaning of **sich aufregen** is *to fuss, to fret, to get worked up about something*. The context helps you decide which is meant. In any case: **Regen Sie sich nicht auf, das ist schlecht für das Herz.** *Don't get worked up, it is bad for your heart.*

***

Answers to Exercise 1

❶ At many borders in Europe, one no longer has to stop. ❷ I kept my fingers crossed for you all morning. ❸ The Germans drive as fast as they can on the motorway. ❹ Don't fret! The traffic jam isn't long. ❺ As soon as Dad sits in front of the TV, he falls asleep.

79 Übung 2 – Ergänzen Sie bitte!

❶ Don't fret (*informal*)! We were lucky again.
... ... nicht ...! ... . noch einmal Glück ....

❷ We['ll] stop at the next service area so that everybody can go to the toilet.
Wir halten .. ... nächsten .... an, ... alle ... .../.... ... gehen können.

❸ If this continues (*so further goes*), we'll never be able to make up the lost time (*can we the lost time never again make-up*).
.... das so ...., können wir ... . nie wieder ....

❹ As soon as we are back from our (*the*) holidays, I['ll] phone you.
...... wir ... ... zurück sind, ... ich Sie ...

❺ Until the border, everything went well; after that there was (*came*) one traffic jam after another.
... ... ging ....; ...... kam ... . nach dem anderen.

Answers to Exercise 2

❶ Reg dich – auf – Wir haben – gehabt ❷ – an der – Raststätte – damit – auf die Toilette/aufs Klo – ❸ Wenn – weiter geht – die verlorene Zeit – aufholen ❹ Sobald – aus den Ferien – rufe – an ❺ Bis zur Grenze – alles gut, danach – ein Stau –

Die Deutschen fahren auf der Autobahn so schnell sie können.

We haven't paid you any compliments lately, yet you deserve them! You're studying new lessons regularly – ideally, daily – and on top of that you're translating previous lessons from English into German. Have you noticed how much you've learned?

Second wave: 30th lesson

80 Achtzigste Lektion

Eine positive oder negative Antwort?

1 **Mann**heim, den 8. (**ach**ten) Sep**tem**ber 2010. ①
2 **Ih**re Be**wer**bung ②
3 Sehr ge**ehr**te ③ Frau **Spreng**er,
4 wir **freu**en uns, dass Sie sich für ④ **ei**ne **Mit**arbeit in **un**serem Unter**neh**men interes**sie**ren.
5 **Lei**der ist je**doch** die **Stel**le ⑤, für die Sie sich be**wor**ben **ha**ben, in**zwi**schen schon be**setzt**.
6 Da ⑥ wir aber in **nah**er **Zu**kunft **wei**tere **Mit**arbeiter für **ähn**liche **Auf**gaben **su**chen, **möch**ten wir Sie **trotz**dem gern **ken**nen **ler**nen.

Pronunciation
... **poh**ziteevuh ... **neh**gateevuh ... **1 man**heim ... tsveitowz'**nt**tsehn **2** ... buh**ver**bung **3** ... guh'**eh**ᵃtuh ... **shpreng**ᵃ **4** ... untᵃ**neh**muhn ... **5** ... ye**dokh** ... buh**vor**buhn ... int**svi**sh'n ... **6** ... **tsoo**kunft ... **ehn**likHuh **owf**gahb'n ...

Notes
① The format for dating a letter is to give the location first, followed by the date, which is normally in the accusative with the article **den**. The day is normally given as an ordinal number, followed by the month. The month can be given as an ordinal number or a word: **Berlin, den 1. 1. 2012** (read **Berlin, den ersten ersten zweitausendzwölf**) or **Berlin, den 1. Januar 2012** (see also lesson 28).

② **die Bewerbung** *application* is a noun derived from **sich bewerben für/um** + acc. *to apply for* (line 5): **Sie bewirbt sich für/um diese Stelle.** *She applies for this position.*

429 • vierhundertneunundzwanzig

Eightieth lesson 80

A positive or negative reply?

1 Mannheim, 8 September 2010
2 Your application
3 Dear Mrs Sprenger (*Very honoured[f.] Mrs Sprenger*),
4 We are glad that you are interested in joining our company (*that you yourself for a collaboration in our company are-interested*).
5 Unfortunately, however, the position for which you applied has already been filled in the meantime (*is ... in-the-meantime already occupied*).
6 But as in the near future we [will be] look[ing] for additional staff (*further workers*) for similar tasks, we would like to meet you nevertheless (*you nevertheless gladly to-know to-learn*).

---

③ **geehrt** is the past participle of **ehren** *to honour, to respect*. If addressing a man, it would be **Sehr geehrter Herr Sprenger!** (Instead of an exclamation mark, one can also use a comma and then continue with a small letter, as in line 3.)

④ Pay attention to the prepositions that accompany certain verbs. In German, *to be interested in* is **sich interessieren für**: **Er interessiert sich für Politik.** *He is interested in politics.* Try to learn these prepositional verbs with the correct preposition.

⑤ **die Stelle(-n)** can have a variety of meanings, such as *place*, *area*, etc. Here, it implies **die Arbeitsstelle** *post, position, job*. Remember **die Tankstelle** *petrol/gas station* (lesson 19)?

⑥ **da** is a conjunction that translates as *as, because, since* (similarly to **weil**). Don't confuse the conjunction **da** with the adverb **da** meaning *there*.

vierhundertdreißig • 430

7 **Könn**ten Sie uns am **Mitt**woch, dem 15. (**fünf**zehnten) Sep**tem**ber, um 10 (zehn) Uhr zu **ei**nem per**sön**licher Ge**spräch** be**su**chen ⑦?

8 Herr Dr. ⑧ Schulz, der **Lei**ter der Ab**tei**lung Infor**ma**tik, hat **die**sen Ter**min** ⑨ für Sie reser**viert**.

9 **Bit**te infor**mie**ren ⑩ Sie uns kurz, ob **Ih**nen **die**ser Ter**min** passt ⑪ **o**der ob Sie **ei**nen **an**deren **vor**ziehen.

10 Selbstver**ständ**lich über**neh**men wir **Ih**re **Aus**lagen ⑫ für die **Rei**se.

11 Mit **freund**lichen **Grü**ßen ⑬

12 **Ih**re Katrin **Zieg**ler Perso**nal**leiterin

---

8 ... **dok**toh{a} shults ... **leit**{a} ... **ap**teilung ... ter**meen** ... **9** ... infor**mee**ruhn ... foh{a}'tsee'n **10** ... **ows**lahg'n ... **12** ... **katrin tseeg**l{a} (perzo**nahl'**leituhrin)

Notes

⑦ **besuchen** *to visit, to call on, to go to see*.

⑧ Careful! **Dr** here doesn't refer to a medical doctor, but is the title used if someone holds a PhD. In formal letters, this title is always included in Germany, preceded by **Herr** for a man or **Frau** for a woman. Remember also that **Herr** is a weak masculine noun (or 'masculine n-noun'), so when it's not in the nominative, it ends in **-n** (lesson 47).

⑨ **der Termin** *appointment, date, deadline*: **ein Termin beim Arzt** *an appointment at the doctor's*.

⑩ **informieren** *to advise, to inform, to let somebody know*.

7	Could you come see (*visit*) us on Wednesday, 15 September at 10 o'clock for (*to*) an interview (*personal conversation*)?
8	(*Mr*) Dr Schulz, the head of the IT department, has reserved this appointment for you.
9	Please advise us in a short note (*briefly*) whether this appointment suits you or whether you prefer another [time].
10	Of course, we [will] reimburse (*take-over*) your travel expenses (*expenses for the journey*).
11	Kind regards,
12	(*Your*) Katrin Ziegler Head of Human Resources (*personnel-leader[f.]*)

Sie haben eine positive Antwort bekommen?

⑪ **passen** *to be suitable*: **Das passt mir.** *That suits (is convenient for) me.* It can also mean *to fit (well)*: **Meine Hosen passen mir wieder.** *My trousers fit me again.*

⑫ **die Auslagen** *expenses*, *costs* (that can be reimbursed).

⑬ **mit freundlichen Grüßen** ('with friendly greetings') is a closing formula used in official correspondence. Don't confuse it with the informal way to sign off a letter, **viele Grüße**! The two may look very similar, but they belong to different registers. Note also that in formal letters, **Ihr** (m.), **Ihre** (f.) *Your* is often placed before the name of the sender.

Übung 1 – Übersetzen Sie bitte!

① Sie haben eine positive Antwort bekommen? Das freut mich! ② Bitte informieren Sie mich, ob die Stelle des Mechanikers schon besetzt ist. ③ Wenn Sie uns besuchen möchten, können wir Ihnen am Donnerstag einen Termin reservieren. ④ Sehr geehrte Frau Ziegler, da ich eine Reise ins Ausland machen muss, passt mir leider der 15. September nicht. ⑤ Ich habe mir jedoch den Freitag reserviert, um Herrn Dr. Schulz zu treffen.

***

Übung 2 – Ergänzen Sie bitte!

① Why don't you (*formal*) apply for the post of head of department?
Warum .... nicht ... ... des Abteilungsleiters?

② Please advise (*formal*) me quickly whether this appointment suits you.
.... mich bitte schnell, ... dieser Termin ....

③ The Head of Human Resources (*personnel-leader[m.]*) would like to meet you (*you gladly to-know to-learn*).
... . möchte Sie gern ....

Answers to Exercise 1

❶ You received a positive reply? I am pleased! ❷ Please let me know whether the post of mechanic is already filled. ❸ If you would like to come in to see us, we can book an appointment for you on Thursday. ❹ Dear Mrs Ziegler, as I have to travel abroad, unfortunately the 15th of September does not suit me. ❺ However, I have reserved Friday to meet Dr Schulz.

***

❹ Our company will be happy to reimburse (*takes-over gladly*) your expenses when you come to see us.

.... übernimmt gern ....
........, wenn Sie uns ....

❺ Even though the post is already filled, Mr Schulz would like to meet you for an interview (*personal conversation*).

Obwohl ... . schon .... ist, möchte Herr Schulz Sie .. ..
.... treffen.

Answers to Exercise 2

❶ – bewerben Sie sich – für die Stelle – ❷ Informieren Sie – ob Ihnen – passt ❸ Der Personalleiter – kennen lernen ❹ Unser Unternehmen – Ihre Auslagen – besuchen ❺ – die Stelle – besetzt – zu einem persönlichen Gespräch –

Second wave: 31st lesson

81 Einundachtzigste Lektion

Ein nicht ganz alltägliches ① Vorstellungsgespräch

1 – **Gu**ten Tag, Herr **Dok**tor Schulz.
2 – **Gu**ten Tag, Frau **Spreng**er. Ich **freu**e mich, Sie **ken**nen zu **ler**nen ②.
3   **Set**zen Sie sich **bit**te!
4   Sie **ha**ben **al**so Elektrotechnik stu**diert** und sich auf Infor**ma**tik speziali**siert** ③?
5 – Ja, nach **Ab**schluss **mei**nes **Stu**diums ④ **ha**be ich mich bei dem **größ**ten **deut**schen **IT-Un**ternehmen ⑤ be**wor**ben.
6   Dort war ich fast fünf **Jah**re **an**gestellt ⑥, ge**nau**er ge**sagt** bis zur Ge**burt mei**ner **Toch**ter.

Pronunciation
... gants al**tehk**lik**Huhs foh**ᵃ**shtelungs-guhsprehkH 4** ... e**lek**tro-tek**Hnik** ... infor**mahtik** shpetsiali**see**ᵃ**t 5** ... ap**shlus** ... **shtoo**diums ... **6** ... **an**guhshtelt

Notes

① **alltäglich** ('all-daily') *everyday, ordinary* by extension implies something that is a little banal or humdrum. **der Alltag** is *everyday life, (daily) routine*.

② **kennen** *to know* – the first infinitive in the double infinitive **kennen lernen** *to meet, to get to know, to become acquainted with* – behaves like a separable prefix of **lernen**. (In fact, it can be written as one word, **kennenlernen**, or two words since the 2006 spelling reform.) Thus, **kennen** separates from **lernen** in the present tense, e.g.: **Wir lernen heute den neuen Chef kennen.** *We're meeting the new boss today.*

435 • vierhundertfünfunddreißig

Eighty-first lesson 81

An unusual job interview
(*A not wholly everyday introduction-conversation*)

1 – Good afternoon, (*Mr*) Dr Schulz.
2 – Good afternoon, Mrs Sprenger. I am pleased to make your acquaintance.
3   Please take a seat!
4   So, you studied electrical engineering and you specialized in computer science?
5 – Yes, after graduating (*conclusion of my studies*), I applied to the largest German IT company.
6   I was employed there [for] almost five years – to be precise (*more accurately said*), until the birth of my daughter.

③ Remember that verbs ending in **-ieren** don't take the **ge-** prefix in the past participle. Also note that *to specialize in something* is a reflexive construction in German: **sich auf etwas spezialisieren**.

④ In the context of education, **der Abschluss** refers to one's final qualification, leaving certificate or graduation: **Bewerber ohne Abschluss bekommen oft keine Stelle.** *Applicants without a qualification often don't get a job.* **Wann hast du deinen Abschluss gemacht?** *When did you graduate?*

⑤ **das Unternehmen** *company, enterprise, business* is neuter as it is the infinitive **unternehmen** *to undertake, to venture* used as a noun, i.e. 'undertaking'. **IT** is, as in English, the abbreviation for 'Information Technology'.

⑥ **angestellt sein** *to be employed*; **der/die Angestellte** *employee*.

7 Nach der Geburt habe ich dann als Selbstständige ⑦ gearbeitet, was mir erlaubte, mich um meine Tochter zu kümmern.

8 Aber jetzt fällt mir langsam ⑧ die Decke auf den Kopf, und außerdem fehlt mir der Austausch mit den Kollegen immer mehr...

9 – Ich hab's ⑨! Laura Busch!

10 – Verzeihung ⑩, was meinen Sie?

11 – Sie sind Laura Busch, nicht wahr?

12 – Ja, in der Tat, mein Vorname ⑪ ist Laura und Busch ist mein Mädchenname. Aber woher wissen Sie das?

(Fortsetzung folgt)

---

*7 ... zelpst-shtendiguh ... kewm*ª*n 8 ... felt ... dekuh ... fehlt ... owstowsh ... 9 ... lowra bush 10 fertseiung ... 12 ... taht ... foh*ª*nahmuh ...*

Notes

⑦ **selbstständig** is used here as a noun to mean *self-employed person* or *freelancer*, but normally it's an adjective that means *independent*: **Die Kinder sind selbstständig; man braucht sich nicht mehr um sie zu kümmern.** *The children are independent; one doesn't have to look after them anymore.* (Note that **sich kümmern** requires the preposition **um**!)

⑧ **langsam** *slow(ly)* can be used to indicate that something is slowly developing, in the sense of 'starting to': **Ich habe langsam Hunger.** *I am starting to get hungry.* **Es wird langsam dunkel.** *It is starting to get dark.*

7   After her (*the*) birth, I was self-employed (*have I then as an independent worked*), which allowed me to look after my daughter.

8   But now I'm starting to get cabin fever (*falls on-me slowly the ceiling on the head*), and, moreover, I increasingly miss the exchange with colleagues …

9 – [Ah], I've got it! Laura Busch!

10 – Pardon, what do you mean?

11 – You are Laura Busch, aren't you?

12 – Yes, indeed, my first name is Laura, and Busch is my maiden name (*girl-name*). But how (*where-from*) do you know this?

(*To be continued*)

> Verzeihung, ich bin ein bisschen nervös.

⑨ **ich hab's** or **ich habe es** *I've got it* is a shorter way of saying **ich hab's gefunden** *I found it*.

⑩ **Verzeihung** *Pardon [me]* is often used interchangeably with **Entschuldigung** *Excuse [me]*, although **verzeihen** means *to forgive* and **(sich) entschuldigen** *to excuse*.

⑪ **der Vorname** *first name*; **der Nachname** *family name* ('after-name'). One can also say **der Familienname**.

81 Übung 1 – Übersetzen Sie bitte!

① Verzeihung, ich bin ein bisschen nervös. ② Er arbeitet als Selbstständiger, um keinen Chef zu haben. ③ Nach der Geburt ihres dritten Kindes hat sie eine Frau angestellt. ④ Unser Personalleiter hat seine Frau bei einem Vorstellungsgespräch kennen gelernt. ⑤ Da er Elektrotechnik studiert hat, bewirbt er sich bei einem IT-Unternehmen.

***

Übung 2 – Ergänzen Sie bitte!

① As she studied computer science, she is employed in an IT company.

.. sie Informatik ...., ist sie in einem IT-Unternehmen ....

② Forgive me! I've forgotten your first name. Ah no, I've got it! Your name is Julia!

.... ! Ich habe .... vergessen. Ach nein, ...' . ! Du heißt Julia!

③ After finishing (*conclusion of*) his studies, he applied to five companies.

Nach .... hat er sich ... . beworben.

④ When he comes home after work, he cooks (*the*) dinner.

Wenn er .... nach Hause kommt, ... er ... .

⑤ My friend (*f.*) looks after my plants while I am on holiday.

.... meine Pflanzen, während ich .. ..

439 • vierhundertneununddreißig

Answers to Exercise 1

❶ Forgive me, I am a little nervous. ❷ He is self-employed (*works as an independent*) in order not to have a boss. ❸ After the birth of her third child, she employed a woman. ❹ Our head of human resources met his wife at a [job] interview. ❺ As he studied electrical engineering, he is applying to an IT company.

***

Answers to Exercise 2

❶ Da – studiert hat – angestellt ❷ Verzeihung – deinen Vornamen – ich hab's – ❸ – Abschluss seines Studiums – bei fünf Unternehmen ❹ – nach der Arbeit – kocht – das Abendessen ❺ Meine Freundin kümmert sich um – in Urlaub bin

Verzeihen Sie uns bitte die Frage, aber vergessen Sie auch nicht, jeden Tag eine Lektion zu übersetzen? Heute ist die Lektion 32 dran ... *Pardon us for asking the question, but you're not forgetting to translate a lesson every day, are you? Today it's lesson 32* ...

Second wave: 32nd lesson

82 Zweiundachtzigste Lektion

Ein nicht ganz alltägliches Vorstellungsgespräch
(Fortsetzung)

1 – **Er**kennst du mich nicht? Ich bin Johannes.
2 – Johannes Schulz. Natürlich! Warum habe ich dich nicht gleich wieder erkannt ①?
3 – Wir sind älter geworden ② und haben uns verändert.
4 – In der Tat! Du scheinst mit deiner Karriere ③ zufrieden zu sein?
5 – Erinnerst du dich noch an das Märchen von Bertolt Brecht?
6 – Du meinst die Geschichte von dem Prinzen ④, der es liebte, auf einer Wiese nahe dem Schloss zu liegen und von weißen, sehr weißen Schlössern mit hohen Spiegelfenstern ⑤ zu träumen?

Pronunciation
1 ... yohanuhs 2 ... erkant 3 ... ferend^{a}t 4 ... kariehruh ...
5 ... bertolt brekHt 6 ... prints'n ... veezuh nahuh ... veiss'n shlœss^{a}n ... shpeeg'l-fenst^{a}n

Notes
① On its own, **erkennen** *to recognize* is used in the sense of identifying something or someone: **Ich habe dich auf dem Foto nicht erkannt.** *I didn't recognize you in the photo.* However, **wieder erkennen** ('to recognize again') is used

Eighty-second lesson 82

An unusual job interview
(Continuation)

1 – Don't you recognize me? I am Johannes.
2 – Johannes Schulz! Of course! Why didn't I recognize you immediately?
3 – We've aged (*are older become*) and have (*ourselves*) changed.
4 – Indeed (*In the deed*)! You seem to be happy (*satisfied*) with your career?
5 – Do you (*still*) remember the fairy tale by Bertolt Brecht?
6 – You mean the story of the prince who (*it*) loved to lie in a meadow near the castle and (*to*) dream of white, very white castles with high mirror windows?

when seeing someone again after time has passed: **Sie haben sich gleich wieder erkannt, obwohl sie sich 5 Jahre nicht gesehen hatten.** *They immediately recognized each other, even though they hadn't seen each other for five years.*

älter/alt werden ('older/old become') *to age, to grow older*. Many verbs can be formed in this way, with an adjective + **werden**: **dick/dicker werden** *to grow big/bigger*, **groß/größer werden** *to grow tall/taller*, **dünner werden** *to become thinner, to lose weight*, etc. (lesson 60, note 5).

die Karriere *career* always implies a glittering, successful career in German.

der Prinz *prince* is a weak masculine noun, hence it takes the ending **-en** in all cases except the nominative.

der Spiegel *mirror*, **das Fenster** *window*.

82   **7** – Ja, … denn auf **die**ser **Wie**se **blüh**ten ⑥ die **Blu**men **größ**er und **schön**er als sonst **ir**gendwo.
- **8** – Dann starb **plötz**lich der **al**te **Kö**nig und der Prinz **wur**de sein **Nach**folger.
- **9** – Und der **jung**e **Kö**nig stand ⑦ nun oft auf den Ter**rass**en von **weiß**en, sehr **weiß**en **Schlöss**ern mit **ho**hen **Spie**gelfenstern…
- **10** – und **träum**te von **ei**ner **klei**nen **Wie**se, auf der die **Blu**men **größ**er und **schön**er **blüh**ten als **sonst**wo ⑧.
- **11** – Siehst du, ich **ha**be **da**mals auf **mei**nem **al**ten, **gel**ben **Fahr**rad davon ⑨ geträumt, die **spie**gelblanken **Fens**ter der **dick**en Limou**si**nen von **in**nen zu **se**hen.
- **12**   Und **heu**te **träu**me ich **hin**ter den **Fens**tern der Limou**si**ne von **mei**nem **gel**ben **Fahr**rad, auf dem ich die **Vö**gel **sing**en **hör**te.

---

7 … blewtuhn … bloomuhn … irg'nt'vo 8 … shtahrp … nakhfolg[a] 11 … limuzeenuhn … 12 … fœg'l zing'n …

Notes

⑥ **blühten** is the third-person plural simple past tense of **blühe** *to bloom, to blossom*. A *flower* is **die Blume**. Here **größe** and **schöner** are comparative adverbs, rather than adjective ('the flowers blossomed bigger and more beautifully'). Th comparative is formed by adding **-er** to the base form of a adjective or adverb + **als** *than* to compare two things.

⑦ This lesson is a good review of the German verbs indicatin positions: **stehen** *to stand*, **liegen** *to lie* and **sitzen** *to sit*. Thes three verbs have a stem vowel change to **-a** in the simple pa tense: **ich stand** *I stood*, **ich lag** *I lay*, **ich saß** *I sat*.

443 • **vierhundertdreiundvierzig**

7 – Yes ... because in this meadow, the flowers were (*blossomed*) bigger and more beautiful than anywhere else (*than else anywhere*).
8 – Then the old king died suddenly and the prince became his successor.
9 – And the young king now often stood on the terraces of white, very white castles with high mirror windows ...
10 – and dreamt of a little meadow where the flowers were bigger and more beautiful than elsewhere.
11 – You see, back then, on my old yellow bike, I dreamt of seeing the mirrorlike (*mirror-shiny*) windows of the big (*fat*) limousines from the inside.
12 And today, behind the windows of my (*the*) limousine, I dream of my yellow bike, on which I heard the birds sing.

Träumen Sie davon, in der Sonne zu liegen, da, wo die Apfelbäume blühen?

3) **sonstwo** is a contraction of **sonst irgendwo** *elsewhere, anywhere else*. The adverb **sonst** here means *else* and **irgendwo** *anywhere, somewhere*.

4) Here **davon** is needed because the prepositional verb is **träumen von** *to dream of*: **Ich träume von der Wiese.** *I dream of the meadow.* **Ich träume davon, auf der Wiese zu sitzen.** *I dream of sitting in the meadow.* ('I dream of-this, on the meadow to sit.')

Übung 1 – Übersetzen Sie bitte!

❶ Träumen Sie auch davon, in der Sonne zu liegen, da, wo die Apfelbäume blühen? ❷ Jeden Samstag wäscht er seine Limousine, bis sie spiegelblank ist. ❸ Irgendwo auf der Welt gibt's ein kleines bisschen Glück für jeden. ❹ Er hat sich gar nicht verändert, obwohl er heute Direktor eines großen Unternehmens ist. ❺ Erinnert ihr euch noch an das weiße Schloss, das wir besichtigt haben?

***

Übung 2 – Ergänzen Sie bitte!

❶ I am looking for my small mirror; it must be somewhere.
Ich suche . . . . ; der muss . . . .

❷ Indeed, I recognized her immediately as she hasn't changed at all.
. . . . , ... sie sofort wieder . . . . , denn . . . . gar nicht . . . .

❸ She seems to be very happy (*satisfied*) with her new post.
. . . . mit ihrer neuen Stelle sehr . . . .

❹ He loves (*it*) to lie in a meadow and dream of faraway countries (*there of distant countries to dream*).
Er liebt es, ... zu liegen und dort . . . fernen Ländern . . . .

❺ Ever since he started cycling every day (*Since he every day with his bicycle travels*), he has lost a lot of weight (*is he much thinner become*).
Seit er jeden Tag . . . . fährt . . . . . viel dünner . . . .

Answers to Exercise 1

❶ Do you also dream of lying in the sun (*there*) where the apple trees blossom? ❷ Every Saturday he washes his limousine until it is gleaming (*is mirror-shiny*). ❸ Somewhere in this (*the*) world there's a little bit of luck for everyone. ❹ He hasn't changed at all even though he is now (*today*) the director of a large company. ❺ Do you still remember the white castle that we visited?

***

Answers to Exercise 2

❶ – meinen kleinen Spiegel – irgendwo sein ❷ In der Tat, ich habe – erkannt – sie hat sich – verändert ❸ Sie scheint – zufrieden zu sein ❹ – auf einer Wiese – von – zu träumen ❺ – mit seinem Fahrrad – ist er – geworden

---

Keep in mind that a list of irregular (strong) verbs is available at the end of the grammatical appendix. If you can't remember the infinitive of a verb, you can easily find it by looking at verbs with the same first letter, as it's the stem vowel that changes ... In any case, it's always useful to review strong verbs, as you'll remember them more easily through regular exposure!

Second wave: 33rd lesson

83 Dreiundachtzigste Lektion

Genial oder verrückt?

1 – Zu dumm! Es **blei**ben ① uns nur zwei **Ta**ge für **Süd**deutschland, be**vor** ② wir nach Brasilien zu**rück**fliegen.
2 Das **nächs**te Mal **müs**sen wir uns mehr Zeit **neh**men.
3 Wo**hin** sol**l**en wir **fah**ren? Was **ra**ten ③ Sie uns?
4 – Oh, da muss ich **ei**nen Mo**ment** laut **nach**denken ④, bevor ich **ant**worten kann: der **Schwarz**wald, der **Bo**densee, **Mün**chen, die **Al**pen, das **Do**nautal… **al**les ist **seh**enswert.
5 **A**ber halt! Na**tür**lich! Falls ⑤ Sie noch nicht die **Schlös**ser von **Lud**wig dem **Zwei**ten be**sich**tigt **ha**ben, dann **müs**sen Sie un**be**dingt **dort**hin ⑥ **fah**ren.

Pronunciation
geniahl … 1 … buhfoh[a] … brazeelyuhn … 4 … nakh-denk'n … shvarts-valt … bohduhn-zeh … dohnow-tahl … zehns-veh[a]t 5 … lootvikH dehm tsveituhn …

Notes
① **bleiben** is in the plural here because the 'real' subject of the phrase is **zwei Tage** rather than **es**. Remember that **es** can occur at the beginning of a phrase to introduce the subject (it acts as a kind of 'false' subject): **Es fehlen fünf Personen.** ('It are missing five people.') *Five people are missing.* If one places the subject at the beginning of the sentence, **es** is eliminated: **Fünf Personen fehlen.** *Five people are missing.*

Eighty-third lesson 83

Brilliant or crazy?

1 – [It's] too bad (*stupid*)! We only have two days left (*It remain to-us only two days*) for southern Germany before we fly back to Brazil.
2 The next time we must take (*to-us*) more time.
3 Where should we go? What do you recommend (*to-us*)?
4 – Oh, (*there*) I have to think out loud (*loudly think-it-over*) for a moment before I can answer: the Black Forest, Lake Constance (*ground-lake*), Munich, the Alps, the Danube Valley … [they] are all worth seeing (*all is seeing-worth*).
5 But wait (*stop*)! Of course! If you haven't yet (*If you still not*) visited the castles of Ludwig II, then you absolutely must go there.

---

② **bevor** *before*. Note that **bevor** is a conjunction that introduces a subordinate clause: **Ich muss essen, bevor ich ins Bett gehe.** *I have to eat before I go to bed.* Don't confuse it with the preposition **vor** *in front of, before*: **fünf Minuten vor sieben** *five minutes before seven*; **Das Schloss steht vor einem Berg.** *The castle stands in front of a mountain.*

③ **raten** here translates as *to advise, to recommend*. It can also mean *to guess*.

④ **denken** *to think*; **nachdenken** *to reflect on, to think something over, to think about something*.

⑤ We've seen the conjunction **falls** with the meaning *in case* (lesson 57). It can also mean *if*, as here.

⑥ Remember that **dorthin** *there(-to)* is used to talk about where you are going (**Ich fahre dorthin.** *I am going there.*) and **dort** *there* to indicate where you are (**Ich wohne dort.** *I live there.*).

vierhundertachtundvierzig • 448

83

6 – Sind das nicht die **Schlös**ser von dem **Kö**nig, der **geis**teskrank war?

7 – Das steht ⑦ in den **Schul**büchern, **a**ber da**rü**ber ⑧ **strei**ten sich die Historiker.

8 Nach**dem** ⑨ **Lud**wig II. **ho**he **Schul**den ge**mach**t **hat**te, um **sei**ne **Schlös**ser zu finan**zie**ren, **hat**te er **vie**le **Fein**de **un**ter **sei**nen Mi**nis**tern.

9 **Si**cher ist, dass die **Bay**ern **die**sem „ver**rück**ten" **Kö**nig **ih**re **schöns**ten **Schlös**ser ver**dan**ken ... ⑩

10 ... und wahr**schein**lich auch **ei**nige **O**pern von **Ri**chard **Wag**ner, **des**sen **Mä**zen er war. □

---

6 ... **geis**tuhs-krank ... 7 ... **shool**-bewkH^an ... histohrik^a
8 nakh**dehm** **loot**vikH deh^a **tsvei**tuh ... **shul**duhn ... finant**see**ruhn ... **fein**duh ... **minist**^en 9 ... fer**dank**'n 10 ...
vahr-**shein**likH ... **rik**Hart **vahgn**^a ... met**sehn** ...

Notes

⑦ **stehen** *to stand* is also used to mean 'is written': **Das steht in der Zeitung.** *That's in the newspaper.*

⑧ **sich streiten darüber** (**über** + acc.) *to disagree on this/about that*, i.e. to disagree about something that has already been referred to; but when **sich streiten** is followed by **um** (+ acc.) it takes on a different meaning: **Die Kinder streiten sich um die Schokolade.** *The children fight over the chocolate.*

⑨ **nachdem** *after*. This sentence uses the past perfect tense which describes events that precede another point in the past that has been established through the present perfect or the simple past tense. The past perfect tense consists of the simple past tense form of **haben** or **sein** and a past participle: **Sie war müde, weil sie am Abend ausgegangen war.** *She was tired because she had gone out in the evening.* **Nachdem wi**

6 – Aren't those the castles of the king who was insane (*mind-ill*)?
7 – That's [what's] (*stands*) in (*the*) schoolbooks, but historians disagree about this (*on-this argue with each other the historians*).
8 After having incurred large debts (*high debts had made*) in order to finance his castles, Ludwig II had many enemies among his ministers.
9 [What is] certain is that the Bavarians owe their most beautiful castles to this 'mad' king ...
10 ... and probably also some operas by Richard Wagner, whose patron he was.

das Schloß besichtigt hatten, gingen wir essen. *After we had visited the castle, we went out to eat.* Note that in spoken German, the present perfect tense is often used, regardless of whether one event precedes another or not: **Nachdem wir das Schloss besichtigt haben, sind wir essen gegangen.**

⑩ **jemandem etwas verdanken** *to owe something to somebody*: **Er verdankt ihm viel.** *He owes a lot to him.* While we're on the subject of gratitude (in German, you can see that **verdanken** *to owe* and **danken** *to thank* are related), remember that **danken** also requires the dative: **jemandem für etwas danken** *to thank someone for something.* **Ich danke Ihnen für Ihre Hilfe.** *I thank you for your help.*

83 Übung 1 – Übersetzen Sie bitte!

① Nach dem Tod seines Vaters wurde Ludwig der Zweite mit 18 Jahren König von Bayern. ② In der Zeitung steht, dass sich die Minister über die Arbeitszeiten streiten. ③ Nachdem sie das Schloss besichtigt hatten, gingen sie im Schlosspark spazieren. ④ Was können wir für Sie tun? Wir verdanken Ihnen so viel! ⑤ Ich rate Ihnen, nicht um Mitternacht in dieses Schloss zu gehen.

***

Übung 2 – Ergänzen Sie bitte!

① Think it over [for] a moment before you reply; take your (*you yourself*) time!

.... einen Moment ...., ... Sie antworten; .... Zeit!

② He advised us to visit the castles of Ludwig II.

Er hat ... geraten, ... von Ludwig dem Zweiten .. ..

③ We have three hours (*It remain us three hours*) until (*before*) our train departs.

.. .. uns drei Stunden, ... unser Zug abfährt.

Answers to Exercise 1

❶ After the death of his father, Ludwig II became King of Bavaria at the age of 18. ❷ In the newspaper it says that the ministers disagree on working times. ❸ After they had visited the castle, they went for a walk in the (*castle*) park. ❹ What can we do for you? We owe you so much! ❺ I advise you not to go into this castle at midnight.

***

❹ I strongly (*absolutely*) advise you to go there, if you are interested in history.
  ... ... unbedingt .... zu gehen,
  ..... du dich für Geschichte ....

❺ After he had incurred (*made*) many debts, Richard Wagner had the great fortune (*big luck*) to meet Ludwig II.
  Nachdem er .... gemacht hatte,
  hatte Richard Wagner ... . ,
  Ludwig den Zweiten ...... zu ....

Answers to Exercise 2

❶ Denken Sie – nach, bevor – nehmen Sie sich – ❷ – uns – die Schlösser – zu besichtigen ❸ Es bleiben – bevor – ❹ Ich rate dir – dorthin – falls – interessierst ❺ – viele Schulden – das große Glück – kennen – lernen

vierhundertzweiundfünfzig • 452

84 | Ludwig II. von Bayern, der Märchenkönig
Ludwig II of Bavaria, the fairy-tale king
After the sudden death of his father, Maximilian II, Ludwig II became King of Bavaria at the age of 18. He reigned for 22 years, until June 1886, when he and his psychiatrist drowned under mysterious circumstances. Ludwig's death came only two days after he had been declared insane and deposed, and his uncle Luitpold was declared the prince regent. Ludwig was something of a legend already during his lifetime. Few other royals in Germany fuelled people's imaginations to the same degree, or sparked as much controversy. His unique personality particularly offended the conservatives around him. He was criticized, among other things, for remaining unmarried, enjoying nightlife, hating official ceremonies and loving art above all else, but mostly for incurring huge debts in order to build his castles.

84 Vierundachtzigste Lektion

Wiederholung – Review

1 Prepositions and case

1.1 Prepositions that require a particular case

Some prepositions always require a particular case.

• **Accusative prepositions**
bis *until*, **durch** *through*, **für** *for*, **gegen** *against*, **ohne** *without*, **um** *around*

• **Dative prepositions**
aus *out of, from*, **bei** *with, at, near*, **mit** *with*, **nach** *after, to*, **seit** *since*, **von** *from, of, by*, **zu** *to*

1.2 Two-way prepositions

Unfortunately, German also has nine so-called 'two-way' prepositions that can take either the accusative or the dative case.

• In their basic meaning, these two-way prepositions are 'spatial'. When **an** *on, at, to*, **auf** *on top of, to*, **hinter** *behind*, **in** *in, into, to*, **neben** *next to, beside*, **über** *over, above, across*, **unter** *under*,

The first castle Ludwig II built (which was never completed) was Neuschwanstein. Only 15 of some 200 rooms were furnished. The work on Neuschwanstein had barely started when Ludwig II decided – after a visit to Versailles – to build his own Versailles: Herrenchiemsee on the lake Chiemsee, the largest lake in Bavaria. All in all, Ludwig II barely stayed there a week! He then started dreaming of a Byzantine palace, but instead built a 'royal villa' named Linderhof. This was the only castle to be completed during his lifetime, and the only one where he actually lived. Yet even if he didn't really benefit from his castles himself, millions of visitors marvel at them today.

Second wave: 34th lesson

Eighty-fourth lesson 84

below, **vor** *in front of*, or **zwischen** *between* refer to positions in space, they take the dative case; when they refer to movement through space, they take the accusative (lesson 49, section 4).

Die Fliege sitzt auf dem Apfel. *The fly is sitting on the apple.*
(position in space: dative)
Die Fliege fliegt auf den Apfel. *The fly flies onto the apple.*
(movement through space: accusative)

Note that the choice of case is not necessarily dependent on whether there is actual movement or not. The accusative is used when a change of location is indicated, answering the question **Wohin?** *Where to?* and the dative when you give a position, answering the question **Wo?** *Where?*

Die Fliege geht auf dem Apfel spazieren. *The fly takes a walk on the apple.* (The fly moves, but it is already on the apple. Hence the question is **Wo geht sie spazieren?** rather than **Wohin?**)

• Some two-way prepositions can also be used in a temporal sense (answering the question **Wann?** *When?*): **an** *on*, *at*, **vor** *before*, **in** *in* and **zwischen** *between* then take the dative.

vierhundertvierundfünfzig • 454

An deinem Geburtstag machen wir ein großes Fest.
On your birthday, we will have a big party.
Vor den Ferien ist kein Termin mehr frei.
Before the holidays, [there] is no appointment available.
Im Oktober fahren wir nach Berlin. *We will go to Berlin in October.*
Zwischen den Osterferien und Pfingsten gibt es viele Feiertage.
Between the Easter holidays and Pentecost, there are many holidays.

- When they accompany verbs, **vor** always takes the dative, and **über** always takes the accusative. However, **an, auf** and **in** can take both. So be careful with the prepositions required by verbs and the cases that follow them:
Erinnerst du dich an ihn? (acc.) *Do you remember him?*
Natürlich, ich hänge an ihm. (dat.) *Of course, I'm attached to him.*

The following section will help you remember some of the prepositional verbs and the cases they take.

2 Prepositional verbs

Prepositional verbs are verbs that require a specific preposition. English has many examples of verbs like this, but be careful, because in German the prepositions might not be the ones you expect. Prepositional verbs should be learned as a unit as neither the choice of preposition nor the case of the noun following two-way prepositions can be easily predicted. Here are some examples. Note that many of these examples are in the imperative:

- **warten auf** (+ acc.) *to wait for*:
  Warten Sie auf mich! *Wait for me!*

- **träumen von** (+ dat.) *to dream of*:
  Sie träumen von dem Meer. *They dream of the sea.*

- **sich erinnern an** (+ acc.) *to remember*:
  Erinnern Sie sich an Herrn Roth? *Do you remember Mr Roth?*

- **sich kümmern um** (+ acc.) *to take care of*:
  Er kümmert sich um alles. *He takes care of everything.*

- **sich interessieren für** (+ acc.) *to be interested in*:
  Interessieren Sie sich für Musik? *Are you interested in music?*

- **aufhören mit** (+ dat.) *to stop* or *to stop doing something*:
  Hört mit eurem Quatsch auf! *Stop this nonsense!*

- **sich bewerben um** or **für** (+ acc.) *to apply for*:
  Er hat sich um/für eine neue Stelle beworben.
  He applied for a new post.
- **sprechen von** (+ dat.) or **über** (+ acc.) *to talk/speak about*:
  Sie sprechen immer von der/über die Arbeit.
  They always talk about their work.
- **denken an** (+ acc.) *to think about/of*:
  Denken Sie an uns! *Think about us!*
- **fragen nach** (+ dat.) *to ask for*:
  Fragen wir jemanden* nach der Adresse!
  Let's ask someone for the address!

* The person you ask is always in the accusative in German!

3 Prepositions and pronouns

In German, pronouns after prepositions normally refer only to people, whereas a **da**-compound consisting of **da-** (or **dar-** before a vowel) + preposition is used to stand in for things and ideas:
Du träumst vom Meer? Ich träume auch davon.
You dream of the sea? I also dream of it.
Ich erinnere mich gut an den Garten unserer Großeltern. Erinnerst du dich auch daran? *I remember our grandparents' garden well. Do you also remember it?*
Er interessiert sich für Autos. Dafür interessiere ich mich gar nicht. *He is interested in cars. I'm not at all interested in this.*

But when referring to a person:
Sie kümmert sich nicht allein um ihren Sohn, ihr Mann kümmert sich auch um ihn. *She doesn't look after her son by herself, her husband also looks after him.*

That's enough about prepositions for the moment!

4 Subordinating and coordinating conjunctions

We've already seen that coordinating conjunctions (e.g. **und** *and*, **aber** *but*, **oder** *or*, **denn** *as, for*) link clauses of the same type (i.e. main clauses or dependent clauses). Hence, they don't affect word order and the conjugated verb is in the second position (if the linked clauses are main clauses). Subordinating conjunctions, in contrast, introduce a subordinate clause that is separated from the main clause by a comma. In the subordinate clause, the conjugated verb moves to the last position. Let's look at some different subordinating conjunctions.

4.1 Temporal conjunctions

• **bevor** *before* and **nachdem** *after*
nachdem and **bevor** are used with a conjugated verb rather than a participle construction, as is often the case in English:
Bevor wir das Schloss besichtigen, können wir einen Spaziergang im Park machen. *Before visiting the castle, we can take a walk in the park.*
Nachdem sie das Schloss besichtigt hatten*, gingen sie in den Park. *After having visited the castle, they went to the park.*

* This is the past perfect tense. It consists of a past tense form of **haben** or **sein** (depending on which auxiliary the main verb takes to form the present perfect tense) and the past participle. After **nachdem**, the past perfect tense is normally used in the subordinate clause, and the simple past in the main clause, as both events occurred in the past, but one precedes the other.

• **bis** *until* and **seit** (or **seitdem**) *since* are conjunctions, but **bis** (+ acc.), **bis zu** (+ dat.) and **seit** (+ dat.) can also function as prepositions.
Wir warten hier, bis der Regen aufhört. *We'll wait here until the rain stops.* (conjunction)
Sie müssen bis nächstes Jahr warten. *You have to wait until next year.* (preposition)
Seit(dem) sie mit ihm zusammen ist, hat sie sich sehr verändert. *Since she got together with him, she has changed a lot.* (conjunction)
Seit wann arbeiten Sie in diesem Unternehmen? *Since when have you been working for this company?* (preposition)

• **sobald** *as soon as* is often used with the present tense, but with a future meaning.
Sobald eine Stelle in unserem Unternehmen frei ist, stellen wir Sie ein. *As soon as a position is available in our company, we will employ you.*

4.2 Some causal conjunctions

- **weil** *because* and **da** *because, as, since*

weil generally answers the question **Warum?** *Why?*; **da** introduces a fairly obvious explanation:

Warum bleibt ihr zu Hause? – Weil draußen ein Sauwetter ist. *Why are you staying at home? – Because the weather is terrible outside.*

Da ein Sauwetter ist, bleiben wir zu Hause. *Since the weather is terrible, we're staying at home.*

- **denn** *for, because* is a coordinating conjunction and therefore doesn't affect word order.

Ludwig II. war der Mäzen von Richard Wagner, denn er liebte seine Opern. *Ludwig II was the patron of Richard Wagner because he loved his operas.*

Note that **denn** introduces an explanation relating to a previous statement, and it can often be replaced by the adverb **nämlich**. But careful, **nämlich** never occurs in the first position and usually occurs in a new sentence:

Ludwig II. war der Mäzen von Richard Wagner. Er liebte nämlich seine Opern. *Ludwig II was the patron of Richard Wagner, for he loved his operas.*

4.3 'although' and 'so that'

- **obwohl** *although, even though* is used as in English.

Obwohl er Karriere gemacht hat, scheint er nicht zufrieden zu sein. *Although he had a good career, he didn't seem to be content.*

- **damit** *so that* is also used in the same way as in English, but don't confuse it with the compound **damit** (**da** + **mit**), used to express *with that/it/them*!

Damit wir uns besser kennen lernen, möchte ich Sie ins Restaurant einladen. *So that we can get to know each other better, I would like to invite you to a restaurant.*

- **damit** can be replaced with **dass** (or **so dass**) in a subordinate clause.

Fahren Sie schneller, (so) dass wir ankommen, bevor es dunkel wird. *Drive faster so that we arrive before it gets dark.*

84 When the subject in the main clause and the subordinate clause is the same, **damit** can be replaced with **um ... zu**:
Was kann man tun, damit man schnell Deutsch lernt? = ..., **um** schnell Deutsch **zu** lernen? *What can one do in order to learn German quickly?*

> *Now it's time to combine work with pleasure and apply what you've learned by reading the following dialogue.*

Review exercise

Mittagspause

1 – Mahlzeit! Ist hier noch ein Platz frei?
2 – Sicher, setz dich, Johannes! Ich freue mich, dich wieder zu sehen.
3 – Nicht möglich, Thomas, du bist's! Ich habe dich nicht wieder erkannt.
4 – Das ist verständlich, seit Abschluss des Studiums haben wir uns nicht mehr gesehen!
5 – Ja, seit mehr als fünfzehn Jahren! Mensch, erzähl mal, was machst du?
6 – Ich arbeite immer noch für das Unternehmen, bei dem ich schon damals während des Studiums angestellt war, und du?
7 – Ich habe mich selbstständig gemacht.
8 Sag mal, ist das dein Magen oder meiner, der so knurrt?
9 – Das ist deiner, der knurrte damals schon immer, wenn du Hunger hattest.
10 – Ja, ich muss unbedingt was essen.
11 Aber erzähl mal weiter, was machen die anderen Studienkollegen? Bachmann, Busch, Schwab?
12 – Bachmann ist noch ganz der Alte, man weiß nie, ob er genial oder einfach verrückt ist,
13 von Busch und Schwab habe ich leider schon lange nichts mehr gehört.

14 – Und Katrin? Erinnerst du dich an sie? Wie war doch ihr Nachname?
15 – Ziegler.
16 – Natürlich, Ziegler, du warst der einzige unter uns, der sich nicht für sie interessierte.
17 Ich dagegen habe oft an sie gedacht.
18 Schade, die verlorene Zeit kann man nicht aufholen.
19 Na ja, sie hat sich sicher inzwischen verändert, ist dicker geworden…
20 – Das finde ich eigentlich nicht.
21 – Warum? Siehst du sie noch?
22 – Jeden Tag… Katrin und ich sind verheiratet und haben eine Tochter.
23 Komm uns doch mal besuchen, wenn du Zeit hast.
24 Katrin wird sich freuen, dich wieder zu sehen.

Translation

Lunchbreak

1 Enjoy your meal! Is there still a seat available here? **2** Certainly, take a seat, Johannes! I'm glad to see you again. **3** [But that's] not possible, Thomas, it's you! I didn't recognize you. **4** That's understandable – we haven't seen each other since we graduated. **5** Yes, for (*since*) more than 15 years! (*Man*) so tell [me], what are you doing? **6** I still work for the company where I was employed during my studies (*at which I already back-then during the studies employed was*), and you? **7** I started my own business (*have myself independent made*). **8** Hey, is that your stomach or mine that['s] growling like that (*so growls*)? **9** That's yours. Even back then it always used to growl (*it growled back-then already always*) when you were hungry. **10** Yes, I really must (*must absolutely*) eat something. **11** But tell [me] more (*once further*); what are our (*the*) other classmates doing? Bachmann, Busch, Schwab? **12** Bachmann is still the same (*wholly the old*); one never knows whether he's brilliant or just crazy, **13** I've unfortunately not heard from Busch and Schwab for a long time (*already long nothing more heard*). **14** And Katrin? Do you remember her? What was her last name again? **15** Ziegler. **16** Of course, Ziegler – you were the only one of (*among*) us who wasn't interested in her. **17** However, I've often thought about her. **18** Too bad, one can't make up for lost time. **19** Well, she's surely changed in the meantime, put on weight … **20** Actually, I don't think so (*That find I actually not*). **21** Why? Do you still see her? **22** Every day … Katrin and I are married, and we have a daughter. **23** Come and visit us when you have time, won't you? **24** Katrin will surely be glad to see you again.

85 Fünfundachtzigste Lektion

Wie wird das Frühstücksei gegessen ①? (Benimmregeln ② zum Köpfen eines weichen Eies)

1 Das Problem mag ③ Ihnen lächerlich erscheinen, aber – glauben Sie uns – es ist todernst.
2 Durch schlechte Manieren kann nämlich eine Karriere brutal beendet werden ④ – oder das Gegenteil!
3 Stellen Sie sich zum Beispiel vor, Sie begleiten Ihren neuen Chef auf einer Geschäftsreise.

Pronunciation
… *frew*-shtewks-ei … bu*nim*-rehg'ln … *kœ*pf'n … *vei*kH'n ei's **1** … *toht*-ernst **2** … ma*nee*ruhn … bru*tahl* buh'*en*duht …

Notes

① Here we have an example of the passive voice. In German the passive is more frequent than in English, so it's a useful construction to know. It is formed with **werden** as an auxiliary verb + a past participle: **Das Ei wird gegessen.** ('The egg becomes eaten.') *The egg is being eaten.* Note that the passive voice assumes that an action is currently taking place, hence

> **Wir werden uns freuen, Sie morgen wieder zu treffen!** And we'll be glad to see you again tomorrow!

Second wave: 35th lesson

Eighty-fifth lesson   85

How to eat a boiled egg
(How becomes [is] the breakfast-egg eaten?)
(Rules of etiquette for the 'decapitation' of a soft-boiled egg)

1 The problem may seem ridiculous to you, but – trust us (*believe you us*) – it is deadly serious (*death-serious*).
2 In fact, a lack of manners (*By bad manners can after-all*) can brutally end a career (*a career brutally ended become*) – or the contrary!
3 Imagine, for example, [that] you accompany your new boss on a business trip.

---

it is often rendered with a progressive (*-ing*) form in English. But be careful not to confuse it with the future tense, which is formed with the present tense of **werden** + infinitive: **Er wird das Ei essen.** *He will eat the egg.* There is another variant of the passive, used to describe states, which uses **sein** as its auxiliary; it is discussed in more detail in the review lesson.

② **der Benimm** is synonymous with **die (guten) Manieren** *(good) manners*. It is also the imperative singular of **sich benehmen** *to behave oneself*: **Benimm dich!** *Behave yourself!*

③ **mögen** *to like, to want* can also mean *may* (i.e. supposition).

④ **beendet werden** *to be ended* is the passive infinitive of **beenden** *to end*.

4 Am **Mor**gen **kom**men Sie na**tür**lich **pünkt**lich zum **Früh**stück, wie es sich ge**hört** ⑤,

5 und da steht es di**rekt** vor **Ih**nen: das **Früh**stücksei!

6 Für **ei**nen **Au**genblick **seh**en Sie das **strah**lende Ge**si**cht **Ih**res **Soh**nes vor sich, als er das **letz**te Mal beim „**Ei**eraufschlagen" ⑥ ge**won**nen hat.

7 Die **Spiel**regeln sind **ein**fach: die **Ei**er **wer**den gegenei**nan**der ge**schla**gen ⑦,

8 und **der**jenige ⑧, **des**sen Ei zu**erst** ka**putt** geht ⑨, hat ver**lo**ren.

9 Doch, **Him**mel, wie wird das **wei**che Ei **an**ständig ge**ges**sen ⑩?

(Fortsetzung folgt)

---

6 ... **shtrah**luhnduh ... **zohn**'s ... **ei**ᵃ-**owfshlag**'n ... **8** ... **deh**ᵃ-**yehn**iguh ... ka**put** ... **9** ... **an**shtendikH ...

Notes

⑤ The expression **das gehört sich** *as one should, as is right and proper* contains the verb **gehören** *to belong to*, though the connection is not very obvious.

⑥ The plural of **das Ei** is **die Eier** *eggs*. The action described by **Eier aufschlagen** *to break eggs* can be turned into a noun and written as one word: **das Eieraufschlagen** ('the eggs-breaking'). This doesn't exactly denote a gentle action: in fact **aufschlagen** derives from **schlagen** (past tense: **schlug**, past participle: **geschlagen**) *to hit, to beat* preceded by **auf**, which indicates opening (e.g. **aufmachen** *to open*).

⑦ This is an example of a plural passive construction: **die Eier werden gegeneinander geschlagen** ('the eggs become against-one-another hit').

4 In the morning, you of course come to breakfast on time, as one should (*as is fitting*),

5 and there it is (*stands*), directly in front of you: the [boiled] (*breakfast-*)egg!

6 For a moment, you see your son's beaming face in front of you the last time he won at 'Break the egg' (*when he the last time with-the eggs-breaking won has*).

7 The rules of the game (*game-rules*) are simple: the [boiled] eggs are knocked against each other (*against-each-other hit*),

8 and the one whose egg gets broken first, loses (*has lost*).

9 But, how on earth (*heaven*) does one eat a soft-boiled egg correctly (*how becomes [is] the soft egg decently eaten*)?

(To be continued)

⑧ The demonstrative pronouns **derjenige, diejenige, dasjenige** refer to a person or thing defined in the relative clause that follows. **Derjenige Bewerber, der gute Manieren hat, wird eingestellt.** *The applicant who has good manners will be employed.* They can occur without a noun if the information in the relative clause makes the overall meaning clear: **Derjenige, der zu viele Eier isst, wird dick.** *He who eats too many eggs will put on weight.* In speech, **derjenige, diejenige, dasjenige** are often replaced by **der, die, das**.

⑨ **kaputt gehen** *to break, to get broken* expresses the action of something breaking. To describe the state of being broken, you say **kaputt sein** *to be broken*. In reference to people, these expressions have a slightly different meaning: **er geht kaputt/er ist kaputt** *he is exhausting himself/he is exhausted*.

⑩ In some contexts, the passive **werden** + past participle translates best in English to the active but impersonal 'one': **wie wird das Ei gegessen** *how does one eat an egg ...?*

85 Übung 1 – Übersetzen Sie bitte!

❶ Es mag dir lächerlich erscheinen, aber so sind die Regeln. ❷ Er wird nicht eingeladen, er hat wirklich keine Manieren. ❸ Stellen Sie sich vor, Sie haben im Lotto gewonnen! ❹ Wie werden Krabben gegessen, wissen Sie das vielleicht? ❺ Das Problem mit Eiern ist, dass sie leicht kaputt gehen.

***

Übung 2 – Ergänzen Sie bitte!

❶ Would you like a soft[-boiled] egg for breakfast?
– Yes (*Gladly*), but not too soft, please.

Möchten Sie ... . zum Frühstück?
– Gern, ... nicht zu ....., bitte.

❷ I find this rather (*quite*) ridiculous, but many people believe in good manners.

Ich finde ... ziemlich ...., aber viele Leute .... an ... .

❸ When I am on a business trip with my colleagues, I am often invited for dinner.

Wenn ich mit meinen Kollegen ... . bin, ... ich oft zum Essen ....

***

In Germany, eggs at breakfast usually come in the form of boiled eggs. You can have either **ein weiches Ei / ein weichgekochtes Ei** *'a soft egg'/'a soft-cooked egg', i.e. a soft-boiled egg, or* **ein hartes Ei / ein hartgekochtes Ei** *a hard-boiled egg. If you're staying with friends or in a hotel, you'll normally be asked how you would like your egg done: that is, how long you'd like it to be cooked: three minutes, three-and-a-half minutes, four minutes, and so on.*

Answers to Exercise 1

❶ It may seem ridiculous to you, but such are the rules. ❷ He won't be invited; he really has no manners. ❸ Imagine you've won the lottery! ❹ How does one eat crabs? Do you know (*that*) by any chance (*perhaps*)? ❺ The problem with eggs is that they break easily.

***

❹ Those who don't arrive punctually won't (*don't*) get anything to eat.

. . . . , . . . nicht . . . . kommen, kriegen nichts . . . .

❺ The rules of the game are very simple: all cards have to be played.

. . . . sind ganz . . . . : alle Karten müssen . . . .

Answers to Exercise 2

❶ – ein weiches Ei – aber – weich – ❷ – das – lächerlich – glauben – gute Manieren ❸ – auf Geschäftsreise – werde – eingeladen ❹ Diejenigen, die – pünktlich – zu essen ❺ Die Spielregeln – einfach – gespielt werden

***

But unless you're there for Easter, you'll most likely not witness (or participate in) an early-morning 'egg contest'. **Eierpecken** *or* **Eiertitschen** *– knocking hard-boiled eggs against each other to see which shell cracks first – is really an Easter custom, particularly in the south of Germany, the Rhineland, Austria and Switzerland.*

Second wave: 36th lesson

86 Sechsundachtzigste Lektion

Wie wird das Frühstücksei gegessen?
(Fortsetzung)

1 Zehn Mi**nu**ten **spä**ter zeigt Ihr Chef **im**mer noch **kei**nerlei ① **Ab**sicht, sein Ei **es**sen zu **wol**len.
2 Er scheint **kei**ne **Ei**er zu **mö**gen, **scha**de!
3 Sie ent**schei**den, auch auf Ihr Ei zu ver**zich**ten.
4 Doch **plötz**lich fällt Ihr Blick auf die **vor**nehme **Da**me am **Nach**bartisch, die ge**ra**de ② ihr Ei isst!
5 **Zuerst** wird von ihr ③ die **Scha**le mit dem **Ei**erlöffel **rund**herum **auf**geschlagen,
6 dann wird **vor**sichtig das **Ei**hütchen **ab**gehoben ④,
7 es ⑤ wird ein **biss**chen Salz da**rauf** ge**streut** und…

Pronunciation
1 … keinuhªlei apzikHt … 3 … fertsikHtuhn 4 … fohªnehmuh … nakhbahªtish … 5 … shahluh … eiª-lœf'l … 6 … foªzikHtikH … ei-hewtkH'n ap'guh-hohbuhn 7 … zalts … guhshtroit …

Notes
① **keinerlei** *no … at all*, *no … whatsoever* doesn't decline.
② When used with a present tense verb, **gerade** *just* often translates as *just now*, *to be in the process of* or simply with the present continuous: **das Auto wird gerade repariert** ('the car becomes just repaired') *the car is just now being repaired*; *the car is being repaired*.
③ To indicate who is carrying out the action in a passive clause, the information is added in a prepositional phrase, using

Eighty-sixth lesson 86

How to eat a boiled egg
(Continuation)

1 Ten minutes later, your boss still shows no intention whatsoever of eating (*wanting to eat*) his egg.
2 He doesn't seem to like eggs – too bad!
3 You decide to also forego your egg.
4 But suddenly, your gaze (*glance*) falls on the distinguished (*refined*) lady at the next table (*neighbour-table*), who is just now eating her egg!
5 First, she cracks the shell (*becomes by her the shell*) with the eggspoon all the way around (*cracked*),
6 then she carefully takes off the top of the egg (*then becomes carefully the little-egg-hat off-lifted*),
7 sprinkles a little salt on it (*it becomes a little salt on-it scattered*) and ...

---

von + dative case: **Die Schokolade wird von den Kindern gegessen.** *The chocolate is eaten by the children.*

④ The particle **ab** usually indicates detachment. On its own, **heben** means *to lift, to raise*: **er hebt den Arm** *he raises his arm*; but **abheben** usually means *to lift off, to take off*.

⑤ Sometimes the passive voice is used in German in ways that do not easily translate into English. For example, the impersonal **es** often begins a passive main clause that denotes general activity: **Es wird getanzt.** *There is dancing going on.* The introductory **es** is particularly common with dative verbs: **Es wird uns geholfen.** *We are being helped.* In some cases, the main clause starts with **es**, but **es** isn't really the subject – like in the example in line 7. The real subject here is **ein bisschen Salz** *a little salt*; one could also say **ein bisschen Salz wird daraufgestreut** *a little salt is sprinkled on top*.

8 Das **Was**ser läuft **Ih**nen im Mund zu**sam**men, **gie**rig **grei**fen ⑥ Sie nach **Ih**rem Ei…

9 **Aber** da hält Sie im **letz**ten Mo**ment** Ihr Chef zu**rück**, in**dem** ⑦ er sagt:

10 „**War**ten Sie, Herr **Schnei**der! **Las**sen Sie ⑧ uns „**Eier**aufschlagen" **spie**len!

11 **Wis**sen Sie, ich **pfei**fe ⑨ auf **Knig**ge und seine **Benimm**regeln.

12 Ich **lie**be **die**ses Spiel und ich **war**ne Sie, ich ge**win**ne **im**mer!"

8 … vass^a loift … geerikH greif'n … 11 … pfeifuh … kniguh … 12 … varnuh …

Notes

⑥ **etwas greifen** *to take something, to grab something*, but **nach etwas greifen** *to reach for something*, as **nach** always denotes movement <u>towards</u> something. The expression **nach den Sternen greifen** *to reach for the stars* ('towards the stars to grab') illustrates this nicely.

⑦ **indem** is a conjunction that starts a clause explaining how something is achieved. It usually translates as *by ….-ing*: **Er warnt seinen Freund, indem er dreimal pfeift.** *He warns his friend by whistling three times.* But note that if the action takes place in the past, in German the **indem** clause is also in the past, e.g. **Er warnte seinen Freund, indem er dreimal pfiff.** 'He warned his friend by having whistled three times.'

8 Your mouth is watering (*The water flows to-you in-the mouth together*) – greedily you reach for your egg …

9 But then (*there*), at the last moment, your boss stops you (*holds you back*) by saying:

10 'Wait, Mr Schneider! Let's play 'Break the egg'!

11 You know, I don't give a damn about (*I whistle on*) Knigge and his rules of etiquette.

12 I love this game, and I'm warning you – I always win!'

> Entschuldigen Sie bitte, ich hatte keinerlei Absicht, zu gewinnen.

⑧ There are two ways to form the first-person plural imperative: we've seen the **wir**-imperative, in which the order of the subject and verb is inverted: **Essen wir!** ('We eat!'). The other way is very similar to the English construction, formed with **lassen** *to let* + the pronoun **uns** *us* + an infinitive. **Lass uns essen!** *Let's eat!* (if addressing one person informally), **Lasst uns essen!** (if addressing several people informally) or **Lassen Sie uns essen!** (formal).

⑨ **pfeifen, pfiff, gepfiffen** *to whistle*; **auf etwas pfeifen** *to not care, to not give a damn*: **ich pfeife darauf** *I don't care.* Note that **auf etwas pfeifen** is a somewhat colloquial expression, so it would be best to avoid in formal contexts.

vierhundertsiebzig • 470

86 Übung 1 – Übersetzen Sie bitte!

❶ Entschuldigen Sie bitte, ich hatte keinerlei Absicht zu gewinnen. ❷ Gierig greift er noch einmal nach der Flasche, aber er wird von seinen Freunden zurückgehalten. ❸ Wenn man die Absicht hat, ein paar Worte zu sagen, wird mit dem Löffel an ein Glas geschlagen. ❹ Zuerst werden die Spaghettis genommen, dann die Tomatensoße, und zuletzt wird Käse daraufgestreut. ❺ Mach das nicht noch einmal oder ich vergesse meine guten Manieren.

***

Übung 2: Ergänzen Sie bitte!

❶ I had no intention at all of buying something when I suddenly saw this sweater.
Ich hatte .... etwas zu kaufen, als ich .... diesen Pullover ....

❷ The tennis ball is hit over the net by the man.
Der Tennisball .... über das Netz ....

❸ Suddenly, the police came, but Thomas warned us by whistling (*has whistled*) loudly.
.... ist die Polizei gekommen, aber Thomas ... uns ...., ... er laut ....

Answers to Exercise 1

❶ Please excuse me, I had no intention at all of winning. **❷** Greedily, he reaches for the bottle once more, but he is held back by his friends. **❸** If one has the intention of saying a few words, one taps a glass with a spoon (*becomes with the spoon on a glass hit*). **❹** First one takes the spaghetti, then the tomato sauce, and last, cheese is sprinkled on top. **❺** Don't do that again, or I['ll] forget my (*good*) manners.

***

❹ Carefully, she glances (*looks*) over to the next (*neighbour-*) table, where the distinguished lady is sitting.

.... sieht sie ....,
wo ... . sitzt.

❺ My mouth was watering (*The water is to-me in-the mouth together-run*), but I decided to forego the chocolate.

... . ist mir .. ....
zusammengelaufen, aber ich habe entschieden,
... die Schokolade .. ..

Answers to Exercise 2

❶ – keinerlei Absicht – plötzlich – gesehen habe **❷** – wird von dem Mann – geschlagen **❸** Plötzlich – hat – gewarnt, indem – gepfiffen hat **❹** Vorsichtig – nach dem Nachbartisch – die vornehme Dame – **❺** Das Wasser – im Mund – auf – zu verzichten

87 | **Freiherr Adolf (von) Knigge** Baron Adolf Knigge
When someone's manners leave something to be desired, Germans often simply say: **er hat Knigge nicht gelesen** *'he hasn't read Knigge', and everyone automatically understands this as 'he is rude'. However, poor Baron Knigge (1751–96) would turn in his grave if he knew that his name has become synonymous with good manners, as contrary to what many believe, he was never really interested in questions of etiquette and manners. The book that made his name is entitled* **Über den Umgang mit Menschen** On Human Relations, *but you won't learn anything from it about table manners or whether you can wear white socks with a suit … Knigge in fact wrote it to give advice on interpersonal relationships, hoping to help common people to better stand up to the aristocracy, whom*

---

87 Siebenundachtzigste Lektion

Willkommen auf der Wies'n ①!

1 – Sieh da! Hier in der **Zei**tung steht ein Be**richt ü**ber das Ok**to**berfest.
2 Das **We**tter soll ② schon **lang**e nicht mehr so schön ge**we**sen sein.

Pronunciation
… *veez'n* **1** … *buhrikHt* …

Notes

① **die Wies'n** is the Munich abbreviation for **die Theresienwiese** *Therese's Meadow*. This is where the Oktoberfest has taken place every year since 1810, when Crown Prince Ludwig I – grandfather of Ludwig II – married Princess Therese of Saxe-Hildeburghausen. The title of the lesson could equally be **Willkommen beim Oktoberfest** *Welcome to the Oktoberfest*.

② **sollen** *'should'*, *to be supposed to* can also be used to report what is heard (or read), as in 'it is said that': **Es soll morgen regnen.** *It's supposed to rain tomorrow.*

he criticized strongly (he removed the particle **von**, *which indicates nobility, from his name).*

How could such confusion arise? Unfortunately for him, his book, which was a great success upon its publication in 1788, was rewritten in the 19th century by a pastor whose aim was to dictate the rules of good conduct to people ... and it worked! It wasn't until 1999, when Knigge's original text was published in a new edition, that the deception was discovered – but it was too late. For a long time, there have been 'Knigges' for everything: an **Urlaubsknigge** for travel advice; the **Bewerbungsknigge** for improving your application letters, and even a **Flirtknigge** to help increase your chances with a love interest.

Second wave: 37th lesson

Eighty-seventh lesson 87

Welcome to the 'meadow'!

1 – Look! There is an article (*report*) about the 'Oktoberfest' in the newspaper.
2 The weather is supposed to have been the best in a long time (*should already a-long-time no more so beautiful to-have-been*).

87

3 „**Gä**ste und **Schau**steller **wur**den ③ beim Ok**to**berfest durch ein **traum**haftes **Wet**ter ver**wöhnt**", steht hier.

4 – **Da**von habe ich nichts ge**merk**t; als ich dort war, hat es **Bind**fäden ge**reg**net ④.

5 – Man kann nicht **im**mer Glück **ha**ben, **a**ber **ra**te mal, wie **vie**le Pers**o**nen da **wa**ren!

6 – **Kei**ne **Ah**nung ⑤, **meh**rere Milli**o**nen ver**mut**lich.

7 – Ja, mehr als 6,5 (sechs **Ko**mma fünf) Milli**o**nen Be**su**cher sind aus der **gan**zen Welt ge**kom**men.

8 **Ins**gesamt **wur**den fast 6 Milli**o**nen Maß ⑥ Bier ge**trun**ken, und 350 000 (**drei**hundert**fünf**zig**tau**send) **Brat**hähnchen, 80 000 (**acht**zig**tau**send) **Schweins**haxen und 80 **Och**sen gegessen ⑦.

---

*3 ge**stuh** ... **show**-shtel[a] ... fer**vœnt** ... 4 ... gu**merkt** ... **bint**-fehd'n ... 6 ... **ah**nung ... mil**yoh**nuhn fer**moot**likH 7 ... zeks **ko**ma fewnf ... 8 ... **braht**-hehnkH'n ... **oks**'n ...*

Notes

③ In the passive, the auxiliary verb (i.e. **werden**) changes tense to indicate when the action took place: **er wird verwöhnt** *he is [being] spoiled*, **er wurde verwöhnt** *he was spoiled*, **er ist von seinem Vater verwöhnt worden** *he has been spoiled by his father*. Remember that **werden** takes **sein** as the auxiliary in the perfect tenses, and note that although the past participle of **werden** is **geworden**, in the passive voice it becomes **worden**. (Another thing to point out is that it is **von seinem Vater** *by his father* because it refers to a person, but **durch das Wetter** *by the weather*. The preposition **durch** is used to describe 'by which means' or 'how' rather than 'who'.)

475 • vierhundertfünfundsiebzig

3 'Visitors (*Guests*) and exhibitors (*showpeople*) at the Oktoberfest were spoiled by fantastic (*dreamlike*) weather,' it says here.

4 – I noticed none of that. When I was there, it was raining cats and dogs (*strings*).

5 – One can't always be lucky, but guess how many people were there?

6 – No idea … several millions presumably.

7 – Yes, more than 6.5 million visitors came from around the world (*the whole world*).

8 In total, almost 6 million litres [of] beer were drunk, and 350,000 roast chickens, 80,000 pork knuckles and 80 oxen were eaten.

---

④ **es regnet Bindfäden** 'it's raining strings'; **der Faden** *thread* and **der Bindfaden** *string* (no umlaut in the singular).

⑤ **keine Ahnung** *no idea*. The noun **die Ahnung** actually means *suspicion*, *hunch*, from **ahnen** *to suspect*, *to guess*.

⑥ In Bavaria, **die Maß** refers to a mug that holds 1 litre of beer. Be careful with the gender of the noun here, as **das Maß** means *measure*, *degree*: **Trinken Sie mit Maßen!** *Drink in moderation* ('with measure')!

⑦ These are simple past forms of the passive: **wurden getrunken** *were drunk*, and **wurden gegessen** *were eaten*.

87 9 Und – na **so** was! – 168 000
(**hund**ert**ach**t**und****sech**zig**tau**send) Be**su**cher
haben ver**sucht** ⑧, **ei**nen **Bier**krug als
Souve**nir mit**gehen zu **la**ssen.
10 **A**ber der Krug **wur**de **ih**nen am **Bier**zelt-
Ausgang **ab**genommen.
11 Sag mal, wo**her** kommt **ei**gentlich der
Bierkrug, aus dem ich **trin**ke?
12 – Tja, wie du selbst ge**ra**de ge**sagt** hast, man
kann nicht **im**mer Glück **ha**ben, aber
manchmal…

---

9 … buhzookh^a … bee^a-krook … zoovuhnee^a … 10 … bee^a-tselt-owsgang … 12 … mankHmahl …

***

Übung 1 – Übersetzen Sie bitte!

❶ In den Ferien wurde ich von meinen Großeltern immer sehr verwöhnt. ❷ Raten Sie mal, wie viel Liter Bier auf dem letzten Oktoberfest getrunken wurden? ❸ Mehrere Millionen Besucher kommen jedes Jahr zum Oktoberfest nach München. ❹ In der Zeitung stand, dass viele Besucher versuchten, einen Bierkrug mitzunehmen. ❺ Nur einen Nachmittag hat es Bindfäden geregnet; an den anderen Tagen ist das Wetter sehr schön gewesen.

9 And – my goodness (*well so something*)! – 168,000 visitors tried to walk off with (*let go- with them*) a beer mug as a souvenir.
10 But the mug was taken away from them at the exit of the beer tent.
11 In fact, tell me, where does the beer mug from which I'm drinking come from?
12 – Well, as you just said yourself, one can't always be lucky, but sometimes …

Notes

⑧ Pay attention to prefixes! **der Besucher** *visitor* derives from **besuchen** *to visit*, but **versuchen** means *to try* and **suchen** *to look for*.

***

Answers to Exercise 1

❶ During the holidays, I was always spoiled a lot by my grandparents. ❷ Guess how many litres of beer were drunk at the last Oktoberfest? ❸ Several million visitors come to Munich every year for the Oktoberfest. ❹ In the newspaper it said that many visitors tried to take a beer mug away with them. ❺ It only rained cats and dogs for one afternoon; on the other days, the weather was very good.

88 Übung 2 – Ergänzen Sie bitte!

❶ How many people came (*are*) to Munich (*come*) to celebrate the Oktoberfest?

... . Leute .... nach München
........, um ... Oktoberfest zu ......?

❷ 80 oxen and several hundred thousand roast chickens were eaten during the celebration – My goodness!

80 Ochsen und .... hunderttausend
Brathähnchen ...... auf dem Fest ....
– .. .. !

❸ Do you know why one cannot always be lucky? – No idea.

Wissen Sie, ... man ..... immer .....
..... kann? – Keine ....

---

88 Achtundachtzigste Lektion

Unsere Vorfahren, die Affen ①

1 – Jetzt ist mir **end**lich klar, wa**rum** wir **Män**ner so viel **ar**beiten **müs**sen ②.
2   Hier steht es schwarz auf weiß:
3   **Un**ser ge**net**isches **Erb**gut ③ ist zu fast 100 Pro**zent** mit dem der Schim**pan**sen i**den**tisch.

Pronunciation
... foh{^a}fahr'n ... af'n 3 ... genehtishuhs erp-goot ... pro**tsent**
... shi'm**pans**'n i**den**tish

Notes
① **der Affe** can refer to a monkey or an ape.

④ Welcome to Munich! You (*formal*) are being spoiled by the nice weather; yesterday it was still raining cats and dogs.
.... in München! ... . durch das schöne Wetter ...., gestern hat es noch ....

⑤ This time, more than 6 million litres [of] beer were drunk by visitors from around the (*from the whole*) world.
Dieses Mal ...... mehr als 6 Millionen Liter Bier ... . aus ... .

Answers to Exercise 2

① Wie viele – sind – gekommen – das – feiern ② – mehrere – wurden – gegessen – Na so was ③ – warum – nicht – Glück haben – Ahnung ④ Willkommen – Sie werden – verwöhnt – Bindfäden geregnet ⑤ – wurden – von Besuchern – der ganzen Welt getrunken

Second wave: 38th lesson

Eighty-eighth lesson 88

Our ancestors, the apes

1 – Now I finally understand (*is to-me finally clear*) why we men have to work so much.
2 Here it is (*stands*) [in] black and (*on*) white:
3 Our genetic make-up is (*to*) almost 100% identical with that of chimpanzees.

② The rule concerning moving the conjugated verb to the last position in a subordinate clause also applies to indirect questions: **Mir ist nicht klar, warum du so viel arbeiten musst.** *I don't understand why you have to work so much.*

③ **das Erbgut** *genotype, genetic make-up* consists of **das Erbe** *inheritance, legacy* and **das Gut** *property, possession, goods.*

vierhundertachtzig • 480

4 – Ja und? Ich verstehe dich nicht. Wo ist der Zusammenhang?

5 – Hast du das Experiment mit den Affen vergessen, das in Amerika ④ durchgeführt worden ist?

6 Bei diesem Experiment konnten sich die Affen Rosinen verdienen ⑤.

7 – Ach ja, jetzt erinnere ich mich wieder, du warst entsetzlich schockiert,

8 weil die Affenmännchen wie die Dummen ⑥ gearbeitet haben, während die Weibchen den ganzen Tag geschlafen haben.

9 – Genau! Und jetzt wissen wir, warum es ewig so weiter gehen wird.

10 – Nicht so schnell! Die Geschichte war damit noch nicht zu Ende!

11 Zwei Forscherinnen kamen auf ⑦ die Idee, die Affen nachts zu beobachten und…

12 sie entdeckten, dass die Männchen so viel arbeiteten, um bei den Weibchen bessere Chancen zu haben!

---

4 … tsoozamuhn-hang 5 … experiment … 6 … rozeenuhn ferdeenuhn 8 … af'n-menkH'n … veipkH'n … 9 … ehvikH … 11 … forsh^arinuhn … buh-ohbakht'n …

Notes

④ In Germany, as in many other places, **Amerika** is often (imprecisely) used to mean the *United States*. Thus, when someone says **Ich bin nach Amerika geflogen**, most people would understand 'I went to the US'. To refer to other parts of the Americas, more specific terms are used: **Südamerika**, **Mittelamerika**, **Kanada**, etc.

4 – So what? I don't understand you. Where is the connection?

5 – Have you forgotten the experiment with the apes that was conducted in the US?

6 In (*With*) this experiment, the apes were able to earn (*themselves*) raisins.

7 – Oh yes, now I remember (*again*), you were awfully shocked

8 because the male apes worked like (*the*) fools while the females slept all day.

9 – Exactly! And now we know why it'll go on like this for eternity (*eternally so further go will*).

10 – Not so quickly! The story didn't end there (*was with-this still not to end*)!

11 Two female researchers came up [with] the idea to observe the apes at night and …

12 they discovered that the males worked so much in order to have better chances with the females!

---

⑤ **etwas verdienen** *to earn something.* Like many other verbs, **verdienen** is often used reflexively, but the reflexive pronoun isn't essential: **Er hat (sich) mit diesem Geschäft Millionen verdient.** *He earned (himself) millions with this deal.*

⑥ Adjectives used as nouns decline! **der Dumme** *fool, idiot, goof* (m.), **ein Dummer** *a fool*, **die Dummen** *the fools*, etc.

⑦ **auf eine Idee kommen** ('on an idea arrive') is synonymous with **eine Idee haben**: **Wie bist du denn auf die Idee gekommen?** *How did you come up with/get that idea?*

88 13 Die ließen ⑧ sich **näm**lich **ihr**e **Lie**besdienste von den **Männ**chen be**zah**len…

14 – Das ist es ja! Seit **An**fang der **Mensch**heit hat sich nichts ge**än**dert, und es ⑨ wird sich nichts **än**dern. □

14 … menshheit …

Notes

⑧ **etwas machen lassen** can mean *to let someone do something* or *to have something done*: **Sie lässt ihn schlafen.** *She lets him sleep.* **Ich lasse mir die Haare schneiden.** *I have my hair cut.*

⑨ **es** *it* is a 'false' subject here; the actual subject is **nichts** *nothing*. One could also say **nichts wird sich ändern** *nothing will [ever] change.* The ideas of this woman's husband don't seem to have evolved much in any case!

***

Übung 1 – Übersetzen Sie bitte!

❶ Seit Anfang der Menschheit hat sich nichts geändert. ❷ Für dieses Experiment sind zwanzig Affen drei Jahre lang von zehn Forschern beobachtet worden. ❸ Die Affenweibchen haben den ganzen Tag geschlafen, aber in der Nacht haben sie hart gearbeitet. ❹ Eines Tages hat er entdeckt, dass man nicht wie ein Dummer zu arbeiten braucht, um viel Geld zu verdienen. ❺ Stimmt es, dass unser genetisches Erbgut fast dasselbe wie das der Schimpansen ist?

13 In fact, the latter had the males pay for their favours (*These let themselves in-fact their love-services by the males pay*) …

14 – Well, there you have it (*That is it yes*)! Nothing has changed since the beginning of humankind, and nothing will [ever] change.

> Unsere Vorfahren, die Affen.

***

Answers to Exercise 1

❶ Nothing has changed since the beginning of humanity. ❷ For this experiment, 20 apes were observed for 3 years by 10 researchers. ❸ The female apes slept all day, but during the night they worked hard. ❹ One day he discovered that one doesn't have to work like a fool to earn a lot of money. ❺ Is it true that our genetic make-up is almost the same as that of chimpanzees?

89 Übung 2 – Ergänzen Sie bitte!

❶ Where do your (*formal*) ancestors come from? – Oh, that's a long story that no one understands.
Woher kommen .... ? – Oh, das ist .... , die niemand ....

❷ Last week we worked day and night – this has to change!
Letzte Woche ..... wir Tag und Nacht ...., das muss sich ...... !

❸ Not so quickly! Where is the connection? The last conclusion (*end*) isn't clear to me.
Nicht so .... ! Wo ist ... . ? Der ...... Schluss ... ... nicht .....

---

89 Neunundachtzigste Lektion

Ein Interview im Radio mit Herrn „Stöffche", dem Apfelwein-König

1 – Zu**erst ein**mal „**herz**liche **Glück**wünsche zum Ge**burts**tag", Herr **Rae**der.

Pronunciation
... intᵉvyoo ... **rah**dyo ... **shtœf**kHuh ... **apf'l**-vein ... **1** ... **herts**likhuh **glewk**-vewnshuh... **rehd**ᵉ

❹ Who discovered (*By whom is discovered become*) that there is only a two percent difference between apes and humans?
Von wem ... ., dass es zwischen ... . und ... . nur .... Unterschied gibt?

❺ Why do you want to earn more? When did you get this idea (*are you on this idea arrived*)?
Warum wollen Sie .... ? Wann sind Sie ... . gekommen?

Answers to Exercise 2

❶ – Ihre Vorfahren – eine lange Geschichte – versteht ❷ – haben – gearbeitet – ändern ❸ – schnell – der Zusammenhang – letzte – ist mir – klar ❹ – ist entdeckt worden – den Affen – den Menschen – zwei Prozent – ❺ – mehr verdienen – auf diese Idee

Second wave: 39th lesson

Eighty-ninth lesson 89

A radio interview with Mr 'Stöffche', the king of cider (*apple-wine-king*)

1 – First of all, Happy Birthday (*warm congratulations to-the birthday*), Mr Raeder!

Pronunciation notes

1 The letter combinations **ae**, **oe**, **ue** are a standard way of representing the umlauts **ä**, **ö**, **ü** and are pronounced in exactly the same way. Before the introduction of the printing press, the sounds now rendered as umlauts were always written like this. However, printers came up with the space-saving measure of replacing the **e** with a superscript **e**, which was later simplified to vertical dashes, and finally to two dots above the other vowel.

89

2 Sie sind **näm**lich **ges**tern 75 (**fünf**undsiebzig) **Jah**re alt ge**wor**den ①, nicht wahr?

3 – Ja, **dan**ke schön, das ist sehr nett von **Ih**nen.

4 – **Sa**gen Sie mal, wo**ran** ② denkt man an so **ei**nem Tag?

5 – Tja, an nichts Be**son**deres, **au**ßer dass man dem **Le**ben **dank**bar ist, dass man trotz des **Al**ters **im**mer noch **ei**ne der **größ**ten und **äl**testen Kelte**rei**en in **Hes**sen **lei**ten kann.

6 **Seh**en Sie, **un**ser Unter**neh**men ist 1799 (**sieb**zehn**hun**dert**neun**und**neun**zig) von **mei**nem **Ur-ur-ur**groß**va**ter ③ ge**grün**det **wor**den.

7 **Heu**te **wer**den von uns **et**wa 25 Milli**o**nen **Li**ter **Ap**felwein und **Ap**felsaft pro Jahr produ**ziert** ④.

8 Dar**auf** ⑤ darf man stolz sein, **mei**nen Sie nicht?

---

4 ... vo**ran** ... **5** ... keltuh**rei**'n ... **hes**'n ... **6** ... **oo**ᵃ-**oo**ᵃ-**oo**ᵃ-grohs-**faht**ᵃ guh**grewn**duht **vor**d'n **7** ... prodoo**tsee**ᵃt
8 ... **shtolts** ...

Notes

① **geworden** *become* is the past participle of **werden**. But remember, in the passive, as in line 6, the **ge-** prefix is dropped: **worden** (see lesson 87, note 3).

② **denken an** (+ acc.) *to think about* is a prepositional verb. When forming a question with these types of verbs, the preposition combines with **wo**: **Ich interessiere mich für Filme. – Wofür intressierst du dich?** *I'm interested in films. – What are you interested in?* ('In-what are you interested?'). **Wo** becomes **wor-** if the preposition starts with a vowel: **Woran denkst du?** *What are you thinking about?* But if the question refers to a person rather than a thing, the preposition is followed by **wen/wem**: **An wen denkst du?** *About whom are you thinking?*

487 • **vierhundertsiebenundachtzig**

2 Because you turned 75 yesterday (*are ... 75 years old become*), didn't you?
3 – Yes, thank you, that's very nice of you.
4 – Tell me, what does one think about on a day like this (*on such a day*)?
5 – Ah well, (*about*) nothing special, except that one is grateful to life that, despite one's age, one is still able to lead one of the largest and oldest fruit-pressing plants in Hesse.
6 You see, our business was founded [in] 1799 by my great-great-great-grandfather.
7 Today we produce (*become by us ... produced*) approximately 25 million litres [of] cider and apple juice per year.
8 One can be proud of that (*Of-this may one proud be*), don't you think?

③ Here used to indicate past generations, the particle **ur** signals that something (or someone) is ancient, original, primitive or archetypal in some way: **die Urzeit(en)** *primeval times*, **uralt** *ancient* (older than **alt** *old*). Don't confuse **ur-** and **die Uhr** *clock, watch* and **die Uhrzeit(en)** *time of day*.

④ **produziert** is the past participle of **produzieren**, as here the statement is in the passive voice: **Wie viel wird von Ihnen pro Jahr produziert?** *How much is* ('becomes') *produced by you per year?* Weak verbs ending in **-ieren** form the past participle without the **ge-** prefix: **produzieren → produziert**; **reparieren → repariert**.

⑤ Just like prepositional verbs, certain adjectives always require a specific preposition: **stolz sein auf** (+ acc.) *to be proud of*. **Worauf sind Sie stolz?** *What are you proud of?* (see note 2) – **Auf unseren Fußballclub.** *[Of] our football club.* – **Ich bin auch stolz darauf.** *I'm also proud of it.* In everyday speech, the preposition is sometimes left out in short answers. However, the prepositional adverb (the **da-**compound) can only be omitted in certain circumstances.

9 – Gewiss! Wenn ich **rich**tig ver**steh**e, **den**ken Sie nicht da**ran** ⑥, in **Ren**te zu **geh**en?

10 – Nein, ich **wer**de ⑦ erst **auf**hören zu **ar**beiten, wenn ich mich alt **füh**le.

11 **Heu**te ist das – toi, toi, toi ⑧ – noch nicht der Fall.

12 – **Ei**ne **letz**te **Fra**ge, Herr **Rae**der: wa**rum wer**den Sie Herr „**Stöff**che" ge**nannt**?

13 – Ach, die **Ant**wort ist ganz **ein**fach, hier in **Hes**sen **sa**gen wir nicht *Apfelwein* wie auf **Hoch**deutsch, **son**dern *Äppelwoi* oder *Stöffche*.

14 – Herr **Stöff**che, ich **dan**ke **Ih**nen ⑨, dass Sie ge**kom**men sind. ☐

---

9 ... *ren*tuh ... **11** ... toi, toi, toi ... **13** ... *ep'l*-voi ...

Notes

⑥ In the phrase **ich denke nicht daran** *I don't think about it*, **daran** *about it* has to be included, even if the verb is followed by an infinitive: **Die Kinder denken nicht daran, ins Bett zu gehen.** *The children aren't thinking about going to bed.* In some contexts, **ich denke nicht daran** takes on the slightly different meaning of *I don't intend to*: **Heiraten? Ich denke gar nicht daran!** *Getting married? No way!*

***

Übung 1 – Übersetzen Sie bitte!

❶ Woran denken Sie? – An nichts Besonderes. ❷ Am Ende des Jahres werde ich aufhören zu arbeiten. ❸ Meine Urgroßmutter hat nicht daran gedacht, Hochdeutsch zu sprechen. ❹ Wenn Hessisch gesprochen worden ist, habe ich nicht viel verstanden. ❺ Mein Vorname ist Hans, aber früher bin ich von allen Hänschen genannt worden.

9 – Certainly! If I understand correctly, you're not thinking about retiring (*in retirement to go*)?

10 – No, I'll only stop working when I feel old.

11 Today – touch wood – that's not yet the case.

12 – One last question, Mr Raeder: why are you called Mr 'Stöffche'?

13 – Ah, the answer is very simple; here in Hesse, we don't say 'Apfelwein', like in 'Hochdeutsch' (*High-German*), but 'Äppelwoi' or 'Stöffche'.

14 – Mr Stöffche, thank you for coming (*that you come are*).

⑦ Did you notice that **werden** is used with an infinitive here? This is the future tense. Remember **werden** + infinitive = future tense.

⑧ **toi, toi, toi** means you're wishing that good luck continues, as in *touch wood*.

⑨ Remember that **danken** *to thank* takes the dative: **ich danke dir/Ihnen** *I thank you*. If mentioning what you're thanking someone for, **danken** is often followed by a subordinate clause introduced by **dass** *that*: **Ich danke Ihnen, dass Sie mir geholfen haben.** *Thank you for helping me.* We see a similar case in line 5 with **man ist dankbar** *one is thankful*.

***

Answers to Exercise 1

❶ What are you thinking about? – Nothing special. ❷ At the end of the year, I'll stop working. ❸ My great-grandmother never thought of speaking standard (*high*) German. ❹ When Hessian was spoken, I didn't understand much. ❺ My first name is Hans, but in the past (*before*) I was called 'Hänschen' by everyone.

89 Übung 2 – Ergänzen Sie bitte!

❶ By whom was the business founded?
– By my great-grandfather.

Von wem ... das Unternehmen ....
......? – ... .

❷ Happy (*Warm congratulations to-the*) Birthday! How old are you (*informal*) actually (*become*)?

.... zum Geburtstag.
Wie alt .... .. eigentlich .... ?

❸ Did I understand correctly that you're giving a radio interview tomorrow?

Habe ich .... verstanden, dass Sie
morgen .. .. ein Interview ..... ?

***

④ I have (*still*) one last question: how many litres [of] cider do you produce each year (*become by you every year produced*)?

Ich habe noch ...., wie viele Liter Apfelwein ...... von Ihnen jedes Jahr ....?

⑤ I am very grateful (*to you*) that you aren't thinking of retiring (*not about-it think in retirement to go*).

... ... Ihnen sehr ...., dass ... nicht ...., in Rente .. ..

Answers to Exercise 2

① – ist – gegründet worden – Von meinem Urgroßvater **②** Herzliche Glückwünsche – bist du – geworden **③** – richtig – im Radio – geben **④** – eine letzte Frage – werden – produziert **⑤** Ich bin – dankbar – Sie – daran denken – zu gehen

***

Sprechen Sie Hochdeutsch? Do you speak Hochdeutsch?
Certainly! In all countries where German is the official language (Germany, Austria, Liechtenstein and the German-speaking parts of Switzerland), the German one learns to read and write in school is (like the German in this course) **das Hochdeutsch** *'high German' or standard German. However, when speaking, many people converse in their regional dialect –* **Dialekt** *or* **Mundart**.

The dialects differ mainly in their accent: **ich**, *for example, is* **ick** *in Berlin,* **isch** *in Saxony and just* **i** *in Bavarian. But there are also differences in vocabulary, especially with regard to food and drink. Thus, a bread roll –* **das Brötchen** *in standard German – is called* **die Semmel** *in Bavaria and Austria,* **der Wecken** *or* **der Weck** *in southwestern Germany,* **die Schrippe** *in Berlin and* **das Rundstück** *in Hamburg. But don't worry! When you're staying in a region, you'll pick up new words, and besides, most people speak* **Hochdeutsch** *to a certain degree. So if you're not following the conversation, just say* **Entschuldigen Sie, ich bin nicht von hier!** *and the person you're speaking to will understand that they have to switch to* **Hochdeutsch**.

Second wave: 40th lesson

90 Neunzigste Lektion

Ein perfekter Plan

1 – **Ach**tung, Jungs ①, in ein paar **Mi**nu**ten** ist es so**weit** ②.
2 Unser **Kön**nen wird **die**ses Mal auf **ei**ne **har**te **Pro**be ge**stellt wer**den ③.
3 – Nur **kei**ne **Pa**nik, Boss! Wir sind **schließ**lich **kei**ne **An**fänger!
4 – Ich weiß schon ④, aber **heu**te **ha**ben wir es zum **ers**ten Mal mit so **ho**hen **Tie**ren zu tun.
5 Es **han**delt sich ⑤ **im**merhin um **ei**nige der **wich**tigsten und **reich**sten Ver**tre**ter aus Poli**tik** und **Wirt**schaft, die im **ers**ten Stock ⑥ ver**sam**melt sind.

Pronunciation
... plahn **1** ... yungs ... **3** ... **pah**nik bos ... **5** ... poli**tik** ... **virt**shaft ... shtok fer**zam**'lt ...

Notes
① **die Jungs** is short for **die Jungen** *boys* and is often used in the sense of *guys*.
② **soweit** can mean *as far as*, but here it is used to signal that it's time for something: **Es ist soweit.** *It's time.* **Ich bin soweit.** *I am ready.*
③ To form the future passive, the auxiliary **werden** is used twice: once for the passive construction and once as an infinitive: **es wird gesungen werden** *there will be singing* ('it becomes sung become'). This repetition can sound rather clunky, especially in subordinate clauses, where the conjugated verb

493 • vierhundertdreiundneunzig

Ninetieth lesson 90

A perfect plan

1 — Get ready, guys, in a few minutes it'll be time (*is it so-far*).
2   This time, our skill will be put to the test (*on a hard test stood become*).
3 — Don't panic (*Only no panic*), boss! After all we're not beginners!
4 — I know very well (*already*), but today, for the first time, we have to deal (*do*) with such big shots (*high animals*).
5   (*It is about*) After all, some of the most important and richest representatives of the political and economic world (*of politics and economy who*) are gathered on the first floor.

---

occurs in the last position: **Sie fragt, wann gesungen werden wird.** *She asks when there will be singing.* So don't hesitate to use the present tense instead of the future if the sentence unambiguously refers to the future (i.e. **morgen, nächstes Jahr** ...). We see this from line 9 on.

④ Note that **ich weiß schon** 'I know already' conveys the meaning *I know very well*.

⑤ Here is another prepositional (and reflexive) verb: **sich handeln um** + acc. *to be about, to concern* ... : **Worum handelt es sich bitte?** *What's this about, please?* Remember that questions are formed with **wo** + the preposition that follows the verb (see lesson 89, note 2).

⑥ **der Stock** *floor* is short for **das Stockwerk**; the plural is **die Stockwerke**. German also uses the French word **die Etage**, pronounced *ehtahzhuh*.

6 Es muss höchst professio**nell vor**gegangen **wer**den, wenn **all**es **kla**ppen soll, wie ge**plant**.
7 – Wird schon **all**es schief **geh**en ⑦!
8 – Mal nicht den **Teu**fel an die Wand!
9 **Al**so, zu**erst** wird 20 Se**kun**den vor **Mit**ternacht von Karl der Strom **ab**gestellt.
10 Von den **an**deren **wer**den die **Tür**en be**wacht** und die **Gäs**te ⑧ in Schach ge**hal**ten.
11 Erst auf mein **Zei**chen **wer**den die **Ker**zen **an**gezündet ⑨.
12 Dann wird schnell **hin**tereinander ⑩ mit der **Tor**te in den Saal ge**lau**fen,
13 und da**bei** wird von **all**en aus **voll**em Hals ⑪ „Zum Ge**burts**tag viel Glück ⑫, Herr Gene**ral**di**rek**tor ⑬" ge**sung**en!
14 **Al**les klar? □

*6 ... profesyo**nel** ... 7 ... sheef ... 8 ... **toif**'l ... vant 9 ... shtrohm ... 10 ... buh**vakht** ... **ges**tuh ... shakh... 11 ... tsei**kH**'n ... **kerts**'n an'**guhts**ewn**duht** 12 ... **hint**ᵉ-einand^a ... zahl ... 13 ... hals ... gene**rahl**-di**rekt**o^a ... guh**zung**uhn*

Notes

⑦ **schief gehen** *to go wrong* is the opposite of **klappen** *to work out, to come off.* The expression **Wird schon schief gehen** or **Es wird schon schief gehen** is based on the idea that voicing the worst outcome will avert misfortune and bring luck. Note that in speech, the initial **es** is often dropped: **(Es) ist nicht so schlimm.** *(It)'s not that bad.*

⑧ The singular of **die Gäste** is **der Gast** *guest*.

⑨ The passive can be used as a polite way to ask for something to be done: **Kinder, jetzt werden endlich die Hausaufgaben**

6 We have to proceed extremely professionally (*It must extremely professionally proceeded become*), if everything is to go as planned (*work-out should as planned*).
7 – It'll turn out all right (*All will already go wrong*)!
8 – Don't tempt fate (*Don't paint the devil on the wall*)!
9 So, first, at 20 seconds to midnight, the electricity is (*becomes*) switched off by Karl.
10 The others guard the doors (*By the others become the doors guarded*) and keep the guests in check (*in check kept*).
11 Only on my signal are (*become*) the candles lit.
12 Then we run quickly into the hall with the cake, one after the other (*becomes fast one-after-the-other with the cake in the hall run*),
13 (*and with-it becomes ... sung*) all singing at the top of our voices (*from full throat*) 'Happy Birthday, (*Mr*) President!'
14 Is everything clear (*All clear*)?

---

gemacht! *Children, now it's time to do your homework* ('now becomes finally the homework done')*!*

⑩ Following the example of **hintereinander** *one after the other*, you can form other adverbs by adding **einander** after a preposition: **miteinander** *with each other/one another*, **gegeneinander** *against one another* (see lesson 85).

⑪ **der Hals** means both *neck* and *throat*.

⑫ The best-known birthday song (**das Geburtstagslied**) in Germany will sound familiar: the melody is the same as 'Happy Birthday to You', but instead of the English lyrics, you sing „Zum Geburtstag viel Glück, zum Geburtstag viel Glück, alles Gute zum Geburtstag, zum Geburtstag viel Glück".

⑬ A **Generaldirektor** is the *president*, *managing director* or *chief executive officer* of a company.

Übung 1 – Übersetzen Sie bitte!

❶ Es wird sicher klappen, ihr seid schließlich keine Anfänger! ❷ Seit heute Morgen wird das Hotel von der Polizei bewacht. ❸ Von wem wird „Zum Geburtstag viel Glück" gesungen? Von allen? ❹ Wenn professionell vorgegangen wird, kann nichts schief gehen. ❺ Achtung, keine Panik! Der Strom wird in ein paar Minuten wieder angestellt werden.

***

Übung 2 – Ergänzen Sie bitte!

❶ For the first time, his skill was put (*stood*) to a difficult test.
... . wurde .... auf eine ..... Probe ....

❷ On which floor do you live? On the ninth? Then we live one on top of the other (*above-one-another*)!
.. .. wohnen Sie? Im neunten? Dann wohnen wir ....!

❸ We're ready, the whole family is gathered: the singing can start (*it can sung become*).
Wir sind ......, die ganze Familie ist ....: es kann ....

❹ When the electricity is switched off, everything will go wrong.
Wenn der Strom ...., wird alles ....

❺ OK guys, we have to talk to (*with*-) each other; you (*pl.*) know very well (*already*) what this is about, don't you?
Also ....., wir müssen .... sprechen, ... schon, worum .. .., nicht wahr?

Answers to Exercise 1

❶ It'll surely work out – after all, you aren't beginners! ❷ Since this morning, the hotel has been (*becomes*) guarded by the police. ❸ Who will sing 'Happy Birthday' (*By whom becomes ... sung*)? (*By*) Everyone? ❹ If one proceeds professionally, nothing can go wrong. ❺ Careful, don't panic! The electricity will be switched on again in a few minutes.

***

Answers to Exercise 2

❶ Zum ersten Mal – sein Können – harte – gestellt ❷ In welchem Stock – übereinander ❸ – soweit – versammelt – gesungen werden ❹ – abgestellt wird – schief gehen ❺ – Jungs – miteinander – ihr wisst – es sich handelt –

> Achtung, keine Panik! Der Strom wird in ein paar Minuten wieder angestellt werden.

Congratulations on your perseverance: the passive is one of the trickiest aspects of German. If it still seems a bit unclear to you, don't worry – you'll gradually pick it up as you come across more examples. And these opportunities will be frequent!

Second wave: 41st lesson

91 Einundneunzigste Lektion

Wiederholung – Review

1 The passive voice

In the active voice, the subject is the agent that performs the action expressed by the verb: *She* lit the candles. This focuses attention on the agent. In contrast, in the passive voice, the subject is acted upon by an expressed or unexpressed agent, so the attention is focused on the receiver of the action: *The candles* were lit.

There are two passives in German, one that relates an action or process, and one that describes a state or result. They are formed using the auxiliary verbs **werden** and **sein** respectively, together with a past participle.

• The passive relating an action or process is formed with **werden** and the past participle. It often corresponds to a progressive/continuous form in English.
Present tense: **Die Kerzen werden um Mitternacht angezündet.** *The candles are being lit at midnight.*
Simple past tense: **Die Kerzen wurden angezündet, als ich in das Zimmer kam.** *The candles were being lit when I came into the room.*

• The passive describing a state or result (the statal or **sein**-passive) is formed with **sein** and the past participle.
Present tense: **Die Kerzen sind angezündet.** *The candles are lit.*
Simple past tense: **Die Kerzen waren schon angezündet, als ich in das Zimmer gekommen bin.** *The candles were already lit when I came into the room.*

Watch out! Although the **sein**-passive looks confusingly like the English passive, which also uses the auxiliary *to be*, the meaning is different. The **sein**-passive describes a <u>result</u> as opposed to an <u>action</u>. Compare these two examples:
Der Tisch wird gedeckt. *The table is being laid.* (action/process)
Der Tisch ist gedeckt. *The table is laid.* (description of a state)

Ninety-first lesson 91

The **sein**-passive is much less common than the **werden-**passive, and the two are rarely interchangeable.

2 Tenses in the passive voice

The passive voice has the same range of tenses as the active voice:
Ich werde gefragt. *I am asked.*
Ich wurde gefragt. *I was asked.*
Ich bin gefragt <u>worden</u>*. *I have been asked.*
Ich war gefragt <u>worden</u>*. *I had been asked.*
Ich werde gefragt werden. *I will be asked.*

* Note that **werden** forms the perfect tense with **sein** and that the past participle **geworden** drops the **ge-** prefix in the passive voice, becoming **worden**.

The tenses you will encounter most frequently in the passive voice are the present and the simple past. The use of the tenses in the active and passive voices is largely the same. However, there is one important qualification. The future tense is not commonly used in the passive, unless it is not clear from the context that the time frame is the future. Thus one would have to say **Das Buch wird gelesen werden.** *The book will be read.* However, if there's an element in the sentence that points to the future, the present tense is generally preferred: **Das Buch wird nächste Woche gelesen.** *The book will be read next week.*

3 The use of the passive voice

The passive voice is generally used more frequently in German than in English. However, this applies more to written language (such as instructions, recipes, manuals and newspapers) than to speech. The usage is often similar, but sometimes the passive occurs in German in cases where it would not be used in English.

• The passive can be used to shift the emphasis from the agent to the recipient of the action (which could be a person or a thing).

fünfhundert • 500

91 **Der Sender sendete das Programm zweimal.**
The channel broadcast the programme twice.

As opposed to:
Das Programm wurde zweimal gesendet.
The programme was broadcast twice.

• It can be used to create a certain distance by leaving the agent of the action (i.e. the subject of the active verb) unspecified:
Das Auto wurde gestohlen. *The car was stolen.*
Die Rechnungen müssen bezahlt werden. *The bills must be paid.*

The passive can be used in the same way in headlines (without the auxiliary) to give concise information:
Auto in der Stadt gestohlen *Car stolen in the city*
Neues Medikament getestet *New medicine tested*

If the agent of the action needs to be specified, it is included in a prepositional phrase introduced by **von** or **durch**, corresponding to the English *by*.
• **von** (+ dat.) is used to indicate the agent of the action:
Neues Medikament von Forschern getestet.
New medicine tested by researchers
Er wurde von zwei Polizeibeamten verhaftet.
He was arrested by two policemen.
• **durch** (+ acc.) indicates by which means the action is carried out, or what intermediary caused the action:
Ich wurde durch den starken Verkehr aufgehalten.
I was held up by the heavy traffic.
Die Stadt wurde durch eine Flut verwüstet.
The city was devastated by a flood.

• The **werden**-passive can be used without a grammatical subject in order to denote an activity in general:
Hier darf nicht geraucht werden! *Smoking isn't allowed here!*

This 'subjectless' passive construction is widely used in spoken and written German and has no direct equivalent in English.

• **es** can be added as a 'dummy subject' if no other word(s) precede the verb in an impersonal passive construction:
Es darf nicht geraucht werden. *Smoking isn't allowed.*

- **es** can also be used to begin an active main clause when there is a grammatical subject:
Es kommen viele Leute zum Oktoberfest nach München.
Viele Leute kommen zum Oktoberfest nach München.
Many people come to Munich for Oktoberfest.
Both sentences mean the same thing, but in the first, the focus is on the subject (**viele Leute**).

- Subjectless (or impersonal) passive constructions can be used to give polite commands:
In 10 Minuten wird gegessen! *We'll eat in ten minutes!*
Jetzt wird gearbeitet! *Let's get down to work now!*

4 The use of *erst* and *nur*

Both **nur** and **erst** can mean *only* in English. The former, **nur**, means *only* in the sense of 'not more than'; i.e. it imposes a quantitative restraint. In contrast, **erst** implies that there is more to come and imposes a temporal constraint.
Ich habe nur ein kleines Haus. *I have only a small house.*
Es ist erst 20 vor 12. *It is only 20 minutes to 12:00.*

Ich weiß nicht, warum ich so müde bin, ich habe nur zwei Maß getrunken! *I don't know why I'm so tired, I only drank two litres of beer!*
Ich habe erst zwei Maß getrunken, ich brauche dringend noch eine dritte! *I've only drunk two litres of beer, I urgently need a third!*

As the last example shows, **erst** is often used subjectively. Its opposite is **schon**.
Was, du hast schon zwei Maß getrunken? Das ist mehr als genug! *What? You've already drunk two litres of beer? That's more than enough!*

Sometimes **erst** indicates time in the sense of *not until*, *only when*:
Nur wenn du kommst, gehe ich auf das Fest.
I will only go to the party if you are coming.
Erst wenn du kommst, essen wir. *We won't eat until you arrive.*

91

> *Now it's time to relax. We invite you to join us to celebrate the birthday of Mr Schulz (even his wife is in on the surprise)!*

Review exercise

Die Rede von Generaldirektor Schulz

1 – Verehrte* Gäste, liebe Freunde!
2 Seien Sie herzlich willkommen!
3 Ich danke Ihnen, dass Sie trotz des entsetzlichen Wetters gekommen sind.
4 Wie Sie wissen, sind wir hier versammelt, um meinen Geburtstag zu feiern, der in ein paar Minuten beginnt.
5 Ich wurde nämlich vor sechzig Jahren in dieser Stadt geboren.
6 Es war an einem Sonntag, und außerdem war das Wetter traumhaft.
7 Von meiner Mutter wurde mir erzählt, dass meine Urgroßmutter sofort gesagt hat:
8 „Dieses Kind ist ein Sonntagskind, es wird viel Glück haben."
9 Und wirklich, ich bin vom Leben sehr verwöhnt worden.
10 Ich hatte zum Beispiel keinerlei Absicht, Karriere zu machen.
11 Im Gegenteil, ich habe auf Geld und Titel gepfiffen.
12 Und heute stehe ich hier vor Ihnen als einer der wichtigsten und reichsten Männer dieser Stadt.
13 Eigentlich verstehe ich selbst nicht, wie ich Generaldirektor geworden bin.
14 Für die Zukunft kann ich nur hoffen, dass mich das Glück weiter auf meinem Weg begleitet – toi toi toi!

15 In einer Minute ist Mitternacht.
16 Lassen Sie uns die Gläser heben und auf unser Glück trinken!
17 Himmel, was ist denn los? Warum ist der Strom abgestellt worden?
18 Machen Sie bitte sofort das Licht wieder an!
19 – Johannes, Liebling, ich habe Angst. Wo bist du denn?
20 – Bitte, bleiben Sie ruhig! Keine Panik! Alles ist in Ordnung!

***

21 – Wir wünschen viel Glück zum Geburtstag, Herr Generaldirektor!

* We've already seen the opening formula usually used for official letters: **Sehr geehrte/r Frau/Herr ...** *Dear* ('Very honoured') *Mrs/Mr ...* (lesson 80). When addressing people in public, **verehrt** is usually used instead of **geehrt**, but the meaning is the same.

Translation
President Schulz's speech

1 Honoured guests, dear friends! **2** Welcome (*Be you warmly welcome*)! **3** I thank you for coming despite the horrible weather. **4** As you know, we're gathered here to celebrate my birthday, which will commence in a few minutes. **5** For I was born in this city sixty years ago. **6** It was (*on*) a Sunday and, in addition, the weather was fantastic. **7** My mother told me that my great-grandmother immediately said: **8** 'This child is a child of fortune (*Sunday-child*), he'll be very lucky.' **9** And truly, I have had a charmed life (*I am by-the life very spoiled become*). **10** For example, I had no intention at all to make [a] career [for myself]. **11** Quite the opposite, I didn't give a damn about money and titles. **12** And today I stand before you as one of the city's most important and richest men. **13** Actually, I don't understand myself how I became managing director. **14** Going forward (*For the future*), I can only hope that luck will continue to accompany me on my way – touch wood! **15** It's one minute to midnight. **16** Let's raise our glasses and toast our luck! **17** Heavens, what's going on? Why has the electricity been switched off? **18** Please turn the light[s] back on immediately! **19** Johannes, darling, I'm afraid. Where are you? **20** Please, stay calm! Don't panic! Everything will be all right (*is in order*)! **21** We wish [you] a very Happy Birthday, (*Mr*) President!

92 Zweiundneunzigste Lektion

Der verständnisvolle ① Blumenhändler

1 – Ent**schul**digen Sie, **hät**ten ② Sie schnell mal **ei**ne Marge**ri**te für mich?

2 – Ja, wir **ha**ben Marge**ri**ten, **wei**ße und **gel**be, **a**ber nur in **Sträu**ßen.

3 – Wie viel **kos**ten die denn?

4 – **Sie**ben **Eu**ro **acht**zig.

5 – **Könn**te ③ ich nicht nur **ei**ne **ein**zige **ha**ben, **bit**te? Ich **ha**be nicht ge**nug** Geld.

Pronunciation
... *fershtentnis-foluh* **bloomuhn-hentl**[a] **1** ... *het'n* ... *marguhreetuh*... **2** ... *shtrois'n* **5** *kœntuh*...

Notes

① The adjective **verständnisvoll** *understanding* derives from the noun **das Verständnis** *understanding, comprehension* and the adjective **voll** *full*. Remember that attributive adjectives take endings depending on the gender, number and case of the noun they modify: **der verständnisvolle Freund** *the understanding friend* (see lesson 56).

② **hätten** is a subjunctive form of **haben**. The subjunctive is a mood rather than a tense. It is used to make conjectural, hypothetical or non-factual statements, wishes or polite requests. There are two types of subjunctive in German: the subjunctive I, used mainly to indirectly report what someone said, and the subjunctive II, used for expressing possibilities,

> *The very fortunate Mr Schulz apparently doesn't feel the need to employ the expression* **Wird schon schief gehen!** *to prevent his luck from taking a turn for the worse. In the same spirit, we also attest that* **Es wird sicher klappen!**

Second wave: 42nd lesson

Ninety-second lesson 92

The understanding flowerseller (*flower-trader*)

1 – Excuse me, could you quickly give me (*would-have you quickly once ... for me*) a daisy?
2 – Yes, we have daisies, white [ones] and yellow [ones], but only in bunches.
3 – How much are (*cost*) they?
4 – 7 euros 80.
5 – Could I not just have a single one, please? I don't have enough money.

uncertain information or for making polite requests or wishes. The second is much more common. Both can refer to things in the present, past or future. The subjunctive II is formed by adding **-e, -est, -e, -en, -et, -en** to the simple past tense stem: **ich kaufte** *I bought* (simple past) → **ich kauft + -e** → **ich kaufte** *I would buy* (subjunctive II), **du arbeitetest** *you worked* → **du arbeitet + -est** → **du arbeitetest** *you would work*. In fact, as you can see, the subjunctive of most regular verbs is indistinguishable from the simple past tense form. Irregular verbs add an umlaut where possible: **ich sah** *I saw* → **ich sähe** *I would see*. **Sie hatten Zeit, ins Kino zu gehen.** *They had time to go to the cinema.* **Sie hätten Zeit, ins Kino zu gehen.** *They would have time to go to the cinema.* Although all verbs have subjunctive forms, only a few are commonly used in written and spoken German.

③ Modal verbs also take an umlaut in subjunctive II: **Sie konnten** *you were able to*, **Sie könnten** *you could*. The only exception is **sollen** *should, to be supposed to*. The umlaut helps differentiate the simple past from the subjunctive II.

fünfhundertsechs • 506

92

6 – Das kann ich **lei**der nicht **ma**chen, dann **wä**ren in **ei**nem Strauß nur noch neun.
7 – **Könn**ten Sie mir dann viel**leicht ei**ne Marge**ri**te **leih**en?
8 – Das **wä**re ④ echt nett von **Ih**nen.
9 – **Ih**nen **ei**ne **leih**en? Wie **mei**nen Sie das? **Blu**men kann man nicht ver**leih**en ⑤.
10 – Ich **brau**che **a**ber ganz **dring**end **ei**ne, ich **bi**tte Sie!
11 – Na ja, **mei**netwegen ⑥ **neh**men Sie sich **ei**ne.
12 – Ich **dan**ke Ihnen **viel**mals:
*Sie liebt mich, von **Her**zen, mit **Schmer**zen, ein **biss**chen, viel, gar nicht...*
13 – Ach, **seh**en Sie, das **ha**be ich be**fürch**tet: sie liebt mich nicht **wirk**lich.
14 – Ich **ho**ffe, Sie sind mir nicht **bö**se ⑦?
15 – Ist schon gut, mein **Jun**ge, ich **wünsch**te ⑧ nur, ich **hä**tte das**sel**be ge**macht**, als ich so jung war wie du! ☐

---

6 ...*vehr'n* ...*strows*... 7 ...*lei-uhn* 8 ...*ekHt*... 11 ...*meinuhtvehg'n*... 13 ...*buhfewrkHtuht*... 15 ...*vewnshtuh*...

Notes

④ The subjunctive **das wäre** *this would be* is formed by adding **-e** and an umlaut to **das war** *this was* (see also line 6).

⑤ etwas <u>ver</u>leihen *to lend something to someone*. However, **leihen** can mean either *to lend* or *to borrow*. **Ich leihe dir Geld.** *I lend you money.* **Ich leihe Geld <u>von</u> dir.** *I borrow money from you.*

⑥ **meintewegen, deinetwegen, seinetwegen, ihretwegen, unsretwegen, euretwegen, ihretwegen, Ihretwegen** *on account of me/you/him/her*, etc. are adverbs. However, only **meinetwegen** can be used as a positive (albeit by no means

507 • **fünfhundertsieben**

6 – I can't do that, unfortunately, [because] then there would be only nine left in a bunch.
7 – Could you perhaps lend me a daisy then?
8 – That would be really (*truly*) nice of you.
9 – Lend you one? What do you mean? One can't lend [someone] flowers.
10 – But I need one really (*completely*) urgently – I'm begging (*asking*) you!
11 – Well, all right, go ahead and take one.
12 – (*I*) Thank you very much (*many-times*): 'She loves me (*from the heart, with pains*), a little, a lot, not at all …'
13 Oh, you see, this is what I was afraid of (*this have I feared*): she doesn't really love me.
14 I hope you aren't angry with me?
15 – Don't worry (*Is already good*), my boy. I just wish (*would-wish*) I had done the same when I was your age (*as young was as you*)!

---

enthusiastic) response, along the lines of 'if you like' or 'I don't mind': **Gehen wir einen trinken?** *Shall we go for a drink?* – **Meinetwegen.** *OK, if you like.*

⑦ **jemandem böse sein** *to be angry with someone*: **Sie war ihm lange Zeit böse.** *She was angry with him for a long time.* Note that the German construction requires the dative case rather than a preposition. And be careful! The adjective **böse** also means *bad, evil, wicked*: **ein böser Mann** *an evil man*.

⑧ **ich wünschte** *I would wish* is a subjunctive II form of **wünschen** *to wish*. As **wünschen** is a regular verb, the subjunctive II and the past tense forms look identical, so **ich wünschte** can mean either *I wished* or *I would wish*. In order to avoid confusion, a different way of expressing the subjunctive mood is frequently employed. We'll have a closer look at this construction in the next lesson. Note also that in this line the speaker switches register from **Sie** to **du** when addressing his interlocutor as 'my boy'.

fünfhundertacht • 508

Übung 1 – Übersetzen Sie bitte!

❶ Hättest du ein bisschen Zeit? Wir könnten auf der Wiese Margeriten suchen. ❷ Ich hätte niemals von ihm Geld leihen sollen. ❸ Sie wäre eine sehr gute Händlerin, sie hat noch nie einen Euro zu viel bezahlt. ❹ Könnten Sie mir bitte morgen Ihr Auto leihen? ❺ Ich wünschte, ich hätte auch einen so freundlichen Blumenhändler getroffen.

***

Übung 2 – Ergänzen Sie bitte!

❶ Please don't be angry with me, but I broke your vase. – Don't worry.

Sei ... bitte nicht ...., aber ich habe deine Vase .... – Ist schon ....

❷ Would you (*pl.*) have time tomorrow to buy a large bunch of flowers for Granny?

.... morgen Zeit, ... großen .... für Oma zu kaufen?

❸ This costs 68 euros. I hope we have enough money.

... . achtundsechzig Euro. ... ., wir haben ..... Geld.

❹ Could you (*informal*) lend me [a] hundred euros? – I (*would*) wish I had (*would-have*) them.

.... mir hundert Euro ......?
– ... ., ich hätte sie.

❺ You (*formal*) have been very understanding, (*I*) thank you very much.

... . sehr .... gewesen, ich .... vielmals.

Answers to Exercise 1

① Would you have a little time? We could look for daisies in the meadow. **②** I should never have borrowed money from him. **③** She would be a very good trader; she has never paid a euro too much. **④** Could you please lend me your car tomorrow? **⑤** I (*would*) wish I had also met such a friendly flower seller.

***

Answers to Exercise 2

① – mir – böse – kaputt gemacht – gut **②** Hättet ihr – einen – Blumenstrauß – **③** Das kostet – Ich hoffe – genug – **④** Könntest du – leihen – Ich wünschte – **⑤** Sie sind – verständnisvoll – danke Ihnen –

93 | **Er liebt mich, er liebt mich nicht …**
He loves me, he loves me not …
*You've probably heard of the daisy petal game, but do you know the most famous literary figure who played it? It was the young Margarete in **Faust** by Goethe, better known by her nickname Gretchen. The young and pious Margarete meets Faust on her way to church with her mother. For Faust, it is love at first sight, and Gretchen also falls in love with him as a result of the pact between Faust and the Devil (see lesson 51). It is on their first walk that Gretchen pulls off the petals of a daisy one by one and has the*

93 Dreiundneunzigste Lektion

Bewahren Sie die Ruhe, wenn möglich!

1 Was **wür**den ① Sie **ma**chen, wenn…
2 wenn Sie **ei**nen **Nach**barn **hät**ten ②, mit dem Sie sich nicht ver**ste**hen **wür**den ③?
3 wenn **die**ser **Nach**bar ④ die **un**möglichsten **Din**ge **ma**chen **wür**de, um Sie zu **är**gern?

Pronunciation
buh**vah**ruhn … **1** … **vewr**duhn … **3** … **erg**ᵃn

Notes

① In conversational German, the subjunctive mood is expressed far more frequently with the construction **würde** + infinitive than with the subjunctive II (see lesson 92): **ich würde das nicht machen, du würdest das nicht machen** *I wouldn't do that, you wouldn't do that*, etc. Note that **würde** is the first- and third-person subjunctive of **werden**. However, the **würde**-construction is avoided for **haben**, **sein** and the modal verbs, which are usually in the subjunctive II (**hätte**, **wäre**, etc.).

② In conditional sentences in which the condition is unreal, the verb in the *if* clause (**wenn**-clause) is normally in the subjunctive II, while the main clause (the consequence) uses

511 • **fünfhundertelf**

misfortune to speak the words **'er liebt mich'** *when plucking off the last petal. Thus reassured, she gives in to his advances, marking the beginning of a series of misfortunes. Gretchen unwittingly poisons her mother with a sleeping potion, finds herself pregnant, and her brother is killed at the hands of Faust and Mephistopheles. Finally, Gretchen strangles her illegitimate child and is convicted of infanticide. Faust tries to free her from prison, but she refuses to escape, prompting voices from heaven to announce that she shall be saved.*

Second wave: 43rd lesson

Ninety-third lesson   93

Keep (*the*) calm, if possible!

1 What would you do, if …
2 if you had (*would-have*) a neighbour with whom you didn't get on (*you yourself not understand would*)?
3 if this neighbour did (*would do*) the most impossible things to annoy you?

either a **würde**-construction or the subjunctive II of the verb: **Wenn ich Zeit hätte, würde ich dich besuchen.** *If I had* (would-have) *time, I would visit you.*

③ **würde** + infinitive tends to be used more often with regular verbs, but it can be used with irregular verbs too: **Sie würden verstehen** *you would understand* means the same as **Sie verständen** (the subjunctive II, formed by adding an umlaut to **Sie verstanden** *you understood*).

④ Here **Nachbar** is in the nominative singular, but remember that in all other cases it takes an **-n** ending as it is a weak masculine noun (see lesson 47, note 2).

fünfhundertzwölf • 512

4 wenn er zum **Bei**spiel **sei**nem Papag**ei bei**bringen ⑤ **wür**de, **hun**dertmal pro Tag **Ih**ren **Na**men zu **schrei**en?

5 Sie **den**ken, so **et**was ⑥ **könn**te nie pass**ie**ren? Falsch!

6 Einem **eng**lischen Ge**schäfts**mann ⑦ **ist die**se Ge**schich**te **wirk**lich pas**siert**.

7 Und da er ein **Gen**tleman war, ist ihm der **Kra**gen erst nach vier **Jah**ren ge**platzt** ⑧.

8 Nach **ei**ner **schlaf**losen Nacht ist er beim **Nach**barn **ein**gebrochen ⑨, **wäh**rend **die**ser bei der **Ar**beit war,

9 und **oh**ne viel **Fe**derlesen zu **ma**chen, hat er dem **ar**men **Vo**gel, der ihn mit **sei**nem **Na**men be**grüß**te, ... den Hals **um**gedreht.

10 Da**nach hat**te er zwar ⑩ **sei**ne **Ru**he, **a**ber die **Ru**he war **teu**er be**zahlt**.

11 Er ist **näm**lich vom Ge**richt** zu **ei**ner **Stra**fe von 1 500 **Eu**ro ver**ur**teilt **wor**den.

---

7 ... *jent*lmuhn ... *krah*g'n ... *guhplatst* 8 ... *ein*-guhbrokh'n ... 9 ... *fehd*ᵉ-lehz'n ... *buhgrews*tuh ... *um*-guhdreht 11 ... *guhrikHt* ... *shtrah*fuh ... *towz'nt-fewnf*hundᵉt *oiro* fer*ur*teilt ...

Notes

⑤ **jemandem etwas beibringen** *to teach someone something*: **Wer hat Ihnen Deutsch beigebracht?** *Who taught you German?*

⑥ **so etwas** *such a thing, anything like this*: **ich habe so etwas noch nie gehört** *I've never heard anything like this.*

⑦ Sometimes sentences can start with elements that aren't the subject. Here, the subject is 'this story', so **einem Geschäftsmann** is in the dative case: *to a businessman...* .

⑧ **es platzt mir der Kragen** or **mir platzt der Kragen** ('to-me bursts the collar') means *I've had enough, I'm going to blow my top*.

4 if, for example, he taught (*would teach*) his parrot to screech your name a hundred times a day?

5 You think that such a thing could never happen? You're wrong (*Incorrect*)!

6 This (*story*) really happened to an English businessman.

7 And as he was a gentleman, he only blew his top (*is to-him the collar burst only*) after four years.

8 After a sleepless night he broke into his (*the*) neighbour's while he was at work

9 and without wasting any time (*much feather-plucking to do*), he wrung the neck of the poor bird who greeted him with his name ...

10 After that it's true he had (*his*) peace [and quiet], but he paid dearly for it,

11 because he was sentenced by the court to [pay] a 1,500 euro fine.

> Wenn ich viel Geld hätte, würde ich mir ein Haus am Meer kaufen.

⑨ **eingebrochen** is the past participle of **einbrechen** *to break in*: **Sie sind beim Juwelier eingebrochen.** *They broke into the jeweller's*. The base verb is **brechen** *to break* (simple past: **brach**, past participle: **gebrochen**).

⑩ **zwar..., aber...**, *admittedly..., but...* , *it's true..., but*, or simply *although ...*: **Deutsch ist zwar nicht leicht, aber man kann es lernen.** *Although German isn't easy, one can learn it.*

fünfhundertvierzehn • 514

93 Übung 1 – Übersetzen Sie bitte!

❶ Mein Vater hat mir das Radfahren beigebracht, und was hat Ihnen Ihr Vater beigebracht? ❷ Wenn ich viel Geld hätte, würde ich mir ein Haus am Meer kaufen. ❸ Wenn dieser verflixte Papagei nicht sofort aufhört zu schreien, drehe ich ihm den Hals um. ❹ Nach einer schlaflosen Nacht platzt vielen Leuten leicht der Kragen. ❺ Du denkst, es ist leicht, in dieses Haus einzubrechen? Falsch!

***

Übung 2 – Ergänzen Sie bitte!

❶ If they kept (*would keep*) calm, that would be better. But unfortunately, they blow their tops easily.

Wenn ... die Ruhe ...., ...
... besser. Aber leider ...... ihnen leicht ...
....

❷ Perhaps you (*formal*) think I wouldn't do this? Wrong! I've already done this many times (*often*).

.... vielleicht, ... das nicht
......? ......! Ich habe das ....
gemacht.

❸ My mother taught me mathematics, and my father how to cook

Meine Mutter ... mir Mathe ....,
und mein Vater, wie man ......

❹ My neighbour is very nice; he always keeps his cool (*the calm*)

.... ist sehr nett, er ....
immer ... .

Answers to Exercise 1

❶ My father taught me to ride a bicycle; and what did your father teach you? ❷ If I had a lot of money, I would buy myself a house by the sea. ❸ If this wretched parrot doesn't stop screeching immediately, I will wring its neck. ❹ After a sleepless night, many people blow their top easily. ❺ You think it's easy to break into this house? Wrong!

***

❺ If someone broke (*would break*) into my place, they (*he*) wouldn't find much they (*one*) could steal.
Wenn jemand bei mir . . . . ,
 . . . . nicht viel . . . . . . , das man stehlen
 . . . .

Answers to Exercise 2

❶ – sie – bewahren würden, wäre das – platzt – der Kragen ❷ Sie denken – ich würde – machen – Falsch – schon oft ❸ – hat – beigebracht – kocht ❹ Mein Nachbar – bewahrt – die Ruhe ❺ – einbrechen würde, würde er – finden – könnte

***

> *Do subjunctive and conditional sentences seem a little tricky?*
> **Keine Panik! Bewahren Sie bitte die Ruhe!** *You'll catch on. The more you come across these forms, the more comfortable you'll be with them. Give yourself time! If you want to practice, you could start by asking yourself every day:* **Wie wäre es, wenn** ... How would it be if ..., **wenn ich heute ein bisschen Deutsch lernen würde?** ... if I learned a little German today?

Second wave: 44th lesson

94 Vierundneunzigste Lektion

Noch einmal Glück gehabt!

1 – **War**ten Sie, wir **dürfen** noch nicht **über** die **Straß**e **geh**en ①, es ist rot!
2 – Ich **geh**e ja ② gar nicht, ich **war**te ja.
3 – Ja, **ab**er ich **wet**te, wenn ich nichts ge**sagt hät**te ③, **wär**en Sie ge**gan**gen.
4 – Na und? Was **wär**e ④ **dar**an schlimm ge**wes**en, es ist kein Auto ge**kom**men.
5 – **Dar**um geht es nicht ⑤.
6 – **Wor**um geht es denn dann?
7 – Bei Rot darf ⑥ man nicht **geh**en.
8   Ge**setz** ⑦ ist Ge**setz**, und Ver**kehrs**regeln sind Ge**setz**e, sie **müss**en be**ach**tet **wer**den.

Pronunciation
8 *guh**zets** ... fer**kehrs**-rehg'ln ... buh**akh**tuht ...*

Notes

① **über die Straße gehen** *to cross the street* is more common than **die Straße überqueren** (*ewbᵃkvehᵃn*), but they mean the same thing. Likewise, **über eine Brücke/einen Platz gehen** *to cross a bridge/square*.

② **ja** translates here as 'but' in the sense of 'but you can see' (see lesson 98).

③ To express hypothetical statements, wishes or unreal conditions in the past, you use the past subjunctive. This is formed using a subjunctive II form of **haben** or **sein** as an auxiliary verb: **Wenn ich nichts gesagt hätte, hätten Sie die Straße überquert.** *If I hadn't* (would not have) *said anything you would have crossed the road.* Remember that in German the subjunctive is used in both parts of a conditional sentence

Ninety-fourth lesson 94

That was lucky!

1 – Wait, we aren't allowed to cross (*go over*) the street yet – it's red!
2 – But I'm not (*at-all*) crossing, I'm waiting.
3 – Yes, but I bet [that] if I hadn't said anything, you would have gone.
4 – So what? What would have been so bad about it; there were no cars (*was no car*) coming.
5 – That's not the point (*About-this goes it not*).
6 – What is the point then?
7 – One isn't allowed to cross at a red light.
8 [The] law is [the] law, and traffic regulations are laws; they have to be respected.

(i.e. also in the clause starting with **wenn**)! The same rule applies in passive sentences: **Wenn sie nicht aufgepasst hätte, wäre sie vom Regen überrascht worden.** *If she hadn't paid attention, she would have been surprised by the rain.*

④ **sein** uses the auxiliary **sein** to form compound tenses: **ich bin gewesen** *I have been, I was*, **ich war gewesen** *I had been*, and in the subjunctive II, **ich wäre gewesen** *I would have been*.

⑤ **es geht um ...** is synonymous with **es handelt sich um ...** *it is about ....* The expression **darum geht es nicht** *it is not about that* is normally used in the sense of 'that's beside the point', 'that's not the point'.

⑥ Remember that **dürfen** always implies permission (or, in the negative, prohibition): *to be allowed to, can, may*.

⑦ **Gesetz** *law* is a neuter noun.

9 Seh**en** Sie, jetzt **dür**fen wir **geh**en, jetzt ist die **Fuß**gängerampel grün.

10 – Halt! **Vor**sicht! Mann, Sie **wä**ren fast über**fah**ren ⑧ **wor**den!

11 **Hab**en Sie mir **ein**en **Schrec**ken **ein**gejagt ⑨!

12 Wie **konn**ten Sie denn den **Last**wagen nicht **seh**en?

13 – Der muss bei Rot **durch**gefahren sein!

14 – Scheint so, **a**ber Gott sei Dank hat **wen**igstens Ihr **Schutz**engel die **Aug**en offen gehalten.

15 An **Ih**rer **Stel**le **wür**de ich ihm ein **herz**liches **Dan**keschön **sa**gen.

---

9 ...foos-geng^a-amp'l grewn 10 ... ewb^afah^an ... 11 ...shrek'n einguhyahkt 12 ... **last**-vahg'n ... 13 ... **durkH**'guhfah^an ... 14 ... **shuts**-eng'l ...

Notes

⑧ The prefix **über** can be separable or inseparable. Which is it in **überfahren** *to run over* ('over-drive')? Two things tell us that it's inseparable: the past participle doesn't take a **ge-** prefix, and **über** isn't stressed. Compare **durchgefahren** (line 13). The prefix separates: **Sieh mal, der fährt bei Rot durch!** *Look, he's going through a red light!* But **Vorsicht! Überfahr nicht die Taube!** *Careful! Don't run over the pigeon!*

***

Übung 1 – Übersetzen Sie bitte!

❶ Erst wenn die Ampel für die Fußgänger grün ist, dürfen wir über die Straße gehen. ❷ Wenn sie nicht geschrien hätte, hätte er nicht den Lastwagen gesehen. ❸ Die Gesetze sind gemacht worden, damit man sie achtet. ❹ An deiner Stelle würde ich nicht bei Rot durchfahren, das ist verboten. ❺ Halten Sie die Augen offen, wenn Sie über die Straße gehen!

9 Look, now we can go: now the pedestrian light is green.
10 – Stop! Careful! Gosh, you almost got yourself run over (*you would-have almost run-over been*)!
11 You gave me a fright!
12 How could you not have seen (*see*) the lorry?
13 – It must have gone through a red light.
14 – So it seems, but thank God [that] at least your guardian angel kept (*held*) its eyes open.
15 If I were you (*In your place*), I would say (*to-it*) a big (*heartfelt*) thank you.

⑨ **jemandem einen Schrecken einjagen** *to scare someone, to give someone a fright*. In contrast to **die Angst**, a pervasive fear or anxiety, **der Schrecken** implies a sudden fright or horror. Note also that starting with a verb reinforces an exclamation: **Hab' ich Angst gehabt!** *Was I frightened!*

> Erst wenn die Ampel für die Fußgänger grün ist, dürfen wir über die Straße gehen.

Answers to Exercise 1

❶ Only when the light for pedestrians is green can we cross the street. ❷ If she hadn't shouted, he wouldn't have seen the lorry/truck. ❸ The laws were made in order to be respected (*so that one respects them*). ❹ If I were you, I wouldn't go through a red light: that's forbidden. ❺ Keep your eyes open when you're crossing the street!

fünfhundertzwanzig • 520

Übung 2 – Ergänzen Sie bitte!

❶ Wait (*informal*), we can't cross the street: the light is red!
..... , ... nicht .... gehen, die Ampel ist ... !

❷ If I were you (*If I in your[formal] place would-be*), I wouldn't do that.
Wenn ich .. .. wäre, ... ich das nicht ....

❸ If his guardian angel hadn't paid attention, he would have been run over by the lorry.
Wenn .... nicht aufgepasst hätte, ... von dem Lastwagen ....

---

95 Fünfundneunzigste Lektion

Wenn sie das gewusst hätte…

1 – Herr **Ober** ①, wir **wür**den gern ② **zah**len!
2 – Selbstver**ständ**lich, **zah**len Sie ge**trennt o**der zu**sam**men?
3 – Zu**sam**men.

Pronunciation
1 ... **ohb**[a] ...

Notes

① **Herr Ober** is used to address waiters only in elegant restaurants. There is no corresponding female form. If you're served by a woman, or if you are in a **Kneipe** *pub, bar*, simply say **hallo** or **Entschuldigung** or just wave your hand. (In normal restaurants, servers are referred to as **der Kellner** *waiter* and **die Kellnerin** *waitress*.)

❹ He no longer respects any law! He must have gone crazy!

.. .. kein Gesetz mehr! .. .... verrückt geworden .... !

❺ What is this about, please? – You went through a red light! – Is that bad?

Worum .... .., bitte? – Sie sind ... ... ! – Ist das .... ?

Answers to Exercise 2

❶ Warte, wir dürfen – über die Straße – rot ❷ – an Ihrer Stelle – würde – machen ❸ – sein Schutzengel – wäre er – überfahren worden ❹ Er achtet – Er muss – sein ❺ geht es – bei Rot durchgefahren – schlimm

Second wave: 45th lesson

Ninety-fifth lesson 95

If she had known that ...

1 – Waiter, we would like to pay.
2 – Of course – are you paying separately or together?
3 – Together.

② We've seen that **gern** (or **gerne**) *gladly* used with a verb expresses 'to like doing something': **ich esse gern** *I like eating*. In the subjunctive this becomes: **ich würde gern essen** *I would like to eat*. When **lieber**, the comparative of **gern**, is used with a verb, this expresses preference: **Ich würde lieber zu Hause bleiben.** *I would prefer to stay at home.*

fünfhundertzweiundzwanzig • 522

95 4 – Gut, ich **bring**e **Ih**nen die **Rech**nung so**fort**.

5 – Hör mal, es kommt **über**haupt ③ nicht in **Frag**e, dass du schon **wie**der be**zahlst**.

6 **Heu**te bin ich dran ④, das war so **un**ter uns **aus**gemacht ⑤.

7 – Das ist mir neu.

8 – Tue nicht so ⑥, als ob du das ver**ge**ssen **hät**test, du hast doch sonst ein so **gu**tes Ge**dächt**nis!

9 – Ich **schwö**re dir, ich kann mich an nichts er**in**nern.

10 – **Hät**te ⑦ ich das ge**wusst**, dann **hät**te ich nichts ge**ge**ssen und schon gar **kei**nen Cham**pa**gner ge**trun**ken!

11 – Das **wä**re **scha**de gewesen, **um**so mehr als ⑧ das **E**ssen **wirk**lich ausge**zeich**net war, **find**est du nicht?

---

5 ... ewbªhowpt ... **6** ... dran ... **8** too-uh ... **he**tuhst ... guh**dekHt**nis

Notes

③ **überhaupt** followed by a negation reinforces the negation (like **gar**): **ich mag ihn nicht** *I don't like him*, **ich mag ihn überhaupt** (or **gar**) **nicht** *I don't like him at all*.

④ The expression **ich bin dran** is a shorter way of saying **ich bin an der Reihe** *it's my turn* ('I am in the row').

⑤ **etwas ausmachen** (or **abmachen**) *to agree something, to arrange something*; **einen Termin ausmachen** *to make an appointment*, but **das Licht ausmachen** *to switch off the light*. As you can see, the meaning of a verb can change completely depending on the object it takes.

523 • fünfhundertdreiundzwanzig

4 – OK, I['ll] bring you the bill immediately.
5 – Listen, it is out of the question (*it comes not at all in question*) that you pay (*already*) again.
6 Today it's my turn, [and] that was agreed (*between us*).
7 – That's new[s] to me!
8 – Stop pretending you forgot (*Don't do so as if you had forgotten this*), you normally (*otherwise*) have such a good memory!
9 – I swear to you, I can't remember anything.
10 – Had I known that, then I wouldn't have eaten anything and certainly not drunk any champagne (*least of all no champagne drunk*)!
11 – That would have been a pity, especially as (*so-much more as*) the food was really excellent, don't you think?

⑥ After **(so) tun, als ob** *to pretend, to act as if*, the verb is in the subjunctive as it expresses something contrary to fact: **Er tut (so), als ob er krank wäre.** *He pretends to be ill* ('as if he would be ill'). Instead of **als ob** one can also just say **als**. In this case, the verb is in the second position after **als**: **Er tut (so), als wäre er krank.** *He pretends to be ill.*

⑦ In conditional sentences, **wenn** can be omitted by starting with the verb: **Wenn es nicht so spät wäre, könnten wir noch spazieren gehen. = Wäre es nicht so spät, könnten wir noch spazieren gehen.** *If it weren't so late, we could go for a walk. = Were it not so late ...* etc.

⑧ **umso mehr als** *all the more so because, especially as*; **umso weniger als** *even less so because, especially as.*

fünfhundertvierundzwanzig • 524

95 **12** – Hol' ⑨ dich der **Teu**fel!
13 – **Lieber** nicht, sonst ⑩ **müss**test du al**lein** zu Fuß nach **Hau**se **geh**en!

13 ... mewsstuhst ...

Notes

⑨ **hol'** is short for **hole**, which is here the third-person singular of the present subjunctive I of **holen** (see lesson 92). The present subjunctive I is formed by adding the subjunctive verb endings **-e, -est, -e, -en, -et, -en** to the stem of the infinitive: **haben** → **hab** + **-e** → **er habe**: **Er sagt, er habe wenig Zeit.** *He says [that] he has little time.* All verbs follow this pattern, with the exception of **sein** *to be*: **Die Präsidentin sagt, sie sei nicht hungrig.** *The president says she isn't hungry.* While the subjunctive I most frequently appears in formal written German to restate what someone has said, it is also used, for example, for third-person commands like **Hol' dich der Teufel!** or **Lang lebe der König!** *Long live the King!*

***

Übung 1 – Übersetzen Sie bitte!

❶ Sie geht gern mit ihm aus, umso mehr als er immer Champagner bestellt. ❷ Es wäre wirklich schade, wenn dich der Teufel holen würde. ❸ Könnten wir für nächste Woche einen Termin ausmachen? ❹ Warum bin ich immer dran, wenn bezahlt werden muss? ❺ Bitte tun Sie nicht so, als ob Sie sich nicht erinnern würden!

12 – To hell with you (*[May] the devil get you*)!
13 – Better not, otherwise you would have to go home on foot all by yourself (*alone*)!

⑩ **sonst** can mean *normally* or *usually* (line 8) as well as *otherwise*, *or else*: **Komisch, die Rechnung ist sonst nicht so teuer.** *Strange, normally the bill isn't this high* ('expensive'). **Ich trinke keinen Champagner mehr, sonst habe ich morgen einen Kater.** *I won't drink any more champagne, or else I'll have a hangover tomorrow.* **Was wünschen Sie sonst?** *What else would you like?*

***

Answers to Exercise 1

❶ She likes going out with him, especially as he always orders champagne. ❷ It would really be a pity if you went to hell (*the devil were to get you*). ❸ Could we arrange an appointment for next week? ❹ Why is it always my turn when [the bill] has to be paid? ❺ Please don't pretend you can't remember!

Übung 2 – Ergänzen Sie bitte!

❶ We had arranged an appointment for 3 o'clock today, but I would prefer to come tomorrow.

... . für heute 15 Uhr einen Termin ...., aber ... . morgen ....

❷ She has an excellent memory; she remembers everything.

Sie hat ... .;
... . sich .. alles.

❸ He swears (*that*) he saw the devil in person at midnight last night.

.. .., dass er gestern um Mitternacht ... . in Person ....

---

96 Sechsundneunzigste Lektion

Auf Regen folgt Sonnenschein ①

1 – Du, ich **ha**be **ei**ne **gu**te und **ei**ne **schlech**te **Nach**richt, mit **wel**cher soll ich **an**fangen?
2 – **Lie**ber mit der **schlech**ten.
3 – Gut, wie **aus**gemacht **ha**be ich **heu**te **Mor**gen im Ho**tel Ad**lon **an**gerufen, um für Sil**ves**ter und **Neu**jahr ein **Zim**mer zu reser**vie**ren.

Pronunciation
3 ... *ahdlon* ... *zilvest*[a] ...

❹ He pretends to be ill, but he just wants attention.
.. .., als ob er krank ...., aber ..
.... nur Aufmerksamkeit.

❺ It is out of the question that you pay the bill again, all the more so as you have hardly eaten anything.
.. .. nicht .. .., dass Sie schon
wieder ... . bezahlen, ...
... Sie fast nichts ....

Answers to Exercise 2

❶ Wir hatten – ausgemacht – ich würde lieber – kommen ❷ – ein ausgezeichnetes Gedächtnis; sie erinnert – an ❸ Er schwört – den Teufel – gesehen habe ❹ Er tut so – wäre – er will – ❺ Es kommt – in Frage – die Rechnung – umso mehr als – gegessen haben

Second wave: 46th lesson

Ninety-sixth lesson 96

Every cloud has a silver lining
(On rain follows sunshine)

1 – I have good news and bad news (*a good and a bad piece-of-news*) – which should I start with?
2 – Preferably (*More-gladly*) with the bad [news].
3 – Well, as agreed, I phoned the Hotel Adlon this morning to book a room for New Year's Eve and New Year's Day.

Notes

① **der Schein** *light* derives from the verb **scheinen**, which can mean both *to shine* and *to seem*, *to appear*: **die Sonne scheint** *the sun is shining*.

fünfhundertachtundzwanzig • 528

4 Leider wurde mir gesagt, dass alle Doppelzimmer schon belegt seien ②.

5 – Das kann nicht sein! Petra und Max haben erzählt, sie hätten ③ erst Ende des Jahres reserviert.

6 – Ja, aber der Herr am Empfang hat mir erklärt, dass das Hotel dieses Jahr schon seit langem für Silvester ausgebucht sei,

7 und dass man das nie im Voraus wissen könne ④.

8 – Das ist wirklich schade, ich habe mich so darauf ⑤ gefreut, ein paar Tage im Luxus zu schwimmen.

9 Weißt du, im Adlon stehen ein Schwimmbad und ein Fitness-Studio kostenlos zur Verfügung ⑥.

10 Ich hätte ein bisschen Hintern ⑦ verlieren können ⑧ und du ein bisschen Bauch…

---

*4 … buh**lehkt zei**uhn **7** … fo**rows** … **kœ**nuh **8** … **luk**sus …*
*9 … **fit**nes-**shtoo**dyo … fer**few**gung **10** … **hint**ᵉn … bowkh …*

Notes

② **sie seien** is the present subjunctive I of **sie sind** *they are*. The subjunctive I is traditionally used in reported speech (see lesson 95, note 9): **er sagt, dass er müde sei** *he says that he is tired.* However, in everyday language in the present tense, people often simply use the indicative these days: **er sagt, er ist krank** *he says he's ill.*

③ The verb is in the subjunctive here because this is reported speech. As the forms of the present subjunctive I are often identical to the present indicative, the subjunctive II is sometimes used instead (as here) in indirect (reported) speech, particularly in the third-person plural.

4 Unfortunately, I was told that all double rooms were already booked (*already full were [subj.]*).

5 – That can't be! Petra and Max told [me] [that] they (*have [subj.]*) only booked at the end of the year.

6 – Yes, but the gentleman at reception explained to me that this year, the hotel has long been *[subj.]* booked up for New Year's Eve,

7 and that one could *[subj.]* never know (*this*) in advance.

8 – That's really a pity; I was so looking forward to bathing in luxury for a couple of days.

9 You know, in the Adlon, a swimming pool and a gym are (*stand*) available free of charge.

10 I could have lost a little [off my] bottom, and you a little [off your] stomach …

---

④ This is a regular present subjunctive I form consisting of the stem of the infinitive + the third-person singular ending **-e**: **er/sie/es könne** *he/she/it can/could*.

⑤ **sich freuen auf** (+ acc.) *to look forward to*: **Ich freue mich auf Ihren Besuch.** *I look forward to your visit.* However, if you're happy about something already in progress: **sich freuen über** (+ acc.): **Ich freue mich über Ihren Besuch.** *I am pleased about your visit.*

⑥ **zur Verfügung stehen** *to be available*: **Im Hotel steht Ihnen ein Schwimmbad zur Verfügung.** *In the hotel, a swimming pool is at your disposal.*

⑦ **der Hintern** *bottom, backside, rear end.*

⑧ Do you remember double infinitive constructions (lesson 76, note 9)? The past participle of a modal verb turns into an infinitive when it comes after an infinitive: **er hat nicht schlafen können** (not **gekonnt**!) *he couldn't sleep.*

11 Na ja, was soll's! Aber sag mal: was ist die **gu**te **Nach**richt?

12 – **A**lles ist nicht ver**lor**en: ich **ha**be **um**gehend **ei**ne Pau**schal**reise nach Gran Ca**na**ria ge**bucht**.

13 Du wirst **seh**en, wir **wer**den in **Top**-Form ins **neu**e Jahr **rut**schen ⑨!

---

12 ... **um**geh-uhnt ... pow**shahl**-reizuh ... 13 ... **top**-form ... **rut**sh'n

***

The Hotel Adlon is located in Berlin, in front of the Brandenburg Gate on Pariser Platz. Founded in the early 20th century by Lorenz Adlon, with the help of Kaiser Wilhelm II, it soon became the most prestigious address in Berlin (Unter den Linden 1), not least because all its rooms had 'electricity and hot water' when it opened in 1907. It seems that some customers even preferred the hotel to their own palaces! Almost all the VIPs of the early 20th century stayed there: kings, tsars and maharajas, politicians, artists, scientists, and so forth. In 1929, one could read in a Berlin newspaper: 'In the lobby

***

Übung 1 – Übersetzen Sie bitte!

❶ Leider kann man nie im Voraus wissen, was passiert. ❷ Für Neujahr sind alle Einzelzimmer belegt, aber wir haben noch ein Doppelzimmer frei. ❸ Er hat mir erzählt, dass er ins Fitness-Studio geht, um ein bisschen Bauch zu verlieren. ❹ Wie am Telefon ausgemacht, steht Ihnen unser Haus für Silvester zur Verfügung. ❺ Sie schreiben, sie würden uns einen „Guten Rutsch ins Neue Jahr" wünschen.

11 Ah well, so what (*what should-it*)! But tell me: what's the good news?
12 – All is not lost – I immediately booked a package holiday to Gran Canaria.
13 You'll see, we'll start (*slide into*) the new year on top form!

Notes

⑨ To wish someone a happy new year, you can say **Gutes, neues Jahr** *Happy New Year* or **Guten Rutsch ins neue Jahr!** 'Good slide into the new year!' The word for *New Year's Eve* is **Silvester**, commemorating the feast day held on the anniversary of the death of Pope Sylvester I in 335.

***

of the Hotel Adlon, one hears all the languages of the rich nations at once.'

Used as a military hospital during World War II, the Adlon became a hotel again after being restored, but was then turned into a home for apprentices in the 1970s, before regaining its former glory in 1997. It is worth a visit, as much for its illustrious history as for its marble staircases, winter garden, gourmet restaurant ... and of course, the chance to mingle with guests as famous as those of the past.

***

Answers to Exercise 1

❶ Unfortunately, one can never know in advance what will happen (*happens*). ❷ All the single rooms are booked for New Year's Day, but we still have a double room available. ❸ He told me that he goes to the gym in order to lose a little [off his] stomach. ❹ As agreed on the telephone, our house will be available to you on New Year's Eve. ❺ They write that they wish us a 'Happy New Year'.

97 Übung 2 – Ergänzen Sie bitte!

❶ We have some bad news (*a bad piece-of-news*) for you. Should we tell you (*it to-you*) immediately? – Preferably later.
Wir haben .... für Sie. Sollen wir sie ..... sofort ..... ?
– ...... später.

❷ No, we don't pay for the swimming pool. They told me on the telephone [that] it is free of charge.
Nein, wir bezahlen nicht für ... .
Sie haben mir am Telefon gesagt, es sei
....

❸ Why haven't you (*informal*), as agreed, booked a room in the hotel for me?
Warum .... .. nicht, ..., ein Zimmer im Hotel für mich .... ?

---

97 Siebenundneunzigste Lektion

Wenn es doch nur ① schneien würde!

1 – Im **Wet**terbericht **ha**ben sie vo**raus**gesagt, dass es noch **wär**mer **wer**den wird ②.
2 **Scha**de, **Weih**nachten **oh**ne Schnee ist kein **rich**tiges **Weih**nachten!

Pronunciation
... *shnei'n* ... **2** ... **vei**nakhtuhn ...

Notes

① **doch nur** is used to express a wish. However, one could also simply use one of the two words to convey the same thing. **Wenn es doch schneien würde!** or **Wenn es nur schneien würde!** *If it would only snow!*

533 • fünfhundertdreiunddreißig

❹ They said that they were (*would-be*) very much looking forward to flying to Madrid soon.
.. .., dass ... sich sehr darauf
...., bald nach Madrid .. ..

❺ The report is available to you.
Der Bericht ..... Ihnen ... .

Answers to Exercise 2

❶ – eine schlechte Nachricht – Ihnen – sagen – Lieber – ❷ – das Schwimmbad – kostenlos ❸ – hast du – wie ausgemacht – reserviert ❹ Sie haben gesagt – sie – freuen würden – zu fliegen ❺ steht – zur Verfügung

---

Second wave: 47th lesson

Ninety-seventh lesson   97

If only it would snow!

1 – In the weather forecast (*weather-report*) they said (*predicted*) that it will get even warmer.
2 [What a] pity, Christmas without snow isn't a proper (*correct*) Christmas!

② In the previous lesson, we saw that the subjunctive I is used to indirectly report the words of others – but also that this rule isn't always applied in everyday language. Here's proof! In formal (written) German one would have to say **..., dass es wärmer werden würde** (not **wird**).

3 – Tja ③, das **Kli**ma ist nicht mehr so wie es **ein**mal war.
4 Hast du be**merkt**, dass die **Blau**meisen, die **ei**gentlich **Zug**vögel sind, **diesen Win**ter hier ge**blie**ben sind ④?
5 – Ja, und es wird da**mit** ge**rech**net ⑤, dass die Er**wär**mung der **Er**de **wei**ter zu**nimmt**.
6 In ein paar **Jah**ren **fei**ern wir **drau**ßen im **Ba**deanzug Heilig**a**bend!
7 – **Um**so **bes**ser, das Meer ist dann viel**leicht** auch schon **näh**er, wo doch ⑥ das **Was**ser in den **O**zeanen steigt…
8 – Ja, **un**sere **Zu**kunft sieht **ro**sig aus.
9 Aber wie dem auch sei ⑦, wir **las**sen uns nicht die **Lau**ne ver**der**ben!
10 Wir **wis**sen ja, der Mensch passt sich **al**lem ⑧ an.

---

3 tya … **klee**ma … **4** …**blow**-meizuhn … **5** … er**ver**mung …
6 … heilikH-**ahb**'nt **7** … **oht**seahnuhn shteikt **8** … **rohz**ikH …

Notes

③ **tja** conveys a certain resignation, as in 'oh well', 'never mind' or 'too bad'. **Tja, ich gehe nicht nach draußen, es schneit!** *Oh well, I'm not going outside, it's snowing!*

④ The speaker got this a bit wrong. Most blue tits are resident in Germany, as well as the rest of temperate Europe, although some population movements have been seen in central Europe.

⑤ **rechnen mit** ('calculate with') *to expect, to reckon on*: **Am Sonntag wird auf der Autobahn mit Stau gerechnet.** *On Sunday, traffic jams are expected on the motorway.*

⑥ **wo… doch…** is close in meaning to **da** *as, since*: **Hören wir auf zu tanzen, wo du doch keine Lust mehr hast.** *Let's stop dancing since you don't feel like it anymore.* However,

3 – Well, the climate isn't what it used to be (*is not more like how it once was*).
4 Did you notice that the blue tits, which are actually migratory birds, stayed here this winter?
5 – Yes, and it is expected that global warming (*the warming of-the Earth*) will continue to increase (*further increases*).
6 In a few years, we'll be celebrating (*we celebrate*) Christmas Eve outside in [our] swimsuit[s].
7 – All the better! Perhaps the sea will be (*is*) closer as well then, as the water [level] of the oceans rises …
8 – Yes, our future is looking rosy!
9 But be that as it may, we won't (*don't*) let it spoil our (*the*) mood!
10 We know well that humankind adapts to everything.

it can also mean *even though*: **Warum ziehst du den dicken Pullover an, wo es doch heute so warm ist?** *Why are you putting on the thick sweater even though it is so warm today?*

⑦ Note that **auch** *also* can't be omitted in this expression, or indeed in two other similar ones: **wer es auch sei** *whoever it may be*, **was es auch sei** *whatever it may be*…

⑧ **sich anpassen** is followed by the dative case: **Er passt sich nie den anderen an.** *He never adapts to others.* Sometimes it is used with the preposition **an** + accusative (in this case, **an** occurs twice – as the separable prefix and the preposition): **Wir müssen uns <u>an</u> das neue Klima <u>an</u>passen.** *We have to adapt to the new climate.*

97 11 Die Entwicklung der **Mensch**heit hat es ge**zeig**t: je **we**niger ⑨ der Mensch **kle**tterte, **des**to **kür**zer **wur**den **sei**ne **Ar**me.
12 **O**der **an**dersrum ge**sag**t: Je mehr er **lau**fen **muss**te, **um**so **läng**er **wur**den **sei**ne **Bei**ne.
13 Die Na**tur fin**det **im**mer **ei**ne Strate**gie**, die dem **Men**schen das Über**le**ben er**mög**licht.
14 – Na ja, ich weiß nicht recht ⑩, ich **wür**de ja gern **dei**nen Opti**mis**mus **tei**len, **a**ber stell dir mal den **Weih**nachtsmann in der **Ba**dehose vor!

*11 … ent**vik**lung … yeh … **klet**ªtuh **des**to … 13 … shtrateg-**ee** … 14 … opti**mis**mus …*

Notes

⑨ **je** (+ comparative) … **desto/umso** (+ comparative) *the more/less … the more/less*: **Je mehr ich denke, desto/umso weniger weiß ich.** *The more I think, the less I know.* Note that after **je** (*yeh*), the verb is in the last position and the word order is inverted after **desto** or **umso**.

***

Übung 1 – Übersetzen Sie bitte!

❶ Je wärmer die Erde wird, desto höher steigt das Wasser in den Ozeanen. ❷ Wenn ich Sie recht verstehe, müssen wir damit rechnen, dass das Klima sich in den nächsten Jahren ändert? ❸ Wer sich nicht anpassen kann, hat keine rosige Zukunft. ❹ Warum bist du schlechter Laune, wo doch das Wetter so schön ist? ❺ Tja, wenn es weiter schneit, dann wird der Weihnachtsmann nicht pünktlich kommen.

11 The evolution of humanity has shown: the less humans climbed, the shorter their arms became.
12 Or (*said*) the other way around: the more they had to run, the longer their legs got.
13 Nature always finds a strategy that allows the survival of humans.
14 – Well, I don't really (*rightly*) know; I'd like to share your optimism, but imagine Father Christmas in swimming trunks!

⑩ **recht** is often used in the sense of **richtig** *right*, *correct*, *proper*: it is used with this meaning in the phrasal verb **recht haben** *to be right*. This is different from its meaning as the opposite of *left*: **die rechte Hand** *the right hand* (from **rechts** *on the right*).

***

Answers to Exercise 1

❶ The warmer the Earth gets, the higher the water level in the oceans rises. ❷ If I understand you correctly, we must expect the climate to change within the coming years? ❸ [He] who can't adapt doesn't have a rosy future. ❹ Why are you in a bad mood even though the weather is so beautiful? ❺ Too bad, if it continues snowing, Father Christmas won't be coming on time.

97 Übung 2 – Ergänzen Sie bitte!

1 Why don't you (*informal*) share my optimism? I swear to you, the future will be beautiful!

Warum .... nicht ....?
Ich schwöre dir, ... wird schön sein!

2 You should buy your food, since your friends will be here in a few days.

Ihr solltet .... einkaufen, ...
eure Freunde .. .. kommen!

3 Be that as it may, whether it snows or is warm, we adapt to every climate.

... ., ob .. .. oder
.... ist, ... uns .. jedes Klima ...

4 We have blue tits in our garden and feed them in winter.

Wir haben ....
und füttern sie .. ..

5 The more vegetables people eat, the less they fall (*become*) ill, have you (*formal*) noticed this?

.. .. die Menschen Gemüse essen, ...
.... werden sie krank, ... das
schon ....?

Answers to Exercise 2

❶ – teilst du – meinen Optimismus – die Zukunft – ❷ – euer Essen – wo doch – in ein paar Tagen – ❸ Wie dem auch sei – es schneit – warm – wir passen – an – an ❹ – Blaumeisen in unserem Garten– im Winter ❺ Je mehr – desto weniger – haben Sie – bemerkt

Der Heiligabend *'the holy evening' is Christmas Eve. On 24 December, once night falls, families gather around the Christmas tree and open their presents. In the north of Germany,* **der Weihnachtsmann** *Father Christmas tends to be in charge of delivering presents, while in the south it is usually* **das Christkind** *the Christ child. In some families, carols are sung, and those with strong willpower wait until Christmas Eve to start eating the cookies and gingerbread baked during* **die Adventszeit** *(the four weeks before Christmas).*

Second wave: 48th lesson

98 Achtundneunzigste Lektion

Wiederholung – Review

1 The subjunctive

The subjunctive mood is used to express something unreal, possible or hypothetical. In German schools, it sometimes used to be called **die Möglichkeitsform** ('the form of possibility') as opposed to **die Wirklichkeitsform** ('the form of reality'), i.e. the indicative mood.

The present subjunctive is formed with distinct verb endings (although in some cases the verb form resembles the indicative). The past and future tenses of the subjunctive are compound forms made using an auxiliary verb. Although there are many subjunctive forms in German, some are used mainly in formal written language.

1.1 Forming the subjunctive

German has two subjunctive moods: subjunctive I and II.

• The present tense of subjunctive I is formed by adding the endings **-e, -est, -e, -en, -et, -en** to the stem of the infinitive: **gehen** *to go, to walk*: **ich gehe, du gehest, er gehe, wir gehen, ihr gehet, sie gehen**

The verb **sein** *to be* is the only exception: **ich sei, du sei(e)st, er sei, wir seien, ihr seiet, sie seien**.

Note: With the exception of **sein**, the first-person singular and plural and the third-person plural forms of present subjunctive I are identical to the corresponding forms of the present indicative.

• The formation of the subjunctive II depends on whether the verb is regular or irregular.

• The subjunctive II of irregular (strong) verbs is formed by adding the endings **-e, -est, -e, -en, -et, -en** to the past tense stem.

Ninety-eighth lesson 98

gehen *to go* → past tense stem **ging** → subjunctive II: **ich ginge, du gingest, er ginge, wir gingen, ihr ginget, sie gingen**

If the past tense stem contains a vowel that can take an umlaut (i.e. **a**, **o**, **u**), this is added in the subjunctive II (except **sollen** *to be supposed to*, *'should'* and **wollen** *to want*):
sein *to be* → past tense stem **war** → subjunctive II: **ich wäre, du wärest, er wäre, wir wären, ihr wäret, sie wären**

• The subjunctive II of regular (weak) verbs is identical to the past tense indicative:
kaufen *to buy*: **ich kaufte, du kauftest, er kaufte, wir kauften, ihr kauftet, sie kauften**

To avoid confusion with the past tense, a different construction with **würde** (the subjunctive II of **werden**) + infinitive is frequently used for the present subjunctive II:
ich würde kaufen, du würdest kaufen, er würde kaufen, wir würden kaufen, ihr würdet kaufen, sie würden kaufen

In everyday speech, the **würde**-construction is used much more frequently, with the exception of **sein**, **haben**, the modal verbs and a few others. Thus, you'll hardly ever hear someone saying: **Wenn ich Zeit hätte, flöge ich nach London,** but: **würde ich ... fliegen.** *If I had time, I would fly to London.* However, you would hear: **Wenn ich größer wäre, müsste ich nicht immer in den selben Kleidergeschäften einkaufen.** *If I were taller, I wouldn't always have to shop in the same clothes shops.*

1.2 Using subjunctive I and II

• **Subjunctive I**

This is traditionally used to report the speech, requests, wishes or suggestions of a third person. However, there is often uncertainty even among native speakers with regard to using it, not least because some forms of present subjunctive I are identical to the present indicative forms. Because of this, those forms are often avoided, and generally the subjunctive I is becoming increasingly rare. (Today it is used almost exclusively in the third-person singular, or with the verb **sein**, whose forms are distinctive.)

It is still used in:
• some common expressions conveying concessions, such as:
es sei denn, dass ... *unless...*; **wie dem auch sei** *be that as it may*
• wishes that have become fixed expressions, such as:
Gott sei Dank! *Thank God!* **Hol' ihn der Teufel!** *To hell with him!*
• instructions (e.g. in cookbooks):
Man nehme zwei Eier, ein Pfund Zucker, 400g Mehl ...
Take 2 eggs, a pound of sugar, 400 g of flour...

But even these are becoming rarer in everyday language, and are increasingly replaced by the indicative. For example, wishes can be rephrased using the modal verb **sollen**: **Soll ihn der Teufel holen!** ('The devil ought to get him'), and orders (e.g. in cookbooks) by using the imperative: **Nehmen Sie...** *Take...*

Wie dem auch ist *Be that as it may*, before you decide to give up on the subjunctive I altogether, read the section a bit further along on reported speech.

• **Subjunctive II**

This is used to express a hypothetical supposition or a possibility. Hence it is first and foremost used in conditional sentences, which consist of a subordinate **wenn** *if* clause that expresses the condition, and a main clause that expresses the consequence.
Wenn wir Zeit hätten, wären wir im Kino.
If we had time, we would be in the cinema.
Wenn ich viel Geld im Lotto gewinnen würde, müsste ich nicht mehr arbeiten. *If I won a lot of money in the lottery, I wouldn't have to work anymore.*
Ich würde mich freuen, wenn du mich besuchen würdest.
I would be glad if you visited me.

Note that:

• The subjunctive II is used in <u>both</u> the **wenn**-clause <u>and</u> the main clause. (English uses the past tense in the *if*-clause, and the conditional in the main clause.)

- Either the subjunctive II form of the verb or a construction with **würde** may be used in both the **wenn**-clause and the main clause. Sentences with **würde** in both clauses are common in spoken German, but they should be avoided in writing.

- The **wenn** may be omitted. The verb in the subordinate clause then moves into the first position, as in English:
Würde die Sonne scheinen, wäre ich glücklich.
Were ('Would-become') the sun to shine, I would be happy.
Conditional sentences without **wenn** are rather literary, and the order of the clauses can be changed:
Ich wäre glücklich, würde die Sonne scheinen.
I would be happy were the sun to shine.

In order to express a hypothetical situation in the past, you use the past subjunctive II (in both the **wenn**-clause and the main clause):
Wenn wir Zeit gehabt hätten wären wir im Kino gewesen.
If we had had time, we would have been in the cinema.
Ich hätte mich gefreut, wenn du mich besucht hättest.
I would have been glad if you had visited me.

The subjunctive II is also used for:

- expressing wishes, often accompanied by **gern**, **lieber**, etc.:
Ich würde jetzt gern ein Eis essen, und du?
I would like to eat an ice cream now, and you?
Ich möchte* lieber einen Kaffee trinken.
I would prefer to have ('drink') a coffee.

* We first saw **ich möchte** *I would like* a long time ago. Now you may be able to recognize that **möchte** is the subjunctive II of **mögen** *to like*. It is formed from the simple past tense **ich mochte** *I liked*, with the addition of an umlaut. So be sure to pronounce the umlaut in the subjunctive II!

- expressing wishes that convey a sense of regret, often accompanied by **doch** or **nur** (or both):
Hätte ich doch nur mehr Geld! *If only I had more money!*
Wäre ich doch zu Hause geblieben! *If only I had stayed at home!*

- expressing a possibility:
Wir könnten nach Dresden fahren. *We could go to Dresden.*

- making a polite request:
  Würden Sie mir bitte das Salz reichen?
  Would you pass me the salt, please?

So the subjunctive II still has a number of uses. It also has a role to play in reported speech.

1.3 Indirect (reported) speech

The subjunctive is used in German to report what someone says or said (someone else or yourself). Subjunctive I should be used if the subjunctive I form is different from the indicative.

If the speech being reported is in the present, the present subjunctive I is used (regardless of whether the main clause – who is saying it – is in the past or present):

direct speech: **Max sagt: „Ich bin in Berlin."**
Max says, 'I am in Berlin.'
reported speech: **Max sagt, dass* er in Berlin sei.**
Max says that he is in Berlin.

direct speech: **Gisela hat gesagt: „Ich habe keine Zeit."**
Gisela said, 'I have no time.'
reported speech: **Gisela hat gesagt, dass* sie keine Zeit habe.**
Gisela said that she has no time.

If the speech being reported is in the past, the past subjunctive I is used:
direct speech: **Max sagt: „Ich bin in Berlin gewesen."**
Max says, 'I was in Berlin.'
reported speech: **Max sagt, dass* er in Berlin gewesen sei.**
Max says that he was in Berlin.

direct speech: **Gisela hat gesagt: „Ich habe keine Zeit gehabt."**
Gisela said, 'I had no time.'
reported speech: **Gisela hat gesagt, dass* sie keine Zeit gehabt habe.** *Gisela said that she had no time.*

* Remember that **dass** can be omitted. In this case, the verb takes its usual place in second position: **Max sagt, er sei in Form.** *Max says he's in good shape.*

If the subjunctive I form is the same as the indicative (i.e. the first-person singular and plural, and the third-person plural forms), subjunctive II should be used.

direct speech: **Sie sagen: „Wir schreiben den Brief."**
They say, 'We are writing the letter.'
reported speech: subjunctive I →
Sie sagen, dass sie den Brief schreiben.
subjunctive II →
Sie sagen, dass sie den Brief schrieben/schreiben würden.

However, in everyday speech, most commonly either the indicative or subjunctive II is used for reported speech. So any of the following are possible:
Peter sagt, er sei/wäre/ist müde. *Peter says he is tired.*

1.4 *als ob* 'as if' clauses

The subjunctive II is used to make hypothetical comparisons, which are usually introduced by **als ob**. In written German, the subjunctive I is sometimes used:
Er benimmt sich, als ob er der Chef sei/wäre.
He behaves as if he were the boss.

als ob can be replaced by **als**, followed immediately by the verb:
Er benimmt sich, als sei/wäre er der Chef.

This also holds true for the expression **(so) tun, als ob** *to pretend, to act as if*:
Er tut so, als ob er das zum ersten Mal hören würde.
He pretends to hear this for the first time.

2 Making comparisons

To make comparisons such as 'the more ... the more ...' / or 'the less ..., the less ...', the construction is:

je + comparative + verb at the end, **desto** or **umso** + comparative + inverted word order:
Je schneller ihr lauft, desto früher kommt ihr an.
The faster you run, the sooner you get there.

Je kälter der Winter ist, umso schöner scheint der Sommer.
The colder the winter, the more beautiful summer seems.

If there's no second adjective, 'more' is translated as **mehr** and 'less' as **weniger**:
Je mehr Wasser ich trinke, desto weniger Durst habe ich.
The more water I drink, the less thirsty I am ('thirst I have').

What a perfect opportunity to review the comparative forms of adjectives (see lesson 63)!

3 Little words with lots of meanings

Let's talk a bit about some useful little words such as **schon** *already* and **ja** *yes*. Their basic meaning is unproblematic, but they can have a variety of other meanings in different contexts.

3.1 *schon*

In its primary sense, it means *already*:
Es ist schon vier Uhr! *It's already 4 o'clock!*
Wir haben schon gegessen. *We have already eaten.*

However, **schon** is also often used instead of (or together with) **seit** *since*:
Ich lerne schon zwei Monate Deutsch. *I've been learning German for two months already.* (implication: a long time!)

It's also found in certain set phrases:
Ist schon gut. *It's OK. It doesn't matter.* ('Is already good.')
Ich trinke wenig Alkohol und schon gar keinen Whisky.
I don't drink much alcohol, and especially no whisky.
Hast du schon wieder Hunger? *Are you hungry again already?*

3.2 *ja*

As you know, **ja** (stressed) alone or in first position means *yes*.
Kommst du mit? – Ja, natürlich!
Are you coming along? – Yes, of course!

It can also be used as a question tag, to prompt an answer after a statement:
Du kommst mit, ja? *You're coming along, aren't you?*

In contrast, in exclamations, **ja** can express the sense of 'as you can see' (often translated as *but*), can express surprise or can intensify a command:
Es ist rot, du musst warten! – Ich warte ja!
It's red, you have to wait! – But I am waiting!
Es schneit ja! *Oh, it's snowing!*
Mach das ja nicht noch einmal!
Just don't do it again! (implication: I'm warning you!)

The meanings of **Na ja!** and **Tja!** depend on the context, ranging from 'well, …' to 'ah well', 'too bad', 'never mind', etc. It's not what you say, but the way that you say it!
Könnte ich bitte eine einzige Margerite haben? – Na ja, nimm dir eine!
Could I please have a single daisy? – Well, go ahead and take one!
Ich sage Ihnen, das ist kein Problem! – Tja, wenn Sie meinen.
I tell you, it's not a problem! – Oh well, if you say so.
Die *Alte Mühle* ist geschlossen. – Tja, dann essen wir eine Pizza beim Italiener!
The 'Old Mill' is closed. – Too bad! Let's have a pizza at the Italian [restaurant] then!

Don't worry, usually the meaning of these little words will be self-explanatory from the accompanying gestures and tone of voice. For example:
• **Ist schon gut** or **schon gut**, like **das ist nicht schlimm** *it isn't serious*, are often spoken with a reassuring tone and a shrug.
• **Schon wieder** is accompanied by an irritated tone and a frown that signals frustration or disapproval: **Es regnet schon wieder!** *It's raining again!*
• **Es regnet ja!** conveys surprise, so may be exclaimed with a wide-eyed expression.
• **Schon gar nicht** is said in a way making it clear that something is completely out of the question: **Ich am Sonntag arbeiten? Das schon gar nicht!** *Me, working on a Sunday? Certainly not!*

Time to put all this theory into practice in the review exercise!

98 Review exercise

Sie denken, es gibt keine verständnisvollen Polizisten? Falsch!

1 – Du, die Ampel war rot!
2 – Welche Ampel? Ich habe keine Ampel gesehen.
3 – Das habe ich bemerkt, Liebling!
4 Ich wünschte nur, die Polizei wäre nicht direkt hinter uns!
5 – Oh nein! Hol sie der Teufel!
6 Ich bin sicher, wenn ich angehalten hätte, wären sie nicht da gewesen!
7 – Mit „hätte" und „wäre" kommen wir nicht weiter, mein Schatz, jetzt brauchen wir dringend unsere gute, alte Strategie!
8 – Guten Tag! Polizei! Könnte ich mal Ihre Papiere sehen?
9 – Selbstverständlich! Hier bitte! Ich hoffe, es ist nichts Schlimmes?
10 – Na ja, Sie sind bei Rot durchgefahren!
11 – Das kann nicht sein! Ich schwöre Ihnen, das ist mir noch nie passiert!
12 – Wie dem auch sei, Sie müssen mit einer hohen Strafe rechnen.
13 – Was heißt das?
14 – Das kostet Sie wenigstens 250 Euro!
15 – Also dieses Mal platzt mir endgültig der Kragen!
16 Hundertmal habe ich dir gesagt, dass Verkehrsregeln genau beachtet werden müssen.
17 Es kommt überhaupt nicht in Frage, dass ich schon wieder für dich bezahle!
18 Außerdem kannst du zu Fuß nach Hause gehen und am besten schnell, bevor ich dir den Hals umdrehe!

19 – Hören Sie mal, so schlimm ist es nun auch nicht, bewahren Sie die Ruhe!
20 Ein Gentleman sind Sie ja nicht gerade!
21 Und Sie, hören Sie auf zu weinen. Die Ampel war ja vielleicht noch gelb!
22 Also auf Wiedersehen und passen Sie in Zukunft besser auf!
23 – Oh, ich danke Ihnen vielmals! Das ist wirklich sehr nett von Ihnen!

***

24 – Na, wie war ich?
25 – Ich würde sagen, fast zu perfekt!
26 Du hast mir wirklich einen Schrecken eingejagt, als du gesagt hast, du würdest mir gern den Hals umdrehen!

Translation
You think there are no understanding policemen? Wrong!

1 (*You*) The light was (*lights were*) red! **2** What light? I didn't see any traffic lights! **3** I noticed that, darling! **4** If (*I would-wish*) only the police weren't (*would not be*) right behind us! **5** Oh no! To hell with them! **6** I am sure if I had (*would-have*) stopped, they wouldn't have been there. **7** 'Would have' and 'would have been' won't get us far (*further*), my treasure; now we urgently need our good old strategy! **8** Good afternoon! Police! Could I see your papers? **9** Of course! Here they are (*please*)! I hope it's nothing serious? **10** Well, you went through a red light! **11** That can't be! I swear to you that's never happened to me before! **12** Be that as it may, you have to expect a high fine. **13** What does that mean? **14** It'll cost you at least 250 euros! **15** Well, that's it, this time I've really had enough (*bursts to-me finally the collar*)! **16** I've told you a hundred times that traffic regulations have to be obeyed carefully (*exactly*)! **17** It's completely out of the question that I'm paying for you again! **18** Furthermore, you can go home on foot, and preferably quickly, before I wring your neck! **19** Listen, it's not that bad now, keep

fünfhundertfünfzig • 550

calm! **20** You aren't exactly a gentleman! **21** And you, stop crying. Maybe the lights were still amber after all! **22** All right, goodbye. And in future pay more attention! **23** Oh, thank you very much! That's really very nice of you! **24** Well, how was I? **25** I'd say almost too perfect! **26** You really gave me a fright when you said you'd like to wring my neck!

Second wave: 49th lesson

That was your last review lesson! But there are still two final lessons to go. **Also, bis morgen!**

99 Neunundneunzigste Lektion

Ohne Fleiß kein Preis

1 – Sei es in **ei**nem Jahr **o**der in zwei, ich **wer**de es **schaf**fen!
2 – Klar doch, so **flei**ßig ① und **tüch**tig wie Sie sind!
3 – Na ja, ich weiß nicht, ob ich be**son**ders **tüch**tig bin, **a**ber ich **wer**de nicht **auf**geben, das ist **si**cher!
4 – Wa**rum soll**ten ② Sie? Es **wä**re **wirk**lich dumm jetzt **auf**zugeben, wo ③ das **Schwer**ste **hin**ter **Ih**nen liegt.
5 – Wo**her wis**sen Sie das?
6 – Es ist ein **of**fenes Ge**heim**nis, dass der **An**fang das **Schwer**ste ist.

Pronunciation
... fleis ... **2** ... fleissikH ... tewkHtikH ...

Ninety-ninth lesson 99

No pain, no gain
(*Without effort no prize*)

1 – Be it in one year or two, I'll make (*manage*) it!
2 – Sure, as diligent and studious as you are!
3 – Ah well, I don't know if I'm particularly studious, but I won't give up, that's [for] sure.
4 – [And] why should you? It would be really stupid to give up now when the most difficult [part] is behind you.
5 – How (*Where-from*) do you know that?
6 – It's an open secret that the beginning is [always] the hardest.

Notes

① **fleißig** and **tüchtig** are virtually synonymous. If somebody is **fleißig** or **tüchtig** (or both), they're diligent, keen, industrious, studious, capable, etc.

② This is the subjunctive II of **sollen** *to be supposed to.* The stem vowel doesn't take an umlaut, so the simple past tense and the subjunctive II forms are identical (see lesson 92, note 3).

③ **wo** is here used as a conjunction, just like **wo doch** (see lesson 97, note 6).

fünfhundertzweiundfünfzig • 552

7 Am **An**fang braucht man viel Mut und **Aus**dauer, weil man auf so **vie**le **Din**ge **gleich**zeitig **auf**passen ④ muss.

8 – **Ko**misch ⑤, das ist mir gar nicht **auf**gefallen ⑥.

9 – **Um**so besser! Die **Haupt**sache ist, am Ball zu **blei**ben und nicht die Ge**duld** zu ver**lie**ren.

10 – Ja, mit der Zeit klärt sich **al**les auf.

11 Mir hat es **je**denfalls **gro**ßen Spaß ge**macht**.

12 Und **des**halb **wer**de ich auch **wei**termachen, e**gal** was ⑦ kommt!

13 **Min**destens **ei**ne **hal**be **Stun**de pro Tag…, so**lan**ge bis ich **flie**ßend Deutsch **spre**che! ☐

7 … dinguh gleikH-tseitikH … 13 … zolanguh … flees'nt …

Notes

④ When **aufpassen** *to pay attention* is used with the preposition **auf**, don't forget the second **auf**: **Passen Sie auf Ihr Geld auf!** *Pay attention to your money!*

***

Übung 1 – Übersetzen Sie bitte!

❶ Die Hauptsache ist, nicht den Mut zu verlieren und weiterzumachen! ❷ Vielen Dank, allein hätte ich das nie geschafft! ❸ Es ist ein offenes Geheimnis, dass ihr Mann nicht besonders tüchtig ist. ❹ Haben Sie bitte ein wenig Geduld, morgen wird sich alles aufklären. ❺ Sie sollten fleißig jeden Tag eine Lektion lesen und übersetzen!

7 In the beginning, one needs a lot of courage and perseverance because one has to pay attention to so many things at the same time!
8 – Strange, I didn't even notice.
9 – All the better! The main thing is to be (*remain*) on the ball and not to lose one's (*the*) patience.
10 – Yes, everything becomes clear (*is cleared up*) with time.
11 In any case, it was great fun for me (*To-me has it anyway big fun made*).
12 And so I'll continue [with it], no matter what happens!
13 At least half an hour per day … until I speak German fluently!

⑤ **komisch** is often used to mean *strange*, *weird*, conveying a sense of surprise, though its basic meaning is *funny*, in the sense of comical.

⑥ **es fällt mir auf, dass …** *I notice that…*

⑦ In everyday speech, **egal was** frequently replaces **was auch** *whatever*, *no matter what*: **Ich mache weiter, was auch/egal was kommt.** (see lesson 97, note 6)

***

Answers to Exercise 1

❶ The main thing is not to lose courage and to continue! ❷ Thank you, I never would have made (*managed*) it alone! ❸ It's an open secret that her husband isn't particularly diligent. ❹ Please be a little patient – tomorrow all will become clear. ❺ You should diligently read and translate a lesson per day.

99 Übung 2 – Ergänzen Sie bitte!

① No matter what happens, I won't give up: that's [for] sure!
Egal ... ., ich werde nicht ...., das ist ......!

② In the beginning, one has to pay attention to so many things; that's really not easy.
.. .. muss man ... so viele Dinge ...., das ist .... nicht leicht.

③ One needs a lot [of] courage and perseverance in order to stay on the ball.
Man braucht .... und ...., um .. .... zu ....

④ It would be a pity not to continue as it is such good fun (*big fun makes*).
.. .... schade nicht ...., wo es doch .... macht.

⑤ He didn't notice that it is particularly hard to learn German.
Es ist ihm nicht ...., dass es .... ist, ... zu lernen.

Answers to Exercise 2

❶ – was kommt – aufgeben – sicher ❷ Am Anfang – auf – aufpassen – wirklich – ❸ – viel Mut – Ausdauer – am Ball – bleiben ❹ Es wäre – weiterzumachen – großen Spaß – ❺ – aufgefallen – besonders schwer – Deutsch –

> Die Hauptsache ist, nicht den Mut zu verlieren und weiterzumachen!

To finish in style, the final lesson contains a variety of the finer points of German grammar: word order in subordinate clauses, the superlative, prepositions, different tenses and, of course, a range of declensions and conjugations! You can review anything you need to in the review lessons or the grammatical appendix.

Second wave: 50th lesson

100 Hundertste Lektion

Als letzte Lektion erzählen wir Ihnen eine wahre Geschichte!

Ende gut, alles gut

1 Hallo Anne, seit mehr als zwei Jahren haben wir nichts voneinander gehört – hoffentlich hat sich deine E-Mail-Adresse inzwischen nicht geändert.
2 Wie geht es dir und deinem Mann ①? Lebt ihr immer noch in der Stadt mit dem höchsten Kirchturm der Welt?
3 Die schöne Zeit, die ich mit euch vor drei Jahren verbracht habe, ist mir unvergesslich geblieben.
4 Umso mehr als ich euretwegen begonnen habe, Deutsch zu lernen.
5 Dafür möchte ich mich bei euch heute herzlich bedanken, denn, ohne es zu wissen, wart ihr meines Glückes Schmied ②!
6 Und das kam so: Im Mai letzten Jahres habe ich am Abend schnell noch Brot holen wollen, bevor die Geschäfte schließen.

Pronunciation
1 ... *ee*mehl ... *5* ... *glew*kuhs shmeet ...

Notes

① Remember that **es geht** is used whether one or more than one person is being addressed. The person after whom you're asking is in the dative case: **Wie geht es Ihrer Frau, Herr Schneider?** *How is your wife, Mr Schneider?*

Hundredth lesson 100

In the last lesson, we'll tell you a true story.

All's well that ends well
(*Ending good, all good*)

1 Hello Anne! It's more than two years we haven't heard from each other – hopefully, your email address hasn't changed in the meantime.
2 How are you and your husband? Are you still living in the city with the highest church tower in the world?
3 The lovely time I spent with you three years ago remains unforgettable (*has to-me unforgettable remained*).
4 All the more as I started learning German because of you.
5 For this, I'd like to say a heartfelt 'thank you' to you today (*with you today cordially thank*), as, unwittingly (*without knowing it*), you were the architects of my fortune (*my luck's smith*).
6 And this is how it happened (*this came thus*): one evening in May last year I wanted to get some bread quickly before the shops closed.

② The full proverb is **Jeder ist seines Glückes Schmied.** *Life is what you make of it. Everyone is the architect of their own fortune.*

100 7 Ich **ha**be vor der **Bäcke**rei ge**parkt** und beim ③ **Aus**steigen ist es pas**siert**!
8 Ein **ar**mer **Rad**fahrer, der ge**ra**de in **die**sem Mo**ment** vor**bei**fuhr ④, **mach**te **ei**nen **Sal**to **ü**ber sein **Lenk**rad!
9 Ich bin **fürch**terlich er**schrock**en und zu dem auf der **Stra**ße **lie**genden ⑤ Mann ge**lau**fen.
10 Und stell dir vor! Ich **wur**de von **ei**nem Schwall **deut**scher **Schimpf**wörter emp**fan**gen! (**Glück**licherweise ver**stand** ich nur „Mist" und „Idi**o**tin"!)
11 To**tal** über**rascht** fiel mir nichts **an**deres ein ⑥ als „Noch **ein**mal Glück ge**habt**!" zu **sa**gen (das war der **Ti**tel **ei**ner Lek**tion** in **mei**nem **Deutsch**buch…).
12 Er **muss**te da**rauf**hin **herz**haft **la**chen und das war der **An**fang von **un**serer **Lie**besgeschichte.

Notes

③ Like most prepositions, **bei** has several meanings. Here it has the temporal meaning 'when', 'while'. **beim** + a verbal noun (a verb used as a noun) usually translates as *in -ing*, *while -ing*: **Er hat sich beim Skilaufen ein Bein gebrochen.** *He broke a leg while skiing.* **Beim Radfahren muss man vorsichtig sein.** *One has to be careful when cycling.*

④ **vorbeifahren** *to pass* (by car, by train, by bike, etc.). The implication is that one goes past quickly. As an adverb, **vorbei** can mean 'past' or 'over': **Alles ist vorbei.** *Everything is over.*

7	I parked in front of the bakery, and when [I was] getting out [of the car] it happened!	100
8	An unfortunate cyclist, who happened to be passing by that very moment, did a somersault over his handlebars!	
9	I got a terrible fright (*was terribly frightened*) and ran over to the man, [who was] lying in the street.	
10	And imagine! I was greeted (*received*) by a stream of German swear words. (Luckily, I only understood 'damn' and 'idiot'!)	
11	Totally surprised, I couldn't think of anything else to say except 'That was lucky!' (this was the title of a lesson in my German book ...).	
12	That made him laugh heartily (*He had-to thereupon heartily to-laugh*), and this was the beginning of our love story.	

⑤ **liegend** is the present participle of **liegen** *to lie*. Present participles can often be used like adjectives in German.

⑥ **einfallen** *to think of something, to remember something, to come to mind*: **Was fällt Ihnen ein, wenn Sie das Wort „Glück" hören?** *What do you think of when you hear the word 'luck'?* But be careful with the reproach **Was fällt Ihnen ein!** *What do you think you're doing?*

100 13 Für **un**seren **nächs**ten **U**rlaub **ha**ben wir vor, die „**Roman**tische **Stra**ße" von **Würz**burg nach **Füs**sen ent**lang** zu **ra**deln ⑦ – 350 **Ki**lometer!
14 **Augs**burg ist **an**scheinend nicht weit von Ulm ent**fernt**. Wir **könn**ten **ei**nen **Ab**stecher **ma**chen und euch be**su**chen.
15 Ich **wür**de mich sehr **freu**en, euch **wie**derzusehen.
16 Lass schnell von dir **hö**ren!

Liebe **Grü**ße an euch **bei**de!

Deine Miriam

---

13 ... vewrts-burk ... 14 ... owksburk ... ulm ...

***

Übung 1 – Übersetzen Sie bitte!

❶ Weißt du noch, wo der höchste Kirchturm der Welt steht? ❷ Wenn man genug Zeit hat, kann man die ganze „Romantische Straße" entlang radeln. ❸ Warum kommen Sie nicht zu einem Glas Wein vorbei? ❹ Glücklicherweise geht es ihm heute viel besser als gestern. ❺ Die wunderschönen Tage, die wir hier verbracht haben, werden uns unvergesslich bleiben.

13 On (*For*) our next holiday, we're planning to cycle along the 'Romantic Route' from Würzburg to Füssen – 350 kilometres!
14 Apparently, Augsburg isn't far away from Ulm. We could make a detour and visit you.
15 I'd be very pleased to see you again.
16 Get in touch soon!

Best wishes (*Dear greetings*) to both of you!

(*Your*) Miriam

Notes

⑦ **radeln** is frequently used instead of **Rad fahren** *to cycle*; **entlang** is a separable prefix here: **Wir wollen mit dem Rad den Rhein entlang fahren.** *We want to cycle along the Rhine.* However, **entlang** can also be a preposition with three case combinations: **entlang** + acc: **Gehen Sie die Straße entlang.** *Walk along the street.* **entlang** + genitive or dative: **Entlang des Rheins** or **Dem Rhein entlang gibt es viele Burgen.** *Along the Rhine there are many castles.*

***

Answers to Exercise 1

❶ Do you remember (*Know you still*) where the highest church tower in the world is? ❷ If one has enough time, one can cycle along the entire 'Romantic Route'. ❸ Why don't you come by (*past*) for a glass [of] wine? ❹ Luckily, he is much better today than yesterday. ❺ The wonderful days we spent here will remain unforgettable for us.

Übung 2 – Ergänzen Sie bitte!

❶ They are planning to visit their friends in Ulm before they continue to Würzburg.

... ., ihre Freunde in Ulm ..
........., ... sie nach Würzburg
weiterfahren.

❷ If you cycle along the 'Romantic Route' you will pass by the Neuschwanstein castle.

Wenn Sie die Romantische Straße ....
......, fahren Sie am Schloss
Neuschwanstein ....

❸ I haven't heard anything from Miriam for (*already*) a long time. I hope she is well.

... . schon lange nichts mehr ...
Miriam .... Ich hoffe, ... ihr ....

❹ When alighting from the train, he somersaulted over his suitcase, but luckily nothing happened to him.

.... aus dem Zug machte er
.... über seinen Koffer, aber
.... ist ... nichts passiert.

❺ She was completely surprised when the man sitting on the street greeted her with a stream of German words.

Sie war total ...., als der ... ...
.... Mann sie mit einem
Schwall .... empfing.

Answers to Exercise 2

❶ Sie haben vor – zu besuchen, bevor – ❷ – entlang radeln – vorbei ❸ Ich habe – von – gehört – es geht – gut ❹ Beim Aussteigen – einen Salto – glücklicherweise – ihm – ❺ – überrascht – auf der Straße sitzende – deutscher Wörter –

Second wave: 51st lesson

Here we are at the end of the book. Congratulations! But carry on with the 'second wave', translating the previous lessons from English into German. This will help to reinforce all you've learned. We hope you've enjoyed our time together!
Auf Wiedersehen!

Grammatical appendix

Contents

1	Nouns	567
2	Articles	568
3	The four cases	569
4	Declension	569
5	Forming plural nouns	570
6	Negation	571
7	Demonstratives	572
8	Possessive adjectives	572
9	Adjectives and adverbs	573
	9.1 Predicate adjectives	573
	9.2 Adjectives used as adverbs	573
	9.3 Attributive adjectives	574
	9.4 Adjectives used as nouns	574
10	Pronouns	574
	10.1 Personal pronouns	574
	10.2 Reflexive pronouns	575
	10.3 Demonstrative pronouns	575
	10.4 Interrogative pronouns	576
	10.5 Relative pronouns	577
	10.6 Indefinite pronouns	577
	10.7 Possessive pronouns	577
11	Verbs	578
	11.1 Regular (weak) verbs	578
	11.2 Irregular (strong) verbs	579
	11.3 Mixed (irregular weak) verbs	580
	11.4 **sein**, **haben**, **werden**	581
	11.5 Perfect tense	584
	11.6 Modal verbs	584
	11.7 Present and past participles	585
	11.8 Verbs used as nouns	585
12	The passive voice	586
13	Conditional sentences	587
14	Separable-prefix verbs	588
15	Transitive and intransitive verbs	589
16	Prepositional verbs	589
	16.1 Verbs with accusative prepositions	590
	16.2 Verbs with dative prepositions	590

fünfhundertsechsundsechzig • 566

	16.3 Verbs with two prepositions	590
	16.4 Verbs with several propositions	591
	16.5 Questions with prepositional verbs	591
17	**Asking 'where'?**	592
18	**Conjunctions**...	593
	18.1 Coordinating conjunctions	593
	18.2 Subordinating conjunctions....................................	593
19	**Relative clauses**	594
20	**Some impersonal expressions**......................................	595

List of irregular verbs.. 596

***

1 Nouns

Nouns in German belong to one of three grammatical genders: masculine, feminine or neuter. Some general rules regarding the gender of German nouns are listed below. However, since these rules don't always apply, it's best to learn a noun with its article, which indicates its gender: **der Tisch** *table* (masculine), **die Reise** *journey* (feminine), **das Buch** *book* (neuter).

Some tips:
- Nouns referring to males are usually masculine, and nouns referring to females are usually feminine. Yet the very young are grammatically neuter: **der Mann** *man*, **der Onkel** *uncle*, **die Frau** *woman*, **die Großmutter** *grandmother*, **der Stier** *bull*, **die Kuh** *cow*; but **das Kind** *child*, **das Kalb** *calf*.

- The days of the week, the names of months and the seasons are all masculine: **der Sonntag** *Sunday*, **der Mai** *May*, **der Winter** *winter*.

- Trees, fruits and flowers are usually feminine: **die Eiche** *oak*, **die Birne** *pear*, **die Rose** *rose* (but **der Baum** *tree*, **der Apfel** *apple*, **der Pfirsich** *peach*).

- Most place names and countries are neuter, with the exception of, for example, **die Schweiz** *Switzerland*, **die Türkei** *Turkey*, **der Libanon** *Lebanon*, **der Iran** and **der Irak**, **die Vereinigten Staaten** (m. pl.) *the United States*, etc.

Sometimes, the ending of a noun may help determine its gender.

- Nouns ending in **-er** that are derived from a verb, and those ending in **-ling** or **-ismus** are masculine:
  löschen *to extinguish* → **der Feuerlöscher** *fire extinguisher*
  der Liebling *darling*
  der Optimismus *optimism*

- Nouns ending in **-ung**, **-heit**, **-keit**, **-schaft** are feminine:
  die Wohnung *flat, apartment*
  die Freiheit *freedom, liberty*
  die Freundlichkeit *friendliness*
  die Wirtschaft *economy*

- Nouns ending in **-chen**, **-lein** and infinitives used as nouns (see section 11.8) are neuter:
  das Mädchen *girl*
  das Tischlein *little table*
  das Essen *meal*

Note that all nouns are capitalized in German.

2 Articles

Unlike English, German has several forms for the definite article *the* (e.g. **der**, **die**, **das**) and the indefinite article *a, an* (e.g. **ein**, **eine**, **ein**). There is also a negative article: **kein**, **keine**, **kein** *no, not a, not any*.

The form of the article depends on the noun's:
- gender (masculine, feminine or neuter)
- number (singular or plural)
- grammatical case.

One of the major differences between English and German is grammatical case. German has four cases, which are used to signal the grammatical function of nouns and pronouns (and certain words associated with them) in a sentence. See section 3 for more information about the cases, and section 4 for a complete table of the different forms of the articles.

fünfhundertachtundsechzig • 568

3 The four cases

The grammatical cases in German are:

- the nominative case (used for the subject)
- the accusative case (used for the direct object)
- the dative case (used for the indirect object)
- the genitive case (used to show possession or a close relationship).

Each of these cases is indicated by changing the ending of certain words, which is called 'declension'. In German, articles, nouns, pronouns, participles and even adjectives can 'decline': that is, take different case endings.

Here is an example with the possessive adjective *mine*, referring to a male friend:

- Nominative: **Mein Freund ist nett.** *My friend is nice.* (subject)
- Accusative: **Er kennt meinen Freund.** *He knows my friend.* (direct object)
- Dative: **Ich gebe meinem Freund das Buch.** *I give the book to my friend.* (indirect object)
- Genitive: **Die Schwester meines Freundes ist nett.** *My friend's sister is nice.* (possession/close relationship)

English uses case markers only for certain pronouns (e.g. *he* [subject pronoun], *him* [direct object pronoun]), so word order is typically used to indicate a noun's grammatical function. In German, different case endings allow word order to be much more flexible. For example, you could say:
Ich gebe meinem Freund das Buch. 'I give my friend the book.'

Or if you wanted to put the emphasis on the book:
Das Buch gebe ich meinem Freund. 'The book give I to my friend.'

4 Declension

Here are all the forms of the articles, with **der Tisch** *table* (m.), **die Reise** *journey* (f.), and **das Buch** *book* (n.).

Singular			
	Masculine	Feminine	Neuter
Nominative	der/ein Tisch	die/eine Reise	das/ein Buch
Accusative	den/einen Tisch	die/eine Reise	das/ein Buch
Dative	dem/einem Tisch	der/einer Reise	dem/einem Buch
Genitive	des/eines Tisch(e)s	der/einer Reise	des/eines Buch(e)s

Plural		
Nominative	die/keine	Tische/Reisen/Bücher
Accusative	die/keine	Tische/Reisen/Bücher
Dative	den/keinen	Tischen/Reisen/Büchern
Genitive	der/keiner	Tische/Reisen/Bücher

As you can see, the declensions mainly affect the articles, but in certain cases, the noun also changes:
- in the genitive singular, masculine and neuter nouns end in **-s** or **-es**
- in the dative plural, nouns end in **-n** (except nouns that already end in **-n** or **-s** in the nominative: **die Autos**, **den Autos**).

Apart from these instances, most nouns don't decline. However, there are some masculine nouns that take an **-n** or **-en** ending in all cases except the nominative. These are called 'masculine n-nouns'. For example:
- **der Junge** *boy*, **den Jungen**, **dem Jungen**, **des Jungen**
- **der Präsident** *president*, **den Präsidenten**, **dem Präsidenten**, **des Präsidenten**.

5 Forming plural nouns

Nouns in German can form plurals in many ways. Some of the most common are:
- by adding an **Umlaut**: **der Bruder** *brother* → **die Brüder**
- by adding an **Umlaut** + **-e**: **die Hand** *hand* → **die Hände**

- by adding **-e**: **der Hund** *dog* → **die Hunde**
- by adding **-er**: **das Kind** *child* → **die Kinder**
- by adding an **Umlaut** + **-er**: **das Rad** *wheel, bike* → **die Räder**
- by adding **-n**: **das Auge** *eye* → **die Augen**
- by adding **-en**: **die Wohnung** *apartment* → **die Wohnungen**
- by not adding anything: **das Zimmer** *room* → **die Zimmer**.

When encountering a new noun, it's a good idea to learn it with its definite article and its plural form!

Note that there is no plural form of the indefinite article **ein**, **eine**, **ein** – the noun just appears on its own: **ein Mann** *a man*, **Männer** *men*. However, the negative article does have a plural form: **kein Mann** *no man*, **keine Männer** *no men, not any men*.

6 Negation

The negative article **kein** (which declines following the same pattern as **ein**) is used to negate a noun that in an affirmative sentence would be preceded by **ein** or no article at all:
Hier gibt es keine U-Bahn. *There isn't a metro station here.*
Ich habe kein Geld. *I have no money.*

The adverb **nicht** is used to negate a verb, a pronoun, an adverb or an adjective:
Ich esse nicht. *I'm not eating./I don't eat.*
Ich sehe ihn nicht. *I don't see him.*
Ich gehe nicht oft ins Kino. *I don't often go to the cinema.*
Thomas ist nicht pünktlich. *Thomas is not punctual.*

Nicht is also used to negate nouns preceded by a definite article or a possessive adjective:
Das ist nicht die Nummer von Klaus. *That's not Klaus's number.*
Das ist nicht meine Nummer. *That is not my number.*

The position of **nicht** is determined by the other elements in a sentence. It always follows:
• the finite verb: **Harry <u>arbeitet</u> nicht.** *Harry doesn't work.*

• nouns used as objects: **Er macht <u>seine Arbeit</u> nicht.** *He doesn't do his work.*

- pronouns used as objects: **Ich glaube es nicht.** *I don't believe it.*

- specific adverbs of time: **Warum arbeitet er heute nicht?** *Why doesn't he work today?*

It precedes most other kinds of elements.

7 Demonstratives

The demonstrative adjective to indicate something relatively near (*this*, sing.; *these*, pl.) also has several forms in German: **dieser** (m.), **diese** (f.), **dieses** (n.), **diese** (pl.). Not only do they have to agree in gender and number with the noun they replace or modify, they also have to decline for case, following the same pattern as the definite article:

Dieser Mann ist wirklich groß.
This man is really tall.
Ich sehe diesen Mann oft am Bahnhof.
I often see this man at the station.
Geben Sie diesem Mann kein Bier mehr!
Don't give any more beer to this man!

To signal something farther away (*that*, *those*), the forms are: **jener**, **jene**, **jenes**, **jene**. They also decline like the definite article.
Dieser Mann ist mein Großvater und jener Mann unser Nachbar. *This man is my grandfather and that man our neighbour.*

However, these days, it is far more common to use the definite article (**der, die, das, die**), stressed, as a demonstrative adjective. So, in everyday German the above would turn into:
Der Mann (da) ist mein Großvater und der Mann (dort) unser Nachbar.

8 Possessive adjectives

Possessive adjectives (*my*, *your*, *his*, *her*, *its*, *our*, *their*) decline following the pattern of the indefinite article **ein/kein**. The form must agree with the gender, number and case of the noun it precedes.

The following table gives an overview of the possessive adjectives in the nominative case.

	What is possessed (when the subject of the sentence)			
Possessor	Masc.	Fem.	Neuter	Plural
my	**mein**	**meine**	**mein**	**meine**
your (inf.)	**dein**	**deine**	**dein**	**deine**
his, its (m.)	**sein**	**seine**	**sein**	**seine**
her, its (f.)	**ihr**	**ihre**	**ihr**	**ihre**
its (neuter)	**sein**	**seine**	**sein**	**seine**
our	**unser**	**unsere**	**unser**	**unsere**
your (inf. pl.)	**euer**	**eure**	**euer**	**eure**
their	**ihr**	**ihre**	**ihr**	**ihre**
Formal				
your (sing. & pl.)	**Ihr**	**Ihre**	**Ihr**	**Ihre**

For the other cases, see the adjective declensions in lesson 56.

9 Adjectives and adverbs

9.1 Predicate adjectives

These are adjectives that occur in the predicate of the sentence – after a form of **sein**, **werden** or **bleiben** – and modify the subject. In German, predicate adjectives do not decline.

Herr Müller ist nett. *Mr Müller is nice.*
Sie wird müde. *She is getting tired.*
Es bleibt morgen kalt. *It will stay cold tomorrow.*

9.2 Adjectives used as adverbs

In most cases, adjectives and adverbs are one and the same word in German. Adverbs don't decline.

Sprechen Sie bitte nicht so schnell!
Don't speak so quickly ('quick')*, please!*
Sie singt sehr gut! *She sings very well* ('good').

9.3 Attributive adjectives

These adjectives directly precede the noun they modify and they decline. Which endings they take depends on two things: 1) the gender, number and case of the noun they modify; 2) whether they are preceded by an article or not. If there is no article to show the gender, number and case of the noun, the adjective must indicate this.

See the tables in lesson 56 for the full adjective declensions.

der nette Mann, ein netter Mann *the/a nice man*
die nette Frau, eine nette Frau *the/a nice woman*
das nette Kind, ein nettes Kind *the/a nice child*

guter Wein *good wine* (masc. sing. nominative)
gute Schokolade *good chocolate* (fem. sing. nominative)
gutes Brot *good bread* (neuter sing. nominative)

9.4 Adjectives used as nouns

Many adjectives can be used as nouns by capitalizing the first letter and putting an article in front of them. They retain adjective endings as if a noun were still there: **der Alte** *the old (man)*, **die Schöne** *the beautiful (woman)*.

10 Pronouns

10.1 Personal pronouns

Nominative	Accusative	Dative
ich *I*	**mich** *me*	**mir** *(to) me*
du *you* (inf. sing.)	**dich** *you*	**dir** *(to) you*
er *he, it*	**ihn** *him, it*	**ihm** *(to) him, it*
sie *she, it*	**sie** *her, it*	**ihr** *(to) her, it*
es *it*	**es** *it*	**ihm** *(to) it*
wir *we*	**uns** *us*	**uns** *(to) us*
ihr *you* (inf. pl.)	**euch** *you*	**euch** *(to) you*
sie *they*	**sie** *them*	**ihnen** *(to) them*
Sie *you* (formal, sing. & pl.)	**Sie** *you*	**Ihnen** *(to) you*

fünfhundertvierundsiebzig

10.2 Reflexive pronouns

Reflexive verbs express an action that acts upon the subject. They do this by using a pronoun. These decline in the accusative and, if there's another object, the dative. Their forms are identical to the personal pronouns in these cases, except in the third-person and the formal, which are **sich**:

	Accusative	Dative
myself	**mich**	**mir**
yourself (inf. sing.)	**dich**	**dir**
himself, herself, itself, oneself	**sich**	**sich**
ourselves	**uns**	**uns**
yourselves (inf. pl.)	**euch**	**euch**
themselves	**sich**	**sich**
yourself, yourselves (formal)	**sich**	**sich**

Er wäscht sich. *He washes (himself).*
Waschen Sie sich die Hände! *Wash your hands!*
Ich möchte mir die Hände waschen. *I'd like to wash my hands.*

10.3 Demonstrative pronouns

There are several demonstrative pronouns (i.e. *this, that, these, those*) in German:

- The pronouns **der**, **die**, **das**, **die** are identical to the definite article, except in the genitive and the dative plural:

	Singular			Plural
	Masc.	Fem.	Neuter	
Nominative	**der**	**die**	**das**	**die**
Accusative	**den**	**die**	**das**	**die**
Dative	**dem**	**der**	**dem**	**denen**
Genitive	**dessen**	**deren**	**dessen**	**deren**

Kennst du die beiden? Denen gehört die halbe Stadt. *Do you know these two? Half the city belongs to them ('To-these belongs …').*

- The pronouns **dieser, diese, dieses, diese** (pl.) *this, these* and **jener, jene, jenes, jene** (pl.) *that, those* are identical to their demonstrative adjective forms (see section 7):
Dieser ist mein Freund, aber jenen dort habe ich nie gesehen.
This one is my friend, but that one I've never seen before.

- **derselbe, dieselbe, dasselbe** *the same (one)* and **derjenige, diejenige, dasjenige** – generally followed by a relative pronoun – decline like the definite article in the first part of the word, and like an adjective in the second part:
Er hat <u>denselben</u> Pullover wie du.
He has the same sweater as you.
Sie wohnt in <u>demselben</u> Haus wie ich.
She lives in the same house as me.
<u>Diejenigen</u>, die zu spät kommen, kriegen nichts mehr.
Those who arrive too late don't get anything.

10.4 Interrogative pronouns (question words)

- **Wer?** *Who?* declines like the masculine definite article. In contrast, **Was?** *What?* doesn't decline and occurs only in the nominative and the accusative:

nom.: **Wer sind Sie?** *Who are you?*
Was machen Sie? *What are you doing?*
acc.: **Wen zeichnen Sie?** *Whom are you drawing?*
Was zeichnen Sie? *What are you drawing?*
dat.: **Wem gehört das neue Auto?**
To whom does the new car belong?
gen.: **Wessen Papiere sind das?** *Whose papers are these?*

- **welcher, welche, welches** *which* can also function as a question word. It declines like the definite article, but rarely occurs in the genitive form these days.
Welcher König hat Neuschwanstein gebaut?
Which king built Neuschwanstein?
Welchen Film haben Sie gestern gesehen?
Which film did you see yesterday?

Ich habe zwei Stück Kuchen. Welches möchtest du?
I have two pieces of cake. Which do you want?

10.5 Relative pronouns

The relative pronouns *who, that, which* are identical to the demonstrative pronouns **der, die, das** (see section 10.3 and lesson 77):
Der Film, den ich sehen möchte, spielt im Kino Panorama.
The film (that) I want to see is showing at the Panorama cinema.
Die Freunde, mit denen wir in Urlaub fahren, sind Amerikaner.
The friends with whom we go on holidays are American.

Note that unlike in English, the relative pronoun cannot be omitted in German.

10.6 Indefinite pronouns

• **einer**, **eine**, **eines** *someone, one* or **keiner**, **keine**, **kein(e)s** *no one, not any, not anyone* decline like the definite article:
Einer von uns beiden muss das machen.
One of the two of us has to do this.
Ich habe kein(e)s von diesen Büchern gelesen.
I haven't read any of these books.
Er kennt keinen hier. *He doesn't know anyone here.*

• **man** *one* (representing people in general) is used only in the nominative.
Man muss aufpassen. *One has to be careful.*

In the dative and the accusative, **einem** and **einen** are used:
Das Fernsehen gibt einem nicht genug Informationen.
The TV doesn't give one enough information.
Das kann einen wirklich krank machen.
That can make one really ill.

10.7 Possessive pronouns

The possessive pronouns **meiner**, **deiner**, **seiner**, etc. (*mine, yours, his, hers,* etc.) are formed by adding the case endings for the definite article to the possessive adjectives (see section 8):
Dein Pullover ist sehr schön, <u>meiner</u> ist nicht so schön.
Your sweater is very nice; mine isn't as nice.

Mit eurem Auto könnt ihr überall parken, mit unserem ist das nicht möglich. *With your car, you can park everywhere. With ours that's not possible.*

11 Verbs

11.1 Regular (weak) verbs

A verb is regular (weak) if the vowel in its stem doesn't change in any of its conjugated forms.

- **hören** *to hear*

Indicative (present tense, lesson 14; perfect tense, lesson 42; future tense, lesson 56; simple past tense, lesson 70)

	Present	Simple past	Perfect	Past perfect	Future
I	ich höre	hörte	habe gehört	hatte gehört	werde hören
you (inf. sing.)	du hörst	hörtest	hast gehört	hattest gehört	wirst hören
he/she/it	er/sie/es hört	hörte	hat gehört	hatte gehört	wird hören
we	wir hören	hörten	haben gehört	hatten gehört	werden hören
you (inf. pl.)	ihr hört	hörtet	habt gehört	hattet gehört	werdet hören
they	sie hören	hörten	haben gehört	hatten gehört	werden hören
you (formal)	Sie hören	hörten	haben gehört	hatten gehört	werden hören

Imperative
Hör(e)! *Listen!* (sing. informal) **Hören wir!** *Let's listen!* **Hört!** *Listen!* (pl. informal) **Hören Sie!** *Listen!* (formal)

fünfhundertachtundsiebzig • 578

Subjunctive (lesson 98)

Present		Past	
Subj. I	Subj. II	Subj. I	Subj. II
ich höre	hörte = würde hören	habe gehört	hätte gehört
du hörest	hörtest = würdest hören	habest gehört	hättest gehört
er/sie/es höre	hörte = würde hören	habe gehört	hätte gehört
wir hören	hörten = würden hören	haben gehört	hätten gehört
ihr höret	hörtet = würdet hören	habet gehört	hättet gehört
sie/Sie hören	hörten = würden hören	haben gehört	hätten gehört

11.2 Irregular (strong) verbs

A verb is irregular (strong) if the stem vowel changes in the simple past tense. There are many irregular verbs that show irregularities in the present or perfect tense as well.

The following is an example, but you'll have to learn the forms of irregular verbs by heart as they aren't always predictable. You'll find a list of the most common irregular verbs at the end of the appendix. For possible stem vowel changes, see lessons 21 (present tense), 63 (past participle) and 70 (simple past tense).

- **sehen** *to see*, *to look*

Indicative

Present	Simple past	Perfect	Past perfect	Future
ich sehe	sah	habe gesehen	hatte gesehen	werde sehen
du siehst	sahst	hast gesehen	hattest gesehen	wirst sehen

er/sie/es sieht	sah	hat gesehen	hatte gesehen	wird sehen
wir sehen	sahen	haben gesehen	hatten gesehen	werden sehen
ihr seht	saht	habt gesehen	hattet gesehen	werdet sehen
sie sehen	sahen	haben gesehen	hatten gesehen	werden sehen
Sie sehen	sahen	haben gesehen	hatten gesehen	werden sehen

Imperative

Sieh! *Look!* (sing. informal) **Sehen wir!** *Let's look/see!* **Seht!** *Look!* (pl. informal) **Sehen Sie!** *Look!* (formal)
Remember that **mal** *once* is often added in the imperative:
Sieh mal! Seht mal! Sehen Sie mal!

Subjunctive (lesson 98)

Present		Past	
Subj. I	Subj. II	Subj. I	Subj. II
ich sehe	sähe = würde sehen	habe gesehen	hätte gesehen
du sehest	sähest = würdest sehen	habest gesehen	hättest gesehen
er/sie/es sehe	sähe = würde sehen	habe gesehen	hätte gesehen
wir sehen	sähen = würden sehen	haben gesehen	hätten gesehen
ihr sehet	sähet = würdet sehen	habet gesehen	hättet gesehen
sie/Sie sehen	sähen = würden sehen	haben gesehen	hätten gesehen

11.3 Mixed (irregular weak) verbs

'Mixed verbs' combine characteristics associated with regular (weak) verbs, such as the past tense endings and the **-t** ending in the past participle, with stem vowel changes associated with irregular (strong) verbs. There are only a few of these. You can find them in lesson 70, section 1.1.

11.4 *sein, haben, werden*

- **sein** *to be*

Indicative

Present	Simple past	Perfect	Past perfect	Future
ich bin	war	**bin gewesen**	war gewesen	werde sein
du bist	warst	**bist gewesen**	warst gewesen	wirst sein
er/sie/es ist	war	**ist gewesen**	war gewesen	wird sein
wir sind	waren	**sind gewesen**	waren gewesen	werden sein
ihr seid	wart	**seid gewesen**	wart gewesen	werdet sein
sie sind	waren	**sind gewesen**	waren gewesen	werden sein
Sie sind	waren	**sind gewesen**	waren gewesen	werden sein

Note that **sein** forms the perfect tense with **sein** as an auxiliary: **Er ist zufrieden gewesen, weil er ein gutes Geschäft gemacht hat.** *He was (has) content (been), because he got a good deal.*

Imperative
Sei froh! *Be glad!* (sing. inf.) **Seien wir froh!** *Let's be glad!* **Seid froh!** *Be glad!* (pl. inf.) **Seien Sie froh!** *Be glad!* (formal)

Subjunctive (see lesson 98)

Present		Past	
Subj. I	Subj. II	Subj. I	Subj. II
ich sei	**wäre = würde sein**	**sei gewesen**	**wäre gewesen**

du seiest	wärest = würdest sein	seiest gewesen	wärest gewesen
er/sie/es sei	wäre = würde sein	sei gewesen	wäre gewesen
wir seien	wären = würden sein	seien gewesen	wären gewesen
ihr seiet	wäret = würdet sein	seiet gewesen	wäret gewesen
sie/Sie seien	wären = würden sein	seien gewesen	wären gewesen

- **haben** *to have*

Indicative

Present	Simple past	Perfect	Past perfect	Future
ich habe	hatte	habe gehabt	hatte gehabt	werde haben
du hast	hattest	hast gehabt	hattest gehabt	wirst haben
er/sie/es hat	hatte	hat gehabt	hatte gehabt	wird haben
wir haben	hatten	haben gehabt	hatten gehabt	werden haben
ihr habt	hattet	habt gehabt	hattet gehabt	werdet haben
sie/Sie haben	hatten	haben gehabt	hatten gehabt	werden haben

As you can see, the **b** of the verb stem disappears in the second- and third-person singular present and in all forms of the simple past tense. Otherwise, the conjugation of **haben** isn't complicated. Even the formation of the imperative is regular.

Imperative

Hab(e) Geduld! *Be patient!* ('Have patience!') (sing. inf.) **Haben wir Geduld!** *Let's be patient!* **Habt Geduld!** *Be patient!* (pl. inf.) **Haben Sie Geduld!** *Be patient!* (formal)

fünfhundertzweiundachtzig • 582

Subjunctive (lesson 98)

Present		Past	
Subj. I	Subj. II	Subj. I	Subj. II
ich habe	hätte = würde haben	habe gehabt	hätte gehabt
du habest	hättest = würdest haben	habest gehabt	hättest gehabt
er/sie/es habe	hätte = würde haben	habe gehabt	hätte gehabt
wir haben	hätten = würden haben	haben gehabt	hätten gehabt
ihr habet	hättet = würdet haben	habet gehabt	hättet gehabt
sie/Sie haben	hätten = würden haben	haben gehabt	hätten gehabt

- **werden** *to become* (also functions as an auxiliary to form the future tense and the passive voice)

Indicative

Present	Simple past	Perfect	Past perfect	Future
ich werde	wurde	bin geworden	war geworden	werde werden
du wirst	wurdest	bist geworden	warst geworden	wirst werden
er/sie/es wird	wurde	ist geworden	war geworden	wird werden
wir werden	wurden	sind geworden	waren geworden	werden werden
ihr werdet	wurdet	seid geworden	wart geworden	werdet werden
sie/Sie werden	wurden	sind geworden	waren geworden	werden werden

Note that the future tense is formed with a present tense form of **werden** and the infinitive of the main verb – even if the main verb is itself **werden**: **Die Menschen werden immer größer werden!** *Human beings will become taller and taller!*

Imperative
Werde nicht frech! *Don't get cheeky!* (sing. inf.) **Werdet nicht frech!** (pl. inf.), **Werden Sie nicht frech!** (formal)

Subjunctive (lesson 98)

Present		Past	
Subj. I	Subj. II	Subj. I	Subj. II
ich werde	würde*	sei geworden	wäre geworden
du werdest	würdest	seiest geworden	wärest geworden
er/sie/es werde	würde	sei geworden	wäre geworden
wir werden	würden	seien geworden	wären geworden
ihr werdet	würdet	seiet geworden	wäret geworden
sie/Sie werden	würden	seien geworden	wären geworden

* würde = würde werden, würdest = würdest werden etc.

11.5 Perfect tense

The perfect tense is a two-word (or compound) tense formed with a conjugated present tense form of **sein** *to be* or **haben** *to have* + the past participle of the main verb. How do you know which one to use? As a rule of thumb:

• **haben** is used to form the perfect tense of transitive verbs (those that take a direct object), reflexive verbs, modal verbs and verbs indicating a position: **Ich habe ihn gesehen.** *I have seen him.*

• **sein** is used with verbs signalling movement, verbs that indicate a change of place or state and **sein, bleiben** and **werden**: **Ich bin ins Schwimmbad gegangen.** *I have gone to the swimming pool.*

11.6 Modal verbs

In German, there are six modal verbs (auxiliary verbs that indicate ability, permission, obligation or attitude towards an action):

müssen *to have to, 'must'*, **sollen** *to be supposed to, 'should'*, **können** *to be able to, 'can'*, **dürfen** *to be allowed to, 'may'*, **wollen** *to want*, **mögen** *to like*.

In a statement, the conjugated modal verb occurs in the second position (or, in a question, the first). The verb it assists or 'modifies' (an infinitive) appears at the end of a clause:
Kann ich mitkommen? *Can I come along?*
Wir müssen heute bis 19 Uhr arbeiten.
We have to work until 7 pm today.

In a subordinate clause, the modal verb occurs in the last position:
Das ist das Kleid, das ich haben will.
This is the dress that I want to have.

Careful! The infinitive used with a modal verb is never preceded by **zu**! For more about modal verbs, see lesson 35.

11.7 Present and past participles

The present participle is normally formed by adding **-d** to the infinitive: **weinen** *to cry* → **weinend** *crying*.
Das Kind kommt weinend nach Hause.
The child comes home crying.

The past participle can take a number of forms. However, most verbs take the present tense stem of the verb and add the **ge-** prefix and the ending **-t** or **-et**.
schmücken *to decorate* → **geschmückt** *decorated*
Wer hat den Weihnachtsbaum geschmückt?
Who decorated the Christmas tree?

Both participles can also be used as adjectives:
Er gibt dem weinenden Kind Schokolade.
He gives chocolate to the crying child.
der geschmückte Weihnachtsbaum *the decorated Christmas tree*

11.8 Verbs used as nouns

The infinitive of a verb, as well as the present or past participle, can be used as a noun by capitalizing its first letter:
lachen *to laugh* → **Lachen tut gut.** *Laughing does you good.*

reisend *travelling* → **Der Reisende stiegt in Hamburg aus dem Zug.** *The traveller* ('travelling-one') *left the train in Hamburg.*

All nouns derived from infinitives are neuter; nouns derived from participles decline like the corresponding adjective.

12 The passive voice

There are two passive forms in German:

- The statal passive or **sein**-passive (**sein** + past participle) describes a state or result:
Der Baum ist geschmückt. *The tree is decorated.*

- The **werden**-passive (**werden** + past participle) relates to an action or process. It often corresponds to an *-ing* form in English:
Der Baum wird geschmückt. *The tree is being decorated.*
The **werden**-passive can be used to emphasize the action rather than the agent: **Der Baum ist von mir allein geschmückt worden.** *The tree was decorated by me alone.*

Note that the past participle of **werden** – when used to form the passive – is **worden** (without **ge-**!).

Here's **schmücken** *to decorate* in the indicative passive:

Present	Simple past	Future
ich werde geschmückt	**wurde geschmückt**	**werde geschmückt werden**
du wirst geschmückt	**wurdest geschmückt**	**wirst geschmückt werden**
er/sie/es wird geschmückt	**wurde geschmückt**	**wird geschmückt werden**
wir werden geschmückt	**wurden geschmückt**	**werden geschmückt werden**
ihr werdet geschmückt	**wurdet geschmückt**	**werdet geschmückt werden**
sie/Sie werden geschmückt	**wurden geschmückt**	**werden geschmückt werden**

Perfect	Past perfect
ich bin geschmückt worden	**war geschmückt worden**
du bist geschmückt worden	**warst geschmückt worden**
er/sie/es ist geschmückt worden	**war geschmückt worden**
wir sind geschmückt worden	**waren geschmückt worden**
ihr seid geschmückt worden	**wart geschmückt worden**
sie/Sie sind geschmückt worden	**waren geschmückt worden**

The passive subjunctive is formed by putting **werden** in the subjunctive (see 11.4) and adding the past participle of the verb: **sei geschmückt (worden)**, **wäre geschmückt (worden)**, etc. You'll find detailed explanations of the passive voice in lesson 91.

13 Conditional sentences

Conditional sentences indicate that a certain condition must be met before an action can be realized. The condition is usually expressed in a subordinate clause introduced by **wenn** *if*, and the action in a main clause:
Wenn ich Zeit habe, komme ich mit. *If I have time, I'll come along.*
Wenn es morgen regnen wird, bleibe ich zu Hause.
If it rains ('will rain') *tomorrow, I'll stay* ('I stay') *at home.*

The consequence in the main clause can be, but doesn't necessarily have to be, preceded by **dann** *then*. This can be inserted at the beginning of the main clause to emphasize the statement, if the conditional clause precedes it:
Wenn du wieder meinen Geburtstag vergisst, dann verlasse ich dich! *If you forget my birthday again, (then) I'll leave you!*

If the action is hypothetical, implausible or impossible, the subjunctive II (the **würde** + infinitive construction) is used <u>in both parts</u> of the sentence:
Wenn es regnen würde, würde ich zu Haus bleiben.
If it was raining, I would stay at home. (But it isn't raining!)
Wenn ich ein Auto hätte, würde ich nach Italien fahren.
If I had a car, I would drive to Italy. (But I don't have a car!)

For actions contrary to fact in the past, the past subjunctive II is used <u>in both parts</u> of the sentence:
Wenn es geregnet hätte, wäre ich zu Haus geblieben.
If it had rained, I would have stayed at home. (But it didn't rain!)

For more information, see lesson 98.

14 Separable-prefix verbs

Some German verbs can be preceded by prefixes that can modify the basic meaning of the verb:
gehen *to go* → **weggehen** *to go away*
sprechen *to speak* → **aussprechen** *to pronounce.*

Sometimes, a prefix can change the meaning of a verb completely:
fangen *to catch* → **anfangen** *to start, to begin*
kommen *to come, to arrive* → **bekommen** *to get, to receive.*

There are two kinds of prefixes.

• Separable prefixes separate from the base verb when the verb is conjugated: **Ich gehe weg.** *I go away.*

• Inseparable prefixes don't separate from the verb under any circumstances: **Er bekommt einen Brief.** *He receives a letter.*

How do you distinguish between a separable and an inseparable prefix? Practice! However, here are some rules that might help:

• In speech, separable prefixes can be recognized by the stress on the prefix; inseparable prefixes are never stressed.

• Generally, separable prefixes have a meaning of their own, e.g. as prepositions, while inseparable prefixes don't. Some of the most common separable prefixes are: **ab-, an-, auf-, aus-, bei-, mit-, nach-, zu-, zurück-**.

• There are five prefixes that can combine with a verb as either separable prefixes or inseparable prefixes. All of these dual prefixes are stressed when separable and unstressed when inseparable. They are: **wieder, um, durch, über, unter**.
Unterbrechen Sie mich nicht! *Don't interrupt me!*
Das Boot geht unter! *The boat sinks* ('goes under').

• The use (or not) of **ge-** in the past participle indicates whether a prefix is separable or inseparable.

With separable prefixes, the **ge-** occurs between the prefix and the verb:
Der Film hat schon angefangen.
The film has already started.

Inseparable-prefix verbs form the past participle without **ge-**:
Ich habe heute keine E-Mail bekommen.
I didn't receive an email today.

For more information, see lessons 21 and 49.

15 Transitive and intransitive verbs

A transitive verb requires a direct object. This is because the verb expresses an action towards someone or something that is named in the sentence. The word or phrase that receives the action of a transitive verb is the direct object.
Er kennt diese Stadt sehr gut. *He knows this city very well.*
Die Kellnerin bringt den Kaffee. *The waitress brings the coffee.*

An intransitive verb doesn't have a direct object because the action is not directed towards someone or something in the sentence.
Kommen Sie! *Come!*
Wir lachen. *We laugh.*

Some verbs can be used intransitively or transitively:
Wir essen. *We're eating.* (intransitive)
Wir essen Pasta. *We eat pasta.* (transitive)

Only transitive verbs can form the passive:
Der Kaffee wird von der Kellnerin gebracht.
The coffee is brought by the waitress.

16 Prepositional verbs

Like in English, there are a large number of verbs in German that are always used with a particular preposition, e.g. **glauben an** *to believe in*, **warten auf** *to wait for*. Some verbs can be used with more than one preposition, such as **bestehen auf** *to insist on* and **bestehen aus** *to consist of*. The prepositions in turn require certain cases to follow them. Thus German prepositional verbs need to be learned as: verb + preposition + case. Here are a few examples.

16.1 Verbs with accusative prepositions

Some prepositional verbs have prepositions that require the use of the accusative case:
denken an *to think of/about*, **bitten um** *to ask for*, **danken für** *to thank for*, **sich erinnern an** *to remember*, **lachen über** *to laugh at*, **schreiben an** *to write to*, **sich verlieben in** *to fall in love with*, **warten auf** *to wait for*, etc.

16.2 Verbs with dative prepositions

Some prepositional verbs have prepositions that require the use of the dative case:
abhängen von *to depend on*, **anfangen/aufhören mit** *to start/stop doing something*, **fragen nach** *to ask after/for*, **sich beschweren bei** *to complain to*, **teilnehmen an** *to participate in*, **sich fürchten vor** *to be afraid of*, **zweifeln an** *to doubt something*, etc.

16.3 Verbs with two prepositions

Some prepositional verbs use two prepositions, each requiring a specific case:

- **sich erkundigen bei jemandem** (dative) **nach etwas** (dative) *to ask someone about something*:
Er erkundigt sich bei dem Verkäufer nach den Öffnungszeiten.
He asks the salesperson about the opening times.

- **sich unterhalten mit jdm** (dative) **über etwas** (acc.) *to talk to someone about something*:
Wir haben uns die ganze Nacht mit unseren Freunden über Politik unterhalten.
We talked about politics with our friends all night.

16.4 Verbs with several prepositions

Some prepositional verbs can take different prepositions, changing the meaning of the verb:

- **sich freuen auf** *to look forward to* (something that will or might happen):
Sie freut sich auf den Sommer. *She's looking forward to summer.*

- **sich freuen über** *to be glad about* (something that has happened):
Sie freut sich über den Sommer. *She's glad about the summer.*

- **kämpfen um** *to fight for/over*:
Sie kämpfen um eine Flasche Champagner. *They fight [each other] over a bottle of champagne.*

- **kämpfen für/gegen/mit** *to fight for/against/with*:
Wir kämpfen für mehr Gerechtigkeit. *We fight for more justice.*
Sophie Scholl hat gegen den Nationalsozialismus gekämpft. *Sophie Scholl fought against National Socialism.*
Sie kämpfen mit unehrlichen Mitteln. *They fight dishonestly* ('with dishonest means').

16.5 Questions with prepositional verbs

When forming questions with prepositional verbs:

- If the question concerns a person, use the preposition followed by **wer** *who* declined in the case required by the preposition:
<u>**An wen**</u> **denken Sie?** *Who are you thinking of?*
<u>**Auf wen**</u> **warten Sie?** *Who are you waiting for?*
<u>**Von wem**</u> **sprechen Sie?** *Who are you talking about?*
<u>**Vor wem**</u> **fürchten sich die Kinder?** *Of whom are the kids afraid?*

When answering, the preposition is followed by a noun or pronoun:
Ich denke oft <u>an</u> unseren Großvater. Denkst du auch manchmal <u>an ihn</u>? *I often think about our grandfather. Do you also sometimes think about him?*

Wir sprechen <u>von</u> Frau Bach, sprechen Sie auch <u>von ihr</u>?
We're talking about Mrs Bach – are you also talking about her?

- If the question concerns a thing rather than a person, use a construction of **wo** + preposition (**wor-** + preposition, if the preposition starts with a vowel):
Woran denken Sie? *What are you thinking of?*
Worauf warten Sie? *What are you waiting for?*
Wovon sprechen Sie? *What are you talking about?*
Wovor fürchten sich die Kinder? *What are the kids afraid of?*

When answering, the preposition is followed by an object, or a construction with **da(r)-** + preposition:
Ich denke an das Wochenende, und Sie, denken Sie auch daran?
I'm thinking of the weekend; and are you thinking of it as well?
Wir sprechen von dem Streik, und Sie, sprechen Sie auch davon?
We're talking about the strike. Are you talking about it as well?

Any questions? Lesson 84 might help you …

17 Asking 'where?'

German has two question words for asking *Where?* (lesson 49).

- **Wo?** is used to ask the location of something or someone.
Wo wohnen Sie? – In Ulm. *Where do you live – In Ulm.*
Wo steht die Weinflasche? – Auf dem Tisch.
Where is the bottle of wine? – On the table.

- **Wohin?** (or **wo … hin**) is used to form questions about direction or movement ('Where to?').
Wohin gehen Sie?/Wo gehen Sie hin? – Ins Kino.
Where are you going? – To the cinema.
Wohin stelle ich die Flasche?/Wo stelle ich die Flasche hin? – Auf den Tisch. *Where do I put the bottle? – On the table.*

When answering **wo** and **wohin** questions, some prepositions always require a particular case to follow them:
Wo wohnst du? – Bei meiner Freundin. *Where do you live? – At my girlfriend's.* (**bei** always requires the dative case)
Wohin gehst du? – Durch die Stadt. *Where are you going? – Across the city.* (**durch** always requires the accusative case)

fünfhundertzweiundneunzig • 592

With other prepositions, the choice of case depends on whether you're giving a position or a direction. These are called two-way prepositions. (There are nine two-way prepositions altogether: **an** *at, on, to*; **auf** *at, to, on, upon*; **hinter** *behind*; **in** *in, into*; **neben** *next to, beside, near*; **über** *above, across, over, about*; **unter** *under, below, among*; **vor** *in front of*; **zwischen** *between*.)

• Two-way prepositions take the dative case to indicate position:
Er ist schon im (= in dem) Büro. *He's already in the office.* (**Wo?**)

• They take the accusative case to indicate motion or direction:
Er fährt ins Büro. *He's going to the office.* (**Wohin?**)

18 Conjunctions

Conjunctions are linking words. There are two kinds of conjunctions (see lesson 84).

18.1 Coordinating conjunctions

These conjunctions, such as **und** *and*, **aber** *but*, **oder** *or*, **denn** *as, for*, simply 'slip' in between two main clauses and don't affect the word order:
Wir essen und danach sehen wir fern.
We eat and afterwards we watch TV.
Er wartet, aber seine Freundin kommt nicht.
He's waiting, but his girlfriend isn't coming.

18.2 Subordinating conjunctions

As the name suggests, subordinating conjunctions introduce subordinate clauses. They provide a transition between two ideas in a sentence, indicating relationships of:

• time: **als** *when*, **bevor** *before*, **bis** *until*, **nachdem** *after*, **seit** *since*, **sobald** *as soon as*, **solange** *as long as*, **während** *while*, **wenn** *when* (lesson 63)

- cause: **weil** *because*, **da** *as*
- concession, comparison: **obwohl**, **obgleich** *even though*
- goal: **damit**, **dass** *so that*, *in order to.*

Subordinating conjunctions do affect word order. They cause the conjugated verb to move into the last position in the subordinate clause:
Ich habe in Heidelberg gewohnt, als ich Kind war.
I lived in Heidelberg when I was a child.
Macht Ordnung, bevor Mama kommt!
Tidy up before Mum arrives!
Iss dein Müsli, damit du groß und stark wirst!
Eat your muesli so that you'll be tall and strong.
Sie trinkt ein Bier, obwohl sie kein Bier mag.
She drinks a beer even though she doesn't like beer.

19 Relative clauses

Relative clauses are subordinate clauses introduced by a relative pronoun (e.g. *that*, *who*). They modify a noun, pronoun or sometimes even a whole phrase (called the antecedent); the relative pronoun establishes the link between the antecedent and the relative clause.

A relative pronoun reflects gender, number and case. Its gender and number depend on the antecedent:
Die Frau, die ich um 17 Uhr treffe, arbeitet mit mir.
The woman whom I'm going to meet at 5 pm works with me.
Der Mann, der im Café wartet, ist ihr Freund.
The man who is waiting in the café is her boyfriend.
Warum sind die Kinder, die dort spielen, noch nicht zu Hause?
Why are the children who are playing over there not at home yet?
Diejenigen, die nach Hause wollen, können jetzt gehen.
Those who want to go home can go now.

However, the case of a relative pronoun is determined by its function in the subordinate clause:
Die Frau, der sie die Stadt zeigt, ist Spanierin.
The woman to whom she showed the city is Spanish.
Der Wagen, den sie gekauft hat, ist groß.
The car that she bought is big.

Die Kinder, mit <u>denen</u> sie spielt, sind glücklich.
The children with whom she plays are happy.
Diejenigen, <u>deren</u> Arbeit zu Ende ist, dürfen gehen.
Those whose work is done may go home.

There are three other important differences to English:

• As in all subordinate clauses, the conjugated verb occurs in the last position of the relative clause.

• The relative pronoun cannot be omitted.

• A relative pronoun that is part of a prepositional phrase always stays with the preposition (**mit denen sie spielt**).

The forms of the relative pronouns can be found in lesson 77.

20 Some impersonal expressions

Some German expressions use the third-person singular pronoun **es** as their subject. They're usually called impersonal expressions because **es** doesn't specify a particular person or thing:
es gibt *there is/there are*; **es dreht sich um…/es handelt sich um** *it concerns*; **es hängt davon ab** *it depends on*; **es schmeckt** *it tastes good*; **es regnet** *it's raining*; **es schneit** *it's snowing*; **es tut mir Leid** *I'm sorry* ('it does me sorrow'), etc.

Another important example to remember: **Wie geht es Ihnen/dir?** *How are you?* (formal/informal) ('How goes it to you?')
And the reply: **Es geht mir …** *I am …* ('It goes to me'), to which you can add **(sehr) gut** *(very) well, fine*, **schlecht** *not well*, **ausgezeichnet** *[doing] excellently*, **miserabel** *miserable*, **blendend** *splendid*, etc.

If you need more information on any grammatical points, the grammatical index will refer you to the relevant lesson.

List of irregular verbs

This list of irregular verbs gives the infinitive, followed by the first-person singular simple past tense and the past participle. If a verb is irregular in the second- and third-person singular present tense, we've also given the third-person singular present tense in parentheses. Note that the conjugations of modal verbs and of **wissen** *to know* are particularly irregular in the present tense (lesson 35).

anbieten, bot an, angeboten *to offer*
beginnen, begann, begonnen *to start, to begin, to commence*
beißen, biss, gebissen *to bite*
bekommen, bekam, bekommen *to receive*
benehmen (sich ~), (benimmt), benahm, benommen *to behave*
beschließen, beschloss, beschlossen *to decide*
besitzen, besaß, besessen *to possess*
betrügen, betrog, betrogen *to cheat, to deceive*
bewerben (sich ~), (bewirbt), bewarb, beworben *to apply*
binden, band, gebunden *to bind, to tie*
bitten, bat, gebeten *to ask for*
bleiben, blieb, geblieben *to stay, to remain*
brechen (bricht), brach, gebrochen *to break*
brennen, brannte, gebrannt *to burn*
denken, dachte, gedacht *to think*
dürfen (darf), durfte, gedurft *may; to be allowed to*
einladen (lädt ein), lud ein, eingeladen *to invite*
empfangen (empfängt), empfing, empfangen *to receive*
empfehlen (empfiehlt), empfahl, empfohlen *to recommend*
entkommen, entkam, entkommen *to escape*
entscheiden, entschied, entschieden *to decide*
erkennen, erkannte, erkannt *to recognize*
erscheinen, erschien, erschienen *to appear, to seem*
erschrecken (erschrickt), erschrak, erschrocken *to get a fright, to give someone a fright*
essen (isst), aß, gegessen *to eat*
fahren (fährt), fuhr, gefahren *to drive, to go (by train/bike/car)*
fallen (fällt), fiel, gefallen *to fall*
fangen (fängt), fing, gefangen *to catch*

fünfhundertsechsundneunzig • 596

finden, fand, gefunden *to find*
fliegen, flog, geflogen *to fly*
fliehen, floh, geflohen *to escape, to take flight*
fließen, floss, geflossen *to flow*
frieren, fror, gefroren *to freeze*
geben (gibt), gab, gegeben *to give*
gefallen (gefällt), gefiel, gefallen *to please*
gelingen, gelang, gelungen *to succeed*
gelten (gilt), galt, gegolten *to be valid*
geschehen (geschieht), geschah, geschehen *to happen*
gewinnen, gewann, gewonnen *to gain*
gießen, goss, gegossen *to pour*
graben (gräbt), grub, gegraben *to dig*
greifen, griff, gegriffen *to take, to grab*
haben (hat), hatte, gehabt *to have*
halten (hält), hielt, gehalten *to hold, to stop*
hängen, hing, gehangen *to hang, to be hanging*
hauen, haute, gehauen *to hit*
heben, hob, gehoben *to lift*
heißen, hieß, geheißen *to be named*
helfen (hilft), half, geholfen *to help*
kennen, kannte, gekannt *to know*
klingen, klang, geklungen *to sound (like), to ring*
kommen, kam, gekommen *to come*
können (kann), konnte, gekonnt *can; to be able to*
kriechen, kroch, gekrochen *to crawl*
laden (lädt), lud, geladen *to load, to charge*
lassen (lässt), ließ, gelassen *to let*
laufen (läuft), lief, gelaufen *to walk, to run*
leiden, litt, gelitten *to suffer*
lesen (liest), las, gelesen *to read*
liegen, lag, gelegen *to lie, to be lying down*
lügen, log, gelogen *to lie, to tell a lie*
meiden, mied, gemieden *to avoid*
messen (misst), maß, gemessen *to measure*
mögen (mag), mochte, gemocht *to like*
müssen (muss), musste, gemusst *must; to have to*
nehmen (nimmt), nahm, genommen *to take*
nennen, nannte, genannt *to call*
pfeifen, pfiff, gepfiffen *to whistle*
raten (rät), riet, geraten *to advise*

597 • fünfhundertsiebenundneunzig

reißen, riss, gerissen *to tear, to crack*
riechen, roch, gerochen *to smell*
rufen, rief, gerufen *to call, to cry*
schaffen, schuf, geschaffen *to create*
scheinen, schien, geschienen *to shine, to seem*
schlafen (schläft), schlief, geschlafen *to sleep*
schlagen (schlägt), schlug, geschlagen *to hit*
schließen, schloss, geschlossen *to close*
schmelzen (schmilzt), schmolz, geschmolzen *to melt*
schneiden, schnitt, geschnitten *to cut*
schreiben, schrieb, geschrieben *to write*
schreien, schrie, geschrien *to cry, to shout*
schweigen, schwieg, geschwiegen *to remain silent*
schwimmen, schwamm, geschwommen *to swim*
schwören, schwor, geschworen *to swear*
sehen (sieht), sah, gesehen *to see*
sein (ist), war, gewesen *to be*
senden, sandte, gesandt *to send*
singen, sang, gesungen *to sing*
sitzen, saß, gesessen *to sit, to be seated*
sollen (soll), sollte, gesollt *to be supposed to*
spinnen, spann, gesponnen *to spin; to be mad*
sprechen (spricht), sprach, gesprochen *to speak, to talk*
springen, sprang, gesprungen *to spring*
stechen (sticht), stach, gestochen *to sting*
stehen, stand, gestanden *to stand, to be standing*
stehlen (stiehlt), stahl, gestohlen *to steal*
steigen, stieg, gestiegen *to climb*
sterben (stirbt), starb, gestorben *to die*
streiten, stritt, gestritten *to argue*
tragen (trägt), trug, getragen *to carry; to wear*
treffen (trifft), traf, getroffen *to meet*
treten, trat, getreten *to tread*
trinken, trank, getrunken *to drink*
tun, tat, getan *to do*
unterhalten (unterhält), unterhielt, unterhalten *to maintain, to entertain*; and **sich unterhalten** *to talk, to converse, to enjoy oneself*
unterscheiden, unterschied, unterschieden *to distinguish, to differentiate*
verbieten, verbot, verboten *to forbid*

verderben (verdirbt), verdarb, verdorben *to spoil*
vergehen, verging, vergangen *to pass*
vergessen (vergisst), vergaß, vergessen *to forget*
verleihen, verlieh, verliehen *to lend, to rent out*
verlieren, verlor, verloren *to lose*
verschwinden, verschwand, verschwunden *to disappear*
versprechen (verspricht), versprach, versprochen *to promise*
verstehen, verstand, verstanden *to understand*
verzeihen, verzieh, verziehen *to forgive*
wachsen (wächst), wuchs, gewachsen *to grow*
waschen (wäscht), wusch, gewaschen *to wash*
werben (wirbt), warb, geworben *to advertise*
werden (wird), wurde, geworden *to become*
wiegen, wog, gewogen *to weigh*
wissen (weiß), wusste, gewusst *to know*
wollen (will), wollte, gewollt *to want*
ziehen, zog, gezogen *to pull*
zwingen, zwang, gezwungen *to force*

Grammatical index

The reference numbers for each entry occur in pairs: the first number refers to the lesson (GA refers to the grammatical appendix), the second to the note or section in which the explanation can be found. Reference numbers in bold indicate review lessons.

Accusative case GA 3
    articles 16.8; **21.2**; GA 2; GA 4
    personal pronouns 24.7; **28.1**
    prepositions requiring the accusative **84.1**
    prepositions with accusative or dative **49.4**; **84.1**; GA 17
Adjectives
    attributive 18.5; 29.8; 31.1; **35.3**; 50.3–4; 51.2; **56.1**; GA 9.3
    comparative forms 57.3–5; 60.9; 62.7; **63.2**
    demonstrative 43.5; **49.5**; 85.8; GA 7
    possessive 23.3; 25.7; **28.2**; **56.3**; GA 8
    predicate 3.7; GA 9.1
    superlative forms 57.3–5; 60.9; 62.7–8; **63.2**
    used as adverbs **7.4**; 8.5; GA 9.2
    used as nouns 53.8; 69.4; 76.1; 88.6; GA 9.4; by adding **-keit** 52.1
Adverbs 8.5; GA 9.2
    comparative forms **63.2**; 82.6
    superlative forms 62.8; **63.2**
    -weise ending 10.7
Age, asking someone's 22.5
Apostrophe 12.1
Articles GA 2
    case, accusative 16.8; **21.2**; GA 4
    case, dative 40.4; **42.1**; GA 4
    case, nominative **7.2**; **14.2**; GA 4
    definite GA 2; GA 4
    demonstrative GA 7
    indefinite 3.2; GA 4
    negative 9.6; **14.2–3**; GA 2
Auxiliary verbs GA 11.4; **sein** and **haben** (present tense) **14.1**; (simple past tense) **49.3**
beim + infinitive (to express an ongoing action) 59.2; 100.3
Capitalization of nouns 1.1; GA 1

sechshundert • 600

Case, grammatical GA 3
Cities and their inhabitants 64.4
Commands (see 'Imperative')
Comparative forms of adjectives/adverbs 60.9; **63.2**
Comparisons
    of adjectives **63.2**
    of adverbs **63.2**
    of equality (**so … wie**) 60.2; **63.2.2**
    of inequality (**als**) 58.5; 60.2; **63.2.2**
    more and more … (**immer** + comparative) 60.5
    the more … /the less … (**je … desto/umso**) 97.9; **98.2**
Conditional sentences 38.6; 39.3; 59.5; 65.5; 83.5; 93.2; 94.3; 95.7; **98.1.2**; GA 13
Conjunctions 31.6; **84.4**; GA 18
    causal (**denn/weil**) GA 18.2; (**da**) 80.6; **84.4.2**
    concessive (**obwohl**) 72.1; **84.4.3**; GA 18.2
    final goal (**damit/dass**) 66.5; 79.2; **84.4.3**; GA 18.2
    how something is achieved (**indem**) 86.7
    temporal 38.6; 52.10; 57.2; **63.3**; **84.4.1**; GA 18.2
Countries and nationalities 50.5; 67.4–5; **70.3**
da(r)- + preposition (to stand in for things or ideas) 74.11; **84.3**; GA 16.5
Dates 22.7; **28.5.2**; 44.1; 64.2; 80.1
Dative case GA 3
    articles **42.1**; GA 2; GA 4
    personal pronouns 37.2–3 & 7–8; 38.1; **42.1**
    possessive adjectives in the dative 39.4 & 9
    prepositions requiring the dative **84.1**
    prepositions with accusative or dative **49.4**; **84.1**; GA 17
    von + dative (as alternative to the genitive case) 47.1
Days of the week and times of day 25.4; 30.7; **35.5**
Declension GA 3; GA 4
    adjectives **56.1**
    nouns **14.2**; **49.1**; GA 4
Demonstratives 43.5; **49.5**; 85.8; GA 7; GA 10.3
Diminutives 4.3; 8.2; (gender of) GA 1
doch (as response) 19.3
Double infinitives 76.9; 96.8
-einander (*one another, each other*) 90.10

es
    'false'/'dummy' subject 83.1; 88.9; **91.3**
    impersonal subject 6.1
    neuter personal pronoun 4.8
    passive voice 86.5; **91.3**
Exclamations (with **doch**) 97.1
Formal address 1.2; 2.4; 47.3
Future tense 55.5; **56.2**; GA 11
Gender, grammatical 2.3; **7.2**; 55 (note); GA 1
Genitive case GA 3
    articles 47.1; 48.5 & 7; **49.1**; GA 2–4
    in set expressions 67.1
    of proper names 64.1; 78.8
    von + dative (as alternative to the genitive case) 47.1
gern + verb (*to like to, with pleasure*) 62.3; 95.2
hin and **her** (direction particles) 37.1 & 6; GA 17
how (**wie**) 9.2; 22.5
How are you? 6.2–3; 100.1; GA 20
if (**wenn** or **ob**) **77.3**
Imperative 11.1
    first-person plural ('**wir**'-imperative) 19.7; (with **lassen**) 86.8
    formal 5.6; 11.1; 15.1; GA 11
    informal plural ('**ihr**'-imperative) 13.2
    informal singular ('**du**'-imperative) 11.1; 16.3 & 5 & 7; 18.7; 36.2
    of **sein** GA 11.4
Impersonal expressions GA 20
Indicative mood 23.1; GA 11
    future tense **56.2**
    perfect tense 20.2; 36.5; **42.2**
    present tense **14.1**
    simple past tense **49.3**; **70.1**
Indirect (reported) speech **98.1.3**
Infinitives 1.3; **7.1**
    dependent infinitive 8.4; 26.4; **28.4.3**
    double infinitive 76.9; 96.8
    used as nouns 27.2; 79.8; GA 11.8
    with **zu** 26.2 & 4; 31.7; 41.5; 64.10; 65.8; 66.3–4 & 7
let (to ~) (**lassen**) 32.6; 72.2; 76.9; 88.8
Letter writing (business) 80; (personal) 18

like (to ~) (**mögen**) 23.1; 33.8; **35.1–2**; *like to (to ~), with pleasure* (**gern** + verb) 62.3; 95.2
Masculine **n**-nouns 47.2; 65.6; 93.4; GA 4; nationalities **70.3**
Modal 'flavouring' particles (to reflect/reinforce mood or attitude) **denn** 10.4; **doch** 30.2; 39.5; **ja** 32.5; 43.8; 67.6; **98.3.2**
Modal verbs 29.1; GA 11.6
    forms **35.1**
    meanings **35.2**
Nationalities 67.4–5; **70.3**
Negation 5.4; **14.3**; GA 6
Nominative case GA 3
    articles **14.2**; GA 4
    personal pronouns **28.1**; GA 10.1
Nouns GA 1
    capitalization of 1.1
    compound nouns 5.1; 8 (pronunciation note); 22.1; 24.2; 73.1
    diminutives 4.3; 8.2
    from adjectives 52.1; 69.4; 81.7; 88.6
    from verbs 5.2; 25.5; 27.2; 80.2; 100.3; GA 11.8
    masculine **n**-nouns 47.2; 65.6; 93.4; GA 4; nationalities **70.3**
    plural forms 6.4; 8.6; 29.4; 50.1; GA 5
Numbers
    cardinal 16.2; 17 (pronunciation note); 17.3; **21.3**
    ordinal 22.7; **28.5**
    writing fractions 78.4
one another, each other (**-einander**) 90.10
only (**erst** and **nur**) **91.4**
Passive voice 85.1 & 10; 90.9; **91.1–3**; GA 12
    future passive 90.3; **91.2**
    impersonal constructions **91.3**
    simple past tense 87.3 & 7; **91.2**
    uses **91.3**
    von + dat. and **durch** + acc. **91.3**
    with **sein** or **werden 91.1**
Past participles
    inseparable-prefix verbs 40.7; **49.2**
    irregular verbs 10.6; 43.1 & 3; 44.5; 45.5–6 & 9; 46.1 & 5; **49.2**; **63.1**
    regular verbs 36.5 & 7; 40.7; **42.2**; GA 11.7
    separable-prefix verbs 43.1 & 3
    verbs ending in **-ieren** 46.2; 89.4

Perfect tense
    past perfect 83.9; **84.4.1**
    present perfect 46.3; **49.2**; 53.3; GA 11.5; of **sein** 53.3; 94.4
Plural forms of nouns 6.4; 8.6; 29.4; 50.1; GA 5
Position/location, verbs indicating 44.3 & 6; **56.4**; 82.7
Possession
    possessive adjectives 23.3; 25.7; **28.2**; **56.3**; GA 8
    possessive pronouns 32.8; 37.8; GA 10.7
    showing possession (with **von**) 12.2; (genitive) 47.1; 64.1
Preference, *would rather* (**lieber** + verb) 62.5; 95.2
Prefixes
    inseparable 46.1; GA 14
    separable 11.7; **21.1.2**; GA 14
    separable or inseparable 94.8
    with past participles **42.2**; **49.2**
Prepositional verbs **84.2**; GA 16; GA 17
Prepositions
    contraction with definite article: **im** 2.1; **ins** 26.3; **zum** 31.3; **aufs** 54.1
    two-way (+ acc. or dat.) 41.4; **49.4**; **84.1.2**; GA 17
    with accusative **84.1**
    with dative **84.1**
Present participles 61.1; 73.2; 100.5; GA 11.7
Present tense **14.1**; GA 11; future meaning 10.2; 23.6; expressing continuous action 4.9; 19.1
Pronouns GA 10
    demonstrative GA 10.3; **der/die/das** 13.5; 32.3; 40.2; **dieser/jener 49.5**; **derselbe/dieselbe/dasselbe** 30.9; 48.2; **derjenige/diejenige/dasjenige** 85.8
    direct object 16.8; 24.7; **28.1**
    indefinite GA 10.6; **keiner** 69.3
    indirect object 37.2–3; **42.1**
    interrogative 23.2; **28.3**; **70.2**; GA 10.4
    personal **7.3**; **28.1**; **42.1.2**; GA 10.1
    possessive 32.8; 37.8; GA 10.7
    reflexive 37.4; 39.1; 45.7; **77.2**; GA 10.2
    relative 33.7; 34.1; 72.4; **77.1**; GA 10.5; GA 19
Questions
    asking questions 2.2; 5.4; 22.5; 23.2; **28.3**; **42.3**; **70.2**; GA 10.4; GA 17; with prepositional verbs GA 16.5
    indirect questions **70.2**; 76.5; 88.2

Reflexive verbs 37.4; 39.1; 45.7; **77.2**; GA 10.2
Relative clauses GA 19
Sentence structure (see 'Word order')
Separable-prefix verbs 11.7; **21.1.2**; GA 14
Simple past tense
    irregular (strong) verbs 64.3; 68.2–4 & 8–10; **70.1**; GA 11.2
    mixed (irregular weak) verbs **70.1**; GA 11.3
    modal verbs 52.4; 64.5; **70.1.1**; GA 11.6
    regular (weak) verbs 64.6; **70.1.1**; GA 11.1
    sein, **haben** 45.1 & 3; 46.6; **49.3**; GA 11.4; **werden** 64.9; GA 11.4
    verbs ending in -**ieren** 68.11
Stress (word stress)
    in numbers 17 (pronunciation note)
    primary/main stress 8; 15 (pronunciation note)
    separable-prefix verbs 16; 20; 43 (pronunciation note)
Subjunctive mood **98.1**; GA 11
    alternative form (**würde** + infinitive) 93.1–3
    forms 92.2–3; 93.1–3; 94.3–4; 95.9; 96.2–4; **98.1**; GA 11
    passive 94.3
Superlatives (see 'Adjectives' and 'Adverbs')
there is/there are (**es gibt**) 15.3; 41.5; GA 20
Time, asking and giving the 16.2; 17.5; 20.6; 44.2; 52.2 & 5–6; 71.2; 78.2–4
Umlaut 4 (pronunciation note); 89 (pronunciation note)
Units and measures 9.4
Verb stem **7.1**; insertion of **e** 11.4; 13.3; 26.5
Verbs GA 11 (see also 'Auxiliary verbs', 'Future tense', 'Imperative', 'Indicative mood', 'Infinitives', 'Modal verbs', 'Passive voice', 'Past participles', 'Perfect tense', 'Present participles', 'Present tense', 'Simple past tense', 'Subjunctive mood')
    indicating a position 44.3; **56.4**; 68.9; 82.7
    indicating action/movement to a position 44.6; **56.4**; 59.1
    intransitive GA 15
    irregular (strong) verbs **63.1**; GA 11.2
    mixed (irregular weak) verbs GA 11.3
    prepositional **84.2**; GA 16; GA 17
    reflexive verbs 37.4; 39.1; 45.7; **77.2**; GA 10.2
    regular (weak) verbs GA 11.1
    separable-prefix verbs 11.7; **21.1.2**; GA 14
    transitive GA 15
    used as nouns 25.5; 27.2; 80.2; 100.3; GA 11.8

von + dative (to show possession) 64.1
what (**was**) 22.2; **28.3**; 34.1; **70.2**; **77.1.2**
when (**als/wenn/wann**) 38.6; 52.10; 57.2; 58.5; **63.3**
where (**wo/woher/wohin**) 36.4 & 8; 41.4; **42.3**; **49.4**; **84.1.2**; GA 17
which/what (**welcher**) 20.3; **28.3**; **70.2**
who (**wer**) 22.2; **28.3**; 33.7; 39.2; 68.6; **70.2**; **77.1.2**
why (**wozu/warum**) 19.8
wo(r)- + preposition (forming questions with prepositional verbs) 89.2; 90.5; GA 16.5
Word order
    dependent infinitives **28.4.3**
    direct and indirect objects 41.2
    in commands **28.4.1**
    in indirect questions 88.2
    in main (independent) clauses 2.2; 25.3; **28.4.2**
    in questions **28.4.1–2**
    in subordinate (dependent) clauses 33.7; 34.4; **35.4**; 38.6; 39.3; 44.7; 52.10; GA 18.2; GA 19; conditional sentences 65.5; 95.7; GA 13; relative clauses **77.1**
    inversion 12.3; 15.4; 43.7
    time – manner – place 51.10
yes in response to a negative question (**doch**) 19.3; 39.5

Glossaries

We've provided a two-way glossary in which you'll find all the German words used in this book.
- German – English
- English – German

The glossary lists only the meanings found in the lessons; it is not a dictionary that lists all possible meanings.

Each German noun is given in the nominative case and its gender is indicated. Its plural form is also given in parentheses: e.g. **Stadt** (¨**-e**) indicates that **die Stadt** becomes **die Städte** in the plural. If the plural form doesn't differ from the singular, this is shown with (-). Irregular verbs are marked with an asterisk (*). Separable-prefix verbs are indicated with an apostrophe between the separable prefix and the rest of the verb, e.g. **auf'stehen**. Adjectives are listed in their uninflected form (e.g. **klein**) unless they are only (or mostly) used attributively. In the latter case, they are listed with the masculine, feminine and neuter forms in the nominative case: e.g. **letzter/letzte/letztes** (m./f./n.).

Key to abbreviations:

(m.) masculine	*(f.)* feminine
(n.) neuter	*(coll.)* colloquial
(sing.) singular	*(pl.)* plural
(acc.) accusative	*(dat.)* dative
(adj.) adjective	*(adv.)* adverb
(conj.) conjunction	*(abb.)* abbreviation

Each word is followed by the number of the lesson in which it first appears. The reference GA refers to the Grammatical Appendix. Certain words refer to more than one lesson if they are used with a different meaning or in a different context, or if an additional explanation is given.

German–English

A

ab'fahren*	to depart, to leave 16
ab'hängen* von	to depend on GA16
ab'hauen *(coll.)*	to beat it (clear off), to get lost 55
ab'heben*	to lift/take off 86
ab'holen	to get (fetch), to pick someone up 20
ab'nehmen*	to take away (from) 87
ab'stellen	to switch off 74
ab'stürzen	to crash, to plunge 62
Abend *(m.)* (-e)	evening 2
Abendessen *(n.)* (-)	dinner 47
aber	but 6
Abschied nehmen*	to take leave of 12
Abschluss *(m.)* (¨-e)	conclusion, graduation, qualification (following studies) 81
Absicht *(f.)* (-en)	intention 86
Abstecher *(m.)* (-)	detour 100
Abteilung *(f.)* (-en)	department 80
ach	ah 15
Ach so!	I see! 15
Acht nehmen* (sich in ~)	to take care of oneself, to be careful 69
achten	to respect 94
Achtung *(f.)* (-)	attention (caution) 16
Achtung!	Careful! 16; Get ready! 90
Acker *(m.)* (¨)	field (of crops) 59
Adresse *(f.)* (-n)	address 84
Affe *(m.)* (-n)	ape 88
ahnen	to guess, to suspect 87
ähnlich	similar 80
Ahnung *(f.)* (-en)	idea, suspicion 87
Akzent *(m.)* (-e)	accent 75
alle	everyone 23
alle Welt	everyone 79
allein	alone 2
allerdings	however 74
alles	all 9; everything 31; anything 34
allgemein	general (common) 68
Alltag *(m.)*	daily life 73; daily routine 81
alltäglich	everyday, ordinary 81
Alpen *(pl.)*	Alps 83
als	when 57; than (comparison) 58; as 72
als ob	as if 95
also	so 9; well then 19

sechshundertacht • 608

alt	old 22
älter	older 82
alt/älter werden*	to age, to grow old/older 82
Altstadt *(f.)* (¨-e)	old town (historic centre) 33
am (an dem)	at the 20; on the (+ date) 51
Ampel *(f.)* (-n)	traffic light 94
Amt *(n.)* (¨-er)	office (agency) 69
an	at 16; on 22; to 24; from 54
an'bieten*	to offer 37
an'fangen*	to begin 45; to start 45, 55
an'halten*	to stop 29, 79
an'kommen*	to arrive 20, 46
an'machen	to switch on 43
an'passen (sich ~)	to adapt to 97
an'rufen*	to call/ring someone 11; to phone 66
an'sehen*	to look at 10; to watch 76
an'sprechen*	to speak to 37
an'stellen	to switch on 74; to employ 81
an'strengen (sich ~)	to make an effort 66
an'ziehen* (sich ~)	to get dressed 59
an'zünden	to light 90
andere (das ~)	the other (thing) 38
anderer/andere/anderes (ein/eine/ein ~) *(m./f./n.)*	another 55
anderer/andere/anderes *(m./f.&pl./n.)*	other 5
ändern (sich ~)	to change, to modify 39
Anfang *(m.)* (¨-e)	beginning 88
Anfänger *(m.)* (-) / Anfängerin *(f.)* (-nen)	beginner 90
Angebot *(n.)* (-e)	offer 62
Angelegenheit *(f.)* (-en)	affair 54
angestellt sein*	to be employed 81
Angestellte (der *m.* / die *f.*) (-n)	employee 81
Angst *(f.)* (¨-e)	anxiety, fear 59, 94
Angst haben*	to worry 59; to be scared 76
Ankunft *(f.)* (¨-e)	arrival 30
Ankunftszeit *(f.)* (-en)	arrival time 30
Annonce *(f.)* (-n)	advertisement 50
Anrufbeantworter *(m.)* (-)	answering machine 12
ans (an + das)	to the 24
anscheinend	apparent 100
Anschluss *(m.)* (¨-e)	connection 20
anständig	correct, decent 85
anstrengend	tiring 26
Anstrengung *(f.)* (-en)	effort 66

Antwort *(f.)* (-en)	answer 68; reply 80
antworten	to reply 11; to answer 83
Anzeige *(f.)* (-n)	advertisement 50
Anzug *(m.)* (¨-e)	suit (clothing) 38
Apfel *(m.)* (¨)	apple 24
Apfelsaft *(m.)* (¨-e)	apple juice 24
Apfelwein *(m.)* (-e)	apple cider 33
Arbeit *(f.)* (-en)	work 78
arbeiten	to work 19
Arbeiter *(m.)* (-) / Arbeiterin *(f.)* (-nen)	worker 33
Arbeitsstelle *(f.)* (-n)	job, position 80
Arbeitszeit *(f.)* (-en)	working hours 78
ärgern	to annoy 93
Argument *(n.)* (-e)	argument 61
arm	poor 53
Arm *(m.)* (-e)	arm 97
Arzt *(m.)* (¨-e) / Ärztin *(f.)* (-nen)	doctor (medical) 50
au	oh 26
Au(a)!	Ouch! 32
auch	also 6; too 53
auch nicht	neither/not either 27; not even 78
auch/selbst wenn	even though 76
auf	on 29; of 50
Auf Wiederhören!	Goodbye! (on the telephone) 5
Auf Wiedersehen!	Goodbye! 5
auf'fallen*	to be noticeable 99
auf'geben*	to give up 99
auf'halten*	to hold up 91
auf'holen	to make up 79
auf'hören	to cease, to stop 51
auf'hören (zu)	to end 51
auf'klären (sich ~)	to become clear 99
auf'machen	to open 21, 74
auf'passen (auf)	to pay attention (to) 99
auf'regen (sich ~)	to fret, to get worked up 79
auf'schlagen*	to break 85
auf'stehen*	to get up 30, 55
auf'wachen	to wake up 71
Aufgabe *(f.)* (-n)	task 80
aufgeregt	excited, nervous 18
Aufmerksamkeit *(f.)* (-en)	attention 95
Auge *(n.)* (-n)	eye 54
Augenblick *(m.)* (-e)	moment 47
Augenblick (im ~)	at the moment 53
August *(m.)*	August 22

sechshundertzehn • 610

aus (+ *dat.*)	from 3; for, of 48; out 71
aus'geben*	to spend 21
aus'machen	to switch off 43; to agree 95
aus'machen (etwas ~)	to arrange something 95
aus'sehen*	to look 18
aus'sprechen*	to pronounce GA14
aus'steigen*	to alight, to get out/off 16
Ausdauer *(f.)*	perseverance 99
Ausfahrt *(f.)* (-en)	exit (for cars) 48
Ausgang *(m.)* (¨-e)	exit (way out) 87
ausgezeichnet	excellent 27
Auskunft *(f.)* (¨-e)	information 15
Auslage *(f.)* (-en)	expense 80
Ausland *(n.)*	abroad 80
Ausnahme *(m.)* (¨-e)	exception 62
außer	apart (from), besides, except (for) 39
außerdem	in addition, besides 50; moreover 81
außergewöhnlich	exceptional 64
Aussicht *(f.)* (-en)	view 50
Austausch *(m.)* (-e)	exchange 81
Auto *(n.)* (-s)	car 40
Autobahn *(f.)* (-en)	motorway 79
Automechaniker *(m.)* (-) / Automechanikerin *(f.)* (-nen)	car mechanic 67

B

Baby *(n.)* (-s)	baby 35
Bäckerei *(f.)* (-en)	bakery 100
Bad *(n.)* (¨-er)	bathroom 50
Badeanzug *(m.)* (¨-e)	swimsuit 97
Badehose *(f.)*	swimming trunks 97
Bahn *(f.)* (-en)	road, track, train 15
Bahnhof *(m.)* (¨-e)	train station 20
bald	soon 12
Balkon *(m.)* (-s)	balcony 50
Ball bleiben* (am ~)	to be on the ball 99
Bankier *(m.)* (-s) / Bankierin *(f.)* (-nen)	banker 67
Bär *(m.)* (-en)	bear 53
Bärenhunger *(m.)* (~ haben*)	to be ravenous 53
barock	baroque 41
Baskenmütze *(f.)* (-n)	beret 72
Bauch *(m.)* (¨-e)	stomach 96
bauen	to construct 57
Bauer *(m.)* (-n) / Bäuerin *(f.)* (-nen)	farmer 75

611 · **sechshundertelf**

Baum *(m.)* (¨-e)	tree 82
Bayer *(m.)* (-n) / Bayerin *(f.)* (-nen)	Bavarian (person) 75
bayerisch	Bavarian *(adj.)* 75
bedanken für (sich ~)	to thank for 100
bedeutend	important 51
beeilen (sich ~)	to hurry up 71
beeindruckend	impressive 74
beendet werden*	to come to an end 85
befürchten	to be afraid of 92
begeistern	to excite 73
beginnen*	to begin 63
begleiten	to accompany 85
Begrenzung *(f.)* (-en)	limitation 79
begrüßen	to greet 93
bei (+ *dat.*)	at 34; by, to, with 51
bei'bringen* (jdm etwas ~)	to teach someone something 93
beide	both 72
beim (+ *infinitive used as a noun*)	to be ...-ing 59; while ...-ing 100
Bein *(n.)* (-e)	leg 58
Beispiel *(n.)* (-e)	example 75
Beispiel (zum ~)	for example 75
beißen*	to bite 32
bekannt	known 69
bekommen*	to get (receive) 33
belegt	booked 96
bemerken	to notice 97
Bemühen *(n.)* (-)	effort 51
benehmen* (sich ~)	to behave oneself 85
Benimm *(m.)*	manners 85
Benzin *(n.)* (-e)	gasoline, petrol 29
Benzinuhr *(f.)* (-en)	petrol/gas gauge 29
beobachten	to observe 88
Berg *(m.)* (-e)	mountain 46
Bericht *(m.)* (-e)	article, report 87
Berliner *(m.)* (-) / Berlinerin *(f.)* (-nen)	Berlin inhabitant 64
beruhigen	to calm (down) 59
berühmt	famous 51
Bescheid *(m.)* (-e)	notification 58
Bescheid sagen (*or* geben*)	to let someone know, to notify 58
beschließen*	to decide 71
beschweren bei (sich ~)	to complain to GA16
besetzt	busy (telephone), engaged (occupied) 66; filled 80
besichtigen	to visit 33
Besichtigung *(f.)* (-en)	visit 33

sechshundertzwölf • 612

besitzen*	to own 56
Besitzer *(m.)* (-) / Besitzerin *(f.)* (-nen)	owner 48
Besonderes *(n.)* (etwas/nichts ~)	something/nothing special 89
besonders	particularly 99
besser	better 27
Beste (das ~)	the best (thing) 27
bestehen* auf	to insist on GA16
bestehen* aus	to consist of GA16
bestellen	to order 95
besuchen	to come/go see, to visit 80
Besucher *(m.)* (-) / Besucherin *(f.)* (-nen)	visitor 87
betrunken	drunk (inebriated) 34
Bett *(n.)* (-en)	bed 56
Beute *(f.)* (-n)	prey 36
bevor	before 83
bewachen	to guard 90
bewahren	to keep 93
bewegen (sich ~)	to move 64
bewerben* bei (+ *dat.*) (sich ~)	to apply for/to 80
Bewerbung *(f.)* (-en)	application 80
bezahlen	to pay 9
Bibliothek *(f.)* (-en)	library 56
Bier *(n.)* (-e)	beer 8
Bild *(n.)* (-er)	picture 54
Bildung *(f.)*	education (learning) 68
billig	cheap 40
Binde *(f.)* (-n)	bandage, tie (necktie) 54
binden*	to attach, to link 54
Bindfaden *(m.)* (¨)	string 87
bis	until 12; to 60
bis (zu + *dat.*)	until 45
Bis bald!	Bye for now! 12
bis jetzt	so far 79
Bis später!	See you soon! 12; See you later! 78
bisschen (ein ~)	a little 18
bitte	please, my pleasure 4
Bitte!	You're welcome! 4
bitten*	to ask (request) 30
blau	blue 46
Blaumeise *(f.)* (-n)	blue tit 97
bleiben*	to stay 11; to remain 71
blendend	splendid GA20
Blick *(m.)* (-e)	glance 86
blockieren	to block 48

613 • **sechshundertdreizehn**

blond	blonde 36
blühen	to bloom (blossom) 82
Blume *(f.)* (-n)	flower 82
Boden *(m.)* (¨)	ground 83
Boot *(n.)* (-e)	boat GA14
böse	evil 92
böse sein*	to be angry 92
Brasilien *(n.)*	Brazil 37
Brathähnchen *(n.)* (-)	roast chicken 87
Bratwurst *(f.)* (¨-e)	fried sausage 9
brauchen	to need 24
brechen*	to break 49, 93
brennen*	to burn 70
Brief *(m.)* (-e)	letter 39
bringen*	to bring 8, 68; to deliver 46
Brot *(n.)* (-e)	bread 4
Brötchen *(n.)* (-)	bread roll 4
Brücke *(f.)* (-n)	bridge 94
Bruder *(m.)* (¨)	brother 23
Buch *(n.)* (¨-er)	book 28
buchen	to book, to reserve (e.g. a ticket/room/flight) 62
Bundesregierung *(f.)* (-en)	Federal Government 64
Bundesrepublik *(f.)* (-en)	Federal Republic 64
Bundestag *(m.)* (-e)	Parliament (German) 64
Burg *(f.)* (-en)	castle 100
Büro *(n.)* (-s)	office 6
Bus *(m.)* (-se)	bus 59

C

Café *(n.)* (-s)	café 4
Champagner *(m.)* (-)	champagne 24
Chance *(f.)* (-n)	chance 88
Chef *(m.)* (-s) / Chefin *(f.)* (-nen)	boss 30
Chinesisch	Chinese (language) 73
Computer *(m.)* (-)	computer 25

D

da	here, there 6; then 58; as, because, since 80
dagegen	however 60; in contrast 67; whereas 71
damals	then 74; back then 82
Dame *(f.)* (-n)	lady 33
Damen (meine ~)	ladies (address) 33
damit	with/by that 58; so that 66
danach	afterwards 51; later (after that) 79

sechshundertvierzehn • 614

Dank *(m.)* (-)	thanks (gratitude) 15
dankbar	grateful 89
danke (nein ~)	no thanks 27
Danke!	Thank you! 4
danken jdm *(dat.)* für (+ *acc.*)	to thank someone for 61
dann	then 15; so 54
daran	about this 79
darüber	about that 75; about this 83
darum	about this 94
Darum geht es nicht.	That's not the point. 94
darunter	underneath 74
das	that, the *(n.)*, this 3; it *(n.)* 32
dass	that *(conj.)* 31; so that 79
Daumen *(m.)* (-)	thumb 79
Daumen drücken (die ~)	to cross one's fingers 79
davon	of that 78
dazu	with it 75
Decke *(f.)* (-n)	ceiling 54
Deckel *(m.)* (-)	lid 57
decken (den Tisch ~)	to lay/set the table 91
dein *(m./n.)* / deine *(f.&pl.)*	your *(sing. informal)* 11
denken*	to think 46, 70, 74
denken* (daran ~)	to think about 79
denken* (sich ~)	to think to oneself 75
Denkmal *(n.)* (-er)	monument (statue) 70
denn	but (conveying surprise), now (surely), then 10; in that case 15; because 54
der	the *(m.)* 3; he, it *(m.)* 32; that (which), who *(relative pronoun)* 85
derjenige/diejenige/dasjenige *(m./f./n.)*	the person who/whose 85
derselbe/dieselbe/dasselbe *(m./f./n.)*	the same (thing) 30, 48
deshalb	therefore, thus 65; because (of this) 79; so 99
Deutsch *(n.)*	German (language) 1
Deutscher *(m.)* / Deutsche *(f.&pl.)*	German (person) 50
Deutschland *(n.)*	Germany 64
Dezember *(m.)*	December 44
Dialekt *(m.)* (-e)	dialect 89
dich *(acc. of* du*)*	you *(sing. informal)* 16
Dichter *(m.)* (-) / Dichterin *(f.)* (-nen)	poet, writer 51
dick	big 82
dick/dicker werden*	to grow big/bigger 82
die	the *(f.)* 3; the *(pl.)* 6; these, they 13; it *(f.)*, she 32
Dienst *(m.)* (-e)	service 25; duty 30

615 • sechshundertfünfzehn

Dienstag *(m.)* (-e)	Tuesday 25
dieser/diese/dieses *(m./f./n.)*	this 43
Ding *(n.)* (-e)	thing 76
Diplom *(n.)* (-e)	diploma (qualification) 65
dir *(dat. of* du)	to you *(sing. informal)* 37
direkt	direct 85
doch	yes (in response to a negative question) 19; after all 40
doch (+ *verb*)	do/just (+ verb) (used for emphasis), … will you? (question tag) 30
Doktor (Herr *m.* / Frau *f.*) (-en)	doctor/Dr (title) 25
Dom *(m.)* (-e)	cathedral 33
Donner *(m.)* (-)	thunder 25
Donnerstag *(m.)* (-e)	Thursday 25
Doppelzimmer *(n.)* (-)	double room 96
dort	there 10
dorthin	there (movement away from speaker) 42
dran (ich bin ~)	it's my turn 95
draußen	outside 61
drehen um (+ *acc.*) (sich ~)	to centre on, to revolve around 57
dreimal	three times 9
dringend	urgent 69
drinnen	inside 78
drücken	to press 79
du	you *(sing. informal)* 8
dumm	stupid 10
Dummer *(m.)* (-n)	fool, idiot 88
dunkel	dark 33
Dunkel *(n.)*	dark *(noun)* 76
Dunkelheit *(f.)* (-en)	darkness 76
dünn	thin 82
durch	by 64
durch'fahren*	to go through a red light 94
durch'führen*	to conduct 88
durchaus	absolutely (thoroughly) 51
Durchschnitt *(m.)* (-e)	average 79
Durchschnitt (im ~)	on average 79
dürfen*	may 32; to be allowed to 35
dürfen* (nicht ~)	to not be allowed to, may/must not 32
Durst *(m.)*	thirst 19
Durst haben*	to be thirsty 19

E

ebenso	just as 63
echt	really, truly 92
egal	no matter 99

sechshundertsechzehn • 616

egal sein*	to not care 48
Ehe *(f.)* (-n)	marriage (married life) 66
Ehemann *(m.)* (¨-er)	husband 66
eher	more likely 31
Ehre *(f.)* (-n)	honour 72
ehren	to honour, to respect 80
Ei *(n.)* (-er)	egg 4
eigentlich	actually (in fact) 22
ein *(m./n.)* / eine *(f.)*	a(n) 1
ein'brechen*	to break in 93
ein'fallen*	to remember something, to think of something 100
ein'kaufen	to shop 24; to go shopping 48
ein'laden*	to invite 23; to treat someone (pay for) 75
ein'leben (sich ~)	to adapt, to settle in 75
ein'schlafen*	to fall asleep 71
ein'steigen*	to board, to get in/on 16
ein'stellen*	to tune in 74
eineinhalb	one and a half 17
einfach	easy 31; just 71; simple 85
Einfahrt *(f.)* (-en)	entrance 48
Einfluss *(n.)* (¨-e)	influence 51
Einheit *(f.)* (-en)	unity 64
einige	some 62
einmal	once 9
eins	one (thing) 38
einverstanden	all right, OK (agreed) 58
einziges Mal (ein ~)	just once 79
Eis *(n.)* (-)	ice, ice cream 57
eisern	iron *(adj.)* 68
eklig	disgusting 75
Elektrotechnik *(f.)*	electrical engineering 81
Eltern *(pl.)*	parents 40
Empfang *(m.)* (¨-e)	reception 96
empfangen*	to greet 100
empfehlen*	to advise 65
Ende *(n.)* (-n)	end(ing) 13, 48
Ende (am ~)	at the end 68
Ende sein* (zu ~)	to be finished 67
endgültig	final 98
endlich	at last 32; finally 43
Engel *(m.)* (-)	angel 72
Engländer *(m.)* (-) / Engländerin *(f.)* (-nen)	English (person) 50
Englisch	English (language) 73
entdecken	to discover 88

entfernt	far 100
entkommen*	to escape 43
entlang	along 100
entscheiden*	to decide 86
entschuldigen (sich ~)	to excuse 5, 81
Entschuldigung *(f.)* (-en)	apology 5
Entschuldigung ...	Excuse (me) ... 5; Pardon (me) ... 81
entsetzlich	terribly 88
enttäuscht	disappointed 66
Entwicklung *(f.)* (-en)	evolution 97
er	he 3; it *(m.)* 24
Erbe *(m.)*	legacy 88
Erbe *(n.)*	inheritance 88
Erbgut *(n.)*	genetic make-up 88
Erdbeere *(f.)* (-n)	strawberry 57
Erde *(f.)* (-n)	earth 97
erfinden*	to invent 57, 68
erinnern an (+ *acc.*) (sich ~)	to remember 74, 82
erkennen*	to recognize 72
erklären	to explain 71
erkundigen (sich ~)	to enquire GA16
erlauben	to allow 34; to permit 49
erleben	to experience, to undergo 64
ermöglichen	to allow 97
eröffnen	to open 65
erscheinen*	to seem 85
Erschöpfung *(f.)*	exhaustion 60
erschrecken*	to get a fright 100
erst	only (temporal) 52; first 53; just (merely) 74
erstaunlich	astonishing 74
erste (der/die/das ~) *(m./f./n.)*	the first 46
ersticken	to choke 58
Erwärmung *(f.)* (-en)	warming 97
erwidern	to reply 58
erzählen	to tell 42
Erzählung *(f.)* (-en)	story 72
es	it *(n.)* 4
es geht (um)	it is about 94
es gibt	there is/are 15
es handelt sich um (+ *acc.*)	it is about 94
es sei denn	unless 98
Essen *(n.)* (-)	meal 27; food 95
essen*	to eat 8, 47
Etage *(f.)* (-n)	floor (storey) 90
etwa	approximately 89

etwas	something 8; a little 61
euch *(acc. of* ihr)	you *(pl. informal)* 27
euch *(dat. of* ihr)	to you *(pl. informal)* 41
euer *(m./n.)* / eure *(f.&pl.)*	your *(pl. informal)* 55
euretwegen	because of you 100
Euro *(m.)* (-s)	euro 9
Europa *(n.)*	Europe 37
ewig	eternal 88
Experiment *(n.)* (-e)	experiment 88

F

Faden *(m.)* (¨)	string 54; thread 87
fahren*	to drive 16; to go (by means of transport) 41
Fahrrad *(n.)* (¨-er)	bicycle 34
Fahrrad fahren*	to cycle 34
Fahrt *(f.)* (-en)	trip 62
Fahrzeug *(m.)* (-e)	vehicle 48
Fall *(m.)* (¨-e)	case 76
Fälle (auf alle ~)	in any case 76
fallen*	to fall 24, 55, 64
fallen* auf (+ *acc.*)	to fall on 81
falls	in case 57; if 83
falsch	wrong 5
Familie *(f.)* (-n)	family 23
Familienname *(m.)* (-n)	last name, surname 81
fangen*	to catch 45
fantastisch	fantastic 18
Farbe *(f.)* (-n)	colour 74
fast	almost 58; nearly 71
Feder *(f.)* (-n)	feather 74
Federlesen machen	to waste time 93
fehlen	to lack 65; to miss/be missing (be lacking) 81
feiern	to celebrate 23
Feind *(m.)* (-e)	enemy 83
Feld *(n.)* (-er)	field 58
Felsen *(m.)* (-)	rock 68
Fenster *(n.)* (-)	window 53
Ferien *(pl.)*	holiday(s) 13
fern	far 55; distant 82
fern'sehen*	to watch TV 55
Fernsehapparat *(m.)* (-e)	television set 74
fertig	ready 13
Fest *(n.)* (-e)	celebration 22
festlich	festive, formal 38

619 • **sechshundertneunzehn**

Feuer *(n.)* (-)	fire GA1
Film *(m.)* (-e)	film, movie 53
finanzieren	to finance 83
finden*	to find 19, 58; to think 76
Firma *(f.)* (*pl.* Firmen)	firm 47; company 75
Flasche *(f.)* (-n)	bottle 44
Fleisch *(n.)* (-)	meat 24; flesh 74
Fleiß *(m.)* (-)	effort 99
fleißig	diligent 99
flexibel	flexible 78
fliegen*	to fly 25
fließen*	to flow 73
fließend	flowing, fluent 73
Flöte *(f.)* (-n)	flute 68
Flug *(m.)* (¨-e)	flight 62
Flughafen *(m.)* (¨)	airport 24
Flugzeug *(n.)* (-e)	airplane 62
Fluss *(m.)* (¨-e)	river 57
flüstern	to whisper 45
Flut *(f.)* (-en)	flood 91
folgen	to follow 52, 75
folgend	following 68
Form (in ~)	on form (well/fit) 96
Forscher *(m.)* (-) / Forscherin *(f.)* (-nen)	researcher 88
Fortsetzung *(f.)* (-en)	continuation 52
Foto *(n.)* (-s)	photo 3
Frage *(f.)* (-n)	question 15
fragen jdn (*acc.*) nach (+ *dat.*)	to ask someone for/about 38, 58
fragen ob (sich ~)	to ask oneself whether 76
Frankreich *(n.)*	France 30
Frau *(f.)* (-en)	wife, woman 3; Ms/Mrs 6
frech	cheeky, insolent 48
frei	free 2
frei'halten*	to save 78
Freiheit *(f.)* (-en)	freedom GA1
Freitag *(m.)* (-e)	Friday 25
fremd	foreign 73
freuen (sich ~)	to be glad, to be happy 20; to be pleased 26
freuen auf (sich ~)	to look forward to 66
Freund *(m.)* (-e)	friend 3; boyfriend 23; lover (enthusiast) 73
Freundin *(f.)* (-nen)	friend 3; girlfriend 23; lover (enthusiast) 73
freundlich	friendly 40
Frieden *(m.)*	peace 55
frisch	fresh 63

frisieren	to style (hair) 65
Frisör *(n.)* (-e) / Frisörin *(f.)* (-nen)	hairdresser 50
Frisörsalon *(m.)* (-s)	hairdressing salon 65
froh	glad 53
früh	early 30
Frühling *(m.)* (-e)	spring (the season) 28
Frühstück *(n.)* (-e)	breakfast 4
fühlen (sich ~)	to feel 89
funktionieren	to work (function) 25
für (+ *acc.*)	for 2
Furche *(f.)* (-n)	furrow 59
fürchterlich	terribly 66
Fuß *(m.)* (¨-e)	foot 33
Fuß (zu ~)	on foot 33
Fußgänger *(m.)* (-) / Fußgängerin *(f.)* (-nen)	pedestrian 33
Fußgängerzone *(f.)* (-n)	pedestrian zone 33
füttern	to feed 97

G

Gang (im ~)	in motion, in progress 76
ganz	complete, really 37; whole 81
gar	at all 73
gar keins *(n.)*	none at all 73
gar nicht	not at all 76; not even 99
garantieren	to assure, to guarantee 75
Garderobe *(f.)* (-n)	coat rack 56
Garten *(m.)* (¨)	garden 23
Gast *(m.)* (¨-e)	guest, visitor 87
geben*	to give 16, 22
geboren	born 51
Geburt *(f.)* (-en)	birth 65
Geburtstag *(m.)* (-e)	birthday 22
Gedächtnis *(n.)* (-se)	memory 95
Geduld *(f.)*	patience 99
gedulden (sich ~)	to be patient 47
geehrter/geehrte/geehrtes *(m./f./n.)*	dear (address in a letter) 80
Gefahr (in ~)	in danger, at risk 61
gefährlich	dangerous 32
gefallen*	to like 40; to appeal to, to enjoy 53
gefüllt	filled 78
gegen	against 77
Gegenteil *(n.)* (-e)	opposite 85
Gegenteil (im ~)	the opposite 69
gegenüber (von)	opposite (of) (facing) 33
Geheimnis *(n.)* (-se)	mystery, secret 65

gehen*	to go 6
gehen* (über die Straße/Brücke ~)	to cross the street/bridge etc. 94
gehören (+ *dat.*)	to belong to 74
gehört (wie es sich ~)	as is proper, as one should 85
Gehweg *(m.)* (-e)	sidewalk 65
Geist *(m.)* (-er)	mind, spirit 83
geisteskrank	insane 83
gelb	yellow 82
Geld *(n.)* (-er)	money 9
Geldschrank *(m.)* (¨-e)	safe (for valuables) 49
gelegen (liegen*)	located 50
Gelegenheit *(f.)* (-en)	occasion 38
Gemüse *(pl.)*	vegetables 97
genau	exact 20; precise 81
Generaldirektor *(m.)* (-en) / Generaldirektorin *(f.)* (-nen)	president (of a company) 90
Generation *(f.)* (-en)	generation 51
genial	brilliant (ingenious) 83
genug	enough 9
genug haben*	to have enough 46
gerade	just (now), straight 47
gerade (+ *present tense verb*)	to be in the process of 86
gerade (+ *simple past verb*)	just ... -ed 87
geradeaus	straight ahead 15
Gerechtigkeit *(f.)*	justice 72
Gericht *(n.)* (-e)	court 93
gern	gladly, please 8
gern (+ *verb*)	to like (doing something) 62
Geschäft *(n.)* (-e)	business, shop, store 10
Geschäftsmann *(m.)* (¨-er) / Geschäftsfrau *(f.)* (-en)	businessperson 93
Geschäftsreise *(f.)* (-n)	business trip 85
geschehen*	to happen 76
Geschichte *(f.)* (-n)	history, story 41
geschlossen	closed 10
Geschrei *(n.)*	shouting, yelling 55
Geschwindigkeit *(f.)* (-en)	speed 79
Geschwister *(pl.)*	siblings 23
Geselle *(m.)* (-n) / Gesellin *(f.)* (-nen)	assistant 57
Gesetz *(n.)* (-e)	law 94
Gesicht *(n.)* (-er)	face 54
Gespräch *(n.)* (-e)	conversation 5; interview 80
gestern	yesterday 36
gestorben (sterben*)	died 51
Gesundheit *(f.)*	health 65
Getränk *(n.)* (-e)	drink (beverage) 8

sechshundertzweiundzwanzig • 622

getrennt	separate 95
gewinnen*	to win 58
gewiss	certainly 89
gewöhnen (sich an etwas (+ *acc.*) ~)	to adjust to, to get used to 75
gierig	greedy 86
gießen*	to pour 54
Glas *(n.)* (¨er)	glass 33
glauben	to believe 20; to think 45
glauben (an + *acc.*)	to believe (in) 74
gleich	immediately 6; right away 47
gleichgültig	indifferent 72
gleichzeitig	both, simultaneous 64
Gleis *(f.)* (-e)	platform 16
Glück *(n.)* (-e)	happiness, luck 1
Glück haben*	to be lucky 79
glücklich	happy, lucky 10
glücklicherweise	fortunately 10
Glückwunsch *(m.)* (-e)	congratulations 89
Gott *(m.)* (¨-er)	god 29
Grad *(m.)* (-e)	degree 57
gratulieren jdm *(dat.)* zu (+ *dat.*)	to congratulate on 38
greifen*	to reach 86
Grenze *(f.)* (-n)	border 79
Grieche *(m.)* (-n) / Griechin *(f.)* (-nen)	Greek (person) 68
grillen	to barbecue 22
groß	big 1; tall 36; great 40; large 57
groß/größer werden*	to grow tall/taller 82
Großeltern *(f. pl.)*	grandparents 68
Großmarkt *(m.)* (¨-e)	superstore 48
Großvater *(m.)* (¨) / Großmutter *(f.)* (¨)	grandfather/grandmother 39
grün	green 94
Grund *(m.)* (¨-e)	reason 48
gründen	to found 89
Gruß *(m.)* (¨-e)	greeting 18
Grüße (freundliche ~)	kind regards 80
Grüße (viele ~)	best wishes 80
grüßen	to greet 18
gucken *(coll.)*	to look 36
günstig	cheap, favourable, reasonable 38
gut	good 1; fine 8
gut gehen*	to be/go well 59
Gute Nacht!	Good night! 43
Guten Abend!	Good evening! 2
Guten Morgen!	Good morning! 6
Guten Tag!	Good afternoon! 1

H

Haar *(n.)* (-e)	hair 68
haben*	to have 2, 9, 14, GA11
halb	half 52
halbe Stunde	half an hour 48
Hälfte *(f.)* (-n)	half 76
hallo	hello 11
Hals *(m.)* (¨-e)	neck, throat 90
Halt!	Wait! 58
halten*	to stop 24, 29
halten* (in Schach ~)	to hold in check 90
Haltestelle *(f.)* (-n)	stop (e.g. of a bus or tram) 15
Hand *(f.)* (¨-e)	hand 54
handeln um (+ *acc.*) (sich ~)	to be about, to concern 90
Händler *(m.)* (-) / Händlerin *(f.)* (-nen)	merchant 92
Handy *(n.)* (-s *or* -ies)	mobile phone 11
hängen* (an + *dat.*)	to hang (on/from) 54
hart	hard (solid) 85
Hase *(m.)* (-n)	hare, rabbit 58
hassen	to hate 62
hässlich	ugly 36
haupt-	main 27
Haupt *(n.)* (¨-er)	head 27
Hauptbahnhof *(m.)* (¨-e)	main station 27
Hauptrolle *(f.)* (-n)	leading role 72
Hauptsache *(f.)* (-n)	the main thing 99
Hauptspeise *(f.)* (-n)	main course 27
Hauptstadt *(f.)* (¨-e)	capital city 27
Haus *(n.)* (¨-er)	house 11; home 53
Haus(e) (nach ~)	going/coming home 11
Haus(e) (zu ~)	at home 11
Hausaufgaben *(pl.)*	homework 90
hausgemacht	homemade 78
Hausmeister *(m.)* (-) / Hausmeisterin *(f.)* (-nen)	caretaker 69
heben*	to lift, to raise 86
heilig	holy 97
Heiligabend *(m.)* (-e)	Christmas Eve 97
heiraten	to get married 38
heiß	hot 7; fervent 51
heißen*	to be called/named 3
helfen*	to help 38
helfen* jdm *(dat.)*	to help someone 59
hell	pale 33; bright 50

her	here (movement towards speaker) 37; from (movement towards speaker) 48
her'bringen*	to bring here 37
heraus	out 46
Herbst *(m.)* (-e)	autumn/fall 28
Herr *(m.)* (-en)	Mr 5; gentleman 51
Herren (meine ~)	gentlemen (address) 33
herrlich	splendid, wonderful 46; magnificent 50
herum'fahren* (*or* rum'fahren*)	to drive around 52
herunter	down 43
Herz *(n.)* (-en)	heart 18
herzlich	affectionate 18; cordial 51; warm 89
heute	today 1
heute Abend	this evening, tonight 11
hier	here 4
hierher	here (this way), over (here) 37
hierhin	here 45
Hilfe *(f.)* (-n)	help 45
Himbeere *(f.)* (-n)	raspberry 57
Himmel *(m.)* (-)	heaven, sky 24
hin-	there (movement away from speaker) 31
hin'fahren*	to go there (by means of transport) 37
hin'gehen*	to go there 31, 37
hinter	behind 54
hinterlassen*	to leave (behind) 12
Hintern *(m.)* (-)	backside, bottom 96
Historiker *(m.)* (-) / Historikerin *(f.)* (-nen)	historian 83
Hitze *(f.)* (-n)	heat 22
Hitzewelle *(f.)* (-n)	heatwave 22
hoch	high(ly) 54, 57
Hochdeutsch *(n.)*	standard German 89
höchst	extremely 90
Hochzeit *(f.)* (-en)	wedding 66
Hochzeitstag *(m.)* (-e)	wedding anniversary 66
Hof *(m.)* (¨-e)	court, yard 20
hoffen	to hope 25, 45
hoffentlich	hopefully 45
höflich	polite 52
Höflichkeit *(f.)* (-en)	politeness 52
hoher/hohe/hohes *(m./f./n.)* *(attributive adj.)*	high 82
hohes Tier *(n.)* (-e)	big shot 90
holen	to fetch, to go and get 24
Hölle *(f.)* (-n)	hell 67
hören	to hear GA11; to listen 34

625 • **sechshundertfünfundzwanzig**

hören an (+ *dat.*)	to hear (something) in 75
Hose *(f.)* (-n)	trousers 75
Hotel *(n.)* (-s)	hotel 2
Hund *(m.)* (-e)	dog 12
Hunger *(m.)*	hunger 19
Hunger haben*	to be hungry 19
Hut *(m.)* (¨-e)	hat/cap 86
Hütchen *(n.)* (-)	little hat/cap 86

I

ich	I 2
Idee *(f.)* (-n)	idea 26
identisch	identical 88
Idiot *(m.)* (-en) / Idiotin *(f.)* (-nen)	idiot 100
Igel *(m.)* (-)	hedgehog 58
ihm *(dat. of* er)	to him, to it *(m./n.)* 37
ihn *(acc. of* er)	him, it *(m.)* 24
ihnen *(dat. of* sie)	to them 37
Ihnen *(dat of* Sie)	to you *(formal)* 38
ihr	you *(pl. informal)* 10
ihr *(m./n.)* / ihre *(f.&pl.)*	her, its *(f.)* 23; their 25
Ihr *(m./n.)* / Ihre *(f.&pl.)*	your *(formal)* 5
im (in dem)	in the 2
immer	always 6
immer (+ *comparative*)	more and more / -er and -er 60
immer noch	still 84
immer noch kein…	still no 75
in	at, in, into 2
inbegriffen	included, inclusive 62
indem	by … -ing 86
Informatik *(f.)*	information technology (IT) 80
informieren	to advise, to inform 80
Inhalt *(m.)* (-e)	content 57
innen	inside 82
insgesamt	in total 87
interessant	interesting 36
interessieren für (+ *acc.*) (sich ~)	to be interested in 80
inzwischen	in the meantime 80
irgend-	some … or other 76
irgendwo	anywhere, somewhere 82
irren (sich ~)	to be mistaken 54
Italien *(n.)*	Italy 30
Italienisch *(n.)*	Italian (language) 73

J

ja	yes 2; but (conveying surprise) 32
Ja und?	So what? 88

sechshundertsechsundzwanzig • 626

Jahr *(n.)* (-e)	year 17
Jahrhundert *(n.)* (-e)	century 68
jammern	to moan (lament) 59
je (+ *comparative*)… desto/umso (+ *comparative*)	the more/less... the more/less 97
jedenfalls	anyway, in any case 99
jeder/jede/jedes *(m./f.&pl./n.)*	every 30; everyone 65
jedoch	however 80
jemand	anyone, someone 34
jetzt	now 11
jung	young 51
Junge *(m.)* (-n)	boy 7
Jungs	guys 90
Juni *(m.)*	June 46
Jura *(m.)*	law (at university) 51

K

Kabel *(n.)* (-)	cable 73
Kaffee *(m.)* (-s)	coffee 4
Kaffeekanne *(f.)* (-n)	coffee pot or press 8
Kaiser *(m.)* (-) / Kaiserin *(f.)* (-nen)	emperor/empress 68
Kakao *(m.)* (-s)	cocoa 57
Kalender *(m.)* (-)	calendar 25
kalt	cold 8, 57
Kälte *(f.)*	cold *(noun)* 78
Kamm *(m.)* (¨-e)	comb 65
kämmen	to comb 68
kämpfen	to fight GA16
Kännchen *(n.)* (-)	small coffee pot or press 8
Kanzler *(m.)* (-) / Kanzlerin *(f.)* (-nen)	chancellor 68
kapieren	to catch on, to get it 54
Kapital *(n.)* (-)	capital (funds) 65
kaputt gehen*/sein*	to get/be broken 85
Karriere *(f.)* (-n)	successful career 82
Karte *(f.)* (-n)	card 85
Kartoffel *(f.)* (-n)	potato 24
Käse *(m.)* (-)	cheese 4
Kasse *(f.)* (-n)	checkout (cash register) 24
Kater *(m.)* (-)	tomcat 13; hangover 54
Katze *(f.)* (-en)	cat 13
Kauf *(m.)* (¨-e)	purchase 40
kaufen	to buy 19
kaum	scarcely 46
kein *(m./n.)* / keine *(f.&pl.)*	no, none, not a(n), not any 9
Keine Ursache!	You're welcome! 15

keinerlei	no ... whatsoever 86
Kellner *(m.)* (-) / Kellnerin *(f.)* (-nen)	waiter/waitress 95
Kelterei *(f.)* (-en)	fruit-pressing plant 89
kennen*	to know (be familiar with) 32
kennen* lernen	to get to know 41; to meet 66
Kerze *(f.)* (-n)	candle 90
Kilo *(n.)* (-s) *(abb. of* Kilogramm)	kilogram 9
Kilometer *(m.)* (-)	kilometer 29
Kind *(n.)* (-er)	child 6
Kino *(n.)* (-s)	cinema, movie theatre 74
Kirche *(f.)* (-n)	church 41
Kirchturm *(m.)* (¨-e)	church tower 100
kitzeln	to tickle 76
klappen	to go as planned, to work out 90
klar	clear 31
klar *(coll.)*	of course 9
Klasse *(f.)* (-n)	class 40
Klasse!	Great! 40
Klasse (große ~)	really fantastic 40
Klassik *(f.)* (-en)	classical period 51
Kleid *(n.)* (-er)	dress 74
klein	small 42
klettern	to climb 97
Klima *(n.)* (-s)	climate 97
klingen*	to sound 50
Klo *(n.)* (-s) *(abb. of* Klosett)	bathroom, toilet 45
Kloß *(m.)* (¨-e)	dumpling 78
klug	intelligent 51
Kneipe *(f.)* (-n)	pub 16
Knödel *(m.)* (-)	dumpling 78
knurren	to growl, to snarl 78
Koch *(m.)* (¨-e) / Köchin *(f.)* (-nen)	chef 59; cook 67
kochen	to boil, to cook 59
Koffer *(m.)* (-)	suitcase 13
Kollege *(m.)* (-n) / Kollegin *(f.)* (-nen)	colleague 6
Köln	Cologne 20
komisch	funny, strange 76; weird 99
kommen*	to arrive 4; to come 4, 14
kommen* nach Hause	to come home 11
komponieren	to compose 68
Konditor *(m.)* (-en) / Konditorin *(f.)* (-nen)	confectioner 57
König *(m.)* (-e)	king 52
konkret	concrete 73
Können *(n.)* (-)	skill 90

können*	can 26; to be able to 26, 35; to know how to 29
kontrollieren	to check, to inspect 30
Konzert *(n.)* (-e)	concert 53
Kopf *(m.)* (¨-e)	head (body part) 54
köpfen	to decapitate 85
kosten	to cost 50
kostenlos	free (of charge) 96
köstlich	delicious 27
Krabbe *(f.)* (-n)	crab 13
Kragen *(m.)* (-)	collar 93
krank	ill 83
Krawatte *(f.)* (-n)	tie (necktie) 54
Kreditkarte *(f.)* (-n)	credit card 12
Krieg *(m.)* (-e)	war 72
kriegen	to catch, to get, to receive 40
Krimi *(abb. of* Kriminalfilm/ Kriminalroman) *(m.)* (-s)	detective film/novel 76
Krug *(m.)* (¨-e)	mug (for beer) 87
krumm	crooked 58
Küche *(f.)* (-n)	kitchen 50
Kuchen *(m.)* (-)	cake 27
Kuh *(f.)* (¨-e)	cow 63
kühl	cool 44
Kühlschrank *(m.)* (¨-e)	refrigerator 44
kümmern um (+ *acc.*) (sich ~)	to look after 81
Kunde *(m.)* (-n) / Kundin *(f.)* (-nen)	customer 25; client 65
kurz	brief 34; short 60
Kuss *(m.)* (¨-e)	kiss 16
Küste *(f.)* (-n)	coast 50

L

lächeln	to smile 54
lachen	to laugh 37
Lachen *(n.)*	laughter 58
lächerlich	ridiculous 85
Laden *(m.)* (¨)	shop 48
Lampe *(f.)* (-n)	lamp 43
Land *(n.)* (¨-er)	country 5; land 57
lang(e)	for long 22; a long time 29
langem (seit ~)	in a long time 76
langsam (+ *verb*)	starting to … 81
langweilen (sich ~)	to be bored 76
langweilig	boring 76
lassen*	to leave 12; to leave (behind) 26

lassen* (+ *verb*)	to allow, to have something done 26; to let (permit) 32
Lastwagen *(m.)* (-)	lorry, truck 94
laufen*	to go, to run, to walk, to work (function) 18
Laune *(f.)* (-n)	mood 31
laut	loud, noisy 34; according to 62
leben	to live 13
Leben *(n.)* (-)	life 51
Lebensart *(f.)* (-en)	lifestyle 75
Leberwurst *(f.)* ("-e)	liver sausage 78
lebhaft	lively 53
Leder *(n.)* (-)	leather 75
ledig	single (unmarried) 36
leer	empty 53
legen	to lay (something down), to put 54; to place 56
leicht	easy 54
Leid *(n.)* (-en)	agony, distress, sorrow 51
leider	unfortunately 12
leihen*	to borrow, to lend 92
leise	quiet 34
leisten	to accomplish 74
leiten	to lead 89
Leiter *(m.)* (-) / Leiterin *(f.)* (-nen)	head (of a department) 80
Lektion *(f.)* (-en)	lesson 1
lenken	to direct 46
Lenkrad *(n.)* ("-er)	handlebars 100
lernen	to learn 1
Lesen *(n.)* (-)	reading 27
lesen*	to read 27
letzter/letzte/letztes *(m./f./n.)*	last 40
Leute *(pl.)*	people 48
Licht *(n.)* (-er)	light 43
lieb	dear, kind 18
Liebe *(f.)* (-n)	love 74
lieben	to love 16
lieber	preferably 96
lieber (+ *verb*)	to prefer to, would rather 62
Liebesdienst *(m.)* (-e)	favour 88
Liebhaber *(m.)* (-) / Liebhaberin *(f.)* (-nen)	lover 67
Liebling *(m.)* (-e)	darling 26
liegen*	to be located, to be situated 41; to lie 44
links	on the left 15
Löffel *(m.)* (-)	spoon 86
logisch	logical 76

sechshundertdreißig • 630

lohnen	to pay 41
lohnen (sich ~)	to be worthwhile 41
los (+ *modal verb*)	to leave 71
Los!	Come on!, Hurry up!, Let's go! 55
los'fahren*	to go (by means of transport) 59
los'fliegen*	to fly 62
los'laufen*	to start running 60
löschen	to extinguish GA1
Lösung *(f.)* (-en)	answer 72
Luft *(f.)* (¨-e)	air 78
Lüge *(f.)* (-n)	lie 69
Lust *(f.)* (¨-e)	desire 26
Lust haben* (zu)	to feel like (doing something) 26
lustig	amusing, fun, funny 23
Luxus *(m.)* (-)	luxury 50

M

machen	to do, to make 9
machen (+ *adj.*)	to make one ... 17
machen lassen*	to have something done, to let someone do something 88
Mädchen *(n.)* (-)	girl 36
Mädchenname *(m.)* (-n)	maiden name 81
Magen *(m.)* (-)	stomach 53
Mahlzeit *(f.)* (-en)	meal 78
Mahlzeit!	Enjoy your meal! 78
Mai *(m.)*	May 22
mal (*abb. of* einmal)	once 11
Mal *(n.)* (-e)	time (occasion) 43, 60
Mal (jedes ~)	every time, whenever 76
Mal (nicht ein einziges ~)	not once (not one single time) 71
malen	to paint 90
Mama	Mum/Mom 18
man	one (impersonal pronoun) 17
manchmal	sometimes 87
Manieren *(pl.)*	manners 85
Mann *(m.)* (¨-er)	man 3; husband 23
Männchen *(n.)* (-)	male (animal) 88
Mantel *(m.)* (¨)	coat 56
Märchen *(n.)* (-)	folktale 58; story 82
Margerite *(f.)* (-n)	daisy 92
Markt *(m.)* (¨-e)	market 19
März *(m.)*	March 51
Maschine *(f.)* (-n)	machine 25
Maß *(f.)* (-)	litre of beer 87
Maß *(n.)* (-e)	measure 87

631 • **sechshunderteinunddreißig**

Mauer *(f.)* (-n)	wall 64
Mauerfall *(m.)*	fall of the Berlin Wall 64
Mäzen *(m.)* (-e) / Mäzenin *(f.)* (-nen)	patron 83
Medikament *(n.)* (-e)	medication 91
Medizin *(f.)*	medicine 51
Meer *(n.)* (-e)	sea 24
Mehl *(n.)* (-e)	flour 98
mehr	more 83
mehrere *(pl.)*	several 87
mein *(m./n.)* / meine *(f.&pl.)*	my 5
meinen	to think 26; to believe, to mean, to be of the opinion 67
meiner/meine/meins *(m./f.&pl./n.)*	mine 32
meinetwegen	all right (OK) 92
meinetwegen/deinetwegen/ seinetwegen etc.	on account of me/you/him/her etc. 92
Meinung *(f.)* (-en)	opinion 67
meist	most 77
Meister *(m.)* (-) / Meisterin *(f.)* (-nen)	master 24
melden	to announce 47
Mensch *(m.)* (-en)	humankind 17; human being 46
Mensch!	Man!/Boy! 17
Menschenfreund *(m.)* (-e) / Menschenfreundin *(f.)* (-nen)	philanthropist 73
Menschheit *(f.)*	humanity 88
merken	to notice 76
Methode *(f.)* (-n)	method 73
mich *(acc. of* ich)	me 11
Mieter *(m.)* (-) / Mieterin *(f.)* (-nen)	tenant 68
Milch *(f.)*	milk 12
Milchkaffee *(m.)* (-s)	coffee with milk 8
Million *(f.)* (-en)	million 18
mindestens	at least 72
Minister *(m.)* (-) / Ministerin *(f.)* (-nen)	minister (government) 83
Minute *(f.)* (-n)	minute 16
mir *(dat. of* ich)	to me 16
mischen (sich ~)	to meddle 54
miserabel	miserable GA20
Missverständnis *(n.)* (-se)	misunderstanding 32
Mist *(m.)* (-)	dung 9
Mist!	Damn! 9
mit (+ *dat.*)	with 4
mit'bringen*	to bring along 23, 46
mit'kommen*	to come along/with 12
mit'kriegen	to catch on, to get (understand) 76

mit'nehmen*	to take along 26
Mitarbeit *(f.)* (-)	collaboration, participation 80
Mittag *(m.)* (-e)	midday, noon 35
Mittagessen *(n.)* (-)	lunch 47
Mittagspause *(f.)* (-n)	lunchbreak 78
Mitte *(f.)* (-n)	middle 25
Mittel *(n.)* (-)	means (method) 73
Mitternacht *(f.)* (¨-e)	midnight 44
Mittwoch *(m.)* (-e)	Wednesday 25
mögen*	to like 4, 23, 35; to want 8; may 85
möglich	possible 13
Moment *(m.)* (-e)	moment 12
Moment (im ~)	at the moment 12
Monat *(m.)* (-e)	month 17
Mond *(m.)* (-e)	moon 25
Montag *(m.)* (-e)	Monday 25
Mord *(m.)* (-e)	murder 76
morgen	tomorrow 10
Morgen *(m.)* (-)	morning 6
Mücke *(f.)* (-n)	mosquito 43
müde	tired 17
müde machen	to make tired 17
Mühle *(f.)* (-n)	mill 78
mühsam	arduous 65
Mund *(m.)* (¨-er)	mouth 53
Mundart *(f.)* (-en)	dialect 89
Museum *(n.)* (*pl.* Museen)	museum 74
Musik *(f.)* (-en)	music 34
Müsli *(n.)* (-s)	muesli cereal 4
müssen*	must 10; to have to 10, 30, 35; to need to 30
Mut *(m.)*	courage 99
mutig	brave 74
Mutter *(f.)* (¨)	mother 18
Mutti	Mum/Mom 18
Mütze *(f.)* (-n)	hat/cap 72

N

na	well … 27
Na so was!	My goodness! 87
nach	to (+ destination) 11; past (+ hour) 20
nach (+ *dat.*)	after 46
nach'denken*	to think over 53; to reflect 83
nach'kommen*	to be there, to follow 78
nach'sehen*	to check, to look (verify) 44
Nachbar *(m.)* (-n) / Nachbarin *(f.)* (-nen)	neighbour 67

633 • **sechshundertdreiunddreißig**

nachdem	after 83
Nachfolger *(m.)* (-) / Nachfolgerin *(f.)* (-nen)	successor 82
Nachmittag *(m.)* (-e)	afternoon 25
Nachname *(m.)* (-n)	last name, surname 81
Nachricht *(f.)* (-en)	message 11; news 96
Nachspeise *(f.)* (-n)	dessert 27
nächste Mal (das ~)	the next time 83
nächster/nächste/nächstes *(m./f./n.)*	next 18
Nacht *(f.)* (¨-e)	night 17
Nachtisch *(m.)* (-e)	dessert 27
nachts	at night 88
nackt	naked 74
nah(e)	close 37; near 80
nahe (bei + *dat.*)	near 82
Name *(m.)* (-n)	name 5
nämlich	after all 57; in fact 85
Nase *(f.)* (-n)	nose 54
Nase voll haben* (die ~)	to be fed up 54
Nationalität *(f.)* (-en)	nationality 67
Natur *(f.)*	nature 97
natürlich	of course 8
neben	next to 37
nee *(coll.)*	no 55
negativ	negative 80
nehmen*	to take 4, 20
nein	no 5
nennen*	to call (designate) 68
nervös	nervous 31
nett	nice 18
neu	new 40
Neujahr *(n.)* (-e)	New Year 96
nicht	not 5
nicht (ein)mal	not even 71
nicht mehr	no longer, not anymore/any longer 22
Nicht wahr?	Isn't it? Doesn't it? Aren't you? etc. (question tag) 40
nichts	nothing 19
nicken	to nod 59
nie(mals)	never 53
niemand	no one 39; not … anyone 52
noch	still 6
noch ein *(m./n.)* / eine *(f.)*	another 16
noch nicht	not yet 6
nord	north(ern) 68

Norden *(m.)*	north 42
normalerweise	normally 46
nötig	necessary 79
Nudel *(f.)* (-n)	noodle 78
Null *(f.)* (-en)	zero 29
Nummer *(f.)* (-n)	number 5
nun	now 82
nur	only 15; nothing but 46
nützen	to be of use 60

O

ob	whether 76
oben	above, upstairs 45
oben (an + *dat.*)	at the top (of) 59
obwohl	although, even though 72
och	oh 26
Ochse *(m.)* (-n)	ox 87
oder	or 4
offen	open 99
öffnen	to open 74
oft	often 72
ohne	without 35
Ohr *(n.)* (-en)	ear 76
Öl *(n.)* (-e)	oil 44
Olivenöl *(n.)* (-e)	olive oil 44
Onkel *(m.)* (-)	uncle 39
Oper *(f.)* (-n)	opera 11
Optimismus *(m.)*	optimism 97
Orangensaft *(m.)* (¨-e)	orange juice 24
Orchester *(n.)* (-)	band (musical) 23
Ordnung *(f.)* (-en)	order (organization) 52
Ordnung (in ~)	fine (all right) 52
Organisation *(f.)* (-en)	organization 23
ost	east(ern) 64
Osten *(m.)*	east 41
Ozean *(m.)* (-e)	ocean 97

P

Paar *(n.)* (-e)	couple, pair 60
paar (ein ~)	a few 60
Paket *(n.)* (-e)	parcel 24
Panik *(f.)* (-en)	panic 90
Papa *(m.)* (-s)	Dad 48
Papagei *(m.)* (-en)	parrot 73
Papier *(n.)* (-e)	paper 98
Paradies *(n.)* (-e)	paradise 67

parken	to park 48
Parkplatz *(m.)* (¨-e)	parking space/lot 52
Partie *(f.)* (-n)	match 36
Party *(f.)* (-s)	party 22
passen	to be convenient, to fit (well), to be suitable 80
passieren	to happen 46
pauschal	all inclusive 96
Pause *(f.)* (-n)	break 4; interval (intermission) 45
Pazifist *(m.)* (-en) / Pazifistin *(f.)* (-nen)	pacifist 72
Pech *(n.)*	bad luck 39; pitch (tar) 69
Pelle *(f.)* (-n)	peel (skin) 78
perfekt	perfect 90
Person *(f.)* (-en)	person 2
Personal *(n.)*	personnel 80
persönlich	personal 30; in person 69
Pfanne *(f.)* (-n)	pan (skillet) 64
pfeifen*	to whistle 86
pfeifen* auf (+ *acc.*)	to not care (about) 86
Pferd *(n.)* (-e)	horse 68
Pflanze *(f.)* (-n)	plant 81
Pfund *(n.)* (-e)	pound (weight) 98
Pizza *(f.)* (-s *or* Pizzen)	pizza 26
Plan *(m.)* (¨-e)	plan 39
planen	to plan 90
Platz *(m.)* (¨-e)	place, seat 11; town square 51
platzen	to burst 93
plötzlich	sudden 82
Polen *(n.)*	Poland 68
Politik *(f.)*	politics 80
Polizei *(f.)*	police 48
Polizeiwagen *(m.)* (-)	police car 48
Polizist *(m.)* (-en) / Polizistin *(f.)* (-nen)	police officer 67
Pommes *(pl.)*	chips (fries) 9
Portion *(f.)* (-en)	portion 8
positiv	positive 80
Postkarte *(f.)* (-n)	postcard 18
praktisch	practical 29
Preis *(m.)* (-e)	price 38; prize 99
Prima!	Great! 20
Prinz *(m.)* (-en)	prince 82
Prinzessin *(f.)* (-nen)	princess 82
pro	per 17
Probe *(f.)* (-n)	test 90

sechshundertsechsunddreißig • 636

probieren	to try 75
Problem *(n.)* (-e)	problem 22
produzieren	to produce 89
Professor *(m.)* (-en) / Professorin *(f.)* (-nen)	professor 18
Programm *(n.)* (-e)	programme 74
Prozent *(n.)* (-e)	percent 88
Pullover *(m.)* (-)	sweater 77
Punkt *(m.)* (-e)	point 52
pünktlich	punctual 6
Pünktlichkeit *(f.)*	punctuality 52
Puppe *(f.)* (-n)	doll 56

Q

Quatsch *(m.)*	nonsense 55

R

Rad *(n.)* (¨-er)	bike, wheel 34
Rad fahren*	to cycle 100
radeln	to cycle 100
Radio *(n.)* (-s)	radio 74
Rast *(f.)* (-en)	rest 79
Rastplatz *(m.)* (¨-e)	rest stop (without food outlets) 79
Raststätte *(f.)* (-n)	motorway service area 79
Rat *(m.)* (*pl.* Ratschläge)	piece of advice 31
raten*	to guess 72; to recommend 83
Ratte *(f.)* (-n)	rat 13
rauchen	to smoke 72
rauchig	husky 72
raus *(abb. of* heraus)	out 46
raus'gehen*	to go out(side) 46, 78
rechnen	to calculate, to count 61
rechnen mit	to expect 97
Rechnung *(f.)* (-en)	bill (check), calculation 61
Recht *(n.)*	the law 73
Recht *(n.)* (-e)	right 73
recht haben*	to be right 73
rechts	on the right 15
reden	to speak, to talk 36
reden über (+ *acc.*)	to talk about 36
Regel *(f.)* (-n)	rule 85
Regen *(m.)* (-)	rain 26
Regenschirm *(m.)* (-e)	umbrella 26
Regenwetter *(n.)*	rainy weather 48
Regisseur *(m.)* (-e) / Regisseurin *(f.)* (-nen)	film/theatre director 72

regnen	to rain 26
reich	rich 36
reichen	to pass (to someone) 98
Reihe *(f.)* (-n)	row (line) 45
Reihe. (Ich bin an der ~)	It's my turn. 95
rein *(abb. of* herein/hinein)	in 52
Reise *(f.)* (-n)	journey 16; trip 62
Reisebüro *(n.)* (-s)	travel agency 62
reisen	to travel 62
reißen*	to tear 54
rennen*	to run 70
Rente *(f.)* (-n)	retirement 89
reparieren	to repair 25
reservieren	to book, to reserve 61
Rezept *(n.)* (-e)	recipe 57
richtig	correct 73; right 74; proper 97
Rivale *(m.)* (-n) / Rivalin *(f.)* (-nen)	rival 74
Roman *(m.)* (-e)	novel 51
romantisch	romantic 100
rosig	rosy 97
Rosine *(f.)* (-n)	raisin 88
rot	red 34
Rot (bei ~)	at a red light 34
rufen*	to call out 58; to shout 59
Ruhe *(f.)*	silence 45; calm, peace (and quiet) 93
ruhig	calm, patient 60
rund	round 57
rundherum	all the way round 86
runter *(abb. of* herunter)	down 43
runter'fallen*	to fall down 43
runter'gehen*	to go down 43
runter'gucken	to look down 43
rutschen	to slide 96

S

's *(abb. of* es)	it 12
Saal *(m.)* (*pl.* Säle)	hall 90
Saft *(m.)* (¨-e)	juice 24
sagen	to say 11
Sahne *(f.)*	cream 8
Salat *(m.)* (-e)	salad 78
Salto *(m.)* (-s)	somersault 100
Salz *(n.)* (-e)	salt 78
Samstag *(m.)* (-e)	Saturday 22
Sand *(m.)* (-)	sand 54
Sandale *(f.)* (-n)	sandal 34

satt	full (fed to satisfaction) 27
Satz *(m.)* (¨-e)	sentence 58
Sau *(f.)* (¨-e)	sow (female pig) 78
Sauwetter *(n.)*	bad weather 78
Saxofon *(n.)* (-e)	saxophone 34
Schachtel *(f.)* (-n)	box 57
schade	what a pity, what a shame 20; too bad 86
schaffen (es ~)	to achieve, to cope with, to manage to 29
Schale *(f.)* (-n)	shell 86
schämen (sich ~)	to be ashamed 54
Schatz *(m.)* (¨-e)	darling, treasure 66
schauen	to look 38
Schauspieler *(m.)* (-) / Schauspielerin *(f.)* (-nen)	actor/actress 72
Schausteller *(m.)* (-) / Schaustellerin *(f.)* (-nen)	exhibitor (at a show) 87
Schein *(m.)* (-e)	light 96
scheinen*	to appear (to be) 31; to seem 31, 76; to shine 96
schicken	to send 39
schief gehen*	to go wrong 90
Schiff *(n.)* (-e)	ship 68
Schimpanse *(m.)* (-n)	chimpanzee 88
Schimpfwort *(n.)* (¨-er)	swear word 100
Schlacht *(f.)* (-en)	battle 70
schlafen*	to sleep 17
schlaflos	sleepless 93
Schlafzimmer *(n.)* (-)	bedroom 50
schlagen*	to hit 55; to defeat 70; to beat 85
Schlägerei *(f.)* (-en)	fight 76
Schlagsahne *(f.)*	whipped cream 8
Schlange *(f.)* (-n)	queue (line), snake 24
Schlange stehen*	to stand in line, to queue up 24
schlau	clever 62
schlecht	bad 31
schließen*	to close 10
schließlich	finally 52; after all 62
schlimm	bad 69
Schloss *(n.)* (¨-er)	castle 82
Schluss *(m.)* (¨-e)	closure, end 29
Schluss (zum ~)	finally 33
schmecken	to taste (good) 27
Schmerz *(m.)* (-en)	pain 92
Schmied *(m.)* (-e) / Schmiedin *(f.)* (-nen)	smith 100
schmücken	to decorate GA11

Schnäppchen *(n.)* (-)	bargain, deal 62
schnappen	to grab, to snap up 62
Schnaps *(m.)* (¨-e)	schnapps 30
Schnee *(m.)* (-)	snow 97
schneiden*	to cut 79
schneien	to snow 97
schnell	quick 11
Schnitt (im ~)	on average 79
schockiert	shocked 88
Schokolade *(f.)* (-n)	chocolate 23
schön	beautiful 3; nice 46
schon	already 15
schon lange	a long time since 53
schon wieder	again 95
Schrank *(m.)* (¨-e)	cupboard 44
Schreck *(m.)* (-e)	fright, horror 94
Schrecken einjagen (jdm einen ~)	to scare someone 94
schrecklich	terrible 36
schreiben*	to write 39
Schreibtisch *(m.)* (-e)	desk 72
schreien*	to shout 45; to cry out 49; to shriek 60
Schriftsteller *(m.)* (-) / Schriftstellerin *(f.)* (-nen)	writer 72
Schritt *(m.)* (-e)	step (stride) 60
Schuh *(m.)* (-e)	shoe 73
Schulbuch *(n.)* (¨-er)	schoolbook 83
Schuld *(f.)* (-en)	debt 83
Schule *(f.)* (-n)	school 51
Schüler *(m.)* (-) / Schülerin *(f.)* (-nen)	schoolchild 22
schütteln	to shake one's head 59
Schutz *(m.)* (-)	protection 94
schwach	weak 63
Schwall *(m.)* (-e)	torrent 100
Schwan *(m.)* (¨-e)	swan 74
schwarz	black 83
Schwein *(n.)* (-e)	pig, pork 75
Schweinerei *(f.)* (-en)	rubbish 75
Schweinshaxe *(f.)* (-n)	pork knuckle 75
Schweiz *(f.)*	Switzerland 68
schwer	difficult, heavy 57; hard (arduous) 71
Schwester *(f.)* (-n)	sister 23
schwierig	difficult 48
Schwimmbad *(n.)* (¨-er)	swimming pool 96
schwimmen*	to swim 96
schwören*	to swear (vow) 41

sechshundertvierzig • 640

See *(m.)* (-n)	lake 83
sehen*	to see 10, GA11; to look 37
sehenswert	worth seeing 83
sehr	very 3
Seide *(f.)* (-n)	silk 54
seiden	silken 54
sein *(m./n.)* / seine *(f.&pl.)*	his, its *(m./n.)* 23
sein*	to be 1, 2, 14, GA11
seit	since 29
Seite *(f.)* (-n)	side 50
seither	since then 64
Sekt *(m.)* (-e)	sparkling wine 24
Sekunde *(f.)* (-n)	second 90
selber/selbe/selbes *(m./f./n.)*	same 48
selbst	myself/yourself/himself/herself etc., in person 61
Selbstmord *(m.)* (-e)	suicide 76
selbstständig	independent, self-employed 81
selbstverständlich	of course (self-evident) 61
selten	rare 35
senden*	to send 70; to broadcast 91
Sendung *(f.)* (-en)	transmission (shipment or broadcast) 51; programme (radio/TV) 74
Sessel *(m.)* (-)	armchair 55
setzen	to place, to put, to set down 56
setzen (sich ~)	to sit (down) 37, 45
sich	oneself/himself/herself/itself/themselves/yourself *(formal)* 47
sicher	sure 6; certain 19; safe 62
Sicher!	Sure! 41
sie	she 3; they 6; her, it *(f.)* 24
Sie	you *(formal)* 1
sie	them 28
Sieh da!	Look! 87
Silvester *(m./n.)* (-)	New Year's Eve 96
singen*	to sing 82
Sitte *(f.)* (-n)	custom 5
sitzen*	to sit 25, 68; to be sitting 43
sitzen bleiben*	to stay seated 60
Sitzung *(f.)* (-en)	meeting 25
Smoking *(m.)* (-s)	tuxedo 38
so	so 16
so (etwas)	such (a thing) 93
so viel	so much 88
so… wie	as … as 60
sobald	as soon as 79

Socke *(f.)* (-n)	sock 34
sofort	immediately 4; at once 55
sogar	even 37
Sohn *(m.)* (¨-e)	son 85
solange	as long as GA18; until 99
sollen*	should 31; to be supposed to 31, 35; to be meant to 36
Sommer *(m.)* (-)	summer 28
sondern	but (rather), on the contrary 30
Sonnabend *(m.)* (-e)	Saturday 25
Sonne *(f.)* (-n)	sun 25
sonnig	sunny 50
Sonntag *(m.)* (-e)	Sunday 10
sonst	otherwise 71; or else, normally, usually 95
sonst irgendwo	anywhere else 82
sonstwo (*abb. of* sonst irgendwo)	elsewhere 82
Sorge *(f.)* (-n)	concern, worry 52
Souvenir *(n.)* (-s)	souvenir 87
soweit (es ist ~)	it is time 90
sowieso	anyway 48
Spanien *(n.)*	Spain 50
Spanier *(m.)* (-) / Spanierin *(f.)* (-nen)	Spanish (person) 50
Spanisch	Spanish (language) 50
spannend	captivating 76
sparen	to save (economize) 10
Spaß *(m.)* (¨-e)	pleasure 49; fun 99
Spaß machen	to be fun 99
spät	late 6
später	later 12
spätestens	at the latest 71
spazieren gehen*	to go for a walk 34
Spaziergang *(m.)* (¨-e)	walk (a stroll) 26
Speise *(f.)* (-n)	dish (food) 27
Speisekarte *(f.)* (-n)	menu 8
spezialisieren auf (+ *acc.*) (sich ~)	to specialize in 81
Spiegel *(m.)* (-)	mirror 82
spiegelblank	gleaming (mirrorlike) 82
Spiel *(n.)* (-e)	game 31
spielen	to play 34
Spinne *(f.)* (-n)	spider 55
spinnen*	to be crazy, to spin 55
Sprache *(f.)* (-n)	language 73
sprechen*	to speak 8
sprechen* (+ *acc.*)	to speak to 47
sprechen* (von)	to speak/say (about) 62

sechshundertzweiundvierzig • 642

Sprudel *(m.)* (-)	sparkling mineral water 33
Stadt *(f.)* (¨-e)	town 10; city 41
Stadtbesichtigung *(f.)* (-en)	sightseeing 33
Stamm *(m.)* (¨-e)	trunk (of tree) 55
stammen (aus)	to come from (originate from) 68
stark	strong 63
Station *(f.)* (-en)	station 15
Statistik *(f.)* (-en)	statistic 62
Stätte *(f.)* (-n)	place, site 79
Stau *(n.)* (-s)	traffic jam 79
stehen*	to stand 24, 82; to be standing 44; to be written 83
stehlen*	to steal 91
steigen*	to rise 97
Stelle *(f.)* (-n)	place 15; area, position 80
stellen	to place (upright), to put (upright) 44; to stand (upright) 56
sterben*	to die 51
Stern *(m.)* (-e)	star 86
still	quiet 45
Stimme *(f.)* (-n)	voice 72
stimmen	to be correct, to be right, to be true 40
stimmt	that's true 24, 40; that's right 40
Stock *(m.)* (*pl.* Stockwerke)	floor (storey) 90
stolz	proud 89
stören	to bother 34
Strafe *(f.)* (-n)	fine (penalty) 93
strahlend	beaming 85
Strand *(m.)* (¨-e)	beach 79
Straße *(f.)* (-n)	street 15
Straßenbahn *(f.)* (-en)	tram 15
Strategie *(f.)* (-n)	strategy 97
Strauß *(m.)* (¨-e)	bunch 92
streicheln	to stroke 32
streiten über/um (+ *acc.*) (sich ~)	to disagree on/about 83
stressig	stressful 65
streuen	to strew 54; to sprinkle 86
Strich *(m.)* (-e)	line (stroke) 61
Strom *(m.)* (¨-e)	electricity (current) 90
Stück *(n.)* (-e)	piece 4; play (theatre) 45
Stück *(n.)* (ein ~)	a bit 64
Student *(m.)* (-en) / Studentin *(f.)* (-nen)	student 3
Studienkollege *(m.)* (-n) / Studienkollegin *(f.)* (-nen)	classmate 84
studieren	to study 51

Studium *(n.)* *(pl.* Studien)	studies (at university) 81
Stuhl *(m.)* (¨-e)	chair 55
Stunde *(f.)* (-n)	hour 17
stürzen	to fall, to topple 62
suchen	to look for, to search for 19
süd	south(ern) 50
Süden *(m.)*	south 42
Supermarkt *(m.)* (¨-e)	supermarket 19
Suppe *(f.)* (-n)	soup 78
süß	cute 28; sweet 32
Symbol *(n.)* (-e)	symbol 64

T

Tag *(m.)* (-e)	day 1
Tankstelle *(f.)* (-n)	service station 19
Tante *(f.)* (-n)	aunt 39
tanzen	to dance 86
Tasche *(f.)* (-n)	bag 32
Tasse *(f.)* (-n)	cup 8
Tat *(f.)* (-en)	action 81
Tat (in der ~)	indeed 81
Tausend *(n.)* (-e)	thousand 18
Taxi *(n.)* (-s)	taxi 13
Tee *(m.)* (-s)	tea 4
teil'nehmen an	to participate in GA16
teilen	to divide 64; to share 97
teilen (sich ~)	to be divided into 35
Telefon *(n.)* (-e)	telephone 5
Telefongespräch *(n.)* (-e)	telephone call/conversation 5
Teller *(m.)* (-)	plate 56
Termin *(m.)* (-e)	appointment, date, deadline 25
Terrasse *(f.)* (-n)	terrace 82
teuer	expensive 23; dear 93
Teufel *(m.)* (-)	devil 90
Theater *(n.)* (-)	theatre 26
theoretisch	theoretical 29
tief	deep 58
Tier *(n.)* (-e)	animal 73
Tisch *(m.)* (-e)	table 27
Titel *(m.)* (-)	title 100
tja	well … 87
Tochter *(f.)* (¨)	daughter 81
Tod *(m.)* (-e)	death 83
todernst	deadly serious 85
Toi! Toi! Toi!	Touch wood! 89
Toilette *(f.)* (-n)	toilet 45

sechshundertvierundvierzig • 644

Toll!	Great! 20
Tor *(n.)* (-e)	gate 68
Torte *(f.)* (-n)	cake/tart 57
tot	dead 57
tot um'fallen*	to drop dead 60
tot'lachen (sich ~)	to die of laughter 58
total	total 27; complete 37
Tourist *(m.)* (-en) / Touristin *(f.)* (-nen)	tourist 38
tragen*	to wear 34, 38, 72, 74
Traum *(m.)* (¨-e)	dream 53
träumen	to dream 82
traumhaft	fantastic (dreamlike) 53
traurig	sad 54
treffen*	to meet 25, 58
trennen	to separate 95
Trennung *(f.)* (-en)	separation 64
trinken*	to drink 4
Trinkschokolade *(f.)* (-n)	hot chocolate 8
trotzdem	even so (all the same) 46; nevertheless 80
Tschüs(s)!	Bye!, See you! 12
tüchtig	capable, studious (hard-working) 99
tun*	to do 32
tun* als ob	to pretend 95
Tür *(f.)* (-en)	door 16
Turm *(m.)* (¨-e)	tower 63
Tut mir Leid!	I'm sorry! 32
tut weh (das ~)	that hurts 32
typisch	typical 33

U

U-Bahn *(f.)* (-en)	subway, underground train 15
über	about, above 36; over (more than) 57
über'schnappen	to go crazy 37
überall	everywhere 44
überfahren*	to run over 94
überhaupt nicht	not at all 95
Überleben *(n.)*	survival 97
Überlegung *(f.)* (-en)	reflection 65
übermorgen	the day after tomorrow 62
übernehmen*	to reimburse 80
überqueren	to cross 34
überraschen	to surprise 76
überrascht	surprised 100
übersetzen	to translate 1
überzeugen	to convince, to persuade 61

überzeugend	convincing 61
Übung *(f.)* (-en)	exercise 1
Ufer *(n.)* (-)	shore 68
Uhr *(f.)* (-en)	clock/o'clock, time (an exact time i.e. hours/minutes) 16; watch (wristwatch) 17
um	at (+ time) 16; around 33
Um wie viel Uhr?	At what time? 16
um… zu (+ *infinitive*)	in order to 50
um'drehen	to wring 93
um'fallen*	to fall over 60
Umgang *(m.)* (¨-e)	relations 86
umgehend	immediate 96
umso besser	all the better 99
umso mehr/weniger als	especially as 95
Umwelt *(f.)* (-en)	environment 40
umweltfreundlich	environmentally friendly 40
unbedingt	absolute 41
unbekannt	unknown 69
und	and 3
ungefähr	about (approximately) 29; around (approximately) 57
Ungerechtigkeit *(f.)* (-en)	injustice 72
Uni *(f.)* (-s) *(coll.)*	uni (abb. for university) 18
Universität *(f.)* (-en)	university 18
unmöglich	impossible 77
Unrecht *(n.)* (-)	injustice, wrong 73
unrecht haben*	to be wrong 73
uns	us 22
unten	below, downstairs 45; down 59
unter (+ *dat.*)	between 69; among, under(neath) 75
unterbrechen	to interrupt GA14
Untergrund *(m.)* (¨-e)	underground 15
unterhalten* (sich ~)	to talk to (each other) 37; to discuss/converse 69
Unterkunft *(f.)* (¨-e)	accommodation 62
Unternehmen *(f.)* (-)	company 80; business 89
Unterschied *(m.)* (-e)	difference 29
unvergesslich	unforgettable 100
uralt	ancient 89
Urgroßvater *(m.)* (¨) / Urgroßmutter *(f.)* (¨)	great-grandfather/great-grandmother 89
Urlaub *(m.)* (-e)	holiday, vacation 37
Ursache *(f.)* (-n)	cause 15
Urzeit *(f.)* (-en)	primeval times 89

V

Vater *(m.)* (¨)	father 18
Vati	Dad 18
verabredet sein (*or* sich verabreden)	to arrange to meet 52
Verabredung *(f.)* (-en)	appointment 47
verändern	to change 82
verbieten*	to forbid, to prohibit 34
verboten	forbidden 34
verbringen*	to spend (time) 37, 46
verdanken (+ *dat.*)	to owe 83
verderben*	to spoil 65
verdienen (sich ~)	to earn 31, 88
Verehrter/Verehrte/Verehrtes *(m./f.&pl./n.)*	dear (address in a speech) 91
Vereinigte Staaten *(pl.)*	United States 70
Vereinigung *(f.)* (-en)	unification 64
Verflixt!	Darn! 29
Verfügung *(f.)* (-en)	disposition (availability) 96
Verfügung stehen (zur ~)	to be available 96
Vergangenheit *(f.)* (-en)	past 64
vergehen*	to pass 16
vergessen*	to forget 16
Vergnügen *(n.)* (-)	pleasure 1; amusement 60
vergnügt	merry 60
vergöttern	to adore 72
verhaften	to arrest 91
verheiratet	married 38
verkaufen	to sell 40
Verkäufer *(m.)* (-) / Verkäuferin *(f.)* (-nen)	salesperson 62
Verkehr *(m.)*	traffic 91
verlassen*	to leave (desert) GA13
verleihen*	to award someone 72; to lend 92
verletzen	to hurt 58
verlieren*	to lose 54, 96
verloren	lost 72
vermieten	to rent (let) 50
vermutlich	presumably 87
verpassen	to miss (fail to catch) 20
verraten*	to reveal 65
verrückt	crazy 32
verrückt werden*	to go crazy 79
versammeln	to gather (assemble) 90
versprechen*	to promise 54
Verstand *(m.)*	mind, reasoning, common sense 60

647 • **sechshundertsiebenundvierzig**

verständlich	comprehensible/comprehensibly, understandable 61
Verständnis *(n.)*	comprehension, understanding *(noun)* 32
verständnisvoll	understanding *(adj.)* 92
verstecken (sich ~)	to hide 59
verstehen*	to understand 27, 54
verstehen* (sich ~)	to get on/along 93
verstopfen	to jam/block 52
Versuch *(m.)* (-e)	attempt 65
versuchen	to try 61
vertraulich	confidential 69
Vertreter *(m.)* (-) / Vertreterin *(f.)* (-nen)	representative 25
verurteilen	to sentence 93
Verwandte *(pl.)*	relatives 39
verwechseln (mit)	to confuse (mistake) 74
Verwechslung *(f.)* (-en)	confusion (mistake) 77
verwirrt	baffled, confused 60
verwöhnen	to spoil (indulge) 87
verwüsten	to devastate 91
verzeihen*	to forgive 69
Verzeihung …	Pardon (me) … 81
verzichten auf (+ *acc.*)	to do without 75; to forego 86
verzweifelt	desperate 54
Vesperbrot *(n.)* (-e)	sandwich 47
viel	much 1; a lot 18
viele	many 18
Vielen Dank!	Many thanks! 15
vielleicht	maybe, perhaps 29
vielmals	many times 92
vielseitig	versatile (many-sided) 60
Viertel *(n.)* (-)	quarter 52
Viertelstunde *(f.)* (-n)	quarter of an hour 47
Vogel *(m.)* (¨)	bird 82
voll	full 25
Vollpension *(f.)*	full board 62
vom (von dem)	of them 47
von (+ *dat.*)	of 3; from 33; by 82
von … bis	from … to 74
vor	before, to (+ hour) 20; ago 66; to 68
vor'gehen*	to proceed 90
vor'stellen (+ *acc.*) (sich ~)	to introduce 37, 62
vor'stellen (+ *dat.*) (sich ~)	to imagine 62
vor'ziehen*	to prefer 80
Voraus (im ~)	in advance 96
voraus'sagen	to predict 97

sechshundertachtundvierzig • 648

vorbei	over (finished) 22; past 100
vorbei'fahren	to pass (by car/bike/train etc.) 100
Vorfahr *(m.)* (-en)	ancestor 88
Vormittag *(m.)* (-e)	morning 25
vorn	at the front 45
Vorname *(m.)* (-n)	first name 81
vornehm	distinguished 86
Vorsicht *(f.)*	care (caution) 13
Vorsicht!	Careful! 13
vorsichtig	careful 86
Vorspeise *(f.)* (-n)	first course (starter/appetizer) 27
Vorstellungsgespräch *(n.)* (-e)	job interview 81
Vorteil *(m.)* (-e)	advantage 78
Vorzimmer *(n.)* (-)	waiting room 47

W

wagen	to dare 69
Wagen *(m.)* (-)	car 40
Wahl *(f.)* (-en)	choice 31
wahr	true 37
Wahrheit *(f.)* (-en)	truth 69
wahrscheinlich	probably 48
Wald *(m.)* (¨-er)	forest 65
Wand *(f.)* (¨-e)	wall 54
wann	when 11
warm	warm 97
warnen	to warn 86
warten	to wait 13, 14
warten auf (+ *acc.*)	to wait for 59
warum	why 1
was	what 4; that (which) 34
was (*abb. of* etwas)	something 19
was auch kommt	whatever may happen 99
Was für ein/eine…!	What (a/an) ...! 22
Was für ein/eine…?	What kind of ...? 22
Was ist los?	What's going on? 55; What's up?, What's wrong? 71
was/etwas anderes	something different 78
was/wer es auch sei	whatever/whoever it may be 97
waschen* (sich ~)	to wash 71, 77
Wasser *(n.)* (-)	water 97
wechseln	to change 75
wecken (jemanden ~)	to wake (someone) 71
Wecker *(m.)* (-)	alarm clock 71
weder… noch	neither ... nor 34
weg	away 52

Weg *(m.)* (-e)	way 38
weg'fahren*	to drive away 48
weg'fliegen*	to fly away 43
weg'gehen*	to go away, to leave 52
weg'laufen*	to run away 73
weh'tun*	to ache 78
Weibchen *(n.)* (-)	female (animal) 88
weich	soft 85
Weihnachten *(n.)* (-)	Christmas 97
Weihnachtsmann *(m.)*	Father Christmas 97
weil	because 57
Wein *(m.)* (-e)	wine 35
weinen	to cry 98
Weise *(f.)* (-n)	manner, way (mode) 10
weiß	white 82
Weißbier *(n.)* (-e)	wheat beer 75
Weißwurst *(f.)* (¨-e)	veal and pork sausage 75
weit	far 18; wide 29
weit (von)	far (from) 55
weiter (+ *verb*)	to continue to (do something) 17
weiter *(adv.)* / weitere *(adj./pl.)*	further 80
weiter'gehen*	to continue 33
weiter'machen	to continue 99
welcher/welche/welches *(m./f./n.)*	which 20; what 61
Welt *(f.)* (-en)	world 57
Weltgeschichte *(f.)*	world history 64
wem *(dat. of* wer)	to whom 39
wen *(acc. of* wer)	whom 23
wenden*	to turn 70
wenig	little 30; few 65
wenig (ein ~)	a little 30
wenigstens	at least 57
wenn	if 32; when, whenever 38
wer	whoever 33
Wer?	who 3
werden*	to become 22, 51, 64, GA11
werden* *(+ adj./adv.)*	to get/become ... 23, 60
werden* *(+ infinitive)*	will (future tense auxiliary) 55
Werk *(n.)* (-e)	work 51
Wert *(m.)* (-e)	value, worth 41
wert sein*	to be worth 41
weshalb	why 65
wessen	whose 68
west	west(ern) 64
Westen *(m.)*	west 42
wetten	to bet 58

sechshundertfünfzig • 650

Wetter *(n.)*	weather 46
Wetterbericht *(m.)* (-e)	weather forecast 97
Wettlauf *(m.)* (¨-e)	race 58
wichtig	important 73
wie	how, what 5; like 46; as 48
Wie alt bist du?	How old are you? 22
Wie bitte?	What? 27; Excuse me? (Sorry?), Pardon? 71
wie dem auch sei	be that as it may 97
Wie gefällt dir…?	How do you like ...? 76
Wie geht's?	How are you? 66
Wie lange?	How long? 62
Wie spät ist es?	What time is it? 78
wie viel	how much 9, 61
wie viele	how many 61
wieder	again 54
wieder erkennen*	to recognize (after time has passed) 82
wieder'sehen*	to see again 100
Wiederaufbau *(f.)* (-)	reconstruction 64
wiederholen	to repeat 65
Wiederholung *(f.)* (-en)	review 7
wiegen*	to weigh 57
Wiese *(f.)* (-n)	meadow 82
Wille *(m.)* (-n)	will (volition) 65
willkommen	welcome 51
winken	to wave 37
Winter *(m.)* (-)	winter 28
wir	we 1
wirklich	really 27
Wirklichkeit *(f.)* (-en)	reality 56
Wirtschaft *(f.)* (-en)	economy 90
wissen*	to know 22, 30, 31
Witwe *(f.)* (-n)	widow 68
wo	where 11
wo doch	as, even though, since 97
wo… (doch)	when 99
Woche *(f.)* (-n)	week 18
Wochenende *(n.)* (-n)	weekend 33
Wochentag *(m.)* (-e)	weekday 25
woher	where from 36; how 81
wohin	where to 36
wohl	probably 56; well 77
wohnen	to live 37
Wohnung *(f.)* (-en)	apartment, flat 50
Wohnzimmer *(n.)* (-)	living room 50
wollen*	to wish 27; to want 27, 31, 35, 36

Wort *(n.)* (¨-er *or* -e)	word 58
Wozu?	What for?, Why? 19
Wunder *(n.)* (-)	miracle 73
Wundermittel *(n.)* (-)	magic formula 73
wunderschön	lovely 50
wünschen	to desire, to wish 1
Wurst *(f.)* (¨-e)	cooked meat(s), sausage 4
Würstchen *(n.)* (-)	small sausage 4
Wut *(f.)*	anger, fury 60
wüten	to rage 60
wütend	enraged 60

Z

Zahl *(f.)* (-en)	number (numeral) 17
zahlen	to pay 9
zählen	to count 60
Zahn *(m.)* (¨-e)	tooth 50
Zahnarzt *(m.)* (¨-e) / Zahnärztin *(f.)* (-nen)	dentist 50
Zauber *(m.)*	magic 68
Zeichen *(n.)* (-)	signal 90
zeichnen	to draw GA10
zeigen	to show 13
Zeit *(f.)* (-en)	time 12
Zeit haben*	to be available, to have time 12
Zeit haben* (keine ~)	to be busy, to not have time 12
Zeitung *(f.)* (-en)	newspaper 43
Zelt *(n.)* (-e)	tent 87
Zentrum *(n.)* (*pl.* Zentren)	centre 41
Zerstörung *(f.)* (-en)	destruction 64
ziehen*	to pull 70
ziemlich (+ *adj.*)	quite 31
Zimmer *(n.)* (-)	room 2
zischen	to hiss 21
zögern	to hesitate 64
Zone *(f.)* (-n)	zone 33
zu (+ *adj./adv.*)	too 22
zu (+ *dat.*)	for, to 37
zu (+ *infinitive*) (es ist ~)	it is enough to … 79
zu viel	too much 23
zu'machen	to close 74
Zucker *(m.)* (-)	sugar 98
zuerst	first 33; at first 74
zufrieden	satisfied 82
Zug *(m.)* (¨-e)	train 16
Zugvogel *(m.)* (¨)	migratory bird 97

Zukunft *(f.)* (¨-e)	future 80
zukünftig	future *(adj.)* 38
zuletzt	last 86
zunehmen	to increase 97
zurück	back, behind 12
zurück sein*	to be back 47
zurück'fliegen*	to fly back 83
zurück'gehen*	to go back 12
zurück'halten*	to hold back 32; to detain 86
zurück'kommen*	to come back 12, 25, 47
zurück'rufen*	to call back 12
zusammen	together 9
Zusammenhang *(m.)* (¨-e)	connection 88
zuverlässig	reliable 52
Zuverlässigkeit *(f.)*	reliability 52
zwar… aber	admittedly … but 75
zweifeln an	to doubt something GA16
zweimal	twice 9
zweiter/zweite/zweites *(m./f./n.)*	second 45
zweites Mal (ein ~)	a second time 76
Zwerg *(m.)* (-e)	dwarf 68
zwischen	between 29
zwölf	twelve 44

English–German

A

a lot	viel 18
a(n)	ein *(m./n.)* / eine *(f.)* 1
able to (to be ~)	können* 26, 35
about	über 36
about (approximately)	ungefähr 29
about (it is ~)	es geht (um), es handelt sich um (+ *acc.*) 94
about (to be ~)	sich handeln um (+ *acc.*) 90
above	über 36; oben 45
abroad	Ausland *(n.)* 80
absolute	unbedingt 41
absolutely (thoroughly)	durchaus 51
accent	Akzent *(m.)* (-e) 75
accommodation	Unterkunft *(f.)* (¨-e) 62
accompany (to ~)	begleiten 85
accomplish (to ~)	leisten 74
according to	laut 62
account of me/you/him/her etc. (on ~)	meinetwegen/deinetwegen/seinetwegen etc. 92
ache (to ~)	weh'tun* 78
achieve (to ~)	es schaffen 29
action	Tat *(f.)* (-en) 81
actor/actress	Schauspieler *(m.)* (-) / Schauspielerin *(f.)* (-nen) 72
actually (in fact)	eigentlich 22
adapt (to ~)	sich ein'leben 75
adapt to (to ~)	sich an'passen 97
addition (in ~)	außerdem 50
address	Adresse *(f.)* (-n) 84
adjust to (to ~)	sich an etwas (+ *acc.*) gewöhnen 75
admittedly … but	zwar… aber 75
adore (to ~)	vergöttern 72
advance (in ~)	im Voraus 96
advantage	Vorteil *(m.)* (-e) 78
advertisement	Annonce *(f.)* (-n), Anzeige *(f.)* (-n) 50
advice (piece of ~)	Rat *(m.)* (*pl.* Ratschläge) 31
advise (to ~)	empfehlen* 65; informieren 80
affair	Angelegenheit *(f.)* (-en) 54
affectionate	herzlich 18
afraid of (to be ~)	befürchten 92
after	nach (+ *dat.*) 46; nachdem 83
after all	doch 40; nämlich 57; schließlich 62
afternoon	Nachmittag *(m.)* (-e) 25

sechshundertvierundfünfzig • 654

afterwards	danach 51
again	wieder 54; schon wieder 95
against	gegen 77
age (to ~)	alt/älter werden* 82
ago	vor 66
agony	Leid *(n.)* (-en) 51
agree (to ~)	aus'machen 95
ah	ach 15
air	Luft *(f.)* (¨-e) 78
airplane	Flugzeug *(n.)* (-e) 62
airport	Flughafen *(m.)* (¨) 24
alarm clock	Wecker *(m.)* (-) 71
alight (to ~)	aus'steigen* 16
all	alles 9
all right	einverstanden 58
all right (OK)	meinetwegen 92
all the better	umso besser 99
allow (to ~)	lassen* (+ *verb*) 26; erlauben 34; ermöglichen 97
allowed to (to be ~)	dürfen* 35
allowed to (to not be ~)	nicht dürfen* 32
almost	fast 58
alone	allein 2
along	entlang 100
Alps	Alpen *(pl.)* 83
already	schon 15
also	auch 6
although	obwohl 72
always	immer 6
among	unter (+ *dat.*) 75
amusement	Vergnügen *(n.)* (-) 60
amusing	lustig 23
ancestor	Vorfahr *(m.)* (-en) 88
ancient	uralt 89
and	und 3
angel	Engel *(m.)* (-) 72
anger	Wut *(f.)* 60
angry (to be ~)	böse sein* 92
animal	Tier *(n.)* (-e) 73
anniversary (wedding ~)	Hochzeitstag *(m.)* (-e) 66
announce (to ~)	melden 47
annoy (to ~)	ärgern 93
another	noch ein *(m./n.)* / eine *(f.)* 16; ein/eine/ein anderer/andere/anderes *(m./f./n.)* 55
answer	Antwort *(f.)* (-en) 68; Lösung *(f.)* (-en) 72
answer (to ~)	antworten 83
answering machine	Anrufbeantworter *(m.)* (-) 12

655 • **sechshundertfünfundfünfzig**

anyone	jemand 34
anything	alles 34
anyway	sowieso 48; jedenfalls 99
anywhere	irgendwo 82
anywhere else	sonst irgendwo 82
apart (from)	außer 39
apartment	Wohnung *(f.)* (-en) 50
ape	Affe *(m.)* (-n) 88
apology	Entschuldigung *(f.)* (-en) 5
apparent	anscheinend 100
appeal to (to ~)	gefallen* 53
appear (to be) (to ~)	scheinen* 31
apple	Apfel *(m.)* (¨) 24
apple cider	Apfelwein *(m.)* (-e) 33
apple juice	Apfelsaft *(m.)* (¨-e) 24
application	Bewerbung *(f.)* (-en) 80
apply for/to (to ~)	sich bewerben* bei (+ *dat.*) 80
appointment	Termin *(m.)* (-e) 25; Verabredung *(f.)* (-en) 47
approximately	etwa 89
arduous	mühsam 65
area	Stelle *(f.)* (-n) 80
argument	Argument *(n.)* (-e) 61
arm	Arm *(m.)* (-e) 97
armchair	Sessel *(m.)* (-) 55
around	um 33
around (approximately)	ungefähr 57
arrange something (to ~)	etwas aus'machen 95
arrange to meet (to ~)	verabredet sein (*or* sich verabreden) 52
arrest (to ~)	verhaften 91
arrival	Ankunft *(f.)* (¨-e) 30
arrival time	Ankunftszeit *(f.)* (-en) 30
arrive (to ~)	kommen* 4; an'kommen* 20, 46
article	Bericht *(m.)* (-e) 87
as	wie 48; als 72; da 80; wo doch 97
as … as	so… wie 60
as if	als ob 95
ashamed (to be ~)	sich schämen 54
ask (to ~) (request)	bitten* 30
ask oneself whether (to ~)	sich fragen ob 76
ask someone for/about (to ~)	fragen jdn (*acc.*) nach (+ *dat.*) 38, 58
assistant	Geselle *(m.)* (-n) / Gesellin *(f.)* (-nen) 57
assure (to ~)	garantieren 75
astonishing	erstaunlich 74
at	in 2; an 16; bei (+ *dat.*) 34
at (+ time)	um 16
at all	gar 73

at all (none ~)	gar keins *(n.)* 73
at the	am (an dem) 20
attach (to ~)	binden* 54
attempt	Versuch *(m.)* (-e) 65
attention	Aufmerksamkeit *(f.)* (-en) 95
attention (caution)	Achtung *(f.)* (-) 16
August	August *(m.)* 22
aunt	Tante *(f.)* (-n) 39
autumn/fall	Herbst *(m.)* (-e) 28
available (to be ~)	Zeit haben* 12; zur Verfügung stehen 96
average	Durchschnitt *(m.)* (-e) 79
average (on ~)	im Durchschnitt, im Schnitt 79
award someone (to ~)	verleihen* 72
away	weg 52

B

baby	Baby *(n.)* (-s) 35
back	zurück 12
back then	damals 82
backside	Hintern *(m.)* (-) 96
bad	schlecht 31; schlimm 69
bad weather	Sauwetter *(n.)* 78
baffled	verwirrt 60
bag	Tasche *(f.)* (-n) 32
bakery	Bäckerei *(f.)* (-en) 100
balcony	Balkon *(m.)* (-s) 50
ball (to be on the ~)	am Ball bleiben* 99
band (musical)	Orchester *(n.)* (-) 23
bandage	Binde *(f.)* (-n) 54
banker	Bankier *(m.)* (-s) / Bankierin *(f.)* (-nen) 67
barbecue (to ~)	grillen 22
bargain	Schnäppchen *(n.)* (-) 62
baroque	barock 41
bathroom	Klo *(n.)* (-s) *(abb. of* Klosett) 45; Bad *(n.)* (¨-er) 50
battle	Schlacht *(f.)* (-en) 70
Bavarian (person)	Bayer *(m.)* (-n) / Bayerin *(f.)* (-nen) 75
Bavarian *(adj.)*	bayerisch 75
be (to ~)	sein* 1, 2, 14, GA11
be ...-ing (to ~)	beim (+ *infinitive used as a noun*) 59
be back (to ~)	zurück sein* 47
be that as it may	wie dem auch sei 97
be there (to ~)	nach'kommen* 78
beach	Strand *(m.)* (¨-e) 79
beaming	strahlend 85
bear	Bär *(m.)* (-en) 53
beat (to ~)	schlagen* 85

beat it (to ~) (clear off)	ab'hauen *(coll.)* 55
beautiful	schön 3
because	denn 54; weil 57; da 80
because (of this)	deshalb 79
because of you	euretwegen 100
become (to ~)	werden* 22, 51, 64, GA11
bed	Bett *(n.)* (-en) 56
bedroom	Schlafzimmer *(n.)* (-) 50
beer	Bier *(n.)* (-e) 8
beer (wheat ~)	Weißbier *(n.)* (-e) 75
before	vor 20; bevor 83
begin (to ~)	an'fangen* 45; beginnen* 63
beginner	Anfänger *(m.)* (-) / Anfängerin *(f.)* (-nen) 90
beginning	Anfang *(m.)* (¨-e) 88
behave oneself (to ~)	sich benehmen* 85
behind	zurück 12; hinter 54
believe (in) (to ~)	glauben (an + *acc.*) 74
believe (to ~)	glauben 20; meinen 67
belong to (to ~)	gehören (+ *dat.*) 74
below	unten 45
beret	Baskenmütze *(f.)* (-n) 72
Berlin inhabitant	Berliner *(m.)* (-) / Berlinerin *(f.)* (-nen) 64
besides	außer 39; außerdem 50
best (thing) (the ~)	das Beste 27
bet (to ~)	wetten 58
better	besser 27
between	zwischen 29; unter (+ *dat.*) 69
bicycle	Fahrrad *(n.)* (¨-er) 34
big	groß 1; dick 82
big shot	hohes Tier *(n.)* (-e) 90
big/bigger (to grow ~)	dick/dicker werden* 82
bike	Rad *(n.)* (¨-er) 34
bill (check)	Rechnung *(f.)* (-en) 61
bird	Vogel *(m.)* (¨) 82
birth	Geburt *(f.)* (-en) 65
birthday	Geburtstag *(m.)* (-e) 22
bit (a ~)	ein Stück *(n.)* 64
bite (to ~)	beißen* 32
black	schwarz 83
block (to ~)	blockieren 48
blonde	blond 36
bloom (to ~) (blossom)	blühen 82
blue	blau 46
blue tit	Blaumeise *(f.)* (-n) 97
board (to ~)	ein'steigen* 16
boat	Boot *(n.)* (-e) GA14

sechshundertachtundfünfzig • 658

boil (to ~)	kochen 59
book	Buch *(n.)* (¨-er) 28
book (to ~)	reservieren 61; buchen 62
booked	belegt 96
border	Grenze *(f.)* (-n) 79
bored (to be ~)	sich langweilen 76
boring	langweilig 76
born	geboren 51
borrow (to ~)	leihen* 92
boss	Chef *(m.)* (-s) / Chefin *(f.)* (-nen) 30
both	gleichzeitig 64; beide 72
bother (to ~)	stören 34
bottle	Flasche *(f.)* (-n) 44
bottom	Hintern *(m.)* (-) 96
box	Schachtel *(f.)* (-n) 57
boy	Junge *(m.)* (-n) 7
boyfriend	Freund *(m.)* (-e) 23
brave	mutig 74
Brazil	Brasilien *(n.)* 37
bread	Brot *(n.)* (-e) 4
bread roll	Brötchen *(n.)* (-) 4
break	Pause *(f.)* (-n) 4
break (to ~)	brechen* 49, 93; auf'schlagen* 85
break in (to ~)	ein'brechen* 93
breakfast	Frühstück *(n.)* (-e) 4
bridge	Brücke *(f.)* (-n) 94
brief	kurz 34
bright	hell 50
brilliant (ingenious)	genial 83
bring (to ~)	bringen* 8, 68
bring along (to ~)	mit'bringen* 23, 46
bring here (to ~)	her'bringen* 37
broadcast (to ~)	senden* 91
broken (to get/be ~)	kaputt gehen*/sein* 85
brother	Bruder *(m.)* (¨) 23
bunch	Strauß *(m.)* (¨-e) 92
burn (to ~)	brennen* 70
burst (to ~)	platzen 93
bus	Bus *(m.)* (-se) 59
business	Geschäft *(n.)* (-e) 10; Unternehmen *(f.)* (-) 89
business trip	Geschäftsreise *(f.)* (-n) 85
businessperson	Geschäftsmann *(m.)* (¨-er) / Geschäftsfrau *(f.)* (-en) 93
busy (telephone)	besetzt 66
busy (to be ~)	keine Zeit haben* 12
but	aber 6

but (conveying surprise)	denn 10; ja 32
but (rather)	sondern 30
buy (to ~)	kaufen 19
by	bei (+ *dat.*) 51; durch 64; von (+ *dat.*) 82
by ... -ing	indem 86
Bye for now!	Bis bald! 12
Bye!	Tschüs(s)! 12

C

cable	Kabel *(n.)* (-) 73
café	Café *(n.)* (-s) 4
cake	Kuchen *(m.)* (-) 27
cake/tart	Torte *(f.)* (-n) 57
calculate (to ~)	rechnen 61
calculation	Rechnung *(f.)* (-en) 61
calendar	Kalender *(m.)* (-) 25
call (to ~) (designate)	nennen* 68
call back (to ~)	zurück'rufen* 12
call out (to ~)	rufen* 58
call/ring someone (to ~)	an'rufen* 11
called/named (to be ~)	heißen* 3
calm	ruhig 60; Ruhe *(f.)* 93
calm (down) (to ~)	beruhigen 59
can	können* 26
candle	Kerze *(f.)* (-n) 90
capable	tüchtig 99
capital (funds)	Kapital *(n.)* (-) 65
capital city	Hauptstadt *(f.)* (¨-e) 27
captivating	spannend 76
car	Auto *(n.)* (-s), Wagen *(m.)* (-) 40
car mechanic	Automechaniker *(m.)* (-) / Automechanikerin *(f.)* (-nen) 67
card	Karte *(f.)* (-n) 85
care (about) (to not ~)	pfeifen* auf (+ *acc.*) 86
care (caution)	Vorsicht *(f.)* 13
care (to not ~)	egal sein* 48
care of oneself (to take ~)	sich in Acht nehmen* 69
career (successful ~)	Karriere *(f.)* (-n) 82
careful	vorsichtig 86
careful (to be ~)	sich in Acht nehmen* 69
Careful!	Vorsicht! 13; Achtung! 16
caretaker	Hausmeister *(m.)* (-) / Hausmeisterin *(f.)* (-nen) 69
case	Fall *(m.)* (¨-e) 76
case (in ~)	falls 57
case (in any ~)	auf alle Fälle 76; jedenfalls 99

sechshundertsechzig • 660

case (in that ~)	denn 15
castle	Schloss *(n.)* (¨-er) 82; Burg *(f.)* (-en) 100
cat	Katze *(f.)* (-en) 13
catch (to ~)	kriegen 40; fangen* 45
catch on (to ~)	kapieren 54; mit'kriegen 76
cathedral	Dom *(m.)* (-e) 33
cause	Ursache *(f.)* (-n) 15
cease (to ~)	auf'hören 51
ceiling	Decke *(f.)* (-n) 54
celebrate (to ~)	feiern 23
celebration	Fest *(n.)* (-e) 22
centre	Zentrum *(n.)* (*pl.* Zentren) 41
centre on (to ~)	sich drehen um (+ *acc.*) 57
century	Jahrhundert *(n.)* (-e) 68
certain	sicher 19
certainly	gewiss 89
chair	Stuhl *(m.)* (¨-e) 55
champagne	Champagner *(m.)* (-) 24
chance	Chance *(f.)* (-n) 88
chancellor	Kanzler *(m.)* (-) / Kanzlerin *(f.)* (-nen) 68
change (to ~)	sich ändern 39; wechseln 75; verändern 82
cheap	günstig 38; billig 40
check (to ~)	kontrollieren 30; nach'sehen* 44
checkout (cash register)	Kasse *(f.)* (-n) 24
cheeky	frech 48
cheese	Käse *(m.)* (-) 4
chef	Koch *(m.)* (¨-e) / Köchin *(f.)* (-nen) 59
child	Kind *(n.)* (-er) 6
chimpanzee	Schimpanse *(m.)* (-n) 88
Chinese (language)	Chinesisch 73
chips (fries)	Pommes *(pl.)* 9
chocolate	Schokolade *(f.)* (-n) 23
choice	Wahl *(f.)* (-en) 31
choke (to ~)	ersticken 58
Christmas	Weihnachten *(n.)* (-) 97
Christmas Eve	Heiligabend *(m.)* (-e) 97
church	Kirche *(f.)* (-n) 41
church tower	Kirchturm *(m.)* (¨-e) 100
cinema	Kino *(n.)* (-s) 74
city	Stadt *(f.)* (¨-e) 41
class	Klasse *(f.)* (-n) 40
classical period	Klassik *(f.)* (-en) 51
classmate	Studienkollege *(m.)* (-n) / Studienkollegin *(f.)* (-nen) 84
clear	klar 31
clear (to become ~)	sich auf'klären 99

clever	schlau 62
client	Kunde *(m.)* (-n) / Kundin *(f.)* (-nen) 65
climate	Klima *(n.)* (-s) 97
climb (to ~)	klettern 97
clock/o'clock	Uhr *(f.)* (-en) 16
close	nah(e) 37
close (to ~)	schließen* 10; zu'machen 74
closed	geschlossen 10
closure	Schluss *(m.)* (¨-e) 29
coast	Küste *(f.)* (-n) 50
coat	Mantel *(m.)* (¨) 56
coat rack	Garderobe *(f.)* (-n) 56
cocoa	Kakao *(m.)* (-s) 57
coffee	Kaffee *(m.)* (-s) 4
coffee pot or press	Kaffeekanne *(f.)* (-n) 8
coffee pot or press (small ~)	Kännchen *(n.)* (-) 8
coffee with milk	Milchkaffee *(m.)* (-s) 8
cold	kalt 8, 57
cold *(noun)*	Kälte *(f.)* 78
collaboration	Mitarbeit *(f.)* (-) 80
collar	Kragen *(m.)* (-) 93
colleague	Kollege *(m.)* (-n) / Kollegin *(f.)* (-nen) 6
Cologne	Köln 20
colour	Farbe *(f.)* (-n) 74
comb	Kamm *(m.)* (¨-e) 65
comb (to ~)	kämmen 68
come (to ~)	kommen* 4, 14
come along/with (to ~)	mit'kommen* 12
come back (to ~)	zurück'kommen* 12, 25, 47
come from (to ~) (originate from)	stammen (aus) 68
come home (to ~)	kommen* nach Hause 11
Come on!	Los! 55
company	Firma *(f.)* (*pl.* Firmen) 75; Unternehmen *(f.)* (-) 80
complain to (to ~)	sich beschweren bei GA16
complete	ganz, total 37
compose (to ~)	komponieren 68
comprehensible/ comprehensibly	verständlich 61
comprehension	Verständnis *(n.)* 32
computer	Computer *(m.)* (-) 25
concern	Sorge *(f.)* (-n) 52
concern (to ~)	sich handeln um (+ *acc.*) 90
concert	Konzert *(n.)* (-e) 53
conclusion	Abschluss *(m.)* (¨-e) 81
concrete	konkret 73

sechshundertzweiundsechzig • 662

conduct (to ~)	durch'führen* 88
confectioner	Konditor *(m.)* (-en) / Konditorin *(f.)* (-nen) 57
confidential	vertraulich 69
confuse (to ~) (baffle)	verwirren 60
confuse (to ~) (mistake)	verwechseln (mit) 74
confused	verwirrt 60
confusion (mistake)	Verwechslung *(f.)* (-en) 77
congratulate on (to ~)	gratulieren jdm (*dat.*) zu (+ *dat.*) 38
congratulations	Glückwunsch *(m.)* (-e) 89
connection	Anschluss *(m.)* (¨-e) 20; Zusammenhang *(m.)* (¨-e) 88
consist of (to ~)	bestehen* aus GA16
construct (to ~)	bauen 57
content	Inhalt *(m.)* (-e) 57
continuation	Fortsetzung *(f.)* (-en) 52
continue (to ~)	weiter'gehen* 33; weiter'machen 99
continue to (do something) (to ~)	weiter (+ *verb*) 17
contrary (on the ~)	sondern 30
contrast (in ~)	dagegen 67
convenient (to be ~)	passen 80
conversation	Gespräch *(n.)* (-e) 5
convince (to ~)	überzeugen 61
convincing	überzeugend 61
cook	Koch *(m.)* (¨-e) / Köchin *(f.)* (-nen) 67
cook (to ~)	kochen 59
cooked meat(s)	Wurst *(f.)* (¨-e) 4
cool	kühl 44
cope with (to ~)	es schaffen 29
cordial	herzlich 51
correct	richtig 73; anständig 85
correct (to be ~)	stimmen 40
cost (to ~)	kosten 50
count (to ~)	zählen 60; rechnen 61
country	Land *(n.)* (¨-er) 5
couple	Paar *(n.)* (-e) 60
courage	Mut *(m.)* 99
court	Hof *(m.)* (¨-e) 20; Gericht *(n.)* (-e) 93
cow	Kuh *(f.)* (¨-e) 63
crab	Krabbe *(f.)* (-n) 13
crash (to ~)	ab'stürzen 62
crazy	verrückt 32
crazy (to be ~)	spinnen* 55
crazy (to go ~)	über'schnappen 37; verrückt werden* 79
cream	Sahne *(f.)* 8
credit card	Kreditkarte *(f.)* (-n) 12

crooked	krumm 58
cross (to ~)	überqueren 34
cross one's fingers (to ~)	die Daumen drücken 79
cross the street/bridge etc. (to ~)	über die Straße/Brücke gehen* 94
cry (to ~)	weinen 98
cry out (to ~)	schreien* 49
cup	Tasse *(f.)* (-n) 8
cupboard	Schrank *(m.)* (¨-e) 44
custom	Sitte *(f.)* (-n) 5
customer	Kunde *(m.)* (-n) / Kundin *(f.)* (-nen) 25
cut (to ~)	schneiden* 79
cute	süß 28
cycle (to ~)	Fahrrad fahren* 34; Rad fahren*, radeln 100

D

Dad	Vati 18; Papa *(m.)* (-s) 48
daily life	Alltag *(m.)* 73
daisy	Margerite *(f.)* (-n) 92
Damn!	Mist! 9
dance (to)	tanzen 86
danger (in ~)	in Gefahr 61
dangerous	gefährlich 32
dare (to ~)	wagen 69
dark	dunkel 33
dark *(noun)*	Dunkel *(n.)* 76
darkness	Dunkelheit *(f.)* (-en) 76
darling	Liebling *(m.)* (-e) 26; Schatz *(m.)* (¨-e) 66
Darn!	Verflixt! 29
date	Termin *(m.)* (-e) 25
daughter	Tochter *(f.)* (¨) 81
day	Tag *(m.)* (-e) 1
dead	tot 57
dead (to drop ~)	tot um'fallen* 60
deadline	Termin *(m.)* (-e) 25
deadly serious	todernst 85
deal	Schnäppchen *(n.)* (-) 62
dear	lieb 18; teuer 93
dear (address in a letter)	geehrter/geehrte/geehrtes *(m./f./n.)* 80
dear (address in a speech)	Verehrter/Verehrte/Verehrtes *(m./f.&pl./n.)* 91
death	Tod *(m.)* (-e) 83
debt	Schuld *(f.)* (-en) 83
decapitate (to ~)	köpfen 85
December	Dezember *(m.)* 44
decent	anständig 85
decide (to ~)	beschließen* 71; entscheiden* 86

sechshundertvierundsechzig • 664

decorate (to ~)	schmücken GA11
deep	tief 58
defeat (to ~)	schlagen* 70
degree	Grad *(m.)* (-e) 57
delicious	köstlich 27
deliver (to ~)	bringen* 46
dentist	Zahnarzt *(m.)* (¨-e) / Zahnärztin *(f.)* (-nen) 50
depart (to ~)	ab'fahren* 16
department	Abteilung *(f.)* (-en) 80
depend on (to ~)	ab'hängen* von GA16
desire	Lust *(f.)* (¨-e) 26
desire (to ~)	wünschen 1
desk	Schreibtisch *(m.)* (-e) 72
desperate	verzweifelt 54
dessert	Nachspeise *(f.)* (-n), Nachtisch *(m.)* (-e) 27
destruction	Zerstörung *(f.)* (-en) 64
detain (to ~)	zurück'halten* 86
detective film/novel	Krimi *(abb. of* Kriminalfilm/ Kriminalroman*) (m.)* (-s) 76
detour	Abstecher *(m.)* (-) 100
devastate (to ~)	verwüsten 91
devil	Teufel *(m.)* (-) 90
dialect	Dialekt *(m.)* (-e), Mundart *(f.)* (-en) 89
die (to ~)	sterben* 51
die of laughter (to ~)	sich tot'lachen 58
died	gestorben (sterben*) 51
difference	Unterschied *(m.)* (-e) 29
difficult	schwierig 48; schwer 57
diligent	fleißig 99
dinner	Abendessen *(n.)* (-) 47
diploma (qualification)	Diplom *(n.)* (-e) 65
direct	direkt 85
direct (to ~)	lenken 46
director (film/theatre ~)	Regisseur *(m.)* (-e) / Regisseurin *(f.)* (-nen) 72
disagree on/about (to ~)	sich streiten über/um (+ *acc.*) 83
disappointed	enttäuscht 66
discover (to ~)	entdecken 88
discuss/converse (to ~)	sich unterhalten* 69
disgusting	eklig 75
dish (food)	Speise *(f.)* (-n) 27
disposition (availability)	Verfügung *(f.)* (-en) 96
distant	fern 82
distinguished	vornehm 86
distress	Leid *(n.)* (-en) 51
divide (to ~)	teilen 64
divided into (to be ~)	sich teilen 35

do (to ~)	machen 9; tun* 32
do without (to ~)	verzichten auf (+ *acc.*) 75
do/just (+ verb) (used for emphasis)	doch (+ *verb*) 30
doctor (medical)	Arzt *(m.)* ("-e) / Ärztin *(f.)* (-nen) 50
doctor/Dr (title)	Doktor (Herr *m.* / Frau *f.*) (-en) 25
dog	Hund *(m.)* (-e) 12
doll	Puppe *(f.)* (-n) 56
door	Tür *(f.)* (-en) 16
double room	Doppelzimmer *(n.)* (-) 96
doubt something (to ~)	zweifeln an GA16
down	herunter, runter (*abb. of* herunter) 43; unten 59
downstairs	unten 45
draw (to ~)	zeichnen GA10
dream	Traum *(m.)* ("-e) 53
dream (to ~)	träumen 82
dress	Kleid *(n.)* (-er) 74
dressed (to get ~)	sich an'ziehen* 59
drink (beverage)	Getränk *(n.)* (-e) 8
drink (to ~)	trinken* 4
drive (to ~)	fahren* 16
drive around (to ~)	herum'fahren* (*or* rum'fahren*) 52
drive away (to ~)	weg'fahren* 48
drunk (inebriated)	betrunken 34
dumpling	Kloß *(m.)* ("-e), Knödel *(m.)* (-) 78
dung	Mist *(m.)* (-) 9
duty	Dienst *(m.)* (-e) 30
dwarf	Zwerg *(m.)* (-e) 68

E

ear	Ohr *(n.)* (-en) 76
early	früh 30
earn (to ~)	sich verdienen 31, 88
earth	Erde *(f.)* (-n) 97
east	Osten *(m.)* 41
east(ern)	ost 64
easy	einfach 31; leicht 54
eat (to ~)	essen* 8, 47
economy	Wirtschaft *(f.)* (-en) 90
education (learning)	Bildung *(f.)* 68
effort	Bemühen *(n.)* (-) 51; Anstrengung *(f.)* (-en) 66; Fleiß *(m.)* (-) 99
effort (to make an ~)	sich an'strengen 66
egg	Ei *(n.)* (-er) 4
electrical engineering	Elektrotechnik *(f.)* 81
electricity (current)	Strom *(m.)* ("-e) 90

else (or ~)	sonst 95
elsewhere	sonstwo (*abb. of* sonst irgendwo) 82
emperor/empress	Kaiser *(m.)* (-) / Kaiserin *(f.)* (-nen) 68
employ (to ~)	an'stellen 81
employed (to be ~)	angestellt sein* 81
employee	Angestellte (der *m.* / die *f.*) (-n) 81
empty	leer 53
end	Schluss *(m.)* (¨-e) 29
end (at the ~)	am Ende 68
end (to ~)	auf'hören (zu) 51
end (to come to an ~)	beendet werden* 85
end(ing)	Ende *(n.)* (-n) 13, 48
enemy	Feind *(m.)* (-e) 83
engaged (occupied)	besetzt 66
English (language)	Englisch 73
English (person)	Engländer *(m.)* (-) / Engländerin *(f.)* (-nen) 50
enjoy (to ~)	gefallen* 53
Enjoy your meal!	Mahlzeit! 78
enough	genug 9
enough (to have ~)	genug haben* 46
enough to ... (it is ~)	es ist zu (+ *infinitive*) 79
enquire (to ~)	sich erkundigen GA16
enraged	wütend 60
entrance	Einfahrt *(f.)* (-en) 48
environment	Umwelt *(f.)* (-en) 40
environmentally friendly	umweltfreundlich 40
escape (to ~)	entkommen* 43
especially as	umso mehr/weniger als 95
eternal	ewig 88
euro	Euro *(m.)* (-s) 9
Europe	Europa *(n.)* 37
even	sogar 37
even so (all the same)	trotzdem 46
even though	obwohl 72; auch/selbst wenn 76; wo doch 97
evening	Abend *(m.)* (-e) 2
evening (this ~)	heute Abend 11
every	jeder/jede/jedes *(m./f.&pl./n.)* 30
every time	jedes Mal 76
everyday	alltäglich 81
everyone	alle 23; jeder/jede/jedes *(m./f.&pl./n.)* 65; alle Welt 79
everything	alles 31
everywhere	überall 44
evil	böse 92
evolution	Entwicklung *(f.)* (-en) 97
exact	genau 20

667 • **sechshundertsiebenundsechzig**

example	Beispiel *(n.)* (-e) 75
example (for ~)	zum Beispiel 75
excellent	ausgezeichnet 27
except (for)	außer 39
exception	Ausnahme *(m.)* (¨-e) 62
exceptional	außergewöhnlich 64
exchange	Austausch *(m.)* (-e) 81
excite (to ~)	begeistern 73
excited	aufgeregt 18
Excuse (me) …	Entschuldigung … 5
excuse (to ~)	sich entschuldigen 5, 81
Excuse me? (Sorry?)	Wie bitte? 71
exercise	Übung *(f.)* (-en) 1
exhaustion	Erschöpfung *(f.)* 60
exhibitor (at a show)	Schausteller *(m.)* (-) / Schaustellerin *(f.)* (-nen) 87
exit	Ausfahrt *(f.)* (-en) 48; Ausgang *(m.)* (¨-e) 87
expect (to ~)	rechnen mit 97
expense	Auslage *(f.)* (-en) 80
expensive	teuer 23
experience (to ~)	erleben 64
experiment	Experiment *(n.)* (-e) 88
explain (to ~)	erklären 71
extinguish (to ~)	löschen GA1
extremely	höchst 90
eye	Auge *(n.)* (-n) 54

F

face	Gesicht *(n.)* (-er) 54
fact (in ~)	nämlich 85
fall (to ~)	fallen* 24, 55, 64; stürzen 62
fall asleep (to ~)	ein'schlafen* 71
fall down (to ~)	runter'fallen* 43
fall of the Berlin Wall	Mauerfall *(m.)* 64
fall on (to ~)	fallen* auf (+ *acc.*) 81
fall over (to ~)	um'fallen* 60
family	Familie *(f.)* (-n) 23
famous	berühmt 51
fantastic	fantastisch 18
fantastic (dreamlike)	traumhaft 53
fantastic (really ~)	große Klasse 40
far	weit 18; fern 55; entfernt 100
far (from)	weit (von) 55
farmer	Bauer *(m.)* (-n) / Bäuerin *(f.)* (-nen) 75
father	Vater *(m.)* (¨) 18
Father Christmas	Weihnachtsmann *(m.)* 97

favour	Liebesdienst *(m.)* (-e) 88
favourable	günstig 38
fear	Angst *(f.)* (¨-e) 59, 94
feather	Feder *(f.)* (-n) 74
fed up (to be ~)	die Nase voll haben* 54
Federal Government	Bundesregierung *(f.)* (-en) 64
Federal Republic	Bundesrepublik *(f.)* (-en) 64
feed (to ~)	füttern 97
feel (to ~)	sich fühlen 89
feel like (doing something) (to ~)	Lust haben* (zu) 26
female (animal)	Weibchen *(n.)* (-) 88
fervent	heiß 51
festive	festlich 38
fetch (to ~)	holen 24
few	wenig 65
few (a ~)	ein paar 60
field	Feld *(n.)* (-er) 58
field (of crops)	Acker *(m.)* (¨) 59
fight	Schlägerei *(f.)* (-en) 76
fight (to ~)	kämpfen GA16
filled	gefüllt 78; besetzt 80
film	Film *(m.)* (-e) 53
final	endgültig 98
finally	zum Schluss 33; endlich 43; schließlich 52
finance (to ~)	finanzieren 83
find (to ~)	finden* 19, 58
fine	gut 8
fine (all right)	in Ordnung 52
fine (penalty)	Strafe *(f.)* (-n) 93
finished (to be ~)	zu Ende sein* 67
fire	Feuer *(n.)* (-) GA1
firm	Firma *(f.)* (*pl.* Firmen) 47
first	zuerst 33; erst 53
first (at ~)	zuerst 74
first (the ~)	der/die/das erste *(m./f./n.)* 46
first course (starter/appetizer)	Vorspeise *(f.)* (-n) 27
fit (well) (to ~)	passen 80
flat	Wohnung *(f.)* (-en) 50
flesh	Fleisch *(n.)* (-) 74
flexible	flexibel 78
flight	Flug *(m.)* (¨-e) 62
flood	Flut *(f.)* (-en) 91
floor (storey)	Etage *(f.)* (-n), Stock *(m.)* (*pl.* Stockwerke) 90
flour	Mehl *(n.)* (-e) 98
flow (to ~)	fließen* 73

flower	Blume *(f.)* (-n) 82
flowing	fließend 73
fluent	fließend 73
flute	Flöte *(f.)* (-n) 68
fly (to ~)	fliegen* 25; los'fliegen* 62
fly away (to ~)	weg'fliegen* 43
fly back (to ~)	zurück'fliegen* 83
folktale	Märchen *(n.)* (-) 58
follow (to ~)	folgen 52, 75; nach'kommen* 78
following	folgend 68
food	Essen *(n.)* (-) 95
fool	Dummer *(m.)* (-n) 88
foot	Fuß *(m.)* (¨-e) 33
foot (on ~)	zu Fuß 33
for	für (+ *acc.*) 2; zu (+ *dat.*) 37; aus (+ *dat.*) 48
forbid (to ~)	verbieten* 34
forbidden	verboten 34
forego (to ~)	verzichten auf (+ *acc.*) 86
foreign	fremd 73
forest	Wald *(m.)* (¨-er) 65
forget (to ~)	vergessen* 16
forgive (to ~)	verzeihen* 69
form (on ~) (well/fit)	in Form 96
formal	festlich 38
fortunately	glücklicherweise 10
forward to (to look ~)	sich freuen auf 66
found (to ~)	gründen 89
France	Frankreich *(n.)* 30
free	frei 2
free (of charge)	kostenlos 96
freedom	Freiheit *(f.)* (-en) GA1
fresh	frisch 63
fret (to ~)	sich auf'regen 79
Friday	Freitag *(m.)* (-e) 25
friend	Freund *(m.)* (-e), Freundin *(f.)* (-nen) 3
friendly	freundlich 40
fright	Schreck *(m.)* (-e) 94
fright (to get a ~)	erschrecken* 100
from	aus (+ *dat.*) 3; von (+ *dat.*) 33; an 54
from (movement towards speaker)	her 48
from ... to	von ... bis 74
front (at the ~)	vorn 45
fruit-pressing plant	Kelterei *(f.)* (-en) 89
full	voll 25
full (fed to satisfaction)	satt 27

full board	Vollpension *(f.)* 62
fun	lustig 23; Spaß *(m.)* (¨-e) 99
fun (to be ~)	Spaß machen 99
funny	lustig 23; komisch 76
furrow	Furche *(f.)* (-n) 59
further	weiter *(adv.)* / weitere *(adj./pl.)* 80
fury	Wut *(f.)* 60
future	Zukunft *(f.)* (¨-e) 80
future *(adj.)*	zukünftig 38

G

game	Spiel *(n.)* (-e) 31
garden	Garten *(m.)* (¨) 23
gasoline	Benzin *(n.)* (-e) 29
gate	Tor *(n.)* (-e) 68
gather (to ~) (assemble)	versammeln 90
general (common)	allgemein 68
generation	Generation *(f.)* (-en) 51
genetic make-up	Erbgut *(n.)* 88
gentleman	Herr *(m.)* (-en) 51
gentlemen (address)	meine Herren 33
German (language)	Deutsch *(n.)* 1
German (person)	Deutscher *(m.)* / Deutsche *(f.&pl.)* 50
German (standard ~)	Hochdeutsch *(n.)* 89
Germany	Deutschland *(n.)* 64
get (to ~)	kriegen 40
get (to ~) (fetch)	ab'holen 20
get (to ~) (receive)	bekommen* 33
get (to ~) (understand)	mit'kriegen 76
get (to go and ~)	holen 24
get in/on (to ~)	ein'steigen* 16
get it (to ~)	kapieren 54
get lost (to ~)	ab'hauen *(coll.)* 55
get on/along (to ~)	sich verstehen* 93
get out/off (to ~)	aus'steigen* 16
get up (to ~)	auf'stehen* 30, 55
get worked up (to ~)	sich auf'regen 79
get/become ... (to ~)	werden* *(+ adj./adv.)* 23, 60
girl	Mädchen *(n.)* (-) 36
girlfriend	Freundin *(f.)* (-nen) 23
give (to ~)	geben* 16, 22
give up (to ~)	auf'geben* 99
glad	froh 53
glad (to be ~)	sich freuen 20
gladly	gern 8
glance	Blick *(m.)* (-e) 86

glass	Glas *(n.)* (¨er) 33
gleaming (mirrorlike)	spiegelblank 82
go (to ~)	gehen* 6; laufen* 18
go (to ~) (by means of transport)	fahren* 41; los'fahren* 59
go as planned (to ~)	klappen 90
go away (to ~)	weg'gehen* 52
go back (to ~)	zurück'gehen* 12
go down (to ~)	runter'gehen* 43
go out(side) (to ~)	raus'gehen* 46, 78
go there (to ~)	hin'gehen* 31, 37
go there (to ~) (by means of transport)	hin'fahren* 37
go through a red light (to ~)	durch'fahren* 94
god	Gott *(m.)* (¨-er) 29
good	gut 1
Good afternoon!	Guten Tag! 1
Good evening!	Guten Abend! 2
Good morning!	Guten Morgen! 6
Good night!	Gute Nacht! 43
Goodbye!	Auf Wiedersehen! 5
Goodbye! (on the telephone)	Auf Wiederhören! 5
goodness! (My ~)	Na so was! 87
grab (to ~)	schnappen 62
graduation	Abschluss *(m.)* (¨-e) 81
grandfather/grandmother	Großvater *(m.)* (¨) / Großmutter *(f.)* (¨) 39
grandparents	Großeltern *(f. pl.)* 68
grateful	dankbar 89
great	groß 40
Great!	Prima!, Toll! 20; Klasse! 40
great-grandfather/ great-grandmother	Urgroßvater *(m.)* (¨) / Urgroßmutter *(f.)* (¨) 89
greedy	gierig 86
Greek (person)	Grieche *(m.)* (-n) / Griechin *(f.)* (-nen) 68
green	grün 94
greet (to ~)	grüßen 18; begrüßen 93; empfangen* 100
greeting	Gruß *(m.)* (¨-e) 18
ground	Boden *(m.)* (¨) 83
growl (to ~)	knurren 78
guarantee (to ~)	garantieren 75
guard (to ~)	bewachen 90
guess (to ~)	raten* 72; ahnen 87
guest	Gast *(m.)* (¨-e) 87
guys	Jungs 90

H

hair	Haar *(n.)* (-e) 68
hairdresser	Frisör *(n.)* (-e) / Frisörin *(f.)* (-nen) 50

sechshundertzweiundsiebzig • 672

hairdressing salon	Frisörsalon *(m.)* (-s) 65
half	halb 52; Hälfte *(f.)* (-n) 76
half an hour	halbe Stunde 48
hall	Saal *(m.)* (*pl.* Säle) 90
hand	Hand *(f.)* (¨-e) 54
handlebars	Lenkrad *(n.)* (¨-er) 100
hang (on/from) (to ~)	hängen* (an + *dat.*) 54
hangover	Kater *(m.)* (-) 54
happen (to ~)	passieren 46; geschehen* 76
happiness	Glück *(n.)* (-e) 1
happy	glücklich 10
happy (to be ~)	sich freuen 20
hard (arduous)	schwer 71
hard (solid)	hart 85
hare	Hase *(m.)* (-n) 58
hat/cap	Mütze *(f.)* (-n) 72; Hut *(m.)* (¨-e) 86
hat/cap (little ~)	Hütchen *(n.)* (-) 86
hate (to ~)	hassen 62
have (to ~)	haben* 2, 9, 14, GA11
have something done (to ~)	lassen* (+ *verb*) 26; machen lassen* 88
have to (to ~)	müssen* 10, 30, 35
he	er 3; der 32
head	Haupt *(n.)* (¨-er) 27
head (body part)	Kopf *(m.)* (¨-e) 54
head (of a department)	Leiter *(m.)* (-) / Leiterin *(f.)* (-nen) 80
health	Gesundheit *(f.)* 65
hear (something) in (to ~)	hören an (+ *dat.*) 75
hear (to ~)	hören GA11
heart	Herz *(n.)* (-en) 18
heat	Hitze *(f.)* (-n) 22
heatwave	Hitzewelle *(f.)* (-n) 22
heaven	Himmel *(m.)* (-) 24
heavy	schwer 57
hedgehog	Igel *(m.)* (-) 58
hell	Hölle *(f.)* (-n) 67
hello	hallo 11
help	Hilfe *(f.)* (-n) 45
help (to ~)	helfen* 38
help someone (to ~)	helfen* jdm *(dat.)* 59
her	ihr *(m./n.)* / ihre *(f.&pl.)* 23; sie 24
here	hier 4; da 6; hierhin 45
here (movement towards speaker)	her 37
here (this way)	hierher 37
hesitate (to ~)	zögern 64
hide (to ~)	sich verstecken 59

673 • **sechshundertdreiundsiebzig**

high	hoher/hohe/hohes *(m./f./n.) (attributive adj.)* 82
high(ly)	hoch 54, 57
him	ihn *(acc. of* er) 24
him (to ~)	ihm *(dat. of* er) 37
his	sein *(m./n.)* / seine *(f.&pl.)* 23
hiss (to ~)	zischen 21
historian	Historiker *(m.)* (-) / Historikerin *(f.)* (-nen) 83
history	Geschichte *(f.)* (-n) 41
hit (to ~)	schlagen* 55
hold back (to ~)	zurück'halten* 32
hold in check (to ~)	in Schach halten* 90
hold up (to ~)	auf'halten* 91
holiday	Urlaub *(m.)* (-e) 37
holiday(s)	Ferien *(pl.)* 13
holy	heilig 97
home	Haus *(n.)* (¨-er) 53
home (at ~)	zu Haus(e) 11
home (going/coming ~)	nach Haus(e) 11
homemade	hausgemacht 78
homework	Hausaufgaben *(pl.)* 90
honour	Ehre *(f.)* (-n) 72
honour (to ~)	ehren 80
hope (to ~)	hoffen 25, 45
hopefully	hoffentlich 45
horror	Schreck *(m.)* (-e) 94
horse	Pferd *(n.)* (-e) 68
hot	heiß 7
hot chocolate	Trinkschokolade *(f.)* (-n) 8
hotel	Hotel *(n.)* (-s) 2
hour	Stunde *(f.)* (-n) 17
house	Haus *(n.)* (¨-er) 11
how	wie 5; woher 81
How are you?	Wie geht's? 66
How do you like ...?	Wie gefällt dir…? 76
How long?	Wie lange? 62
how many	wie viele 61
how much	wie viel 9, 61
How old are you?	Wie alt bist du? 22
however	dagegen 60; allerdings 74; jedoch 80
human being	Mensch *(m.)* (-en) 46
humanity	Menschheit *(f.)* 88
humankind	Mensch *(m.)* (-en) 17
hunger	Hunger *(m.)* 19
hungry (to be ~)	Hunger haben* 19
hurry up (to ~)	sich beeilen 71
Hurry up!	Los! 55

sechshundertvierundsiebzig • 674

hurt (to ~)	verletzen 58
hurts (that ~)	das tut weh 32
husband	Mann *(m.)* (¨-er) 23; Ehemann *(m.)* (¨-er) 66
husky	rauchig 72

I

I	ich 2
I see!	Ach so! 15
ice	Eis *(n.)* (-) 57
ice cream	Eis *(n.)* (-) 57
idea	Idee *(f.)* (-n) 26; Ahnung *(f.)* (-en) 87
identical	identisch 88
idiot	Dummer *(m.)* (-n) 88; Idiot *(m.)* (-en) / Idiotin *(f.)* (-nen) 100
if	wenn 32; falls 83
ill	krank 83
imagine (to ~)	sich vor'stellen (+ *dat.*) 62
immediate	umgehend 96
immediately	sofort 4; gleich 6
important	bedeutend 51; wichtig 73
impossible	unmöglich 77
impressive	beeindruckend 74
in	in 2; rein (*abb. of* herein/hinein) 52
in order to	um… zu (+ *infinitive*) 50
in the	im (in dem) 2
included	inbegriffen 62
inclusive	inbegriffen 62
inclusive (all ~)	pauschal 96
increase (to ~)	zunehmen 97
indeed	in der Tat 81
independent	selbstständig 81
indifferent	gleichgültig 72
influence	Einfluss *(n.)* (¨-e) 51
inform (to ~)	informieren 80
information	Auskunft *(f.)* (¨-e) 15
information technology (IT)	Informatik *(f.)* 80
inheritance	Erbe *(n.)* 88
injustice	Ungerechtigkeit *(f.)* (-en) 72; Unrecht *(n.)* (-) 73
insane	geisteskrank 83
inside	drinnen 78; innen 82
insist on (to ~)	bestehen* auf GA16
insolent	frech 48
inspect (to ~)	kontrollieren 30
intelligent	klug 51
intention	Absicht *(f.)* (-en) 86
interested in (to be ~)	sich interessieren für (+ *acc.*) 80

675 • **sechshundertfünfundsiebzig**

interesting	interessant 36
interrupt (to ~)	unterbrechen GA14
interval (intermission)	Pause *(f.)* (-n) 45
interview	Gespräch *(n.)* (-e) 80
interview (job ~)	Vorstellungsgespräch *(n.)* (-e) 81
into	in 2
introduce (to ~)	sich vor'stellen (+ *acc.*) 37, 62
invent (to ~)	erfinden* 57, 68
invite (to ~)	ein'laden* 23
iron *(adj.)*	eisern 68
Isn't it? Doesn't it? Aren't you? etc. (question tag)	Nicht wahr? 40
it	's (*abb. of* es) 12
it *(f.)*	sie 24; die 32
it *(m.)*	er, ihn (*acc. of* er) 24; der 32
it *(m./n.)* (to ~)	ihm (*dat. of* er) 37
it *(n.)*	es 4; das 32
Italian (language)	Italienisch *(n.)* 73
Italy	Italien *(n.)* 30
its *(f.)*	ihr *(m.,/n.,)* / ihre *(f.&pl.)* 23
its *(m./n.)*	sein *(m./n.)* / seine *(f.&pl.)* 23

J

jam/block (to ~)	verstopfen 52
job	Arbeitsstelle *(f.)* (-n) 80
journey	Reise *(f.)* (-n) 16
juice	Saft *(m.)* (¨-e) 24
June	Juni *(m.)* 46
just	einfach 71
just (merely)	erst 74
just (now)	gerade 47
just ... -ed	gerade (+ *simple past verb*) 87
just as	ebenso 63
justice	Gerechtigkeit *(f.)* 72

K

keep (to ~)	bewahren 93
kilogram	Kilo *(n.)* (-s) (*abb. of* Kilogramm) 9
kilometer	Kilometer *(m.)* (-) 29
kind	lieb 18
king	König *(m.)* (-e) 52
kiss	Kuss *(m.)* (¨-e) 16
kitchen	Küche *(f.)* (-n) 50
know (to ~)	wissen* 22, 30, 31
know (to ~) (be familiar with)	kennen* 32
know (to get to ~)	kennen* lernen 41

know how to (to ~)	können* 29
known	bekannt 69

L

lack (to ~)	fehlen 65
ladies (address)	meine Damen 33
lady	Dame *(f.)* (-n) 33
lake	See *(m.)* (-n) 83
lamp	Lampe *(f.)* (-n) 43
land	Land *(n.)* (¨-er) 57
language	Sprache *(f.)* (-n) 73
large	groß 57
last	letzter/letzte/letztes *(m./f./n.)* 40; zuletzt 86
last (at ~)	endlich 32
late	spät 6
later	später 12
later (after that)	danach 79
latest (at the ~)	spätestens 71
laugh (to ~)	lachen 37
laughter	Lachen *(n.)* 58
law	Gesetz *(n.)* (-e) 94
law (at university)	Jura *(m.)* 51
law (the ~)	Recht *(n.)* 73
lay (something down) (to ~)	legen 54
lay/set the table (to ~)	den Tisch decken 91
lead (to ~)	leiten 89
leading role	Hauptrolle *(f.)* (-n) 72
learn (to ~)	lernen 1
least (at ~)	wenigstens 57; mindestens 72
leather	Leder *(n.)* (-) 75
leave (behind) (to ~)	hinterlassen* 12; lassen* 26
leave (to ~)	lassen* 12; ab'fahren* 16; weg'gehen* 52; los (+ *modal verb*) 71
leave (to ~) (desert)	verlassen* GA13
left (on the ~)	links 15
leg	Bein *(n.)* (-e) 58
legacy	Erbe *(m.)* 88
lend (to ~)	leihen*, verleihen* 92
lesson	Lektion *(f.)* (-en) 1
let (to ~) (permit)	lassen* (+ *verb*) 32
let someone do something (to ~)	machen lassen* 88
let someone know (to ~)	Bescheid sagen (*or* geben*) 58
Let's go!	Los! 55
letter	Brief *(m.)* (-e) 39
library	Bibliothek *(f.)* (-en) 56

lid	Deckel *(m.)* (-) 57
lie	Lüge *(f.)* (-n) 69
lie (to ~)	liegen* 44
life	Leben *(n.)* (-) 51
lifestyle	Lebensart *(f.)* (-en) 75
lift (to ~)	heben* 86
lift/take off (to ~)	ab'heben* 86
light	Licht *(n.)* (-er) 43; Schein *(m.)* (-e) 96
light (to ~)	an'zünden 90
like	wie 46
like (doing something) (to ~)	gern (+ *verb*) 62
like (to ~)	mögen* 4, 23, 35; gefallen* 40
limitation	Begrenzung *(f.)* (-en) 79
line (stroke)	Strich *(m.)* (-e) 61
line (to stand in ~)	Schlange stehen* 24
link (to ~)	binden* 54
listen (to ~)	hören 34
litre of beer	Maß *(f.)* (-) 87
little	wenig 30
little (a ~)	ein bisschen 18; ein wenig 30; etwas 61
live (to ~)	leben 13; wohnen 37
lively	lebhaft 53
living room	Wohnzimmer *(n.)* (-) 50
located	gelegen (liegen*) 50
located (to be ~)	liegen* 41
logical	logisch 76
long (for ~)	lang(e) 22
long as (as ~)	solange GA18
long time (a ~)	lang(e) 29
long time (in a ~)	seit langem 76
long time since (a ~)	schon lange 53
look (to ~)	aus'sehen* 18; gucken *(coll.)* 36; sehen* 37; schauen 38
look (to ~) (verify)	nach'sehen* 44
look after (to ~)	sich kümmern um (+ *acc.*) 81
look at (to ~)	an'sehen* 10
look down (to ~)	runter'gucken 43
look for (to ~)	suchen 19
Look!	Sieh da! 87
lorry	Lastwagen *(m.)* (-) 94
lose (to ~)	verlieren* 54, 96
lost	verloren 72
loud	laut 34
love	Liebe *(f.)* (-n) 74
love (to ~)	lieben 16
lovely	wunderschön 50

lover	Liebhaber *(m.)* (-) / Liebhaberin *(f.)* (-nen) 67
lover (enthusiast)	Freund *(m.)* (-e), Freundin *(f.)* (-nen) 73
luck	Glück *(n.)* (-e) 1
luck (bad ~)	Pech *(n.)* 39
lucky	glücklich 10
lucky (to be ~)	Glück haben* 79
lunch	Mittagessen *(n.)* (-) 47
lunchbreak	Mittagspause *(f.)* (-n) 78
luxury	Luxus *(m.)* (-) 50

M

machine	Maschine *(f.)* (-n) 25
magic	Zauber *(m.)* 68
magic formula	Wundermittel *(n.)* (-) 73
magnificent	herrlich 50
maiden name	Mädchenname *(m.)* (-n) 81
main	haupt- 27
main course	Hauptspeise *(f.)* (-n) 27
main station	Hauptbahnhof *(m.)* (¨-e) 27
main thing (the ~)	Hauptsache *(f.)* (-n) 99
make (to ~)	machen 9
make one ... (to ~)	machen (+ *adj.*) 17
make up (to ~)	auf'holen 79
male (animal)	Männchen *(n.)* (-) 88
man	Mann *(m.)* (¨-er) 3
Man!/Boy!	Mensch! 17
manage to (to ~)	es schaffen 29
manner	Weise *(f.)* (-n) 10
manners	Benimm *(m.)*, Manieren *(pl.)* 85
many	viele 18
many times	vielmals 92
March	März *(m.)* 51
market	Markt *(m.)* (¨-e) 19
marriage (married life)	Ehe *(f.)* (-n) 66
married	verheiratet 38
married (to get ~)	heiraten 38
master	Meister *(m.)* (-) / Meisterin *(f.)* (-nen) 24
match	Partie *(f.)* (-n) 36
may	dürfen* 32
May	Mai *(m.)* 22
may/must not	nicht dürfen* 32
maybe	vielleicht 29
me	mich *(acc. of* ich) 11
me (to ~)	mir *(dat. of* ich) 16
meadow	Wiese *(f.)* (-n) 82
meal	Essen *(n.)* (-) 27; Mahlzeit *(f.)* (-en) 78

mean (to ~)	meinen 67
means (method)	Mittel *(n.)* (-) 73
meant to (to be ~)	sollen* 36
meantime (in the ~)	inzwischen 80
measure	Maß *(n.)* (-e) 87
meat	Fleisch *(n.)* (-) 24
meddle (to ~)	sich mischen 54
medication	Medikament *(n.)* (-e) 91
medicine	Medizin *(f.)* 51
meet (to ~)	treffen* 25, 58; kennen* lernen 66
meeting	Sitzung *(f.)* (-en) 25
memory	Gedächtnis *(n.)* (-se) 95
menu	Speisekarte *(f.)* (-n) 8
merchant	Händler *(m.)* (-) / Händlerin *(f.)* (-nen) 92
merry	vergnügt 60
message	Nachricht *(f.)* (-en) 11
method	Methode *(f.)* (-n) 73
midday	Mittag *(m.)* (-e) 35
middle	Mitte *(f.)* (-n) 25
midnight	Mitternacht *(f.)* (¨-e) 44
migratory bird	Zugvogel *(m.)* (¨) 97
milk	Milch *(f.)* 12
mill	Mühle *(f.)* (-n) 78
million	Million *(f.)* (-en) 18
mind	Verstand *(m.)* 60; Geist *(m.)* (-er) 83
mine	meiner/meine/meins *(m./f.&pl./n.)* 32
minister (government)	Minister *(m.)* (-) / Ministerin *(f.)* (-nen) 83
minute	Minute *(f.)* (-n) 16
miracle	Wunder *(n.)* (-) 73
mirror	Spiegel *(m.)* (-) 82
miserable	miserabel GA20
miss (to ~) (fail to catch)	verpassen 20
miss/be missing (to ~) (be lacking)	fehlen 81
mistaken (to be ~)	sich irren 54
misunderstanding	Missverständnis *(n.)* (-se) 32
moan (to ~) (lament)	jammern 59
mobile phone	Handy *(n.)* (-s *or* -ies) 11
modify (to ~)	sich ändern 39
moment	Moment *(m.)* (-e) 12; Augenblick *(m.)* (-e) 47
moment (at the ~)	im Moment 12; im Augenblick 53
Monday	Montag *(m.)* (-e) 25
money	Geld *(n.)* (-er) 9
month	Monat *(m.)* (-e) 17
monument (statue)	Denkmal *(n.)* (-er) 70
mood	Laune *(f.)* (-n) 31

sechshundertachtzig • 680

moon	Mond *(m.)* (-e) 25
more	mehr 83
more and more / -er and -er	immer (+ *comparative*) 60
more likely	eher 31
more/less... the more/less (the ~)	je (+ *comparative*)... desto/umso (+ *comparative*) 97
moreover	außerdem 81
morning	Morgen *(m.)* (-) 6; Vormittag *(m.)* (-e) 25
mosquito	Mücke *(f.)* (-n) 43
most	meist 77
mother	Mutter *(f.)* (¨) 18
motion (in ~)	im Gang 76
motorway	Autobahn *(f.)* (-en) 79
motorway service area	Raststätte *(f.)* (-n) 79
mountain	Berg *(m.)* (-e) 46
mouth	Mund *(m.)* (¨-er) 53
move (to ~)	sich bewegen 64
movie	Film *(m.)* (-e) 53
movie theatre	Kino *(n.)* (-s) 74
Mr	Herr *(m.)* (-en) 5
Ms/Mrs	Frau *(f.)* (-en) 6
much	viel 1
muesli cereal	Müsli *(n.)* (-s) 4
mug (for beer)	Krug *(m.)* (¨-e) 87
Mum/Mom	Mama, Mutti 18
murder	Mord *(m.)* (-e) 76
museum	Museum *(n.)* (*pl.* Museen) 74
music	Musik *(f.)* (-en) 34
must	müssen* 10
my	mein *(m./n.)* / meine *(f.&pl.)* 5
myself/yourself/himself/herself etc.	selbst 61
mystery	Geheimnis *(n.)* (-se) 65

N

naked	nackt 74
name	Name *(m.)* (-n) 5
name (first ~)	Vorname *(m.)* (-n) 81
name (last ~)	Familienname *(m.)* (-n), Nachname *(m.)* (-n) 81
nationality	Nationalität *(f.)* (-en) 67
nature	Natur *(f.)* 97
near	nah(e) 80; nahe (bei + *dat.*) 82
nearly	fast 71
necessary	nötig 79
neck	Hals *(m.)* (¨-e) 90
need (to ~)	brauchen 24

need to (to ~)	müssen* 30
negative	negativ 80
neighbour	Nachbar *(m.)* (-n) / Nachbarin *(f.)* (-nen) 67
neither ... nor	weder... noch 34
neither/not either	auch nicht 27
nervous	aufgeregt 18; nervös 31
never	nie(mals) 53
nevertheless	trotzdem 80
new	neu 40
New Year	Neujahr *(n.)* (-e) 96
New Year's Eve	Silvester *(m./n.)* (-) 96
news	Nachricht *(f.)* (-en) 96
newspaper	Zeitung *(f.)* (-en) 43
next	nächster/nächste/nächstes *(m./f./n.)* 18
next time (the ~)	das nächste Mal 83
next to	neben 37
nice	nett 18; schön 46
night	Nacht *(f.)* (¨-e) 17
night (at ~)	nachts 88
no	nein 5; kein *(m./n.)* / keine *(f.&pl.)* 9; nee *(coll.)* 55
no ... whatsoever	keinerlei 86
no longer	nicht mehr 22
no matter	egal 99
no one	niemand 39
nod (to ~)	nicken 59
noisy	laut 34
none	kein *(m./n.)* / keine *(f.&pl.)* 9
nonsense	Quatsch *(m.)* 55
noodle	Nudel *(f.)* (-n) 78
noon	Mittag *(m.)* (-e) 35
normally	normalerweise 46; sonst 95
north	Norden *(m.)* 42
north(ern)	nord 68
nose	Nase *(f.)* (-n) 54
not	nicht 5
not ... anyone	niemand 52
not a(n)	kein *(m./n.)* / keine *(f.&pl.)* 9
not any	kein *(m./n.)* / keine *(f.&pl.)* 9
not anymore/any longer	nicht mehr 22
not at all	gar nicht 76; überhaupt nicht 95
not even	nicht (ein)mal 71; auch nicht 78; gar nicht 99
not yet	noch nicht 6
nothing	nichts 19
nothing but	nur 46
notice (to ~)	merken 76; bemerken 97

sechshundertzweiundachtzig • 682

noticeable (to be ~)	auf'fallen* 99
notification	Bescheid *(m.)* (-e) 58
notify (to ~)	Bescheid sagen (*or* geben*) 58
novel	Roman *(m.)* (-e) 51
now	jetzt 11; nun 82
now (surely)	denn 10
number	Nummer *(f.)* (-n) 5
number (numeral)	Zahl *(f.)* (-en) 17

O

observe (to ~)	beobachten 88
occasion	Gelegenheit *(f.)* (-en) 38
ocean	Ozean *(m.)* (-e) 97
of	von (+ *dat.*) 3; aus (+ *dat.*) 48; auf 50
of course	natürlich 8; klar *(coll.)* 9
of course (self-evident)	selbstverständlich 61
of them	vom (von dem) 47
offer	Angebot *(n.)* (-e) 62
offer (to ~)	an'bieten* 37
office	Büro *(n.)* (-s) 6
office (agency)	Amt *(n.)* (¨-er) 69
often	oft 72
oh	au, och 26
oil	Öl *(n.)* (-e) 44
OK (agreed)	einverstanden 58
old	alt 22
old town (historic centre)	Altstadt *(f.)* (¨-e) 33
old/older (to grow ~)	alt/älter werden* 82
older	älter 82
olive oil	Olivenöl *(n.)* (-e) 44
on	an 22; auf 29
on the (+ date)	am (an dem) 51
once	einmal 9; mal *(abb. of* einmal) 11
once (at ~)	sofort 55
once (just ~)	ein einziges Mal 79
once (not ~) (not one single time)	nicht ein einziges Mal 71
one (impersonal pronoun)	man 17
one (thing)	eins 38
one and a half	eineinhalb 17
oneself/himself/herself/ itself/themselves/ yourself *(formal)*	sich 47
only	nur 15
only (temporal)	erst 52
open	offen 99

open (to ~)	auf'machen 21, 74; eröffnen 65; öffnen 74
opera	Oper *(f.)* (-n) 11
opinion	Meinung *(f.)* (-en) 67
opinion (to be of the ~)	meinen 67
opposite	Gegenteil *(n.)* (-e) 85
opposite (of) (facing)	gegenüber (von) 33
opposite (the ~)	im Gegenteil 69
optimism	Optimismus *(m.)* 97
or	oder 4
orange juice	Orangensaft *(m.)* (¨-e) 24
order (organization)	Ordnung *(f.)* (-en) 52
order (to ~)	bestellen 95
ordinary	alltäglich 81
organization	Organisation *(f.)* (-en) 23
other	anderer/andere/anderes *(m./f.&pl./n.)* 5
other (thing) (the ~)	das andere 38
otherwise	sonst 71
Ouch!	Au(a)! 32
out	heraus, raus (*abb. of* heraus) 46; aus (+ *dat.*) 71
outside	draußen 61
over (finished)	vorbei 22
over (here)	hierher 37
over (more than)	über 57
owe (to ~)	verdanken (+ *dat.*) 83
own (to ~)	besitzen* 56
owner	Besitzer *(m.)* (-) / Besitzerin *(f.)* (-nen) 48
ox	Ochse *(m.)* (-n) 87

P

pacifist	Pazifist *(m.)* (-en) / Pazifistin *(f.)* (-nen) 72
pain	Schmerz *(m.)* (-en) 92
paint (to ~)	malen 90
pair	Paar *(n.)* (-e) 60
pale	hell 33
pan (skillet)	Pfanne *(f.)* (-n) 64
panic	Panik *(f.)* (-en) 90
paper	Papier *(n.)* (-e) 98
paradise	Paradies *(n.)* (-e) 67
parcel	Paket *(n.)* (-e) 24
Pardon (me) …	Entschuldigung …, Verzeihung … 81
Pardon?	Wie bitte? 71
parents	Eltern *(pl.)* 40
park (to ~)	parken 48
parking space/lot	Parkplatz *(m.)* (¨-e) 52
Parliament (German)	Bundestag *(m.)* (-e) 64

sechshundertvierundachtzig • 684

parrot	Papagei *(m.)* (-en) 73
participate in (to ~)	teil'nehmen an GA16
participation	Mitarbeit *(f.)* (-) 80
particularly	besonders 99
party	Party *(f.)* (-s) 22
pass (to ~)	vergehen* 16
pass (to ~) (by car/bike/train etc.)	vorbei'fahren 100
pass (to someone) (to ~)	reichen 98
past	Vergangenheit *(f.)* (-en) 64; vorbei 100
past (+ hour)	nach 20
patience	Geduld *(f.)* 99
patient	ruhig 60
patient (to be ~)	sich gedulden 47
patron	Mäzen *(m.)* (-e) / Mäzenin *(f.)* (-nen) 83
pay (to ~)	bezahlen, zahlen 9; lohnen 41
pay attention (to) (to ~)	auf'passen (auf) 99
peace	Frieden *(m.)* 55
peace (and quiet)	Ruhe *(f.)* 93
pedestrian	Fußgänger *(m.)* (-) / Fußgängerin *(f.)* (-nen) 33
pedestrian zone	Fußgängerzone *(f.)* (-n) 33
peel (skin)	Pelle *(f.)* (-n) 78
people	Leute *(pl.)* 48
per	pro 17
percent	Prozent *(n.)* (-e) 88
perfect	perfekt 90
perhaps	vielleicht 29
permit (to ~)	erlauben 49
perseverance	Ausdauer *(f.)* 99
person	Person *(f.)* (-en) 2
person (in ~)	selbst 61; persönlich 69
personal	persönlich 30
personnel	Personal *(n.)* 80
persuade (to ~)	überzeugen 61
petrol	Benzin *(n.)* (-e) 29
petrol/gas gauge	Benzinuhr *(f.)* (-en) 29
philanthropist	Menschenfreund *(m.)* (-e) / Menschenfreundin *(f.)* (-nen) 73
phone (to ~)	an'rufen* 66
photo	Foto *(n.)* (-s) 3
pick someone up (to ~)	ab'holen 20
picture	Bild *(n.)* (-er) 54
piece	Stück *(n.)* (-e) 4
pig	Schwein *(n.)* (-e) 75
pitch (tar)	Pech *(n.)* 69
pity (what a ~)	schade 20

685 • **sechshundertfünfundachtzig**

pizza	Pizza *(f.)* (-s *or* Pizzen) 26
place	Platz *(m.)* ("-e) 11; Stelle *(f.)* (-n) 15; Stätte *(f.)* (-n) 79
place (to ~)	legen, setzen 56
place (upright) (to ~)	stellen 44
plan	Plan *(m.)* ("-e) 39
plan (to ~)	planen 90
plant	Pflanze *(f.)* (-n) 81
plate	Teller *(m.)* (-) 56
platform	Gleis *(f.)* (-e) 16
play (theatre)	Stück *(n.)* (-e) 45
play (to ~)	spielen 34
please	bitte 4; gern 8
pleased (to be ~)	sich freuen 26
pleasure	Vergnügen *(n.)* (-) 1; Spaß *(m.)* ("-e) 49
pleasure (my ~)	bitte 4
plunge (to ~)	ab'stürzen 62
poet	Dichter *(m.)* (-) / Dichterin *(f.)* (-nen) 51
point	Punkt *(m.)* (-e) 52
Poland	Polen *(n.)* 68
police	Polizei *(f.)* 48
police car	Polizeiwagen *(m.)* (-) 48
police officer	Polizist *(m.)* (-en) / Polizistin *(f.)* (-nen) 67
polite	höflich 52
politeness	Höflichkeit *(f.)* (-en) 52
politics	Politik *(f.)* 80
poor	arm 53
pork	Schwein *(n.)* (-e) 75
pork knuckle	Schweinshaxe *(f.)* (-n) 75
portion	Portion *(f.)* (-en) 8
position	Arbeitsstelle *(f.)* (-n), Stelle *(f.)* (-n) 80
positive	positiv 80
possible	möglich 13
postcard	Postkarte *(f.)* (-n) 18
potato	Kartoffel *(f.)* (-n) 24
pound (weight)	Pfund *(n.)* (-e) 98
pour (to ~)	gießen* 54
practical	praktisch 29
precise	genau 81
predict (to ~)	voraus'sagen 97
prefer (to ~)	vor'ziehen* 80
prefer to (to ~)	lieber (+ *verb*) 62
preferably	lieber 96
president (of a company)	Generaldirektor *(m.)* (-en) / Generaldirektorin *(f.)* (-nen) 90
press (to ~)	drücken 79

presumably	vermutlich 87
pretend (to ~)	tun* als ob 95
prey	Beute *(f.)* (-n) 36
price	Preis *(m.)* (-e) 38
primeval times	Urzeit *(f.)* (-en) 89
prince	Prinz *(m.)* (-en) 82
princess	Prinzessin *(f.)* (-nen) 82
prize	Preis *(m.)* (-e) 99
probably	wahrscheinlich 48; wohl 56
problem	Problem *(n.)* (-e) 22
proceed (to ~)	vor'gehen* 90
process of (to be in the ~)	gerade (+ *present tense verb*) 86
produce (to ~)	produzieren 89
professor	Professor *(m.)* (-en) / Professorin *(f.)* (-nen) 18
programme	Programm *(n.)* (-e) 74
programme (radio/TV)	Sendung *(f.)* (-en) 74
progress (in ~)	im Gang 76
prohibit (to ~)	verbieten* 34
promise (to ~)	versprechen* 54
pronounce (to ~)	aus'sprechen* GA14
proper	richtig 97
proper (as is ~)	wie es sich gehört 85
protection	Schutz *(m.)* (-) 94
proud	stolz 89
pub	Kneipe *(f.)* (-n) 16
pull (to ~)	ziehen* 70
punctual	pünktlich 6
punctuality	Pünktlichkeit *(f.)* 52
purchase	Kauf *(m.)* (¨-e) 40
put (to ~)	legen 54; setzen 56
put (upright) (to ~)	stellen 44

Q

qualification (following studies)	Abschluss *(m.)* (¨-e) 81
quarter	Viertel *(n.)* (-) 52
quarter of an hour	Viertelstunde *(f.)* (-n) 47
question	Frage *(f.)* (-n) 15
queue (line)	Schlange *(f.)* (-n) 24
queue up (to ~)	Schlange stehen* 24
quick	schnell 11
quiet	leise 34; still 45
quite	ziemlich (+ *adj.*) 31

R

rabbit	Hase *(m.)* (-n) 58
race	Wettlauf *(m.)* (¨-e) 58

radio	Radio *(n.)* (-s) 74
rage (to ~)	wüten 60
rain	Regen *(m.)* (-) 26
rain (to ~)	regnen 26
rainy weather	Regenwetter *(n.)* 48
raise (to ~)	heben* 86
raisin	Rosine *(f.)* (-n) 88
rare	selten 35
raspberry	Himbeere *(f.)* (-n) 57
rat	Ratte *(f.)* (-n) 13
rather (would ~)	lieber (+ *verb*) 62
ravenous (to be ~)	Bärenhunger *(m.)* haben* 53
reach (to ~)	greifen* 86
read (to ~)	lesen* 27
reading	Lesen *(n.)* (-) 27
ready	fertig 13
ready! (Get ~)	Achtung! 90
reality	Wirklichkeit *(f.)* (-en) 56
really	wirklich 27; ganz 37; echt 92
reason	Grund *(m.)* (¨-e) 48
reasonable	günstig 38
reasoning	Verstand *(m.)* 60
receive (to ~)	kriegen 40
reception	Empfang *(m.)* (¨-e) 96
recipe	Rezept *(n.)* (-e) 57
recognize (to ~)	erkennen* 72
recognize (to ~) (after time has passed)	wieder erkennen* 82
recommend (to ~)	raten* 83
reconstruction	Wiederaufbau *(f.)* (-) 64
red	rot 34
red light (at a ~)	bei Rot 34
reflect (to ~)	nach'denken* 83
reflection	Überlegung *(f.)* (-en) 65
refrigerator	Kühlschrank *(m.)* (¨-e) 44
regards (kind ~)	freundliche Grüße 80
reimburse (to ~)	übernehmen* 80
relations	Umgang *(m.)* (¨-e) 86
relatives	Verwandte *(pl.)* 39
reliability	Zuverlässigkeit *(f.)* 52
reliable	zuverlässig 52
remain (to ~)	bleiben* 71
remember (to ~)	sich erinnern an (+ *acc.*) 74, 82
remember something (to ~)	ein'fallen* 100
rent (to ~) (let)	vermieten 50
repair (to ~)	reparieren 25

sechshundertachtundachtzig • 688

repeat (to ~)	wiederholen 65
reply	Antwort *(f.)* (-en) 80
reply (to ~)	antworten 11; erwidern 58
report	Bericht *(m.)* (-e) 87
representative	Vertreter *(m.)* (-) / Vertreterin *(f.)* (-nen) 25
researcher	Forscher *(m.)* (-) / Forscherin *(f.)* (-nen) 88
reserve (to ~)	reservieren 61
reserve (to ~) (e.g. a ticket/room/flight)	buchen 62
respect (to ~)	ehren 80; achten 94
rest	Rast *(f.)* (-en) 79
rest stop (without food outlets)	Rastplatz *(m.)* (¨-e) 79
retirement	Rente *(f.)* (-n) 89
reveal (to ~)	verraten* 65
review	Wiederholung *(f.)* (-en) 7
revolve around (to ~)	sich drehen um (+ *acc.*) 57
rich	reich 36
ridiculous	lächerlich 85
right	Recht *(n.)* (-e) 73; richtig 74
right (on the ~)	rechts 15
right (that's ~)	stimmt 40
right (to be ~)	stimmen 40; recht haben* 73
right away	gleich 47
rise (to ~)	steigen* 97
risk (at ~)	in Gefahr 61
rival	Rivale *(m.)* (-n) / Rivalin *(f.)* (-nen) 74
river	Fluss *(m.)* (¨-e) 57
road	Bahn *(f.)* (-en) 15
roast chicken	Brathähnchen *(n.)* (-) 87
rock	Felsen *(m.)* (-) 68
romantic	romantisch 100
room	Zimmer *(n.)* (-) 2
rosy	rosig 97
round	rund 57
round (all the way ~)	rundherum 86
routine (daily ~)	Alltag *(m.)* 81
row (line)	Reihe *(f.)* (-n) 45
rubbish	Schweinerei *(f.)* (-en) 75
rule	Regel *(f.)* (-n) 85
run (to ~)	laufen* 18; rennen* 70
run away (to ~)	weg'laufen* 73
run over (to ~)	überfahren* 94
running (to start ~)	los'laufen* 60

S

sad	traurig 54
safe	sicher 62

safe (for valuables)	Geldschrank *(m.)* (¨-e) 49
salad	Salat *(m.)* (-e) 78
salesperson	Verkäufer *(m.)* (-) / Verkäuferin *(f.)* (-nen) 62
salt	Salz *(n.)* (-e) 78
same	selber/selbe/selbes *(m./f./n.)* 48
same (thing) (the ~)	derselbe/dieselbe/dasselbe *(m./f./n.)* 30, 48
sand	Sand *(m.)* (-) 54
sandal	Sandale *(f.)* (-n) 34
sandwich	Vesperbrot *(n.)* (-e) 47
satisfied	zufrieden 82
Saturday	Samstag *(m.)* (-e) 22; Sonnabend *(m.)* (-e) 25
sausage	Wurst *(f.)* (¨-e) 4
sausage (fried ~)	Bratwurst *(f.)* (¨-e) 9
sausage (liver ~)	Leberwurst *(f.)* (¨-e) 78
sausage (small ~)	Würstchen *(n.)* (-) 4
sausage (veal and pork ~)	Weißwurst *(f.)* (¨-e) 75
save (to ~)	frei'halten* 78
save (to ~) (economize)	sparen 10
saxophone	Saxofon *(n.)* (-e) 34
say (to ~)	sagen 11
scarcely	kaum 46
scare someone (to ~)	jdm einen Schrecken einjagen 94
scared (to be ~)	Angst haben* 76
schnapps	Schnaps *(m.)* (¨-e) 30
school	Schule *(f.)* (-n) 51
schoolbook	Schulbuch *(n.)* (¨-er) 83
schoolchild	Schüler *(m.)* (-) / Schülerin *(f.)* (-nen) 22
sea	Meer *(n.)* (-e) 24
search for (to ~)	suchen 19
seat	Platz *(m.)* (¨-e) 11
seated (to stay ~)	sitzen bleiben* 60
second	zweiter/zweite/zweites *(m./f./n.)* 45; Sekunde *(f.)* (-n) 90
second time (a ~)	ein zweites Mal 76
secret	Geheimnis *(n.)* (-se) 65
see (to ~)	sehen* 10, GA11
see (to come/go ~)	besuchen 80
see again (to ~)	wieder'sehen* 100
See you later!	Bis später! 78
See you soon!	Bis später! 12
See you!	Tschüs(s)! 12
seem (to ~)	scheinen* 31, 76; erscheinen* 85
self-employed	selbstständig 81
sell (to ~)	verkaufen 40
send (to ~)	schicken 39; senden* 70
sense (common ~)	Verstand *(m.)* 60

sentence	Satz *(m.)* (¨-e) 58
sentence (to ~)	verurteilen 93
separate	getrennt 95
separate (to ~)	trennen 95
separation	Trennung *(f.)* (-en) 64
service	Dienst *(m.)* (-e) 25
service station	Tankstelle *(f.)* (-n) 19
set down (to ~)	setzen 56
settle in (to ~)	sich ein'leben 75
several	mehrere *(pl.)* 87
shake one's head (to ~)	schütteln 59
shame (what a ~)	schade 20
share (to ~)	teilen 97
she	sie 3; die 32
shell	Schale *(f.)* (-n) 86
shine (to ~)	scheinen* 96
ship	Schiff *(n.)* (-e) 68
shocked	schockiert 88
shoe	Schuh *(m.)* (-e) 73
shop	Geschäft *(n.)* (-e) 10; Laden *(m.)* (¨) 48
shop (to ~)	ein'kaufen 24
shopping (to go ~)	ein'kaufen 48
shore	Ufer *(n.)* (-) 68
short	kurz 60
should	sollen* 31
should (as one ~)	wie es sich gehört 85
shout (to ~)	schreien* 45; rufen* 59
shouting	Geschrei *(n.)* 55
show (to ~)	zeigen 13
shriek (to ~)	schreien* 60
siblings	Geschwister *(pl.)* 23
side	Seite *(f.)* (-n) 50
sidewalk	Gehweg *(m.)* (-e) 65
sightseeing	Stadtbesichtigung *(f.)* (-en) 33
signal	Zeichen *(n.)* (-) 90
silence	Ruhe *(f.)* 45
silk	Seide *(f.)* (-n) 54
silken	seiden 54
similar	ähnlich 80
simple	einfach 85
simultaneous	gleichzeitig 64
since	seit 29; da 80; wo doch 97
since then	seither 64
sing (to ~)	singen* 82
single (unmarried)	ledig 36
sister	Schwester *(f.)* (-n) 23

sit (to ~)	sitzen* 25, 68
sit (down) (to ~)	sich setzen 37, 45
site	Stätte *(f.)* (-n) 79
sitting (to be ~)	sitzen* 43
situated (to be ~)	liegen* 41
skill	Können *(n.)* (-) 90
sky	Himmel *(m.)* (-) 24
sleep (to ~)	schlafen* 17
sleepless	schlaflos 93
slide (to ~)	rutschen 96
small	klein 42
smile (to ~)	lächeln 54
smith	Schmied *(m.)* (-e) / Schmiedin *(f.)* (-nen) 100
smoke (to ~)	rauchen 72
snake	Schlange *(f.)* (-n) 24
snap up (to ~)	schnappen 62
snarl (to ~)	knurren 78
snow	Schnee *(m.)* (-) 97
snow (to ~)	schneien 97
so	also 9; so 16; dann 54; deshalb 99
so far	bis jetzt 79
so much	so viel 88
So what?	Ja und? 88
sock	Socke *(f.)* (-n) 34
soft	weich 85
some	einige 62
some … or other	irgend- 76
someone	jemand 34
somersault	Salto *(m.)* (-s) 100
something	etwas 8; was (*abb. of* etwas) 19
something different	was/etwas anderes 78
sometimes	manchmal 87
somewhere	irgendwo 82
son	Sohn *(m.)* (¨-e) 85
soon	bald 12
soon as (as ~)	sobald 79
sorrow	Leid *(n.)* (-en) 51
sorry! (I'm ~)	Tut mir Leid! 32
sound (to ~)	klingen* 50
soup	Suppe *(f.)* (-n) 78
south	Süden *(m.)* 42
south(ern)	süd 50
souvenir	Souvenir *(n.)* (-s) 87
sow (female pig)	Sau *(f.)* (¨-e) 78
Spain	Spanien *(n.)* 50
Spanish (language)	Spanisch 50

sechshundertzweiundneunzig • 692

Spanish (person)	Spanier *(m.)* (-) / Spanierin *(f.)* (-nen) 50
sparkling mineral water	Sprudel *(m.)* (-) 33
sparkling wine	Sekt *(m.)* (-e) 24
speak (to ~)	sprechen* 8; reden 36
speak to (to ~)	an'sprechen* 37; sprechen* (+ *acc.*) 47
speak/say (about) (to ~)	sprechen* (von) 62
special (something/nothing ~)	etwas/nichts Besonderes *(n.)* 89
specialize in (to ~)	sich spezialisieren auf (+ *acc.*) 81
speed	Geschwindigkeit *(f.)* (-en) 79
spend (time) (to ~)	verbringen* 37, 46
spend (to ~)	aus'geben* 21
spider	Spinne *(f.)* (-n) 55
spin (to ~)	spinnen* 55
spirit	Geist *(m.)* (-er) 83
splendid	blendend GA20; herrlich 46
spoil (to ~)	verderben* 65
spoil (to ~) (indulge)	verwöhnen 87
spoon	Löffel *(m.)* (-) 86
spring (the season)	Frühling *(m.)* (-e) 28
sprinkle (to ~)	streuen 86
square (town ~)	Platz *(m.)* (¨-e) 51
stand (to ~)	stehen* 24, 82
stand (upright) (to ~)	stellen 56
standing (to be ~)	stehen* 44
star	Stern *(m.)* (-e) 86
start (to ~)	an'fangen* 45, 55
starting to …	langsam (+ *verb*) 81
station	Station *(f.)* (-en) 15
statistic	Statistik *(f.)* (-en) 62
stay (to ~)	bleiben* 11
steal (to ~)	stehlen* 91
step (stride)	Schritt *(m.)* (-e) 60
still	noch 6; immer noch 84
still no	immer noch kein… 75
stomach	Magen *(m.)* (-) 53; Bauch *(m.)* (¨-e) 96
stop (e.g. of a bus or tram)	Haltestelle *(f.)* (-n) 15
stop (to ~)	halten* 24, 29; an'halten* 29, 79; auf'hören 51
store	Geschäft *(n.)* (-e) 10
story	Geschichte *(f.)* (-n) 41; Erzählung *(f.)* (-en) 72; Märchen *(n.)* (-) 82
straight	gerade 47
straight ahead	geradeaus 15
strange	komisch 76
strategy	Strategie *(f.)* (-n) 97
strawberry	Erdbeere *(f.)* (-n) 57
street	Straße *(f.)* (-n) 15

stressful	stressig 65
strew (to ~)	streuen 54
string	Faden *(m.)* (¨) 54; Bindfaden *(m.)* (¨) 87
stroke (to ~)	streicheln 32
strong	stark 63
student	Student *(m.)* (-en) / Studentin *(f.)* (-nen) 3
studies (at university)	Studium *(n.)* (*pl.* Studien) 81
studious (hard-working)	tüchtig 99
study (to ~)	studieren 51
stupid	dumm 10
style (hair) (to ~)	frisieren 65
subway	U-Bahn *(f.)* (-en) 15
successor	Nachfolger *(m.)* (-) / Nachfolgerin *(f.)* (-nen) 82
such (a thing)	so (etwas) 93
sudden	plötzlich 82
sugar	Zucker *(m.)* (-) 98
suicide	Selbstmord *(m.)* (-e) 76
suit (clothing)	Anzug *(m.)* (¨-e) 38
suitable (to be ~)	passen 80
suitcase	Koffer *(m.)* (-) 13
summer	Sommer *(m.)* (-) 28
sun	Sonne *(f.)* (-n) 25
Sunday	Sonntag *(m.)* (-e) 10
sunny	sonnig 50
supermarket	Supermarkt *(m.)* (¨-e) 19
superstore	Großmarkt *(m.)* (¨-e) 48
supposed to (to be ~)	sollen* 31, 35
sure	sicher 6
Sure!	Sicher! 41
surname	Familienname *(m.)* (-n), Nachname *(m.)* (-n) 81
surprise (to ~)	überraschen 76
surprised	überrascht 100
survival	Überleben *(n.)* 97
suspect (to ~)	ahnen 87
suspicion	Ahnung *(f.)* (-en) 87
swan	Schwan *(m.)* (¨-e) 74
swear (to ~) (vow)	schwören* 41
swear word	Schimpfwort *(n.)* (¨-er) 100
sweater	Pullover *(m.)* (-) 77
sweet	süß 32
swim (to ~)	schwimmen* 96
swimming pool	Schwimmbad *(n.)* (¨-er) 96
swimming trunks	Badehose *(f.)* 97
swimsuit	Badeanzug *(m.)* (¨-e) 97
switch off (to ~)	aus'machen 43; ab'stellen 74
switch on (to ~)	an'machen 43; an'stellen 74

sechshundertvierundneunzig • 694

Switzerland	Schweiz *(f.)* 68
symbol	Symbol *(n.)* (-e) 64

T

table	Tisch *(m.)* (-e) 27
take (to ~)	nehmen* 4, 20
take along (to ~)	mit'nehmen* 26
take away (from) (to ~)	ab'nehmen* 87
take leave of (to ~)	Abschied nehmen* 12
talk (to ~)	reden 36
talk about (to ~)	reden über (+ *acc.*) 36
talk to (each other) (to ~)	sich unterhalten* 37
tall	groß 36
tall/taller (to grow ~)	groß/größer werden* 82
task	Aufgabe *(f.)* (-n) 80
taste (good) (to ~)	schmecken 27
taxi	Taxi *(n.)* (-s) 13
tea	Tee *(m.)* (-s) 4
teach someone something (to ~)	jdm etwas bei'bringen* 93
tear (to ~)	reißen* 54
telephone	Telefon *(n.)* (-e) 5
telephone call/conversation	Telefongespräch *(n.)* (-e) 5
television set	Fernsehapparat *(m.)* (-e) 74
tell (to ~)	erzählen 42
tenant	Mieter *(m.)* (-) / Mieterin *(f.)* (-nen) 68
tent	Zelt *(n.)* (-e) 87
terrace	Terrasse *(f.)* (-n) 82
terrible	schrecklich 36
terribly	fürchterlich 66; entsetzlich 88
test	Probe *(f.)* (-n) 90
than (comparison)	als 58
thank for (to ~)	sich bedanken für 100
thank someone for (to ~)	danken jdm *(dat.)* für (+ *acc.*) 61
Thank you!	Danke! 4
thanks (gratitude)	Dank *(m.)* (-) 15
thanks (no ~)	nein danke 27
thanks! (Many ~)	Vielen Dank! 15
that	das 3
that (about ~)	darüber 75
that (of ~)	davon 78
that (so ~)	damit 66; dass 79
that (which)	was 34; der 85
that (with/by ~)	damit 58
that *(conj.)*	dass 31
That's not the point.	Darum geht es nicht. 94
the *(f.)*	die 3

the *(m.)*	der 3
the *(n.)*	das 3
the *(pl.)*	die 6
theatre	Theater *(n.)* (-) 26
their	ihr *(m./n.)* / ihre *(f.&pl.)* 25
them	sie 28
them (to ~)	ihnen (*dat. of* sie) 37
then	denn 10; dann 15; da 58; damals 74
theoretical	theoretisch 29
there	da 6; dort 10
there (movement away from speaker)	hin- 31; dorthin 42
there is/are	es gibt 15
therefore	deshalb 65
these	die 13
they	sie 6; die 13
thin	dünn 82
thing	Ding *(n.)* (-e) 76
think (to ~)	meinen 26; glauben 45; denken* 46, 70, 74; finden* 76
think about (to ~)	daran denken* 79
think of something (to ~)	ein'fallen* 100
think over (to ~)	nach'denken* 53
think to oneself (to ~)	sich denken* 75
thirst	Durst *(m.)* 19
thirsty (to be ~)	Durst haben* 19
this	das 3; dieser/diese/dieses *(m./f./n.)* 43
this (about ~)	daran 79; darüber 83; darum 94
thousand	Tausend *(n.)* (-e) 18
thread	Faden *(m.)* (¨) 87
three times	dreimal 9
throat	Hals *(m.)* (¨-e) 90
thumb	Daumen *(m.)* (-) 79
thunder	Donner *(m.)* (-) 25
Thursday	Donnerstag *(m.)* (-e) 25
thus	deshalb 65
tickle (to ~)	kitzeln 76
tie (necktie)	Binde *(f.)* (-n), Krawatte *(f.)* (-n) 54
time	Zeit *(f.)* (-en) 12
time (an exact time i.e. hours/minutes)	Uhr *(f.)* (-en) 16
time (it is ~)	es ist soweit 90
time (occasion)	Mal *(n.)* (-e) 43, 60
time (to have ~)	Zeit haben* 12
time (to not have ~)	keine Zeit haben* 12
time? (At what ~)	Um wie viel Uhr? 16

sechshundertsechsundneunzig • 696

tired	müde 17
tired (to make ~)	müde machen 17
tiring	anstrengend 26
title	Titel *(m.)* (-) 100
to	an 24; zu (+ *dat.*) 37; bei (+ *dat.*) 51; bis 60; vor 68
to (+ destination)	nach 11
to (+ hour)	vor 20
to the	ans (an + das) 24
today	heute 1
together	zusammen 9
toilet	Klo *(n.)* (-s) (*abb. of* Klosett), Toilette *(f.)* (-n) 45
tomcat	Kater *(m.)* (-) 13
tomorrow	morgen 10
tomorrow (the day after ~)	übermorgen 62
tonight	heute Abend 11
too	zu (+*adj./adv.*) 22; auch 53
too bad	schade 86
too much	zu viel 23
tooth	Zahn *(m.)* (¨-e) 50
top (of) (at the ~)	oben (an + *dat.*) 59
topple (to ~)	stürzen 62
torrent	Schwall *(m.)* (-e) 100
total	total 27
total (in ~)	insgesamt 87
Touch wood!	Toi! Toi! Toi! 89
tourist	Tourist *(m.)* (-en) / Touristin *(f.)* (-nen) 38
tower	Turm *(m.)* (¨-e) 63
town	Stadt *(f.)* (¨-e) 10
track	Bahn *(f.)* (-en) 15
traffic	Verkehr *(m.)* 91
traffic jam	Stau *(n.)* (-s) 79
traffic light	Ampel *(f.)* (-n) 94
train	Bahn *(f.)* (-en) 15; Zug *(m.)* (¨-e) 16
train station	Bahnhof *(m.)* (¨-e) 20
tram	Straßenbahn *(f.)* (-en) 15
translate (to ~)	übersetzen 1
transmission (shipment or broadcast)	Sendung *(f.)* (-en) 51
travel (to ~)	reisen 62
travel agency	Reisebüro *(n.)* (-s) 62
treasure	Schatz *(m.)* (¨-e) 66
treat someone (to ~) (pay for)	ein'laden* 75
tree	Baum *(m.)* (¨-e) 82
trip	Fahrt *(f.)* (-en), Reise *(f.)* (-n) 62
trousers	Hose *(f.)* (-n) 75
truck	Lastwagen *(m.)* (-) 94

697 • **sechshundertsiebenundneunzig**

true	wahr 37
true (that's ~)	stimmt 24, 40
true (to be ~)	stimmen 40
truly	echt 92
trunk (of tree)	Stamm *(m.)* (¨-e) 55
truth	Wahrheit *(f.)* (-en) 69
try (to ~)	versuchen 61; probieren 75
Tuesday	Dienstag *(m.)* (-e) 25
tune in (to ~)	ein'stellen 74
turn (it's my ~)	ich bin dran 95
turn (to ~)	wenden* 70
turn. (It's my ~)	Ich bin an der Reihe. 95
tuxedo	Smoking *(m.)* (-s) 38
twelve	zwölf 44
twice	zweimal 9
typical	typisch 33

U

ugly	hässlich 36
umbrella	Regenschirm *(m.)* (-e) 26
uncle	Onkel *(m.)* ( ) 39
under(neath)	unter (+ *dat.*) 75
undergo (to ~)	erleben 64
underground	Untergrund *(m.)* (¨-e) 15
underground train	U-Bahn *(f.)* (-en) 15
underneath	darunter 74
understand (to ~)	verstehen* 27, 54
understandable	verständlich 61
understanding *(adj.)*	verständnisvoll 92
understanding *(noun)*	Verständnis *(n.)* 32
unforgettable	unvergesslich 100
unfortunately	leider 12
uni (abb. for university)	Uni *(f.)* (-s) *(coll.)* 18
unification	Vereinigung *(f.)* (-en) 64
United States	Vereinigte Staaten *(pl.)* 70
unity	Einheit *(f.)* (-en) 64
university	Universität *(f.)* (-en) 18
unknown	unbekannt 69
unless	es sei denn 98
until	bis 12; bis (zu + *dat.*) 45; solange 99
upstairs	oben 45
urgent	dringend 69
us	uns 22
use (to be of ~)	nützen 60
used to (to get ~)	sich an etwas *(+ acc.)* gewöhnen
usually	sonst 95

sechshundertachtundneunzig • 698

V

vacation	Urlaub *(m.)* (-e) 37
value	Wert *(m.)* (-e) 41
vegetables	Gemüse *(pl.)* 97
vehicle	Fahrzeug *(m.)* (-e) 48
versatile (many-sided)	vielseitig 60
very	sehr 3
view	Aussicht *(f.)* (-en) 50
visit	Besichtigung *(f.)* (-en) 33
visit (to ~)	besichtigen 33; besuchen 80
visitor	Besucher *(m.)* (-) / Besucherin *(f.)* (-nen), Gast *(m.)* (¨-e) 87
voice	Stimme *(f.)* (-n) 72

W

wait (to ~)	warten 13, 14
wait for (to ~)	warten auf (+ *acc.*) 59
Wait!	Halt! 58
waiter/waitress	Kellner *(m.)* (-) / Kellnerin *(f.)* (-nen) 95
waiting room	Vorzimmer *(n.)* (-) 47
wake (someone) (to ~)	jemanden wecken 71
wake up (to ~)	auf'wachen 71
walk (a stroll)	Spaziergang *(m.)* (¨-e) 26
walk (to ~)	laufen* 18
walk (to go for a ~)	spazieren gehen* 34
wall	Wand *(f.)* (¨-e) 54; Mauer *(f.)* (-n) 64
want (to ~)	mögen* 8; wollen* 27, 31, 35, 36
war	Krieg *(m.)* (-e) 72
warm	herzlich 89; warm 97
warming	Erwärmung *(f.)* (-en) 97
warn (to ~)	warnen 86
wash (to ~)	sich waschen* 71, 77
waste time (to ~)	Federlesen machen 93
watch (to ~)	an'sehen* 76
watch (wristwatch)	Uhr *(f.)* (-en) 17
watch TV (to ~)	fern'sehen* 55
water	Wasser *(n.)* (-) 97
wave (to ~)	winken 37
way	Weg *(m.)* (-e) 38
way (mode)	Weise *(f.)* (-n) 10
we	wir 1
weak	schwach 63
wear (to ~)	tragen* 34, 38, 72, 74
weather	Wetter *(n.)* 46
weather forecast	Wetterbericht *(m.)* (-e) 97
wedding	Hochzeit *(f.)* (-en) 66

Wednesday	Mittwoch *(m.)* (-e) 25
week	Woche *(f.)* (-n) 18
weekday	Wochentag *(m.)* (-e) 25
weekend	Wochenende *(n.)* (-n) 33
weigh (to ~)	wiegen* 57
weird	komisch 99
welcome	willkommen 51
welcome! (You're ~)	Bitte! 4
welcome! (You're ~)	Keine Ursache! 15
well	wohl 77
well (to be/go ~)	gut gehen* 59
well …	na 27; tja 87
well then	also 19
west	Westen *(m.)* 42
west(ern)	west 64
what	was 4; wie 5; welcher/welche/welches *(m./f./n.)* 61
What (a/an) ...!	Was für ein/eine…! 22
What for?	Wozu? 19
What kind of ...?	Was für ein/eine…? 22
What time is it?	Wie spät ist es? 18
What?	Wie bitte? 27
What's going on?	Was ist los? 55
What's up?	Was ist los? 71
What's wrong?	Was ist los? 71
whatever may happen	was auch kommt 99
whatever/whoever it may be	was/wer es auch sei 97
wheel	Rad *(n.)* (¨-er) 34
when	wann 11; wenn 38; als 57; wo… (doch) 99
whenever	wenn 38; jedes Mal 76
where	wo 11
where from	woher 36
where to	wohin 36
whereas	dagegen 71
whether	ob 76
which	welcher/welche/welches *(m./f./n.)* 20
while …-ing	beim (+ *infinitive used as a noun*) 100
whipped cream	Schlagsahne *(f.)* 8
whisper (to ~)	flüstern 45
whistle (to ~)	pfeifen* 86
white	weiß 82
who	Wer? 3
who *(relative pronoun)*	der 85
who/whose (the person ~)	derjenige/diejenige/dasjenige *(m./f./n.)* 85
whoever	wer 33
whole	ganz 81

siebenhundert • 700

whom	wen *(acc. of* wer) 23
whom (to ~)	wem *(dat. of* wer) 39
whose	wessen 68
why	warum 1; weshalb 65
Why?	Wozu? 19
wide	weit 29
widow	Witwe *(f.)* (-n) 68
wife	Frau *(f.)* (-en) 3
will (future tense auxiliary)	werden* (+ *infinitive*) 55
will (volition)	Wille *(m.)* (-n) 65
… will you? (question tag)	doch (+ *verb*) 30
win (to ~)	gewinnen* 58
window	Fenster *(n.)* (-) 53
wine	Wein *(m.)* (-e) 35
winter	Winter *(m.)* (-) 28
wish (to ~)	wünschen 1; wollen* 27
wishes (best ~)	viele Grüße 80
with	mit (+ *dat.*) 4; bei (+ *dat.*) 51
with it	dazu 75
without	ohne 35
woman	Frau *(f.)* (-en) 3
wonderful	herrlich 46
word	Wort *(n.)* (¨-er *or* -e) 58
work	Werk *(n.)* (-e) 51; Arbeit *(f.)* (-en) 78
work (to ~)	arbeiten 19
work (to ~) (function)	laufen* 18; funktionieren 25
work out (to ~)	klappen 90
worker	Arbeiter *(m.)* (-) / Arbeiterin *(f.)* (-nen) 33
working hours	Arbeitszeit *(f.)* (-en) 78
world	Welt *(f.)* (-en) 57
world history	Weltgeschichte *(f.)* 64
worry	Sorge *(f.)* (-n) 52
worry (to ~)	Angst haben* 59
worth	Wert *(m.)* (-e) 41
worth (to be ~)	wert sein* 41
worth seeing	sehenswert 83
worthwhile (to be ~)	sich lohnen 41
wring (to ~)	um'drehen 93
write (to ~)	schreiben* 39
writer	Dichter *(m.)* (-) / Dichterin *(f.)* (-nen) 51; Schriftsteller *(m.)* (-) / Schriftstellerin *(f.)* (-nen) 72
written (to be ~)	stehen* 83
wrong	falsch 5; Unrecht *(n.)* (-) 73
wrong (to be ~)	unrecht haben* 73
wrong (to go ~)	schief gehen* 90

Y

yard	Hof *(m.)* (¨-e) 20
year	Jahr *(n.)* (-e) 17
yelling	Geschrei *(n.)* 55
yellow	gelb 82
yes	ja 2
yes (in response to a negative question)	doch 19
yesterday	gestern 36
you (to ~) *(formal)*	Ihnen *(dat. of* Sie) 38
you (to ~) *(pl. informal)*	euch *(dat. of* ihr) 41
you (to ~) *(sing. informal)*	dir *(dat. of* du) 37
you *(formal)*	Sie 1
you *(pl. informal)*	ihr 10; euch *(acc. of* ihr) 27
you *(sing. informal)*	du 8; dich *(acc. of* du) 16
young	jung 51
your *(formal)*	Ihr *(m./n.)* / Ihre *(f.&pl.)* 5
your *(pl. informal)*	euer *(m./n.)* / eure *(f.&pl.)* 55
your *(sing. informal)*	dein *(m./n.)* / deine *(f.&pl.)* 11

Z

zero	Null *(f.)* (-en) 29
zone	Zone *(f.)* (-n) 33

ASSiMiL

German
With Ease

Available soon from Assimil:

German Phrasebook

Edition number 3364 : GERMAN
Printed in Slovenia - october 2014